D1067653

SOUL MATTERS

WRITINGS FROM THE GRECO-ROMAN WORLD
SUPPLEMENT SERIES

Clare K. Rothschild, General Editor

Number 22

SBL PRESS

Atlanta

Copyright © 2023 by Society of Biblical Literature

Library of Congress Control Number: 2023946424

The editors wish to express gratitude to the Bruce Frier Fund of the Department of Classical Studies and to the Chairs of the Department, Artemis Leontis and Celia Schultz, as well as to the College of Literature, Science, and the Arts at the University of Michigan, for making this publication possible.

SOUL MATTERS

Plato and Platonists on the Nature of the Soul

Edited by

Sara Ahbel-Rappe, Danielle A. Layne, and Crystal Addey

SBL PRESS

Contents

Part 5. Christian and Pagan Perspectives

Foreword

The present volume is the outcome of a conference organized by Sara Ahbel-Rappe at the University of Michigan (Ann Arbor) to celebrate the impending retirement of John Finamore as professor of classics and chair of the Department of Classics at the University of Iowa. Although the occasion was a very happy one for all concerned, a look of embarrassment could occasionally be caught on the face of the honorand. A modest man, more used to praising others than of being praised himself, he seemed at times to wonder what all this ado was about. If only for this reason, it seems appropriate here to recall some of the reasons that prompted his closest colleagues to organize a celebration of this particularly significant point of his career.

A pioneer of the study of Neoplatonism in the English-speaking world, Finamore came to his preferred author, Iamblichus, through a long, direct, and studious route. His undergraduate and graduate studies in both philosophy and classics, first at the University of Maryland (BA in philosophy, 1968–1972), then at Tufts (MA in philosophy, 1972–1975), then at Rutgers (MA and PhD in classics, 1975–1977 and 1977–1983, respectively), gave him a solid grounding in the techniques of analytical philosophy and developed his incipient interest in the history of philosophy. At the time, the two disciplines were not easily combined—indeed, they were not uncommonly perceived as antagonistic—and it is much to John's credit that he succeeded in combining them through his career. It was during those years of study on the East Coast that John met Susan McLean, who was to become his lifelong partner. Susan, a poet and a translator,[1] later joined him in the Midwest when she took up a post as professor of English at Southwest Minnesota State University.

---

1. Her publications include *The Best Disguise* (Evansville, IN: University of Evansville Press, 2009) and *The Whetstone Misses the Knife* (West Chester, PA: Story Line Press,

In a not uncharacteristic case of serendipity, in the course of his MA studies, it was suggested to John that he write an essay on Iamblichus, an author who at the time was but rarely thought to be a fit object of philosophical interest. The essay was the spark that determined the course of his professional life. As he would often say in later years, he decided that "this fascinating fellow" would be an excellent topic for his PhD. The serendipity was compounded by the fact that he soon discovered that, at the opposite end of the country, at Berkeley, a young Irish scholar, John Dillon, had recently published the results of his own doctoral research on the same author's commentaries on the *Timaeus* in a book titled *Iamblichi Chalcidensis in Platonis dialogos commentariorum fragmenta* (1973).[2] Finamore, thus encouraged to devote his doctoral energies to Iamblichus, embarked on a thesis that would, in turn, be published under the title of *Iamblichus and the Theory of the Vehicle of the Soul* (1985). The highly positive recommendation that Dillon had written to the publisher to whom Finamore had sent his manuscript soon made the two men collaborators as well as friends. Indeed, it would be no exaggeration to say that, between them, the two Johns succeeded in raising the status of the Sage of Apamea to that of one of the main voices of pre-Procline Neoplatonism.

John's attitude to scholarship is one of sober detachment, grounded in the conviction that the belief system of the exegete should always be kept separate from that of his/her author. Accordingly, his main concern is to reconstruct the thought of his author, based on the writings that have come down to us, and, once that task is complete, to articulate its presuppositions and core values so as to make them understandable to modern audiences. It is neither to endorse his author's views nor to expand on them. The distinction between describing and endorsing is crucial in the study of the philosopher who introduced the practice of theurgy (divine working) as an aid to self-purification and ascent to the Neoplatonic higher principles. For Iamblichus, theurgy involved the use of nonrational ways to reach out to the transcendent and included such practices as the recitation of hymns to the sun as a symbol of the highest divine principle as well as sacrifices, rituals, and invocations to various deities. To be sure, John would not deny the relevance of theurgy to Iamblichus. What he

---

2014). For her translations, see *Martial, Selected Epigrams* (Madison: University of Wisconsin Press, 2014).

2. For the timing of John Dillon's Iamblichean studies in the United States, see "An Interview with Professor John Dillon," in *IJPT* 12 (2018): 197–202.

characteristically does is to highlight the difference between Iamblichus and his predecessors Plotinus and Porphyry, in whose systems theurgy plays no significant part, before explaining how and why it came to form an integral and valuable part of that of Iamblichus. And if, by chance, of an early morning on the days of the annual conference, some of his wilder and more doctrinally playful colleagues would sometime decide ritually to invoke the sun, John would always find some other tasks with which to occupy himself.

So much for John's intellectual virtues and achievements. But we must not leave the matter there. Adapting to modern times and circumstances Aristotle's distinction between intellectual and moral virtues, it is appropriate also to record the virtues that have enabled John to become the expert administrator and the skillful organizer that he is. The virtues in question are generosity and inclusiveness. His generosity manifests itself in a willingness to devote a great amount of his time to causes that serve the common good. The following episode is a case in point. Some twenty years ago, it had become clear that the International Society for Neoplatonic Studies, set up by R. Baine Harris in 1973, had become dormant and that its dedicated organ, *The Journal of Neoplatonic Studies*, attracted but few worthwhile submissions. Action was needed, and under John's leadership action was soon taken. At a meeting of a conference organized ad hoc by Jay Bregman at the University of Maine,[3] John convened a meeting in which he outlined his plans for revitalizing the moribund society and its journal. A committee of younger, energetic, and dedicated international scholars would be formed to oversee the development and the day-to-day business of a renamed International Society for the Study of Neoplatonism. A new journal, *The International Journal of the Platonic Tradition*, would be set up, for which the reputable auspices of Brill would be sought.

To outline a plan and to bring it to maturity are two different things. Not for John, it seems, for a year later, the new society had come into existence, due to meet annually, and Brill was looking favorably on the plan for a new journal. *The International Journal of the Platonic Tradition* duly came into existence in 2006 and, after somewhat hesitant beginnings, is now going from strength to strength, attracting sound

---

3. Those who are old enough to have attended that conference may remember that it featured the world premiere of one of Jay's jazz compositions, "I Dig the One."

individual submissions as well as welcoming single-themed issues, such as the latest to date, devoted to the scholarship of Werner Beierwaltes. To the organization of the yearly conference and the main editorship of the journal, John brought his demonic energy and capacity for selfless hard work. The organization of the yearly conference in particular is a mammoth task that involves negotiating with the host university, agreeing with it the details of financial planning, vetting the submissions, and securing all parties' agreement in the setting up of the day-to-day schedule of the conference. Of all these tasks, John takes the lion's share, while continuing to fulfill his own departmental responsibilities and honoring his research commitments.

If John can so successfully prepare our annual conferences, it is because he practices a virtue that is currently more praised than cultivated in academic contexts, namely, inclusiveness. To be inclusive, we are told, is to disregard as irrelevant such features in a candidate's background that do not pertain directly to the function one wishes to entrust them with. More practically, it is to resist discrimination on grounds of age, background, or prestige of affiliation. As the coeditor of the society's journal, I have seen John practice that virtue by not outright rejecting the submissions of young, inexperienced, or unaffiliated scholars without first helping them to improve their article or to suggest other possible outlets for it. Even more relevantly, I have seen him willingly enter into dialogue with young and seemingly inexperienced scholars hoping to persuade him to choose their university as a venue for the next conference. That some of the suggested venues proved to host our most successful conferences shows his shrewdness of judgment in the choice of his interlocutors.

Long may John continue to practice those virtues of generosity and inclusiveness for the benefit of us all.

Suzanne Stern-Gillet
Manchester (UK)
August 2022

Abbreviations

1 Succ.	Cyril, *First Letter to Succensus*
2 Succ.	Cyril, *Second Letter to Succensus*
Abst.	Porphyry, *De abstinentia*
AC	*L'Antiquité Classique*
ACO	Schwartz, Eduard, ed. *Acta consiliorum oecunenicorum.* Berlin: de Gruyter. 1922.
Acut.	Hippocrates, *De ratione victus in morbis acutis*
Aff.	Hippocrates, *De affectionibus*
AGP	*Archiv für Geschichte der Philosophie*
AJP	*American Journal of Philology*
[Alc. maj.]	Plato, *Alcibiades major*
Alex. fort.	Plutarch, *De Alexandri magni fortuna aut virtute*
An.	Tertullian, *De anima*
AN	*Ancient Narrative*
An. post.	Aristotle, *Analytica posteriora*
An. procr.	Plutarch, *De animae procreatione in Timaeo*
AncPhil	*Ancient Philosophy*
Aneb.	Porphyry, *Epistula ad Anebonem*
Anth.	Vettius Valens, *Anthologia*
Antr. nymph.	Porphyry, *De antro nympharum*
Ap. John	NHC II 1 Secret Book of John
Apoc. Adam	NHC V 5 Revelation of Adam
Apol.	Plato, *Apologia*; Pamphilus, *Apologia pro Origene*
Apot.	Hephaestio, *Apotelesmatica*
APR	Ancient Philosophy and Religion
Arith.	Nicomachus, *Arithmetike eisagoge*
Ars med.	Galen, *Ars medica*
Atr. bil.	Galen, *De atra bile*
AW	*The Ancient World*
Beat.	Gregory of Nyssa, *De beatitudinibus*

Bell. civ.	Lucan, *De Bello Civili*
BETL	Bibliotheca Ephemeridum Theologicarum Lovaniensium
BGU	Berliner Griechische Urkunden
BHM	*Bulletin of the History of Medicine*
Bibl.	Photius, *Bibliotheca*
BICS	*Bulletin of the Institute of Classical Studies*
BLC	Bardaisan, *The Book of the Laws of Countries*
BMCR	*Bryn Mawr Classical Review*
ByzZ	*Byzantinische Zeitschrift*
Cael. hier.	Pseudo-Dionysius the Areopagite, *De caelesti hierarchia*
CAT	Companions to Ancient Thought
CC	*Culture and Cosmos*
CCAG	*Catalogus Codicum Astrologorum Graecorum*
Cels.	Origen, *Contra Celsum*
Chald. Or.	Chaldean Oracles
Charm.	Plato, *Charmides*
Cher.	Philo, *De cherubim*
Civ.	Augustine, *De civitate Dei*
CJ	*Classical Journal*
ClO	*Classical Outlook*
ClQ	*Classical Quarterly*
ClRev	*Classical Review*
CLS	*Comparative Literature Studies*
C. Boeth.	Porphyry, *Against Boethus on the Soul*
Comm. cael.	Simplicius, *In Aristotelis De Caelo commentaria*
Comm. Cant.	Origen, *Commentarius in Canticum*
Comm. Crat.	Proclus, *In Platonis Cratylum commentaria*
Comm. harm.	Porphyry, *Eis ta harmonika Ptolemaiou hypomnēma*
Comm. in R.	Proclus, *In Platonis rem publicam commentarii*
Comm. Jo.	Origen, *Commentarii in evangelium Joannis*; Cyril, *Commentariorum in Joannem*
Comm. math. sc.	Iamblichus, *De communi mathematica scientia liber*
Comm. Matt.	Origen, *Commentarium in evangelium Matthaei*
Comm. Metaph.	Alexander of Aphrodisias, *In Aristotelis Metaphysica commentaria*
Comm. Rom.	Origen, *Commentarii in Romanos*
Comm. ser. Matt.	Origen, *Commentarium series in evangelium Matthaei*

Comm. somn.	Macrobius, *Commentarii in somnium Scipionis*
Comm. Tim.	Proclus, *In Platonis Timaeum commentaria*
Conf.	Augustine, *Confessionum libri XIII*
CP	*Classical Philology*
CPS	Clarendon Plato Series
Crat.	Plato, *Cratylus*
CRLM	Cambridge Readings in the Literature of Music
CW	*Classical World*
CZ	Collection Zêtêsis
De an.	Alexander of Aphrodisias, *De anima*; Aristotle, *De anima*; Gregory of Nyssa, *De anima*; Iamblichus, *De anima*
De arte	Hippocrates, *De arte*
De fat.	Pseudo-Plutarch, *De fato*
De in.	Alexander of Aphrodisias, *De intellectu*
De opif. hom.	Gregory of Nyssa, *De opificio hominum*
Diaet.	Hippocrates, *De diaeta in morbis acutis*
Dial.	Origen, *Diologus cum Heraclide*
Didasc.	Alcinous, *Didascalicus*
Diis mund.	Sallust, *De diis et mundo*
Diss.	Maximus of Tyre, *Dissertationes*
Div.	Cicero, *De divinatione*
Div. nom.	Pseudo-Dionysius the Areopagite, *De Divinis Nominibus*
DK	Diels, H., and W. Kranz, ed. *Die Fragmente der Vorsokratiker*. 6th ed. Zürich: Weidmann, 1951–1952.
Dogm. Plat.	Apuleius, *De dogma Platonis*
Ecl.	Stobaeus, *Eclogae*
Elem. theol.	Proclus, *Elementatio theologica*
Enn.	Plotinus, *Enneades*
Ep.	*Epistula(e)*; Seneca, *Epistulae morales*
Ep. Afr.	Origen, *Epistula ad Africanum*
Ep. Mel.	Evagrius, *Epistula ad Melaniam*
Epoché	*Epoché: A Journal for the History of Philosophy*
Eth. Eud.	Aristotle, *Ethica Eudemia*
Eth. Nic.	Aristotle, *Ethica Nicomachea*
Eun.	Gregory of Nyssa, *Contra Eunomium*
Euthyd.	Plato, *Euthydemus*
Euthyphr.	Plato, *Euthyphro*

Exc.	Clement of Alexandria, *Excerpta ex Theodoto*
Fac.	Plutarch, *De facie in orbe lunae*
Fort.	Plutarch, *De fortuna*
frag(s).	fragmentum, fragmenta
Frag. Ep.	Julian, *Fragmentum Epistolae*
Gaur.	Porphyry, *Ad Gaurum*
GCS	Die griechischen christlichen Schriftsteller der ersten [drei] Jahrhunderte
Gen. Socr.	Plutarch, *De genio Socratis*
GNO	Gregorii Nysseni Opera
Gorg.	Plato, *Gorgias*
Gos. Eg.	NHC III 2 Gospel of the Egyptians
Gos. Jud.	Tchacos 3 Gospel of Judas
GRBS	*Greek, Roman, and Byzantine Studies*
Haer.	Irenaeus, *Adversus haereses*; Ephrem, *Contra haereses*
HDAC	Histoire des doctrines de l'Antiquité classique
Hel.	Gorgias, *Helena*
HH	Hypomnemata Heft
Hist.	Herodotus, *Historiae*
Hist. an.	Aristotle, *Historia animalium*
Hist. nov.	Zosimus, *Historia nova*
Hom. Cant.	Gregory of Nyssa, *Homiliae in Canticum*; Origen, *Homiliae in Canticum*
Hom. Exod.	Origen, *Homiliae in Exodum*
Hom. Ezech.	Origen, *Homiliae in Ezechielem*
Hom. Gen.	Origen, *Homiliae in Genesim*
Hom. Jer.	Origen, *Homiliae in Jeremiam*
Hom. Lev.	Origen, *Homiliae in Leviticum*
Hom. Ps.	Origen, *Homiliae in Psalmos*
HS	Hellenic Studies
HTR	*Harvard Theological Review*
Hymn	Ephrem, *Hymns against Heresies*
IJPT	*International Journal of the Platonic Tradition*
Il.	Homer, *Ilias*
Immort. an.	Augustine, *De immortalitate animae*
In Alc.	Olympiodorus, *In Platonis Alcibiadem*; Proclus, *Alcibiades Commentary*
In Epict.	Simplicius, *Commentaria In Epicteti Encheiridion*
In Parm.	*In Platonis Parmenidem commentaria*

In Phaed.	Damascius, *In Platonis Phaedum commentarii*
In. Phileb.	Damascius, *In Platonis Philebum commentarius*
In. Phys.	Simplicius, *In Aristotelis Physicorum libros quattuor priores/posteriores*
In Tim.	Proclus, *In Platonis Timaeum commentaria*
Int.	Hippocrates, *De affectionibus internis*
IPQ	*International Philosophical Quarterly*
Is. Os.	Plutarch, *De Iside et Osiride*
JBR	*Journal of Bible and Religion*
JCoptS	*Journal of Coptic Studies*
JECS	*Journal of Early Christian Studies*
JFSR	*Journal of Feminist Studies in Religion*
JGRChJ	*Journal of Greco-Roman Christianity and Judaism*
JHMAS	*Journal of the History of Medicine and Allied Sciences*
JHP	*Journal of the History of Philosophy*
JNS	*Journal of Neoplatonic Studies*
JP	*Journal of Philosophy*
JTS	*Journal of Theological Studies*
JVI	*Journal of Value Inquiry*
KJV	King James Version
Lach.	Plato, *Laches*
LCL	Loeb Classical Library
Leg.	Plato, *Leges*
LM	Laks, André, and Glenn W. Most. *Early Greek Philosophy*. Cambridge: Harvard University Press, 2016.
Loc. hom.	Hippocrates, *De locis in homine*
LXX	Septuagint
Mal. sub.	Proclus, *De malorum subsistentia*
Marsanes	NHC X Marsanes
Math.	Sextus Empiricus, *Adversus mathematicos*
Mens.	John Lydus, *De mensibus*
Metam.	Apuleius, *Metamorphoses*
Metaph.	Aristotle, *Metaphysica*; Theophrastus, *Metaphysica*
Metaphr.	Priscianus, *Metaphrasis*
MHCP	*Medicine, Health Care and Philosophy*
MHNH	*MHNH: revista internacional de investigación sobre magia y astrología antiguas*
Mnemosyne	*Mnemosyne: A Journal of Classical Studies*
MnemSup	Mnemosyne Supplements

Mor.	Plutarch, *Moralia*
Mos.	Philo, *De vita Mosis*
MP	*Mediterranean Perspectives*
Myst.	Iamblichus, *De mysteriis*
Nat. d.	Cicero, *De natura deorum*
Nat. hom.	Hippocrates, *De natura hominis*
NDPR	*Notre Dame Philosophical Reviews*
NHC	Nag Hammadi Codex
NHS	Nag Hammadi Studies
Nicom. arithm.	Iamblichus, *In Nicomachi arithmeticum introductionem*
NIV	New International Version
NTS	*New Testament Studies*
Numen	*Numen: International Review for the History of Religions*
OCD	Hornblower, Simon, and Antony Spawforth, eds. *Oxford Classical Dictionary*. 4th ed. Oxford: Oxford University Press, 2012.
OCT	Oxford Classical Texts
Od.	Homer, *Odyssea*
OED	*Oxford English Dictionary*
Op.	Hesiod, *Opera et dies*
Or.	Julian, *Orationes*
OrChrAn	Orientalia Christiana Analecta
OSAP	*Oxford Studies in Ancient Philosophy*
Parm.	Plato, *Parmenides*
PAS	*Proceedings of the Aristotelian Society*
PBCAP	*Proceedings of the Boston Area Colloquium on Ancient Philosophy*
PDM	*Papyri Demoticae Magicae*. Demotic texts in PGM corpus as collated in Betz, Hans Dieter, ed. *The Greek Magical Papyri in Translation, including the Demotic Spells*. Chicago: University of Chicago Press, 1996
Periph.	Eriugena, *Periphyseon*
PG	Patrologia Graeca [= *Patrologiae Cursus Completus: Series Graeca*]. Edited by Jacques-Paul Migne. 162 vols. Paris, 1857–1886.
PGM	Preisendanz, Karl, ed. *Papyri Graecae Magicae: Die*

	griechischen Zauberpapyri. 2nd ed. Stuttgart: Teubner, 1973–1974.
PhA	Philosophia Antiqua
Phaed.	Plato, *Phaedo*
Phaedr.	Plato, *Phaedrus*
Phil	*Philologus*
Phileb.	Plato, *Philebus*
Philoc.	Origen, *Philocalia*
PhilRev	*Philosophical Review*
PHP	Galen, *De placitis Hippocratis et Platonis*
Phys.	Aristotle, *Physica*
PLATO	*PLATO, The Electronic Journal of the International Plato Society*
Pol.	Plato, *Politicus*: Aristotle, *Politica*
PQ	*The Philosophical Quarterly*
PR	Ephrem, *Prose Refutations*
Princ.	Damscius, *De principiis*: Origen, *De principiis* (*Peri archōn*)
Probl. gnos.	Evagrius of Pontus, *Problemata gnostica*
Procl.	Marinus, *Proclus, or On Happiness*
Prot.	Plato, *Protagoras*
PT	*Political Theory*
PTSPP	Proceedings of the Tenth Symposium Platonicum Pragense, Prague, 12–14 November 2015
Pyth.	Pindar, *Pythionikai*
QAM	Galen, *Quod animi mores corporis temperamenta sequantur*
QSI	*Quaderni di Studi Indomediterranei*
Quaest. Thal.	*Quaestiones ad Thalassium*
RAC	Klauser, Theodor, et al., eds. *Reallexikon für Antike und Christentum.* Stuttgart: Hiersemann, 1950–.
RBPH	*Revue Belge de Philologie et d'Histoire*
Res.	Origen, *De resurrectione libri ii*
Res gest.	Ammianus Marcellinus, *Res gestae*
ResOr	*Res Orientales*
Resp.	Plato, *Respublica*
RevMet	*Review of Metaphysics*
RevPhilos	*Revue Philosophique*

RGRW	Religions in the Graeco-Roman World
RhM	*Rheinisches Museum für Philologie*
RPL	*Recherches de philologie et de linguistique*
SAP	Studies in Ancient Philosophy
SBLTT	Society of Biblical Literature Texts and Translations
SC	Sources chrétiennes
ScEs	*Science et esprit*
Sent.	Porphyry, *Sententiae ad intelligibilia ducentes*
SGA	*Studia graeco-arabica*
Soph. elench.	Aristotle, *Sophistici elenchi* (*Top.* 9)
SPhiloA	*Studia Philonica Annual*
SPNPT	Studies in Platonism, Neoplatonism, and the Platonic Tradition
STDJ	Studies on the Texts of the Desert of Judah
StPatr	Studia Patristica
Strom.	Clement of Alexandria, *Stromateis*
SyllC	*Syllecta Classica*
Symp.	Plato, *Symposium*
TAPS	*Transactions of the American Philosophical Society*
TSBPCP	Theandrites: Studies in Byzantine Platonism and Christian Philosophy
Tetr.	Ptolemy, *Tetrabiblos*
Theaet.	Plato, *Theaetetus*
Theog.	Hesiod, *Theognia*
Thras.	Galen, *Thrasybulus*
Tim.	Plato, *Timaeus*
VC	*Vigiliae Christianae*
VCS	Variorum Collected Studies
VCSup	Vigiliae Christianae Supplements
Vet. med.	Hippocrates, *De vetere medicina*
Vict.	Hippocrates, *De victu*
Vit. phil.	Diogenes Laertius, *Vitae philosophorum*
Vit. Plot.	Porphyry, *Vita Plotini*
Vit. Pyth.	Porphyry, *De vita pythagorica*
Vit. soph.	Eunapius, *Vitae sophistarum*
WCR	*Women: A Cultural Review*
WUNT	Wissenschaftliche Untersuchungen zum Neuen Testament

WWBJ	*Walking the Worlds: A Biannual Journal of Polytheism and Spiritwork*
ZKG	*Zeitschrift für Kirchengeschichte*
Zost.	NHC VII 1 Zostrianos
ZPE	*Zeitschrift für Papyrologie und Epigraphik*
ZPF	*Zeitschrift für philosophische Forschung*

Introduction

Sara Ahbel-Rappe

The legacy of John F. Finamore, professor emeritus of classics at the University of Iowa and president of the International Society for Neoplatonic Studies, precedes him. Over the course of decades, Finamore has organized international conferences, edited or coedited twelve volumes of collected essays as well as the *International Journal of the Platonic Tradition*, authored four volumes (three translations and an original monograph), served as the chief editor for the Brill Studies in Platonism, Neoplatonism and the Platonic Tradition Series, personally authored dozens of essays, supervised graduate dissertations, and above all inspired, mentored, and rallied scholars of Platonism literally all over the globe. The proliferation of scholarship on Neoplatonism witnessed in recent years, together with the publication of significant scholarly works and translations of ancient texts never before translated into English, owes no small credit to Finamore's consistent nurturing of this field, disseminating texts, and presiding over the International Society for Neoplatonic Studies, its meetings, publications, and membership. To celebrate Finamore's retirement and seventieth birthday, the following hopes to collect essays that reflect both his long-time research interests and the diversity of inspiration he fostered, gathering together work of senior and junior scholars on issues of Platonic psychology, epistemology, spirituality, and so on.

The essays in this volume range in subject matter over the many centuries of speculation on the nature of the soul within the Platonic tradition, from Plato's dialogues composed in the fourth century BCE to the early Academy and the late Neoplatonic period alongside even his reception in the Renaissance. Perhaps there is no other topic more central to this tradition and yet more variegated in its ramifications than the psyche, an entity that proves both elusive and ubiquitous in the texts of Platonism. The psyche does duty for what today we would call the mind as the seat of intelligence, knowledge, and sentience in the individual person, but it also is conceived as an immortal substance, source of life, and intelligence for a living cosmos. Thus in the texts of Plato we encounter the soul as both macrocosmic and microcosmic: as the animating force of the universe as a whole as well as the source of competing drives within humans beings who transmigrate over the course of innumerable possible embodiments. Although Plato defines the soul in the *Phaedrus*, calling it the *arche* (the beginning, the principle) of motion (246a3), in fact in various other texts he uses a series of contradictory terms to unpack its nature. From the *Phaedo* to the *Republic* new images emerge, demanding that we ask, Is the soul tripartite or simple, winged or mired in the dirt, cosmic or terrestrial, unchanging and akin to the Forms or driven by sensibility markedly witnessed in our sexual and corporeal appetites? and so on. Some ancient Platonists asked questions about the soul that still might resonate today: What are the parameters of knowledge, of healing, of performing gender? Others concerned themselves with issues that are very difficult for contemporary academics to approach, as the concerns reach past our own accepted worldviews: What is the so-called (ethereal) vehicle of the soul; when is the best time to reincarnate; how does the soul relate to other ontological principles such as the so-called indefinite dyad; how does one effect the elevation of the soul in ritual practices? Further complicating the question of the soul are the Platonic tradition's competing exegeses of Plato's dialogues, which were the subject of specific commentaries made in late antiquity, or of topical treatises that embraced doctrinal and interpretive questions. The consensus over what exactly constitutes Platonism seems wanting.

As we saw above, Platonism extends from the dialogues of Plato through to the Renaissance. Given this expanse of time, it can be helpful to recognize distinct periods of development within which the interpretation and application of Plato's views about the soul evolved, sometimes beyond recognition. Thus we can delineate the period right after Plato's death, the early Academy under the direction of Speusippus and then Xenocrates, as well as the Hellenistic Academy of Polemon. Although the doctrines formulated under the early scholarchs offer radical interpretations of the original dialogues, most of this work is unfortunately lost and survives only in the form of fragments. Imperial Platonism, roughly spanning the first to second centuries CE (usually referred to as Middle Platonism and represented in this volume by the Chaldean Oracles, Apuleius, and Moderatus), often fuses indigenous religious traditions with Platonist mysticism, allegory, and/or doctrine. Neoplatonism, often thought to begin with the writings of Plotinus (d. 270 CE) and ending in the late antique Academies of Proclus (ca. 540 CE) and of Damascius (fl. 525 CE) represents the highwater mark of Platonist speculative metaphysics and results in a proliferation of commentarial works. We can also recognize various representatives of Christian Platonism whose thought developed right alongside polytheist Platonists. In this volume, the earliest such theologian is Bardaisan (d. 220 CE).

Owing to the variegated nature of the texts, authors, and questions pursued, and stemming directly from the complexity of the soul as it appears in Plato's original texts, the essays in this volume reflect the depth of the controversies and debates within the tradition. We have grouped them thematically with the understanding that the emergent differences of perspective will allow the reader to come to a multidimensional and multifaceted appreciation of the topics. Accordingly, to bring out the richness and polymorphism of Platonist work on the soul, the author's voices encountered in this volume have not been limited by editorial directions and represent the views of the individual authors of these essays. Necessarily, then, within each subsection, the reader will encounter perspectives that challenge, complement, respond to, but ultimately coexist within a pluralistic interpretive enterprise. There are five parts: (1) "Madness, Irrationality, and Healing"; (2) "Ontologies and Epistemologies"; (3) "Hermeneutics and Methodologies"; (4) "Ritual Contexts, Inspiration, and Embodied Practices"; and (5) "Christian and Pagan Perspectives." In what follows, we adumbrate the themes developed as well as the rationale for each section.

Part 1, "Madness, Irrationality, and Healing," treats a fundamental dichotomy deployed within Plato's psychic taxonomies, the question of what belongs to the rational soul and what belongs to the irrational soul. Not wholly distinctive to Platonism but certainly highly characteristic of Platonic psychology is the thesis that this dichotomy inheres within different parts of the mind and that both are connate. At the same time, Plato's own texts together with the tradition affirm that rationality per se can confine the soul to narrower channels of experience. In addition to the valorization of rationality, Plato and his successors celebrate moments of heightened awareness as *mania*, as hyperrationality or suprarationality, even as ecstasy. Lloyd P. Gerson's "Irrationality in the Platonic Tradition" begins this segment with a discussion of the paradox inherent in Plato's positing irrationality of beings (i.e., human beings) who at the same time,

Plato affirms, are intrinsically rational and whose rationality affords them a unique nisus toward their own good. In attributing the thesis of fungible subjectivity to Plato's psychology, Gerson points the way forward to issues involving embodiment and the true identity of the person that will challenge subsequent thinkers. We might then view Suzanne Stern-Gillet's essay, "Plato on the Manic Soul," as the complement to Gerson's opening bid. Stern-Gillet also explores the paradoxes associated with irrationality and uses the generic term *mania* as a catch-all device that signals, paradoxically, both mental illness and vice. In pursuing the competing threads of culpability versus disease for one's vicious states, Stern-Gillet hits on the example of Oedipus's overweening anger in the murder of his own father, nicely dovetailing with Gerson's own discussion of Oedipus's self-contradictory intellectual responses to the Delphic Oracle's warning of the impending patricide. Together, these essays demonstrate the complexities of Plato's moral psychology in ways that are rarely explored in contemporary analytic literature. Svetla Slaveva-Griffin's "Plato and Plotinus on Healing: Why Does the Art of Medicine Matter?" in turn responds to Stern-Gillet's discussion of mental illness to focus on mental healing. Her approach resonates with the previous essays as it negotiates the implications of Platonist dualism on models of medicine. Does philosophy alone suffice to restore the patient's health? Slaveva-Griffin's novel approach involves reading Plato's *Charmides* alongside the last chapters of Plotinus's treatise "Problems concerning the Soul" (*Enn.* 4.4), where Plotinus discusses the susceptibility of souls to harm from external factors. The subtle interaction between psychic and physiological changes, the normative health of the cosmos as a whole, and the entangled skein of causal direction all are enlisted to explore the art of medicine as an auxiliary to philosophy proper. The final essay, John Dillon's "Intellect Sober and Intellect Drunk: Some Reflections on the Plotinian Ascent Narrative," also studies Plotinus (*Enn.* 6.7, "On the One and on the Good") in light of the implications of mind-body dualism. Dillon facilitates this discussion by placing the visionary or mystical experiences described by Plotinus alongside contemporary narratives offered by those who have had near-death experiences or otherwise, in the words of Slaveva-Griffin, undergone liminal states that border between life and death.

Taken together, the first section allows us to glimpse Platonists' subtle inquiries into the relationship between mind and body (or embodiment, in the words of Gerson). Part 2, "Ontologies and Epistemologies," then surveys aspirational ways of knowing and being, highlighting the psyche's negotiations with affiliated realities, that is, objects of knowledge, Forms, other minds, or even stations of being. We begin with two essays that set forth the parameters of what constitutes the soul in Plato's dialogues, Luc Brisson's "Soul in Plato" and Van Tu's "Is the Soul a Form? The Status of the Soul in the Final Argument of the *Phaedo*, Again." Brisson offers a reading of Plato's psyche *in toto* by relying on the mythical passages of *Phaedr.* 245–248 and of the *Timaeus*, an approach he defends by arguing that only myth is capable of conveying the soul's nature, which is neither a Form nor a material object but an intermediary between the two kinds of reality. Agreeing with Tu, Brisson asserts that only Soul as a whole is immortal, while individual souls must be recycled every ten thousand years, a process that allows Soul to function as the repository of individual karma and thus belong to a moral vision of the universe as a whole. Brisson's essay, which details the processes of transmigration and birth, operates as a touchstone for other essays in the volume that allude to the ontological status of the soul and its cosmic and temporal journeying. Tu's essay belongs to the analytic camp of Plato scholarship, yet it agrees remarkably with many of Brisson's major conclusions, as we saw: that the individual soul is not necessarily immortal and that the soul is something other than a Form. Tu and Brisson leave us with the question of what Plato means when he theorizes soul as "something else" (ἄλλο τι), but both remind us that modern two-substance dualisms do not easily map onto the Platonic construction of the soul. The next two essays, those of Kevin Corrigan, "Against the Stereotype of Abstract Knowledge in Plato: Scientific Perception or Sharp Seeing in the Middle and Late Dialogues," and of Robert Berchman, "Of Orioles, Owls, and Aviaries: Rethinking the Problem of Other Minds," delineate some of the same questions raised by Brisson and Tu: whereas those essays ask about the murky status of the soul as an ontological entity, Corrigan and Berchman ask about the soul's knowledge. Corrigan's essay joins a chorus of contemporary Plato scholars (Mary-Louise Gill, Gail Fine, and Charles Kahn) who emphasize the model of scientific, or at least natural, philosophy in examining the epistemology of even so-called Middle dialogues such as the *Republic* and *Phaedo*. Berchman surveys the Platonic tradition as a whole but starts with Plato's *Theaetetus* and asks whether Platonic epistemology can solve the problem of knowing other minds. Both Corrigan and Berchman thus try to bring ancient epistemology into dialogue with contemporary issues in epistemology, such as knowledge of the natural world (Corrigan) or the problems of solipsism that might be entailed by forms of idealism

(Berchman). The late John D. Turner wished his essay, perhaps the last piece written by this prolific scholar of Gnosticism and Platonism, to be included in this volume in honor of Professor Finamore. "Initial Stages on the Ladder of Ascent to the Intelligible World: The Metempsychotic Aeons in Zostrianos and Related Sethian Literature" fathoms the unfathomable realms traversed by one "Zostrianos," a psychonaut whose experiences of the stations of the real, revealed in a mystical ascent, once more complicate the dichotomies that are often reduced to rigid taxonomies between the material and spiritual worlds. Zostrianos, Allogenes, and Marsanes, known as the Sethian Platonizing Treatises, together add an enriched vision of dimensions of human consciousness and experience that even the great visionary Plotinus has trouble countenancing, as Turner shows.

Altogether the essays in the section on ontology and epistemology run the gamut from the mythical to the natural but everywhere show that the realm of the soul is distinctive, irreducible, even sui generis, and thus essential to the complex legacy of Platonism. In part 3, "Hermeneutics and Methodologies," we enter into the sphere of what it means to read Plato. Central to the project of late antique Platonism, Platonists over the centuries devised sometimes elaborate ways of entering into Plato's dialogues not only in terms of their linguistic or even argumentative structure but rather in the terms of a reification wherein the remarkable literary devices of the dialogues are conceived as coming alive in the world as such and effecting the profound transformations that Platonists undertake as students of the tradition. Danielle A. Layne's "The Indefinite Dyad and The Platonic Equality of the Male and Female Ruling Principles" reveals this seamless dynamism between the world of the dialogues and the world of the individual, resonating as it does within the multiple registers of gender, metaphysics, and feminism. Layne invokes the metaphysical principle of the earliest Academy, the Dyad, and shows how this structure informs and skews the metaphysics of essence as revealed in individuals, in philosophical discourse, and in philosophical method. The soul emerges as the human equivalent of the Dyad, with the implication that every soul partakes of both members of any potentially opposing or dualistic distinctions. Harold Tarrant's "Soul in the Earliest Multilevel Interpretations of the *Parmenides*" is a detective story, among other things. It also provides a statistical stylistic analysis of Porphyry's paraphrases of first-century philosopher Moderatus of Gades, whose Pythagorean-influenced interpretation of Plato's *Parmenides* initiates the major interpretive development for all subsequent Platonist readings of the dialogue. In particular, Tarrant shows how competing interpretations of the Parmenidean hypotheses resulted in distinctive views about the soul's status as a metaphysical principle. Sara Ahbel-Rappe's piece, "Apuleius's Platonic Laboratory," discusses another second-century philosopher, Apuleius of Madaurus. His novel, *The Golden Ass*, offers a reading of Plato's *Phaedrus* that translates the famous myth of the soul into a vivid narrative and in this way offers the reader insight into how to engage the myth. John F. Finamore's "Proclus Interprets Hesiod: The Procline Philosophy of the Soul" derives from his studies on Proclus's *Commentary on the Republic*, specifically the thirteenth essay of this commentary, where Proclus embarks on an eighty-page discussion of the discourse of the Muses in book 8 of the *Republic*. Finamore's aim is to illustrate a principle of Neoplatonic interpretation, wherein disparate texts (in this case, Orphic texts and Hesiod's *Works and Days*) are recruited into a Platonizing allegory. His article concentrates on Proclus's contemplative reading of Plato's myth of the metals. Each of these essays is concerned with Platonist hermeneutics, which, to the outsider, might threaten a vicious circle, since Platonists assume the truth of Platonic doctrine and then seek to discover realities (the Dyad, the incarnation of the soul, the third hypothesis of the *Parmenides*, the composition of the soul based on its metallic rank) that correspond to the texts, often mythical, often only mentioned in passing. Yet what appears to be a closed hermeneutic process breaks open in the contemplative praxes also integrated into the exegetical productions of Platonism.

Part 4, "Ritual Contexts, Inspiration, and Embodied Practices," indeed offers such a complement to purely textual methodologies, exemplifying just how imbricated theory is with practice in the Platonic traditions of what we might call soul work. The first essay in the section is by Crystal Addey and Jay Bregman: "Julian and Sallust on the Ascent of the Soul and Theurgy," where we see the fusion between ritual and text realized in the theurgic hymns of the Emperor Julian and of Sallust. Theurgy, in the works of Julian and of Sallust, is at once rooted in Platonic conceptions of the soul's ascent to the divine and incorporates traditional Mediterranean religions and myth. Addey and Bregman read Julian and Sallust as esoteric ritualists who, perhaps paradoxically, invent systems of mythic interpretation that are ideologically poised to find popular appeal. Dirk Baltzly and Dorian Gieseler Greenbaum's essay, "The Optimal Times for Incarnation: Let Me Count the Ways," treats, as does Finamore's, Proclus's *Commentary on the Republic* (book 2). They demonstrate the intricate relationship between

exegesis and practice by showing how the failure of the Guardians to calculate the nuptial number at R.546d2 is related by late antique Platonists to
astrological calculations, in particular, the katarchic time, or astrological
configuration at a child's conception. Yet at the same time, the astrological
figurations are shown by Proclus to adhere to Pythagorean cosmological
number systems, so that Proclus's reading of the nuptial number relies
both on astrological practice and on ancient interpretive traditions that
focus on Platonic numerology. The upshot is that Proclus is able to explain
what goes wrong in the Guardians' calculations such that Kallipolis is destined (it is in the stars) to come to an end. Elizabeth Hill's "Prophets and
Poets: Plato and the Daimonic Nature of Poetry" begins with intuitions
that might seem more familiar to students of Neoplatonism concerning
Plato's possible critique of the limits of discursive reason but returns the
reader to an early context, Plato's *Ion* and its treatment of poetry. For Hill,
the *Ion*'s theory of rhapsodic possession shares much in common with
the *Symposium*: just as Eros is a daimon, mediating between humans and
gods, so poetry itself reveals a daimonic influence and must be understood as a gift of the gods, facilitating human assimilation to the divine.
Therefore, Hill's essay once more illustrates the links between exegesis and
ritual, here highlighting the ritual aspect of poetic *techne* in the *Ion* and
showing its implications for the overall status of poetry in Plato's corpus
as a whole. In all of this ritual—in theurgic rites of elevation, in astrological observations, in visionary exercises, or in inspired poetry—exegesis of
Plato's texts is married with techniques that extend human seeing beyond
the immediacy of submersion in the physical-temporal stretch that seems
to confine the soul.

If in the last section of the volume, part 5, "Christian and Pagan Perspectives," we consider polytheist religiosity and set Platonism within that
framework, it is equally true that the first centuries of Christianity were
also profoundly shaped by Platonist doctrines of the soul. The first two
essays in this section discuss the soul's identity and its relationship to the
divine, understood in Christian Platonism as Logos or Nous, the eternal
wisdom in which even human souls have a share. Ilaria L. E. Ramelli's
"The Soul in Bardaisan, Origen, and Evagrius: Between Unfolding and
Subsumption" surveys the origin and destiny of the soul in three Christian
Platonists: Bardaisan of Edessa, Origen of Alexandria, and Evagrius. In a
development that might be considered an application of the *Phaedrus*'s
myth of the soul, these theologians understand soul to be a manifestation
or unfolding of intellect on descent into the body. The reverse is also to be

expected, namely that the soul's destiny is ultimately subsumption into a truer and more divine identity. In Sarah Klitenic Wear's essay, titled "Proclus, Hermias, and Cyril of Alexandria on the Embodied Soul," the soul's irrational dimensions, its emotions and desires, are shown to belong to the complex essence of the soul. In Cyril's *Scholia on the Incarnation*, we find that these same irrational elements, the emotions and passions, belong intrinsically to Christ as the incarnation of the Logos, such that they aid, rather than counter, the deification not just of this one particular entity but all of human beings. The final essay in this section, Gregory Shaw's "Christian and Pagan Neoplatonism," challenges the fundamental claim that Christian Platonists can truly be Platonists. Despite the evidence that both Ramelli and Wear present, that at least some Christian Platonists fully affirm the possibility that the human being is divinized, not ultimately separate from God, not a mere creature who must somehow call on divine grace, Shaw points to the Augustinian version of Platonism. Here, according to Shaw, we see a dogmatic formulation of a truth that must conform to orthodoxy, a way of thinking that is totally inimical to the Platonic practices of aporia. Further, as Shaw so vividly states, in Augustine's Christian Platonism, we find a God whose grace redeems us from the sin of being human, embodied and fallen. But the genuinely Platonic orientation to the human condition, the human soul, sees this state as a gift, an opening onto divinity, an expression of creative intelligence that never, even in the midst of embodiment, loses its true identity.

Throughout the course of centuries, Platonist discourses about the soul are not merely doctrinal deliverances or abstract arguments. Instead, the essays in this volume trace the Platonic legacy of the soul as a deliverance about the true purpose of human life. Not all Platonists would confine themselves to Plotinus's succinct but eloquent exhortation that "our concern is not merely to be sinless, but to be God" (*Enn.* 1.2), but all Platonists agree that the human soul—as it journeys within birth and death, in knowing and in all forms of experience, in its ultimate identity as no other than divine intelligence—matters profoundly.

Part 1
Madness, Irrationality, and Healing

Irrationality in the Platonic Tradition

Lloyd P. Gerson

Let us start with an operational definition of *rationality*: the ability to make and understand universal statements. According to this definition, someone (principally a member of the species *Homo sapiens*) who lost or never had this ability would be deemed to be irrational. This sense of the word *irrational* has very little relevance to the great debates in antiquity about deviant or vicious human behavior. I will leave it aside. But that leaves us with the very considerable puzzle of how someone *with* this ability, that is, with this ability activated, can be said to be irrational. After all, human beings have rational souls. That is the kind of souls we have. To be or to act irrationally seems, at least on the face of it, to be an impossibility, much as it would be an impossibility to be or to act as an animal would act that does not have a rational soul. If a person were to hop around on all fours and eat only lettuce, he would not thereby become a rabbit; he would only be a stupid human acting like a rabbit.

It is often said that Plato introduced irrationality into human behavior by his tripartitioning of the soul.[1] Thus, in the *Republic*, the calculative part of the soul (τὸ λογιστικόν) is distinguished from the spirited part (τὸ θυμοειδές) and from the appetitive part (τὸ ἐπιθυμητικόν), the source of appetitive behavior (see *Resp.* 4 [436a–439c5]). This "part" (μέρος) or "kind" (εἶδος) of the soul is indeed said to be ἀλόγιστόν, which is widely

---

1. See, e.g., Terry Penner, "The Historical Socrates and Plato's Early Dialogues: Some Philosophical Questions," in *New Perspectives on Plato, Modern and Ancient*, ed. Julia Annas and Christopher Rowe (Cambridge: Harvard University Press, 2003), 189–212, esp. 194. Eric R. Dodds just assumes that tripartition marks the introduction of irrationality (occasionally called by Dodds "non-rationality") into Plato's philosophy. See Dodds, *The Greeks and the Irrational* (Berkeley: University of California Press, 1966), ch. 7, "Plato, the Irrational Soul, and the Inherited Conglomerate."

held to be translated correctly as "irrational," indicating, roughly, that it is bereft of rationality or nonrational. Such a translation, however, is at best misleading, for in book 9 Plato gives us as a paradigm case of some-one driven by his appetites, a lover of money.[2] To justify calling a lover of money irrational in the sense of having no rationality, one would have to explain how someone could love money without understanding what money is, that is, without being sufficiently rational to grasp the universal, money. In fact, only rational beings can love money. So, how shall we char-acterize the individual, such as the wretched Leontius, who acts counter to the deliverances of the calculative part of his soul? If he is indeed irratio-nal, it would seem to be in a sense different from that according to which he could not even conceptualize the object of his appetite.

Clearly, what Leontius is doing is acting counter to a standard of behav-ior as determined by his calculative faculty. He thinks that he ought not to gaze on the naked bodies even though he wants to do so. The irrationality apparently consists in acting consciously against a normative standard of some sort, even if it is a standard that would not be universally shared. Many of us would like to think that anyone who disagrees with us is irra-tional, but again we typically, ruefully or not, agree that this is not so. It is not irrational in any sense for A to disagree with B. No, the acting counter to a standard of behavior must be the acting against *one's own* standard of behavior. As puzzling as this may be, it seems downright impossible if we add the Platonic premise that everyone, without qualification, acts to achieve their own good.[3] So, if my standard of behavior is a rule or

---

2. See Plato, *Resp.* 9 (555a1–6, 562b1–2), where the appetite for money is for a good, instrumental to the acquisition of other goods. Many English translators (e.g., Shorey, Cornford, Bloom, Sterling and Scott, Grube, Reeve) succumb to the tempta-tion to translate ἀλόγιστόν as "irrational." Rowe has "unreasoning," which is slightly better. An exception is Allen, who, more accurately in my view, translates it as "unre-flective." The temptation is owing to a contextual ambiguity in a term that is contrasted with a term, λογιστικόν, that is most frequently translated as "rational" or "calcula-tive." To be noncalculative is not necessarily to be irrational or nonrational. Hence the ambiguity. When the terms *rational* and *calculative* are treated as synonymous, the tendency is to take its opposite as indicating an absence of rationality. The term ἄνους ("mindless") can conceal a similar ambiguity. See Plato, *Phaedr.* 257a2.

3. See Plato, *Resp.* 6 (505d5–9). This passage, strictly speaking, says that while most people would select the seemingly beautiful or just even if they were really not so, no one would select merely apparent goods. The question is left open whether "real goods" could be real even if others were adversely affected by one possessing them.

precept formulated to guide behavior aimed at achieving my own good, it does not seem possible that I could, while acknowledging or asserting this standard, act contrary to it. And yet, it seems discouragingly possible that that is exactly what happens all the time. Anyone who has ever been tempted to do something that they think is not in their own best interest and nevertheless does it presents living testimony to the reality of the phenomenon known in antiquity as incontinence or weakness of the will (ἀκρασία). To deny that people sometimes succumb to temptation seems about as plausible as the denial of the reality of consciousness. One must add—if additional confirmation is necessary—that to deny the reality of giving in to temptation means also the denial of the reality of resisting temptation (ἐγκράτεια), since the idea of resisting only makes sense if it is at least possible that one failed to resist.[4] A denial such as this seems to amount to such an impoverishment of our conceptual framework for dealing with human psychology that, wanting to avoid such impoverishment, we might perhaps be open to Plato's radical explanation for the possibility of acratic behavior.

The tripartitioning of the soul, which is the key to Plato's strategy for explaining the above behavior, is challengeable from a number of perspectives. But the biggest challenge comes from the fact that the standard of behavior against which the acratic acts is not the only standard of behavior involved. For, say, the lover of money, who is sufficiently rational to be able to understand what money is, is, too, acting according to a standard of behavior. That standard is effectively the major premise in a practical syllogism. That premise is, approximately, that the acquisition of money is good for me. In this case, it is not clear why one should follow the standard that prohibits the action as opposed to the standard that enjoins it. When faced with conflicting standards of behavior, it is far from obvious which one ought to be selected. In the case of Leontius, his thinking that gazing on dead, naked, corpses is ignoble is up against a standard according to which gazing on these corpses is a good thing for him to do because it is pleasurable in some way. It is a mistake to say that his precipitous or impetuous behavior consisting of corpse gazing is irrational because there is no standard according to which he is acting. For if this were the case, he would not be acting at all but rather moving reflexively. And in that case,

---

4. Oscar Wilde's quip, "I can resist anything except temptation," is amusing because temptation is the *only* thing we can resist within our own thinking processes.

he would not be an acratic. There would be no real conflict between his reason and his appetite.

How, then, is it possible to believe something is bad for you and at the same time also believe that it is not bad for you? In fact, it is not possible, as Aristotle explains in detail in his *Metaphysics* (see *Metaph.* Γ 4 [1008a30–b31]). It is, however, apparently possible to believe a proposition and to act as if the proposition were false. Consider Oedipus, who evidently believes the oracle's pronouncement that he is going to kill his father and marry his mother. But if he believes that, what point is there in acting on the belief that he can escape the oracle? After all, the oracle's pronouncement is not conditional; for example, you will kill your father and marry your mother unless you escape. By contrast, if Oedipus did not believe the oracle, then why did he leave town? The irrationality of Oedipus does not consist in his acting in the way that a nonrational animal acts. Far from it. It consists in acting as if he were two distinct persons: the one who believes that he is doomed and the one who believes that he can act to avoid his doom. But how is it possible for one person to act as if he were two?

The Platonic answer to this question depends on seeing how persons are identified. Plato never maintains the crude identification of a person with an ἄνθρωπος, a human being composed of a body and a soul. He does not do this not just because souls are immortal and we are identified with our souls alone, but because human beings, like everything else in the sensible world, are constantly changing. If it is true that Plato identified the person with the soul, that simply shifts the problem into one of identifying the soul. A soul is identified minimally by a state (πάθος) and a subject of that state. That state can be a cognitive state or an affective state such as an emotion or an appetite or a sensation. In the case of the cognitive state, there is in addition always an intentional object helping us to identify the subject.[5] For example, there is a subject who believes that 2 + 2 = 4 and a subject who believes that 2 + 2 = 5. There is a subject who believes that his good is achieved by acting virtuously and a subject who believes that it is achieved by acting viciously. There is a subject who desires to eliminate a sensation of pain and believes that doing so-and-so

---

5. There is a case to be made that for Plato, all embodied states of which we are aware are cognitive states, and all cognitive states have intentional objects. If I am in pain, the intentional object is not the pain but rather me-in-pain. If there is no intentional object, then I cannot be aware of the state, e.g., a state of my autonomic nervous system. I will not pursue this claim here.

will achieve that goal. And there is a subject who believes that the pain must be borne in the light of other considerations. What all these subjects have in common is their ephemeral nature. The subject who desires to eliminate the pain is gone when the pain is gone. The subject who has a false belief is gone when she comes to have the contradictory belief (*Meno* 97e6–98a4). It may seem far-fetched to maintain that a person who has her false belief corrected has become a different person. But that is the case only if one finds it difficult to separate the person from the composite of body and soul, the human being.

Because the ephemeral subjects of the cognitive, affective, appetitive, and sensitive states are identified by these states (and, where appropriate) by their intentional objects, their commitment, we might say, to their real as opposed to apparent good is fundamentally compromised by the fact that these states are presented to oneself as constitutive of one's good.[6] At least this is the case insofar as one acts to achieve one's own good. To Leontius, it appears that corpse gazing is good because he has an appetite to do so, and what appetites do is present their satisfaction as the means to one's good.[7] I feel hungry and I think that my good is achieved by satisfying that hunger. Oedipus is in a troubled emotional state, and he believes that eliminating this state requires him to flee. When he flees, he is a subject or person not in contact with the person who is the subject of the belief that he is doomed. That, thinks Plato, is what embodiment does to a person. It shatters him into a myriad of ephemeral subjects, all of whom are rational subjects manifesting a rational soul, but none of whom

---

6. In *Alc.* 1 (131b5), self-knowledge is identified with being self-controlled (σώφρων). As one increasingly identifies with the subject of one's rational faculty, control over the ephemeral subjects of the appetites increases until the point when they are completely under rational control.

7. It is sometimes claimed (e.g., by Irwin) that Plato's explanation for the phenomenon of incontinence involves the introduction of "good-independent desires." See Terence Irwin, *Plato's Ethics* (Oxford: Oxford University Press, 1995), 223–43. That is, while the calculative faculty tries to determine what is good for the person, the appetitive faculty acts on desires that are independent of that determination. I think this is a mistake, easily made by overlooking a distinction between the appetite as a state and the awareness of the appetites, which is cognitive and, since it is the awareness of a rational animal, always oriented to what is good (see *Phileb.* 35b3–4; see also 41c4–7). An appetite qua state is indeed only related to its object without consideration of whether the object is good (see *Resp.* 4 [437d9–438a2]). But the desire to satisfy the appetite is a desire for a good, namely, the satisfaction of the appetite.

are able to guarantee the identity of what appears to them to be good with their real good. Even an ordinary, virtuous embodied person for whom what appears to be good is in fact good cannot change this calculus. What is really good for him is not entailed by what appears to be good for him; these are adventitiously identified, like Justin Trudeau and the present prime minister of Canada.

At least part of the reason Plato radically separates belief (δόξα) and knowledge (ἐπιστήμη) is that *no* belief state can guarantee that what appears to be good for oneself is really so. Even a *true* belief that something is good for oneself, though that belief logically entails that that something is good for oneself, does not psychologically guarantee it. The truth of the belief is not internal to the belief. What makes it true has nothing to do with the content of the belief as such. Knowledge, however, as we learn in the *Republic*, is only possible when one has connected all intelligible objects with the superintelligible object that is the Idea of the Good (see *Resp.* 6 [511b2–c2]). The feature of this extraordinary claim that I want to focus on here is that knowledge of one's own good is here seen to be identical with knowledge of the Good. That is, one's own good is insepa-rable from the good of everyone and everything else. Stated otherwise, it is not possible to achieve what is good for me by doing something that is not good for someone else any more than it is possible for me to arrive at the correct answer to a mathematical problem different from another answer to the same problem given by someone else. One of us is wrong. Achieving one's own good is therefore not a zero-sum game. And though this does not, unfortunately, give us a straightforward answer to specific problems in moral behavior, it does give us a substantial guideline for determining nonstarters.

Only the person with knowledge reliably gets what he really wants, namely, his own good. But his own good is identical with the Good. The way that one possesses that is by knowing all that is knowable. The stan-dard of behavior is just that, the Idea of the Good. The ephemeral subjects can at best offer up an apparent good for the consideration of the sub-ject possessed of the knowledge of the real good. Indeed, an embodied subject with this knowledge is still weighted down by pursuing apparent goods, but in her case this apparent good is presented in the light of the knowledge of the real good, and if there is still no guarantee of matching these up, there is the best chance of doing so that any embodied person could have. Instantiations or manifestations or expressions of the Idea of the Good—alternative ways of indicating participation—will still appear to one who knows as good. It is just that the appearance will be veridical, not nonveridical.

Plato uses the term ἄλογον principally to indicate explicit or implicit behavior that violates a logical standard.[8] For example, it is irrational (ἄλογον) to think that if you cure sickness in the eyes, you will not be left with healthy eyes (*Gorg.* 496b1). Or, it is irrational to say that a part of the Form of Largeness makes something Large (which is what we would seemingly be led to say if many things that are large participates in Largeness; *Parm.* 131d2). Let us note that the violation or disregard for logic here is different from the disregard of a standard of behavior found in the acratic.[9] Leontius is not cured by getting him to admit that he ought not to gaze. He *already* accepts that. By contrast, Socrates frequently gets his interlocutors to cede their position by pointing out to them its illogical, that is, irrational nature.[10]

Plato believes that it is a permanent endowment of living beings with rational souls that they desire their own good (see *Resp.* 6 [505d5–9]). Most people most of the time are satisfied with the apparently beautiful and the apparently just, but no one is satisfied with anything but real goods. Someone might believe that what is in fact only an apparent good is her own real good. But if it turns out not to be her real good, then she will no longer desire it. This seems to be a straightforward implication of this passage. But then Plato adds,

> Every soul pursues [good] and does everything on account of this, divining [ἀπομαντευομένη] it to be something [τι εἶναι], but is puzzled about it and is not able to grasp adequately what it is or to have the sort of stable beliefs it has about other things, and for this reason it fails to acquire the benefit, if any, that these things have. (*Resp.* 6 [505e1–5; Grube and Reeve, slightly modified])

There is no doubt that what Socrates is talking about here is the Idea of the Good, which less than a page earlier is said to be that which makes

---

8. See, e.g., *Phaed.* 62b2, c6, 68d12; *Theaet.* 199a3, 203d6; *Parm.* 131d2, 144b3; *Gorg.* 496b1, 519e3; *Resp.* 10 (609d9–11).

9. Indeed, in the case of Leontius, the term used is ἀλόγιστόν, not ἄλογον.

10. Vlastos made a great deal of Socrates's search for "elenctic knowledge." See Gregory Vlastos, *Socrates: Ironist and Moral Philosopher* (Ithaca, NY: Cornell University Press, 1991), 107–31. This is knowledge acquired by showing the falsity (usually logical falsity) of his interlocutors' positions.

just deeds and so on beneficial (*Resp.* 6 [505a2–4]). So, people want what is good for themselves. They intuit that there is a Good that makes anything really good for them, but they are puzzled about it. But without knowing this Good, they are unable to acquire the benefit or goodness that they pursue.

I would like to suggest that Plato's use of the word *divine* (ἀπομαντευο-μένη) should be treated just the way Socrates treats the natural ability of rational beings to mentally see a logical mistake. It is irrational to maintain a position when you have been shown that that position could not logically be true. Analogously, if you have divined that the Good is something and that it is the Good that makes activities and states and possessions good, then it is irrational to act as if this were not so. It is irrational to think that, in pursuing my real good, I can do so by simultaneously instantiating the Good and failing to instantiate it or, in other words, instantiate its opposite. This is exactly what tyrants think they can do with impunity and, more to the point, with complete success in achieving their goal of having what is really good for themselves.

Why is Plato so confident that everyone divines that the Good is something? The implicit argument seems to go like this. Everyone wants their real, not apparent, good. But the mere fact that something can appear to be good even though it is not means that one cannot infer that it is good just because it appears to be so. So, our own self-reflective awareness that we seek our real good, not what appears to be our real good, is sufficient for us to be able to divine that the good is something. But why suppose further that the good that we seek is provided by a superordinate Idea of the Good? Because for anything we propose for ourselves as the real good, we can ask whether it is so or merely apparent. For example, if we are hedonistically inclined, we can ask whether pleasure is our real good. But this is not the question of whether pleasure is pleasant but whether pleasure participates in the Good, that is, whether pleasure is beneficial because it participates in the Good. We can continue to ask the exact sort of question for anything we propose to ourselves as good. But this question cannot be answered substantively, so to speak, by adducing some definite property or essence which makes things good. That is why the Idea of the Good has to be "beyond οὐσία" (*Resp.* 6 [509b5–9]). Because it is beyond οὐσία, it has to be unique; otherwise it, along with a putative second Good, would have to have a property or nature that distinguished it from the other. But in that case, the Good would be over and above the putative two Goods, and that would be the real Good.

Everyone divines that there is a Good. Since we desire its real instantiation in our lives, to act as if we did not believe that the Good were something and that it is not instantiated in our lives by instantiating its opposite anywhere is as irrational as someone who believes that something is destroyed by an evil that does not belong to it or someone who believes that what makes someone brave is cowardly fear.[11] An interesting question naturally arises. How is this sort of irrationality related to the irrationality of the acratic? The acratic is irrational because he acts as if his belief that not acting is good for him were not true. But as we have seen, his belief that not acting is good for him does not entail that it really is good for him not to act. He may, after all, just be a neurotic acratic, tempted to act against what he incorrectly thinks is his own good. If, however, someone, such as the successful graduates of Plato's philosophy school, knew the Good and so knew that his own good and the Good were identical, then he would be least likely to act acratically because he would be least likely ever to identify himself with the subject of the appetites whose fulfillment is bad for himself, simply because they are bad, not good.

This account still leaves us with the problem of how an embodied soul is supposed to have access to the eternal truths, the disregard of which is irrational. In book 10 of the *Republic*, Socrates says,

> Yet our recent argument and others as well compel us to believe that the soul is immortal. But to see the soul as it is in truth, we must not study it as it is while it is maimed by its association with the body and other evils—which is what we were doing earlier—but as it is in its pure state, that's how we should study the soul, thoroughly and by means of logical reasoning. (*Resp.* 10 [611b9–c; Grube and Reeve])

From this we can infer, I think, that the embodied soul is in an impure state owing to embodiment. If one could "see" it in a disembodied state, one could see its true nature. Why does embodiment have this effect? The answer to this question will turn out also to be the answer to the question of how it is possible for a rational being to act irrationally.

The embodied soul has a dispersed or scattered essence (σχεδαστὴ οὐσία; see *Tim.* 37a5–6).[12] What this seems to mean, among other things, is

---

11. For these two examples see *Resp.* 10 (609d9–11); *Phaed.* 68d12.

12. See Banner, who nicely describes the point as "indeterminate identity." Nicholas Banner, *Philosophical Silence and the "One" in Plotinus* (Cambridge: Cambridge University Press, 2018), 190–92.

that the embodied soul is spread out among the various psychical faculties
and their subjects. Thus, the pure soul takes on the subjectivity of discursive thinking, or an appetite or a bodily sensation or an emotion, and so
on. When liberated from the body, this soul reverts to its original and true
nature, that of a subject of nonbodily activity. The principal and perhaps
only nonbodily activity is that of thought (see *Tim.* 90b–c).[13] So, we must
not suppose that embodiment, though it obviously involves the addition
of a body, does not do more than that. It also involves the multiplication
of subjects or selves, episodic and transient though they be. It produces
a psychological hall of mirrors. But the multiple subjects are, in all cases,
manifestations of a rational soul. The many times that Plato speaks about
controlling or resisting or succumbing to appetites are incorrectly assimilated to an interpersonal struggle. They are also incorrectly assimilated to
a struggle that one might have with a bodily state such as a melanoma or
a torn muscle. What in fact Plato is focusing on is an internal struggle in
a compromised immortal and rational soul owing to its embodiment. The
famous exhortations to "become immortal" and to "assimilate to god" are
not exhortations to become what we already are or to become something
other than what we are, namely, a god (see *Tim.* 90b6–c6; *Theaet.* 176b1–
2). They are exhortations to recover or to embrace our true identity, an
identity that we have lost because of embodiment.

An inclination to identify irrationality with the objective operation
of the parts of the soul other than τὸ λογιστικόν should also be resisted
by the recognition that the subjects of appetite and emotion are "parts"
of the rational soul. When the lower parts of the soul are said to "have
the same beliefs" (ὁμοδοξῶσι) as τὸ λογιστικόν, it is thought to follow that
the non-rational or irrational parts of the soul can have beliefs (see *Resp.*
4 [442c9–d2]; see also 9 [574d–e]; *Phaedr.* 255e–256a; *Tim.* 69d; *Leg.*
1 [644c–d, 645a]). No one who holds this view has, to my knowledge,
been able to explain how if A has the same belief as B, B can be held to
be rational while A not. It is not surprising that the subject of embodied states is a feeble rational agent, but it is a rational agent nonetheless.
An appetite itself cannot agree or disagree with anyone, except perhaps

---

13. In this passage, b3–4, we learn that if someone is engrossed in appetites, "all
his thoughts [τὰ δόγματα] are bound to become mortal." I take it that mortal thoughts
are the thoughts accompanying appetites including the conceptualization of the appetite, the identification of its object, and the means for satisfying it. The thoughts are
mortal because the subject of the thoughts is mortal, indeed, ephemeral.

metaphorically; but the subject of the appetite can. When the tyrant lusts after power and also thinks that lusting after power is a good thing, the "having the same belief" is unremarkable if disreputable. The reason we can call this an agreement is the divided subjectivity of the rational soul when embodied.

Incontinence is a dramatic example of the divided embodied self. But incontinence is not vice. Our account of irrationality, understood as acting as if a proposition were true at the same time as believing that it is false, should be able to explain vice too. It should also be able to explain the sort of self-delusion of an Oedipus or of the anonymous virtuous individual in *Republic* 10 who, given the opportunity to choose his next life, opts for the life of a tyrant. He does not do this because he is vicious—this is explicitly excluded by the text—or because he is acratic. He is self-deluded, the habitual state, it would seem, of one who is "without philosophy" (ἄνευ φιλοσοφίας, *Resp.* 10 [619c7–d1]). The subject matter of philosophy is, for Plato, the intelligible world. But the therapeutic value of philosophy is that it alone enables one to overcome the irrationality caused by embodiment.

Every subject of every embodied state thinks it has immediate and transparent access to its own identity. After all, what else could I be but the one who is doing or thinking or feeling whatever it is that I am doing or thinking or feeling now? Why is Plato so confident that persons are not after all just a collection of such subjects? Why think that the transitory subjects are not the real self? The short answer to this question is that the rational soul, as it takes up the subjectivity of embodied states, including the embodied state of discursive thinking, could not do what it does, namely, think practically, if it could not access the subject of theoretical thinking. And by *access* I mean being able to make and understand universal statements or, as I should prefer to say, cognize form universally. This is, I maintain, the true import of the doctrine of recollection that we find in *Meno* and *Phaedrus*. Being a subject of understanding, so to say, is a condition for the possibility of embodied thinking. As a result, we should have good hope of being able to discover that we are really the permanent subject of understanding and not any ephemeral subject of embodied states.[14]

---

14. As Plato says in *Phaedr.* 249b5–6, there could be no incarnation of a human being who did not possess a vision of Forms. See Aristotle, *Eth. Nic.* K 1178a7, who agrees that a human being is "especially" (μάλιστα) an intellect.

Irrationality inevitably arises when there is a confusion about subject identity. There are no doubt numerous avenues of explanation for the ubiquitous phenomenon of persons with strong religious or political or ethical convictions who regularly act in a way that is patently inimical to these. There is a gospel song the refrain of which is "You don't love God if you don't love your neighbor." The point of the song is that many people profess a love of God but in fact do not, as evidenced by the fact that they do not love their neighbors. It is hard to identify the problem here as incontinence or as vice. The Platonic analysis of this situation, which is more like that of Oedipus than it is like that of an acratic or a vicious individual, is of someone who believes that God commands the love of neighbors but who acts as if this were not true. *Why* someone would act in such a manner may ultimately be beyond explanation, which should not surprise us if we are really dealing with irrationality. In any case, the phenomenon is at least relatively clear. It is the phenomenon of two subjects that are in fact avatars of one subject. The two subjects are the one who believes in the divine commandment and the other who believes that acting in a nonloving way toward one's neighbors is the right way to act. The one subject of which the other two are avatars is the disembodied intellect, or at least, the intellect capable of being disembodied. In *this* subject there is no conflict, and indeed, there is no belief, only knowledge.

The operation of theoretical or disembodied rationality does not, of course, guarantee success. It is possible to embrace, against all efforts at dislodgement by others, a false universal claim. It may well be irrational in the normative sense to prefer money to love, but it is not irrational in the straightforward sense of rationality according to which only a rational animal could think that money is preferable to love. The embodied subject of thinking, the subject of the faculty of τὸ λογιστικόν, is in a way in the middle between the subject of a disembodied intellect and the subjects of the transitory bodily states. It aims to access the knowable or purely intelligible and apply this knowledge to our embodied lives. In the interstice between the embodied effort to access the knowable and the disembodied, knowing itself is exactly where philosophy operates, according to Plato.[15]

---

15. See Plato, *Resp.* 4 (439d1), where the resistance to appetite in the individual comes ἐκ λογισμοῦ, that is, from a process of practical reasoning. In practical reasoning, there must be a normative premise. It is philosophy that is tasked with arriving at correct normative premises. See 441b6–c2: τὸ ἀναλογισάμενον περὶ τοῦ βελτίονός τε καὶ χείρονος.

This is exactly what Plotinus points out when answering the question, "Where is the real 'we'?" (*Enn.* 1.1.7.16–24). The "we" is found in the subject of discursive thinking and above in the undescended intellect that is eternally contemplating eternal being.[16] Plotinus follows Plato in thinking that there are potentially two ways of being irrational. The first is when our discursive reasoning conflicts with the deliverances of intellect, as in a blatant violation of logic.[17] Oedipus seems to be an example of someone who makes an intellectual error, albeit a fairly subtle one. The second is when the subject of bodily states acts as if the deliverances of embodied discursive reasoning, that is, beliefs held to be true, were not in fact true.[18] The reason this second type of irrationality can occur at all is that we actually are the subjects of the appetitive and emotional states the satisfaction of which requires the operation of reason and the acquisition of beliefs, which, along with the desire, puts the agent at the threshold of action. Most people, most of the time, are sufficiently ignorant regarding who they really are that they act on beliefs arrived at in this way, even when the beliefs, formally speaking, contradict the beliefs that they have arrived at independently of appetites and emotions.

On a spectrum ranging from a technical error in logic to the utmost personal depravity, it is far from clear what moral responsibility amounts to. If "no one does wrong willingly" encapsulates the starting point for the explanation for irrational behavior, it is not even entirely clear what sort of scale of moral responsibility follows, although it is plausible that we should be held morally responsible for some types of behavior more than for others. Indeed, it is not obvious that the heinousness of the crime is an index of moral responsibility; a small lapse may in certain circum-

---

16. On the undescended intellect, see Plotinus, *Enn.* 3.4.3.24; 4.4.3.5–6, 12.3–4; 4.7.10.32–33, 13.1–3; 4.8.4.31–35, 8.8; 6.4.14.16–22; 6.7.5.26–29, 17.26–27; 6.8.6.41–43.

17. See, e.g., Plotinus, *Enn.* 1.2.1.23; 2.3.3.19, 4.1; 2.9.5.16; 3.1.4.13; 6.3.18.4.

18. See, e.g., Plotinus, *Enn.* 1.2.5.21–31. In this passage, Plotinus explains in vivid detail how a person, having ignoble bodily desires, might come to be ashamed when confronted with his own reasoning (see, e.g., 1.4.2.26; 1.8.4.6–12). Here are two examples of later Platonists whose account of irrationality is along the same lines: (1) Proclus, *In Alc.* 292.2–13 (Segonds), says that the irrational (ἄλογον) in the soul is that which is incapable of science (ἐπιστήμη), implying that the subject of appetites and emotions is, nevertheless, otherwise capable of cognition. (2) Simplicius, *In Epict.* 31.27–32.3, identifies the ἄλογον in us with a child who seeks gratification to the exclusion of any other motive. Education is directed to this child.

stances be more morally blameworthy than a larger one, particularly if the consequences of our behavior are considered. If anyone is going to be held morally responsible for anything—as opposed to being merely legally liable—the responsibility is going to have to be focused on something such as culpable ignorance, that is, ignorance of the conflict of beliefs between those that impel behavior and those that should form behavior's theoretical background. When we say of someone that "he should have known better," we are appealing not to laws of logic that any rational person can see or to one's own deliberative steps up to the threshold action; rather, we are appealing to the fact that "everyone divines that the Good is something," where this intuition entails the awareness that certain behavioral acts egregiously defy this awareness. This divination is what is sometimes called in modern contexts a moral sense, though it would be highly misleading to use the term *moral sense* to recruit Plato to those who make a sharp distinction between the moral and the prudential. Plato's whole philosophy is, in a way, based on a rejection of any attempt to split these two apart. You will, Plato thinks, come to see the inseparability of morality and prudence when you come to have a firmer grasp on your own identity, firmer than the grasp that embodiment habitually allows.

Returning again to Oedipus, is he culpably ignorant of the irrationality of his behavior? Should he have been held morally responsible for the results of his thinking that he can escape the revelations of an oracle? Or should we say that in his case blame is a trivial footnote to the disaster that befalls him because of his irrationality? It seems that both Plato and Plotinus have an admirably cautious view about the assigning of moral responsibility, though Plato, particularly in *Laws*, is still struggling at the end of his life with gradations of strict liability (see *Leg.* 9).[19]

Culpable ignorance does not refer to a logical error per se. It refers to a logical error committed at the same time as affirming the truth that makes it an error to commit. The very possibility of this simultaneity is owing to the travails of embodiment. It is hardly overgenerous to say that Oedipus acts unwillingly since he was manifestly ignorant of the consequences that his actions would have. At the same time, he acted irrationally because he planned and carried out a series of actions that a responsible use of his reasoning ability could have told him was pointless. Sometimes we are culpably ignorant in this way, and nothing bad happens as a result. But that

---

19. See Trevor Saunders, *Plato's Penal Code* (Oxford: Clarendon, 1991), part 2.

is just luck. When something catastrophic happens, that is just the sort of inexplicable thing that the gods are adduced to explain.

Human beings could not engage in a single action without making appeal to the deliverances of their discursive reasoning faculty. To habitually make appeal to our reasoning faculty and at the same time to make it an instrument of our appetites rather than authoritative over them is the result of the identity crisis that Plato and all Platonists see as a uniquely human burden. Animals do not have a reasoning faculty that they regard as more or less alien from themselves. Assigning blame for the culpable ignorance of misidentifying our true selves is a secondary issue. Here is another job that Plato gladly hands off to the gods, I think. The primary issue is how to remedy ignorance. This is, of course, a critical issue in a political framework. The answer of all Platonists is clear: the practice of philosophy is the cure. In doing philosophy, one gradually detaches the embodied self from the body and rediscovers its true identity if only by a practiced intercourse with the intelligible world. For those incapable of philosophy, the best hope is to live under the aegis of those enlightened individuals who know that the Good is one and the same for everyone.

Bibliography

Primary Sources

Proclus. *Proclus sur le premier Alcibiade de Platon*. Edited and translated by Alain-Philippe Segonds. Paris: Belles Lettres, 2003.

Secondary Sources

Banner, Nicholas. *Philosophical Silence and the "One" in Plotinus*. Cambridge: Cambridge University Press, 2018.

Dodds, Eric R. *The Greeks and the Irrational*. Berkeley: University of California Press, 1966.

Irwin, Terence. *Plato's Ethics*. Oxford: Oxford University Press, 1995.

Penner, Terry. "The Historical Socrates and Plato's Early Dialogues: Some Philosophical Questions." Pages 189–212 in *New Perspectives on Plato, Modern and Ancient*. Edited by Julia Annas and Christopher Rowe. Cambridge: Harvard University Press, 2003.

Saunders, Trevor. *Plato's Penal Code*. Oxford: Clarendon, 1991.

Vlastos, Gregory. *Socrates: Ironist and Moral Philosopher*. Ithaca, NY: Cornell University Press, 1991.

Plato on the Manic Soul

Suzanne Stern-Gillet

The roots of unreason held considerable interest for Plato: with the possible exception of the *Hippias Major* and the *Hippias Minor*, no dialogue is without a mention of some form or other of psychic impairment or imbalance. The conceptual array with which he expressed his interest includes the following terms: ἄνοια, παραφροσύνη, παρανοία, πτόησις, ὕβρις, μανία, βακχεῖα, κατοκωχή, ἐνθουσιασμός, ἔρως, θύμος, τὸ ἀφρόν, and the condition of being ἐμμανής or ἔκφρων, as well as the mental state censored as φιλεραστία. The semantic spread covered by these terms is wide, ranging as it does from general ineptitude, epistemic or practical, to full-blown clinical madness. Of these terms, none is more evenly spread throughout the corpus than μανία, none bears as heavy a weight of theory, and none has had as rich and varied a *nachleben*. An untidy concept, it proved resistant to whatever distinctions and classifications Plato tried to introduce in his own usage.

Although he almost unfailingly connotates μανία negatively, there are occasions in which he seemingly uses it to praise. Two such occasions are worth noting. In the *catalogue raisonné* of the sources, symptoms, and manifestations of μανία that he provides in the *Phaedrus*, the μανία granted by the Muses is said to enable lyric poets "to glorify the countless mighty deeds of ancient times for the instruction of posterity" (*Phaedr.* 245a4–5 [Hackforth]). This seems praise enough. However, the fact that

---

It gives me great pleasure to dedicate this essay to John Finamore, with whom I have been shepherding *The International Journal of the Platonic Tradition* these last twelve years—a collaboration that has unfailingly been harmonious and productive.

Earlier versions of this paper were read at Emory University and at the University of Michigan at Ann Arbor. On both occasions I benefited from the discussion that ensued, for which special thanks are due to Crystal Addey and Richard Parry.

three Stephanus pages later (248d2–e3), Socrates downgrades the lives of poets and other imitative artists to the sixth level in the order of merit of lives, as determined by the extent of their souls' antenatal vision of the Forms, makes his earlier endorsement of poetic μανία seem more like faint than genuine praise. For the ranking puts poets and other μιμητικοὶ just ahead of farm laborers, Sophists, and tyrants. For a more positive evaluation of μανία, we must turn to the elaborate elenchus that Diotima mounts in the *Symposium* to refute Agathon's claim that Erōs is king of the gods (*Symp.* 195a1). Erōs, she retorts, is but a *daimōn*, whose function is to mediate between the divine and the human orders. This involves passing on divine messages to persons who find themselves in less than fully conscious states, or suffer a temporary loss of their mental faculties, or operate below the threshold of rational control, or indeed, as the Pythia is traditionally held to be, are the passive object of some form of divine possession.[1]

Having recorded Plato's tergiversations on the merit of μανία, including his one positive assessment of its effects, I now turn to the forms and manifestations of it that he classifies as stemming from "human ailments" (νοσημάτων ἀνθρωπίνων, *Phaedr.* 265a9–10). To set the scene, I begin with the informal distinction to be found in the corpus between the forms of μανία that are ethically connotated and therefore potentially curable and those that are so deep-seated as to be wholly incapacitating.

Μανία Severe and Less Severe

In its severe form, μανία overlaps with modern concepts of psychosis, involving as it does loss of contact with reality or a severe pathology of the affectivity. Thus, in the opening section of the *Republic*, in the context of an attempted definition of justice (*Resp.* 1 [331e–332a5] and 2 [382c9–e2]), μανία denotes full-blown clinical madness. As Socrates is made to remark to Polemarchus, mad people lack σωφροσύνη and should be dealt with in a manner appropriate to their condition. They are unfit to be told the truth, and it would not be "just" (μὴ δίκαιος) to hand them back the dangerous weapon that they had been lent while sane (σωφρονοῦντος, *Resp.* 1 [331c6; see also 331e9 and 332a4–5], 9 [573c3–5]). In the *Theaetetus*,

---

1. A detailed account of Diotima's argument is provided in Suzanne Stern-Gillet, "Poets and Other Makers: Agathon's Speech in Context," *Dionysius* n.s. 26 (2008): 9–29.

too, μανία covers a variety of delusional states liable to cause what Plato calls "lying perceptions" (ψευδεῖς αἰσθήσεις) in which "of the things which appear, not one of them is" (*Theaet.* 157e1–158a3). In the closing page of the *Statesman* (310d–f), when discussing how best to weave courageous and bold elements in the public and private spheres, Plato mentions the fits of total madness (παντάπασι μανίαι) that are liable to overwhelm bold and intrepid people whose nature is not tempered by an admixture of the virtue of moderation (σωφροσύνη). As will presently be seen, in book 9 of the *Laws*, Plato uses μανία to denote the extreme of blind rage (μανίαις ὀργῆς, *Leg.* 869a3) that may drive someone to kill a parent, an act of impiety (ἀσέβεια) for which, in the opinion of the Athenian Stranger, a penalty most just (δικαιότατον) would be "a great many deaths" (θανάτων πολλῶν). In this severe form, *mania* is conveniently rendered as "madness," "insanity," or "lunacy."

It will have been noted that in some of the passages quoted above μανία is used in the plural, either to refer to different kinds of μανία (see, e.g., *Leg.* 6 [783a2]) or, more significantly and more often, to denote such fits of μανία or ὀργή as might, in extreme circumstances, overwhelm people otherwise sane and lead them to commit criminal acts (see, e.g., *Pol.* 310d–e; *Phileb.* 38e5–6; *Leg.* 9 [869a and 881b4]). From these passages, which come mostly from dialogues conventionally classified as late, it may be inferred that Platonic μανία, unlike its modern equivalent, can denote either a long-term disposition or one or several isolated episodes in the life of a person.[2]

The second form of μανία is milder, being nondelusional and less aggressive. In most dialogues in which the subject arises, with the possible exception of the *Timaeus*, this form of μανία is said to stem from a failure on the part of reason (τὸ λογιστικόν) to control one or the other of the two elements that coexist with it in the soul, namely, spirit (θύμος) and appetite (ἐπιθυμία). In the *Protagoras*, for example, it is the overassertiveness of spirit, referred to as θύμος or μανία, that is said to separate dispositions such as confidence, which can be used both virtuously and nonvirtuously, from dispositions such as courage, which are virtuous by definition. Although the distinction between the two kinds of disposition is made by Protagoras, it bears the stamp of Platonic psychology:

---

2. As noted by Richard D. Parry, *Plato's Craft of Justice* (Albany: State University of New York Press, 1996), 401 n. 13.

I neither here nor anywhere else admit that the capable are strong, but
rather that the strong are capable; for capability [δύναμις] and strength
[ἰσχύς] are not the same thing, but the former comes from knowledge
[ἐπιστήμη] indeed, and also from madness and animal boldness [ἀπὸ
μανίας γε καὶ θυμοῦ], while strength results from a good natural condition and nurture of the body. And similarly in the other case daring
[θάρσος] and courage [ἀνδρεία] are not the same, so that it happens that
the courageous are daring, but that not all the daring are courageous.
For daring results both from skill and from animal boldness and madness [ἀπὸ τέχνης ... καὶ ἀπὸ θυμοῦ καὶ ἀπὸ μανίας], like capability, but
courage from a good natural disposition and nurture of the soul. (*Prot.*
350e6–351b1 [Taylor])

More often than not, however, it is the failure of the appetites (ἐπιθυμίαι)
to submit to rational control that Plato associates with μανία (see, e.g.,
Resp. 1.4036–4010; *Leg.* 6 [783a2], 8 [839a7]), either as its source or as its
outcome. Unsurprisingly, the clearest evidence for such association comes
from discussions on the nature of pleasure in the *Philebus*. Consider, to
begin with, the value-loaded terminology used to express the claim that
μανία almost invariably ensues from excessive indulgence in unnecessary pleasures: "Moderate people [τοὺς μὲν ... σώφρονας] somehow always
stand under the guidance of proverbial maxim 'nothing too much' and
obey it. But, as to foolish people and those given to debauchery, the excess
of their pleasures [τὸ δὲ τῶν ἀφρόνων τε καὶ ὑβριστῶν] drive them near
madness [μέχρι μανίας] and to shrieks of frenzy" (*Phileb.* 45d7–e4).[3]
    Even more pointed in that respect is the speech that Plato ascribes in
the same dialogue to "intelligence and reason" (φρόνησις καὶ νοῦς, *Phileb.*
63c5–6), in answer to the question as to which kind of pleasure they would
prefer to be associated with. Would it be the pleasures earlier identified as
"true and pure" or those now described as "the greatest and most intense"
(τὰς μεγίστας ἡδονὰς ... καὶ τὰς σφοδροτάτας, *Phileb.* 63d3–4)? Recognizing
that the inquiry is question-begging, intelligence and reason reply:

"Why on earth should we need them?" Socrates, they might reply, "They
are a tremendous impediment to us, since they infect the souls in which
they dwell with madness [ταράττουσαι διὰ μανικὰς] or even prevent our
own development altogether. Furthermore, they totally destroy most of

---

3. All quotations from the *Philebus* follow Dorothea Frede, trans., *Philebus* (Indianapolis: Hackett, 1993).

our offspring, since neglect leads to forgetfulness. But as to the true and pure pleasures [ἀληθεῖς καὶ καθαρὰς] you mentioned, those regard as our kin. And besides, also add the pleasures of health and of temperance [μεθ᾽ ὑγιείας καὶ τοῦ σωφρονεῖν], and all those that commit themselves to virtue as to their deity and follow it around everywhere." (*Phileb.* 63d1–7)

Last, evidence comes from the *Statesman* that Plato took whatever can correctly be described as *manikos* to be objectionable by definition: "When keenness, speed, and persistence turn out to be unseasonable, we call it 'wanton' and 'mad' [ὑβριστικά καὶ μανικά]" (*Pol.* 307b9–c1 [Skemp, rev. Ostwald]).

From the texts so far considered, it is clear that the nature and variety of psychic states covered by μανία in its nondelusional form make it inappropriate to render the word as "madness." Since the English word *mania* denotes a particular kind of psychological abnormality that is no adequate match for the semantically more diverse Greek μανία, I shall here refer to the latter in its transliterated form.

Μανία: Disease or Vice?

As described above, μανία, in whichever form it comes, is a state of passivity: anyone whom Plato describes as μαινόμενος, μανικός, or ἐμμανής is in the grip of a force that debilitates or altogether overwhelms their reasoning faculty. The last four quoted examples show, in addition, that Plato tends to rely on heavily value-loaded terminology to characterize the less severe, nondelusional species of common μανία. His frequent use of σωφροσύνη (moderation)[4] as a concept with which to contrast μανία strongly suggests that he may long have regarded μανία as the vice corresponding to the virtue of σωφροσύνη. What, at any rate, is beyond doubt is that he believed μανία to be an obstacle to virtue, either because it leads to or results from

---

4. Like a number of other names of traditional Greek virtues, σωφροσύνη is not readily translatable into modern vernaculars. The usual renderings, i.e., "moderation" and "temperateness," although not actually wrong, are very far from conveying the full meaning of the Greek term. To be Platonically σώφρων is to have set oneself into a way of life that is both rational and reasonable and thus to enjoy a state of being largely devoid of inner turmoil and conflict. The moderate person is one who consistently gives each aspect of one's soul (or personality) its due: reason is in control, but not so much in control that the appetites are denied their legitimate satisfaction or that the task of the θυμός in assisting reason is made excessively hard.

the kind of excess detrimental to the harmony and well-being of the soul. Not unlike his modern readers, Plato takes μανία to be inimical to knowledge and good counsel, and likely, therefore, to have an adverse effect not only on composure but also on the ability to judge matters theoretical and practical. Unlike his modern readers, however, at any rate until he turned to writing the *Timaeus* and the *Laws*, Plato did not view μανία as a debilitating psychological condition for which sufferers are to be pitied or that can mitigate the moral responsibility that they would otherwise bear for their actions. Platonic μανία of the nondelusional variety can thus be viewed as a nefarious condition whose sufferers are guilty agents rather than victims.

Μανία in the *Republic*

To account for such disparity between Plato's views and our own, we turn to the doctrine of the tripartition of the soul, as expounded in the *Republic*. In passages of book 4 too well known to require quoting at length, three elements or parts are distinguished in the human soul (τὸ λογιστικόν, θυμός, and ἐπιθυμία), and the natural supremacy and authority of the rational element asserted over that of the other two. It is the ability of the rational element to control the appetitive side of our nature (ἐπιθυμία), albeit with the (effective) assistance of spirit (θυμός) that renders a soul wise. Correspondingly, it is the state of inner harmony prevailing in it "when the ruler and its two subjects share the belief that the rationally calculating element should rule, and do not engage in faction against it" (*Resp.* 4 [442c10–d1]) that ensures that the soul as a whole is σώφρων.[5] So comprehensively understood, Platonic σωφροσύνη does not come alone but goes hand in

---

5. By presenting σωφροσύνη as a virtue of the soul as a whole rather than a virtue of the appetitive element in it, I take up a position on a controversial issue. Just as each class in the ideal city has a virtue specific to itself, so, too, has each element in the soul. Σωφροσύνη, therefore, so it has been argued, is both the virtue of the artisan class in the city and the virtue of the appetitive element in the individual soul. Restrictions on space prevent me from outlining here the reasons I do not share this view. While members of the lowest class can be taken to be capable of reasonableness and self-restraint in the interest of the well-being of the community as a whole, the same cannot be true of the appetites within the soul, which Plato consistently describes as nonrational "by nature" (*Resp.* 4 [440–441]). If, therefore, as Plato claims, the appetites are to be educated, it cannot but be by some authoritative agency other than their own. All quotations of the *Republic* follow C. David C. Reeve, trans., *Republic* (Indianapolis: Hackett, 2004).

hand with wisdom and courage insofar as no soul can be moderate unless it is also wise and courageous. Last, it is through its possession of all three virtues that the soul as a whole also possesses the virtue of justice, a virtue that Plato presents as the bloom of a soul in good order, a soul in which each part is exercising its due function of ruling and being ruled.

Vice, by contrast, is presented as the inevitable by-product of civil strife in a soul in which reason is in thrall to the passions, and spirit ineffective in its role as ally of reason (*Resp.* 4 [444d–e]). A Platonically vicious soul, therefore, is a disordered soul in which the natural order of ruler and ruled has been reversed and which as a result is capable of only the crudest form of instrumental rationality. It is a soul that lacks all four cardinal virtues.[6] While most social-service practitioners would nowadays describe such a soul as dysfunctional, Plato regards it as diseased as well as vicious. His diagnosis of the tyrannical condition in book 9 of the *Republic* highlights his conception of μανία as a manifestation of both vice and disease.

The Tyrannical Man as Sufferer of μανία

As will be recalled, the account of the stages of political decadence in books 8 and 9 of the *Republic* ends with the description of tyranny, as instantiated in both the city and the individual. Tyranny represents the final stage of the ever-worsening process of decline that began as the ruling order of the once-perfect city became weakened by dissensions and miscalculations of various kinds. Furthest removed from the ideal of the just citizen, the tyrannical man is Plato's paradigm of vice (ἀδίκους γε ὡς οἷόν τε μάλιστα, *Resp.* 9 [576a10]), a man whose soul is entirely ruled by those appetitive elements in it that are least fit to rule, namely, the appetites and pleasures that Plato classifies as lawless, a subcategory of those he had earlier identified as "unnecessary."[7] Lawless appetites, of which he gives a somewhat proto-Freudian account, manifest themselves for the most part in dreams in which the most illicit fantasies are entertained, including incest, murder

---

6. I describe the vicious soul as "capable of only the crudest form of instrumental rationality" rather than "irrational" since in many cases such a soul presumably remains capable of identifying means to bring about the satisfaction of its appetitive wants and needs. This, of course, does not amount to a denial that its enslavement to the passions has rendered it incapable of exercising theoretical or even full practical rationality.

7. For "unnecessary pleasures," see *Resp.* 9 (559a3–6), recalled in 9 (571b4); for the lawless ones, see 9 (571b5).

most foul, and other acts of "extreme shamelessness and folly" (οὔτε ἀνοίας οὐδὲν ἐλλείπει οὔτ ἀναισχυντίας, *Resp.* 9 [571d3–4]). Although probably innate in all of us, such lawless desires must be kept in check lest they erode and finally altogether incapacitate the rational principle and undermine the sense of shame. Great care, therefore, should be taken to eradicate those appetites in childhood, or at least to discipline them by training and education (*Resp.* 9 [559a3–4]). The tyrannical man is Plato's graphic and terrifying portrait of someone in whom this has not been done.

As Plato describes it, the disorder in the tyrannical soul is the product not so much of the tyrannical man's own earlier choices and decisions but of factors largely outside his control. These factors, which Plato outlines in some detail, include deficient political and social arrangements (see *Resp.* 8 [563e–565a]) as well as, more directly, the deplorable upbringing that the tyrannical man had received at the hand of his father, the democratic man. Characteristically, the democratic man, rather than attempting to curb or to educate his young son's desires and appetites, allowed them all to seek fulfillment and thus inevitably to become discrepant and unruly in the process (*Resp.* 8 [551b–c]). As a result, the adolescent grew up with a warped conception of the good as pleasure and any budding practical rationality and ability to withstand the dominance of passion that he may have had earlier on were soon extinguished in his soul. His tendency to lawlessness was encouraged by unscrupulous boon companions. These, acting as τυραννοποιοὶ (*Resp.* 9 [572e4–5]), succeeded in implanting in the young man's soul some overwhelming passion (ἔρωτά τινα, *Resp.* 9 [572e5]), to which his other wants and desires would soon be made to defer, a master passion that Plato colorfully compares to a great-winged drone. And so, what had started as an undisciplined soul, prey to multifarious wants, was transformed into a soul dominated by an insatiable and irresistible need. While Plato's own examples are lust, drink, and the kind of madness that leads sufferers to think that they can lord it over men and gods, heroin addiction is the modern example that springs to mind. Being insatiable by nature, all such needs are prone to become frantic or, in Plato's colorful metaphor, to enlist μανία as his "armed guard" (δορυφορεῖταί, *Resp.* 9 [573a9–b1]). The kind of μανία that becomes the drone's assistant is to be conceived as a craving so obsessive that it incapacitates reason and corrodes the will to the point of rendering its victim incapable of even the most elementary calculation of self-interest (see also *Resp.* 9 [578a10–12]).[8] Indeed, once the drone

---

8. As Parry, referring to the portrait of the tyrannical soul, says well, "madness has

has developed the ability to sting and thus literally to infuriate, its power over the tyrannical soul is complete: whatever power of agency and respect for other humans had so far remained in it are effectively destroyed. At this point, even conventional values and common decencies, including vestigial respect for parents and city, have lost the power to restrain the tyrannical man, who by then has come to consent to his own enslavement. This, however, does not lessen his guilt since, in the context of the *Republic*, the tyrannical man's inability to act otherwise than he does is itself a manifestation of injustice.

Such, according to Plato, is the manner in which the drone, with the help of μανία, completed the process of psychic enslavement that had unwittingly been started in the tyrannical man's infancy by his parents. The process, as Plato describes it, has a most paradoxical outcome: the man who would one day be master to a whole city and preside over the worst possible form of government is a man "who has in his soul the greatest and strongest tyrant of all" (*Resp.* 9 [575c8–d1]). Slave to himself though master to others, Plato's tyrannical man "never gets a taste of freedom or true friendship" (*Resp.* 9 [576a5–6]). He is the antithesis of the just man of the *Republic*, whose freedom and happiness are guaranteed by the ability of his rational principle to exercise forethought on behalf of the soul as a whole (τὴν ὑπὲρ ἁπάσης τῆς ψυχῆς προμήθειαν, *Resp.* 4 [441e5]) and thus to give spirit and appetite each their due while also harnessing them to the service of soul and state. Clearly, this particular paradox of tyranny, meant to counter Thrasymachus's earlier claims regarding the pleasures of tyranny, is also Plato's most vivid argument in support of the thesis that injustice does not pay.

In the eyes of his modern readers, Plato's description of the tyrannical man generates a second paradox. How, they want to know, can Plato describe this character as the paradigm of the worst possible form of injustice while, at the same time, presenting him as being to a large extent the victim of circumstances independent of his control? Insofar as this second paradox highlights a mismatch between Plato's conception of μανία and ours, we may wonder why it has no place in the *Republic*.

If, as we must, we agree with Plato that the tyrannical man lacks inner freedom, must we also endorse the view that he is guilty of the worst form of injustice? After all, as Plato will later recognize, the bonds that keep him

---

a dramatic role analogous to that of the false and bold beliefs" (*Plato's Craft of Justice*, 398).

prisoner are not all of his own making. His unfortunate upbringing has left him without either the motivation or the inner resources to seek the good, or even to resist the forces that would progressively erode his rational capacities. Does his upbringing not mitigate the blame that we might otherwise be inclined to apportion him for his later depravity? Did Plato not consider the possibility that the tyrannical man's upbringing explains why he later fell prey to the τυραννοποιοί who filled his soul with the μανία of a master passion?

The short answer to these questions is no. There is no indication in the *Republic* that Plato did entertain the view that the tyrannical man—or indeed anyone else in a similar condition of inner slavery—deserves less than full blame for his condition. More generally, there is no indication in the so-called middle dialogues that the degree of moral responsibility ascribed to someone like the tyrannical man should be proportional to his ability to act independently of internal, or indeed external, constraints. However paradoxical it may seem to us, Plato, as Richard Stalley aptly remarks, "does not see freedom in his sense [independence from the passions] as a necessary condition of responsibility."[9]

Even so, the question remains as to why Plato did not see what seems so blatantly obvious to us, namely that moral responsibility presupposes, at the very least, some degree of freedom. The question is large and complex, involving as it does fundamental differences between ancient and modern ethics. To the extent that we take it as axiomatic that ought implies can, anxiously debate problems generated by the putative autonomy of morals, and do not consider rationality to be a sufficient bulwark against vice, we find ourselves at a far cry from Plato's expressed views in the *Republic* regarding individual responsibility and the nature of moral norms. This particular gap between ancient and modern views raises issues too complex to be explored in the present framework. Accordingly, all I will do here is draw attention, very tentatively, to such features of Plato's use of the analogy between health and virtue as might have influenced his thinking on this and related matters at the time of writing the *Republic*. My argument will be that the analogy carries greater theoretical weight than Plato himself, as well as his latter-day interpreters, has generally recognized. Analogies, however, are no innocent aids to understanding but come laden with theo-

---

9. So Richard Stalley, "Persuasion and the Tripartite Souls in Plato's Republic," *OSAP* 32 (2007): 153, to whom I am here indebted.

retical assumptions, not all of which are immediately apparent, least of all to their author. Plato's analogy between virtue and health is no exception, highlighting as it does a profound ambiguity at the heart of his thinking on what he calls vice or injustice.

The Analogy between Virtue and Health

The fullest and, from our point of view, most helpful formulation of the analogy between virtue and health comes from the *Republic*:

> To produce health is to put the elements that are in the body in their *natural* [κατὰ φύσιν] relations of mastering and being mastered by one another; while to produce disease is to establish a relation of ruling and being ruled by one another that is *contrary to nature* [παρὰ φύσιν].... Doesn't it follow, then, that to produce justice is to establish the elements in the soul in a natural relation of mastering and being mastered by one another, while to produce injustice is to establish a relation of ruling and being ruled by one another that is contrary to nature? (*Resp.* 4 [444d3–e2])

Upon Glaucon's affirmative answer, Socrates concludes: "Virtue, then, so it seems, is a sort of health [ὑγίειά ... τις], a fine [κάλλος] and good state [εὐεξία] of the soul; whereas vice seems to be a shameful disease and weakness [νόσος τε καὶ αἶσχος καὶ ἀσθένεια]." The analogy takes us to the very heart of Plato's conception of virtue at the time that the tripartite conception of the soul dominated his moral psychology. Even though he was aware of the limitations of the analogy—so much is clear from his use of ὡς ἔοικεν and ὑγίειά τις at line 4 (444d13)—there are reasons to think that he found it convenient to ground his conception of vice and virtue on it. First, the analogy sanctions a conception of virtue as an objectively identifiable state, independent of human wishes, customs, and values; correspondingly, it presents vice as an adverse psychic condition with well-defined symptoms and a foreseeable evolution. In the same way that an overactive thyroid, for instance, inevitably disrupts metabolic function and, if left untreated, leads to kidney failure, vice in the soul inevitably disrupts the power of rational agency and, if left rampant, leads to its subjection to the appetites. Just as there is no scope for medical disagreement over the effects of hyperthyroidism, so there is no disputing the paralyzing effects that unchecked appetites have on the soul as a whole. Second, the analogy reinforced his inclination to think that there are specialists

in morality: just as a somatic disease calls for specialist medical intervention, vice in the soul calls for treatment by an expert. Third, the analogy
specifies that in the case of virtue as in that of health, the natural (κατὰ
φύσιν) condition, which is also the optimal condition, provides all the
guidance that one may wish for. To deal with sick bodies and souls, the
best way is to bring in those who are experts in matters of the natural. In
the same way, therefore, as advice on hyperthyroidism and other endo-
crinological matters should be sought from someone with the relevant
specialized knowledge, namely, a physician, so advice on matters of both
political organization and individual psychic health should come from
those whom Plato labels the "good physicians" of the state. From Plato's
viewpoint, as we know, these are the philosophers who, during their long
years of training, have been taught to reach out to and draw guidance
from "the eternal and unchanging" Forms. Subsequently, during their
period of active service as guardians of the state, these good doctors of
the body politic (ἀγαθὸν ἰατρόν τε καὶ νομοθέτην, Resp. 8 [564c1])[10] will
ensure that it functions harmoniously as a whole and that those of their
fellow citizens whose rational principle is naturally weak can nonetheless
live their lives contentedly and usefully in a position suited to their dispositions and capabilities.

In the conduct of an individual life, the expert physician is the
λογιστικόν, whether one's own or that of the guardians of the state. Like
a good physician concerned to establish a state of equilibrium in the
patient's body, the λογιστικόν coordinates the other two elements in the
soul, thereby ensuring that they function as organic parts rather than as a
mere assemblage of discrete elements, each of which would otherwise be
liable to pull in a separate direction (Resp. 4 [443e1]). Last, when things
go wrong, errors made or crimes committed, the analogy suggests a cura-
tive cum educational theory of punishment, of a kind that we find Plato
advocating in the Gorgias as well as in a number of passages in the Laws.
In the same way that we readily subject ourselves to medical treatment in
the hope of being cured of a bodily ailment, so the analogy goes, we should
accept without resentment whatever punishment we are given to help rid
our soul of the vicious condition that led us to commit a crime.[11] Seen in

---

10. The analogy between the lawgiver and the physician is older than the *Republic*. In the *Gorgias*, we find Socrates already maintaining that "the counterpart of medicine is justice" (*Gorg.* 464b8).

11. See *Gorg.* 476a–480e, especially 480a8–b1, where the judge is compared to

the light of the analogy between virtue and health, Plato's description of the tyrannical man's decline into unbridled licentiousness and inner slavery is not unlike a case study in a medical textbook.

However, for all its rhetorical force and pedagogic value, the analogy has the drawback of blurring some very real differences between the terms of the comparison. Somatic diseases, for the most part, strike sufferers unawares; since they do not generally stem from any deliberate action or blameworthy disposition on their part, the sick deserve pity as opposed to censure.[12] By contrast and barring strongly mitigating circumstances, vices such as cowardice, intemperance, and dishonesty are agreed to result, for the most part, from the repeated and intentional performance of cowardly, intemperate, and dishonest actions. The severest penalties, therefore, are reserved for crimes premeditated and deliberately carried out by persons otherwise sane, who as a result deserve censure, not pity.

Plato's silence on the disanalogy between diseases of the body and diseases of the soul suggests that the problem of identifying the grounds of moral responsibility at the individual level did not greatly preoccupy him at the time of writing the *Republic*. Since his main concern in the dialogue is with the virtue and the well-being of the state, he may have considered the virtue and the well-being of individual citizens only insofar as they are likely to affect the whole of which they are parts. If so, he should not have been expected to devote full attention to the extent or the degree of blame merited by each of the vicious characters portrayed in book 9. More relevant, from his point of view in that context, was the description of their effects on the body politic as a whole. In his portrait of the tyrannical man, most particularly, Plato is at pains to argue that vicious dispositions, especially when present in the soul of a ruler, threaten the common good: "there is no city," he wrote, "more wretched than a tyrannical one" (*Resp.* 9

---

a doctor, and evil in the soul to a festering ulcer (ὕπουλος). See also *Leg.* 9 (862c), in which punishment is described in terms of therapy.

12. It might here be objected that some diseases, such as pancreatitis and cirrhosis of the liver, which almost always result from an excessive consumption of alcohol, are self-inflicted and that those who suffer from these conditions therefore are to be blamed for the heavy demands that they make on medical resources. The analogy, it might then be concluded, was even closer than Plato knew. This objection, however, carries less weight than might appear at first since (1) the majority of somatic diseases result from factors other than wrong "lifestyle" choices, and (2) it is the cause of the cirrhosis of the liver, i.e., the vice of intemperance, that we blame rather than the condition itself.

[576e3–4]). The vice in the tyrant's soul, once allowed to spread, becomes a dangerous and spreading canker at the heart of the state. Compared to the risk that such a canker poses, it is of little consequence whether the disease originated in the morally wrongful choices that the tyrannical man made earlier in life or in conditions for which he could not be held responsible, such as a poor early education and upbringing, a deviant political constitution, or possibly even an endogenic disease of the mind.

From Plato's lack of concern in the *Republic* with the conditions of individual moral responsibility, it should not be assumed, however, that he would always remain insensitive to the cluster of problems involved in specifying those conditions. As will now be seen, the *Timaeus* and the *Laws* prove otherwise.

Agents or Victims? The *Timaeus*

The account of μανία that Timaeus gives at the end of the work has a claim to being the midpoint in Plato's reflections on diseases of the soul. It systematizes the view put forward in the *Republic* regarding the state of unfreedom in the tyrant's soul while anticipating the recommendation that the Athenian Stranger will introduce in the *Laws* that μανία be regarded as an extenuating circumstance in the sentencing of those guilty of murder or manslaughter.

Upon completion of his account of the formation and location of mortal nature, Timaeus turns to accounting for the "terrible and inevitable affections" (παθήματα, *Tim.* 69c8–d1) to which it is subject and the diseases to which it is prone. After giving a lengthy aetiology of somatic ailments, he moves on to diseases of the soul, at which point he puts forward the following striking claim:

> So much for the way in which diseases of the body occur; we go on to diseases of the soul caused by bodily condition. It will be granted that folly [ἄνοιαν] is a disease of the soul, and of folly there are two kinds, madness [μανίαν] and ignorance [ἀμαθίαν]. Any affection which brings on either must be called a disease and so we must rank excessive pleasures and pains as the worst diseases of the soul. For when a man enjoys great pleasure or conversely when he suffers from pain, he is incapable of seeing or hearing anything correctly but hurries to grab one thing and avoid another; being in a state of frenzy, his reasoning power is at this time at its lowest ... being for most of his life in a state of madness [ἐμαννὴς ... γιγνόμενος] induced by the greatest pleasures and pains, his

soul is deprived of health and judgment by his bodily constitution, and he is commonly regarded not as a sick man but as deliberately wicked [ἑκὼν κακός]. But the truth is that sexual incontinence is for the most part a disease of the soul caused by the condition of a single substance, which overflows and floods the body because of the porousness of the bones. And indeed it is generally true that it is unjust to blame over-indulgence in pleasure as if wrongdoing were voluntary; no one is bad voluntarily [κακὸς μὲν γὰρ ἑκὼν οὐδείς], but a bad man becomes bad because of a pernicious bodily condition and an uneducated upbring-ing, evils which nobody wants to befall him [ἄκοντι προσγίγνεται].... Besides, when the constitutions that men with these flaws live under are bad and the way people speak in the city, in private and in public, is bad and they pursue no learning from an early age with the power to cure them, you have the conditions in which all those of us who are bad become so through *two involuntary factors. The responsibility always lies with* the parents rather than the offspring, and with those who educate them rather than their pupils; but we must all try with all our might by education, by practice and by study to avoid evil and grasp its contrary. (*Tim.* 86b1–87b8 [Lee, rev. Johansen])

The passage has not found favor with commentators, who have variously described it as "notoriously puzzling" and "particularly bizarre ... even by the standards of the *Timaeus*."[13] There is no doubt that the passage con-tains a number of claims that are baffling, at any rate at first sight. Coming from Plato, the extreme reductivism that underlies the claim that somatic dysfunctions are the sole cause of psychic disorders is certainly perplex-ing.[14] Yet, once the claim is taken in its context, the oddity lessens; it becomes clear that it stems directly from Timaeus's physicalist and deter-ministic conception of the mortal ingredients in the human soul, each of

---

13. Christopher Gill, "The Body's Fault? Plato's *Timaeus* on Psychic Illness," in *Reason and Necessity: Essays on Plato's Timaeus*, ed. M. Rosemary Wright (Swansea: Classical Press of Wales, 2000), 59; Christopher Rowe, review of *Reason and Necessity: Essays on Plato's* Timaeus, by M. R. Wright, *Classical Review* 54 (2004): 316.

14. I here deliberately leave aside the question as to whether Plato's claim in that passage is that *all* or only *some* forms of psychological imbalance stem from somatic conditions. Cornford holds that in the human composite living being, either the soul or the body can set up disorders in the other. See Francis M. Cornford, *Plato's Cosmology* (Indianapolis: Hackett, 1935), 346. Lautner denies this. See Peter Lautner, "Plato's Account of the Diseases of the Soul in *Timaeus* 86b1–87b9," *Apeiron* 44 (2011): 23.

which is housed in its own bodily part and is the seat of specific emotions. Being spatial and mortal, these elements, so Timaeus is made to argue, are liable to be disturbed by the body and the irrational motions produced by the circle of the different that enters into their composition. Timaeus's endorsement of the Socratic thesis that no one errs, or does wrong, willingly (ἑκούσιος), which is made clear in the passage, further explains why he can be made to infer from it that stupidity or ignorance (ἀμαθία) is a disease of the soul (*Tim.* 86b4). Indeed, so runs Timaeus's unspoken inference at this point, what other reason could there be for people choosing to be ignorant of what is in their self-interest, when it is correctly conceived?

More deeply puzzling is Timaeus's advice to sufferers of mental diseases as to the measures that they might take in order to lessen the impact of such conditions on their daily life. To take the precautionary measures recommended, they would first have to realize that they are sick, not only in body but also in mind. Since Plato's endorsement of the Socratic thesis that no one does wrong willingly makes it a matter of definition that sufferers of mental diseases are unable to take the full measure of their impairment, such advice could not but be pointless.

By far the most intriguing and interesting aspect of the passage is the correction made in it to the concept of psychic disorder that Plato had presented in the *Republic*. There, as will be recalled, the tyrannical man had repeatedly been stigmatized for allowing his appetites to become so pressing as to make him lose control over his appetitive drive. There, no allowance had been made for the force of circumstance—lax upbringing, unfavorable political structures—that had made it well-nigh impossible for him to withstand the forces that would progressively make him a slave to his passions. There, the budding tyrant had been presented as the epitome of vice and injustice, with no mitigating conditions being allowed to lessen his guilt. By contrast, Plato's standpoint in the *Timaeus* on this particular kind of μανία is more complex and balanced. The position defended in the *Republic* is now presented as a common mistake. While most people are of the opinion that those who suffer from diseases of the soul are deliberately bad (ἑκὼν κακὸς δοξάζεται), the truth of the matter (τὸ δὲ ἀληθές), Timaeus is made to state, is that they are better described as victims, primarily of a sick body, but also, in most cases, of an unenlightened upbringing (ἀπαίδευτον τροφὴν) as well as of defective political and educational arrangements (*Tim.* 87a7–b4). While injustice had been described in the *Republic* as a psychic disposition analogous to somatic ill health, it is now presented as for the most part the product of somatic ill health. Furthermore, parents and the state are now explicitly ascribed responsibility for their children's vicious or manic dispositions of soul.

Admittedly, the change of doctrine from the *Republic* to the *Timaeus* is doubly theory-driven, being accountable in terms of Timaeus's physicalist conception of the human body and his endorsement of Socratic intellectualism. Even so, Plato's departure from views he had defended in the *Republic* is striking. It shows that, by the time he wrote the *Timaeus*, he had come to believe that moral responsibility was conditional on the ability to act otherwise and could thus be mitigated by circumstances restricting the agent's freedom of action. A close reading of book 9 of the *Laws* will reveal that Plato's concept of mitigating circumstances would undergo further developments in the years following the composition of the *Timaeus*.

In between Voluntary and Nonvoluntary Killings: μανία in the *Laws*

Although the concept of μανία does not play a prominent role in the *Laws*, one of the examples that Plato classifies as a case of a μανία-inspired killing gives rise to a conundrum that takes us to the heart of the most philosophically challenging part of the dialogue. In book 9, which is devoted to a discussion of issues related to the establishment of an optimal code of law for the small city of Magnesia, the Athenian Stranger is prompted by Cleinias to outline his conception of justice. As a preliminary to devising a penal system best suited to the implementation of his conception of justice as impartiality between the parties concerned, the Stranger spells out the distinction between voluntary and involuntary actions that informs the commonly held view that an offender's guilt is to be assessed not only by the injury inflicted but also by his/her state of mind at the time of committing the offense. From that viewpoint, premeditation compounds the guilt, while unplanned and unintended violence justifies a more lenient sentence. The Athenian does not share this view, since he holds that "no one does evil willingly," a view that Socrates had been made to put forward in earlier dialogues, most notably in the *Protagoras* (*Prot.* 345c4–e6). The philosophical conundrum arises at this point. To counter the common view, the Athenian Stranger begins by redrawing the distinction between voluntary and nonvoluntary to reflect the difference that he takes to obtain between, on the one hand, human souls who succeed in conquering the force of passion or the pull of desire and those who, on the other hand, let themselves be mastered by them. This more specific distinction underlies the Athenian's definition of injustice as the mastery of the soul by anger, fear, pleasure, pain, envy and desires, whether they lead to any actual damage [τι βλάπτη] or not. But no matter how states and individuals think they can achieve the good, it is the conception of what the good is that should govern every man and hold sway in his soul, *even if he is a little mistaken*. If it does, every action done in accordance with it, and any part of a man's nature that becomes subject to such control, we have to call "just," and best for the entire life of mankind—and this in spite of the popular belief that damage done in such circumstances is an "involuntary" injustice. (*Leg.* 9 [863e5–864a8])[15]

If evil deeds committed under the impetus of passion were to be classed as involuntary, the Athenian argues, the administration of justice would be gravely impeded. This being so, he continues, "If someone hurts someone else involuntarily and without intending it ... I will not legislate so as to make this an involuntary act of injustice" (*Leg.* 9 [862a3–5]). Passion-driven and anger-fueled acts, he concludes, should not be treated more leniently than planned actions committed in cold blood. From a Socratic point of view, the position is understandable insofar as it is inconceivable that someone would choose deliberately to perform an act that s/he recognizes to be evil.

Since the Athenian will not give up his position, a compromise has to be sought between the Socratic tenet, as expressed above, and the popular belief in the possibility of involuntarily doing evil (*Leg.* 9 [860c4–5]). The compromise, to which an allusion is made in the first of the above two quotations, had earlier been introduced in the form of a distinction between the guilty act considered in itself and the guilty act taken in the context of the agent's state of mind at the time of acting:

What we must do, before we legislate, is somehow make clear that there are two categories, but that the distinction between them is a different one. Then, when one imposes the penalty on either, everybody will be able to appreciate the arguments for it, and make some kind of judgment whether it is the appropriate penalty to have imposed or not. (*Leg.* 9 [860c2–6])[16]

---

15. Unless otherwise stated, all quotations of the *Laws* follow the translation of Trevor J. Saunders, trans., *The Laws* (Harmondsworth, UK: Penguin, 1970).

16. I am indebted to Trevor Saunders for the interpretation of this complex passage. See Saunders, "Paradoxes in Plato's *Laws*: A Commentary on 859c–864b," *Hermes* 96 (1968): 362–75.

Somewhat contrived if not captious as the distinction may appear today, it would not have seemed outlandish to Plato's contemporaries, most of whom had attended performances of *Oedipus Tyrannos* in the course of the regularly held dramatic festival of the Great Dionysia. As will be recalled, the play narrates the fate of Oedipus, who, prior to becoming *tyrannos* in Corinth, had slain an elderly stranger who had angrily blocked his way on a mountain pass. The retaliation would have seemed justified in the mind of both Oedipus himself and the play's audience since none of them could have known that the irate stranger was Oedipus's father. Oedipus's parricide remains a paradigm of an evil act performed involuntarily by an agent whose state of mind at the time was one of (largely) nonblameworthy ignorance. As the play unfolds, Oedipus's ignorance of the identity of the stranger makes no difference to the pollution that the murder inflicts on the city and the ensuing sentence of exile that Creon metes out to him. Although nonvoluntarily caused, the pollution remains an objective fact. Since Sophocles wrote the play in circa 429 BCE and the *Laws* were left unfinished at Plato's death in 347 BCE, it is highly likely that in the eighty or so intervening years, Plato's audience would have had occasions to see the drama performed.

However, if the Athenian, in conformity with the Socratic motto, would prize acts of violence from the intention that initiated them, he recommended a broader and more sensitive handling of the culprit's state of soul. The lawgiver, he explained, after exacting a precise retribution calculated to compensate the plaintiff for the injury or the damage sustained, "must try by his laws to make the criminal and the victim, in each separate case of injury, friends instead of enemies" (*Leg.* 9 [862c3–4]). To that effect, the lawgiver may use "absolutely any means to make him [the offender] hate injustice and embrace true justice—or at any rate not hate it" (*Leg.* 9 [862d6–8]). However, the Athenian concluded, returning to his more usual severity, if the offender proves beyond cure, "the best thing for him is to cease to live" (*Leg.* 9 [862e4–5]).

How do the Athenian Stranger's distinctions and recommendations bear on his proposals for dealing with cases of involuntary homicide? More specifically, to continue with the main theme of the present investigation, which penalties does he propose to inflict on offenders whose uncontrolled anger or manic rage (μανία) has led to murder? Does he entertain the possibility that passion in the form of μανία, for instance, which lessens or even obliterates self-control, does constitute a mitigating circumstance that a sentencing judge would do well to take into account?

Bringing his customary analytical precision to the issue, the Athenian begins by making an internal distinction between two kinds of killing in anger. On the one hand: "anger is common to those who kill a man by blows or similar means, owing to a sudden impulse: here the action is immediate, there is no previous intention to kill, and regret for the deed follows at once" (*Leg.* 9 [866d7–e3]). Because the anger of this man bursts uncontrollably, the Athenian explains, he "resembles an involuntary killer" (ὁμοῖος ἀκουσίῳ, *Leg.* 9 [867a6]). From his use of ὁμοῖος, we infer that the Athenian considers that although the murder retains a residual element of voluntariness, the defendant should get a lighter sentence on the ground that the crime was mostly unpremeditated. On the other hand, there are murderers "who have been stung by insults or opprobrious actions and who pursue their vengeance until, sometime later, they kill somebody: they intend to kill, and the deed causes no repentance" (*Leg.* 9 [866e3–6]). The latter deserves comparatively more severe penalties than the former, the reason being that their act had been premeditated. Clearly, from Plato's viewpoint at that point of his writing life, the presence of passion and the (almost total) absence of premeditation do constitute extenuating circumstances.

A feature of Plato's penology is that the status of the victim should be reflected in the sentencing. Thus, it is a worse offense to hit a citizen than a resident alien or to injure someone else's slave than one's own. In the terms of that particular scale, assault against one's parents is a particularly heinous crime, which twice retains Plato's attention in the *Laws*. At the conclusion of book 9, a list of detailed penalties, both civil and religious, are outlined to be meted out at those guilty of such offenses:

> Whosoever shall dare to lay hands on father or mother, or their progenitors, and to use outrageous violence, fearing neither the wrath of the gods above nor that of the Avengers (as they are called) of the underworld, but scorning the ancient and world-wide traditions (thinking he knows what he knows not), and shall thus transgress the law,—for such a man there is needed the some most severe deterrent. (*Leg.* 9 [80e6–81a3; Bury])

Be it noted that, even in this case, which rates particularly high in his scale of heinousness, the Athenian regards μανία as an extenuating circumstance: in the course of the detailed provisions he outlines for dealing with the offense, he notes that the punishment will be alleviated if "it so happens that he [the offender] is afflicted with madness" (τύπτειν μὴ μανίαις ἐχόμενος, *Leg.* 9 [881b4]). No mitigating circumstances, however, can lessen the guilt of one who "gets into such an ungovernable temper [ἀκρατὴς θυμοῦ] with his parents and begetters that in his insane fury [μανίαις ὀργῆς] he dares to kill one of them" (*Leg.* 9 [869a2–4]). Such a one should be put to death. However, since nothing is ever entirely straightforward in Plato's *Laws*, a puzzling escape clause is sounded at that point: the offender can be let off responsibility for parricide or matricide by "a voluntary statement of the deceased before death" (*Leg.* 9 [869a4–5]). So puzzling is the clause that it should be left for a separate investigation.

By Way of a Conclusion

The terminological liberality that Plato deploys in his use of the vocabulary of psychological impairment did not prevent him from repeatedly trying to demarcate the field of its central concept, μανία. Unfortunately, as we have seen, the principles on which he based his classification did not remain steady from one dialogue to another. Should this be considered to be a failing on his part? Not really, I here conclude, for he squarely addressed the problem in the *Phaedrus* (263c) by taking care to explain how and why our evaluative concepts are prone to carry fluctuating, if not questionable or even contradictory, connotations. Having noted in an early dialogue (*Euthyphr.* 7c10–d5) that it is a fact that predicates such as good and evil tend to be subject to disagreements and controversies, he went on much later to develop the point in his discussion of the uses of rhetoric as a method of persuasion. In the concluding pages of the *Phaedrus*, he groups μανία as well as σωφροσύνη, which he presented as its contrary in the *Republic*, together with the normative concepts that he identified in the *Euthyphro*. This led him to claim, in turn, that since none of these concepts should be taken to refer to "a single objective form existing in human beings" (ἕν ἐν ἡμῖν πεφυκὸς εἶδος, *Phaedr.* 266a2–3), the mental state of μανία should in effect be divided off into a common or garden variety, which stems from human faults or ailments, and a rare because transcendent kind, which stems from "a divine disturbance of our conventions," to which Diotima draws attention in the elenchus she directed at Agathon in the *Symposium*.

Bibliography

Primary Sources

Plato. *Laws*. Translated by Robert G. Bury. Cambridge: Harvard University Press, 1926.

―――. *The Laws*. Translated by Trevor J. Saunders. Harmondsworth, UK: Penguin, 1970.

―――. *Phaedrus*. Translated by Reginald Hackforth. Cambridge: Cambridge University Press, 1952.

―――. *Philebus*. Translated by Dorothea Frede. Indianapolis: Hackett, 1993.

―――. *Protagoras*. Translated by Christopher C. W. Taylor. Oxford: Oxford University Press, 1996.

―――. *Republic*. Translated by C. David C. Reeve. Indianapolis: Hackett, 2004.

―――. *Statesman*. Translated by Martin Ostwald. Indianapolis: Hackett, 1992.

Secondary Sources

Cornford, Francis M. *Plato's Cosmology*. Indianapolis: Hackett, 1935.

Gill, Christopher. "The Body's Fault? Plato's *Timaeus* on Psychic Illness." Pages 59–84 in *Reason and Necessity: Essays on Plato's Timaeus*. Edited by M. Rosemary Wright. Swansea: Classical Press of Wales, 2000.

Lautner, Peter. "Plato's Account of the Diseases of the Soul in *Timaeus* 86b1–87b9." *Apeiron* 44 (2011): 22–39.

Parry, Richard D. *Plato's Craft of Justice*. Albany: State University of New York Press, 1996.

Rowe, Christopher. Review of *Reason and Necessity: Essays on Plato's Timaeus*, by M. R. Wright. *ClRev* 54 (2004): 316–17.

Saunders, Trevor. "Paradoxes in Plato's *Laws*: A Commentary on 859c–864b." *Hermes* 96 (1968): 421–34.

Stalley, Richard. "Persuasion and the Tripartite Souls in Plato's Republic." *OSAP* 32 (2007): 63–89.

Stern-Gillet, Suzanne. "Poets and Other Makers: Agathon's Speech in Context." *Dionysius* n.s. 26 (2008): 9–29.

Plato and Plotinus on Healing:
Why Does the Art of Medicine Matter?

Svetla Slaveva-Griffin

Introduction

It is no surprise that the art of medicine has remained under the radar in the study of (Neo)Platonic psychology.[1] If health is an afterthought of wholeness, which, once had, is lost, then we can turn to the (Neo)Platonist understanding of healing only after its psychosomatic dualism has been examined inside out.[2] Diagnosing the vertical relationship between soul and body has been the first order of our priority until not long ago, and rightly so.[3] Consequently, medicine as the art (*technē*) that provides

I am grateful to the honoree of this collection for teaching me how much soul matters when I studied with him all those years ago.

1. This applies more to Plotinus than Plato. The dialogue, started by King, Pigeaud, Vegetti, Ferrari, and Allen, is ready to be extended from Plato to the Neoplatonists. See Linda S. King, "Plato's Concepts of Medicine," *JHMAS* 9 (1954): 38–48; Jackie Pigeaud, *La maladie de l'âme: Étude sur la relation de l'âme et du corps dans la tradition médico-philosophique antique* (Paris: Les Belles Lettres, 2006); Mario Vegetti, *La Medicina in Platone* (Venice: Il Cardo, 1995); Giovanni R. F. Ferrari, *City and Soul in Plato's Republic* (Chicago: University of Chicago Press, 2005); and James Allen, "The Soul's Virtue and the Health of the Body in Ancient Philosophy," in *Health: A History*, ed. Peter Adamson (New York: Oxford University Press, 2019), 75–94.

2. On the grades of Plato's soul-body dualism, see Thomas M. Robinson, *Plato's Psychology*, 2nd ed. (Toronto: University of Toronto Press, 1995). For a less polar view, see Colleen P. Zoller, *Plato and the Body: Reconsidering Socratic Asceticism* (Albany: State University of New York Press, 2018).

3. On Plato, see Robinson, *Plato's Psychology*. On Plotinus, see Henry Blumenthal, *Plotinus' Psychology* (The Hague: Nijhoff, 1971); Eyjólfur K. Emilsson, *Plotinus on Sense-Perception: A Philosophical Study* (Cambridge: Cambridge University Press,

knowledge and treatment of the physiological aspect of the human being matters less. Or so it seems.

In this chapter, I follow Plato's lead in the *Timaeus*, juxtaposing the body of the universe to the body of the individual, to uncover Plato's and Plotinus's understanding of healing in the context of the soul-body dualism of (Neo)Platonic psychology. The *Timaeus* is Plato's penultimate dialogue. It presents the subject of natural philosophy in two clearly defined acts. *Actus primus* explains the composition of the complete living being of the universe by the Demiurge as its intelligible cause. *Actus secundus* explains the composition of the individual human being on the Demiurge's instructions to the younger gods to imitate his composition of the complete living being of the universe. The macrocosm-microcosm relation between the two acts of the *Timaeus* offers low-hanging fruits. The dialogue is the final destination of Plato's dualism and becomes a staple of (Neo)Platonist natural philosophy and psychology.

Instead of continuing on the beaten track, I turn to one of Plato's earlier dialogues, the *Charmides*, to uncover the roots of his understanding of healing of the human being before the macrocosm-microcosm parallel of Plato's natural philosophy looms large. I examine two patients' cases, which form their own microcosm-macrocosm relation. The first is the case of young Charmides, who suffers from morning headaches (*Charm.* 155b–157d). The second is the universe and its health (*Enn.* 4.4.40–45). The former opens Socrates's examination of moderation, temperance, or sound-mindedness (*sōphrosynē*) in Plato's eponymous dialogue (*Charm.* 155e2–156a2, 156b3–c5, 156d8–e6); the latter closes Plotinus's discussion of magic in *Enn.* 4.4.[4] If, in the fallen physical

---

1988); Pauliina Remes, *Plotinus on Self: The Philosophy of the "We"* (Cambridge: Cambridge University Press, 2007); Damian Caluori, *Plotinus on the Soul* (Cambridge: Cambridge University Press, 2015).

4. On the semantic spectrum of *sōphrosynē*, see Charles H. Kahn, *Plato and the Socratic Dialogue: The Philosophical Use of a Literary Form* (Cambridge: Cambridge University Press, 1996), 188–91; Christopher Moore and Christopher C. Raymond, trans., *Plato: Charmides* (Indianapolis: Hackett, 2019), xxviii–xxxvii; on its nontranslatability, see Benjamin Jowett, trans., "Charmides," in *Plato, The Collected Dialogues Including the Letters*, ed. Edith Hamilton and Huntington Cairns (Princeton: Princeton University Press, 1989), 99. Considering the medical theme in the *Charmides*, I adopt Christopher Rowe's translation of "sound-mindedness." See Rowe, *Plato and the Art of Philosophical Writing* (Cambridge: Cambridge University Press, 2007), 36–37 and n. 113. On the organization of *Enn.* 4.4, see Gary M. Gurtler, SJ, trans.,

world, the soul matters more than the body for Plato, why does he begin his investigation of *sōphrosynē* by making Socrates choose the good doctors' treatment protocol as the starting point of his investigation? And if the art of medicine indeed does not matter for Plotinus on the background of his top-down metaphysics, why does he talk about the health of the whole (ἵνα ὑγιαίνοι τὸ πᾶν) or even consider surgical amputation and pharmaceutical treatment for certain souls, as diseased parts in the complete living being of the universe (*Enn.* 4.4.45)? What do Plato and Plotinus think about healing?

First Patient: The Individual Human Being

The *Charmides* is one of Plato's later Socratic dialogues. Its perceived lateness presupposes Socrates to have perfected his aporetic method of philosophizing. In fact, it is the opposite.[5] Socrates gives up on the question he sets out to answer, while the recipient of his investigative method eagerly commits to it (*Charm.* 175e5–176b8). The question concerns the sound-mindedness or the health of the soul (*sōphrosynē*). This scenario seeds ambiguity. Why is Socrates's tried and true aporetic method currently deficient?[6] And why is Charmides so enthused about Socrates's prescription, despite Socrates's failure?

The question of health sets the dramatic stage of the dialogue. On it, Socrates has just returned from the battlefield at Potidaea and is hanging out at Taureas's palestra—one of his old haunts—telling his friends the latest on the military front at which Athens continues to lose (*Charm.* 153b9–c1).[7] His own motive, however, is to learn the latest on the philosophical front at which

---

Plotinus: Ennead IV.4.30–45 and IV.5: Problems Concerning the Soul (Las Vegas: Parmenides, 2015).

5. The dialogue is often considered Socrates's less-than-satisfying display of his aporetic method. See Joan Crexells, trans., *Plato: Diàlegs; Carmides; Lisis; Protàgoras*, vol. 2 (Barcelona: Fundació Bernat Metge, 1925), 4; William K. C. Guthrie, *History of Greek Philosophy*, 155; Charles H. Kahn, "Plato's *Charmides* and the Proleptic Reading of Socratic Dialogues." *JP* 85 (1968): 541–49; Kahn, *Plato and the Socratic Dialogue*.

6. The *Charmides* is in the category of zetetic dialogues, in the subcategory of training dialogues, and in the subgroup of testing dialogues, together with the *Euthyphro*, *Meno*, *Ion*, and *Theaetetus*. See Diogenes Laertius, *Vit. phil.* 3.49–51.

7. On the dramatic date of the dialogue, see Crexells, *Plato: Diàlegs; Carmides; Lisis; Protàgoras*, 3–4; Guthrie, *History of Greek Philosophy*, 155; Moore and Raymond, *Plato: Charmides*, xx–xxi.

Athens remains a stronghold (153a1–d1).[8] He wants to know whether there
are any young men "who had become distinguished for wisdom or beauty
or both" (153d4–5).[9] Socrates, it turns out, is in the right place and at the
right time, just as a group of young men, covered in dust and sweat, emerge
from the arena. In their lead is Charmides, admired by all for his beauty, "as
if he were a statue" (154c8). Socrates, too, is taken by the young man's looks
and cannot resist the proposition of Charmides's guardian and cousin, Critias, to consult the young man on an ongoing medical matter.[10] A couple of
days ago, Critias confides in Socrates, the beautiful youth complained to him
about waking up with a heavy head (155b1–5). Critias describes Charmides's
current physical state in the proper medical jargon as "weakness" (astheneia)
and heaviness in the head (barynesthai).[11] Critias is so concerned about
Charmides's condition that he asks Socrates to pretend in front of his cousin
to know (epistasthai) a remedy (pharmakon) for it (155b5–6).[12] Socrates proceeds to examine his patient with a medically attuned eye and assures him
of having a remedy for his suffering (155d3–e2). In the opening scene of

8. On the relation between the social context of the dialogue and Socrates's investigation of sōphrosynē, see Thomas M. Tuozzo, "What's Wrong with These Cities? The
Social Dimension of Sophrosune in Plato's Charmides," JHP 39 (2001): 321–50.

9. Hereafter the text is according to John Burnet, ed., Platonis Opera, vols. 2–4
(Oxford: Clarendon, 1903–1909), and the translation is according to Rosamond Kent
Sprague, trans., "Charmides," in Plato: Complete Works, ed. John M. Cooper (Indianapolis: Hackett, 1997), 639–63, with my alterations and in consultation with Moore
and Raymond, Plato: Charmides.

10. On the characters of the dialogue, see Moore and Raymond, Plato: Charmides,
xxii–xxvii; and Debra Nails, The People of Plato: A Prosopography of Plato and Other
Socratics (Indianapolis: Hackett, 2002).

11. In the medical literature, ἀσθενεία denotes the weakened state of the body by
disease. See Hippocrates, Aff. 22.17; Acut. 2.11.66; Loc. hom. 43.1. On the medical state
of "heaviness," see Hippocrates, Int. 39.4. On weakness in the head, see Loc. hom. 28.6.
Hereafter all references to the medical treatises are according to Émile Littré, ed. and
trans., Oeuvres complètes d'Hippocrate, 10 vols. (Paris: Baillière, 1839–1861).

12. This is not the first time Plato casts Socrates in a medical role. E.g., Socrates's
participation as a doctor in a contest with a chef in the Gorgias (464d3–e2), his self-
identified role of a midwife in the Theaetetus (150c7–d2), and his midwife practice in
the Alcibiades (103a1–119c; see also Olympiodorus, In Alc. 11.7–8). On the maieutic
character of the Alcibiades, see Harold Tarrant, Plato's First Interpreters (Ithaca, NY:
Cornell University Press, 2000), 121–22. On midwifery's medical status, see Vivian
Nutton, Ancient Medicine (London: Routledge, 2004), 101–2; Herbert Bannert,
"Medical Education," in A Companion to Ancient Education, ed. W. Martin Bloomer
(London: Wiley-Blackwell, 2015), 424–25.

the dialogue, the two cousins think of Socrates as a knowledgeable medical practitioner, while Socrates goes along with their impression. From here on, the three main characters of the dialogue are entangled in a medically staged philosophical examination, which ends at the closing scene, having Charmides ready to write down the charm rolling off Socrates's lips. His readiness seals their doctor-patient relationship (158d7–158e7).[13]

In the long exchange between Socrates and Critias about what knowledge (*epistēmē*) is, in the central section of the dialogue, Plato makes Socrates define the art of medicine as "knowledge of what is healthy and what is diseased."[14] Medical treatment protocol is based on knowledge. Socrates considers it essential and yet incomplete. For this reason, he adds another step. For his treatment to work, Socrates explains, he has to apply a certain leaf (*ti philon*) to Charmides's body at the same time as an incantation (*epōidē*) to his soul. He is emphatic about the treatment's necessary condition. The leaf will not heal the body unless its application is accompanied by an incantation for the soul.[15] The full disclosure of the necessary condition for the treatment to work introduces Socrates's new, holistic protocol for healing. Plato presents its rationale in three parts. In part 1, Socrates analyzes the current medical protocol:

> Its nature, Charmides, is not such as to be able to cure the head alone. You have probably heard this about good doctors [ἀγαθῶν ἰατρῶν], that if you go to them with a pain in the eyes, they are likely to say that they cannot undertake to cure the eyes by themselves, but it will be necessary to treat the head at the same time if things are also to go well with the eyes. And again it would be very foolish to suppose that one could even

---

13. Allen, "Soul's Virtue," 77. On the Hippocratic doctor-patient relation, see Chiara Thumiger, "Doctors and Patients," in *The Cambridge Companion to Hippocrates*, ed. Peter E. Pormann (Cambridge: Cambridge University Press, 2018), 263–91.

14. *Charm.* 171a8–9: ἡ ἰατρικὴ δὴ ἑτέρα εἶναι τῶν ἄλλων ἐπιστημῶν ὡρίσθη τῷ τοῦ ὑγιεινοῦ εἶναι καὶ νοσώδους ἐπιστήμη. Also see *Charm.* 165c10–11. On the semantic register of *epistēmē* and its interchangeability with *technē* in Plato, see Robert Bolton, "Science and Scientific Inquiry in Aristotle: A Platonic Provenance," in *The Oxford Handbook of Aristotle*, ed. Christopher Shields (New York: Oxford University Press, 2012), 46–60. On medical epistemology, see Jacques Jouanna, *Hippocrates*, trans. Malcolm B. DeBevoise (Baltimore: Johns Hopkins University Press, 1999), 243–58; Lorenzo Perilli, "Epistemologies," in *The Cambridge Companion to Hippocrates*, ed. Peter E. Pormann (Cambridge: Cambridge University Press, 2018), 119–51.

15. On the importance of prognosis, see Hippocrates, *De arte* 3, 8; Joel E. Mann, *Hippocrates: On the Art of Medicine* (Leiden: Brill, 2012).

treat the head by itself without treating the whole body. In keeping with this principle [ἐκ δὴ τούτου τοῦ λόγου], they plan a regime for the whole body [διαίταις ἐπὶ πᾶν τὸ σῶμα] with the idea of treating and curing the part along with the whole [μετὰ τοῦ ὅλου τὸ μέρος]. (*Charm.* 156b3–c5)

In part 2, Socrates exposes a gap in it:

I learned [the incantation] while I was with the army, from one of the Thracian doctors of Zalmoxis, who are also said to make men immortal. And this Thracian said that the Greek doctors [(ἰατροὶ) οἱ Ἕλληνες] were right to say what I told you just now. "But our king Zalmoxis," he said, "who is a god, says that just as one should not attempt to cure the eyes apart from the head [ὀφθαλμοὺς ἄνευ κεφαλῆς], nor the head apart from the body [κεφαλὴν ἄνευ σώματος], so one should not attempt to cure the body apart from the soul [οὐδὲ σῶμα ἄνευ ψυχῆς]. And this, he says, is the very reason why most diseases are beyond the Greek doctors [παρὰ τοῖς Ἕλλησιν ἰατρούς], that they fail to recognize the whole that should be the object of their care [τὸ ὅλον ἀγνοοῖεν], since if the whole is not in a good condition, it is impossible that the part should be." (156d4–e6)[16]

In part 3, Socrates learns how to fill in the gap from a Thracian doctor:

"So it is necessary first and foremost to cure the soul if the parts of the head and of the rest of the body are to be healthy. And the soul," he said, "my dear friend, is cured by means of certain charms, and these charms consist of beautiful words [τοὺς λόγους εἶναι τοὺς καλούς]. It is a result of such words that sound-mindedness [σωφροσύνην] arises in the soul, and when the soul acquires and possesses sound-mindedness, it is easy to provide health both for the head and for the rest of the body [τὴν ὑγίειαν καὶ τῇ κεφαλῇ καὶ τῷ ἄλλῳ σώματι].... Don't let anyone persuade you to treat his head with this remedy who does not first submit his soul to you for treatment with the charm. Because nowadays ... this is the mistake in treating human beings, that some try to be doctors of the one apart from the other, the health of the soul apart from the health of the body [χωρὶς ἑκατέρου, σωφροσύνης τε καὶ ὑγιείας]." (157a1–b7)[17]

---

16. With Murphy and Moore and Raymond, I read τοῦ ὅλου ἀμελοῖεν as τὸ ὅλον ἀγνοοῖεν. See David J. Murphy, "Critical Notes on Plato's *Charmides*," *Mnemosyne* 60 (2007): 217; Moore and Raymond, *Plato: Charmides*, xlii.

17. With Burnet and Kent Sprague, and *pace* Murphy and Moore and Raymond, I retain σωφροσύνης τε καὶ ὑγιείας at *Charm.* 157b6 (Burnet, *Platonis Opera*; Kent

Socrates's explanation has been in the center of scholarly attention for a long time. In an often-cited study, Drew Hyland diagnoses the young man's condition as *veisalgia*, commonly known as hangover.[18] Some scholars consider the pathology of the condition less relevant to Plato's emphasis on the soul.[19] Others interpret Plato's use of Socratic elenchus as therapy for the soul in analogy with the therapeutic methods of medicine for the body.[20] Their interpretations do not focus on Plato's understanding of healing as inseparable from and sequential to the soul. Only if both parts of the treatment are administered, Socrates insists, will the outcome be successful. Instead of underscoring the polarity between soul and body, Plato draws the therapeutic methods of medicine and Socrates together in healing not the body or the soul but the human being.[21]

Each part is a step in Plato's rationale for the holistic nature of healing. The first part contains Socrates's analysis of the medical understanding of the body as an interrelated system of parts in a whole.[22] By systematically diagnosing and treating the eyes, the head, and the entire body, to use Socrates's example, the doctors treat the body as a complex but unified

---

Sprague, "Charmides," 643; Murphy, "Critical Notes," 217; Moore and Raymond, *Plato: Charmides*, xlii).

18. Drew A. Hyland, *The Virtue of Philosophy: An Interpretation of Plato's Charmides* (Athens: University of Ohio Press, 1981).

19. Robinson, *Plato's Psychology*, 3–20.

20. Alvaro Vallejo, "Maieutic, *epôdê*, and Myth in the Socratic Dialogues," in *Plato: Lysis, Charmides*, ed. Thomas M. Robinson and Luc Brisson, Proceedings of the V Symposium Platonicum (Sankt Augustine: Akademia, 2000), 324–36; Brisson, *Plato the Mythmaker* (Chicago: University of Chicago Press, 2000).

21. Robinson also interprets Plato's holistic understanding to refer to the psychosomatic compound, not to the body. See Thomas M. Robinson, "The Defining Features of Mind-Body Dualism in the Writings of Plato," in *Psyche and Soma: Physicians and Metaphysicians on the Mind-Body Problem from Antiquity to Enlightenment*, ed. John P. Wright and Paul Potter (Oxford: Clarendon, 2000), 39–40; see also Allen, "Soul's Virtue," 77. On the integrative model of healing in folk medicine, using natural substances and incantations, see Richard Gordon, "The Healing Event in Graeco-Roman Folk-Medicine," in *Ancient Medicine in Its Socio-cultural Context*, ed. Philip van der Eijk, Manfred Horstmanshoff, and Petrus H. Schrijvers (Amsterdam: Rodopi, 1995), 2:363–76.

22. On history of holism in medicine, see William E. Stempsey, "Plato and Holistic Medicine," *MHCP* 4 (2001): 202–3; Chiara Thumiger, "Holism: Methodological and Theoretical Perspectives," in *Holism in Ancient Medicine and Its Reception*, ed. Thumiger (Leiden: Brill, 2021), 25–46.

system of organization. For their holistic method, they earn Socrates's approbation for being good (*agathoi iatroi, Charm.* 156b5).[23] But Plato sets the bar higher. Even though the current medical protocol is holistic, it is incomplete.

The second passage exposes its incompleteness. Its method, Socrates warns, treats the body, not the human being. While the body is a composite whole, it is a part of the composite whole of the human being (*Tim.* 87e5–6; see also *Symp.* 209b4–c2).[24] The good doctors' protocol treats holistically the composite unity of the body, but it does not treat holistically the composite unity of the human being because, on Socrates's new treatment protocol, the body cannot be healed "without the soul" (*Charm.* 156e2).[25]

The third passage concludes Socrates's discussion of healing with the words of a Thracian doctor and a follower of the legendary Zalmoxis. What Socrates learns from him does not annul but expands the current medical protocol to include the soul. It would be hasty, I think, to conclude that Socrates's proposed method makes medicine's treatment protocol on the body redundant. There is no hint of it in his criticism of the doc-

---

23. On the medical content of the passage, Hynek Bartoš, *Philosophy and Dietetics in the Hippocratic on Regimen: A Delicate Balance of Health* (Leiden: Brill, 2015), 12. On the history of the scholarly interpretations, see Giouli Korobili and Konstantinos Stefou, "Plato's *Charmides* on Philosophy as Holistic Medical Practice," in Thumiger, *Holism in Ancient Medicine*, 201–19. On holistic evaluation of eye ailments, see, e.g., Hippocrates, *Nat. hom.* 4.3; *Loc. hom.* 10. The appreciation of the current medical protocol in the *Charmides* is later amplified by Plato's praise of Hippocrates's method in the *Phaedrus* (270c10–d1) as the blueprint for how "to think systematically about the nature of anything."

24. Since the *Charmides* precedes Plato's definition of the human being as a soul-*cum*-body compound (*synamphoteron*) in the *Timaeus* and the instrumental relation between soul and body in the *Alcibiades*, his introduction of the soul-and-body method of healing in the *Charmides* could be considered an early intimation of it. On the soul's instrumental use of the body, see *Alc.* 130a9–e5; Nicholas Denyer, ed., *Plato: Alcibiades* (Cambridge: Cambridge University Press, 2001), 214–15. On the relation between the *Charmides* and the *Alcibiades*, see Robinson, *Plato's Psychology*, 3–20.

25. On the soul's responsibility for the health and disease of the body, see *Charm.* 156e6–157a3. On the medical view of soul and body as two distinct but related aspects of human nature, see Beate Gundert, "Soma and Psyche in Hippocratic Medicine," in Wright and Potter, *Psyche and Soma*, 13–35. On Plato's understanding of health, see Julius Moravcsik, "Health, Healing, and Plato's Ethics," *JVI* 34 (2000): 7–26; Stempsey, "Plato and Holistic Medicine," 203–8.

tors' oversight of the soul in their protocol. On the contrary, he insists that, in order for the treatment to be successful, the body and the soul have to be treated simultaneously with their appropriate remedies. On his understanding, the head as the anatomical and physiological locus of Charmides's rationality and his lack of sound-mindedness are correlated (*Charm.* 157a4–5).[26] If one cannot be healed without the other, it follows that one cannot be diseased without the other. Since one cannot be diseased without the other, Socrates's proposed method casts a doubt on the efficacy of the good doctors' current protocol. They cannot heal the body without the proper treatment protocol for the soul, provided by those who have expert knowledge in treating the soul.[27]

If Socrates challenges the efficacy of the medical art on grounds that the doctors, however good they are, do not treat the soul, why does then Plato go out of his way to introduce Socrates's treatment protocol of the soul as a foreign lore? He could simply point to Socrates's art of philosophizing as providing what the doctors' art cannot. Three possibilities come to mind: (1) because Socrates learns his holistic method during the siege of Potidaea, which is itself ectopic to his cultural milieu, primary occupation, and Athens; (2) because, at the battlefield, Socrates firsthand witnesses the liminal experiences of life and death, health and injury, wholeness and fracture; (3) because Socrates's exposure to Zalmoxis's use of incantations taps in the time-honored medicinal use of incantations, prayers, amulets, and magic.[28] No single possibility is the sole reason, I suggest, but all three

---

26. If we consider, with Hyland (*Virtue of Philosophy*), Charmides's condition as a case of hangover, the necessary moderation of his soul is apparent. On *sōphrosynē* as order in the soul, see *Gorg.* 504c–507c. On the soul-body relation in the *Charmides*, see Robinson, *Plato's Psychology*, 4–8; Kahn, "Plato's *Charmides*"; Kahn, *Plato and the Socratic Dialogue*, 183–209; Richard E. Stalley, "*Sôphrosunê* in the *Charmides*," in Robinson and Brisson, *Plato: Euthydemus, Lysis, Charmides*, 265–77; Sara Ahbel-Rappe, *Socratic Ignorance and Platonic Knowledge in the Dialogues of Plato* (Albany: State University of New York Press, 2018), 35–46; Moore and Raymond, *Plato: Charmides*, xxviii–xl; Allen, "Soul's Virtue."

27. In Plato's psychosomatic classifications of the arts in the *Gorgias* and the *Alcibiades*, medicine is closely related to the arts of the soul. Socrates's protocol is supported by the place of medicine as a correlative to justice in the *Gorgias* and its intermediate position between the art of self-knowledge and the banausic arts in the *Alcibiades*.

28. Zalmoxis's connection with the medical profession is unattested in the doxographical tradition. Our earliest source is Herodotus (*Hist.* 4.94–95), who recounts

of them contribute to promoting Socrates's proposed method as appropriate. Socrates himself does not invent the method during his philosophizing at the palestra but adopts it from another practice while he himself is in a liminal position between life and death at the battlefield. In this liminal position, I further suggest, his "beautiful words" (*kalloi logoi*) acquire their healing power.[29] His experience at the battlefield and his encounter with Zalmoxis's holistic approach unlock the enchanting power of his investigative method, searching to define the virtue of the soul.[30] "Don't let anyone persuade you," Plato makes the Thracian doctor stress, "to treat his head with this remedy who does not first submit his soul to you for treatment with the charm" (*Charm.* 157b2–4). The salubrious effect of Socrates's words on Charmides proves that they are the healing incanta-

---

a Thracian and a Greek version of the legend. Neither one involves a medical treatment or a healing cult. In the Thracian version, Zalmoxis is said to spend four years in an underground chamber in order to convince his tribesmen of his immortality. The interpretations of Socrates's reference to Zalmoxis are numerous; e.g., Francis P. Coolidge Jr., "Relation of Philosophy to σωφροσύνη: Zalmoxian Medicine in Plato's *Charmides*," *AncPhil* 13 (1993): 23–36; Brisson, *Plato the Mythmaker*; David J. Murphy, "Doctors of Zalmoxis and Immortality in the *Charmides*," in Robinson and Brisson, *Plato: Euthydemus, Lysis, Charmides*, 287–95; Robinson, "Defining Features of Mind-Body Dualism"; Tuozzo, "What's Wrong with These Cities"; Louis-André Dorion, *Platon: Charmide; Lysis* (Paris: Flammarion, 2004), 117 n. 32. Edelstein remains standard on the relation between scientific and religious healing. See Ludwig Edelstein, "Greek Medicine and Its Relation to Religion and Magic," in *Ancient Medicine: Selected Papers of Ludwig Edelstein*, ed. Owsei Temkin and C. Lilian Temkin, trans. C. Lilian Temkin (Baltimore: Johns Hopkins University Press, 1967), 205–46. *On The Sacred Disease* (*Morb. Sacr.* 2) distinguishes the two forms of healing.

29. Socrates's soul-body parallel is a *topos* of the Sophists too. Gorgias considers the power of speech as having the same relationship to the order of soul (*taxis psychēs*) as does the order of drugs (*pharmakōn taxis*) to the nature of bodies (*sōmatōn physin, Hel.* 14). See *Gorg.* 456b1–c8; Eric R. Dodds, trans., *Plato: Gorgias* (Oxford: Clarendon, 1959), 227; Robinson, *Plato's Psychology*, 7; Maria Plastira-Valkanou, "Medicine and Fine Cuisine in Plato's *Gorgias*," *AC* 67 (1998): 201.

30. Dorion, *Platon: Charmide; Lysis*, 116 n. 27. See also Plato, *Euthyd.* 290a; Pindar, *Pyth.* 3.47–53. On medical incantations in Pythagorean practice, see Iamblichus, *Vit. Pyth.* 163.4–164.6. On incantations in Plato, see Brisson, *Plato the Mythmaker*; and Robinson, "Defining Features of Mind-Body Dualism"; on the therapeutic use of words in Plato and Socrates, see Robinson, *Plato's Psychology*, 7–8; Pedro Laín Entralgo, *The Therapy of the Word in Classical Antiquity*, ed. and trans. Lelland J. Rather and John M. Sharp (New Haven: Yale University Press, 1970), 108–38; Vladislav Suvák, "Sókratovská *Therapeia*: Platónov *Charmidés* 153a–158d," *Filosofia* 71 (2016): 362–65.

tion he recommends.[31] Socrates's tripartite explanation of his rationale is itself the charm, setting Charmides on his path of healing.

That Plato makes Socrates insist on the use of incantations is not ectopic to the art of medicine. It echoes the popular use of incantations in medical practices, recited in the Greek magical papyri or inscribed on the walls of the Asclepieia.[32] Although Plato's linguistic choice of "incantation" (*epōidē*) is unattested in the medical literature, the adjuvant use of prayer (*euchē*) and clinical therapy are well documented (Hippocrates, *Ep.* 9.328.21, 9.344.9; *Loc. hom.* 6.342.10; *Diaet.* 6.642).[33] The cultural evidence suggests that Greek doctors are not unaware of the use of incantations, but that the use of incantations does not comport with the ratiocinative nature of their treatment protocol. They rely on a different kind of *logoi*, aimed at explaining the nature of either the body, according to Socrates's definition of the art of medicine in the *Gorgias*, or the human being, according to the self-definitions of the art in the medical literature of the fifth century BCE (*Gorg.* 501a1–3).[34] While medical definitions mention the human being,

---

31. On incantation as a metaphor of Socrates's *elenchos*, see Dorion, *Platon: Charmide; Lysis*, 119 n. 37. On Socrates as a magician, see *Meno* 80b. On the *Charmides* as "a dialogue of definition," see Moore and Raymond, *Plato: Charmides*, xviii–xix.

32. On the contending relation between medicine and magic in the Greco-Roman world, see Eric R. Dodds, *Pagan and Christian in an Age of Anxiety* (New York: Norton, 1965), 44–46; Edelstein, "Greek Medicine"; Jouanna, *Hippocrates*, 181–209; Nutton, *Ancient Medicine*; Louis Cilliers and F. Pieter Retief, "Dream Healing in Asclepieia in the Mediterranean," in *Dreams, Healing, and Medicine in Greece from Antiquity to Present*, ed. Steven M. Oberhelman (Farnham, UK: Ashgate, 2013), 69–92. The ancient sources on this relation are collected in *PDM* and Emma J. Edelstein and Ludwig Edelstein, eds., *Asclepius: Collection and Interpretation of the Testimonies*, 2 vols. (Baltimore: Johns Hopkins University Press, 1998). On the Mesopotamian origin of the idea to distinguish between a practicing doctor and an exorcist, see Markham J. Geller, *Ancient Babylonian Medicine: Theory and Practice* (Oxford: Wiley-Blackwell, 2010); Troels P. Arbøll, *Medicine in Ancient Assur: A Microhistorical Study of the Neo-Assyrian Healer Kiṣir Aššur* (Leiden: Brill, 2021).

33. Nutton, *Ancient Medicine*, 66; David C. Lindberg, *The Beginnings of Western Science: The European Scientific Tradition in Philosophical, Religious, and Institutional Context, Prehistory to A.D. 1450*, 2nd ed. (Chicago: University of Chicago Press, 2007), 113–19.

34. Admittedly, Socrates's view of the body as the object of medicine is less sophisticated than the views in his contemporary medical literature. In it, the suffering human (Hippocrates, *De arte* 3), the human being (Hippocrates, *Vet. med.* 3.6), or the human nature (*Nat. hom.* 1) are identified as the object of the art.

they conspicuously omit the soul as a part of it.[35] Plato approves of medicine's holistic method of healing but calls it out for not including the soul. Many diseases escape the good Greek doctors' notice because they neglect to treat the whole, "not the body without the soul" (οὐδὲ σῶμα ἄνευ ψυχῆς, *Charm.* 156e1–6).

The therapeutic success can be considered a pointed case of Socratic irony, drawing on the characteristic of medicine as a stochastic art that aims at a goal within a range of unknown and changing particulars.[36] Charmides is healed not because Socrates knows what *sōphrosynē* is but because Socrates has shown him how to search for it.[37] In this light, Socrates successfully fulfills his role of a doctor, offering a medical consultation to Charmides (*Charm.* 175e2–176b4).[38] His protocol is empirically effective. Like the good doctors' protocol, praised by him at the onset of his investigation, his protocol achieves its goal. While the former holistically treats the parts within the body, the latter holistically treats the body and the soul within the human being. The health of one entails the health of the other.[39]

The *Charmides* is Plato's work in progress at integrating medicine and philosophy to collaborate in healing not the soul or the body but the psychosomatic compound of the individual human being. Can we consider Socrates's expansion of the good doctors' treatment protocol as Plato's critique of medicine's deficiency? I do not think so. Plato's insistence that the body cannot be healed without healing the soul indeed determines the top-down priority of the process. But its top-down designation does not make either healing the body or medicine's contribution to the holistic healing of the human being unnecessary. Plato's insistence

---

35. An exception is the explanation of the physiological nature of the soul in *Regimen* (Hippocrates, *Vict.* 25).

36. On the difficulty of precision in medical knowledge, see Hippocrates, *Vet. med.* 9–12, and Mark J. Schiefsky, *Hippocrates: On Ancient Medicine* (Leiden: Brill, 2005), 33–36.

37. Here I follow Ahbel-Rappe's (*Socratic Ignorance*, 37–46) analysis of Socrates's search for definition as an expression of what she calls the epistemic self. On the presence of the Thracian as Plato's commentary on the political and epistemological state of affairs in Athens, see Tuozzo, "What's Wrong with These Cities," 325–30.

38. On Socrates's dialectical examination as "doctoring," see Allen, "Soul's Virtue," 77.

39. In Robinson's words, "head and body entail each other as concave does convex, and the same can be said of body and soul" (*Plato's Psychology*, 6).

on including the soul in his understanding of healing is not surprising. In fact, the opposite would be anomalous. I do not think Plato would begin his argument for holistic psychosomatic healing from the bottom-up perspective of the body, unless he considers medicine's participation essential. If anything, beginning from the top down would be the shortest way for him to expose the good doctors' mistaken protocol. This case could be made if Plato said anywhere in the *Charmides* that the soul heals the body. But he does not say this, explicitly or implicitly. Rather, he insists that the soul and the body are simultaneously healed by the remedies suitable to each.

For Plato, healing is a top-down yet bidirectional process. Since the soul and the body weld the compound of the human being into a composite whole, in order for healing to be successful, the therapeutic action must jointly work from two directions: applying natural substances to the body at the bottom and Socrates's "beautiful words" to the soul at the top (*Charm.* 157a4–5). Although Plato's psychosomatic dualism is gestational in the *Charmides*, his holistic understanding of healing anticipates its final goal. According to Plato, the art of medicine and the aporetic art of Socrates have to work together in healing the individual human being. Healing is one of the earliest subjects in which Plato begins to shape his understanding of the correlation between soul and body in the human being. His fully developed view of the microcosmic organization of the individual soul-body compound in the *Timaeus* contains a distant echo of Socrates's protocol in the *Charmides*. The only way for the human being to preserve themselves is "not to exercise the soul without the body, nor the body without the soul, so that each may be balanced by the other and so be healthy" (*hygiē, Tim.* 6c1). Plato begins his argument from the bottom up in the *Charmides* by insisting on not treating "the body without the soul." Plato does not explain how and why the joint application of natural substance and incantation work together to heal. To understand the joint nature of the healing process, we have to turn to Plotinus, who directs his attention to healing the living being of the universe.

Second Patient: The Living Being of the Universe

Plotinus addresses the topic of the universe as a functioning organism in the closing movement of *Enn.* 4.4. The tractate is the second installment in the tripartite series, titled *Problems Concerning the Soul*, according to Porphyry's thematical arrangement (*Vit. Plot.* 5.3–4, 25.19–20).[40] It belongs to Plotinus's middle writing period, when Porphyry attended his lectures in Rome and insisted Plotinus elaborated on his view of exactly how "the soul was 'in' the body" (*Vit. Plot.* 13.10–11). The last five chapters of the work (*Enn.* 4.4.40–45) offer Plotinus's answer concerning the embodied souls' susceptibility to harm or benefit.

His explanation begins on the same note as Socrates's observation about the good doctors' understanding of the holistic relation between parts and whole in the *Charmides*, but from a metaphysical perspective. The individual living beings are interconnected parts of the universe as a whole that contains them all (see *Enn.* 3.3.6.1–15). In the background of Plotinus's premise is the Demiurge's composition of the living being of the universe in the *Timaeus*, complemented by Plato's understanding of Nature and the arts auxiliary to it, such as medicine, agriculture, and physical training, as propounded in the *Laws* (respectively, *Tim.* 29e, 30a–35a, 41d; *Leg.* 889a–d).[41]

Much has happened in the philosophical landscape between Plato and Plotinus. One direction of these developments elicits the relation between the individual living being and the order (*kosmos*) of the universe. The Stoics, especially, take to heart the interwoven relation between soul and body in Plato's cosmology in the *Timaeus* and laboriously work out a physicalistic and deterministic explanation for it on the principle that "the world … is in sympathy with itself" (Pseudo-Plutarch, *De fat.* 574d; see also Sextus Empiricus, *Math.* 9.79, Cicero, *Nat. d.* 2.19).[42] On this principle, the entities within the world are in sympathy with each other, individual being with individual being, soul with body, body with soul. Everything about this idea is appealing to Plotinus, except its materialistic underpinnings. One of his goals in *Enn.* 4.4 is to rectify them on proper metaphysical grounds. He does so while engaging with recent scientific developments in astronomy, astrology, and medicine.[43] Behind his inter-

---

40. Gurtler, *Plotinus: Ennead IV.4.30–45 and IV.5*, 15–25.

41. See Gurtler, *Plotinus: Ennead IV.4.30–45 and IV.5*, 18–22.

42. A recent overview of sympathy in Stoicism is found in René Brouwer, "Stoic Sympathy," in *Sympathy: A History*, ed. Eric Schliesser (Oxford: Oxford University Press, 2015), 15–35.

43. On Plotinus's engagement with Ptolemy and Galen, see Gurtler, *Plotinus: Ennead IV.4.30–45 and IV.5*, 17. On Galen's understanding of *sympatheia*, see Brooke Holmes, "Galen's Sympathy," in Schliesser, *Sympathy*, 61–69.

est is the motivation to explain the interconnectedness of all things in the universe by the power of the world-soul to bring everything in an unified whole.[44] Plato's reference to the contagious nature of yawning in the *Charmides* has come on the scholarly radar as an early notion of *sympatheia*, but its role in his holistic psychosomatic understanding of healing has remained unnoticed, even though, as examined in the first section of the chapter, Socrates's treatment protocol intimates the sympathetic nature of healing of the individual with the help of medicine and the incantation of Socrates's words (*Charm.* 169c3–6).[45]

Between Plato and Plotinus, the intellectual standing of magic and medicine has reversed. Plotinus criticizes "the arts of magic" in favor of medicine as one of "the arts of nature."[46] As Plato in the *Charmides*, he considers the arts of incantation and medicine in relation to the health of the human being. He diverts his rationale from Plato's, however, on their healing effect. His view shows significant leaps in understanding the holistic nature of healing, medicine's contribution to it, and the countereffect of magic on it:

Each thing in the universe [ἑκάστον τῶν ἐν τῷ παντί] contributes to the whole, and acts or is acted on according to its nature and disposition [φύσεως καὶ διαθέσεως], just as does each part in the case of a single living being [ἕκαστον τῶν μέρων]; it contributes to the universe [πρὸς τὸν ὅλον], serves it, and is held to be worth a place in the order and a role [τάξεως καὶ χρείας] in it in accordance with its nature and structure [φύσεως καὶ κατασκευῆς]. Each both makes its own contribution and receives as many things that come from elsewhere as its nature is capable

44. On *sympatheia* in Plotinus and his differences with the Stoics and Galen, see Eyjólfur K. Emilsson, "Plotinus on *Sympatheia*," in Schliesser, *Sympathy*, 36–60. On the world-soul in Stoicism and Platonism, respectively, see Ricardo Salles, "The Stoic World Soul and the Theory of Seminal Principles," in *World Soul: A History*, ed. James Wilberding (Oxford: Oxford University Press, 2021), 44–66 and James Wilberding, "The World Soul in the Platonic Tradition," in Wilberding, *World Soul*, 15–43.

45. Brouwer, "Stoic Sympathy," 17–18. On holism and *sympatheia* in medicine and philosophy, see Emilsson, "Plotinus on *Sympatheia*."

46. The question of Plotinus's treatment of magic, as reported in *Vit. pyth.* 10.3–13, is examined in Philip Merlan, "Plotinus and Magic," *Isis* 44 (1953): 341–48; Arthur Hilary Armstrong, "Was Plotinus a Magician?," *Phronesis* 1 (1955): 73–79; Wendy E. Helleman, "Plotinus as Magician," *IJPT* 4 (2010): 114–46.

of receiving; and the whole has the kind of self-awareness of the whole [συναίσθησις πάντος πρὸς πᾶν]. (*Enn.* 4.4.45.2–8)[47]

In his exposition of the harmful effects of magic, Plotinus's explanation is medically exact, referring to natures, dispositions, structures, proper order, giving and receiving powers.[48] Even though he does not discuss the healing method of medicine specifically, he couches the interrelation between parts and whole in the living being of the universe in the conceptual framework of medicine and in the same rationale as the good doctors' healing method, commended by Socrates in the *Charmides*. The difference is a matter of scale, between the microcosm of the individual and the macrocosm of the universe.[49] While Plato argues that it is impossible to heal one part without healing the whole, Plotinus argues that it is impossible to affect one part in an organism without affecting all the other parts within the whole. Plato and Plotinus agree that healing is a form of affect in which one part acts on another. But their agreement ends here.

Unlike Socrates's innovative method in the *Charmides*, which relies on the joint healing effects of incantation and medicine on the individual human being, Plotinus does not consider all such effects salubrious.[50] For him, the interconnectedness of all parts is double-edged. The kinship between things, he reasons, makes them susceptible to beneficial as well as harmful effects. He is particularly cautious about magic (*goēteia*,

---

47. Hereafter the translation of *Enn.* 4.4 is according to Lloyd P. Gerson, ed., *Plotinus: The Enneads* (Cambridge: Cambridge University Press, 2018), with my alternations and in consultation with Gurtler's translation (*Plotinus: Ennead IV.4.30–45 and IV.5*). The Greek text is according to Paul Henry and Hans-Rudolf Schwyzer, eds. *Plotini Opera*, 3 vols. (Oxford: Clarendon, 1964–1983).

48. The medical content of the terms can be illustrated in any medical treatise by Galen or any early medical author.

49. On the medical microcosm-macrocosm relation, see Hippocrates, *De victu*; Laura R. Schluderer, "Imitating the Cosmos: The Role of Microcosm-Macrocosm Relationships in the Hippocratic Treatise *On Regimen*," *ClQ* 68 (2018): 31–52. On the universe as an organism and the power of soul's *sympatheia*, see Emilsson, "Plotinus on *Sympatheia*," 39–43.

50. The ritualistic element in the healing process supplies a vital vein of interest for the post-Plotinian Neoplatonists. On their use of dreams, prayers, and incantations, see James Wilberding, "Neoplatonism and Medicine," in *The Routledge Handbook of Neoplatonism*, ed. Pauliina Remes and Svetla Slaveva-Griffin (London: Routledge, 2014), 362–64. On astral influence, magic, and prayer, see Emilsson, "Plotinus on *Sympatheia*," 44–52.

mageia) and distinguishes three ways in which it works: (1) by sympathy
(*sympatheia*), (2) by the natural tendency of harmony (*symphōnia*) among
similar things and their opposites, and (3) by the diversity (*poikilia*) of
powers contributing to the perfection of a living being (*Enn.* 4.4.40.1–4).
The number of possibilities opens the door for different results not all beneficial to their recipient.

Plotinus examines each of the possibilities in order. He relates *sympatheia* to the principle of Love (*Philia*), pertaining to Empedocles's cosmic
pair of Love and Strife.[51] Accordingly, Love for him is "the first magician
and pharmacist [γοὴς and φαρμακεύς] whom men observed well, using
his drugs and spells [τοῖς φαρμάκοις καὶ τοῖς γοητεύμασι] on one another"
(*Enn.* 4.4.40.5–9).[52] His explanation blurs the boundaries between magic
and medicine more than Plato's holistic psychosomatic method of healing
that joins medicine and incantation in the *Charmides*. While Plotinus's use
of "magician" (*goēs*) delimits its meaning to the arts of magic, his choice
of *pharmakeus* broadens it to include both magic and medicine. Consequently, the dual meaning of *pharmakon* as drug and poison underpins
the dual meaning of *pharmakeus* as "one who prepares drugs to heal or
potions to bewitch."[53] The healing or harming effect of Love then is conveyed through the power of *sympatheia* among things. "When one prays
to a heavenly being," Plotinus adds, "something emanates from that being
to him or to someone else" (*Enn.* 4.4.40.32).[54] The emanated power of *sympatheia*, it can be concluded, pertains to the nature of the universe and
Soul as its organizing principle. It permeates all beings, aware or not.

Take young Charmides as an example. On Plotinus's understanding,
he begins to heal because Socrates's "beautiful words" have already activated the innate power of *sympatheia* within his individual being as a part
of the universe. The speculative example of Charmides points us to Plotinus's understanding of soul as the third organizing principle of reality

---

51. Empedocles frag. D73 Laks and Most. Gurtler, *Plotinus: Ennead IV.4.3–45 and
IV.5*, 85 n. 12.

52. On personal love and *sympatheia*, see *Enn.* 4.9.3.1–4.

53. Robert Beekes, ed., *Etymological Dictionary of Greek* (Leiden: Brill, 2010),
1554; Pierre Chantraine, ed., *Dictionnaire étymologique de la langue grecque*, 2nd ed.
(Paris: Klincksieck, 1999), 1177–79. On the history of the term, see Gurtler, *Plotinus:
Ennead IV.3–45 and IV.5*, 187.

54. On the soul's controlling the faculties of growth and generation, see Plotinus,
Enn. 2.3.17.1–9.

which expresses the intelligible realm in the physical world. Accordingly, the world-soul and the individual soul can be considered respectively the macrocosmic and microcosmic power that binds the universe and the individual being together. Sympathy works on the binding power of the world-soul and the individual soul, while healing belongs to the nature of the living being of the universe that binds all parts in a whole. This places the former in a powerful position, which Plotinus carefully qualifies. While *sympatheia* affects the individual being within it, he clarifies, the universe itself remains unaffected (*apathes*).[55] By analogy, even within the individual being, the governing part (*to hegoumenon*) of the soul of the individual remains unaffected.[56] Affected only is the outer layer of the human being. Because of its proximity to other living beings as parts of the universe, Plotinus explains, the outer layer of the human being is susceptible to external influences.[57] He elaborates:

> And one part benefits from another or is harmed by it because they are of this nature, and by the skills of doctors and of those who sing incantations [καὶ τέχναις ἰατρῶν καὶ ἐπαοιδῶν], one part is forced to make something of its power [τι τῆς δυνάμεως] available to another. (*Enn.* 4.4.42.8–10)[58]

And in the next chapter:

> And even as the non-rational part [τὸ ἄλογον] is affected by incantations [ἐπῳδαῖς], so the [virtuous person] himself can undo the forces that come from them by chanting against them and singing counter-incantations [ἀντεπᾴδων]. But [that person] might suffer death [θάνατον], disease

---

55. Plotinus, *Enn.* 4.4.42.19: οὔκουν δοτέον τὸ πᾶν πάσχειν.

56. Plotinus, *Enn.* 4.4.40.31: ἀπαθὲς δ᾽αὐτῷ τὸ ἡγούμενόν ἐστιν.

57. The tension, inherited from Plato's division of rational/immortal and nonrational/mortal part of the individual soul at *Tim.* 69c5–71e2, forces Plotinus to allow the possibility for the nonrational part of the soul to be influenced externally through its immediate proximity to the body.

58. See Plotinus, *Enn.* 3.3.6.29–38: "The inferior is related to the inferior as the better is to the better; for example, as eye is to eye, so is foot to foot, one thing to the other, and if you wish, as virtue is to justice, so is vice to injustice.... And if heaven acts upon things here, it does so in the way that the parts in every living being act on each other, not as one thing generating another—for they are generated simultaneously—but each thing experiences in accordance with its own nature whatever contributes to its own nature and because a thing has a particular nature, what it experiences is of this nature, too."

[νόσους], or other things that are to do with the body [τὰ σωματικά], from such things; for the part of the whole [τὸ μέρος τοῦ παντός] could be affected either by another part of it, or by the whole [ὑπὸ μέρους ἄλλου ἢ τοῦ παντός], but the person himself remains unharmed [ἀβλαβής]. (*Enn.* 4.4.43.7–11)

In the first passage, Plotinus groups together medicine and magic, as influencing the relations between the different parts of the body through *sympatheia*, drawing them in a constant give-and-take relation with their environment. In the second passage, he distinguishes medicine and magic by singling out the harmful effects of magic.[59] To the harmful effects of the arts of magic, he juxtaposes "the arts of nature" (οὐ μάγων τέχναις, ἀλλὰ τῆς φύσεως), one of which is the art of medicine, together with agriculture and physical training, that attend to the well-being of the body and thereby engage closely with the nonrational part of the soul (*Enn.* 4.4.43.22–23; see 5.9.11.17–21). Here Plotinus considers the nonrational part of the soul to be affected by incantations because it is the closest to the body and thus the external environment of the human being. This proximity makes it susceptible to outside influence, whether it is aware of it or not. In the tractate titled "Against the Gnostics" (*Enn.* 2.9 [33]), composed not long after *Enn.* 4.4, Plotinus modifies his earlier pronouncement about the relation between diseases and incantation. Contrary to those who claim that diseases occur when daemons invade the body, he promotes the medically informed theory of the origin of diseases in "exhaustion, excess, and deficiency of nourishment, decay, and in general processes that have their starting point either inside or outside of the body" (*Enn.* 2.9.14.13–20).[60] His understanding separates the arts of magic and medicine and relates each of them to Nature.

In "What Is the Living Being and What Is the Human Being?" (*Enn.* 1.1), the tractate Porphyry deemed important to place first in his edition of Plotinus's works, Plotinus identifies the part of soul that is influenced by magic with the generative and vegetative faculties of the soul (*Enn.*

---

59. Under the influence of Plato (*Tim.* 89b2–4), Plotinus acknowledges the harmful effects of drugs, e.g., the use of drugs to induce death at *Enn.* 1.9.1.14–15, the hallucinogenic power of drugs at *Enn.* 6.8.2.7–8.

60. Discussed in Wilberding, "Neoplatonism and Medicine," 360–61. See also Plotinus, *Enn.* 3.8.39–40. On Plato's understanding of diseases and their causes, see *Tim.* 81e6–89d1.

1.1.9.20–23; see 2.3.17.6–7). In *Enn.* 4.4, this faculty is responsible for the self-sustainability and self-preservation of the human being as a living organism: some actions of the human being are stimulated nonrationally, he elaborates, "for the sake of needs, seeking to fill a natural deficiency [χάριν τὴν τῆς φύσεως ἔνδειαν … ἀποπληροῦν], clearly have as their origin the force of nature [τὴν τῆς φύσεως βίαν πρὸς τὸ ζῆν] which adapts us for life as something that is our own";[61] other actions, such as the care for children, the urge for marriage, and the drive for positions of authority are stimulated "due to the force of human nature [τῇ τῆς φύσεως τῆς ἀνθρωπίνης βίᾳ] and [the human being's] own concern for the life of others, or even of his own [πρὸς τὸ ζῆν τῶν ἄλλων ἢ καὶ αὐτοῦ οἰκειώσει]…, he does become subject to sorcery" (*Enn.* 4.4.44.6–24). The art of medicine does not have anything to do with the political or otherwise social life of the human being, but, insofar as the nonrational part of the soul is responsible for the biological life of the body, the art of medicine serves in an auxiliary capacity to nature itself.

The association of medicine with the vegetative power of nature determines Plotinus's distinction between the harmful effects of magic and the salubrious effects of medicine. In his discussion of the different products of the arts early in the treatise, he classifies medicine, together with agriculture, as an auxiliary art (ὑπηρετικὴ τέχνη), "helping natural things be in natural state" (κατὰ φύσιν).[62] In the discussion under examination here, he understands the human being to be ultimately subject to the sorcery of Nature itself and, by extension, to medicine as the auxiliary art of Nature and ultimately of the world-soul as the caretaker of the universe.[63] What is more, he considers Nature the most potent magician and *pharmakeus*

---

61. The natural deficiency is caused by the ontologically decompensated state of the body and, as such, it is the object of the art of medicine (Plato, *Resp.* 341e5–6).

62. Plotinus, *Enn.* 4.4.3.18–19: ἰατρικὴ δὲ καὶ γεωργία καὶ αἱ τοιαῦται ὑπηρετικαὶ καὶ βοήθειαν εἰς τὰ φύσει εἰσφερόμεναι, ὡς κατὰ φύσιν ἔχειν. In coining the term *auxiliary*, Plotinus echoes Galen's reference to medicine and agriculture as providing auxiliary service to nature (*Thras.* 5.834.11–16). See also *Thras.* 5.862.6–8: ἡ γὰρ φύσις οὕτω γε καὶ ποιεῖ τὸ σῶμα καὶ αὖθις ἐπανορθοῦνται κάμνον ὡς ἡ περὶ τὴν ἐσθῆτα τέχνη. ταύτης δ' ὑπηρετική τίς ἐστιν ἡ νῦν ζητουμένη; *Ars med.* 1.378.11–12: ἁπάντων δ' αὐτῶν [μορίων] ἡ μὲν φύσις ἐστὶ δημιουργός, ὁ δ' ἰατρὸς ὑπηρέτης. Hereafter all references to Galen are according to Karl G. Kühn, *Galeni Opera Omnia*, 20 vols. (Leipzig: Cnobloch, 1819–1933). The notion of auxiliary arts as a category of arts is originally detected in Aristotle, *Metaph.* 982a14–17.

63. Plotinus, *Enn.* 4.4.44.29–30: τοῦτο δὲ ἡ τῆς φύσεως γοητεία ποιεῖ.

because its actions are imperceptible and unavoidable. This sort of action, according to him, infatuates the nonrational part of the soul because its faculties of growth and generation (*to phytikon* and *to gennētikon*) are akin to Nature as the universal principle of growth and generation through the imperceptible channels of *sympatheia*. For this reason, he concludes, the nonrational part is pulled "by the drawing strings of Nature."[64] The antidote to this most powerful form of spell, he advises, is to realize that we do these actions when we are turned outwardly, away from our true self. Medicine then works on the outer layer of the self, namely, the body as the product of the world-soul in the natural world.

Again, take young Charmides, for example. Socrates plays the role of both the doctor, who is applying a leaf as a remedy (*pharmakon*) to his body, and a magician, who is applying an incantation (*epōidē*) to his soul. According to Plotinus, both applications work because the remedy and the incantation are akin to Charmides's condition. Socrates's treatment protocol succeeds because its joint application activates the power of *sympatheia* between Charmides as a part of the universe and the universe as a whole. Although the outcome is beneficial to Charmides, there is an implicit danger in how *sympatheia* works. What if the practitioner of the arts of magic or medicine would not have Socrates's salubrious intention? Charmides would be still affected by the binding power of *sympatheia*, Plotinus would elaborate, with or without Socrates's intent because of the natural tendency of harmony (*symphōnia*) among similar things and their opposites. For this, Plotinus provides his own example. Anger, yellow bile, and the liver, he points out, all share the quality of bitterness. The bitter quality of the affection of anger is drawn along with the bitter quality of bile and the bitter quality of the nature of the liver as the organ, closely related to the bodily humor of bile (*Enn.* 4.4.41.9–11).[65] The affections of anger, yellow bile, and liver are bound together by the quality of bitterness and thus are sympathetic. Although when we are

---

64. Plotinus, *Enn.* 4.4.45.26: ἐκ μηρίνθων ὁλκαῖς τισι φύσεως μετατιθεμένων. See also, e.g., *Enn.* 1.1.8.20–23; 2.3.17.1–9; 3.6.4.38–39; 4.9.3.10–16.

65. See also Plotinus's previous discussion (*Enn.* 4.4.4.28) of the origin of anger from the faculties of growth and reproduction and the individual's physical constitution. On the contrast between Plotinus and Galen on the faculty of growth, see Courtney A. Roby, "Animal, Vegetable, Metaphor: Plotinus' Liver and the Roots of Biological Identity," in *The Comparable Body: Analogy and Metaphor in Ancient Mesopotamian, Egyptian, and Greco-Roman Medicine*, ed. John Z. Wee (Leiden: Brill, 2017), 387–414.

angry, we do not intend to harm our liver, the production of bile and the individual constitution of our liver make us susceptible to harm, according to Plotinus, because the constitution of the body is predisposed to the boiling of bile.[66] His medically informed example explains how the parts within the human being affect each other through the *sympatheia* of their natures. But he does not stop here and, on the same principle, envisions involuntary adverse effects of bile on the cosmic stage:

> This thing [that comes from soul itself] is indeed a living being, but a rather imperfect one, and one which finds its own life disgusting inasmuch as it is the worst, ill-conditioned, savage, made of worse matter, this matter being a sort of sediment of the prior realities, bitter and embittering [πικρᾶς καὶ πικρά]. (*Enn.* 2.3.17.20–24)

Plotinus identifies bitterness, produced by the excess of yellow bile, as one of the defining characteristics of the living being of the universe.[67] Since the universe is a single living organism, held together by unity of soul (*psychē mia*), its parts give and receive something of their powers to the extent their nature allows. The arts of magic and medicine work as catalysts, directing or speeding up the effects of this global exchange.[68] Plotinus considers the two principal elements in Plato's understanding of healing—medicine and incantations—to operate under the same denominator, without the need to introduce the idea of their collaboration through the tale of the foreign Zalmoxis. His explanation is straightforward. With its earthly substances and methods of manipulation, medicine

---

66. The effects of bile on its adjacent parts are discussed at *Enn.* 2.3.12.27; the physiology of bile at 1.1.5.24–25; the excess of bile as a cause of disease at 1.8.14.24.

67. On bitterness and yellow bile, see Hippocrates, *Vet. med.* 19.20–21. On the difference between black and yellow bile, see Galen, *Atr. bil.* 5.108.8, 5.129.6–7. On the origin of the term in Prodicus and Plato, see Galen, *PHP* 8.6.48. On Galen's interpretation of Plato's account of the influence of bile and the constitution of the body on the soul, see *QAM* 4.789. See also Plato, *Tim.* 86e5–87a8.

68. Plotinus, *Enn.* 4.9.3.4–9: "And if spells and magical procedures [ἐπῷδαὶ καὶ ὅλως] in general serve to bring people together and cause them to connect sympathetically [συμπαθεῖς] from considerable distances, this must at all events result from a unity of soul [διὰ ψυχῆς μιᾶς]. And an utterance pronounced quietly has an effect on what is far distant from it and has caused an attentive reaction from something vastly removed in space. From such phenomena, one may conclude the unity of all things [ἑνότητα μαθεῖν ἁπάντων], by reason of the unity of soul [ψυχῆς μιᾶς οὔσης]." On *sympatheia* and nonadjacent parts, see Emilsson, "Plotinus on *Sympatheia*," 46–47.

does to the body what magic does to the nonrational part of the soul, with potions, prayers, and incantations. They both operate on the sympathetic channels of natural attraction in the universe.

But here Plotinus's joined attention to magic and medicine parts. He does not discuss the beneficial or harmful effects of medicine, only of magic. Magic affects only the nonrational part of the soul, while her rational part, he emphasizes, remains unaffected, because "only that which is focused on itself is immune to sorcery [ἀγοήτευτον]" (*Enn.* 4.4.43.18). He prescribes contemplation as the best antidote for magic. When turned inwardly, we are attuned to our true self, seeking to uncover our own channel of well-being, centripetally retracing the nested organization of the human being and the universe from body to soul to intellect and ultimately to the One. In "Against the Gnostics" (*Enn.* 2.9), Plotinus acknowledges the use of incantation in medicine.[69] Those who claim to purge diseases with incantations (*epaoidai*) would be right, he qualifies, "if what they mean is that purging is due to sound-mindedness [*sōphrosynē*] and an ordered way of life [κοσμία διαίτη]." They would be right, he concludes, "since this is what philosophers say."[70]

His observation treats philosophy both as a form of incantation and medical prescription for a certain regimen of life. It fuses the boundaries between medicine and philosophy, giving us a new insight about the outcome of Socrates's treatment of Charmides. According to it, Socrates's "beautiful words," investigating what *sōphrosynē* is, charm Charmides because his soul is turned outwardly toward the body. Charming Charmides, however, is the first stage of Socrates's therapy. It prepares him for the second and essential stage, which orients him inwardly on the path of the virtuous human being, as promoted by Plotinus in *Enn.* 4.4. At the second stage, Socrates deploys his own set of medical skills, inherited from his midwife mother and empirically illustrated in the *Alcibiades*, which is

69. Under gnostic influence are ritual bowls from the fifth century CE, depicting healing incantations, written centripetally on the inside surface and personifying diseases by daemons' names. Plotinus's reference to incantations, figures, and exorcist practices reflects an early stage of this development. See Dan Levene, *Curse or Blessing: What Is in the Magic Bowl?*, The Ian Karten Lecture 2002 (Southampton: Print Centre University of Southampton, 2002).

70. Plotinus, *Enn.* 2.9.14.11–13: καθαίρεσθαι δὲ νόσων λέγοντες αὐτούς, λέγοντες μὲν ἂν σωφροσύνῃ καὶ κοσμίᾳ διαίτῃ, ἔλεγον ἂν ὀρθῶς, καθάπερ οἱ φιλόσοφοι λέγουσι.

named after another of Socrates's patients who suffer from an imbalance. In Socrates's practice, medicine and philosophy work jointly.

In the *Charmides*, Plato's understanding of healing relies on the time-honored relation between medicine and magic. In his discussion of magic in *Enn.* 4.4, Plotinus's goal is more ambitious. It extends beyond the soul-body compound of the individual being to explain its permeable relation with the universe. His investigation of magic does not stop with the discussion of its harmful effects on the body and how the virtuous person can remain immune to them. While he warns against the dangers of magic, performed either by a practitioner or nature itself, he remains positive about the global salubrious effect of medicine. Plotinus does not praise medicine for its systematic treatment protocol of the individual body, as Plato does in the *Charmides*, but analogously applies medicine's procedures to explain how the universe maintains its health. For Plotinus, the outer layer of the individual is an inner layer in the universe.

In the *Timaeus*, Plato explains why the Demiurge creates the body of the universe in the way he does: spherical, smooth, without organs of sense perception, free of old age and disease, self-sufficient (*Tim.* 33a6–d3). In his explanation of why the universe as a whole remains unaffected by magic, Plotinus reinstates Plato's principal position that the universe is always healthy: "no element of the universe as a whole is contrary to nature" (παρὰ φύσιν) because it is directed to itself (*Enn.* 4.4.42.22–23). Accordingly, he considers the universe to have its own self-healing method, which exhibits "power and order, with everything happening 'by a silent progress, in accordance to justice,' which none can escape."[71] The universe, then, maintains its health even when some parts of it, such as the human beings, are harmed by the charms of magic or their nature, entangled in the biological necessities of the body and in political life. To explain, he describes the anatomy of the living being of the universe in analogy to the parts-and-wholes anatomy of a small animal:

> So, it is not unreasonable to say that souls change places [τὰς ψυχὰς μετατίθεσθαι] and do not always retain the identical character, but are ordered in a way analogous [ταττομένας δὲ ἀνάλογον] to what has happened to them and what they do, some receiving a position in the order like that of a head [τάξιν οἷον κεφαλῆς], while others receive one

---

71. Plotinus, *Enn.* 4.4.45.27–29: ἔχει δυνάμεως καὶ τάξεως τόδε τὸ πᾶν γινομένων ἀπάντων ἀψόφῳ κελεύθῳ κατὰ δίκην, ἣν οὐκ ἔστι φυγεῖν οὐδενί.

like that of feet [οἷον ποδῶν], in concord with the universe [πρὸς τὸ πᾶν σύμφωνον].... As for punishments, they correspond to treatments of parts that are diseased [ὥσπερ νενοσηκότων μερῶν]; some involve styptics, along with drugs [ἐπιστύψεις φαρμάκοις], other extractions or modifications [ἐξαιρέσεις ἢ καὶ ἀλλοιώσεις], so that the whole may be healthy [ἵνα ὑγιαίνοι τὸ πᾶν] when each part is disposed where it should be. But the health of the whole [τὸ δ᾽ὑγιεινὸν τοῦ πάντος] comes about when one part is modified and another is removed from its place, because it is diseased where it is, and put where it will not be diseased. (*Enn.* 4.4.45.40–52)

This is Plotinus's view of what happens to the soul after her embodiment. When the body has run its physical course, the part of the soul that has descended in it and thus has been in contact with its sense-perceptible experiences returns to her permanent dwelling place, but only after she has been healed from the mark these experiences have made on her. Plotinus, I suggest, conceives of this process of earthly decontamination of the soul as an inversion of the healing process Plato envisions in the *Charmides*. Without the body, the soul herself undergoes the full range of medical procedures, available for the body, but applied to her by the self-healing principle of order and justice in the universe. To carry out his medically informed analogy, Plotinus maps the anatomy of the human body part by part on the anatomy of the universe as a living organism, distinguishing between souls, which are allocated in the order (*taxis*) of the head or the feet (aka *ab capite ad calces* in medical jargon), depending on their embodied way of life. The soul of the virtuous person is ranked with the head for choosing neither the better nor the worse in the sensible world, but exchanging the things here for a different place there, whereas the soul of the person who has not been able to remain immune to the charms of the sensible world is assigned to the feet, where they receive medically corrective treatments by the power and order of the universe.[72]

Plotinus's correlation between universal justice and medicine harks back to Plato's correlation between the political art of justice and the somatic art of medicine in the psychosomatic classification of the arts and Socrates's self-professed role of a medical doctor, who cuts, burns, and prescribes lifestyle regimen to the souls of the young Athenians in the *Gorgias*

---

72. Plotinus echoes motifs in Galen's discussion of the different types of treatments for the deficient bodily parts, e.g., in *Ars med.* 1.378. His cosmological undertone is anticipated by Galen's observation that "nature is the demiurge of all these; the doctor is merely the servant."

(464b2–465c3, 504c7–d3, 521e6–522a7).[73] For Plato and Plotinus, health is order (*taxis*), which is maintained in the body by the art of medicine and in the soul by the art of justice, political and universal. This correlation presents healing as a holistic process that requires the health of the universe to include a health-check of the individual souls. In the footsteps of Plato who interweaves the nature of the universe and the nature of the human being in the *Timaeus*, Plotinus interweaves medicine and cosmology in his understanding of the living organism of the universe in *Enn.* 4.4.

The (Neo)Platonic understanding of healing, despite the top-down architecture of its worldview, elicits and redeems the importance of the art of medicine in maintaining the health of the individual and the health of the universe. In neither patient is the health of the soul considered without the body. From this perspective, the concept of health, although a medical construct, acquires a genuinely Platonic facelift with two tributary ideas: (1) that the healing process is holistic in nature, and (2) that it includes both the art of medicine and the art of the Platonic way of life, healing through philosophizing and searching for the essence of existence. Medicine matters for the well-being of the individual and the universe.

This examination has come a long way from Charmides's hangover to the global healing of the universe. But Platonic psychology itself has its charming beauty, fusing the boundaries between the individual and the universal. Does the vertical axis in the (Neo)Platonic understanding of healing negate the holistic therapeutic method of the art on the ground? I think not. Neither Plato nor Plotinus denies the efficacy of medicine's holistic part-and-whole treatment of what is diseased. Plato simply insists that the soul, too, needs to be treated, because, as he says, doctors "cannot heal the body without the soul" (*Charm.* 156e2). Plotinus, on the other hand, approaches the healing process from the other way around. He cannot envision the healing of the individual souls as parts of the universe without medicine's therapeutic methods for the body.

Conclusion

Plato and Plotinus offer two different explanatory models of the Platonic understanding of health and healing in which the participation of the soul

---

73. See Plato's explanation that doctors and physical trainers give "order and organization to the body" (κοσμοῦσί που τὸ σῶμα καὶ συντάττουσιν, *Gorg.* 504a3–4), the product of which is the greatest good for mankind, health (ὑγιεία, *Gorg.* 452a9–10).

in the healing of the individual body matters as much as the participation of the body in the healing of the soul in the single living being. Instead of offering another example of the standard interpretation of the psychosomatic dichotomy in which the soul gets all the credit and the body gets all the blame, the Platonic understanding of healing offers a moderate view.[74] It envisions a vertical yet holistic model. Medicine and philosophy work together to heal not the body but the being either of the individual or the universe, simultaneously from below and from above. Here Plato's advice in the *Republic* is instructive: "We mustn't hug the hurt part and spend our time weeping and wailing like children when they trip. Instead, we should always accustom our souls to turn as quickly as possible to healing the disease [πρὸς τὸ ἰᾶσθαι] and putting the disaster right, replacing lamentation with cure [ἰατρικῇ]" (*Resp.* 604c7–d2).[75]

Medicine matters since it offers a knowledgeable treatment protocol that restores the wholeness of the individual being and the universe. For Plato and Plotinus, healing is not an afterthought to "a broken pot," as is for us. It pertains to the order of the universe and of the human being. Consequently, neither philosophy nor medicine can heal without the other.

Bibliography

Primary Sources

Burnet, John, ed. *Platonis Opera*. Vols. 2–4. Oxford: Clarendon, 1903–1909.

Crexells, Joan, trans. *Plato: Diàlegs; Carmides; Lisis; Protàgoras*. Vol. 2. Barcelona: Fundació Bernat Metge, 1925.

Denyer, Nicholas, ed. *Plato: Alcibiades*. Cambridge: Cambridge University Press, 2001.

Dodds, Eric R., trans. *Plato: Gorgias*. Oxford: Clarendon, 1959.

Dorion, Louis-André, trans. *Platon: Charmide; Lysis*. Paris: Flammarion, 2004.

---

74. Pauliina Remes, "Olympiodorus on the Human Being: A Case of Moderate Embodiment," in *Lovers of the Soul, Lovers of the Body: Philosophical and Religious Perspectives in Late Antiquity*, ed. Svetla Slaveva-Griffin and Ilaria L. E. Ramelli (Washington, DC: Center for Hellenic Studies, 2022), 171–91.

75. Trans. George M. A. Grube, *Plato: Republic*, rev. C. D. C. Reeve (Indianapolis: Hackett, 1992).

Edelstein, Emma J., and Ludwig Edelstein, eds. *Asclepius: Collection and Interpretation of the Testimonies.* 2 vols. Baltimore: Johns Hopkins University Press, 1998.

Gerson, Lloyd P., ed. *Plotinus: The Enneads.* Cambridge: Cambridge University Press, 2018.

Grube, George M. A., trans. *Plato: Republic.* Revised by C. D. C. Reeve. Indianapolis: Hackett, 1992.

Gurtler, Gary M., SJ, trans. *Plotinus: Ennead IV.4.3–45 and IV.5: Problems Concerning the Soul.* Las Vegas: Parmenides, 2015.

Henry, Paul, and Hans-Rudolf Schwyzer, eds. *Plotini Opera.* 3 vols. Oxford: Clarendon, 1964–1983.

Jowett, Benjamin, trans. "Charmides." Pages 99–122 in *Plato, The Collected Dialogues Including the Letters.* Edited by Edith Hamilton and Huntington Cairns. Princeton: Princeton University Press, 1989.

Kent Sprague, Rosamond, trans. "Charmides." Pages 639–63 in *Plato: Complete Works.* Edited by John M. Cooper. Indianapolis: Hackett, 1997.

Kühn, Karl G., ed. *Galeni Opera Omnia.* 20 vols. Leipzig: Cnobloch, 1819–1933.

Laks, André, and Glenn W. Most, eds. and trans. *Early Greek Philosophy: Western Greek Thinkers.* Part 2. Cambridge: Harvard University Press, 2016.

Littré, Émile, ed. and trans. *Oeuvres complètes d'Hippocrate.* 10 vols. Paris: Baillière, 1839–1861.

Mann, Joel E., trans. *Hippocrates: On the Art of Medicine.* Leiden: Brill, 2012.

Moore, Christopher, and Christopher C. Raymond, trans. *Plato: Charmides.* Indianapolis: Hackett, 2019.

Schiefsky, Mark J. *Hippocrates: On Ancient Medicine.* Leiden: Brill, 2005.

Secondary Sources

Ahbel-Rappe, Sara. *Socratic Ignorance and Platonic Knowledge in the Dialogues of Plato.* Albany: State University of New York Press, 2018.

Allen, James. "The Soul's Virtue and the Health of the Body in Ancient Philosophy." Pages 75–94 in *Health: A History.* Edited by Peter Adamson. New York: Oxford University Press, 2019.

Arbøll, Troels P. *Medicine in Ancient Assur: A Microhistorical Study of the Neo-Assyrian Healer Kiṣir Aššur.* Leiden: Brill, 2021.

Armstrong, Arthur Hilary. "Was Plotinus a Magician?" *Phronesis* 1 (1955): 73–79.

Bannert, Herbert. "Medical Education." Pages 413–29 in *A Companion to Ancient Education*. Edited by W. Martin Bloomer. London: Wiley-Blackwell, 2015.

Bartoš, Hynek. *Philosophy and Dietetics in the Hippocratic on Regimen: A Delicate Balance of Health*. Leiden: Brill, 2015.

Beekes, Robert, ed. *Etymological Dictionary of Greek*. Leiden: Brill, 2010.

Blumenthal, Henry. *Plotinus' Psychology*. The Hague: Nijhoff, 1971.

Bolton, Robert. "Science and Scientific Inquiry in Aristotle: A Platonic Provenance." Pages 46–60 in *The Oxford Handbook of Aristotle*. Edited by Christopher Shields. New York: Oxford University Press, 2012.

Brisson, Luc. *Plato the Mythmaker*. Chicago: University of Chicago Press, 2000.

Brouwer, René. "Stoic Sympathy." Pages 15–35 in *Sympathy: A History*. Edited by Eric Schliesser. Oxford: Oxford University Press, 2015.

Caluori, Damian. *Plotinus on the Soul*. Cambridge: Cambridge University Press, 2015.

Chantraine, Pierre, ed. *Dictionnaire étymologique de la langue grecque*. 2nd ed. Paris: Klincksieck, 1999.

Cilliers, Louise, and F. Pieter Retief. "Dream Healing in Asclepieia in the Mediterranean." Pages 69–92 in *Dreams, Healing, and Medicine in Greece from Antiquity to Present*. Edited by Steven M. Oberhelman. Farnham, UK: Ashgate, 2013.

Coolidge, Francis P., Jr. "Relation of Philosophy to σοφροσύνη: Zalmoxian Medicine in Plato's *Charmides*." *AncPhil* 13 (1993): 23–36.

Dodds, Eric R. *Pagan and Christian in an Age of Anxiety*. New York: Norton, 1965.

Edelstein, Ludwig. "Greek Medicine and Its Relation to Religion and Magic." Pages 205–46 in *Ancient Medicine: Selected Papers of Ludwig Edelstein*. Edited by Owsei Temkin and C. Lilian Temkin. Translated by C. Lilian Temkin. Baltimore: Johns Hopkins University Press, 1967.

Emilsson, Eyjólfur K. *Plotinus on Sense-Perception: A Philosophical Study*. Cambridge: Cambridge University Press, 1988.

———. "Plotinus on *Sympatheia*." Pages 36–60 in *Sympathy: A History*. Edited by Eric Schliesser. Oxford: Oxford University Press, 2015.

Ferrari, Giovanni R. F. *City and Soul in Plato's Republic*. Chicago: University of Chicago Press, 2005.

Geller, Markham J. *Ancient Babylonian Medicine: Theory and Practice.* Oxford: Wiley-Blackwell, 2010.

Gordon, Richard. "The Healing Event in Graeco-Roman Folk-Medicine." Pages 363–76 in *Ancient Medicine in Its Socio-cultural Context.* Vol. 2. Edited by Philip van der Eijk, Manfred Horstmanshoff, and Petrus H. Schrijvers. Amsterdam: Rodopi, 1995.

Gundert, Beate. "Soma and Psyche in Hippocratic Medicine." Pages 13–35 in *Psyche and Soma: Physicians and Metaphysicians on the Mind-Body Problem from Antiquity to Enlightenment.* Edited by John P. Wright and Paul Potter. Oxford: Clarendon, 2000.

Guthrie, William K. C. *A History of Greek Philosophy.* Vol. 4. Cambridge: Cambridge University Press, 1975.

Helleman, Wendy E. "Plotinus as Magician." *IJPT* 4 (2010): 114–46.

Holmes, Brooke. "Galen's Sympathy." Pages 61–69 in *Sympathy: A History.* Edited by Eric Schliesser. Oxford: Oxford University Press, 2015.

Hyland, Drew A. *The Virtue of Philosophy: An Interpretation of Plato's Charmides.* Athens, OH: University of Ohio Press, 1981.

Jouanna, Jacques. *Hippocrates.* Translated by Malcolm B. DeBevoise. Baltimore: Johns Hopkins University Press, 1999.

Kahn, Charles H. *Plato and the Socratic Dialogue: The Philosophical Use of a Literary Form.* Cambridge: Cambridge University Press, 1996.

———. "Plato's *Charmides* and the Proleptic Reading of Socratic Dialogues." *JP* 85 (1968): 541–49.

King, Linda S. "Plato's Concepts of Medicine." *JHMAS* 9 (1954): 38–48.

Korobili, Giouli, and Konstantinos Stefou. "Plato's *Charmides* on Philosophy as Holistic Medical Practice." Pages 201–19 in *Holism in Ancient Medicine and Its Reception.* Edited by Chiara Thumiger. Leiden: Brill, 2021.

Laín Entralgo, Pedro. *The Therapy of the Word in Classical Antiquity.* Edited and translated by Lelland J. Rather and John M. Sharp. New Haven: Yale University Press, 1970.

Levene, Dan. *Curse or Blessing: What Is in the Magic Bowl?* The Ian Karten Lecture 2002. Southampton: Print Centre University of Southampton, 2002.

Lindberg, David C. *The Beginnings of Western Science: The European Scientific Tradition in Philosophical, Religious, and Institutional Context, Prehistory to A.D. 1450.* 2nd ed. Chicago: University of Chicago Press, 2007.

Merlan, Philip. "Plotinus and Magic." *Isis* 44 (1953): 341–48.

Moravcsik, Julius. "Health, Healing, and Plato's Ethics." *JVI* 34 (2000): 7–26.

Murphy, David J. "Critical Notes on Plato's *Charmides.*" *Mnemosyne* 60 (2007): 213–34.

———. "Doctors of Zalmoxis and Immortality in the *Charmides.*" Pages 287–95 in *Plato: Euthydemus, Lysis, Charmides.* Proceedings of the V Symposium Platonicum. Edited by Thomas M. Robinson and Luc Brisson. Sankt Augustine: Akademia, 2000.

Nails, Debra. *The People of Plato: A Prosopography of Plato and Other Socratics.* Indianapolis: Hackett, 2002.

Nutton, Vivian. *Ancient Medicine.* London: Routledge, 2004.

Perilli, Lorenzo. "Epistemologies." Pages 119–51 in *The Cambridge Companion to Hippocrates.* Edited by Peter E. Pormann. Cambridge: Cambridge University Press, 2018.

Pigeaud, Jackie. *La maladie de l'âme: Étude sur la relation de l'âme et du corps dans la tradition médico-philosophique antique.* Paris: Les Belles Lettres, 2006.

Plastira-Valkanou, Maria. "Medicine and Fine Cuisine in Plato's *Gorgias.*" *AC* 67 (1998): 195–201.

Remes, Pauliina. "Olympiodorus on the Human Being: A Case of Moderate Embodiment." Pages 171–91 in *Lovers of the Soul, Lovers of the Body: Philosophical and Religious Perspectives in Late Antiquity.* Edited by Svetla Slaveva-Griffin and Ilaria L. E. Ramelli. Washington, DC: Center for Hellenic Studies, 2022.

———. *Plotinus on Self: The Philosophy of the "We."* Cambridge: Cambridge University Press, 2007.

Robinson, Thomas M. "The Defining Features of Mind-Body Dualism in the Writings of Plato." Pages 37–55 in *Psyche and Soma: Physicians and Metaphysicians on the Mind-Body Problem from Antiquity to Enlightenment.* Edited by John P. Wright and Paul Potter. Oxford: Clarendon, 2000.

———. *Plato's Psychology.* 2nd ed. Toronto: University of Toronto Press, 1995.

Roby, Courtney A. "Animal, Vegetable, Metaphor: Plotinus' Liver and the Roots of Biological Identity." Pages 387–414 in *The Comparable Body: Analogy and Metaphor in Ancient Mesopotamian, Egyptian, and Greco-Roman Medicine.* Edited by John Z. Wee. Leiden: Brill, 2017.

Rowe, Christopher. *Plato and the Art of Philosophical Writing.* Cambridge: Cambridge University Press, 2007.

Salles, Ricardo. "The Stoic World Soul and the Theory of Seminal Principles." Pages 44–66 in *World Soul: A History*. Edited by James Wilberding. Oxford: Oxford University Press, 2021.

Schluderer, Laura R. "Imitating the Cosmos: The Role of Microcosm-Macrocosm Relationships in the Hippocratic Treatise *On Regimen*." *ClQ*
68 (2018): 31–52.

Stalley, Richard F. "*Sôphrosunê* in the *Charmides*." Pages 265–77 in *Plato:
Euthydemus, Lysis, Charmides*. Proceedings of the V Symposium Pla-
tonicum. Edited by Thomas M. Robinson and Luc Brisson. Sankt
Augustine: Akademia, 2000.

Stempsey, William E. "Plato and Holistic Medicine." *MHCP* 4 (2001):
201–9.

Suvák, Vladislav. "Sókratovská *Therapeia*: Platónov *Charmidés* 153a–
158d." *Filosofia* 71 (2016): 357–68.

Tarrant, Harold. *Plato's First Interpreters*. Ithaca, NY: Cornell University
Press, 2000.

Thumiger, Chiara. "Doctors and Patients." Pages 263–91 in *The Cambridge
Companion to Hippocrates*. Edited by Peter E. Pormann. Cambridge:
Cambridge University Press, 2018.

———. "Holism: Methodological and Theoretical Perspectives." Pages
25–46 in *Holism in Ancient Medicine and Its Reception*. Edited by
Chiara Thumiger. Leiden: Brill, 2021.

Tuozzo, Thomas M. "What's Wrong with These Cities? The Social Dimension of *Sophrosune* in Plato's *Charmides*." *JHP* 39 (2001): 321–50.

Vallejo, Alvaro. "Maieutic, *epôdê* and Myth in the Socratic Dialogues."
Pages 324–36 in *Plato: Euthydemus, Lysis, Charmides*. Edited by
Thomas M. Robinson and Luc Brisson. Proceedings of the V Sympo-
sium Platonicum. Sankt Augustine: Akademia, 2000.

Vegetti, Mario. *La Medicina in Platone*. Venice: Il Cardo, 1995.

Wilberding, James. "Neoplatonism and Medicine." Pages 356–71 in *The
Routledge Handbook of Neoplatonism*. Edited by Pauliina Remes and
Svetla Slaveva-Griffin. London: Routledge, 2014.

———. "The World Soul in the Platonic Tradition." Pages 15–43 in *World
Soul: A History*. Edited by James Wilberding. Oxford: Oxford University Press, 2021.

Zoller, Coleen P. *Plato and the Body: Reconsidering Socratic Asceticism*.
Albany: State University of New York Press, 2018.

Intellect Sober and Intellect Drunk:
Some Reflections on the Plotinian Ascent Narrative

John Dillon

This paper, which is necessarily highly speculative and which may well seem outrageous to many of Plotinus's admirers—of whom I would certainly count myself as one, even as our honorand is another—is provoked, on the one hand, by discussions with colleagues in the field of neurology in Trinity College[1] and, on the other hand, by the reading of two most stimulating books. The first is *A Smell of Burning*, by Colin Grant, which is a lively and learned account of the treatment of epilepsy down the ages serving as a background to his experiences with his younger brother Christopher, who was afflicted with the condition; the second is a rather more controversial but still most interesting one, *Proof of Heaven*, by American neurologist Eben Alexander.[2]

It is a great pleasure to dedicate this paper to an old friend, who has done so much for the development of Neoplatonic studies and in particular for our understanding of later Platonist theories of the soul. I hope that it will amuse him.

1. I might mention in that connection a fine book by my colleague Kevin Mitchell, *Innate: How the Wiring of Our Brains Shapes Who We Are* (Princeton: Princeton University Press, 2018). I can also recommend a book by two Canadian scholars, Mario Beauregard and Denyse O'Leary, *The Spiritual Brain: A Neuroscientist's Case for the Existence of the Soul* (New York: HarperCollins, 2007).

2. Colin Grant, *A Smell of Burning: The Story of Epilepsy* (London: Cape, 2016); Eben Alexander, *Proof of Heaven: A Neurosurgeon's Journey into the Afterlife* (New York: Simon & Schuster, 2012). I should also not omit to mention an authoritative account of near-death experiences in Raymond Moody, *Life after Life: The Investigation of a Phenomenon—Survival of Bodily Death* (Atlanta: Mockingbird Books, 1975). I should not omit to mention in this connection the remarkable discussion of epilepsy that comes down to us from the ancient world, the treatise on *The Sacred Disease*, included in the Hippocratic Corpus. In this work, however, the author is primarily

My particular focus of interest in this paper is to explore the following question: Might there be any excuse for postulating, in not only the case of Plotinus but of any of those whom one might term natural mystics, that the visions they experience of another realm of existence may result from a distinctive brain condition—specifically, a condition of the temporal lobes—that, while not itself being a disease, has affinities to aspects of the disease of epilepsy, notably the proneness of certain epileptics to experiencing visions, or auras, as prelude to a seizure? These visions typically involve the experience of bright light, which is regarded as benign and even lovable, with the sensation of being transported to some other realm of existence. What one experiences in that other realm is conditioned, not surprisingly, by the intellectual or religious traditions in which one has been brought up; for example, those of Christian faith might well experience visions of angels and saints, or even of Christ himself, or his Blessed Mother, while Sufi mystics, let us say, or Buddhist ones, would find themselves confronted with appropriate figures or scenarios from their cultural environments. Among such figures Colin Grant, in a fine chapter of his book titled *Ticket to Heaven*, gives good arguments for including Paul of Tarsus, Muhammad, Joan of Arc, and novelist Fyodor Dostoevsky. All of these manifested some symptoms analogous to epilepsy, though without—except perhaps in the case of Dostoevsky—suffering from that disease in its normal or chronic form.

There are records of similar phenomena being reported by those who have undergone near-death experiences, and that is what was experienced by American surgeon Dr. Eben Alexander as a result of a bad case of bacterial meningitis, which almost killed him and had him in a medically induced coma for a full week in 2008. His background would seem to have been pretty firmly secular and materialist, so that his visions give off an aura rather of Disney World than of a Christian or Muslim heaven, but they are nonetheless interesting for that. What I would like to do here is to run through the chief features of his near-death experience and then see how they relate to any hints that Plotinus may drop, in particular in the tractate *Enn.* 6.7 (38): "How the Multitude of the Forms Came into Being, and on the Good," but also elsewhere, in the slightly earlier treatise 5.8 (31): "On Intelligible Beauty," as to the nature of his personal experiences.[3]

---

concerned with debunking the notion that this disease is sacred, in the sense of being sent by the gods, and so gives no attention to the question of auras.

3. Another key passage would be *Enn.* 6.9.7–11, but 6.7 will do for the present purpose. I have derived some inspiration here, I may say, from rereading a paper by an

Alexander begins his spiritual adventure in a murky darkness.[4] He seems to be surrounded by roots or blood vessels in a womb. He hears a grim, rhythmic pounding. He feels that he no longer has a body, no memory of prior existence or of the passage of time.

> Then something impinges on the darkness, something "radiating filaments of white-gold light," which at the same time emits "a new sound, a *living* sound, like the richest, most complex, most beautiful piece of music you've ever heard"—this in place of the previous mechanical pounding associated with the darkness. Then, at the very center of the light, something else appeared … an opening. I was no longer looking *at* the slowly spinning light at all, but *through* it. The moment I understood this, I began to move up. Fast. There was a whooshing sound,[5] and in a flash I went through the opening and found myself in a completely new world—the strangest, most beautiful world I'd ever seen.[6]

Now, so far, the analogy to this account is not so much anything in Plotinus's work, but rather the allegory of the cave in Plato's *Republic*—though admittedly life in the cave-like dwelling is a good deal more structured than in Alexander's primeval dark, which is more reminiscent of the "barbaric ooze" (βόρβορος βαρβαρικός) in which the "eye of the soul" is described as being sunk in *Resp.* 7 (533d1). But the emerging of the released prisoner into the light of the "real" world (and then his ultimate contemplation of the sun itself)—as well, of course, as certain features of the Myth of Er, in the same dialogue—does accord with the general pattern of recorded

---

old friend, now sadly long dead, Richard Wallis, in which he explores this same topic but without indulging in the outrageous suggestions that I am proposing here. See Wallis, "*Nous* as Experience," in *The Significance of Neoplatonism*, ed. R. Baine Harris (Albany: State University of New York Press, 1976), 121–54. On the role of light in Plotinian thought and imagery, one may consult Werner Beierwaltes, "Die Metaphysik des Lichtes in der Philosophie Plotins," *ZPF* 15 (1961): 334–62.

4. Alexander, *Proof of Heaven*, 29–32.

5. This is interestingly reminiscent of the Greek word ῥοῖζος, used not by Plotinus but by Iamblichus in the *De Mysteriis* (e.g., 3.9, 119), to characterize the sounds of the heavenly bodies moving through the heavens; this, he tells us elsewhere (*Vit. Pyth.* 15, 65.3), was imitated by Pythagoras to "purify the confused minds" of his disciples, sending them into a prophetic sleep. He himself, Iamblichus tells us, was able to hear the music of the spheres and suitably transpose it for his pupils.

6. Alexander, *Proof of Heaven*, 38–39.

near-death experiences and provokes one to wonder whether Plato himself may not have enjoyed some quantum of mystical experience.

However, that is by the way: we are concerned here with Plotinus.
Before we turn to consider what he is prepared to let slip for us, though,
we must allow Alexander to finish his story. I select out only features of
his rather ecstatic narrative that seem to me to have some particular relevance to Plotinus's characterization of the intelligible realm, specifically
concerning interpenetration of all the objects of that realm, and even the
lack of distinction between subject and object of perception. In chapter 9,
then, we find the following:

> Seeing and hearing were not separate in this place where I now was. I
> could *hear* the visual beauty of the silvery bodies of those scintillating
> beings above, and I could see the surging, joyful perfection of what they
> sang. It seemed that you could not look at or listen to anything in this
> world without becoming a part of it—without joining with it in some
> mysterious way. Again, from my present perspective, I would suggest
> that you couldn't look *at* anything in that world at all, for the word *at*
> implies a separation that did not exist there. Everything was distinct,
> yet everything was also a part of everything else, like the rich and inter-
> mingled designs on a Persian carpet—or a butterfly's wing.[7]

I find this most significant, from a man who can have no inkling of the
philosophy of Plotinus or of his attempts to convey the quality of the intelligible realm. Let us recall, in this connection, just two notable passages
from *Enn.* 6.7. First, the image that closes chapter 12, where he is trying to
describe a situation where "all things are filled full of life, and we may say,
boiling with life":

> They all flow, in a way, from a single spring, not like one particular breath
> or one warmth, but as if there were one quality which held and kept
> intact all the qualities in itself, of sweetness along with fragrance, and
> was at once the quality of wine and the character of all tastes, the sights
> of colors, and all the awareness of touch, and all that hearings hear, all
> tunes and every rhythm.[8]

---

7. Alexander, *Proof of Heaven*, 45–46.
8. All following translations from the *Enneads* are from *Plotinus*, trans. A. H.
Armstrong, LCL (Cambridge: Harvard University Press, 1966–1988), with in some
cases minor modifications.

And then the remarkable passage from 15.25–34, where he is trying to describe the complexity involved in the vision of the bright life of the intelligible realm—which he contrasts with the darkness (σκότος) here below:

> And so, if one likens it to a living, richly varied sphere, or imagines it as a thing all faces [παμπρόσωπόν τι χρῆμα], shining with living faces, or as all the pure souls running together into the same place, with no deficiencies, but having all that is their own, and universal Intellect sitting on their summits, so that the region is illuminated by intellectual light—if one imagined it like this, one would be seeing it somehow as one sees another from outside. *But one must become that, and make oneself the contemplation.*

Here it seems to me that Plotinus is attempting to give a coherent account, compatible with his Platonist philosophical education, of an experience very similar to that of Alexander (who is himself representative of many attested near-death experiences): all the objects of one's experience seem to blend together, in a timeless environment, and one feels oneself to be somehow united with those objects.[9]

But this is not the end, or the summit, of the adventure. Alexander now approaches a level of being he calls "the Core":

> I continued moving forward and found myself entering an immense void, completely dark, infinite in size, yet also infinitely comforting. Pitch black as it was, it was also brimming with light: a light that seemed to come from a brilliant orb that I now sensed near me. An orb that was living and almost solid.[10]

---

9. One might also adduce a significant passage from *Enn.* 5.8.4.5–9: "For all things there are transparent [διαφανῆ], and there is nothing dark or opaque; everything and all things are clear to the inmost part to everything; for light is transparent to light. Each there has everything in itself and sees all things in every other, so that all are everywhere, and each and every one is all, and the brilliance is unbounded [ἄπειρος ἡ αἴγλη]."

10. Alexander, *Proof of Heaven*, 46–48. Interestingly, God, as supreme principle, is described as "darkness" (σκότος) not by Plotinus but by his older contemporary Origen (the Christian), in his *Comm. Jo.* 2.172, arising out of the exegesis of John 1:5, where precisely God is declared to be "a light shining in darkness." This is also a feature of the mystical theology of Dionysius the Areopagite, who, at *Myst. Theol.* 1.1, concocts the notable phrase ὑπέρφωτος γνόφος, "darkness beyond/above light," to characterize the quality of this ultimate vision. Many later mystics also, such as Jacob Boehme, Heinrich Suso, and Jan van Ruysbroek, attest to this paradoxical sensation of a "dazzling obscurity."

He describes himself as feeling somehow "like a fetus in a womb," floating and nourished by an invisible mother:

> In this case, the "mother" was God, the Creator, the Source who is responsible for making the universe and all in it. This Being was so close that there seemed to be no distance at all between God and myself. Yet at the same time, I could sense the infinite vastness of the Creator, could see how completely miniscule I was by comparison.[11]

He now proposes to denominate this ultimate Being *Om*, and we may humor him in that. What I find particularly interesting in this passage, however, is his testimony that he finds Om both intimately close and remotely vast; this surely accords well with Plotinus's testimony (e.g., 5.3.14–17; 6.7.36) that the One is both near—indeed, within us—and infinitely remote.

The other remarkable sensation that he experiences, which seems to me to relate significantly to an important aspect of Plotinus's view of both the intellectual realm and the One itself, is that of both the *lovingness*, and the *lovability*, of this supreme Being. He reveals a basic intuition that he acquired from his contact with Om:

> It came in three parts, and to take one more shot at putting it into words (because of course it was initially delivered wordlessly), it would run something like this:
>> *You are loved and cherished*
>> *You have nothing to fear*
>> *There is nothing you can do wrong*
> If I had to boil this entire message down to one sentence, it would run this way:
>> *You are loved*
> And if I had to boil it down further to just one word, it would (of course) be simply
>> *Love*
> Love is, without a doubt, the basis of everything. Not some abstract, hard-to-fathom kind of love, but the day-to-day kind that everyone knows—the kind of love we feel when we look at our spouse and our children, or even our animals. In its purest and most powerful form, this love is not jealous or selfish, but unconditional. This is the reality of realities, the incomprehensibly glorious truth of truths that breathes at the core of everything that exists or that ever will exist, and no remotely

---

11. Christos Retoulas, *God's Gift, World's Deception* (Münster: LIT, 2022), 302.

accurate understanding of who and what we are can be achieved by anyone who does not know it, and embody it in all of their activity.[12]

Now, this may all come across as absurdly effusive and sentimental, but I think that we must give it due attention as an—admittedly amateurish—version of a truth into which a long succession of serious mystics down the ages, not least Plotinus, have gained insight, namely, that there is, at the core of the universe, an entity, or force, that is both enormously attractive, or lovable, and which itself radiates love for its creation—which may indeed be the reason for its profound attraction.

If we turn to the later chapters of *Enn.* 6.7, we can, I think, see some significant evidence of this. The question that arises, from chapter 18 onward, is why the intelligible world is so beautiful, so *attractive*—after all, mere perfection of form and structure does not necessarily generate attractiveness. The answer develops over the next few chapters, but the essence of it, stated at the outset, is that it is *infused with the Good*—giving this interpretation to the adjective ἀγαθοειδὲς, which is rather difficult to render adequately in this context. That involves being suffused with a sort of spiritual light and beauty, emanating from a source higher than itself. The characterization of this comes to a head in chapter 22:

> When anyone, therefore, sees this light, then truly he is also moved to the Forms, and longs for the light that plays upon them and delights in it [γλιχόμενος εὐφραίνεται], just as with the bodies here below our desire is not for the underlying material things, but for the beauty imaged upon them.[13] For each is what it is by itself, but it becomes desirable when the Good colors it, giving a kind of grace to them and passionate love to the desirers. Then the soul, receiving into itself an outflow from thence, is moved and dances wildly and is all stung with longing and becomes love.
>
> Before this it is not moved even toward Intellect, for all its beauty; the beauty of Intellect is inactive (ἀργόν) till it catches a light from the Good, and the soul by itself "falls flat on its back" and is completely inactive and, though Intellect is present, is unenthusiastic about it. But when a kind of warmth (ὥσπερ θερμασία) from thence comes upon it, it gains strength and wakens and is truly winged, and though it is moved with passion for that which lies close by it, yet all the same it rises higher to

---

12. Alexander, *Proof of Heaven*, 70–71.
13. This is a thought that Plotinus develops in *Enn.* 1.6 and 5.8.

something greater which it seems to remember. And as long as there
is anything higher than that which is present to it, it naturally goes on
upwards, lifted by the giver of its love. (6.7.22.1–4)

As Armstrong notes à propos this last phrase: "This is the clearest statement by Plotinus of something implicit in his whole system, that our
desire to return to the Good is given by the Good." But this whole passage,
I think, when read against the background of Alexander's testimony, gives
evidence of the degree of personal experience informing Plotinus's concept of the Good, both of the love that it emanates and the love in return
that it inspires.[14]

It is interesting that Alexander wishes to characterize the ultimate principle, that which is in some way *beyond* the timeless but structured world
of interpenetrating essences, as both "completely dark" and "brimming
over with light," infinite in size, and with no discernible features—though
at the same time "infinitely comforting."[15] It is something like this, it seems
to me, that Plotinus is making a heroic effort to describe in chapters 35–36
of 6.7, to some features of which I wish now to draw our attention.

Let us look first at the beginning of chapter 35, noting how, in the
approach to the One, the soul actually transcends intellection—while, of
course, retaining some mode of immediate apprehension:

And the soul is so disposed then as even to despise intelligence, which
at other times it welcomed, because intelligence is a kind of movement, and the soul does not want to move. For it says that he[16] whom

---

14. Another significant passage occurs at 6.8.15.1–5, the treatise following 6.7,
where Plotinus characterizes the One, or Good, as follows: "And he, that same self,
is loveable and love and love of himself, in that he is beautiful only from himself and
in himself. For surely his keeping company [συνεῖναι] with himself could not be in
any other way than if what keeps company and what it keeps company with were
one and the same." On the basis of such a passage, it is certainly tempting to suppose
that Plotinus has repeatedly enjoyed experiences analogous to that of Alexander. One
might also, for that matter, adduce the striking passage at the beginning of 4.8, where
Plotinus describes what must have been for him a fairly regular occurrence, "waking
up out of the body into myself," "seeing a beauty wonderfully great," with which he
feels an identity. This is fairly plainly a purposefully adduced vision of what Alexander
came upon accidentally.

15. Alexander, *Proof of Heaven*, 46–47.

16. We may note here the switch from neuter to masculine that is characteristic of
Plotinus's treatment of his first principle.

it sees does not move either; yet when this soul has become intellect it contemplates, when it has been, so to speak, made intellect [οἷον νοωθεῖσα] and has come to be in "the intelligible place";[17] but when it has come to be in it and moves about in it, it possesses the intelligible and thinks, but when it sees that god it at once lets everything go [πάντα ἀφίησιν].[18]

We are now treated to the image of one entering a fine mansion and admiring all the furniture and ornaments but, when at last the master of the house appears, forgetting all about the fine fittings and focusing solely on him. Furthermore, as it emerges, the vision of the master of the house has a curious quality:

and then, as he looks and does not take his eyes away, by the continuity of his contemplation he no longer sees a sight, *but mingles his seeing with what he contemplates,* so that what was seen before has now become sight in him, and he forgets all other objects of contemplation. And perhaps the image would better preserve the analogy [τάχα ἂν σῴζοι τὸ ἀνάλογον ἡ εἰκών] if it was not a mortal who encountered the viewer of the contents of the house but one of the gods, and one who did not appear visibly but filled the soul of the beholder. (6.7.35.1–3 [trans. Armstrong, slightly emended])

Here, in the best tradition of Plotinian dynamic imagery, the master of the house is first transformed from a human into a god and then somehow blended with the beholder! We may recall here the testimony of Alexander that the Being he encountered "was so close that there seemed to be no distance at all between God and myself"—and this is an experience testified to by many mystics down the ages.

Plotinus now goes on to make the well-known distinction that inspires the title of this paper:

Intellect[19] also, then, has one power for thinking, by which it looks at the things in itself, and one by which it looks at what transcends it by a direct awareness and reception [ἐπιβολῇ τινι καὶ παραδοχῇ], by which

---

17. A significant reference here to Plato, *Resp.* 7 (508c1, 517b5).

18. A phrase interestingly reminiscent of the last sentence of *Enn.* 5.3: ἄφελε πάντα.

19. *Nous* here, I think, may be taken to refer both to the hypostasis Intellect and to our own particular intellect at its highest level of insight, so I do not capitalize it.

also before it saw only, and by seeing acquired intellect and is one.[20] And
that first one is the contemplation of intellect in its right mind, but the
other is intellect in love, when it goes out of its mind "drunk with the
nectar"; then it falls in love, simplified into happiness by having its fill
[ἀπλωθεὶς εἰς εὐπάθειαν τῷ κόρῳ]; and it is better for it to be drunk with
a drunkenness like this than to be more respectably sober. (6.7.35.5–8)

The significant evocation of the myth of Poros and Penia from the *Symposium* (203b–c) is actually being used rather inappropriately, as Poros
in the myth did not gain any vision of supra-intellectual reality through
becoming drunk; he simply left himself open to seduction by Penia—but
no matter. It would not be by any means the only creative misappropria-
tion of a myth, Platonic or traditional, perpetrated by Plotinus. What is
significant here is the connection of drunkenness, in the sense of a special,
suprarational state of intellect, and love—both the feeling of love for a special kind of object, and the sensation that one is oneself suffused by the
love emanating from that object—which is attested to by Alexander and,
once again, by a long succession of mystics in various ages and cultures.
Plainly, Plotinus is here conveying to us a personal experience, which he is
seeking to fit into the structure of his Platonist universe.[21]

For the rest of chapter 35 and the whole of 36, he is concerned to
attempt to specify the peculiar quality of our apprehension of the supra-
intellectual First Principle, the One or the Good. At 35.34–43, he produces
the following:

> But the soul sees by a kind of confusing and annulling [οἷον συγχέασα
> καὶ ἀφανίσασα] the intellect which abides within it—or rather its intellect
> sees first, *but then the vision actually enters into it, and the two become
> one.* But the Good is spread out over them and fitted in to the union of
> both, playing upon them and uniting the two, it rests upon them and
> gives them a blessed perception and vision, lifting them so high as not to

---

20. This distinction between the two levels of activity by Intellect is made, interestingly, in such a passage as *Enn.* 5.3.11, where, however, the contrast is between
Intellect's preintellectual turning back to the One, which actually constitutes it as
Intellect, and its proper activity as Intellect. Here, however, the two activities are both
within the capacity of the individual intellect, in no particular sequence.

21. He employs the imagery of "drunkenness on the nectar," we may note, also in
5.8.10.32–45, to express the phenomenon of contemplating an object of sight that is
also within us.

be in place at all, nor in anything other, among things where it is natural for one thing to be in another—for he[22] is not anywhere either; the "intelligible place" is in him, but he is not in anything else.

We see here Plotinus valiantly striving to characterize the peculiar mode of apprehension proper to intellect in relation to the first principle, or Good. In the following chapter, we find him expanding on this (36.10–15):

> But whoever has become at once contemplator of himself and everything else and object of his own contemplation [θεατής τε καὶ θέαμα αὐτὸς αὐτοῦ], and since he has become substance [οὐσία] and intellect and "the complete living being,"[23] no longer looks at it from outside—when he has become this he is near [ἐγγύς], and that Good is next above him [ἐφεξῆς], and already close by, shining upon all the intelligible world.

This is in turn followed by a remarkable passage in which he describes how, first, one abandons—or transcends—all study and learning, and is lifted up on high "by a kind of swell" (οἷον κύματι), "and sees suddenly [ἐξαίφνης], not seeing how, and the vision fills his eyes with light and does not make him see something else by it, but the light itself is what he sees." This is all eerily reminiscent of the testimony of Alexander, that the Being with whom he was confronted "was so close that there seemed to be no distance at all between God and myself" and that it was "brimming with light."

I feel that all this indicates pretty clearly that the basis of Plotinus's account of the structure of the noetic, and supranoetic, world is personal experience. My final question is whether there is any evidence that, in order to attain these insights, Plotinus resorted to any ritualistic practices, analogous to those copiously attested in other mystical traditions, such as the Buddhist or Islamic ones. This is something that Plotinus is not at all inclined to be specific about, but it seems to me that in this same chapter of 6.7 he does, rather coyly, suggest that he has an adequate supply of these. At 36.2–5, at any rate, we find the following:

---

22. We may note, once again, the switch from neuter to masculine, in referring to the First Principle.

23. Plato, *Tim.* 31b1, suggesting the mystic's effective union with the Paradigm, or totality of the noetic world.

We are taught about it [sc. Plato's "greatest study"] by analogies and
negations and knowledge of the things which come from it, and certain
methods of ascent by degrees, but we are put on the way to it by purifications and virtues and adornings [καθάρσεις καὶ ἀρεταὶ καὶ κοσμήσεις],
and by gaining footholds [ἐπιβάσεις] in the intelligible and settling ourselves firmly [ἱδρύσεις] there and feasting [ἑστιάσεις] on its contents.
(6.7.36.2–5)

This last, presumably, a reference to the *Phaedrus* myth (247e2). The earlier
list here corresponds to the various dialectical methods of ascent to the First
Principle outlined, for instance, by Alcinous in his *Didaskalikos* (ch. 10),
ἀναλογία, ἀφαίρεσις, and ὑπεροχή, and thus attested for the earlier Platonist
tradition. I am particularly interested, however, in the καθάρσεις, ἀρεταί, and
κοσμήσεις. What practices might be concealed behind these terms?

Under the heading of "purifications," I suppose that one might
include ascetic dietary practices, such are attested in chapter 2 of Porphyry's *Life*, but really all that Porphyry tells us is that Plotinus observed
a strictly vegetarian diet, and no doubt he was frugal with that—and
avoided baths. Under the heading of "virtues," one might perhaps
include the systematic ascent through levels of virtue envisaged in *Enn.*
1.2, where one may ascend from the civic level of virtue to the purificatory, and then to the paradigms of the virtues residing at the level of
intellect (ch. 7). Attainment of this paradigmatic level of virtue effectively makes us gods; for it is to them, says Plotinus, and not to good
men, that we are to liken ourselves. This process of ascent, which inevitably involves meditative practices of some sort, is attested for Plotinus,
most interestingly, by Porphyry in a later section of the *Life* (ch. 23),
where he is conducting an exegesis of the oracle from Delphi commis-
sioned by Amelius:

So to this godlike man above all, who often raised himself in thought,
according to the ways Plato teaches us in the *Symposium*,[24] to the first
and transcendent God [εἰς τὸν πρῶτον καὶ ἐπέκεινα θεὸν], that God
appeared who has neither shape nor any intelligible form, but is throned
above Intellect and all the intelligible. (*Vit. Plot.* 23.1–3)

---

24. That is to say, Diotima's Ladder of Ascent, Plato, *Symp.* 210a–211b. We may
assume, therefore, I take it, that Plotinus used this or some analogous meditative technique to generate mystical visions.

Porphyry goes on, rather coyly, to attest that he himself, on at least one occasion, "drew near" to this god, while asserting that Plotinus achieved this union four times "while I was with him ... *in an unspeakable actuality, and not in potency only."* I have often wondered, rather irreverently, how these occasions were recorded. Did the great man perhaps emerge from his study, with a beatific smile on his face, and announce, "I've done it again!"? Or might it be the case, rather, on four occasions, that Porphyry finds him prostrated on the floor of his study, and, on rousing him, learns that that is where he has been? We will never know; but surely *something* remarkable happened that leads Porphyry to make this claim.

Furthermore, Porphyry records, quoting the Oracle, that "the gods often set him straight when he was going on a crooked course, 'sending down a solid shaft of light,' which means that he wrote what he wrote under their inspection and supervision."[25] I find it most interesting that it is actually Apollo, through his oracle, that attests to all this. Perhaps we may give some credence to the suggestion that Amelius, who ordered the oracle, in fact marked the cards of the Delphic priests rather thoroughly, when putting in his order.

To return for a moment to the question of possible aids to mystical vision, apart from exercises based on Diotima's ladder, I would suggest the consideration of a number of Plotinus's "dynamic images," such as, for instance, the striking ones in 5.1.2 and 5.8.9, of soul "lighting up" the physical universe (first all is darkness, then the light pours in, illuminating all the features of the globe), or, better, 5.8.9.4, where we are exhorted to call to mind the whole physical cosmos and then think away its spatial extension—calling on God to assist us in this. It is surely spiritual exercises such as this that Plotinus employs to bring on mystical insights, in the form of ascent to the noetic world; but if so, he is certainly not going to tell us.

As for the third category of aids, κοσμήσεις, I can only suggest that, in the sense of structurings or orderings, rather than adornments of the soul, Plotinus might in fact be referring to the spiritual exercises just mentioned. Plato, I note, uses the term in the *Gorgias* (504d2) to denote the

---

25. This accords interestingly with the evidence of St. Teresa of Ávila, and other mystics, that they wrote what they wrote at the bidding of a power superior to themselves. For St. Teresa, see G. Cunninghame Graham, *Santa Teresa* (London, 1907), 1:202. It seems plausible to me that such a document as 6.7, in whole or in part, might qualify as such a piece of writing.

qualities of soul that make men orderly and law-abiding, which is not too far away from the meaning suggested here.

With that, then, I rest my case. My suggestion is that Plotinus, like many another remarkable figure in human history, such as Saint Paul, Muhammad, Joan of Arc, Teresa of Ávila, or Fyodor Dostoievsky, was endowed (rather than afflicted) with a disorder of the temporal lobes of the brain, which enabled him to access other realms of reality, and since his training was in the Platonist philosophical tradition, he strove to fit the mystical insights with which he was blessed into the framework of that tradition. This he did, in general, with great dexterity, though retaining a few distinctive features, of which he is himself conscious, such as the postulation of that aspect of the human soul that remains above, in the noetic world—a conviction that stems directly from his personal experience and that he is not prepared to surrender, despite its interference with the general distinction he wishes to draw, for dogmatic reasons, between the levels of intellect and soul.

In conclusion, I would like to quote a passage from that great chronicler of mysticism, Evelyn Underhill:

In mysticism that love of truth which we saw as the beginning of all philosophy leaves the merely intellectual sphere, and takes on the assured aspect of a personal passion. Where the philosopher guesses and argues, the mystic lives and looks; and speaks, consequently, the disconcerting language of first-hand experience, not the neat dialectic of the schools. Hence, whilst the Absolute of the metaphysicians remains a diagram— impersonal and unattainable—the Absolute of the mystics is lovable, attainable, alive.[26]

Now Plotinus is undoubtedly a first-rate philosopher, in the Platonist tradition, but I think it is undeniable that he is also, and perhaps primarily, a mystic—though one who is at every stage concerned to structure his mystical insights within the framework of his philosophy.

---

26. Evelyn Underhill, *Mysticism: A Study in the Nature and Development of Man's Spiritual Consciousness* (Cleveland: World Publishing, 1955), 24.

Bibliography

Primary Sources

Hippocrates. *Hippocratic Writings*. Edited by G. E. R. Lloyd. London: Penguin Books, 1978.

Iamblichus. *De Mysteriis*. Translated with introduction and notes by Emma C. Clarke, John M. Dillon, and Jackson P. Hershbell. Leiden: Brill, 2004.

Plotinus. *Plotini Opera*. Edited by P. Henry and H. R. Schwyzer. 3 vols. Oxford: Oxford University Press, 1964–1983.

———— *Plotinus*. Translated by Arthur H. Armstrong. LCL. Cambridge: Harvard University Press, 1966–1988.

Secondary Sources

Alexander, Eben. *Proof of Heaven: A Neurosurgeon's Journey into the Afterlife*. New York: Simon & Schuster, 2012.

Beauregard, Mario, and Denyse O'Leary. *The Spiritual Brain: A Neuroscientist's Case for the Existence of the Soul*. New York: HarperCollins, 2007.

Beierwaltes, Werner. "Die Metaphysik des Lichtes in der Philosophie Plotins." *ZPF* 15 (1961): 334–62.

Graham, G. Cunninghame. *Santa Teresa*. Vol. 1. London, 1907.

Grant, Colin. *A Smell of Burning: The Story of Epilepsy*. London: Cape, 2016.

Mitchell, Kevin. *Innate: How the Wiring of Our Brains Shapes Who We Are*. Princeton: Princeton University Press, 2018.

Moody, Raymond. *Life after Life: The Investigation of a Phenomenon—Survival of Bodily Death*. Atlanta: Mockingbird Books, 1975.

Retoulas, Christos. *God's Gift, World's Deception*. Münster: LIT, 2022.

Underhill, Evelyn. *Mysticism: A Study in the Nature and Development of Man's Spiritual Consciousness*. Cleveland: World Publishing, 1955.

Wallis, Richard. "*Nous* as Experience." Pages 121–54 in *The Significance of Neoplatonism*. Edited by R. Baine Harris. Albany: State University of New York Press, 1976.

Part 2
Ontologies and Epistemologies

Soul in Plato

Luc Brisson

The passages on the soul I will evoke pertain for the most part to *mythos*, as narrative, and not to *logos*, taken in the strict sense of "argued discourse." This seems inevitable to me because of the very nature of that reality known as the soul in Plato. As such, the soul is a reality intermediate between the sensible and the intelligible (see *Tim.* 35a–b). It cannot therefore be the object either of the Intellect (*nous*), since it is not a Form (*eidos*), nor of any sense organ, since it is not a sensible particular. From this perspective, only one type of discourse can be held about it, which cannot be declared true or false, and this type of discourse is myth.[1] According to the interpretation I defend, the soul cannot, moreover, be reduced to a process or an activity;[2] it is an autonomous entity that has a personality and a history. We must take seriously the "description" of the mixture, carried out by the Demiurge in the *Timaeus*, that is at the origin first of the soul of the world (*Tim.* 35a–b) and then of the soul of other living beings (*Tim.* 41d). In order for a retributive system, such as that proposed by Plato, to work, it is necessary that an autonomous entity survive death, that is, when the separation from the body it moves for a time intervenes, and that this entity be transported from one body to another.

The Two Traditional Models of the Soul

In ancient Greece, the soul is associated with a body, which it moves and to which it provides spontaneous movement, thus establishing an opposition between the living and the nonliving. In this context, we find two models

---

1. See Luc Brisson and Gerard Naddaf, *Plato, the Mythmaker* (Chicago: University of Chicago Press, 1999), 91–111.

2. Monique Dixsaut, *Platon: Le désir de comprendre* (Paris: Vrin, 2003), 196–214.

of the soul. The first and most widespread one is surely that which associates the soul with a motive force of the body, from which it detaches itself at death to become a feeble image, an image that does not regain vigor until it is placed in contact with a corporeal element (for instance, breath or blood). The second one, in contrast, presents the soul as a temporary guest that travels independently of the body it animates.

The Invisible Motor

We find the first model in the *Iliad* and the *Odyssey*. In these two poems, the soul, which is not directly perceptible as such during life, is observable only when it leaves the body. Here is the formula that, in the *Iliad*, describes two famous deaths: that of Patroclus, killed by Hector (*Il.* 16.505), and that of Hector, killed by Achilles (22.362): "Scarcely had he spoken: death, which finishes all things, already enveloped him. His soul left his limbs, and went flying to Hades, weeping over its fate, abandoning strength and youth" (my trans.). The soul is associated with a breath (23.98), which may exit from the mouth (9.409), or with a vapor that rises from the blood flowing from a wound in the chest (16.505) or in the side (14.518). This is why Achilles can complain that he "risks his soul" (9.322); elsewhere, in order to cheer up his companions, Agenor points out that Achilles has only one soul (21.569). When Achilles is pursuing Hector around the walls of Troy, he remarks that the soul of his enemy will be the prize of his victory (22.61).

Once abandoned by the soul, the body is no more than a cadaver, a decomposing heap of flesh. The soul, for its part, is presented as an image (*eidolon*) of the deceased (*Il.* 13.72, 11.476, 24.14; *Od.* 11.83, 20.355), or its alter ego, as Achilles reveals when he evokes the soul of Patroclus, which comes to ask him to organize a funeral for him: "Ah! There is no doubt something, I know not what, that still lives in Hades, a soul, a shadow, but in which the spirit [φρένες] no longer dwells.[3] All night long, the soul of unfortunate Patroclus stood before me, lamenting, despairing, multiplying its injunctions. It resembled him prodigiously" (*Il.* 23.103–106). Although this image is his alter ego, once it has abandoned the body it animated, it is bereft of strength, not only physical, since it lacks coherence, but also

---

3. See Richard B. Onians, *The Origins of European Thought: About the Body, the Mind, the Soul, the World, Time, and Fate* (Cambridge: Cambridge University Press, 1988), 23–43.

psychic, for it loses its thought. Achilles can no more seize Patroclus's soul (*Il.* 23.99–102) than Odysseus can embrace the soul of his mother (*Od.* 11.205); while in the *nekyia*, the seer Tiresias can predict the future to Odysseus only once he has drunk the blood of slaughtered sacrificial victims (*Od.* 11.90–96), allowing him to interrogate the other souls, including his mother.

In this context, death represents a considerable diminution for the individual, even if something of him can survive indirectly in his children, ones who have received his genetic capital. As such, however, this individual continues his existence only in the form of an evanescent double, a piece of air that vegetates underground for an indeterminate time. Reduced to the state of a flimsy image of the deceased, the soul seems to lose its faculty of thinking, with the one exception of Tiresias, the exemplary seer. As a result, the soul, with its indefinite duration of survival, finds itself practically bereft of all individuality and therefore cannot take its place within a retributive system intended to correct in another world the injustices suffered or committed in this world. In the Homeric poems, moreover, only the souls of great criminals are punished and delivered over to exemplary tortures.

The Traveling Entity

The second model presents the soul as an autonomous entity that can travel outside the body it animates. Already in Homer, the soul travels in a certain way when separated from the body. It goes to Hades, which is an inhospitable place, whence it can return to converse with the living, like the soul of Patroclus and the souls conjured up by Odysseus. However, these voyages are limited and not very significant. By contrast, there are stories that speak of personages (in particular Aristeas, Abaris, Epimenides, and Phormion) who are able to separate their soul from their body and make it travel while leaving their body in situ, often for long periods of time. The following anecdote illustrates the subject admirably. The soul of Hermotimus,[4] it was told, could abandon its body and go traveling, returning to its body later. One day, his enemies, taking advantage of his wife's treason, threw his body in flames:

---

4. See Marcel Detienne, "Les origines religieuses de la notion de l'intellect: Hermotime et Anaxagore," *RevPhilos* 89 (1964): 167–78.

Among such souls you have doubtless heard of that of Hermotimus[5] of Clazomenae—how night and day it used to leave his body entirely and travel far and wide, returning after it had encountered and witnessed many things said and done in remote places, until his wife betrayed him and his enemies found his body at home untenanted by his soul and burnt it. (*Gen. Socr.* 22.592c–d [de Lacy and Einarson])

In this context, the individual's soul has its own life, independent from the body it moves, and a genuine personality, which enables it to experience specific adventures.

The Platonic Synthesis

The interest of Plato's position resides in that he associates these two models in his representation of the soul. The model of the soul attached to the body it animates appears in the *Timaeus*, whereas that of the traveling entity appears in the *Phaedrus*. Above all, however, this position should be situated within a specific philosophical context. Plato defends a paradoxical philosophical doctrine, characterized by a twofold reversal. (1) The world of the things perceived by the senses, in which we live, is a mere image of a world of intelligible realities (or Forms), which, as the models of sensible things, constitute genuine reality. Unlike sensible things, the Forms possess their principle of existence within themselves. (2) Man cannot be reduced to his body, and his genuine identity coincides with what we designate by means of the term *soul*, whatever may be the definition proposed of this entity, which accounts not only in man but also in the totality of the universe, for all motion, both material (growth, locomotion, etc.) and spiritual (feelings, sense perception, intellectual knowledge, etc.). Throughout the history of philosophy, this twofold reversal has enabled the specificity of Platonism to be defined.

The Soul as Invisible Motor of the Body in the *Timaeus*

In the *Timaeus*, we find the model of the soul as the invisible motor of the body understood in two senses.

---

5. A correction proposed by Xylander, for the text has Hermodorus. Hermotimus is the third reincarnation of Pythagoras according to Porphyry in his *Vit. Pyth.* 45.

The Soul as a Reality Intermediate between the Sensible and the Intelligible

The soul is invisible because it is incorporeal, situated at a level that is intermediate between the sensible and the intelligible. This is what Plato implies in this passage from the *Timaeus*, where we find a description of the mixture from which all souls derive, whether the soul of the world, of the gods, of demons, men, or animals, and even plants:[6]

> The components from which he made the soul and the way in which he made it were as follows: In between the Being that is indivisible and always changeless, and the one that is divisible and comes to be in the corporeal realm, he mixed a third, intermediate form of being, derived from the other two. Similarly,[7] he made a mixture of the Same, and then one of the Different, in between their indivisible and their corporeal, divisible counterparts.[8] And he took the three mixtures and mixed them together to make a uniform mixture, forcing the Different, which was hard to mix, into conformity with the Same. (*Tim.* 34e–35b)[9]

The description of the "fashioning" of the soul of the world by the Demiurge does not necessarily imply an origin in time. It merely illustrates the status of the soul, as a reality intermediate between the realm of intelligible forms, on which it depends, and that of sensible things, whose orderly motion it ensures, whether in the case of the circular motions of the heavenly bodies or the rectilinear motions of sublunary realities. In the passage cited above, Plato expresses the following two ideas: the soul is made of the same constitutive features (Being, Same, and Other) as all other realities, and it is a reality intermediate between the intelligible and the sensible.

From this initial mixture there results a substance that serves to form particular souls:[10] on the one hand, the soul of the world, which

---

6. Luc Brisson, "How to Make a Soul in the *Timaeus*," in *Plato*'s Timaeus, ed. Chad Jorgenson, Filip Karfík, and Štěpán Špinka, PTSPP (Leiden: Brill, 2021), 70–91.

7. I maintain *au peri*, widely attested in the direct and the indirect tradition.

8. I consider *auton*, attested by all the manuscripts, to be a partitive genitive governed by *en mesoi*, which represents both the nature of the Same and that of the Other.

9. Quotations from Plato follow Plato, *Complete Works*, ed. John M. Cooper (Indianapolis: Hackett, 1997).

10. Luc Brisson, "Le corps des dieux," in *Les dieux de Platon*, ed. Jérôme Laurent (Caen: Presses de l'Université de Caen, 2003), 11–23.

accounts for the motion of the celestial bodies, as is illustrated by the continuation of the text on the Demiurge's construction of an armillary sphere (see *Tim.* 40d), that is, a globe made up of rings or circles, representing the motion of the heavens and the stars. The Demiurge, who works like a blacksmith, laminates the mass of the mixture he has realized to transform it into a plate, into which he introduces a certain number of divisions. He begins by cutting this plate lengthwise, to obtain two bands, which he calls the band of the "Same" and that of the "Other" (although each of these bands is made up of a mixture of Being, Same, and Other). The technical operation carried out by the Demiurge accounts on a metaphorical level for the distinction observed between the fixed stars, which move from east to west, and the planets, which move from west to east. Just as Same and Other are contraries, so the celestial bodies that move along the circle of the Same and on that of the Other move in a contrary direction. The Demiurge continues his work by cutting the band of the Other into seven parts, which allows the fashioning of circles along which the seven planets known at the time will move (from west to east). Plato gives this band the name Other, thereby opposing it to the band of the Same, representing the apparently regular motion of the fixed stars, which move from east to west. This operation constitutes a preliminary to the fashioning of two circles along which the celestial bodies will move with the permanence ensured by the perfect symmetry of the circle in a two-dimensional space. On the other, it forms the souls of the gods and demons, as we can observe by reading the beginning of the speech by the Demiurge to the gods he has just fashioned (see *Tim.* 41a–d).

Soul (the human soul as well as the world soul) also has a mathematical structure similar to musical harmony. It may seem bizarre to attribute to the soul a mathematical structure, corresponding to a musical harmony (*Tim.* 35b–36b). Historically, however, it seems that Plato was impressed by the discovery, attributed to the Pythagoreans (in *Resp.* 7 [530e–531c]), of the relation between mathematical ratios and material sounds: if the length of the strings of a musical instrument is in a given mathematical *ratio*, it is possible to produce a given sound. In other words, the recourse to mathematical ratios enabled to produce in the physical world a phenomenon that could be perceptible by the eyes in the form of motion of the celestial bodies. Thus, the incorporeal could have an effect on the body.

After completing his study of the soul of the world and of the gods and demons,[11] Plato moves on to that soul of other living beings.

> When he had finished this speech, he turned again to the mixing bowl he had used before, the one in which he had blended and mixed the soul of the universe. He began to pour into it what remained of the previous ingredients and to mix them in somewhat the same way, though these were no longer invariably and constantly pure, but of a second and third grade of purity. (*Tim.* 41d)

Whereas the first mixture was reserved for the immortal beings, in the sense that they are endowed with an indestructible body,[12] this one is intended for the other living beings, men, animals, and even plants.

The Soul as Motor of the Body

From a Platonic perspective, all souls, the soul of the world, those of the gods, those of the demons, those of human beings and of animals, derive from the same mixture, whose degree of purity may vary but which always contains the same elements. One part of the initial mixture serves to constitute the soul of the world, which the Demiurge associates with the body of the world. This operation is described in two passages (*Tim.* 34a–b, 36d–e), which adopt different viewpoints. However, the idea is the same in both cases: the soul is the principle of all psychic and physical motion in this universe, and particularly that of the celestial bodies (*Tim.* 34a–b). In addition, part of the second mixture serves to constitute a human soul, principle of all psychic and physical motion in a given human being, which enters the human body, under difficult conditions, in an initial period (*Tim.* 43a–b). It may be interesting to note that the soul of mankind is constituted by the same interweaving of rings as the soul of the world and that this interweaving of rings is found again in the head of human beings (*Tim.* 76a–b), where they leave traces, and of the other animals, whose form they explain (*Tim.* 91e). These two remarks

---

11. If we consider the Demiurge's speech, we must associate the soul of the world with that of the gods, both visible—that is, the celestial bodies—and invisible—that is, the gods of tradition—who only manifest themselves from time to time, and those of the demons who come from the gods.

12. See Brisson, "Le corps des dieux," 11–23.

show to what extent the soul in Plato is close to the living body, of which
it is the motive force. Thus, although he proposes a radically new ontological system, Plato is very close here to Homer.

The Soul as Temporary Guest of a Human Body

It is above all in the central myth of the *Phaedrus* (245c–246b) that the
soul is described as a traveling entity (see also *Tim.* 41e–42a). In this mag-
nificent passage, Plato describes the ascent of the human souls, which
follow the troop of the gods and demons to take their place on the external
envelope of the sphere that constitutes the body of the world, in order
to contemplate the intelligible realities. The soul exhibits the following
features: (1) As a reality (*ousia*), the soul can by definition (*logos*) be considered a principle of motion and hence of life. It can therefore neither be
born nor die. Indeed, if this were the case, all things in the world would
stop or die. (2) The soul is by nature a composite power (*symphytē dyna-
mis*). Both in gods and in men, it includes three elements. In the central
myth of the *Phaedrus*, Plato does not give an argued description of the
structure of the soul; he limits himself to comparing the soul to a chariot
drawn by two horses that are led by a charioteer, who can be identified
respectively with intellect (*nous*), spirit (*thymos*) and desire (*epithymia*).
Intellection (*noēsis*) is the highest faculty of the soul, and Intellect (*nous*)
has the Forms as its objects. There can be no intellect without a soul (*Tim.*
30b), and soul must be directed by its own intellect (*Tim.* 90a–e). In fact,
the history of a soul, whether situated in a terrestrial body or not, is determined by the quality of the exercise of the activity of its intellect. On earth,
this activity finds itself in competition with that of spirit (*thymos*) and of
desire (*epithymia*); but by taking time away from the exercise of the intellect, these two parts of the soul have an influence on the intellect. The term
part does not have a material meaning here but indicates an aspect, or
rather a capacity or faculty, of the soul.

Importantly, the *Timaeus* establishes a hierarchy of being, since, in the
final analysis, any mythical construction whose purpose is to influence
human behavior cannot elude the prior establishment of a value system.
The highest rank in this hierarchy is occupied by gods and demons; then
come human beings, men and women; then the animals that live in the air,
on earth and in the water; while plants are at the bottom. This hierarchy
is based on the two criteria: (1) the relations between the soul and the
intellect, and (2) the nature of the body that the soul enables to move or to

change spontaneously. The first criterion establishes an impassable border between plants and the rest of living beings, whereas the second one establishes another barrier, just as impassable, between the gods and demons on the one hand, and the rest of living beings on the other.

Gods

Phaedrus 246d gives the following definition of god: "an immortal living being, which has a soul and a body, both naturally united forever." Yet there are several kinds of gods. First of all, there is the universe, a sphere made up of the four elements; the celestial bodies, made of fire; and the traditional divinities, also endowed with a body, although we do not know what it is made of. In the middle, between human beings and the gods, are the demons, who are also endowed with a body. The bodies of the gods and the demons are not in themselves indestructible, but they will not be destroyed, as a function of the will of the being who made them (*Tim.* 41a–b). What is more, the gods, whose body cannot be destroyed, cannot take on another appearance; in other words, they cannot metamorphose themselves. The soul of gods and demons is thus always associated with the same body.

The world, which is unique, has a body shaped like a vast sphere, without organs or members. This sphere contains within itself the totality of elements, so that nothing can come from outside to attack it, and it is therefore exempt from sickness and death. In addition, the Demiurge, who is benevolent, does not wish the universe to be subject to corruption. This body is inhabited by a soul, an incorporeal entity between the sensible and the intelligible and endowed with a mathematical structure (*Tim.* 35b–36b). The soul of the world is made up of circles, whose permanent motions are arranged in mathematical ratios, and it is associated with an indestructible body over which it reigns. This soul has a twofold function: a motor function, since it moves all bodies, including celestial bodies, and a cognitive one. The physical motion that animates the universe is as simple as possible: it is that of a sphere rotating around its axis, from east to west, while remaining in place. In addition, the soul of the world is endowed with an intellect, which is perfect and ceaselessly active. This is what guarantees that the physical motions will be as orderly as possible.

The celestial bodies, made of fire (*Tim.* 40a–b), and the Earth (*Tim.* 40b–c), made primarily of earth, are qualified as divine since they meet the criteria stated above. They are indeed living immortals, consisting in a body that cannot be destroyed and a soul that is proper to them, and endowed with an intellect. There is a hierarchy among celestial bodies, according to their motion. The fixed stars follow the course imposed by the circle of Sameness, from east to west, with perfect uniformity, for the motion of their soul does not give rise to any interference. The soul of the wandering stars introduces anomalies with regard to the trajectory of the circle of Otherness, which transports them all. The Earth, for its part, remains at the center of the universe.

Human Beings and Animals

Beneath the gods in the hierarchy are souls that are endowed with an intellect like the gods but liable to be attached to a body, which, unlike that of the gods, is destructible. These inferior souls are subject to temporality; their existence is marked by cycles of ten thousand years, imposed by destiny, which involve a system of retribution based on reincarnation.

In order to account for the soul's relations with a destructible body, Plato, beginning with the *Republic*, distinguishes three powers within the soul, the first of which is in itself immortal, whereas the two others enjoy immortality only so long as the body over which they reign is indestructible. The immortal power of soul, that is, the intellect, contemplates the intelligible realities of which sensible things are mere images. By its means, mankind is akin to a god, or rather to a *daimon*. The other two powers are, on the one hand, spirit (*thymos*), which enables mortal living beings to defend themselves; and desire (*epithymia*), which enables them to ensure they remain alive and can reproduce. Whereas the intellect can be said to be immortal, these two powers are declared to be mortal because they are associated with functions that enable the survival of the sensible body to which the soul is attached, albeit only for a lifetime (*Phaedr.* 248b–249c).

When applied to mortal living beings, and in particular to mankind, the psychic tripartition just mentioned is associated with a tripartition that is corporeal and even social. In the *Timaeus*, Plato associates each power of soul with a place in the body. The lowest or desiring power, which ensures the functions of survival (by provoking the desire for food) and of reproduction (by provoking sexual desire), is situated under the diaphragm in the area of the liver. Above the diaphragm, in the area of the heart, is the spirited power, which enables human beings to remain alive by ensuring defensive functions, both internal and external. This second power enables a mediation between the desiring power and intellect, situated in the head, which is responsible for all the processes of knowledge that can be expressed in speech. In mankind, only intellect is immortal, for the spirited power and the desiring power are restricted to ensuring the functions that enable destructible bodies to maintain themselves in good working order for a specific time. When this body is destroyed, the spirited power and the desiring power associated with it cease their activities, which are, moreover, not preserved in memory,[13] and this is why they are qualified as "mortal" (*Tim.* 69d).

This psychic tripartition, associated with a corporeal one, is in addition related to a functional tripartition in a social context. At the end of book 2 of the *Republic*, Plato proposes an organization in which individuals are distributed in *functional* groups in accordance with this hierarchy, based on the predominance in the human individual of one of the powers: intellect (*nous*), spirit (*thymos*), or desire (*epithymia*). The most numerous group, responsible for ensuring the production of food and of wealth, is made up of farmers and craftsmen. This group is protected by guardians, warriors responsible for ensuring the maintenance of order, both within and outside the city. Insofar as they can possess neither property nor money, the guardians are completely separated from the producers, who, in exchange for the protection they receive from the guardians, must feed them and ensure their upkeep. From these functional groups, a very small number of individuals are chosen, those who are intended for higher education and the government of the city.

The Ten-Thousand-Year Cycle of the Souls

Only soul, as an incorporeal whole, is immortal. Individual souls are recycled every ten thousand years. Throughout these years, a soul can be attached to a given body, which body is subject to destruction. In this way, the soul can be punished or rewarded for its previous lives (punished, for instance, by becoming attached to an inferior animal). Another cycle for this soul then begins, now deprived of its previous individuality. Here, Plato's thought on soul is not very different from oriental doctrines of reincarnation. Since the presence of soul in a body signifies that this body is

---

13. See Luc Brisson, "The Mortal Parts of the Soul, or Death Forgetting the Body," in *Inner Life and Soul: Psyche in Plato*, ed. Maurizio Migliori, Linda M. Napolitano Valditara, and Arianne Fermani (Sankt Augustin: Academia, 2011), 63–70.

temporarily alive, we note that, in this scheme, it is not individual life that persists, but what remains constant is, so to speak, the available pool of souls, almost as if it were the phenomenon of life per se that persists. Let us next consider the soul's wanderings in more detail.

During the first millennium (*Phaedr.* 245d–248c), the soul is separated from all destructible bodies, whereas during the following nine millennia (*Phaedr.* 248c–e), it passes from body to body as a function of the moral value of its previous existence, which depends on the quality of its intellectual activity. At the end of this first millennium of recurring transmigrations, all those souls that are worthy of being associated with a sensible body inhabit the body of a man—that is, a male, even though the sexual organs are still missing—and this association remains valid for the following millennium. A man who loves knowledge or beauty and who has chosen an upright life for three consecutive millennia will be able to escape from the cycle of reincarnations and rise back up to the heavens. The others will voyage from one body to another, beginning with the third millennium (*Tim.* 90e–92c). The first category of bodies mentioned is that of women: whoever displays cowardice enters into the body of a woman, since virility was associated with war in ancient Greece. Not until the course of this millennium does the distinction of the sexes appear, thus allowing sexual reproduction. Then come incarnations in various kinds of what we call animals, although there is no term in ancient Greek to designate this category of living beings. They are classified as a function of the elements (beginning with the air, since fire is reserved for the gods), in a vertical order. At the top, birds fly through the air. Then come the living beings that inhabit the surface of the earth; these are the quadrupeds, insects, and reptiles. Last come the aquatic animals: fish, shellfish, and others; they are the intellectually weakest.

In fact, Plato describes a psychic *continuum*, in which we find a hierarchical order of gods, demons, human beings, and the animals that live in the air, on the earth, and in the water, and even, as we shall soon see, plants. Intellectual activity, conceived as the intuition of Ideas, constitutes the criterion that enables a distinction to be established between all these souls. Gods and demons contemplate the intelligible reality, that is, the Forms, directly and, as it were, incessantly. Human beings share this privilege only during a certain period of their existence, when their souls are separated from all bodies. Once human souls have been incarnated, their contemplation of the Ideas is mediated, since it must pass through the intermediary of the senses; above all, it is more or less uncertain. For their part, animals use their intellect less and less as one goes down the scale of beings.

Within the psychic scale mentioned above, we note two discontinuities: (1) a discontinuity between the souls of gods and of demons, which never fall into a body subject to destruction; and the souls of human beings and of animals, which inhabit destructible bodies with diverse appearances; and (2) a discontinuity between the souls of human beings and of animals, which are endowed with a rational power, and the souls of plants (*Tim.* 76e–77c), which are reduced to the desiring power.

Let us consider one by one the consequences of these two discontinuities.

1. In this hierarchical system, only souls endowed with an intellect are subject to a retributive system, which makes them rise or fall on the scale of souls, incarnated according to the quality of their intellectual activity. Gods and demons are above this class, while plants are below it. Gods and plants thus always remain at their level, at the highest or the lowest extremity.

2. As a result, human beings, who are situated at the uppermost limit of the class of incarnate souls, must have as their goal to become assimilated to the gods and the demons, by seeking contemplation of the Forms. Hence the theme of the assimilation to divinity by the philosopher, who tends toward knowledge, that is, the contemplation of the Forms, or true reality.

3. The hierarchy of human beings and animals, which is a function of the exercise of their intellectual activity, is rendered material by the body.[14] The body in which the soul is situated illustrates the quality of that soul's intellectual activity; in short, the body is a "state of the soul." From this perspective, all human beings and animals that inhabit the air, the earth, and the water constitute a vast system of symbols; symbols from the point of view of appearances, but also from the viewpoint of behavior, which justifies the recourse to a number of comparisons, images, and metaphors in which animals play a role. In the *Timaeus*, these symbols refer to different types of soul, whose moral quality is ultimately determined by their contemplation of the intelligible, according to a

---

14. Amber D. Carpenter, "Embodied Intelligence: Animals and Us in Plato's *Timaeus*," in *Platonism and Forms of Intelligence*, ed. John Dillon and Marie-Élise Zovko (Berlin: Akademie, 2008), 179–90.

number of details that may seem ironic or ridiculous but that can be interpreted only in this sense: birds are naive astronomers, who think that sight is the ultimate source of knowledge; quadrupeds need four feet in order to support their skull, which has been elongated by the deformations of the revolutions of the circles of its rational power. Stupid terrestrial animals crawl; fish are even more stupid, and the worst ignorance is that of shellfish.

Be that as it may, the reproduction and conservation of this material symbol known as the body must be ensured.

4. Sexual reproduction raises serious problems for Plato, as we can observe in the passage from the *Timaeus* that describes the appearance of male and female sexual organs in the third millennium of the cycle undergone by each soul (see *Tim.* 91a–d). The two sexes are kinds of autonomous living beings, grafted onto the bodies of men and women. The male sexual organ emits sperm, which is made of marrow (for a description of marrow, see *Tim.* 74a, 77d, 86c–d), that corporeal substance on which the soul is anchored (*Tim.* 86c–d).[15] Sperm is thus the bearer of invisible living beings that the male, upon ejaculation, deposits in the female's uterus; she, in turn, will supply one of these invisible living beings with the nourishment it needs to grow until the moment when it emerges into the light. This "preformist" theory of the sexual transmission of life is subtle; yet it enters into conflict with the doctrine of reincarnation, because the transmitted soul already has a history, which the male who transmits it and the female who receives it cannot know.

5. Like that of human beings, whether men or women, the soul of animals is endowed with a rational power, and this is true even if animals are what they are because they make little or no use of their intellect. In any case, nothing prevents an animal, whatever it may be, from climbing back up the scale to become a human being. It follows that killing and eating an animal is equivalent to

15. David Sedley, "'Becoming like God' in Plato and Aristotle," in *Interpreting the Timaeus-Critias, Proceedings of the IV Symposium Platonicum*, ed. Tomás Calvo and Luc Brisson (Sankt Augustin: Academia, 1997), 327–39.

killing and eating a man.[16] How, in this case, can the survival of human beings, who need to feed themselves, be ensured, without making an anthropophagus of them? By giving them as food a kind of living being that is not endowed with intellect, namely, plants.

Plants

After mentioning the four types of living beings that populate the universe, the gods associated with fire, the human beings, men or women, the birds that inhabit the air, the animals walking or crawling on the earth, and the aquatic beasts, Timaeus rapidly mentions the origin of plants, which he associates with the third or desiring power of soul in the *Timaeus* (76e–77c).[17]

Plato justifies the existence of plants by the human body's need to reconstitute in order to maintain itself in existence, through consuming beings endowed with a soul like it, but a soul that is absolutely bereft of any intellect (*Tim.* 77c6–7).[18] For man, to eat a human being endowed with an intellect, even if this living being did not make use of this higher faculty, would be an act of cannibalism. This is no longer the case with plants, which possess a soul, but one that is bereft of intellect. The decomposition of plants within the human body enables the constitution of blood, which nourishes all the other tissues. In this way, plants enable the human body—which, unlike the world's body, may be destroyed by the external aggression of fire or of air—to reconstitute itself without consuming living beings endowed with a soul. In short, Plato "invents" plants in order to be able to maintain his scale of living beings. We must insist on the following corollaries: since plants cannot be endowed with an intellect, a human soul cannot be incarnated in a plant.[19]

The consequences Plato derives from this conception of the phenomenon of life are certainly not primarily biological but ethical and political.

---

16. Luc Brisson, "Justifying Vegetarianism in Plato's *Timaeus* (76e–77c)," in *Greek Philosophy in the New Millennium: Essays in Honour of Thomas M. Robinson*, ed. Livio Rossetti, SAP (Sankt Augustin: Academia, 2004), 313–19.

17. Carpenter, "Embodied Intelligence," 281–303.

18. "All the plant kinds, those that are more powerful (that is, the gods) planted them to serve as food for us, who are less powerful."

19. Difference from Empedocles DK 31B.117 = LM 22D.13.

The main purpose seems to be the establishment of a system of retribution that no living being—excepting gods, demons, and plants—are able
to escape. Yet behind this intention, which can lead only to a myth, we
reencounter all the great themes associated with the notion of life. Life is
inseparable from time, which enables the measurement of the change that
affects all sensible things, and hence the introduction of something that
does not change. Thus, life, which, in individual beings, men, animals, and
plants, assumes meaning only as a function of death, presents itself immediately as a universal phenomenon, which has immortality as its goal.[20]

Memory and Immortality

In souls that are not those of a god or of a demon, however, individual
immortality remains limited in time, as we can observe by rereading the
central myth of the *Phaedrus*. Let us take up matters in order. (1) The
excellence of a soul that falls into an earthly body depends on its direct contemplation of the intelligible realities in the course of the first millennium.
(2) When it enters an earthly body, a soul can contemplate intelligible reality only partially and indirectly. Partially, because this soul must ensure
other functions, in particular that of the defense of the body it animates
against the threats that come from within or without, as well as that of
the nutrition necessary for keeping this body alive. In the third millennium, the reproductive function is added to these concerns. Indirectly, for
the human soul, which can no longer directly contemplate the intelligible,
must rediscover its memory thereof, as we can observe by rereading certain passages from the *Meno* and the *Phaedo*. (3) When death, understood
as the separation of the soul from the body, occurs, the exercise of these
functions ceases. (4) The quality of a soul's subsequent existence depends
on the quality of its previous existence, which in turn depends on its ability to contemplate the intelligible. Yet the energy it expends to ensure the
functions of the defense and safekeeping of the body with which it is associated diminishes its capacity to contemplate intelligible reality. (5) Thus,
the sensible can have an influence on the greater or lesser excellence of a
soul, which, as a function of this excellence, rises or falls on the scale of
living beings.

---

20. This immortality is linked to the quality of exercise of the intellect, but it
cannot be reduced to this intellect, precisely insofar as the soul is a substance intermediate between the sensible and the intelligible.

Death and Its Consequences for the Individual Soul

When it is in a body, the soul, by means of one of its activities, namely, the intellect (*nous*), remains in contact with the intelligible, which in fact enables it to concern itself with the body to which it is attached. It must ensure the survival of this body by means of the ingestion of food and drink and of its reproduction. It must also defend this body against aggressions that come from outside, or even from within; this is why spirit and desire are necessary. What happens, however, when this soul is separated from the body? Its higher activity remains what it was, and it maintains the memory of its object, the intelligible, simply because this object is immutable. However, this contemplative activity is qualified by the fact that when the soul was in a body, it paid greater or lesser attention to the sensible; hence the application of a retributive system. When the soul becomes detached from the body for which it cared, its activities in this area cease being exercised, and it loses the memory of the objects and events associated with these activities. This consequence derives from the following observation: in Plato, a soul never recalls empirical events associated with a previous existence, as is the case, for instance, when Pythagoras or the Pythagoreans are mentioned.

In this context one can, it seems to me, declare the functions known as the spirit (*thymos*) and desire (*epithymia*) to be mortal. However, insofar as they are the activities of a soul, these functions share the soul's immortality. That they subsist among the gods without being exercised goes to show, in my view, that the soul must be considered naturally compound. As capacities to act and to suffer, however, as a result of the soul's separation from its body, these functions cease to be exercised, and since no memory of what they have done in the past subsists, they can be qualified as mortal. From this perspective, the "death" that affects the functions of the human soul known as ardor and desire may be defined as a forgetting of the body, consequent upon the soul's separation from this body.

The Immortality of the Soul in Whole or in Part?

This new approach to death involves memory, that is, the preservation of the recollection of certain objects and events. However, even if Plato accepts metensomatosis, he never mentions the memory of an event pertaining to a past empirical existence, as could be done by Pythagoras and the Pythagoreans. Indeed, Diogenes Laertius reports the following anecdote about Pythagoras:

This is what Heraclides of Pontus tells us Pythagoras used to say about himself: that he had once been Aethalides and was accounted to be Hermes' son and Hermes told him he might choose any gift he liked except immortality; so he asked to retain through life and through death a memory of his experiences. Hence in life he could recall everything, and when he died he still kept the same memories. Afterwards in course of time his soul entered into Euphorbus and he was wounded by Menelaus. Now Euphorbus used to say that he has once been Aethalides and obtained the gift from Hermes, and then he told of the wanderings of his soul, how it migrated hither and thither, into that it underwent in Hades, and all that the other souls there have to endure. When Euphorbus died, his soul passed into Hermotimus, and he also, wishing to authenticate the story went up to the temple of Apollo at Branchidae, where he identified the shield which Menalaus, on his voyage home from Troy, had dedicated to Apollo, so he said; the shield being now so rotten through and through that the ivory facing only was left. When Hermotimus died, he became Pyrrhus, a fisherman of Delos, and again he remembered everything, how he was first Aethalides, then Euphorbus, then Hermotimus, and then Pyrrhus. But when Pyrrhus died, he became Pythagoras, and still remembered alle the facts mentioned. (Diogenes Laertius, *Vit. phil.* 8.4–5 [Hicks])

For Plato, by contrast, all that counts is memory of the intelligible. From this perspective, we should recall this text from the *Meno*:

As the soul is immortal, has been born often, and has seen all things here and in the underworld, there is nothing which it has not learned; so it is in no way surprising that it can recollect the things it knew before, both about virtue and other things. As the whole of nature is akin, and the soul has learned everything, nothing prevents a man, after recalling one thing only—a process men call learning—discovering everything else for himself, if he is brave and does not tire of the search, for searching and learning are, as a whole, recollection. We must, therefore, not believe that debater's argument, for it would make us idle, and fainthearted men like to hear it, e whereas my argument makes them energetic and keen on the search. (*Meno* 81c5–e1)

As I have tried to show,[21] this text must be placed in parallel with the *Phaedo* (72e–77a) on the level both of language and of doctrine. The argumentation

---

21. Luc Brisson, "La réminiscence dans le *Ménon* (80e–81e) et son arrière-plan religieux," in *Anamnese e Saber*, ed. José Trindade Santos (Imprensa Nacional-Casa da

used in this passage can be reconstructed as follows. (1) There is nothing of which the soul has not already acquired knowledge. The object of this preliminary knowledge is the intelligible it contemplated when it was separated from all bodies. This is obvious in the *Phaedo* but remains implicit in the *Meno*, where the allusion to Hades and the reference to virtue take on a meaning that is both simple and satisfying only under the hypothesis of the existence of intelligible realities. (2) The same holds true for the whole of nature: sensible things and intelligible realities maintain relations among themselves, and above all, sensible things participate in intelligible realities. (3) Consequently, because sensible things participate in intelligible realities, remembering intelligible realities makes it possible to discover all other things. However, insofar as this is an exercise that consists in taking the sensible as the departure point, in order later to detach oneself from the sensible with a view to reaching the intelligible, this requires courage and bravery, effort and trouble.

From this, however, a paradoxical consequence results: to know oneself is to remember not one's past experiences in the sensible world but the experience one has had of the intelligible. Consequently, to know oneself is to dissolve the individual in the universal. In brief, to know oneself is not to carry out an act of introspection but to be able to judge the quality of one's relations with the intelligible.

After a certain period of time, the soul in question rejoins a body. Its lower functions then adapt to this new body and persist in relation with it, until they separate from it. The identity or individuality of his soul is thus changing with the series of its particular existences. However, this identity or individuality persists for a certain stretch of time, but not for eternity, for it is linked to the history of a soul during a cycle of a thousand years. At the end of this cycle, one may think that this soul loses its identity before resuming its reascent toward the intelligible with the gods and demons, and that it acquires, for another period of a thousand years, a new individuality, which will then be placed in question once again. In other words, it is the entire soul that is immortal, not any particular soul.

There is therefore no longer a contradiction in Plato's dialogues on the question of immortality. In the *Phaedrus* as in the *Timaeus*, it is the soul in its totality that is, by definition, presented as immortal. Certain particular

Moeda: Centro de Filosofia da Universidade de Lisboa, 1999), 23–61; Brisson, "Reminiscence in Plato," in Dillon and Zovko, *Platonism and Forms of Intelligence*, 179–90.

souls, the soul of the world, that of the gods and those of the demons, may be presented as immortal, because their body, although destructible in itself, will not be destroyed, in accordance with the promise of the Demiurge. In the case of the human soul, immortality and mortality are a function of this soul's relations with a body. Because the body it animates is destructible, one may qualify certain functions of this soul as mortal. Nevertheless, the intellect of a soul is individualized, at least for a certain period of time, by the quality of its contemplation of the intelligible, which makes possible a system of retribution. In this context, individuality is associated with the body in a negative way, in the sense that the body reduces the quality of intellectual activity. Individuality is therefore defined by a deficit with regard to the intelligible. What is more, at the end of each thousand-year cycle, this individuality disappears, since the soul must lose all its characteristics before being reintegrated within another cycle. In short, for Plato, the human individual soul has only a relative immortality, limited in time.

Bibliography

Primary Sources

Diogenes Laertius. *Lives of Eminent Philosophers*. Translated by R. D. Hicks. Cambridge , MA: Harvard University Press; London: Heinemann, 1980.

Plato. *Complete Works*. Edited by John M. Cooper. Indianapolis: Hackett, 1997.

Plutarch. *On the Sign of Socrates*. Vol. 7 of *Moralia*. Translated by Ph. H. de Lacy and B. Einarson. Cambridge, MA: Harvard University Press, 1959.

Secondary Sources

Brisson, Luc. "Le corps des dieux." Pages 11–23 in *Les dieux de Platon*. Edited by Jérôme Laurent. Caen: Presses de l'Université de Caen, 2003.

———. "How to Make a Soul in the *Timaeus*." Pages 70–91 in *Plato's Timaeus*. Edited by Chad Jorgenson, Filip Karfík, and Štěpán Špinka. PTSPP. Leiden: Brill, 2021.

———. "Justifying Vegetarianism in Plato's *Timaeus* (76e–77c)." Pages 313–19 in *Greek Philosophy in the New Millennium: Essays in Honour of Thomas M. Robinson*. Edited by Livio Rossetti. SAP. Sankt Augustin: Academia, 2004.

———. "The Mortal Parts of the Soul, or Death Forgetting the Body." Pages 63–70 in *Inner Life and Soul: Psyche in Plato*. Edited by Maurizio Migliori, Linda M. Napolitano Valditara, and Arianne Fermani. Sankt Augustin: Academia, 2011.

———. "La réminiscence dans le *Ménon* (80e–81e) et son arrière-plan religieux." Pages 23–61 in *Anamnese e Saber*. Edited by José Trindade Santos. Imprensa Nacional-Casa da Moeda: Centro de Filosofia da Universidade de Lisboa, 1999.

———. "Reminiscence in Plato." Pages 179–90 in *Platonism and Forms of Intelligence*. Edited by John Dillon and Marie-Élise Zovko. Berlin: Akademie, 2008.

Brisson, Luc, and Gerard Naddaf. *Plato, the Mythmaker*. Chicago: University of Chicago Press, 1999.

Carpenter, Amber D. "Embodied Intelligence: Animals and Us in Plato's *Timaeus*." Pages 179–90 in *Platonism and Forms of Intelligence*. Edited by John Dillon and Marie-Élise Zovko. Berlin: Akademie, 2008.

Detienne, Marcel. "Les origines religieuses de la notion de l'intellect: Hermotime et Anaxagore." *RevPhilos* 89 (1964): 167–78.

Dixsaut, Monique. *Platon: Le désir de comprendre*. Paris: Vrin, 2003.

Onians, Richard B. *The Origins of European Thought: About the Body, the Mind, the Soul, the World, Time, and Fate*. Cambridge: Cambridge University Press, 1988.

Sedley, David. "'Becoming like God' in Plato and Aristotle." Pages 327–39 in *Interpreting the Timaeus-Critias, Proceedings of the IV Symposium Platonicum*. Edited by Tomás Calvo and Luc Brisson. Sankt Augustin: Academia, 1997.

Is the Soul a Form?
The Status of the Soul in the
Final Argument of the *Phaedo*, Again

Van Tu

Among the many theses Plato holds about the nature of the soul, there is perhaps none in which he believes more firmly than the thesis that a person's soul survives the person's death. Plato offers not one but four distinct arguments for the immortality of the soul in the *Phaedo*. This literary masterpiece depicts the last day of Socrates's life, culminating in what is intended to be a conclusive argument that purports to show that the soul is "altogether deathless and imperishable" (παντὸς μᾶλλον ... ἀθάνατον καὶ ἀνώλεθρον, 106e9–107a1).[1] Commentators continue to be vexed by the *Phaedo*'s final argument for the everlastingness of the soul. A significant source of perplexity has to do with the ambiguous ontological status of

This paper has many past lives. Matthew Evans's seminar on Plato on the soul in 2014 at the University of Michigan provided the occasion for its birth. A version of this paper was read at the second Regional Meeting of the International Platonic Society in Taipei, Taiwan, 2015. Another was presented at Soul Matters: Plato and Platonists on the Nature of the Soul, at the University of Michigan, in 2019. I am grateful to members of the audience for their valuable feedback. I owe a debt of a different kind to Sara Ahbel-Rappe, who introduced me to John Finamore and the welcoming community of scholars at the International Society for Neoplatonic Studies headed by John. I would like to dedicate this paper to John and Sara, who have been sources of inspiration for my research on the Platonic tradition and who, through their actions and scholarship, testify that soul indeed matters.

1. I follow the Greek text edited by Rowe; all translations are my own, occasionally drawing from Gallop's or Grube's translations. See Plato, *Phaedo*, ed. Christopher Rowe (Cambridge: Cambridge University Press, 1993); David Gallop, *Plato: Phaedo*, CPS (Oxford: Clarendon, 1975); George M. A. Grube, *Plato's Phaedo* (Indianapolis: Hackett Publishing, 1977).

the soul, which is alleged to shift "from soul as form to soul as possessor of form."[2] At its crudest, the interpretative issue is this: Does the word *soul* (ψυχή) in the final argument of the *Phaedo* refer to an individual substance—a bearer of Forms—or a Form itself?[3]

This paper has another go at this vexing question. It argues that the *Phaedo*'s final argument consistently treats the soul as "something else" (ἄλλο τι) distinct from both the transcendental Form in nature (τὸ ἐν τῇ φύσει) and the immanent form in us (τὸ ἐν ἡμῖν, *Phaed.* 103e9–104a3).[4] In the context of *Phaedo*'s final argument, the soul is persistently taken to be an individual bearer of life: a substance that necessarily imparts life always and everywhere to that to which it is present.[5] The reading to be defended might reasonably be thought to commit Plato to what Richard Archer-

---

2. Reginald Hackforth, *Plato's Phaedo* (Cambridge: Cambridge University Press, 1955), 165. Gallop, too, notes the ambiguity about whether the items mentioned in the final argument—the soul, fire, and snow—are thought of as Forms or ordinary Form-bearing substances (*Plato: Phaedo*, 197). There is a related concern discussed by Keyt, who believes that Plato infers fallaciously from the premise that the soul, which is something like an immanent form, is subordinate to the immanent forms of deathlessness (τὸ ἀθάνατον) and indestructible (τὸ ἀνώλεθρον) to the conclusion that the soul possesses these two forms. See David Keyt, "The Fallacies in 'Phaedo' 102a–107b," *Phronesis* 8 (1963): 171. For responses to this charge of equivocation, see Dorothea Frede, "The Final Proof of the Immortality of the Soul in Plato's 'Phaedo' 102a–107a," *Phronesis* 23 (1978): 27–41; Jerome Schiller, "Is the Soul a Form?," *Phronesis* 12 (1967): 50–58.

3. I will use *Form* to refer to the transcendental Platonic Form and *form* when talking about the immanent form.

4. Here I bypass the interpretative debate concerning whether Plato distinguishes a category of immanent forms with separate ontological status from the Forms in nature. The distinction is accepted by Hackforth in *Plato's Phaedo*; Richard S. Bluck, *Plato's Phaedo* (London: Routledge & Kegan Paul, 1955), 17–18; Gregory Vlastos, "Reasons and Causes in the *Phaedo*," *PhilRev* 78 (1969): 298–301; Daniel Devereux, "Separation and Immanence in Plato's Theory of Forms," *OSAP* 12 (1994): 63–90. It is denied by Willem J. Verdenius, "Notes on Plato's *Phaedo*," *Mnemosyne* (1958): 133–243; Denis O'Brien, "The Last Argument of Plato's *Phaedo*," *ClQ* 17 (1967): 201–3.

5. In defending the conception of the soul as a substance in the *Phaedo*'s final argument, I am in large part agreeing with, and hoping to revive, the reading of the final argument by Frede in "Final Proof of the Immortality" and John Burnet in *The Phaedo of Plato* (Oxford: Clarendon, 1911). More importantly, my aim here is to defend this line of interpretation against challenges recently launched by Brian D. Prince, who follows Richard D. Archer-Hind in insisting that the Form of Soul must be assumed by the internal logic of the argument at issue. See Prince, "The Form of the

Hind dubs a "metaphysical monstrosity," the Form of Soul in which individual souls participate.[6] It might also be supposed that Plato espouses a doctrine of personal immortality: that an individual, such as Socrates, is immortal in virtue of his eternal soul. It is the task of the present paper to show that, once we correctly understand the *Phaedo*'s theory of soul, neither of these consequences must follow from the interpretation of the soul as a substance closely resembling but ontologically distinct from a Form.

Following the structure of the final argument as presented in the *Phaedo*, the paper begins by introducing the threefold division that underlies the argument at issue (§1). The next part of the paper shows that this threefold classification offers Socrates the necessary conceptual framework to articulate his new, sophisticated answer to the question of what makes some x F (§2). It is subsequently argued that, according to Socrates's new sophisticated hypothesis, the soul in the final argument is best read as a substance, rather than a Form in nature or an immanent form, which animates the living body, *pace* Archer-Hind and others.[7] It is further argued that the logical structure of *Phaedo*'s final argument makes no theoretical commitment to a Form of Soul (§3). The paper concludes with reflections on the ensuing psychological theory in light of the conception of the soul emerging from the *Phaedo*. Once we see the restricted scope of the psychological activities and responses the *Phaedo* assigns to the soul, we will also see that we have no license to infer an everlasting existence of the person from the modest conclusion of the final argument (§4).

1. A Threefold Division

The final argument of the *Phaedo* occurs between 102a10 and 107b10. At the start of these passages, Socrates embarks on the main task of showing that the soul is everlasting by making a threefold distinction among (1)

Soul in the *Phaedo*," *PLATO* 11 (2011); Archer-Hind, *The Phaedo of Plato* (London: Macmillan, 1883).

6. Writing in 1894, Archer-Hind makes a note of caution in his commentary on the *Phaedo*, "It is true that an idea of soul is a metaphysical monstrosity; but we cannot escape it here" (*Phaedo of Plato*, 116).

7. In recent years, Archer-Hind's interpretation has been systematically defended by Prince, "Form of the Soul." See n. 5. I want to reverse this trend and argue, along with Burnet, that Plato's final argument for the immortality of the soul need not assume a Form of Soul.

the Forms, (2) the things that share in the Forms, and (3) something other than the Form *F* but that may deserve the same name as *F*. Socrates begins by reiterating (1) that "each of the Forms exists" and (2) that "other things which partake in these get their names from them" (τι ἕκαστον τῶν εἰδῶν καὶ τούτων τἆλλα μεταλαμβάνοντα αὐτῶν τούτων τὴν ἐπωνυμίαν ἴσχειν, *Phaed.* 102a10–b3). The examples he provides are (1) the Form of Tallness and (2) the tallness in Simmias—the feature in virtue of which Simmias is said to be tall relative to Socrates. Having obtained the agreement of his interlocutors that (1) the Form and (2) the immanent form in the subject can never admit and endure their opposite such as to be other than they are, he proceeds to introduce a further addition to the division. Socrates claims (3) there is "something else" (ἄλλο τι, *Phaed.* 103e4) that is not the Form *F* but has *F*'s characteristic wherever it exists.[8] Call members of this new category the carriers of Forms.[9]

However we are to understand the ontological status of these carriers of Forms at this stage of the argument, Plato is clear on the point that a carrier of a particular Form *F* cannot be what it is without exhibiting *F*-ness while being nonidentical to the *F* itself (*Phaed.* 103e4–5). This observation is borne out by the examples of the members of class (3), which include snow, fire, and odd numbers.[10] Considering odd numbers, Socrates notes,

---

8. As I mentioned, scholarly opinions differ concerning whether items in this new class are supposed to be yet some different Forms other than the ones mentioned earlier (e.g., Tallness and Smallness), the immanent forms, or individual substances. This paper follows the interpretation of Gallop, Burnet, and Frede in taking Plato at his words to mean that he is not referring to yet some other Forms by the words ἄλλο τι (Burnet, *Phaedo of Plato*, 105; Gallop, *Plato: Phaedo*, 197; Frede, "Final Proof of the Immortality," 35).

9. I follow several interpreters in calling this third type of item the "carrier" or "bringer" of Forms. Evans used these labels interchangeably in his seminar that took place at the University of Michigan, Ann Arbor, in 2014. Debra Nails also informed me at the regional meeting of the International Plato Society that David Ebrey, too, had referred to the items in category (3) as "carriers" in a talk on his forthcoming book on the *Phaedo*. Prince also refers to these items as "Form-bringers" ("Form of the Soul," 17).

10. For the present, I must put aside the following question: How, exactly, are the items in (3) related to each other such that they form a homogeny? I take for granted that there is some fundamental similarity among the *F*-carriers in virtue of which they subsume under this classification, although I cannot elaborate on just how we should classify items in this class here. For a discussion, see David Bostock, *Plato's Phaedo* (Oxford: Oxford University Press, 1986), 188–89.

"each odd number is always odd though not identified with the Form of Odd" (οὐκ ὢν ὅπερ τὸ περιττὸν ἀεὶ ἕκαστος αὐτῶν ἐστι περιττός, *Phaed.* 104b1). That an odd number, such as the number three, is always odd though not identical to Oddness suggests that it has the property of being odd as an essential, albeit not a sufficient defining characteristic (e.g., while the number three is necessarily an odd number, it is also equally necessarily a prime number and a factor of nine).[11] That three has odd-ness as its essential property, Socrates holds, allows the number three to be called odd, although it is not strictly identical to the Odd (*Phaed.* 104b1).

Indeed, no *F*-carrier can be identical to the Form *F*. Whereas the Form *F* is just *F*-ness and nothing else (αὐτὸ τὸ *F*),[12] the *F*-carrier's essence is not exhausted by that *F*-ness alone. Consider another of Socrates's examples: snow. Just as the number three, although possessing oddness by necessity, is not identical to the Form of Oddness, so too snow is necessarily cold but is not identified with the Form of Coldness. For what it is to be snow is not to be cold simpliciter, but snow must also be in the form of an ice crystal, whose water molecules are lined up in a precise hexagonal array.

Although Plato insists that the *F*-carrier is not to be identified with the *F*, he nonetheless maintains that, like the *F* itself, the *F*-carrier cannot endure the opposite of *F* (*Phaed.* 104a7). Like the Odd, the Form it is inextricably linked to, the number three will not admit the Even lest it perish (*Phaed.* 104c1–3). In this respect, the items in Plato's newly minted category are like the Forms and the immanent forms: "these do not seem to admit that Form which is opposite to that which is in them" (οὐδὲ ταῦτα ἔοικε δεχομένοις ἐκείνην τὴν ἰδέαν ᾗ ἂν τῇ ἐν αὐτοῖς οὔσῃ ἐναντία ᾖ, *Phaed.* 104b9–10). However, it is crucial to observe that Plato simultaneously denies that the *F*-carrier, strictly speaking, has a single opposite. He affirms that the *F*-carriers are "not being opposite to some-thing, while they do not admit the opposite [of *F*]" (οὐκ ἐναντία τινὶ

---

11. O'Brien observes that the examples Plato gives of temperature and numbers are meant to pick out essential, as opposed to accidental, predication ("Last Argument of Plato's *Phaedo*," 95–106). According to Frede, the suggestion is that if something that is not identical to the *F* but has the characteristic of *F* wherever it exists, then that thing has *F*-ness as its essential property ("Final Proof of the Immortality," 29). Burnet also notes that the *F*-carriers have *F*-ness as "an inseparable predicate" (*Phaedo of Plato*, 103).

12. I follow Burnet and Rowe in rendering αὐτὸ τὸ *F* as "*F* and nothing else" (see Burnet, *Phaedo of Plato*, 65; Rowe, *Phaedo*, 141).

ὄντα ὅμως οὐ δέχεται αὐτό, τὸ ἐναντίον, *Phaed.* 104e7–8). This feature
of *F*-carriers may be explained by the fact that their essence cannot be
exhausted by *F*-ness alone. As such, one and the same entity can be both
an *F*-carrier and *G*-carrier, granted that the *F* and the *G* are not opposites. Snow, for example, must be both cold and solid, hence a carrier of
the Forms of Coldness and Solidity. Although snow will resist both the
opposites of the Coldness and the Solidity, it does not have any opposites
of its own since, unlike these Forms, it is not just coldness or just solidity
tout court.

Having articulated the fundamental similarities and differences
between the *F*-carriers and the *F* itself, we must consider why Socrates
postulates a third category of *F*-carriers in his ontology at this stage of
the argument. On this question, the text speaks for itself. The *Phaedo*
makes it clear that the hitherto established conceptual framework allows
Socrates to give his partners in the dialogue a new safe (ἀσφαλὲς) and more
sophisticated (κομψοτέραν) answer to the question of what makes *x F*, as
compared to the previous naive answer introduced in an autobiographical
prelude to the final argument (*Phaed.* 105c1–7). It is time to see how this
threefold division allows Socrates to accomplish this task.

2. A New Safe and Sophisticated Hypothesis

Though the passage is well known, a brief reminder of the autobiographical preliminaries will be useful. In Socrates's intellectual autobiography,
he informs us of his earliest interest in natural science and sketches a
theory of explanation (αἰτία), which he attributes to Anaxagoras (*Phaed.*
95a4–102a9). The appeal of Anaxagoras's theory, Socrates tells us, lies in
his identification of mind (νοῦς) as the cause of all things (*Phaed.* 97c4).[13]
Yet after a deeper engagement, Socrates becomes dissatisfied with Anaxagoras's theory since the entity that Anaxagoras in fact identifies as the
cause is not mind but material entities such as bones and sinews (*Phaed.*

---

13. The underlying assumption here is that if mind is the intelligent generator
of the universe, then things are as they are because it is for the best. As commentators have observed, this model of causal explanation is teleological in nature, which
explains why Socrates finds Anaxagoras's account attractive prima facie. See, e.g.,
James Lennox, "Plato's Unnatural Teleology," in *Platonic Investigations,* ed. Dominic J.
O'Meara (Washington, DC: Catholic University of America Press, 1985), 196; Vlastos,
"Reasons and Causes," 297.

98c8).[14] Rejecting these material causes and the corresponding methods of the natural scientists, Socrates embarks on his second voyage (δεύτερος πλοῦς) in search of the causes (*Phaed.* 99c9–d2).[15] In this second sailing, Socrates employs the method of hypothesis and offers his safe answer: Forms as causes (*Phaed.* 100d10).[16]

Returning to the final argument at issue, the introduction of carriers of Forms enables Socrates to put this safe answer on a new footing, as follows.

> I give an answer beyond that safe answer which I spoke of at first, now that I see another safe reply [ἄλλην ὁρῶν ἀσφάλειαν] deduced from what has just been said. If you should ask me what, coming into a body, makes it hot, I will not give you that safe but ignorant answer and say that it is Heat, but I can now give a more refined [κομψοτέραν] answer, that it is fire; and if you ask, what causes the body in which it is to be ill, I shall not say Illness, but fever; and if you ask what causes a number in which it is to be odd, I shall not say Oddness, but a unit, and so forth. (*Phaed.* 105b8–c6)

---

14. According to most interpreters, Socrates rejects material causation because he demands causes to be teleological. See Julia Annas, "Aristotle on Inefficient Causes," *PQ* 32 (1982): 311–26; Bostock, *Plato's Phaedo*; James Hankinson, *Cause and Explanation in Ancient Greek Thought* (Oxford: Clarendon, 1998); Stephen Menn, "On Socrates' First Objections to the Physicists (*Phaedo* 95E 8–97B 7)," *OSAP* 38 (2010): 37–68; David Wiggins, "Teleology and the Good in Plato's *Phaedo*," *OSAP* 4 (1986): 1–18. Alternatively, David Ebrey argues that Socrates rejects Anaxagoras's material causes because they could explain one effect as much as their opposite, which is an imperfection of material causes given that Socrates is committed to there being only one cause for each *explanandum*. See Ebrey, "Making Room for Matter: Material Causes in the *Phaedo* and the *Physics*," *Apeiron* 47 (2014): 245–65.

15. Yahei Kanayama points out that in general in ancient literature, as well as in the *Phaedo*, the term "second voyage" refers to a more laborious attempt to get to the same destination, rather than to a second best, as Socrates modestly claims. See Kanayama, "The Methodology of the Second Voyage and the Proof of the Soul's Indestructibility in Plato's *Phaedo*," *OSAP* (2000): 41–100. Rowe makes a similar observation in his commentary, writing, "The phrase δεύτερος πλοῦς refers to the use of oars in the absence of fair wind, suggesting the use of a slower and more laborious, but more reliable, method of getting to the same destination, or at least achieving the same objective" (*Phaedo of Plato*, 238).

16. For discussions of the method of hypothesis, see Kanayama, "Methodology of the Second Voyage"; Dom T. J. Bailey, "Logic and Music in Plato's *Phaedo*," *Phronesis* (2005): 95–115.

Consider one of Socrates's new, refined safe answers: a fever. Following the threefold division previously introduced, a fever is a carrier of Illness, distinct from the Form of Illness and the illness inhering in the sick patient. Since a fever accompanies illness always and everywhere, it functions much like Socrates's initial safe answer: the fever's presence explains the illness in a sick body. Moreover, the fever serves as well as, or at times better as, an *explanans* than the Form of Illness for the same *explanandum*. Socrates seems to believe as much insofar as he affirms that the new sophisticated safe answer is an improvement on the old safe answer.[17] Yet, he says surprisingly little about the nature of the improvement. We must endeavor to flesh out an explanation.

One such explanation may be found by examining the larger context in which the final argument is situated. As we have seen, Socrates begins the final argument by laying the necessary conceptual groundwork. He reiterates at the start of the final argument that the Form F and the immanent f in a particular individual can never admit and endure the opposite of F. Now, this statement ushers in an objection to the cyclical argument previously offered in the *Phaedo*:[18] How can opposites be from opposites if any given opposite always flees at the advance of another (*Phaed.* 103a4–10)? The principle presently articulated, the objector maintains, is incompatible with an earlier principle assumed in the cyclical argument: if something is now F, it must be at an earlier time not-F. Socrates points out in response that the objection is founded on an ambiguity between the things that possess the Forms and the Forms themselves (*Phaed.* 103b–c). What he presently asserts is that the Forms themselves cannot venture to be their opposites. However, this claim is compatible with his previous position that an F-thing comes to be from its opposite, such as the living coming to be from the dead (*Phaed.* 70c).

---

17. As Rowe points out, here Socrates recognizes the causes of the sort preferred by scientists. Despite his general dissatisfaction with the natural scientists' method, he appears to acknowledge that some limited aspect of that method seems to yield correct results. This recognition by no means implies that Socrates rejects his original answer: the theory of Forms. Instead, he claims that, on some occasions, there is another answer to the question of why something F is F beyond the explanation offered by the theory of Forms (Rowe, *Phaedo*, 259).

18. The cyclical argument (70c4–72e2) concludes that the souls of the dead must continue in existence on the ground that what has an opposite comes to be from its opposite.

I want to suggest that the introduction of the F-carriers offers Socrates a way to evade this objection altogether. By providing the F-carrier as a sophisticated safe answer, Socrates is in a position to explain why a particular F-thing is F without appealing to F-ness itself.[19] The idea is that a fever qua Illness-carrier will either resist the opposite of Illness or perish in whichever body it occupies. According to this new explanation, a healthy body comes from its opposite, a sick body, when a fever departs from that body. We can now appreciate why the introduction of the F-carriers is an advancement on the old safe answer. For, being immaterial, nonspatial, and atemporal, the Form of Illness—or any Form for that matter—cannot enter and depart from any particular body, nor can it ever perish due to its privileged metaphysical status. The introduction of F-carriers thus allows Socrates to offer a subtler, if not also more naturalistic, explanation to the question of what makes x F.

It might be thought that the immanent illness can play the same role as a fever under the present hypothesis. Certainly, the immanent illness does not persist eternally and can enter a particular body, causing the body to become ill, and later "either withdraw or perish" (ἢ ὑπεξιέναι ἢ ἀπολεῖσθαι) from the same body at the arrival of its opposite (*Phaed.* 103d11). However, it is far from obvious how we should understand an immanent form that withdraws unscathed from a body it previously occupied. To imagine an immanent form in this way requires supposing that the immanent form could have an independent existence.[20] An immanent form f, however, owes its existence to the fact that something participates in the F. There cannot be a free-floating illness in Socrates if the illness is no longer in Socrates. Even if we suppose that the illness in a given body can survive the separation from that body, the fever will remain the preferable explanation over the immanent illness. For it allows Socrates to explain why a sick body is sick without referring to illness, the *explanandum* he seeks to account for in the first place.[21]

---

19. Burnet puts the point differently by clarifying that previously we could only say that participation in the Form of F was the cause of x's being F, but from what has been established by the introduction of the carriers, we may substitute the F-carrier for the F itself since Socrates has acquired the agreement of his partners that the carrier may be called by the same name as F (*Phaedo of Plato*, 123).

20. Frede makes a similar point in her rejection of the suggestion that the soul could be plausibly interpreted as an immanent form ("Final Proof of the Immortality," 35–36).

21. Gallop puts the point slightly different, writing, "The answer 'fire' is not a mere tautology, but is still 'safe.' For since fire is incapable of being cold, it can explain why a body is hot without contradiction" (*Plato: Phaedo*, 101).

Indeed, we see Socrates putting the newly refined explanation to work precisely in this way throughout the remainder of the argument. When confronted with the question about what thing is such that when present in a body makes it a living thing, he no longer responds with the initial safe answer: the Form of Life. Instead, Socrates claims that it is the soul's presence in a body that makes the body a living one (*Phaed.* 105c11). Socrates's answer clarifies that the soul is neither a Form nor an immanent form in us. On the triadic schema he proposed at the beginning of the final argument, the soul is a carrier of Forms, which places it in the newly introduced category along with odd numbers or snow. These individual substances impart one characteristic in a pair of opposites to whatever they meet. Similarly, Socrates argues that the soul always brings one pair of opposites, life (ζωήν), to any subject it occupies. In its capacity as a Life-carrier, the soul will never admit the opposite of life, which is death (θάνατος, *Phaed.* 105c9–d9).

To elucidate and bolster his claim, Socrates enumerates various analogous cases where a thing is called by a negative name after its opposites. His examples include the opposites of justice (δίκαιον) and musical (μουσικὸν), which are injustice (ἄδικον) and unmusical (ἄμουσον), respectively. Using the same alpha privative construction, he claims that the opposite of death (θάνατον) is deathless (ἀθάνατον, *Phaed.* 105e6). Just as the thing that does not admit the musical is unmusical and the thing that does not admit the just is unjust, so too the soul is deathless because it does not admit death. The soul, Socrates concludes, is everlasting.

That, at least, is the most straightforward reading of *Phaedo* 102a10–107b containing the *Phaedo*'s final argument for the immortality of the soul. If we take Plato at his words when he claims that there is "something else" that exists besides the Forms at 103e4, and if we follow him in placing the soul in this category of "something else," then Plato is committed to the view that the soul is something other than a Form. Despite Plato's noncommittal language in calling the category to which the soul belongs "something else" and despite the lack of Form-referring expressions in connection with any items belonging to this class of "something else," commentators have insisted that "the *Phaedo* is best read as assuming the Form of Soul" and that "we cannot escape it [the Form of Soul] here."[22] In the following, I lay out the philosophical motivation behind the suggestion

---

22. Prince, "Form of the Soul," 4; Archer-Hind, *Phaedo of Plato*, 116.

that the Form of Soul is inescapable in the final argument and consider whether the text of the *Phaedo* is implicitly committed to the existence of such a Form.

3. The Necessity of the Form of Soul Reconsidered

Commentators who argue that a Form of Soul is crucially operative in the final argument for the soul's immortality might argue for this reading in two ways. The first possibility is to maintain that the word *soul* used in the final argument refers either (1a) to a Form of Soul or (1b) to an immanent form. The second possibility is to argue that (2) the Form of Soul is implicitly but surely at work in the logic of *Phaedo*'s final argument. I will consider these alternatives, in turn, beginning first with readings of the word *soul* as (1a) a Form or (1b) an immanent form.

Those commentators who maintain that the referent of the word *soul* is something other than an individual substance generally identify the referent of this word with (1b) an immanent form rather than (1a) a Form in nature.[23] Three interpretative concerns drive the preference for (1b) over (1a). First, anyone who reads the word *soul* to be referring to the Form of Soul is obligated to explain why Plato would go through an incredible amount of trouble to argue that the Form of Soul is everlasting. One would expect this conclusion to follow straightforwardly from the theory of Forms, according to which a Form is eternal, divine, intelligible, uniform, and indissoluble (*Phaed.* 80b). Since Socrates already receives an acknowledgment from his interlocutors that they fully accept that there are Forms (*Phaed.* 72e3–77a5) and that these Forms are everlasting (*Phaed.* 78b4–84b8), he need not offer a further argument to show that the Form of Soul is immortal. Second, if Socrates is to be successful in his defense against the fear of death and in proving the paramount importance of the care of the soul in the final argument, then the soul referred to in that argument is best understood as an individual soul rather than

---

23. I am unaware of any commentator who defends the position that the word *soul* ought to be read as a Form of the Soul, although anyone who reads *soul* as an immanent form is committed to there being a transcendental Form of Soul. For the immanent form of *F* owes its existence to the *F* itself. Commentators who prefer the immanent form interpretation include Hackforth, *Plato's Phaedo*, 159, 161–162; Keyt, "Fallacies in 'Phaedo,'" 169; Allan Silverman, *The Dialectic of Essence: A Study of Plato's Metaphysics* (Princeton: Princeton University Press, 2002), 63.

a Form of the soul, something subject to neither change nor perish-
ing, properly speaking. Finally, the soul in the *Phaedo* is said to go away
(οἴχεται), withdrawing (ὑπεχχωρῆσαν) from death (106e). Since the Form
of Soul is immaterial, nonspatial, and atemporal, the soul in the context
of the argument cannot, therefore, be a Form. These various difficulties
render interpretation (1a) untenable.

Nor can the soul plausibly be an immanent form, as interpretation
(1b) claims. In this way of reading the argumentative strategy, it is difficult
to understand why Socrates would endeavor to develop his new safe and
sophisticated hypothesis rather than solely relying on the familiar ontology
of Forms and the things that participate in them. But a close examination
of the text would reveal that the addition of a new class of Form-carriers
is necessary to answer the objection raised by Cebes, in which the soul
is compared to the weaver of a series of cloaks, who although outlives a
single cloak will nonetheless perish before the last one he wears (*Phaed.*
87b). It is this troubling image that provides the impetus for the final argument. For what Cebes demands from Socrates is an argument to sustain
his claim that the soul is altogether deathless and indestructible (*Phaed.*
88b). In fulfilling this challenge, Socrates introduces the Form-carriers to
which he likens the soul, which is something else distinct from the Form
F and the derivative *F*-ness in us. According to the new, refined answer,
what accounts for any living body's aliveness is not the Form of Life but
another entity altogether—the soul—which always carries life to anybody
it occupies (*Phaed.* 105c9). The upshot of this new safe answer is that the
soul is essentially alive without being identified simply with the principle
of life in a living creature *and nothing else*.[24]

Considering the *Phaedo* alone, we get a confirmation for this robust
conception of the soul in Cebes's exchange with Socrates. Having listened
to Socrates's defense of the philosopher's occupation as preparing for dying
(*Phaed.* 64a4–69e5), Cebes confesses he remains doubtful and shares the
following contention.

> Socrates, everything else you said is excellent, I think, but people find it
> very hard to believe what you said about the soul. They think that after
> it has left the body it no longer exists anywhere, but that it is destroyed
> and dissolved on the day the person dies, as soon as it leaves the body;

---

24. Wilfrid Sellars also appears to be attributing the same notion of the soul in
Phaedo. See Sellars, "Substance and Form in Aristotle," *JP* 54 (1957): 699.

and that, on leaving it, *it is dispersed like breath or smoke, has flown away and gone and is no longer anything anywhere* [εὐθὺς ἀπαλλαττομένη τοῦ σώματος, καὶ ἐκβαίνουσα ὥσπερ πνεῦμα ἢ καπνὸς διασκεδασθεῖσα οἴχηται διαπτομένη καὶ οὐδὲν ἔτι οὐδαμοῦ ᾖ]. If indeed it gathered itself together and existed by itself and escaped those evils you were recently enumerating, there would then be much good hope, Socrates, that what you say is true; but to believe this requires a good deal of faith and persuasive argument, *to believe that the soul still exists after a person has died and that it still possesses some capability and intelligence* [ὡς ἔστι τε ψυχὴ ἀποθανόντος τοῦ ἀνθρώπου καί τινα δύναμιν ἔχει καὶ φρόνησιν]. (*Phaed.* 69e7–70b4, emphases added)

Cebes expresses his concern by contrasting the thick notion of the soul, which he takes Socrates to be defending, with the thin notion in the popular imagination. According to the latter, the soul is "like a breath or smoke" that scatters at the moment of death, whereas Socrates defends the view that the soul also "possesses some capacity and wisdom." On Socrates's thick notion, what it is to be a soul is not merely to impart life but also to enable the ensouled creature to exercise a host of mental activities such as knowing, believing, and desiring.[25] This conception of the soul suggests that the soul is not exclusively any singular *F*-ness, such as largeness, beauty, or justice. Instead, the soul must be the kind of entity capable of possessing knowledge in addition to possessing life as one of its many defining characteristics. In this respect, the soul is entirely unlike any Forms—and indeed immanent forms—insofar as a Form *F* (*auto to F*) is just *F* and nothing else.

This observation is in harmony with an accepted view in the literature concerning the range of Forms. According to this interpretation, in the *Phaedo* and other middle-period dialogues, Plato is theoretically committed to the view that Forms are of a particular kind of property: the so-called incomplete properties such as large, small, just, and beautiful.[26]

---

25. I discuss the limited kind of psychological activities and responses the *Phaedo* assigns to the soul in more detail in §4. Beyond the *Phaedo*, the claim that the soul is responsible for a host of mental actions is also borne out, for instance, by the theory of the soul developed in *Resp.* 4, where the soul is divided according to the affections it brings or activities it performs. Moreover, the account of the soul in the *Timaeus* fits with the interpretation that the soul is a substance here since we are told in that dialogue that the demiurge creates the individual soul by mixing various elements (35a–b).

26. This interpretation has been defended by Fine, Irwin, Nehamas, and others. See Gail Fine, *On Ideas: Aristotle's Criticism of Plato's Theory of Forms* (Oxford: Clarendon, 1993); Terence Irwin, "Plato's Heracleiteanism," *PQ* 27 (1977):

For ease of expression, I will refer to this view as the incomplete reading concerning the range of Forms.[27] There is no single formula to specify what commentators call the incomplete properties or incomplete predicates. It is generally held that an incomplete property, p, cannot tell us what S is in the phrase "S is p" without further elucidation about S's nature. "Largeness" fits this description, for instance. The statement "Simmias is large" does not tell us what Simmias is, since the term *largeness* is not connected with the identity of the object to which it applies. Although the property of being large may be said of Simmias, he is, strictly speaking, a human being rather than largeness. For he cannot cease to be a human while maintaining his identity as Simmias, but he can cease to be large. The claim "Simmias is large" must be supplemented with a further description of Simmias's nature, such as "for a human." Indeed, Simmias is not large relative to a plane tree; he is only accidentally, temporarily, and incompletely large. By contrast, I want to suggest that the term *soul* is unlike an incomplete predicate such as *large*. If something is a soul, it is a soul independently of any relation to other things. As long as the soul remains what it is, it is always and everywhere a soul. If the incomplete reading is correct, we should not expect Plato to be theoretically committed to a Form of Soul in the *Phaedo*.

It must be acknowledged at this stage that some scholars have challenged the incomplete reading in recent years, arguing that Plato does not intend to restrict the numbers of Forms he posits. Brian Prince points out that Socrates's "general and sweeping statements about the Forms in the

---

1–13; Irwin, *Plato's Ethics* (New York: Oxford University Press, 1995); Alexander Nehamas, "Predication and Forms of Opposites in the *Phaedo*," *RevMet* 26 (1973): 461–91; Nehemas, "Plato on the Imperfection of the Sensible World," in *Virtues of Authenticity*, ed. Nehamas (Princeton: Princeton University Press, 1999), 138–58.

27. Nehamas presents the incomplete reading as an alternative to what he calls the approximation view, according to which Plato believes that the sensible world is imperfect in comparison to the world of Forms. According to the approximation view, the Form F is the embodiment of the perfection of what we call F, whereas the earthly F-things are copies that strive to be like the F itself. Various expressions of the approximation view can be found in the writings of Taylor, Burnet, and Ross, among others. See Alfred E. Taylor, *Plato* (London: Constable, 1922), 41; Burnet, *Phaedo of Plato*, 41–43; William D. Ross, *Plato's Theory of Ideas* (Oxford: Clarendon, 1951), 25. See also the discussion and rejection of the approximation view in Nehamas, "Plato on the Imperfection."

Phaedo" allow the Forms of Soul to be one of the Forms.[28] Moreover, he cites the fact that Plato explicitly names the Forms of Oddness (*Phaed.* 103e2–104b4) and Life (*Phaed.* 105d5–6) as evidence against the incomplete reading. The thought is that an odd number such as the number three "needs no comparison with anything else to establish its oddness, nor is there any relatum needing to be filled in to complete the thought that three is odd."[29] We thus have an apparent counterexample to the imperfect reading: oddness. Oddness does not appear to be an incomplete predicate, but it is explicitly mentioned in the text as a Form. According to this line of reasoning, if there can be a Form of Odd and a Form of Life, nothing rules out the possibility of a Form of Soul.

Although the reading of the ontological status of the soul this paper defends need not hang on to the incomplete reading, a few remarks may be made in defense of the incomplete reading by considering the manner in which "is odd" behaves similarly to an incomplete predicate in the attributive position.[30] This is not to deny that oddness appears to be connected to the identity of the number to which it applies. For the number three is necessarily odd, possessing oddness irrespectively of its relation to any other numbers. But "is odd" is also importantly unlike complete and logically one-place predicates such as "is a human" or "is a stone," which sufficiently captures the essence of the subject to which it applies. To say that the number three is odd does not supply an exhaustive account of what it is to be the number three, or indeed any odd number. For instance, the number three is also necessarily a prime number and a factor of nine. It is due to this reason that three is an odd *number*, rather than oddness itself, just as Simmias is a large *human* rather than largeness itself. Plato seems to be committed to this position insofar as he claims that the number three "is odd but is not the Odd" (*Phaed.* 104b1).

Suppose, however, along with critics that the Form of Oddness does present a genuine counterexample to the incomplete reading. The following implication is thought to ensue. Since the *Phaedo* is abundantly clear that there is a Form of Oddness, we need not interpret Plato to exclude the possibility of Forms of substantives, such as the Form of Soul. Yet, the *Phaedo* is equally clear about the fact that Plato is reluctant to speak openly

---

28. Prince, "Form of the Soul," 8.

29. Prince, "Form of the Soul," 14.

30. Nehamas expresses the thought that the incomplete predicates are attributive or relational ("Plato on the Imperfection," 177).

about the Form of Soul. To be sure, nothing that is said in the *Phaedo*
explicitly precludes the extension of the range of Forms to include the
Form of Soul. The point is only that we have no license to infer that there is
a Form of Soul from the recognition that there is a Form of Oddness. The
Phaedo is silent about the range of predicates of which there are Forms,
especially the Form of Soul.

Even Prince acknowledges this difficulty, writing, "the *Phaedo* is best-
read as assuming a Form of Soul, *which nevertheless goes unmentioned*."[31]
Nonetheless, the logic of the final argument, he argues, demands that there
be a Form of Soul. This point brings us to interpretation (2) in favor of
positing a Form of Soul. It has been argued that the Form of Soul is not
only a metaphysical possibility in the *Phaedo* but also a necessity, especially if one takes the referent of the word *soul* in the final argument to be
an individual substance, a view the present paper also advocates. Along
with Archer-Hind, one might insist that the Form of Soul is inevitable
by citing a passage in *Republic* 10, where Socrates claims that whenever
a group of particular *F*s is called by the same name, there is a Form of *F*
(*Phaed.* 596a).[32] If we apply this general rule to the inquiry at issue, then
one might reasonably think that since there is a soul, there must be a thing
that is Soul itself by itself—the Form of Soul. Prince puts the point differently, as follows: "If the fact that a thing is a soul were not to be explained
by participation in a Form, this would make souls highly unusual among
the non-Form items in Plato's universe."[33]

Certainly, Plato is willing to recognize Forms of substantives, such as
beds and tables, in the concluding book of the *Republic* (*Resp.* 596b). Yet, in
the *Parmenides*, a dialogue standardly placed in the same period as the *Republic* and *Phaedo*,[34] he professes uncertainty about whether there are Forms of
natural kinds such as human beings, water, and fire in the following passage.

> And is there a Form of Human Being [ἀνθρώπου εἶδος], apart from us
> and all others such as we are, or of fire or water?

---

31. Prince, "Form of the Soul," 4, emphasis original.
32. Archer-Hind, *Phaedo of Plato*, 152.
33. Prince, "Form of the Soul," 1.
34. See this accepted chronology, among others, in Irwin, *Plato's Ethics*, 12; Mary
Louise Gill and Paul Ryan, *Plato: Parmenides* (Indianapolis: Hackett, 1996); Samuel
Rickless, *Plato's Forms in Transition: A Reading of the Parmenides* (Cambridge: Cambridge University Press, 2007).

I often have, he replied, been very much perplexed [ἐν ἀπορίᾳ ...
πολλάκις], Parmenides, to decide whether there are Forms of such things
or not. (*Parm.* 130c1–4)[35]

In this middle-period dialogue, Socrates admits that he is skeptical about
whether there are Forms of Human Being, Fire, and the like.[36] If Socrates
is reluctant to accept that there are Forms of these substances, then souls
would be hardly unusual among the non-Form items. There are theoretically many Formless entities on the basis of the passage at issue: human
beings, fire, and water. While we cannot settle the question of whether
there is a development in Plato's conception of the scope of the theory
of Forms at present, what is clear is that the textual evidence taken col-
lectively is inconclusive at best on the question of whether there is a Form
of Soul.[37]

     If we consider the epistemic motivation for the theory of Forms, then
the fact that Plato is noncommittal on whether there is a Form of Soul
becomes all the more apparent. According to an uncontroversial interpretation of Plato, Forms are the objects of knowledge since sensory
particulars suffer from the compresence of opposites, rendering them
ungraspable by the intellect.[38] In the context of the *Phaedo*, the argument
from recollection asserts that we recollect truths about nonsensible Forms
from imperfect sensible instances (*Phaed.* 74e8–75a3). This is because, in
our capacity as knowers, we require a nonsensible, unwavering Form of
F-ness to acquire the concept of *F*. For the many sensible *F*s are not suitable
to instruct us in anything about the concept of *F*, if they vacillate between
being *F* and not-*F*.

---

35. The Greek text is Plato, *Opera*, ed. John Burnet (Oxford: Oxford University
Press, 1903); the translation is by Gill and Ryan, *Plato: Parmenides*, with minor modi-
fication.

36. Rickless suggests that the problem raised in these lines concerns the fact that
some forms are such that they cannot be conceived as other than sensible: the Forms
of Human Being, Fire, and Mud, for instance (*Plato's Forms in Transition*, 55).

37. Archer-Hind admits that Plato "rectifies" his mistake in assuming that there is
a Form of Soul in later works (*Phaedo of Plato*, 152).

38. See this view expressed, for instance in Gill and Ryan, *Plato: Parmenides*, 22;
Terence Irwin, "The Theory of Forms," in *Plato 1: Metaphysics and Epistemology*, ed.
Gail Fine (Oxford: Oxford University Press, 1999), 143–70; Bostock, *Plato's Phaedo*,
97–98.

However, Socrates affirms in the affinity argument that the soul is more similar in kind to the intelligible, pure, and invariable Forms rather than impure earthly entities suffering from compresence of opposites (*Phaed.* 78b–80b).[39] For our epistemic interests, the claim that souls are akin to Forms implies one of two possibilities: either the properties making something a soul are not revealed by sense perception, or they are fully accessible to the senses such that the senses do not take opposing views on what these properties are.[40] In either case, unlike the many sensible *F*s, there is no *x* such that *x* is both a soul and not a soul, for there is not a single soul that is more or less a soul than another (*Phaed.* 93d1). As we saw, if something is a soul, then it is a soul in a complete and nonrelational way. Since souls resemble the Forms in this metaphysical and epistemological salient way—being insusceptible to the compresence of opposites—Plato is intentionally noncommittal on whether there is a Form of Soul because he lacks an epistemic or metaphysical reason to make such a theoretical commitment.

Are there, however, reasons internal to the logic of the final argument to posit a Form of Soul, as those advocating for interpretation (2) believe? Archer-Hind argues that a Form of Soul is required to carry the Form of Life to individual souls, stating the following rationale. "Now if souls participate in the Form of Life without the mediation of a Form of Soul, it will not have been necessary to invoke Forms in general."[41] It is not obvious

---

39. This argument would seem to present an obstacle to both interpretations (1a) and (1b) since it teaches us that the soul has an affinity with the form, but it is not a Form. If, on Plato's view, the soul is a Form, then he would plainly assert this conclusion rather than the weaker claim that the soul shares salient attributes with the Forms without being one.

40. The latter option has a precedent in an instructive passage in *Resp.* 7, where Socrates claims, "The soul isn't compelled to ask the understanding what a finger is, since sight never suggest to it that a finger is simultaneously the opposite of a finger" (ἡ ψυχὴ τὴν νόησιν ἐπερέσθαι τί ποτ' ἐστὶ δάκτυλος· οὐδαμοῦ γὰρ ἡ ὄψις αὐτῇ ἅμα ἐσήμηνεν τὸν δάκτυλον τοὐναντίον ἢ δάκτυλον εἶναι, 523d4–6). I take it that, since there is nothing such as to be the opposite of a finger, perception cannot render the perceptible object simultaneous as what it is, a finger, and its opposite. Alternatively, Irwin suggests that perception discriminates adequately without summoning thought in this case since we can eliminate doubts about whether something is a finger if we examine the finger more carefully ("Theory of Forms," 162). The text does not appear, however, to rely on any distinction about degrees of specification perception can yield.

41. Archer-Hind, *Phaedo of Plato*, 152.

how the theory of Forms will become obsolete if we deny the existence of a Form of Soul. In agreement with Archer-Hind, Prince offers these elaborations: "The argument's key claim will just be that souls are essentially alive. Putting that claim in a form that mentions the Form of Life cannot show that souls are necessarily or permanently alive."[42] The objection raised in these lines is that, since there appears to be a logical connection neither between souls and life nor souls and the Form of Life, it is easy to imagine a soul that dies or is destroyed. Plato's claim that the soul always carries life with it, therefore, simply begs the question.

If the worry is as I have formulated it, then we cannot escape it by assigning the Form of Soul the task of securing the immortality of individual souls. It is far from obvious why the assertion that the Form of Soul necessarily carries life to itself, and individual souls by extension, is any less question-begging. Those in favor of positing a Form of Soul might insist that the Form of Soul necessarily participates in the Form of Life simply because it is a Form. However, if this supposition were correct, we should expect any individual substance to have a claim to immortality and indestructibility in virtue of its corresponding Form's participation in the Form of Life. We would still lack an explanation to justify why it is that the Form of Soul, and individual souls derivatively, uniquely have a privileged connection to the Form of Life, whereas the remaining Forms, and corresponding individuals, do not. The logical structure of the final argument according to which an individual soul requires the Form of Soul to bring it life appears both unnecessarily rococo and lacking the appropriate explanation for the very point at issue in the argument: that the soul always carries life with it. What, then, can be the justification for this assumption?

I want to suggest that we need not look further than the text of the *Phaedo* itself. In particular, the general rule given in *Phaed.* 104d1–3 clarifies that whenever some F always imparts something else, G, F cannot possess G only as an accidental but as an essential property.[43] This general law preempts the worry that it is logically possible to say there is still a soul in a particular body but that this body is dead. This assumption is problematic since it is the soul, if its existence is granted, that always quickens the body to which it is present. To insist that there can be a dead soul is akin to maintaining that something is affected by snow but does not

42. Prince, "Form of the Soul," 1.

43. Frede observes a similar distinction between essential and accidental property in her reading of the final argument ("Final Proof of the Immortality," 35).

become cold. Just like the snow's possession of coldness, the soul's possession of life cannot be a mere accidental one such that there may be a dead
soul. If the assumption that dead souls are inconceivable appears dubious,
it is not because the argument at issue assumes its conclusion but because
of the application of the general rule given in *Phaed.* 104d1–3 for finding
entities possessing something as an essential property. This, of course, is
not to say that either the general law stated in *Phaed.* 104d1–3 or its application is without problems.[44] The point is just that the logical structure of
the final argument neither depends on nor is ameliorated by positing a
Form of Soul.

4. Immortality of the Soul without Personal Immortality

I have been arguing that Plato regards the soul as a substance having life
essentially, which it imparts to the body to which it is present. Being the
life-bearing entity that it is, the soul is alive for as long as it remains what
it is. It might be thought that the interpretation I favor implies a promise
of personal immortality—that each person persists eternally in virtue of
the immortal soul. After all, Plato's expressed view in the *Phaedo* is that,
when a person dies, her soul passes on to the invisible world, where it
dwells in the company with what is like itself, which is pure, divine, and
intelligible (*Phaed.* 79c–91a). A person's existence can thus be prolonged
indefinitely, even after death. This is precisely the lure of immortality: a
never-ending existence.

A close examination reveals that Plato makes no such promise in the
Phaedo. That the soul currently animating *S*'s body is immortal is insufficient to warrant the inference that the individual *S* will persist after the
destruction of *S*'s body. Plato is silent on whether the person's soul also
contains that person's distinctive psychological responses and activities
(i.e., beliefs, desires, and preferences) as opposed to general knowledge
of the Forms when it separates from the person's body. However, he is
undoubtedly committed to the view that the soul possesses some wisdom
and capacity (*Phaed.* 69e6–70b, 70c12–13). In light of the preceding

---

44. One possible objection might be that the general law says nothing about the
fact that souls exist, a claim Plato takes for granted. It might be thought, in response,
that the cyclical argument at 70c4–72e is proof for the existence of the soul, but all the
argument shows is that the souls of the dead must continue to exist, such that, in a
sense, the living ones can be said to be coming from the dead.

argument from recollection (*Phaed.* 72e3–77a5), we have every reason to believe that the knowledge belonging to the soul is knowledge of Forms.[45] But we have no license to infer that the soul will preserve a person's individual mental life upon leaving the person's body. Even Plato's suggestive remarks about metempsychosis—that all souls participate in an eternal rebirth—are not evidence for this assumption.[46] Plato offers no reason to suppose a continuity of consciousness between one period of incarnation and another. The only secure and textually grounded conclusion that we can draw from the final argument is that the soul, not the individual composite of soul and body, is immortal.

One may, however, be skeptical of this line of conjecture if one reasons in the following way. The central aporia of the *Phaedo* is concerned with the fate of the soul after the destruction of the body, as Socrates is supposed to give reasons for his fearless, even joyful, attitude in the face of death. If the *Phaedo* is supposed to be a continuation of Socrates's apologia—that Socrates has nothing to fear after his death since he has lived a life devoted to philosophy—then we should expect Socrates to survive the death of his body. The final argument of the *Phaedo*, then, must secure Socrates's immortality to justify the optimism he displays at the hands of death.

The objection seems to misplace the locus of Socrates's optimism. Socrates welcomes death because he is a philosopher par excellence, for death is a reward rather than punishment to philosophers. At the beginning of the *Phaedo*, Socrates establishes the following two claims concerning the state of death and the philosopher's occupation. He defines the state of death as "the separation of the soul from the body" (τὴν τῆς ψυχῆς ἀπὸ τοῦ σώματος ἀπαλλαγήν, *Phaed.* 64c4–5) and a philosopher as someone who "more than other people frees the soul from association with the body" (φιλόσοφος ἀπολύων ὅτι μάλιστα τὴν ψυχὴν ἀπὸ τῆς τοῦ σώματος, *Phaed.* 65a1–2). Given this view of death and of the philosopher's aim, we should indeed expect Socrates, qua philosopher, to rejoice at death's advance, as it will liberate his soul from the body to which it is chained (*Phaed.* 66d).

---

45. The effect of the argument from recollection is that not only do souls exist but that they possess intelligence before our birth.

46. I cannot fully defend Plato's belief in reincarnation here, but he alludes to it, inter alias, in the following places: chariot myth (*Phaedr.* 246–254), Myth of Er (*Resp.* 614–621), *Gorgias* myth (*Gorg.* 523E–527), *Phaedo* myth (106e–115a), *Meno* (81), *Cratylus* (400), *Phaedo* (70c–72e, 81c–e), *Timaeus* (41d–42d, 90–91), *Laws* (870d–e, 872e, 881a, 904a–905d).

For the body drags the embodied soul into the changeable region, where it is hindered and confused, unable to come in contact with the unchanged and intelligible Forms. My own view is that Socrates's justification explains why, as a true votary of philosophy, he does not fear death but rather welcomes death. Indeed, Plato writes, "This is how the soul of a philosopher *would* reason" (*Phaed.* 84a).[47] The final argument for the immortality of the soul need not be proof of personal immortality but only immortality of the soul as a possessor of the knowledge of the eternal Forms.

If this result seems unsatisfying, it is because the conception of the soul in the *Phaedo* is significantly narrower than our concept of a mind that preserves a continuation of consciousness. Yet, it is doubtful that this is the conception of the soul as it is conceived of in the *Phaedo*. For Socrates makes it abundantly clear that the soul is not responsible for all of a person's psychological activities and responses, but rather only for a restricted subset of them. In the dialogue at issue, he attributes many mental states not to the soul but the soul welded to the body; these states include beliefs, pleasures, and fears.[48] Unlike the view emerging in another of Plato's extensive treatment of the soul, *Resp.* 4, the psychological theory of *Phaedo* does not assign to a person's soul the desires associated with *Resp.* 4's nonrational parts of the soul, such as those for food or recognition.[49] Instead, the *Phaedo* attributes only a subset of psychological activities and responses to the soul—those concerning the acquisition of knowledge (*Phaed.* 114e). Once we recognize the underpinning psychological framework of the *Phaedo*, we can also recognize that the final

---

47. Emphasis added. Of course, in giving his reason as a philosopher for not fearing death, Socrates is, in my view, encouraging others to follow suit in pursuing a philosophical lifestyle. After all, death is inevitable, and one could adopt a welcoming attitude toward it if one becomes, like Socrates, a lover of knowledge.

48. See, 83d, 94d, and especially 94b7–c1, which goes as follows: "Does it [the soul] comply with the bodily feelings, or does it oppose them? I mean, for example, when heat and thirst are in the body, by pulling the opposite way, away from drinking, and away from eating when it feels hunger; and surely in countless other ways we see the soul opposing bodily feelings, don't we?" (Πότερον συγχωροῦσαν τοῖς κατὰ τὸ σῶμα πάθεσιν ἢ καὶ ἐναντιουμένην; λέγω δὲ τὸ τοιόνδε, οἷον καύματος ἐνόντος καὶ δίψους ἐπὶ τοὐναντίον ἕλκειν, τὸ μὴ πίνειν, καὶ πείνης ἐνούσης ἐπὶ τὸ μὴ ἐσθίειν, καὶ ἄλλα μυρία που ὁρῶμεν ἐναντιουμένην τὴν ψυχὴν τοῖς κατὰ τὸ σῶμα· ἢ οὔ;).

49. See this observation in Hendrik Lorenz, *The Brute Within: Appetitive Desire in Plato and Aristotle* (Oxford: Clarendon, 2006), 37.

argument for the immortality of the soul does not amount to a never-ending existence for the individual.

Despite first appearances, the view this paper favors does not imply an eternal existence for the individual, unless one subscribes to the view that an individual's identity is exhausted by those mental states associated with the knowledge-seeking part of the individual's soul.[50] After all, this result is what we should expect since the *Phaedo* conceives of the soul as a substance possessing life as an essential property, and one that is capable of knowledge and selective psychological functions. If I am not mistaken in my interpretation, we ought not to suppose that the soul participates in the Form of Soul to account for its liveliness. Nor must we conceive of the soul on Plato's conceptual framework as a Form. Indeed, the *Phaedo*'s final argument is an argument for the everlastingness not of the Form or an immanent form of soul but of the individual soul. Yet, the conception of the soul in the *Phaedo* provides no evidence for a more optimistic view according to which a never-ending existence for the person, consisting of the totality of her conscious states rather than a minimal fraction of them, is guaranteed. Whereas we may find this result rather modest, it is sufficient for Plato's purposes in the *Phaedo*. The immortality of the soul, as he understands it, enables the achievement of a godlike rationality and understanding—the philosopher's, and indeed Socrates's, ultimate reward.

Bibliography

Primary Sources

Plato. *Opera*. Edited by John Burnet. Oxford: Oxford University Press, 1903.

———. *Phaedo*. Edited by Christopher Rowe. Cambridge: Cambridge University Press, 1993.

---

50. It is unclear that this is even Plato's conception of personhood since the soul of *Resp.* 4, and even the *Phaedrus*, is a complex of rational and irrational parts, which are responsible for a wide-ranging set of psychological activities beyond knowledge acquisition. Regarding the theory of the immortality of the soul in the *Phaedo*, Rowe makes a similar point and notes it shortcoming, writing, "The only soul which will apparently maintain its identity is the truly philosophical one, which will join the company of the gods ... though the cost of achieving it, if it involves giving up everything except for the search for knowledge, may seem rather high" (*Phaed.* 10).

Secondary Sources

Annas, Julia. "Aristotle on Inefficient Causes." *PQ* 32 (1982): 311–26.
Archer-Hind, Richard D. *The Phaedo of Plato.* London: Macmillan, 1883.
Bailey, Dom T. J. "Logic and Music in Plato's *Phaedo.*" *Phronesis* (2005): 95–115.
Bluck, Richard S. *Plato's Phaedo.* London: Routledge & Kegan Paul, 1955.
Bostock, David. *Plato's Phaedo.* Oxford: Oxford University Press, 1986.
Burnet, John. *The Phaedo of Plato.* Oxford: Clarendon, 1911.
Devereux, Daniel. "Separation and Immanence in Plato's Theory of Forms." *OSAP* 12 (1994): 63–90.
Ebrey, David. "Making Room for Matter: Material Causes in the *Phaedo* and the *Physics.*" *Apeiron* 47 (2014): 245–65.
Fine, Gail. *On Ideas: Aristotle's Criticism of Plato's Theory of Forms.* Oxford: Clarendon, 1993.
Frede, Dorothea. "The Final Proof of the Immortality of the Soul in Plato's 'Phaedo' 102a–107a." *Phronesis* 23 (1978): 27–41.
Gallop, David. *Plato: Phaedo.* CPS. Oxford: Clarendon, 1975.
Gill, Mary Louise, and Paul Ryan. *Plato: Parmenides.* Indianapolis: Hackett, 1996.
Grube, George M. A. *Plato's Phaedo.* Indianapolis: Hackett Publishing Company, 1977.
Hackforth, Reginald. *Plato's Phaedo.* Cambridge: Cambridge University Press, 1955.
Hankinson, James. *Cause and Explanation in Ancient Greek Thought.* Oxford: Clarendon, 1998.
Irwin, Terence. *Plato's Ethics.* New York: Oxford University Press, 1995.
———. "Plato's Heracleiteanism." *PQ* 27 (1977): 1–13.
———. "The Theory of Forms." Pages 143–70 in *Plato 1: Metaphysics and Epistemology.* Edited by Gail Fine. Oxford: Oxford University Press, 1999.
Kanayama, Yahei. "The Methodology of the Second Voyage and the Proof of the Soul's Indestructibility in Plato's *Phaedo.*" *OSAP* (2000): 41–100.
Keyt, David. "The Fallacies in 'Phaedo' 102a–107b." *Phronesis* 8 (1963): 167–72.
Lennox, James. "Plato's Unnatural Teleology." Pages 195–218 in *Platonic Investigations.* Edited by Dominic J. O'Meara. Washington, DC: Catholic University of America Press, 1985.

Lorenz, Hendrik. *The Brute Within: Appetitive Desire in Plato and Aristotle.* Oxford: Clarendon, 2006.

Menn, Stephen. "On Socrates' First Objections to the Physicists (*Phaedo* 95E 8-97B 7)." *OSAP* 38 (2010): 37–68.

Nehamas, Alexander. "Plato on the Imperfection of the Sensible World." Pages 138–158 in *Virtues of Authenticity.* Edited by Alexander Nehamas. Princeton: Princeton University Press, 1999.

———. "Predication and Forms of Opposites in the *Phaedo.*" *RevMet* 26 (1973): 461–91.

O'Brien, Denis. "The Last Argument of Plato's *Phaedo.*" *ClQ* 17 (1967): 198–213; 18 (1968): 95–106.

Prince, Brian D. "The Form of the Soul in the *Phaedo.*" *PLATO* 11 (2011).

Rickless, Samuel. *Plato's Forms in Transition: A Reading of the Parmenides.* Cambridge: Cambridge University Press, 2007.

Ross, William D. *Plato's Theory of Ideas.* Oxford: Clarendon, 1951.

Schiller, Jerome. "Is the Soul a Form?" *Phronesis* 12 (1967): 50–58.

Sellars, Wilfrid. "Substance and Form in Aristotle." *JP* 54 (1957): 688–99.

Silverman, Allan. *The Dialectic of Essence: A Study of Plato's Metaphysics.* Princeton: Princeton University Press, 2002.

Taylor, Alfred E. *Plato.* London: Constable, 1922.

Verdenius, Willem J. "Notes on Plato's *Phaedo.*" *Mnemosyne* (1958): 133–243.

Vlastos, Gregory. "Reasons and Causes in the *Phaedo.*" *PhilRev* 78 (1969): 291–325.

Wiggins, David. "Teleology and the Good in Plato's *Phaedo.*" *OSAP* 4 (1986): 1–18.

Against the Stereotype of Abstract Knowledge in Plato: Scientific Perception or Sharp Seeing in the Middle and Late Dialogues

Kevin Corrigan

Introduction

Plato has often been understood by modern critics to be the originator of a definitive move in the Western world away from ordinary experience to abstract knowing and to the priority of the intelligible universe of pure thought over the ambiguities of ordinary life. According to this common view, knowledge for Plato tidies up the inscrutable difficulties of ordinary experience in favor of the secure but bland haven of abstract, universal knowledge. Here I want to argue two things: (1) that such a view is not warranted by the evidence and (2) that it overlooks a crucial strand of Plato's thought that, as far as I can see, has never been noticed in modern scholarship. I shall call this strand "scientific perception" or sharp seeing. Of course, this is not to claim that Plato held perception to be in some sense knowledge. He did not, as the *Theaetetus* makes clear.[1] Neither

---

1. But see the view of Mary Louise Gill about the *Theaetetus* that knowledge must somehow be constituted by all three together of the rejected candidates, that is, sense perception, true belief, plus an account. See Gill, *Philosophos Plato's Missing Dialogue* (Oxford: Oxford University Press, 2014), 137. Thus, she articulates different "levels of knowledge" employed by the philosopher, the statesman, and even the Sophist. See also Gail Fine, "Knowledge and Belief in *Republic* V," *AGP* 60 (1978): 121–39; Fine, "Knowledge and Belief in *Republic* V–VII," in *Epistemology*, ed. Stephen Everson (Cambridge: Cambridge University Press, 1990), 111: "At [the level of understanding] at the end of *Republic* 6, one no longer uses sensibles, but "Plato does not mean that there is no [understanding] type knowledge of sensibles. He means only that [at the level of understanding] one no longer needs to explain the nature of Forms through

perception nor justified belief, or right opinion with a good account of itself, qualifies as understanding. Understanding something is just what it is: understanding. Nonetheless, Plato was also aware that an approach to knowledge by means of types or stereotypes—and antitypes (though he does not use the word *antitypos*)—is a prosthetic device that requires further tuning by the *accuracy* of knowledge of individuals in concrete circumstances that includes and transforms simple perception into a process of knowing, a process that nonetheless can never completely predict or control the consequences of individual circumstances.

Let me say a few words about terminology and context first. The word *stereotype* or, for that matter, the words *archetype* and *prototype*, does not occur in Plato's dialogues. Because the word στερεός and its cognates signify solidity, especially bodily solidity, and since a "solid type" of anything just on its own pretends a kind of security that I suggest Plato did not believe in or that he thought needed shattering and destroying,[2] the modern stereotype as such was not a philological or philosophical part of Plato's preferences.

Nonetheless, Plato's dialogues abound in stereotypes that provoke deconstruction: to give two examples: First, in the *Republic*, there are the dramatis personae: Cephalus, Polemarchus, Thrasymachus, and Socrates, of course, and then in the genealogies of books 8 and 9, the aristocrat, timocrat, oligarch, democrat, and tyrant—all of whom live in the same "house"; and, second, in the *Symposium*, there are the genres, the layers of narration themselves, through Aristodemus and Apollodorus, as well as the participants: Phaedrus, the ardent beginner; Pausanias, the Sophistic

---

images.... One can speak of them directly, as they are in and of themselves. But once one has done this, one can apply these accounts to sensibles ... [just as] Aristotle believes one can define various species and genera without reference to particular instances of them; but, once one has done this, one can apply the definitions to particulars in such a way as to have knowledge of them." For critique, see Francisco J. Gonzalez, "Propositions or Objects: A Critique of Gail Fine on Knowledge and Belief in *Republic* V," *Phronesis* 41 (1996): 245–75.

2. One might ask how the Platonic solids (in the *Timaeus*) relate to such a critique of solidity. Perhaps one reasonable answer might be that instead of the complete material solidity of the full (that is, being/atoms—with an infinite number of atoms) and the empty (that is, nonbeing/void) of pre-Socratic atomist theory, Plato posits five solids, manifesting an intelligible number of mathematical operations that cannot be understood without the pervasive activity of Soul. In other words, apparent material solidity needs to be shattered or transformed by Soul.

anthropologist; Eryximachus, the doctor who sees everything through the lens of medicine; Aristophanes, the brilliant but dangerous comic poet; Agathon, the "good" golden youth, but in danger of emptiness; Alcibiades, the alcoholic, brilliant student of Socrates and, unwittingly, a good case for the prosecution that Socrates has corrupted the young; and then Socrates himself: saint or destructive menace? Wilfred Cantwell Smith observes that we tend to Platonize our own experience and Aristotelianize that of everybody else. One might add that, while Socrates might have Platonized Plato's own experience, Socrates himself simply breaks the mold: there was nothing Platonic or anything else about him, except for the transformative spirit of inquiry itself.

So one might argue that the Platonic tradition both helps to create the phenomenon we call stereotype and yet calls it radically into question at the same time. Rather than our *stereotype*, Plato prefers simply τύποι, γενή, εἰδή, that is, "types," "kinds," forms, even ἐκμαγεῖα ("molds" or "impressions," as at *Leg.* 7 [800b]),[3] or again, παράδειγμα, a word that can mean an ordinary paradigm or exemplar of anything, or alternatively, a Platonic Form (as in *Parm.* 132d), by contrast with "likeness" (ὁμοίωμα) or "image" (εἴχον), or a living, speaking *logos* (as in *Phaedr.* 276a), by contrast with its brother, written logos, which is an *eidolon* of the former; or in the *Timaeus*, "the intelligible Living Creature" or Paradigm that includes all living beings to be generated in the cosmos. There is a slippage often among different meanings of *form, idea, type, paradigm*: first, there are *concepts* as in defining the "what is" of things; second, there are exemplars, types and classifications of anything such as the classification of types of discourse, and kinds of soul or people in the *Phaedrus* that one must modulate correctly (*Phaedr.* 271b–c: διαταξάμενος τὰ λόγων τε καὶ ψυχῆς γένη καὶ τὰ τούτων παθήματα δίεισι πάσας αἰτίας[4]) or the types/exemplars of lives that the soul before rebirth must choose between in the Myth of Er at the end of the *Republic* (παραδείγματα βίων). Third, there are the Forms themselves, which are not types or stereotypes in the sense that we tend to use the word, nor even primary instances of something to which all kinds of beauty are to be traced,[5]

---

3. For the two words together, *typos ekmageion*, see *Leg.* 801b.

4. *Phaedr.* 271b–c: διαταξάμενος τὰ λόγων τε καὶ ψυχῆς γένη καὶ τὰ τούτων παθήματα δίεισι πάσας αἰτίας, προσαρμόττων ἕκαστον ἑκάστῳ: "Striving to classify the kinds of speeches together with the kinds of souls, as well as the experiences they each undergo, he will traverse all causes, fitting each to each."

5. Though *pros hen* or *aph' henos* equivocity is part of Platonic and Aristotelian

but often just what beauty or justice is *in itself*, forms that give rise to every instance of beauty but are not instances themselves in the sense that they could be aligned with or assimilated to particular kinds of beauty.

In this paper I will deal not with Plato's Forms but rather with classes, concepts, and types, that is, the kinds that can be classified. Speusippus in the early Academy posited a principle of scientific perception (see Sextus Empiricus, *Math.* 7.145–146: τὴν ἐπιστημονικὴν αἴσθησιν), and scholars have no idea where he got the idea. I think he was developing a strand of thought that has not hitherto been noticed in Plato but that this book has shown to be a genuine part of Plato's thought.

So I will, first, indicate what I think is the most likely source of Speusippus's notion of scientific perception and then go on to establish that this is a major theme throughout the middle to late dialogues in order to show that Plato is, in these dialogues at least, not the exponent of abstract knowledge stripped of empirical content but rather a thinker who used types as a means to see through them more sharply into individual experience and deeper understanding. Finally, I will emphasize this scientific strand in Plato's thought that needs to be taken seriously.

Speusippus

Speusippus's notion of scientific perception or cognitive logos is described by Sextus Empiricus as something that "participates in the truth in accordance with reason"—just as a flute player's fingers do not themselves primarily self-produce knowing but "possess an artistic activity that is fully developed as a result of training under the cooperative guidance of reasoning" (*Math.* 7.145–146: ὥσπερ γὰρ οἱ τοῦ αὐλητοῦ ἢ τοῦ ψάλτου δάκτυλοι τεχνικὴν μὲν εἶχον ἐνέργειαν, οὐκ ἐν αὐτοῖς δὲ προηγουμένως τελειουμένην, ἀλλ᾽ ἐκ τῆς πρὸς τὸν λογισμὸν συνασκήσεως ἀπαρτιζομένην),[6] so too "cognitive sense-perception naturally derives from reason the cognitive practice it shares, which leads to the unerring diagnosis of its proper objects" (οὕτω καὶ ἡ ἐπιστημονικὴ αἴσθησις φυσικῶς παρὰ τοῦ λόγου τῆς ἐπιστημονικῆς μεταλαμβάνει τριβῆς πρὸς ἀπλανῆ τῶν ὑποκειμένων διάγνωσιν).

---

usage, this is a part of the completely understandable mystery of later Platonic thought known as Neoplatonism: How can one trace a particular activity to a source that cannot in any way be coordinated or reduced to that activity?

6. Frag. 75 in Leonardo Tarán, *Speusippus of Athens: A Critical Study, with a Collection of the Related Texts and Commentary*, PhA 39 (Leiden: Brill, 1981).

This is an interesting if puzzling passage, but its main notes are apparent; cognitive or scientific perception (1) depends on *logos*, (2) with which it shares an *epistemic practice*, and (3) one that is directed to the correct diagnosis "of its proper objects," namely, the subjects or individual substances in question. The phrase τὰ ὑποκείμενα, the underlying subjects, is certainly ambiguous, for it refers either to the individual subjects themselves or to their underlying natures or to both (according to Aristotelian usage). In the context, I prefer to retain both meanings: *individual things or subjects and underlying natures*, for "diagnosis" evidently refers, if successful—"unerring"—to both. So, in the *Timaeus*, for instance, the works of "Reason and Necessity" are mixed: mind brings the "wandering cause" into a successful focus. Three elements, therefore, stand out as characteristic of scientific perception from Sextus Empiricus's account: (1) logos-dependence, (2) shared epistemic practice,[7] and (3) the diagnosis of individual things and underlying natures.

Phaedrus

This theory of scientific perception can most plausibly be traced to the latter part of Plato's *Phaedrus* in the section devoted to the superiority of the living logos written in the soul over the logos committed to writing. The inner logos is not a purely psychic entity but "ensouled and living," and like the true art (*technē*) of rhetoric, outlined in the immediately preceding section, it is able to take account of "the types of discourses and souls" that need to be addressed because it is able to "see" the "object in respect of which we desire to have scientific knowledge" (270c–d).[8] In other words, in order to see types and the individuals included under

---

7. What is shared in this case is this: not only do artistic fingers, not in themselves epistemic, receive their perfection by the copractice (συνασκήσις) of being guided and fitted to reasoning, but scientific perception itself, naturally "from reason," shares or participates in scientific time well spent. This shared practice derived from reason and guided by reasoning is a collaborative project of artistic fingers, the artist practicing, and reason itself, which results in and is manifest as scientific perception. Since artistic and scientific activity is naturally collaborative and reality based, I suggest that this shared epistemic practice is also intersubjective and world based, as we see immediately below in the example of true rhetoric from the *Phaedrus* and sound, collaborative medical practice in the *Laws*.

8. Translations from the Phaedrus follow Christopher Rowe, *Plato: Phaedrus*. Warminster, UK: Aris & Phillips, 1996.

them, the orator needs more than experience; he must have *technē* (εἰ μέλλεις, μὴ τριβῇ μόνον καὶ ἐμπειρίᾳ ἀλλὰ τέχνῃ); only then will he be able to apply this knowledge to individual souls and circumstances: "All this the orator must fully understand, and next *he must watch it actually occurring*, exemplified in men's conduct, and must cultivate *a sharpness of perception in following it* (271c–e: δεῖ δὴ ταῦτα ἱκανῶς νοήσαντα, μετὰ ταῦτα θεώμενον αὐτὰ ἐν ταῖς πράξεσιν ὄντα τε καὶ πραττόμενα, ὀξέως τῇ αἰσθήσει δύνασθαι ἐπακολουθεῖν). Understanding, together with sharpness of perception (ὀξέως τῇ αἰσθήσει), yields real practical knowledge, even if this is not yet *epistēmē* in the full sense.

So far in our text there is much use of verbs of seeing and knowing with emphasis throughout on *technē*, that is, art or craft, despite the frequent modern mistranslations of *technē* as *epistēmē*, but there is no occurrence of *epistēmē* as such, science or knowledge (except in the verb νοήσαντα—"all this the orator must understand"). For Plato, then, true rhetoric appears to be indistinguishable from philosophy in practice, but it remains a *technē*, no matter how advanced it may be. Only with dialectic, that is, the ability *to see the one and the many together*, does *epistēmē* as such emerge in the following section of the *Phaedrus*: in the living logos that is written in the soul of the farmer, doctor, or musician, that actually knows and sees whom to address and with what kinds of words and why, by contrast with the papyrus-word, or written-down word, that does not actually *see* anything at all and cannot come to its own aid if questioned—only so, as employing dialectical *technē*, does the true rhetorician, musician or farmer "select a soul of the right type and in it plants and sows his words *with epistēmē*" (ὅταν τις τῇ διαλεκτικῇ τέχνῃ χρώμενος, λαβὼν ψυχὴν προσήκουσαν, φυτεύῃ τε καὶ σπείρῃ μετ' ἐπιστήμης λόγους, *Phaedr.* 276e–277a). This is the first instance in the *Phaedrus* of this precise use of *epistēmē* and *logos* linked with dialectic and *technē*, and it is, strikingly so, a proximate source of Speusippus's "scientific perception," for it involves *epistēmē*, logos, aesthetic diagnosis of individuals and their natures through detailed practice and experience[9] of individual cases in which one learns to *see* an individual object. There is need of sharpness of perception, then, to follow with greater precision and accuracy knowledgeable *technē* through, and in, individual cases.

---

9. See *Phaedr.* 273e4–5: it cannot be acquired ἄνευ πολλῆς πραγματείας.

Sharp Perception: *Republic*

This entirely overlooked motif of sharp perception in modern times is in fact an important theme that emerges in the early middle dialogues and culminates in the late *Laws*.[10] Here I shall trace it as briefly as I can in the *Republic* and then pick out its culminating instance in book 12 of the *Laws*.

Generations of critics have thought that Plato's *Republic* is concerned ultimately with abstract ideas or totalitarian, tyrannical aims. Such views go hand in hand with a general condemnation of Plato as an abstract thinker as opposed to the much more empirical, scientific bent of Aristotle and Theophrastus. Yet one of the central methodological principles of the *Republic* is simply the opposite of this, for it is critically involved in the question of what it means to see ordinary, not abstract things, and in the question of how we can see types and individuals more accurately through the lenses of our immediate and ordinary experience. The *Republic* is, in fact, an experiment in learning to see and in recognizing shadows for what they are. Where does this important notion of scientific seeing start?[11] It starts, for our purposes, in book 2 of the *Republic*—at the beginning of the all-important question, why we should be good—not for riches, honors or religious blessings, but just for the good itself. Since we cannot see acutely or sharply—at least, in the immediate present, Socrates argues, we need to develop a microscope in order to see the significance of ordinary, small things by looking at what big things have to tell us, and thereby come to inhabit the proper field of sharp-sightedness. Socrates speaks as follows:

> [Rhythm and harmony] in music and poetry is most important. First, because rhythm and harmony permeate the inner part of the soul more than anything else, affecting it most strongly and bringing it grace, so that if someone is properly educated in music and poetry, it makes him graceful, but if not, then the opposite. Second, because anyone who has been properly educated in music and poetry will *sense it sharply* when

---

10. It also occurs frequently in later writers such as Plotinus and Gregory of Nyssa, but this is not part of my focus here.

11. See Gill, *Philosophos*; Fine, "Knowledge and Belief in *Republic* V–VII," as exceptions in note 1 above. See also Gail Fine, "Plato on the Grades of Perception: Theaetetus 184–186 and the Phaedo," *OSAP* 53 (2017): 65–109, on grades of perception (adopted from Descartes—physiological instinct, effects of mind, mind proper) in the *Theaetetus* and *Phaedo*. I am in agreement with Fine that we cannot completely establish which grades are involved in these dialogues.

something has been omitted from a thing and when it hasn't been finely
crafted or finely made by nature [ὅτι αὖ τῶν παραλειπομένων καὶ μὴ
καλῶς δημιουργηθέντων ἢ μὴ καλῶς φύντων ὀξύτατ' ἂν αἰσθάνοιτο]. And
since he has the right distastes, he'll praise fine things, be pleased by
them, receive them into his soul, and, being nurtured by them, become
fine and good. (*Resp.* 2.401d–e [Grube])

Furthermore, at the beginning of book 6 of the *Republic*, it is agreed that
those who have sharp sight are those who know the truth. The "blind" are
those who are deprived of knowledge. The "sharp-sighted" are "the ones
who have knowledge" (τοὺς ἐγνωκότας). "And isn't it clear that a guardian
who is to keep watch over anything *should be sharp-sighted rather than
blind*?" (Τόδε δέ, ἦν δ' ἐγώ, ἆρα δῆλον, εἴτε τυφλὸν εἴτε ὀξὺ ὁρῶντα χρὴ
φύλακα τηρεῖν ὁτιοῦν; see *Resp.* 6 [375a5–7, 503c2]). Of course, it is clear.

Do you think, then, that there's any difference between the blind and
those who are really deprived of the knowledge of each thing that is?
The latter have no clear model in their souls, and so they cannot—in
the manner of painters—look to what is most true, make constant reference to it, and study it as exactly as possible [Ἦ οὖν δοκοῦσί τι τυφλῶν
διαφέρειν οἱ τῷ ὄντι τοῦ ὄντος ἑκάστου ἐστερημένοι τῆς γνώσεως, καὶ
μηδὲν ἐναργὲς ἐν τῇ ψυχῇ ἔχοντες παράδειγμα, μηδὲ δυνάμενοι ὥσπερ
γραφῆς εἰς τὸ ἀληθέστατον ἀποβλέποντες κἀκεῖσε ἀεὶ ἀναφέροντές τε καὶ
θεώμενοι ὡς οἷόν τε ἀκριβέστατα].

Hence, they cannot establish here on earth conventions about what
is fine or just or good, when they need to be established, or guard and
preserve them, once they have been established. No, by god, there isn't
much difference between them. Should we, then, make these blind
people our guardians or rather those who know each thing that is and
who are not inferior to the others, either in experience or in any other
part of excellence [τοὺς ἐγνωκότας μὲν ἕκαστον τὸ ὄν, ἐμπειρίᾳ δὲ μηδὲν
ἐκείνων ἐλλείποντας μηδ' ἐν ἄλλῳ μηδενὶ μέρει ἀρετῆς ὑστεροῦντας]? It
would be absurd to choose anyone but the ones who have knowledge, if
indeed they're not inferior in these ways, for the respect in which they
are superior is pretty well the most important one. (*Resp.* 6 [484c–d;
Grube, slightly altered])

So, while knowledge and perception are of course clearly distinguished
throughout *Resp.* 6–7, that which gives the power to know is the Good—
dimly in sense perception, more clearly in thought or understanding. The
"one who has knowledge" (τῷ γιγνώσκοντι) or the "sharp-sighted one"

is illuminated by the light of the sun and by that of the Good, since the Good reaches across the divide between sensible and intelligible. In fact, such knowing (*gnōsis, Resp.* 6 [508e5]) is *epistēmē* and *alētheia* (*Resp.* 508e). Sharp-sightedness of this kind, therefore, is the power for epistemic seeing. And it is located along a continuum of seeing from the clearer to the dimmer, a continuum that parallels, first, Socrates's example of the epistemological "divided line" ranging from guesswork through faith/opinion to reasoning and, finally, understanding and, second, his parable of the light of the sun/the Good, the cave and the dialectical ascent in book 7 in the attempt *to see things together* (*synoptikos*).

One might ask the following question: Is not sight in the above passage just a metaphor? Those who have knowledge see a paradigm in their minds; they are not using *aesthesis* at all. There is, indeed, something to this—except for the fact that these knowers are like painters. In other words, their knowledge has to result in a *perceptible work* of the imagination. Their object is to bring knowledge, imagination, and perception *together*. On the other hand, does this mean that sensibles are, in some way, epistemic? Gail Fine argues that at the level of understanding when one no longer needs to understand Forms on the level of images, one can apply one's accounts to a knowledge of sensibles.[12] In his critique of Fine, Francisco Gonzalez rejects Fine's more positive "knowledge of sensibles" on the grounds that "it is inaccurate to say that the objects of this knowledge are the sensibles per se; it is precisely because this knowledge is *not* of sensibles but of the forms, that it can reveal sensibles for what they are: nothing but deficient imitations of these forms."[13] However, this cannot be entirely correct, since, in the first case, not only deficiency but *relative* degrees of perfection are also at stake—and, even more important in the second instance, for *Resp.* 5–7 as a whole, the knowledge that is dialectic is the ability *to see together both the Form and the participants.* This synoptic vision is not simply metaphorical but what perception *in this collaborative focus* really is and strives to be.

Here, then, I want to emphasize that sharp seeing is situated on a continuum: first, it has an intelligible function; second, it is applied ironically to the prisoners in the cave and, at the extreme—with powerful psychological plausibility—to the tyrant who is compelled by his nightmarish

---

12. Fine, "Knowledge and Belief in *Republic* V–VII," 111.
13. Gonzalez, "Propositions or Objects," 273–74.

circumstances to see things sharply. Perception (like desire) depends on the pivot of focus. It "seems" (ἔοικεν) "not to have *nous*," and yet *nous* is somehow there with it, since even the lowest rung on the ladder of cognition, no matter how dimmed, blunted, dark, is still connected along the continuum of seeing (see *Resp.* 6 [508c–d]). First, there is its epistemic function:

> If a nature of this sort had been hammered at from childhood and freed from the bonds of kinship with becoming, which have been fastened to it by feasting, greed, and other such pleasures and which, like leaden weights, pull its vision downwards [τὴν τῆς ψυχῆς ὄψιν]—if, being rid of these, it turned to look at true things, then I say that the *same soul of the same person would see these most sharply*, just as it now does the things it is presently turned towards [ἐκεῖνα ἂν τὸ αὐτὸ τοῦτο τῶν αὐτῶν ἀνθρώπων ὀξύτατα ἑώρα, ὥσπερ καὶ ἐφ' ἃ νῦν τέτραπται]. (*Resp.* 7 [519a–b; Grube])

Second, thinking and perception are symbiotic even in negative circumstances. The fundamental question is the turning around of the soul and waking up the real power of perception that is present remarkably even in defective seeing. Education is not putting sight into dead eyes but orienting the power of sharp-sightedness that is already always there (see *Resp.* 7 [518d–519a]):

> Now, it looks as though the other so-called excellences of the soul are akin to those of the body, for they really aren't there beforehand but are added later by habit and practice. However, *the excellence of thinking* [τοῦ φρονῆσαι] seems to belong above all to something more divine, which never loses its power but is either useful and beneficial or useless and harmful, depending on the way it is turned. Or have you never noticed this about people who are said to be vicious but clever, *how keen the vision* [ὡς δριμὺ μὲν βλέπει τὸ ψυχάριον] of their little souls is and *how sharply it distinguishes* the things it is turned towards [ὀξέως διορᾷ ταῦτα ἐφ' ἃ τέτραπται]? This shows that its sight isn't inferior but rather is forced to serve evil ends, so that *the sharper it sees*, the more evil it accomplishes [ὥστε ὅσῳ ἂν ὀξύτερον βλέπῃ, τοσούτῳ πλείω κακὰ ἐργαζόμενον]. (*Resp.* 7 [518d–519a; Grube])

Third, this applies even to the cave: sharp-sightedness at any level of being can be parodied as a deficiency of real or intelligible keen-sightedness:

> And if there had been any honors, praises, or prizes among them for the one who was *sharpest at identifying* [τῷ ὀξύτατα καθορῶντι] the shadows

as they passed by and who best remembered which usually came earlier, which later, and which simultaneously, and *who could thus best divine the future* [ἐκ τούτων δὴ δυνατώτατα ἀπομαντευομένῳ τὸ μέλλον ἥξειν], do you think that our man would desire these rewards or envy those among the prisoners who were honored and held power? Instead, wouldn't he feel, with Homer, that he'd much prefer to "work the earth as a serf to another, one without possessions," and go through any sufferings, rather than share their opinions and live as they do? (*Resp.* 7 [516c; Grube])

Unlike the positive "divination" of the Good in book 6, here in the guess-work (εἰκασία) and talking points (*doxa*) of the cave, sharp seeing (τῷ ὀξύτατα καθορῶντι) and divination (ἀπομαντευομένῳ) can become distorted images of reality since they take the images cast on the cave wall to be the only reality and suppose their value to be ultimate, closing off everything else to perception.

And finally, this is no longer the parable but the tragic mirror-reality of the tyrant depicted in books 8–9 that he is forced *to see sharply the excellences of those around him and yet, even against his own will, detest and kill them*: "The tyrant will have to do away with all of them if he intends to rule, until he's left with neither friend nor enemy of any worth." Clearly.

He must, therefore, *keep a sharp lookout* for anyone who is brave, large-minded, knowledgeable, or rich [Ὀξέως ἄρα δεῖ ὁρᾶν αὐτὸν τίς ἀνδρεῖος, τίς μεγαλόφρων, τίς φρόνιμος, τίς πλούσιος]. And so happy is he that he must be the enemy of them all, whether he wants to be or not, and plot against them until he has purged them from the city. (*Resp.* 8 [567b–c; Grube])

Keen-sightedness or scientific seeing based on memory and experience is fundamental, then, to the *Republic*. The image also occurs in Alcibiades's speech in the *Symposium*, of the sharp sight of the mind when sense perception wanes; in the *Phaedo* (89a), of Socrates's sharp perception of the effect of Simmias's and Cebes's objections on the assembled group;[14] and in

---

14. *Phaed.* 89a [Grube]: "What I wondered at most in him was the pleasant, kind and admiring way he received the young men's argument, and *how sharply he was aware of* [ὀξέως ᾔσθετο] *the effect the discussion had on us*, and then how well he healed our distress and, as it were, recalled us from our flight and defeat and turned us around to join him in the examination of their argument." Socrates's "sharp" perception/awareness is that of one who comes down from the principles already, as it were,

the *Phaedrus*, of sight as the sharpest of the senses. But the idea of a form of vision that is focused, concrete, and yet anagogic or revelatory is important elsewhere in the dialogues. In fact, it is characteristic of the dialogue form itself that presents a whole range of different characters—or divided continuum of inferior, better, and best personages, stereotypes, or genres—for us to see for ourselves what may be better and best (and worse).

Epistemic Perception: *Laws*

Let me come finally to the culmination of the theme of epistemic perception in the late *Laws* (in twelve books). I have time here for only two points, one a general question about Plato's methodology and the other more specific about the nature of sharp seeing and the role of knowing and seeing in the closing pages of this massive work.

First, an important point of methodology that mirrors the attention to knowledge through individual practice in the case of the positive rhetoric we have seen in the *Phaedrus*. In the later dialogues, laws, however sacred, are only a second-best option to individual choice and personal attention. A good doctor, for instance, in the *Politicus* (295c–d), should not be bound by his prescriptions when the situation changes and the patient inevitably prefers the individual doctor to his prescriptions. In book 4 of the *Laws*, the Athenian Stranger frames the case of legislation as a dilemma between two medical models, a slave-to-slave model based on strict adherence to experience—by which is meant only what has been done previously—and a much more nuanced model of collaborative medicine as ongoing experience, process, knowledge, personal attention, and free choice. The passage runs as follows:

> You are also aware that, as the sick folk in the cities comprise both slaves and free men, the slaves are usually doctored by slaves, who either run round the town or wait in their surgeries; and *not one of these doctors either gives or receives any account of the several ailments of the various domestics, but prescribes for each what he deems right from experience, just as though he had exact knowledge, and with the assurance of a tyrant*; then up he jumps and off he rushes to another sick domestic, and thus he relieves his master in his attendance on the sick. But the free-born doctor

---

before the principles are introduced after the objections of Simmias and Cebes, and this sharp perception is simultaneously based on something real in what is perceptible.

is *for the most part* engaged in visiting and treating the ailments of free men, and he does so *by investigating them from the commencement and according to the course of nature*; he *talks with the patient himself* and *with his friends*, and *thus both learns himself from the sufferers and imparts instruction to them*, so far as possible; and he gives no prescription *until he has gained the patient's consent, and only then, by preparing the sick person as rendered gentle by persuasion*, does he attempt to complete the task of restoring him to health.[15] Which of these two methods of doctoring shows the better doctor, or of training, the better trainer? Should the doctor perform one and the same function in two ways, or do it in one way only and that the worse way of the two and the less humane? (*Leg.* 4 [720c–e; Bury])

The stereotype contrast could not be stronger. The slave doctor imposes an abstract formula on the basis of *past* experience but no proper and prolonged study. The "free doctor," by contrast (1) examines the course of the whole disease; (2) immerses himself in the particular circumstances and environment of the sick person; (3) learns from the sick person and teaches something, if possible, that is, tries to make the sick person *not a patient* but an *active collaborator*; (4) obtains the patient's consent, not as a one-time event but as an ongoing process; and (5) tries to restore health on the basis of knowledge and observation of the sickness in the individual case and its environment with full mutual consent and shared, up-to-date information. For the free doctor, the prescription emerges last on the basis of individual knowledge and personal association. And this is, according to the Athenian Stranger, the case for legislation that should be based, first, on persuasion. There is *no* such thing as abstract knowledge—just the opposite. One has to look through the stereotype to the collaborative, environmental, communal, and individual context.

Let us come then to the end of the *Laws* and to Plato's final representation of epistemic perception in its most communitarian, potentially sustainable form: knowing and seeing or seeing *with* knowing—no longer simply an individual function but, on the community-medical model of *Laws* 4 that

---

15. ὁ δὲ ἐλεύθερος ὡς ἐπὶ τὸ πλεῖστον τὰ τῶν ἐλευθέρων νοσήματα θεραπεύει τε καὶ ἐπισκοπεῖ, καὶ ταῦτα ἐξετάζων ἀπ᾽ ἀρχῆς καὶ κατὰ φύσιν, τῷ κάμνοντι κοινούμενος αὐτῷ τε καὶ τοῖς φίλοις, ἅμα μὲν αὐτὸς μανθάνει τι παρὰ τῶν νοσούντων, ἅμα δὲ καὶ καθ᾽ ὅσον οἷός τέ ἐστιν, διδάσκει τὸν ἀσθενοῦντα αὐτόν, καὶ οὐ πρότερον ἐπέταξεν πρὶν ἄν πῃ συμπείσῃ, τότε δὲ μετὰ πειθοῦς ἡμερούμενον ἀεὶ παρασκευάζων τὸν κάμνοντα, εἰς τὴν ὑγίειαν ἄγων, ἀποτελεῖν πειρᾶται.

we have just examined, an individual-community-political model. Here body posture and organization provide a model for scientific perception

Athenian
One ought to observe, Clinias, in regard to every object, in each of its operations, what constitutes its appropriate savior—as, for example, in an animal, the soul and the head are eminently such by nature.
Clinias
How do you mean?
Athenian
Surely it is the goodness of those parts that provides salvation to every animal.
Clinias
How?
Athenian
By the existence of mind in the soul, in addition to all its other qualities, and by the existence of sight and hearing, in addition to all else, in the head; thus, to summarize the matter, it is *the mixture of mind with the finest senses*, and their union in one, that would most justly be termed the salvation of each animal.[16] (*Leg.* 4 [961d–e])

So now, in our present case, if our settlement of the country is to be finally completed, there must, it would seem, exist in it some element *which knows*, in the first place, *what that political aim*, of which we are speaking, *happens to be*, and, secondly, *in what manner* it may attain this aim, and *which of the laws*, in the first instance, and *secondly of men*, gives it good counsel or bad. But if any State is destitute of such an element, it will not be surprising if, being *thus void of reason and void of sense*, it acts at haphazard always in all its actions. (*Leg.* 4 [962b])

Must we contrive how our wardens shall have a more accurate grasp of virtue, *both in word and deed*, than the majority of men? For otherwise, how shall our State resemble a *wise person's head and senses*, on the ground that it possesses within itself a similar kind of wardenship?
Clinias
What is this resemblance we speak of and wherein does it consist?
Athenian
Evidently we are comparing the State itself to the skull; and, of the wardens, the younger ones, who are selected as the *most intelligent and*

---

16. Compare *Leg.* 12 (961e): ἆρ' οὐκ ἐν νηὶ κυβερνήτης ἅμα καὶ ναῦται τὰς αἰσθήσεις τῷ κυβερνητικῷ νῷ συγκερασάμενοι σῴζουσιναὑτούς τε καὶ τὰ περὶ τὴν ναῦν;

sharpest in every part of their souls, are set, as it were, like the eyes, in the top of the head, and survey the State all round; and **as they watch, they pass on their perceptions to the organs of memory,**—that is, they report to their elders all that goes on in the State,—while the elders, who are likened to the mind because of their eminent wisdom in many matters of account (*logos*), act as counselors, and make use of the young men *as ministers and colleagues also in their counsels,* so that **both these in common** really save the whole city-state. Is this the way, or ought we to contrive some other? (*Leg.* 4 [964d–965a])

(See *Leg.* 4 [965b–c]: "Did we not say that he who is a first-class craftsman or warden, in any department, *must not only be able to pay regard to the many, but must be able also to press towards the one so as to discern it and, on discerning it, to survey and organize all the rest with a single eye to it?*[17] (Bury)

We should note here the implicit reference to *Resp.* 7 (537b–c), where the dialectical method is described as a kind of inductive gathering (συναγωγή) whereby the mind ascends from "the many" particulars to "the one" "idea": a seeing together (σύνοψις) of the whole is what marks the dialectician (ὁ συνοπτικὸς διαλεκτικός).

Here we have precisely, but in a new community key, the sharp perception we have met from the *Phaedo* onward and the combination of knowing and seeing in a single paradigm, namely, scientific perception, that we uncovered in the *Phaedrus* and then the *Republic* above. What is striking here, however, is that epistemic perception is now explicitly dialectical in the manner of the *Republic* (book 7): it both sees the many and simultaneously presses on to the one in order to order everything synoptically (see *Resp.* 7 [537b–c]). *Praxis* or *syntaxis* is inscribed in the whole field of scientific attention. Let me make my own position clear. Knowledge is not perception, as the *Theaetetus* shows. So, I do not agree with the position of Mary Louise Gill, even if I am in sympathy with her instinct (see note 1 above). Nonetheless, perception *is* implicitly cognitive, as Fine has well argued, even if we cannot determine exactly the particular grade of cognition involved (these grades she takes from Descartes: physiological instinct, effects of mind and embodiment, mind proper). Active

---

17. οὐκοῦν ἐλέγομεν τόν γε πρὸς ἕκαστα ἄκρον δημιουργόν τε καὶ φύλακα μὴ μόνον δεῖν πρὸς τὰ πολλὰ βλέπειν δυνατὸν εἶναι, πρὸς δὲ τὸ ἓν ἐπείγεσθαι γνῶναί τε, καὶ γνόντα πρὸς ἐκεῖνο συντάξασθαι πάντα συνορῶντα;

perception linked dialectically and symbiotically in the whole soul is, I suggest, epistemic, as we find reported in Sextus Empiricus.[18] Such a view, I conclude, is that of Plato.

Conclusions

Knowledge for Plato is not the abstract affair in either the middle or the late dialogues that so much modern scholarship has taken it to be. There really does exist a hitherto unknown paradigm of sharp seeing or epistemic perception in these dialogues, a paradigm sensitive to typologies and individuals, to process and dialogue, and one that Speusippus evidently took over from Plato. In the late *Laws* this paradigm is ultimately a community-based form of knowing and seeing that seeks to generate longer-term ecological sustainability in the full understanding that free choice of the best or of what seems the best to us, amid the incommensurabilities of individual circumstances and the catastrophic rise and fall of civilizations, can never guarantee the permanence of anything. This paradigm is not a shift to be found in the later *Laws* only; it also characterizes the earlier *Republic* and *Phaedrus*, traces of which can be found already in the usage of the *Phaedo* and in the possibility of a "true rhetoric" in the *Gorgias* that looks forward to the treatment of rhetoric in the *Phaedrus*.[19]

All of this evidently calls for a complete reappraisal of the question of knowledge in the early to middle dialogues and for a change in our view of the relation between Plato and Aristotle since, for both, things in the sublunary world are only so for the most part, and practical, aesthetic knowing is a methodological necessity even if such seeing-knowing always depends ultimately on contemplative or theoretical insight for its surest footing, and even if this insight is fleeting and open to questioning (as in *Ep.* 7), fragile and liable to deconstruction (as in the *Symposium*)[20]

---

18. By the whole soul, I mean the synergy of all the parts or powers of soul under the cooperative guidance of reason, as in *Resp.* 9 (586e–587a).

19. See also the apparent interest in classification and the study of natural kinds not simply in Aristotle but also in a parody of early Academic practices in a text of Epicrates as well as in the thought of Xenocrates and Speusippus—in István Bodnár, "The Study of Natural Kinds in the Early Academy," in *Plato's Academy: Its Workings and Its History*, ed. Paul Kalligas et al. (Cambridge: Cambridge University Press, 2020), 153–66.

20. In this sketch I focus on the otherwise unnoticed motif of "sharp seeing" that is not prominent as such in the *Symposium*. For further treatment of what this might

and never sufficiently stable to ensure that the best people we can produce will not be corrupted (as in the *Republic*).

Bibliography

Primary Sources

Plato. *Laws*. Translated by Robert G. Bury. LCL. Cambridge: Harvard University Press, 1926.

Rowe, Christopher. *Plato: Phaedrus*. Warminster, UK: Aris & Phillips, 1996.

Secondary Sources

Bodnár, István. "The Study of Natural Kinds in the Early Academy." Pages 153–66 in *Plato's Academy: Its Workings and Its History*. Edited by Paul Kalligas, Chloe Balla, Effie Baziotopoulou-Valvani, and Vassilis Karasmanis. Cambridge: Cambridge University Press, 2020.

Corrigan, Kevin. *A Less Familiar Plato: From Phaedo to Philebus*. Cambridge: Cambridge University Press, forthcoming.

Fine, Gail. "Knowledge and Belief in *Republic* V." *AGP* 60 (1978): 121–39.

———. "Knowledge and Belief in *Republic* V–VII." Pages 85–115 in *Epistemology*. Edited by Stephen Everson. Cambridge: Cambridge University Press, 1990.

———. "Plato on the Grades of Perception: Theaetetus 184–186 and the Phaedo." *OSAP* 53 (2017): 65–109.

Gill, Mary Louise. *Philosophos: Plato's Missing Dialogue*. Oxford: Oxford University Press, 2014.

Gonzalez, Francisco J. "Propositions or Objects: A Critique of Gail Fine on Knowledge and Belief in *Republic* V." *Phronesis* 41 (1996): 245–75.

Grube, George M. A. *Plato's Republic*. Indianapolis: Hackett, 1974.

Tarán, Leonardo. *Speusippus of Athens: A Critical Study, with a Collection of the Related Texts and Commentary*. PhA 39. Leiden: Brill, 1981.

---

mean in a broader sense in the *Symposium*, however, see my *A Less Familiar Plato: From Phaedo to Philebus* (Cambridge: Cambridge University Press, forthcoming).

Of Orioles, Owls, and Aviaries:
Rethinking the Problem of Other Minds

Robert Berchman

Most men live as if their thinking were a private possession.
—Heraclitus, *Fragmentum 2*

[A] Precis

This inquiry is parsed from two similes in the *Theaetetus* where mind is an aviary and each new piece of knowledge is a wild bird caught and caged (*Theaet.* 197d).[1] The aviary is the mind, knowledge is the birds, and when we think, we hold a bird in our hands (*Theaet.* 199a–b).[2] Three metaphors are transposed from these similes:[3] "orioles" stand for indi-

_____

It is a distinct pleasure to participate in this volume in honor of our colleague and friend John F. Finamore.

1. Plato, *Theaet.* 197de [Fowler]: "Now consider whether knowledge is a thing you can possess in that way without having it about you, like a man who has caught some wild birds.... We might say he 'has' them all the time inasmuch as he possesses them ... but in another sense he 'has' none of them though he has got control of them, now that he has made them captive in an enclosure of his own; he can take hold of them whenever he likes by catching any bird he chooses, and let them go again, and it is open to do that as often as he pleases."

2. Plato, *Theaet.* 199a–b: "Thus think of an aviary in which birds are kept. I may be said to possess the birds as long as they are in the aviary, but I may have and hold the birds more closely if I have them in hand. If we have caught the wrong bird we make a false judgment. When hunting for some one kind of knowledge, as the various kinds fly about.... So in one example he thought eleven was twelve, because he caught the knowledge of twelve, which was within him, instead of that of eleven, caught a ring dove instead of a pigeon."

3. To transpose: in mathematics—to transfer a term with a changed sign from one side of an algebraic equation to the other so as not to destroy the equality of the

vidual minds, "owls" for other minds and abstract entities, and "aviaries" for holenmermism, the view that the whole of reality is continuous in its parts. Aristotle and Plotinus[4] claim orioles—indeed, even the most solipsistic of orioles—know owls to some considerable degree if for no other reason than this: orioles and owls share marks of the mental and fly about in aviaries, where the whole is in the part (*holenmermism*) and the world contains genuinely continuous phenomena together (*synechism*). Taken together, holenmermism coupled with synechism constitute an inversion of the egocentric view that orioles and owls know only themselves and live in their own singular aviary ways as well as an invitation to revisiting the problem of other minds.[5]

Horizons

In the *Theaetetus* Plato presents the mind and its constituents as an aviary of birds that leap into flight when our mind attempts to grasp them (*Theaet.*

---

members; in music—to move a chord, melody, composition upward or downward in pitch while retaining its internal interval structure—as said of players or instruments. See *OED*.

4. Aristotle's claim "the whole is in the part" is based on the notion that exclusion is always posterior to inclusion. Consequently, the perfection of divine *nous* thinking itself (καὶ ἔστιν ἡ νόησις νοήσεως νόησις) includes the intellection of individuals: "for to be perfect is to be complete and self-sufficient" and "that from which nothing is wanting." See *Phys.* 3.6 (207a8–15); *Metaph.* 7.8 (1074b33–35); 7.10 (1075b21–24); see also Enrico Berti, "The Intellection of Indivisibles according to Aristotle," in *Aristotle on Mind and Senses: Proceedings of the Seventh Symposium Aristotelicum*, ed. Geoffrey E. R. Lloyd and Gwilym E. L. Owen (Cambridge: Cambridge University Press, 1978), 141–63. The notion that "the whole is in the part" is based on Plotinus's doctrine that every form in Nous contains every other Form by the interiority of its relations to other Forms. Each Form is all the other Forms, and each mind is cognitively identical with each and every Form because the multiplicity of divine intellect is not spatially articulated. See Plotinus, *Enn.* 5.1.19–43; 5.8.3.30–34; 5.9.6; 5.9.8.3–7; see also Frederic M. Schroeder, "Plotinus and Language," in *The Cambridge Companion to Plotinus*, ed. Lloyd P. Gerson (Cambridge: Cambridge University Press, 1996), 336–55; Jean Trouillard, "The Logic of Attribution in Plotinus," *IPQ* 1 (1961): 125–38.

5. Popper contrasts "clouds"—his metaphor for indeterministic systems—with "clocks," meaning deterministic ones. Siding with indeterminism, he comments, "Peirce was right in holding that all clocks are clouds to some considerable degree— even the most precise of clocks. This, I think, is the most important inversion of the mistaken determinist view that all clouds are clocks." See Karl Popper, "Of Clouds and Clocks," in *Objective Knowledge* (Oxford: Oxford University Press, 1972), 215.

199a–b).[6] He is keen to distinguish possession of knowledge from having knowledge. Each new piece of knowledge is caught and caged. Actual knowledge is putting our hands on the bird we want when taking it out of the cage (201d–202c). However, we may put our hands on the wrong bird instead of the one we want, thereby acquiring false knowledge and judgment (201d–210d). The only way to arrive at justified true belief and knowledge is by appeal to logical arguments from justified true belief or mathematical proof (*Meno* 82b–85b).

Several claims frame what justified true belief may be. First, in the aviary simile birds represent functions of thought rather than memories of Forms, and false judgment resides not in our perceptions or thoughts but in the fitting together of perception and thought (*Theaet.* 195a; 197d). The challenge illustrated is—what if we ask what the sum of seven and five is? They could be added correctly such that 7+5=12; and they could be added incorrectly such that 7+5=11, not 12. If added incorrectly, one both has and does not have knowledge of twelve at the same time, which violates the principle of noncontradiction. Second, there are certain kinds of passive knowledge that require some application before knowledge itself becomes active (*Theaet.* 199a). There is a kind of knowledge we potentially have but do not actually possess.[7] Third, Plato proposes there are forms of both ignorance and knowledge in the aviary. Someone who has caught and caged wild birds possesses them all but may not have any in hand—although he can put his hand on them.[8] Fourth, Plato was among the first to parse ἀλήθεια (truth) as ορθότης (the correctness of statements) (*Crat.* 385a–c, 389a–390e). In order to have knowledge (ἐπιστήμη) true judgment (ορθότης) must be accompanied by discourse (logos; *Theaet.* 201d–202c). Fifth, since a distinction exists between simple apprehension

---

6. On uses of this simile with claims of the identity and relation of thinking and being, see Robert M. Berchman, "Of Hunting Doves and Pigeons: Aristotle Reading Plato and Parmenides. On Thinking and Being are the Same," *ScEs* 72 (2020): 31–48.

7. Socrates's example is that until we apply our knowledge of mathematics, even if we know the number twelve, we do not "possess" the knowledge that 7+5=12 (see Plato, *Theaet.* 198d). On this problem, see Myles Burnyeat, *The Theaetetus of Plato*, trans. M. Jane Levett (Indianapolis: Hackett, 1990), 112; Robert J. Roecklein, *Plato versus Parmenides* (Lanham, MD: Lexington Books, 2011), 176–77.

8. Each new piece of knowledge is caught and caged, but actual knowledge is putting our hands on the bird we "know" when taking it out of the cage. But we may put our hands on the wrong bird instead of the one we want, thereby having false knowledge and judgment (see *Theaet*, 197d–e, 199a–b).

and apprehension attended by discourse, knowledge (ἐπιστήμη) is denied to simple apprehension. Beliefs turned into knowledge are secured by providing foundations for them (*Theaet.* 201d–210d).

Three observations should be made before proceeding further. First, in the *Theaetetus* Socrates rejects the idea that a complex of parts such as 7 + 5 has a place in the wax block and denies there is a knowledge bird in the aviary that has parts (*Theaet.* 196a–b).[9] Second, adding Aristotle's claim that mind is a unity or whole distinct from the parts and particularity associated with bodies, it follows that mind as a unity, a whole, and an unformed form with no parts allows for the logical possibility not only that I have a mind but that other minds exist as well.[10] Third, if bodies are located in space and time and subject to the laws of physics, minds are causally different kinds of entities. Since they lack physical properties, minds can be described as incorporeal substances and thus not subject to the laws of physics.[11] If belief in the existence of other minds is warranted, Plotinus proposes that the internalization of the intelligible includes the recognition by my mind of other minds and the intelligible reality discovered within me; it is not merely of or about me, but intentionally of other minds and divine Nous as well (*Enn.* 4.7.10). Significantly, both Plotinus and Aristotle concur that while universals exist only in the mind, they have some foundation in the extramental natures of individuals of the *same class* that exhibit intellect as Nous and Forms do; and intelligibility as "abstract objects" such as mathematicals, meanings, and values do.

---

9. Also in the *Phaedo* (101c) he refuses to allow the form of duality to be divided into two instances of unity, and in the *Republic* (509ab) on the lower portion of the divided line there is the perishable object and its "images," likened to reflections in a mirror or on a surface of a lake, which are not divisible. For the *Sitz im Leben* of Plato's whole and parts argument, see Roecklein, *Plato versus Parmenides*, 146–58.

10. If the activity of *epistēmē* (thinking) is a *theorein* (theorizing) that contemplates ultimate causes and first principles, then *nous* must join *epistēmē* (thought) in *theoria* (contemplation), for it is *nous* that apprehends the causal structure of reality that *epistēmē* contemplates. Moreover, its subject matter is a *noēton* or a-synthetic whole (*asyntheta*), which manifests or constitutes itself in *noēsis* (thinking) as the unity of its *noēseōs* (on thinking; see *Metaph.* 12 [9.1076b34–35, 7.1072b22]).

11. Something is logically possible if it does not involve a contradiction and causally possible if it does not violate the laws of nature. It is logically possible that flying horses exist but logically impossible that Jane is both taller and shorter than Mary. It is causally impossible for a human to live without oxygen or travel faster than the speed of light.

Aristotle tacks further afar and fashions an epistemic regress argument where a set of beliefs is justified if it occurs in an evidential chain including at least two links: a supporting link (e.g., the evidence) and the supported link (e.g., the justified belief). Only chains anchored in foundational beliefs do not derive their justification from other beliefs. On this basis he claims a belief in other minds is justified. More precisely, if we have any justified beliefs, we have some foundational, noninferentially justified beliefs (*An. post.* 2.19 [99b15–100b19]). The epistemic regress argument is central to Aristotle's claim of the existence of other minds. The error implied in a denial of other minds lies in chains that are circular, endless, or ending in unjustified beliefs, or in which the term *mind* is put into the wrong ontological-semantic category, thereby committing a category mistake.[12] A crucial warrant in play here is Aristotle's principle of epistemic fit (*Eth. Nic.* 1 [3.1094b12–1095a12]).[13]

Mental Causality

Mind (νοῦς) is a key to mapping mental causality.[14] Aristotle's "thinking on thinking" (νόησις νοήσεως) is the pure act of thinking itself where the object of

12. See Aristotle concerning the attribute snub and concave in *Metaph.* 7 (1030b14–1031a14.5), esp. 1030b28–37. Interest in category mistakes in the 1930s and 1940s was initially fueled by Aristotle's notion that category mistakes reveal some deep facts about ontological and semantic categories. Following Edmund Husserl, Gilbert Ryle claimed that distinguishing between categories is the primary task of metaphysics. See Ryle, "Categories," *PAS* NS 38 (1937–1938): 189–206. On category mistakes, see Ryle, *The Concept of Mind* (Chicago: University of Chicago Press, 2002), 3.

13. We should fit our epistemic evaluations in an appropriate way to the subject matter under investigation. It is not expected that mathematical claims be evaluated by the kind of arguments that would apply to other epistemologies. Hence, epistemologies of science, history, ethics, aesthetics, and theology do not offer models for epistemology of mathematics. Additionally, just as there are regional ontologies, there are also regional epistemologies of mathematics, including Platonism, mathematical Platonism, logicism, intuitionism, formalism, symbolism, and predicativism.

14. The primitive form of νόησις is *nosis, eos.* In Homer *noos* has several meanings, the most significant being a deeper insight itself. *Noos* penetrates behind the surface appearance to its real nature. In the Homeric poems νοός and νοεῖν are closely related to the sense of vision—ἰδεῖν and γιγνώσκειν. Neither in Homer nor in the Homeric poems, however, do νοός and νοεῖν mean propositional/discursive "reasons" or "reasoning." Nonetheless, each word denotes a thinkable as opposed to a visible disposition. With Xenophanes a different meaning emerges. God is altogether and

thinking is the *concept* of self-contemplation and *noēsis* is the *act* of self-con-templation.[15] Its act and object are different in form but the same in content (*Metaph.* 8.9). An even thicker content of self-contemplation emerges with Alexander's, Alcinous's, and Plotinus's reading of *noēsis noēseōs* (Alcinous, *Ep.* 10.2–5; Alexander, *De an.* 80–92; *De in.* 106.19–108.7). Although Plotinus's *nous* and the self-reflective structure of *noēsis noēseōs* harbor a formal distinction between the concept and act of self-contemplation, "thought thinking itself" does not presuppose phenomenal consciousness because its causal role and intentional context consist in its being thought eternally without interruption (*Enn.* 5.4.2; 5.6.1–2). *Nous* is thus a principle that con-tains the intelligible Forms of all things, including numbers, and its *noēsis* is a self-reflexivity, a self-contemplation, and a self-knowledge.[16] Here, through

---

exclusively νόον and is different in νόημα from mortal beings. The notion that νοός is something exceptional becomes prevalent in the generation after Xenophanes, espe-cially with Heraclitus. In Heraclitus, νοός is still the noun belonging to λέγειν. How-ever, νοός is now what few people possess because it has to do with ἀλήθεια λέγειν, to say true things. Saying true things, in turn, is λόγος, and it has as its focus insight into the divine νόμος that governs everything. By inhaling this λόγος we become νοεροί or acquire νοός. Again, with Heraclitus, νοός is far removed from discursive/propositional "reason" or "reasoning." Associated by Plato with νοῦς (intelligence, understanding), νόησις is not a thinking of extrinsic properties but a thinking of intrinsic properties/ forms (εἰδή). Any thinking via images, representations, calculations, deductions, or discursive propositions is not thinking where thinking and being are numerically the same. See Kurt von Fritz, "*Nous, Noein* and Their Derivatives in Presocratic Philoso-phy (Excluding Anaxagoras)," in *The Pre-Socratics: A Collection of Critical Essays*, ed. Alexander P. D. Mourelatos (Princeton: Princeton University Press, 1993), 23–85, esp. 23–43.

15. See Klaus Brinkmann, "Preface," in *Aristotle and Plotinus on the Intellect*, by Mark J. Nyvlt (Lanham, MD: Lexington Books, 2012), x–xii; Alcinous, *The Hand-book of Platonism*, trans. John Dillon (Oxford: Oxford University Press, 1993), 102–10; Frederic M. Schroeder, "The Analogy of the Active Intellect to Light in the 'de Anima' of Alexander of Aphrodisias," *Hermes* 109 (1981): 215–25.

16. Νοῦς, νόησις, συναίσθησις, and their cognates are best translated as "self-reflex-ivity," not "consciousness." Victor Caston notes that "consciousness" claims in Aris-totle become problematic. See Caston, "Aristotle on Consciousness," *Mind* 111.444 (2002): 752–815. Blumenthal, Gurtler, and Gerson appear to concur in the case of Plotinus. See Blumenthal, *Soul and Intellect*, 203–19; Gary Gurtler, "Plotinus: Self and Consciousness," in *Plato Redivivus*, ed. John Finamore and Robert Berchman (New Orleans: Southern University Press, 2005), 113–30; Lloyd P. Gerson, ed., *Aristotle and Other Platonists* (Ithaca, NY: Cornell University Press, 2005), 131–72. Also see refer-ences to consciousness in Eyjólfur K. Emilsson, *Plotinus on Intellect* (Oxford: Oxford

knowing, understanding, and contemplating, one becomes self-aware or self-reflective of other minds.[17]

Plotinus postulates a particular kind of mental causality, that is, self-knowledge, with claims that sentience has its origins in a hypostatic emanation from the One. In *Enn.* 5.4.2 the One "thinks" the existence of intelligibles. An early work also gives a picture of what Plotinus means (*Enn.* 6.9).[18] Degrees of unity give rise to degrees of being. Plotinus's key point is that being and unity are different, and being requires unity and makes it what it is as the cause of its existence, so that "it is by the One that all beings are beings ... bound together by the One" (*Enn.* 6.9.2.19–20 [Armstrong]). In this sense, mental causality, or what Plotinus calls cognition, is present in a thing's organization and can be traced from Nature to Soul, Intellect, and to the One itself.

Plotinus also claims that the lower realities are within their principle (*Enn.* 5.2.2.13), that the last and lowest things are in the last of those before them, and these are in those prior to them, and one thing is in another up to the first, which is the principle (*Enn.* 5.5.9.5–7).[19] Each of the hypostases has an internal and external activity with the latter following the former. Internal activity is self-contained, while external activity results in a product that is other than itself. Thus while the One is above and prior to *nous* (*Enn.* 6.9.6.50–55), and does not turn on itself in a self-reflexive moment (*Enn.* 6.1.6.15–19) but remains *kata ten noēsin* (*Enn.* 6.9.6.50–55; 5.6.6.8–11), *noēsis* is not the thinking subject but the cause of thinking activity. In nuce, the One's *noēsis* transcends the *noēsis* of *nous*.[20] Indeed, in *Enn.* 5.4.2 the One's *noēsis* is perceived as an object of thought (*noēton*).

University Press, 2007); Emilsson, *Plotinus on Sense Perception* (Cambridge: Cambridge University Press, 1988).

17. *Synaisthomai* is to perceive simultaneously (see Aristotle, *Eth. Nic.* 1170b4; Plotinus, *Enn.* 4.4.24; 6.4.6). Its cognate συναίσθησις refers to being aware of oneself as in self-reflexivity (see *Enn.* 3.8.4).

18. Kevin Corrigan, "Essence and Existence in the Enneads," in *The Cambridge Companion to Plotinus*, ed. Lloyd P. Gerson (Cambridge: Cambridge University Press, 1996), 109–10.

19. Focus of inquiry here involves mapping of the different kinds of self-knowledge and subjectivity beginning with *nous noeseos* in Aristotle and continuing with Plotinus's concepts ranging from κατανόησις and συναίσθησις to παρακολούθησις.

20. Kevin Corrigan, "Enneads 5, 4 [7] 2 and Related Passages: A New Interpretation of the Status of the Intelligible Object," *Hermes* 114 (1986): 195–203.

But an ambiguity remains of the transition of the One to the complete development of *nous*.[21]

While the internal activity of the One is directed toward itself, its external activity or overflowing causes two intellects to emerge: one is a potential *nous* or that which is other than itself, and the other an actualized *nous* in sameness with itself. With the emergence of a potential and actual *nous*, two kinds of plurality arise: one a duality of subject and object of thought, and the other a plurality within objects thought. Plotinus thus maintains that intelligible objects are not without *nous* as subject, for intelligible objects are within *nous* as thinking subject (*Enn.* 5.4.2 .10–12): "Thinking which sees the intelligible and turns toward it and is, in a way, being perfected by it, is itself indefinite like seeing, but is defined by the intelligible. This is why it is said: from the Indefinite Dyad and the One derive the Forms and numbers: that is Intellect" (*Enn.* 5.4.2.7–10).

This level of seeing constitutes a kind of self-reflexivity or a *noēsis* called κατανόσις that differs in kind from *nous*. In this higher or proto-intellection *nous* is fully aware of the intelligibles and the One (*Enn.* 6.9.6.50–55]). Plotinus calls *Nous* a σύνθεσις, a composition just as the number series is a σύνθεσις (*Enn.* 5.4.2.9; 5.3.12.10–11). Both have ontological and epistemological syntax. Here, Plotinus equates numbers and Intellect. Numbers with the Forms that come from the One and Indefinite Dyad are a composition, a structure, a fitting together. Thus the content of *nous* is not simple but many. It manifests composition; it sees many things in a duality of thinking subject and intelligible object—including other minds.

Much of what Plotinus proposes goes back to Aristotle, who argues that thought entails the thinking subject and the apprehended object, and this combination is a single active moment in which the potential intellect and the object apprehended by it are actually united. The salient point is self sees the object of thought as part of itself by the object and form of the object—an activity that *nous* apprehends immediately (*Phys.* 3.3; *De an.* 2.5; 3.3–8). Aristotle's insight influenced Plotinus on rethinking the role of the Indefinite in the emergence of Nous from the One.[22] A duality and plurality of the self emerges here which triggers a *We* and an *I* thinking— both of which are fully formed and actualized visions of the One from

---

21. Nyvlt, *Aristotle and Plotinus*, 146–47.
22. See Corrigan, "Essence and Existence," 109–10; Nyvlt, *Aristotle and Plotinus*, 147–54.

the precipice of *nous*.[23] for it possesses a contemplative force within itself as activity: "We are the activity of nous so that when that is active we are active" (*Enn.* 1.4.9.29–30). Aristotle's concept of intelligible matter is also borrowed by Plotinus, who defines it within the context of geometrical figures as the genus of a definition as a circle is a plane figure (*Metaph.* 8.6 [1045a36]). It is in this sense that intelligible matter covers the rational basis for the emergence of species and individuals[24] characterized by otherness (ἑτερότης), movement (κίνησις), and what is indefinite (ἀόριστος; *Enn.* 2.4.5.32–35; see 6.1.5.7–8). Thus intelligible matter is neither a simple substance like the One or a composite one such as *nous*. Its thinking activity marks the limits of its nature (*Enn.* 6.2.8.22–24). Nonetheless, it is the condition for the possibility of plurality in Intellect. The One's generation of Nous includes both the indefinite and definite aspects of a single eternal movement of the One's unity into the multiplicity of intelligible life—which includes minds and other abstract objects.[25]

Mental Causality and Other Minds

Aristotle's and Plotinus's parsing of mind and mental causality opens access to other minds.[26] First, Aristotle notes humans are animals that can contemplate things in isolation and that reality has an intelligibility that can be

---

23. Emilsson, *Plotinus on Intellect*, 69–123.

24. Alexander and Plotinus later align Aristotle's doctrine with his doctrine of extension. See Alexander of Aphrodisias, *Comm. Metaph.* 510.3; Plotinus, *Enn.* 6.6.3.

25. See Nyvlt, *Aristotle and Plotinus*, 152.

26. Aristotle views the soul as a unity and the form of the body with a set or sum of capacities (see *De an.* 2.3 [414b28–32, 413a3–5]). The psychology of the faculty of the soul begins with mind (*nous*) as "the part of the soul by which it knows and understands" (*De an.* 3.4 [429a9–10]; see also 3.3 [428a5], 3.9 [432b26], 3.12 [434b3]). While not strictly a contradiction (a common objection is the "paradox" of how the active intellect could be separable if it is a capacity of the soul and the soul is not separable), after characterizing mind and its activities, he divides the human soul into five special senses, three inner senses (common sense, imagination, and memory), and two outer senses (active and passive intellect; see *De an.* 3.5 [430a17–18, 430a23]). Later readings of Aristotle and Plotinus include the doctrine of localization of function wherein each faculty has a specific brain function: e.g., those of Galen, Avicenna, Fodor, and localizationalist theories. Alternative theories of mind include mind as a unity with various capabilities: e.g., of Ockham and multiple capabilitalism; unity theory, wherein mind has one function: e.g., those of Descartes, Hume, and associationalism; and distributionist, mass-action, behaviorist, functionalist, identity, and

known and spoken about.[27] As soon as it is asserted that reality has a logical structure and that mind (*nous*) has the capacity to know that structure, it follows that in mapping reality minds become a part of the intelligibility of the cosmos itself.[28] Second, Plotinus proposes that the world-soul and world-intellect are not merely "out there" but that we also find them within ourselves (*Enn.* 6.6.2.10–17; 6.6.16.42).[29] Here Aristotle and Plotinus talk about intellect and its activities as somehow different from soul and its activities.[30] They propose a separable intellect without which there would be no cognition, and a self-reflexive cognition (*noēsis*) requiring incorporeality.[31] Plotinus goes so far as to divide soul into two parts—descended and undescended—with soul's rationality exhibiting two powers, one that is rational and reflective and another that is temporal and erring.[32]

However, by descent into a corporeal and extended being, soul may lose touch with its intelligibility, only to regain contact with its undescended origins with the assistance of judgment, imagination, and memory.[33] Nei-

eliminative materialist theories of the brain: e.g., those of Gall, Skinner, Churchland, and physicalism.

27. John Cleary, "Powers That Be," in *Studies on Plato, Aristotle, and Proclus: The Collected Essays on Ancient Philosophy of John Cleary* (Leiden: Brill, 2013), 19–64.

28. Thomas De Koninck, "La noesis et L'indivisible selon Aristote," in *La naissance de la raisonen Grece: Acts du Congres de Nice Mai 1987*, ed. Jean-François Mattei (Paris: Presses Universitaires de France, 1990), 215–18.

29. See Richard Sorabji, *Time, Creation, and the Continuum* (Bristol: Bristol Classical Press, 2015), 138–39.

30. Henry J. Blumenthal, *Plotinus' Psychology: His Doctrines of the Embodied Soul* (The Hague: Nijhoff, 1971), 109–11; Lloyd P. Gerson, *Plotinus* (London: Routledge, 1994), 254–57; F. P. Hager, "Die Aristotlesinterpretation des Alexander von Aphrodisias und die Aristoteleskritik Plotinus bezüglich der Lehre vom Geist," *AGP* 46 (1964): 174–87.

31. See Henry J. Blumenthal, "On Soul and Intellect," in Gerson, *Cambridge Companion to Plotinus*, 82–104; Lloyd P. Gerson, *God and Greek Philosophy. Studies in the Early History of Natural Theology* (London: Routledge, 1990), 186, 191–201; Gerson, *Aristotle and Other Platonists*, 131–72, 196–200; Michael Wagner, "Veridical Causation in Plotinus," in *The Structure of Being*, ed. R. Baine Harris (Albany: State University of New York Press, 1982), 51–72.

32. With Plotinus's reading Aristotle via Alexander's *De an.* 13.9–24 (see Blumenthal, "On Soul and Intellect," 96–97).

33. Imagination (φαντασία) and memory (ἀνάμνησις) also play key roles in mapping epistemology of aesthetics. Because an immense bibliography exists relating to both faculties, a study of each stands outside the scope of this study. For overviews on both mental states, see Eyjólfur K. Emilsson, "Cognition and Its Object," in Gerson,

ther memory as impressions on wax, nor, imagination which includes
perceptions, entirely suppresses the descended soul's intelligibility, however (*Enn.* 4.7.6.38–50; 3.6.1.4–27). Judgment, together with memory
and imagination, are partless and noncorporeal forms of thought. Thus,
unlike sense perception, whenever judging, remembering, and imagining
occur, the soul's intelligible substance is not adversely affected. Indeed, in
judging, remembering, and imagining what number is, soul reinforces its
connection with its own intelligibility (*Enn.* 4.4.19.13; 4.7.8.10–13).

The Problem of Other Minds

Aristotle's and Plotinus's arguments for other minds take the logical form
of a *modus ponens* argument.

1. If we have *nous*, then *epistēmē* plays an important role in jus-
    tifying our beliefs in other minds.
2. We have *nous*.
Therefore, *epistēmē* plays an important role in justifying our belief
in other minds.

The existence of other minds is tied to two additional notions: (1) identity
theory, that mental states are the same and ultimately are reducible to those
of divine *nous*; and (2) that minds are immaterial thinking substances with
mental properties. Arguments in support of these claims are the conceiv-
ability and intentionality arguments. The first argument rests on the claim
that if we can conceivably find at least one property of minds shared by all
minds, we are entitled to draw the conclusion that other minds exist.[34] The
second proposes that if intentionality is a property of mental states to represent something else, and only minds share this property, we are entitled
to claim other minds exist.[35]

Cambridge Companion to Plotinus, 222–23; Stephen R. L. Clark, "Plotinus: Body and
Soul," in Gerson, *Cambridge Companion to Plotinus*, 280–81.

34. This is a weaker version of Leibniz's law that A and B are identical with each
other if they share *all* properties in common.

35. In standard form this argument appears as follows: (1) I can conceive of
mental properties shared by all minds. (2) I cannot conceive that minds exist without mental states and properties. (3) If minds share at least one mental property, i.e.,
intentionality, then other minds exist. (4) If mental states and properties are ultimately

Plato's arguments for knowledge of whole, not-complex objects constitute the basis for the possibility of other minds. The problem of other minds begins by assuming that everyone knows how to divide the world into the mental (inner) and the physical (outer). Plato suggests an epistemic distinction between two kinds of mental states, outer and inner: "So if the real is the object of knowledge, then the object of belief must be something other than the real" (*Resp.* 478b). Aristotle—a water-diviner pointing out the metaphysical traps of his predecessors—suggests that there is probably *something* to the notion that *nous* is separable even though nothing else about the soul is, and it is on this claim that we have justified true belief in the existence of other minds. First, because as a kind of power (δυνάμει πως) it can think itself; second, because it thinks all things it is unmixed (ἀπαθές); third, because though it is nothing at all until it thinks, it is the power (δύναμις) of becoming all objects of thought (*noēta*) when it thinks (*De an.* 3.4 [429b5–9], 3.4.18–20, 3.5.3); and fourth, since an *epistēmē* of essences or truths as *theoria* is available to *nous*, knowledge (*epistēmē*) provides answers to what my mind and other minds may be.[36] Plotinus ups the ante to propose that the internalization of the intelligible includes the recognition by my mind of other minds and the intelligible reality discovered within me; it is not merely of or about me but of other minds and divine Nous as well (*Enn.* 4.7.10). Significantly, both Aristotle and Plotinus concur that while universals exist only in the mind, they have some foundation in the extramental natures of individuals of the *same class* that exhibit intellect as Nous and Forms do; and intelligibility as abstract objects such as mathematicals, meanings, and values do.

Ego-Identity and Nous-Identity

When Aristotle and Plotinus propose that it is possible to know other minds, they do not argue that *my* mind is not a mind among other minds, or that *I* am not one person among others, or that knowledge

---

reducible to a divine intellect, then all minds and mental states and properties are reducible with the mental states and properties of this divine intellect. Therefore: the states and properties of my mind and other minds exist because they are reducible and identical with those of a divine intellect.

36. Aristotle claims it is not with the body that *nous* is to be contrasted but with particularity. See n. 10, above.

of other minds depends on *my* mind for justification. The fact of *my* intellect, *my* consciousness, or *my* self-consciousness is not simply a subjective mental state, *my* brain activity, or *my* response to external empirical events suggestive of a subjective reception of brute facts tout court—but something rather different. There is no longer only a personal *ego* thinking only internal mental states; there is an interpersonal *nous* thinking other minds—which amounts to the disappearance of a *me* and the acquisition of a *we* knowing. *Ego* (*I*) concepts of self-reference are abandoned, and the subject becomes a *nous* (*We*) self where the potential to think is brought to activity by receiving forms and concepts.

Here Aristotle and Plotinus are keen to stress that when *I* raise myself to Nous and intellection, *I* in no sense lose my identity. *I* merely think as Nous does, thus becoming like *Nous*—a *totum simul*. In an attempt to clarify what self-identity as *ego* and *nous* identity means, Aristotle claims in *Metaphysica* 12 (1072b18–23) that thought thinks itself through "participation" in the object of thought:

> And thought thinking itself deals with that which is best in itself; and that which is thinking in the fullest sense with that which is best in the fullest sense. And thought thinks itself because it shares the nature of the object of thought; for it becomes an object of thought in coming into contact/touch with and thinking its objects, so that thought and object of thought are the same. But it is active when it possesses this object. Therefore the possession rather than the receptivity is the divine element which thought seems to contain, and the act of contemplation is what is most pleasant and best. (*Metaph.* 12 [1072b18–23] [Tredennick and Armstrong])

At *Metaph.* 12.9 (1074b34–35), we are told all forms of cognition are intentionally "of something else" (ἤ ἄλλο) and only incidentally of themselves: "Therefore it must be of itself [αὐτὸν ἄρα νοεῖ] that the divine thought thinks [since it is the most excellent of things] and its thinking is a thinking on thinking" (*Metaph.* 12.9 [1072b34–35]). In *De an.* 3.2 (425b26–27), Aristotle says that the object and the thinking of it are one in *energeia* but different in τὸ εἶναι: "The activity of the sensible object and that of the percipient sense is one and the same activity and yet the distinction between their being remains. Take as illustration actual sound and actual hearing" (*De an.* 3.2 [425b26–27]). Aristotle also claims, in a few broken lines in *De an.* 3.5 (430a14–25), that *nous* ποιητικός makes all things:

Mind ... is what it is by virtue of becoming all things, while there is
another which is what it is by virtue of making all things: this is sort of
a positive state like light; for in a sense light makes potential colors into
actual colors. Mind in this sense is separable, impassible, unmixed, since
it is in its essential nature activity for always the active is superior to the
passive, the originating force to the matter which it forms. Actual knowledge is identical with its object: in the individual, potential knowledge is
in time but in the universe as a whole it is not prior even in time. Mind
is not at one time knowing and another time not. When mind is set free
from its present conditions it appears just as it is and nothing more: this
alone is eternal and immortal ... while mind in this sense is impassible;
mind as passive is destructible and without it nothing thinks. (*De an.* 3.5
[430a14–25])

In nuce, thought actually creates the truths it understands, just as light
may be said to make the colors we see by its aid. This *nous* ποιητικός, he
cryptically adds, is separable from matter, impassive, unmixed, and essentially in its nature an activity that receives universals without embodying
them in matter, thereby acquiring *epistēmē*. A point stressed is not the
survival of *nous* but rather the indestructibility of *epistēmē* based on a
nous identity distinct from an *ego* identity.[37] Plotinus builds on Aristotle's
thought experiment. *Nous* is a thinking of abstract objects that are its own
contents. *Nous* is a hypostasis composed of Forms, or at least every species in the world as well as all moral and mathematical forms.[38] Here the
Forms are not merely self-subsistent universals but beings who think. This
follows from Plotinus's identification of Intellect with the Forms:

Intellect is all things [ὁ δὲ νοῦς πάντα] ... and the whole is universal
intellect and being, Intellect making being exist in thinking it, and being

---

37. It is difficult to say whether one should view *nous* as a special substance
attached to each human body, as a special power (δύναμις) that the body has, or a
single substance that was shared by humans. Aristotle vacillated between the first
two options with later Platonists, and Aristotelians vacillated between the second and
third. Augustine proposes the simplest and most controversial solution of all. The soul
is immortal because it is the subject or seat of reason (*episteme*), which is eternal: "The
human body is mutable and reason is immutable. For all which does not exist always
in the same mode is mutable, but that two and two are four exists always in the same
mode.... This sort of reasoning, then, is immutable. Therefore reason is immutable"
(Augustine, *Immort. an.* 61).

38. Plotinus's starting point is *Soph. elench.* 248e–249a.

giving Intellect thinking and existence by being thought ... but this one
is two things: Intellect and being and thinking and thought; Intellect as
thinking and being as thought. (*Enn.* 5.1.4.26–32)

And with identification of individual Forms and individual intellects:
"Intellect and the intelligible substance; each individual Idea is not other
than Intellect, but each is Intellect. And Intellect as a whole is all the
Forms, and each individual Form is an individual intellect.... We must
assume that the real beings have their place in the thinking subject" (*Enn.*
5.9.8.1–7). And: "This is the kind of thinking that the human intellect may
do when the soul is free from interference from the sensible world and reasoning about it. Plotinus puts it aptly: human intellect [*nous*] is a substance
or being [*ousia*] that accesses Intellect [Nous] by turning toward it" (*Enn.*
5.3.30.27–45). For

> contemplation must be the same as the contemplated, and Intellect the
> same as the intelligible; for if not the same, there will be no truth; for who
> is trying to possess realities will possess an impression different from
> the realities, and this is not truth. For truth ought not to be the truth of
> something else but to be what it says. In this way, Intellect and the intel-
> ligible are one, and this is reality and the first reality, and also the first
> Intellect which possess the real beings, or rather is the same as the real
> beings ... for the intellection will in a way encompass the intelligible or
> be the same as the intelligible.... All together are one, Intellect, intellec-
> tion, the intelligible. If therefore Intellect's intellection is the intelligible,
> and the intelligible is itself, [then] it will itself think itself.... And in a
> turning way from any distractions arising from lower levels of reality....
> The intellectual act is without parts ... the verbal expression unfolds its
> contents and brings it out of the intellectual act into the image making
> power, and so shows the intellectual act as if in a mirror, and this is how
> there is apprehension and persistence and memory of it. The intellectual
> act is one thing and the apprehension of it another, and we are always
> intellectively active but do not always apprehend our activity; and this is
> because that which receives it does not only receive acts of intelligence
> but ... perceptions. (*Enn.* 5.3.30.11–16)

Plotinus makes a significant move here. Corresponding to the state of
the knower's identity with the known by raising ourselves to Nous, we
in no sense lose self-identity but heighten it.[39] By raising *I* to the level

---

39. See, Blumenthal, "On Soul and Intellect."

of *We*, *nous*-identity sublates *ego*-identity and obtains not only attentive-ness (παρακολουθεῖν) but self-awareness (κατανόησις) and self-reflexivity (συναίσθησις). "Often I have woken up out of the body to myself and have entered into myself, going out from all other things; I have seen a beauty wonderfully great and felt assurance that then most of all I belonged to the better part; I have actually lived the best life and come to identify with the divine ... setting myself all the rest of that which is in the intelligible" (*Enn.* 4.8.1.1–7). Aristotle and Plotinus claim that *my* mind (*nous*) is related to other minds because it is dependent on a suprapersonal mind (Nous) that causes my mind and other minds.

Thinking Other Minds

We cannot enter the bone-chilling waters of thinking other minds again without reference to two concepts: (1) "to perceive at the same time," or "to be aware of oneself" (συναισθάνομαι; Aristotle, *Hist. an.* 534b18; *Eth. Nic.* 1170b4; see also Porphyry, *Sent.* 36.12; Plotinus, *Enn.* 4.4.24; 6.4.6); and (2) "self-reflexivity" (συναίσθησις; *Enn.* 3.8.4). Après studies by Pierre Hadot and Walter Beierwaltes, a *Trümmerfeld* of problems concerning the relationship between συναίσθησις, Nous, and the One emerges that cannot be adequately addressed here.[40] However, a reconsideration of sight, illu-mination, touch, and participation while thinking other minds clarifies what intentional self-reflexivity entails. As we have seen, Aristotle and Plotinus claim that sight, illumination, touch, and participation in Nous (or the One) triggers self-awareness and self-reflexivity, and without such self-awareness or self-reflexivity thinking wholes or other minds would be impossible. Such sight, illumination, touch, and participation are not to be taken as mere metaphor or simile. Rather, they are real "abstract entities" or "noetic meanings" akin to "clear and distinct" ideas or mental states we cannot help but giving assent to as *epistēmē* because they meet an indu-

---

40. Pierre Hadot, "Revue of H-S2," *RBPH* 164 (1963): 92–95. Hadot's thesis is that Plotinus would lack precision if he were to assert the subject of *epistrophē* to *nous* rather than to the One—for *nous* is an image and product of the One, and *nous* does not turn toward the One until after (metaphysically posterior) it is generated in order to become actualized, for self-identity involves not only the sticky problem of (1) what the subject is of *epistrophē* (procession) and *prohodos* (return) but also (2) the nature of an inchoate/unfinished and a conscious *nous*. See Walter Beierwaltes, "Die Metaphysik des Lichtes in der Philosophie Plotins," *ZPF* 15 (1961): 334–62.

bitable criterion—what thought thinks is always a universal—a "unity," a "whole" or a "form" (*Parm.* 142c–d).

1. Touching

Aristotle is keen to parse "touch" (contact) to signify a unitary knowledge that guarantees the certainty and truth of what we think: "But [a] truth or falsity is as follows—contact and assertion are truth [assertion is not the same as affirmation] and ignorance is non-contact" (*Metaph.* 9.8 [1051b24–25, 1072b21]). Aristotle claims further that in touching truth a thinker is identical with the object of its thought and thus a knower of truth:[41]

> Truth and falsity are as follows: contact [θίγειν] and assertion [φάναι] are truth [for assertion is not the same as affirmation], and ignorance is non-contact [μὴ θιγγάνειν]. I say ignorance, because it is impossible to be deceived with respect to what a thing is, except accidentally [ἢ κατὰ συμβεβηκός]; and the same applies to in composite substances [τὰς μὴ συνθετὰς οὐσίας], for it is impossible to be deceived about them. And they all exist actually [ἐνεργείᾳ], not potentially [οὐ δυνάμει]; but as it is Being itself is not generated nor destroyed [οὐ γίγνεται οὐδὲ φθείρεται].... With respect, then, to all things which are essences and actual [εἶναί τι καὶ ἐνεργείᾳ], there is no question of being mistaken, but only of thinking or not thinking [ἀλλ᾽ ἢ νοεῖν ἢ μή] them ... truth means to think these objects [τὸ νοεῖν ταῦτα], and there is no falsity or deception. (*Metaph.* 9.10 [1051b25–1052a2])

Aristotle proposes that touch always involves an either/or. A tactile intellect either knows or does not know. This is because in the activity of touch-thinking, *noēsis* is an activity (ἐνεργεία) that results in contemplation, *theoria* rather than movement or a process (κίνησις). In touch-thinking we do not predicate anything of anything (τι κατά τινος; *De an.* 3.6 [430b28]), nor is there any assertion (κατάφασις; *Metaph.* 9.8 [1051b24]), and the

---

41. Aristotle, *Metaph.* 1.5 (986b19–21): "Either as a unity of definition or as materially one: It appears that Parmenides conceived of the Unity as one in definition, but Melissus as materially one. Hence the former says that it is finite, and the latter that it is infinite ... but Xenophanes, the first exponent of Unity [for Parmenides is said to have been his disciple] gave no definite teaching, nor does he seem to have touched [θιγεῖν] either of these conceptions of Unity."

objects of such knowledge are incomposite (ἀσύνθετα; ἀδιαίρετα; *Metaph.* 9.8 [1051b17]; *De an.* 430a26); in that they do not involve matter and form, and in this kind of thinking you cannot be mistaken.

Plotinus also associates thinking and touching but with a caveat. The thinker never remains identical with the object of its thought:

> Therefore the thinker must apprehend one thing different from another and the object of thought in being thought must contain variety; or there will not be a thought of it [*noēsis*] but only a touching and a sort of contact [θίξις ... ἐπαφὴ] without speech or thought, pre-thinking [προνοοῦσα] because Intellect has not yet come into being, and that which touches [*thinganon*] does not think [οὐ νοοῦντος]. But the thinker must not itself remain simple, especially in so far as it thinks itself: for it will duplicate itself, even if it gives an understanding which is silent. (*Enn.* 5.3.10.42–48)

Plotinus holds that the possibility of true and certain knowledge is grasped only if the object known is identical (qualitatively, not numerically) with the subject that knows it—or a divine *nous* whose object of thought is itself (*Enn.* 5.5.2.18–20). In this self-presence of knower and known, there is no spatial distance, no mediating image or representation (*Enn.* 5.5.2.18–20), no separation between knower and known that intervenes so as to turn self-knowledge into an unreliable, unverifiable knowledge of something else. These conclusions require a good deal more explanation than can be provided here. But now that we know what touching truth means, let us see what it means to become one with divine Intellect and thus with other minds as well via participation and identity.

2. Illumination

The analogy between seeing and illumination is a deeply embedded Platonic one—the intelligible light of the Forms is the analog of the light that renders material things visible. Intelligible light emanates from the supreme Form, the Good, to illuminate inferior forms, thus rendering them intelligible; and the mind that understands them like the sun makes other things visible by illuminating them (*Resp.* 509b). Aristotle is keen to associate the mind with light and illumination at the level of perception. But he also claims that active intellect (*nous poietikos*) makes all things into actual colors—just as the presence of light to an object of thought illuminates it.[42] "Mind in the passive sense [*nous pathetikos*] is such because it becomes all things but mind in the active sense [*nous poietikos*] has another aspect in that it makes all things. This is a kind of positive state like light; for in a sense light makes potential into actual colors" (*De an.* 3.5 [430a15–17]). And: "Actual knowledge is identical with its object.... When isolated it is its true self and nothing more and this alone is immortal and everlasting ... and without this nothing thinks" (*De an.* 3.5 [430a20–25]). Alexander reads these passages as the juxtaposition of the subject of reflection and the reflective surface of the mind with self-reflection a joint effect produced by both (*De an.* 42.19–43 [Bruns]).

Light and illumination also provide a meaning mechanism and thus a bridge from Aristotle to Plato. Here Plotinus criticizes Aristotle's and Alexander's analysis of light as a mere extrinsic commonplace, noting that light is an activity (ἐνεργεία) that proceeds from a luminous source, not the effect that arises from the source of illumination and the illuminated object.[43] Reflection as an instance of illumination is a master metaphor in Plotinus.[44] For light to be is for it to be present—as pure intrinsic presence.[45] Behind these claims stands a long tradition of *Lichtmetaphysik* wherein images of the Good as the source of light and intelligibility are employed to parse (1) the derivation of Nous from the One, (2) the One's interior presence to mind, (3) the mind's participation in Nous, and (4) *nous* dwelling in the human soul and teaching it from within noetic illumination.[46] Key claims also include light, and its source is qua luminous (*Enn.* 5.1.7.1–6): that the light we see with our own eyes is incorporeal even if its source is corporeal (*Enn.* 4.5.7.41–42); that since Nous flows from the One like a light from the sun (*Enn.* 5.3.12.40–44), its procession from the One is a shining out or an irradiation (περίλαμψις, ἐπίλαμψις; *Enn.* 5.1.6.26–29). And since the generation of the intelligible world is

---

42. Schroeder, "Plotinus and Language," 341–43.

43. Plotinus's use of Plato's "light" sources and metaphors are many (see Beierwaltes, "Die Metaphysik des Lichtes").

44. Sara Rappe, *Reading Neoplatonism: Non-discursive Thinking in the Texts of Plotinus, Proclus and Damascius* (Cambridge: Cambridge University Press, 2000), 169–70; Frederic M. Schroeder, "Plotinus and Interior Space," in *Neoplatonism and Indian Philosophy*, ed. Paulos Gregorios (Albany: State University of New York Press, 2002), 25–28.

45. The locus classicus is *Enn.* 4.5.7.35–49. For commentary, see Gurtler, *Ennead IV.4.30–45 and IV.5* (Vegas: Parmenides, 2015), 230–70.

46. Corrigan, "Essence and Existence," 118–20.

an act of vision, reflection itself is illumination (*Enn.* 4.5.7.41–41; see 6.4.10.14; 5.8.4.42–43).

Plotinus's claim "reflection is illumination" results in a refinement of Aristotle's focal theory of meaning. Intellect's intentionality, identity, and relation to the One are of pure light and the actualization of light. And once Mind abstracts (ἀφέσει) the objects of its vision (or the Forms) it sees the One—πρὸς ἕν, not πάντα ἕν. Here light not only illuminates focal objects of awareness such as Forms and other minds. It also illuminates the cause of a focal meaning of awareness itself—the One (*Enn.* 5.5.7.16–21).

Participation and Identity

Participation, identity, touch, and sight are also mental marks that *nous* has of Nous and other minds as well. Aristotle claims when inner mental processes meet external criteria, thought and the object of thought are the same. And Nous thinks on itself to the extent that it participates or partakes (*kata metalepsin*) in the object of thought (*noēton*). It becomes the *noēton* when it touches and intuitively apprehends its objects so that thought and the object of thought are the same (ὥστε ταὐτὸν νοῦς καὶ νοητόν; *Metaph.* 12.7 [1072b22–23]). Moreover, such participation and touching is an active possession of thought as thought:

> For that which is capable of receiving the noēton and the *ousia* is Nous. But it is active when it possesses it [ἐνεργεῖ δὲ ἔχων]. Hence it is actuality rather than potentiality that is held to be the divine possession of rational thought [ὁ νοῦς θεῖον ἔχειν] and its active contemplation [*theoria*] is that which is most pleasant and best. (*Metaph.* 12.7 [1072b23–25])

It is in this sense that: "Nous thinks itself [αὑτὸν ἄρα νοεῖ] ... and its thinking is thinking on thinking [ἡ νόησις νοήσεως νόησις]" (12.9 [1074b34–35]).

The crucial difference between divine and human *noēsis* and *theoria* is that God grasps the ἀσύνθετα actually, while the human mind, in potential thinking, is concerned with synthetic things only. But on the few occasions humans enjoy actual *noēsis*, the *nous poietikos* touches (θιγεῖν) the ἀσύνθετα. It is in such noetic activity (ἐνεργεία) that subject-object dichotomy and its complexity are resolved into a subject-object simplicity and unity. And when this occurs there is no longer a gap between knower, knowledge, and object of knowledge. In the activity of thinking the active intellect emerges, which thinks incessantly and forever. It resides both in us and separately from us, it involves no memory, and when the active intellect thinks, its activity (ἐνεργεία) makes things—rather than becomes all things as mere process (κίνησις)—and is identical with its objects. "Actual knowledge is identical with its object ... when isolated it is its true self and nothing more and this alone is immortal and everlasting ... and without this nothing thinks" (*De an.* 3.5 [430a20–25]). But how, on the basis of such claims, does one infer the existence of other minds? Aristotle's answer is that since all forms of intellection (*noēsis*) are "of something else," and only incidentally of themselves, whenever we think Intellect, we think other minds as well. That is to say, the activity of thinking qua Nous points to the existence of other minds. Plotinus offers a similar but more nuanced answer:

> Intellect is all things [ὁ δὲ νοῦς πάντα] ... and the whole is universal intellect and being, Intellect making being exist in thinking it, and being giving Intellect thinking and existence by being thought ... but this one is two things: Intellect and being and thinking and thought; Intellect as thinking and being as thought. (*Enn.* 5.1.4.20, 25–32)

> Contemplation must be the same as the contemplated, and Intellect the same as the intelligible; for if not the same, there will be no truth; for who is trying to possess realities will possess an impression different from the realities, and this is not truth. For truth ought not to be the truth of something else but to be what it says. In this way, Intellect and the intelligible are one, and this is reality and the first reality, and also the first Intellect which possess the real beings, or rather is the same as the real beings ... for the intellection will in a way encompass the intelligible or be the same as the intelligible.... All together are one, Intellect, intellection, the intelligible. If therefore Intellect's intellection is the intelligible, and the intelligible is itself, it will itself think itself. (*Enn.* 5.3.27–45)

Thinking and contemplation point toward beings, intelligibles, and hence other minds.

Conclusion

This inquiry began with a request to reflect on two similes in the *Theaetetus* where mind is an aviary and each new piece of knowledge is a wild bird caught and caged (*Theaet.* 197d–e). The aviary is the mind, knowledge is the birds, and when we think, we hold a bird in our hands (*Theaet.* 199a–b).

Three metaphors were transposed from these similes: "Orioles" stand for individual minds, "owls" for other minds and abstract entities, and "aviaries" for holenmermism—"the whole of reality is continuous in its parts." It was proposed that Aristotle and Plotinus claim orioles—indeed, even the most solipsistic of orioles—know owls to some considerable degree if for no other reason than orioles and owls share marks of the mental and fly about in "aviaries" where the whole is in the part (*holenmermism*) and the world contains genuinely continuous phenomena together (*synechism*)—an inversion of the egocentric view that orioles and owls know only themselves and live in their own singular aviary ways.

Aristotle and Plotinus justify such claims on the basis of arguments from true belief and infinite regress tied to a *holenmermism* where the individual self or mind (*ego*) is continuous with a suprapersonal identity or mind (*nous*). Plotinus also incorporates the Stoic notion of *synechism*—the view that the universe exists as a continuous whole of all of its parts with no part being fully separate, determined, or determinate. Thus, on the metaphysical side, each proposes a hypothetical description of a tightly woven universe woven not within layers of an identical (the same kind) of reality but between layers of reality in a scalar fashion. On the methodological side, each looks for connections and continuous strata between seemingly disconnected entities or events.[47]

Aristotle's holenmermism—that the whole is in the part—is based on the notion that exclusion is always posterior to inclusion. Consequently, the perfection of divine *nous* thinking itself (καὶ ἔστιν ἡ νόησις νοήσεως νόησις) includes an intellection of all individuals, including other minds, for to be perfect is to be complete and self-sufficient and "that from which nothing is wanting"—and certainly not the possibility of other minds.

> For thus we define the whole—that from which nothing is wanting ... what is true of each particular is true of the whole as such—the whole is

---

47. Peirce variously described it as "unbrokenness," "fluidity, the merging of part into part," where "all is fluid and every point directly partakes the being of every other." See Charles Sanders Peirce, *Collected Papers* (Cambridge: Harvard University Press, 1931–1958), 1:163–64, 5:402 n. 2. The mathematical conception of continuity included the notion of infinite divisibility, which Peirce called Kanticity, after Kant, and the notion of an infinite series of points approaching a limit, called Aristotelicity (Peirce, *Collected Papers*, 6:166). A third notion, derived from Cantor, characterized continuity as perfect concatenation (Peirce, *Collected Papers*, 6:164).

that of which nothing is outside. (*Phys.* 3.6 [207a8–15]; see *Metaph.* 12.9 [1074b33–35])

> For this is the sort of principle that constitutes the nature of each ... all must at least come to be dissolved into their elements ... in which all share for the good of the whole. (*Metaph.* 12.10 [1075a23–26])

Plotinus's *holenmermism* and *synechism* rest on the claim that every form in Nous contains every other Form by the interiority of its relations to other Forms. Each Form is in all other Forms, and each mind is cognitively identical with every Form and other minds because the multiplicity of *nous* is not spatially articulated—thus the possibility of other minds (*Enn.* 5.5.1.19–43; 5.8.3.30–34; 5.9.6; 5.9.8.3–7). "Intellect and the intelligible substance; each individual Idea is not other than Intellect, but each is Intellect. And Intellect as a whole is all the Forms, and each individual Form is an individual intellect.... We must assume real beings have their place in the thinking subject" (*Enn.* 5.9.8.1–5, 10–12). When both are brought together, Aristotle and Plotinus reach a precipice from which the problem of other minds is a faux problem and thus dissolved—as a category mistake.

Bibliography

Primary Sources

Alcinous. *The Handbook of Platonism.* Translated by John Dillon. Oxford: Oxford University Press, 1993.

Aristotle. *Metaphysics.* Vol. 2: *Books 10–14. Oeconomica. Magna Moralia.* Translated by Hugh Tredennick and G. Cyril Armstrong. LCL 287. Cambridge: Harvard University Press, 1935.

Plato. *Theaetetus; Sophist.* Translated by Harold North Fowler. LCL 123. Cambridge: Harvard University Press, 1921.

Plotinus. *Enneads VI. 1–5.* Translated by A. H. Armstrong. LCL 445. Cambridge: Harvard University Press, 1988.

Secondary Sources

Beierwaltes, Werner. "Die Metaphysik des Lichtes in der Philosophie Plotins." *ZPF* 15 (1961): 334–62.

Berchman, Robert M. "Of Hunting Doves and Pigeons: Aristotle Reading Plato and Parmenides. On Thinking and Being Are the Same." *ScEs* 72 (2020): 31–48.

Berti, Enrico. "The Intellection of Indivisibles according to Aristotle." Pages 141–63 in *Aristotle on Mind and Senses: Proceedings of the Seventh Symposium Aristotelicum*. Edited by Geoffrey E. R. Lloyd and Gwilym E. L. Owen. Cambridge: Cambridge University Press, 1978.

Blumenthal, Henry J. "On Soul and Intellect." Pages 82–104 in *The Cambridge Companion to Plotinus*. Edited by Lloyd P. Gerson. Cambridge: Cambridge University Press, 1996.

———. *Plotinus' Psychology: His Doctrines of the Embodied Soul*. The Hague: Nijhoff, 1971.

———. *Soul and Intellect*. Abingdon: Routledge, 1993.

Brinkmann, Klaus. "Preface." Pages x–xii in *Aristotle and Plotinus on the Intellect*, by Mark J. Nyvlt. Lanham, MD: Lexington Books, 2012.

Burnyeat, Myles. *The Theaetetus of Plato*. Translated by M. Jane Levett. Indianapolis: Hackett, 1990.

Caston, Victor. "Aristotle on Consciousness." *Mind* 111.444 (2002): 752–815.

Clark, Stephen R. L. "Plotinus: Body and Soul." Pages 280–81 in *The Cambridge Companion to Plotinus*. Edited by Lloyd P. Gerson. Cambridge: Cambridge University Press, 1996.

Cleary, John. "Powers That Be." Pages 251–98 in *Studies on Plato, Aristotle, and Proclus: The Collected Essays on Ancient Philosophy of John Cleary*. Leiden: Brill, 2013.

Corrigan, Kevin. "Enneads 5, 4 [7] 2 and Related Passages: A New Interpretation of the Status of the Intelligible Object." *Hermes* 114 (1986): 195–203.

———. "Essence and Existence in the Enneads." Pages 105–29 in *The Cambridge Companion to Plotinus*. Edited by Lloyd P. Gerson. Cambridge: Cambridge University Press, 1996.

De Koninck, Thomas. "La noesis et L'indivisible selon Aristote." Pages 215–18 in *La naissance de la raisonen Grece: Acts du Congres de Nice Mai 1987*. Edited by Jean-François Mattei. Paris: Presses Universitaires de France, 1990.

Emilsson, Eyjólfur K. "Cognition and Its Object." Pages 222–23 in *The Cambridge Companion to Plotinus*. Edited by Lloyd P. Gerson. Cambridge: Cambridge University Press, 1996.

———. *Plotinus on Intellect*. Oxford: Oxford University Press, 2007.

———. *Plotinus on Sense Perception.* Cambridge: Cambridge University Press, 1988.

Fritz, Kurt von. "*Nous, Noein* and Their Derivatives in Presocratic Philosophy (Excluding Anaxagoras)." Pages 23–85 in *The Pre-Socratics: A Collection of Critical Essays.* Edited by Alexander P. D. Mourelatos. Princeton: Princeton University Press, 1993.

Gerson, Lloyd. P, ed. *Aristotle and Other Platonists.* Ithaca, NY: Cornell University Press, 2005.

———. *God and Greek Philosophy. Studies in the Early History of Natural Theology.* London: Routledge, 1990.

———. *Plotinus.* London: Routledge, 1994.

Gurtler, Gary. *Ennead IV.4.30–45 and IV.5.* Las Vegas: Parmenides, 2015.

———. "Plotinus: Self and Consciousness." Pages 113–30 in *Plato Redivivus.* Edited by John Finamore and Robert Berchman. New Orleans: Southern University Press, 2005.

Hadot, Pierre. "Revue of H-S2." *RBPH* 164 (1963): 92–96.

Hager, F. P. "Die Aristotlesinterpretation des Alexander von Aphrodisias und die Aristoteleskritik Plotinus bezüglich der Lehre vom Geist." *AGP* 46 (1964): 174–87.

Nyvlt, Mark J. *Aristotle and Plotinus on the Intellect.* Lanham, MD: Lexington Books, 2012.

Peirce, Charles Sanders. *Collected Papers.* 8 vols. Cambridge: Harvard University Press, 1931–1958.

Popper, Karl. "Of Clouds and Clocks." Pages 206–55 in *Objective Knowledge.* Oxford: Oxford University Press, 1972.

Rappe, Sara. *Reading Neoplatonism: Non-discursive Thinking in the Texts of Plotinus, Proclus and Damascius.* Cambridge: Cambridge University Press, 2000.

Roecklein, Robert J. *Plato versus Parmenides.* Lanham, MD: Lexington Books, 2011.

Ryle, Gilbert. "Categories." *PAS* n.s. 38 (1937–1938): 189–206.

———. *The Concept of Mind.* Chicago: University of Chicago Press, 2002.

Schroeder, Frederic M. "The Analogy of the Active Intellect to Light in the 'de Anima' of Alexander of Aphrodisias." *Hermes* 109 (1981): 215–25.

———. "Plotinus and Interior Space." Pages 25–28 in *Neoplatonism and Indian Philosophy.* Edited by Paulos Gregorios. Albany: State University of New York Press, 2002.

———. "Plotinus and Language." Pages 336–52 in *The Cambridge Com-

panion to Plotinus. Edited by Lloyd P. Gerson. Cambridge: Cambridge University Press, 1996.

Sorabji, Richard. *Time, Creation, and the Continuum.* Bristol: Bristol Classical Press, 2015.

Trouillard, Jean. "The Logic of Attribution in Plotinus." *IPQ* 1 (1961): 125–38.

Wagner, Michael. "Veridical Causation in Plotinus." Pages 51–72 in *The Structure of Being.* Edited by R. Baine Harris. Albany: State University of New York Press, 1982.

Initial Stages on the Ladder of Ascent to the Intelligible World: The Metempsychotic Aeons in Zostrianos and Related Sethian Literature

John D. Turner †

The Nag Hammadi corpus contains three treatises, Zostrianos, Allogenes, and Marsanes, known as the Sethian Platonizing Treatises, which commemorate the ecstatic ascent of a single exceptional individual, such as Zostrianos (the alleged uncle or grandfather of Zoroaster), Allogenes ("one of another kind, race," a play on Seth as "another seed" in Gen 4:25), and Marsanes (perhaps a contemporary Sethian prophet), who uses a self-performable technique of contemplative ascension into the realms anticipated for the postmortem return of the soul to the intelligible realm from which it originated. The focus of this paper is the stages of the visionary ascent through the preliminary places that lie below the intelligible realms that form the ultimate object of the visionary's quest, in particular the celestial and metempsychotic realms traversed by the seer Zostrianos prior to his entrance into the intelligible world, here called the Aeon of Barbelo.

After an initial description of the failure of Zostrianos's earthly attempts to learn about ultimate reality by means of traditional teaching, he attempts to commit suicide but is rescued by an angel of light, who escorts him on an out-of-the-body ascent into the heavenly realms. He traverses a series of aeonic levels on his way into the intelligible realm, named the Aeon of Barbelo. In order from lowest to highest, these aeonic

For my dear friend and colleague of twenty-five years, with memories of the good times we've had at the Annual Meetings for the International Society for Neoplatonic Studies and the American Academy of Religion/Society of Biblical Literature.

The late John Turner, Cotner Professor of Religious Studies and Mach University Professor of Classics and History at the University of Nebraska-Lincoln, wrote this essay for Professor Finamore's Festschrift shortly before his death on 26 October 2019.

levels are, as can be seen in figure 9.1, the perceptible Earth, the thirteen
cosmic Aeons, the Aetherial or Airy Earth, the aeonic copies (ἀντίτυποι),
the Sojourn (παροίκησις), the Repentance (μετάνοια), and finally at the
very periphery of the Barbelo Aeon, the Self-Generated (αὐτογενεῖς)
Aeons. This paper intends to describe these immaterial levels of reality
encountered by Zostrianos, particularly in light of Plotinus's dismissal of
such entities in *Enn.* 2.5–6.

In an extended passage of treatise 33, the conclusion of Plotinus's anti-
gnostic tetralogy (*Enn.* 3.8 [30]; 5.8 [31]; 5.5 [32]; and 2.9 [33]), he comments:

> But they do not honor this creation or this earth, but say that a "new earth"
> [γῆ καινή] has come into existence for them, to which, say they, they will
> go away from this one: and that this is the rational form of the universe....
> And what ought one to say of the other realities [ὑποστάσεις] they intro-
> duce, their "Exiles" [παροικήσεις] and "Impressions" [ἀντιτύπους] and
> "Repentings" [μετανοίας]? For if they say that these are affections [πάθη]
> of the soul, when it is in repentance and "Impressions" when it is con-
> templating, in a way, images of realities and not the realities themselves,
> then these are the terms of people inventing a new jargon to recommend
> their own school. (*Enn.* 2.9.5.25–26 [Armstrong])

Plotinus's own explanation of these realities introduced by the gnostics
identifies them with certain "experiences" or "passions" (πάθη) of the Soul,
quite possibly on the grounds of the widespread gnostic myth of the fall
of Sophia common to both Valentinian and Sethian thought. In this myth,
the last of the divine Aeons to emerge is Sophia (whom Plotinus tends
to equate with the cosmic Soul), who undertakes a noble but ultimately
futile attempt to apprehend her ultimate forefather, the unknowable First
Principle. Sophia's failure results in her entrance into a state of disordered passion, leading to her consequent fall and exile from the Pleroma,
to which she is only restored after her eventual "repentance."[2] One may
reasonably conclude that the Platonizing Sethians intended these divine
aeonic realities to represent the hypostasized experiences of Sophia at various narrative stages of the classic gnostic myth.

---

2. See the fragmentary version at Zost. 9.16–10.19, but among many other more
classic examples, see also the Sethian-Barbeloite Apocryphon of John (long recension;
NHC III 9.25–14.13 and parallels) and Irenaeus's account of the Ptolemaean-Valen-
tinian system in *Haer.* 1.2.1–3.

Now among other Sethian treatises, Marsanes and the Untitled text of the Bruce Codex mention in passing the Self-Generated, Sojourn and Repentance Aeons,[3] while the Gospel of the Egyptians actually hypostatizes Sophia's personal repentance into a single Repentance Aeon that catalyzes Sethian salvation history.[4] But it is only with the treatise Zostrianos that the function of these realities becomes clearer, mainly as stages or way stations along the course of Zostrianos's heavenly ascent to the intelligible realm of the Barbelo Aeon. Once he begins his ascent, escorted by an angel on a great luminous cloud and having left his body on earth to be

---

3. Marsanes NHC X 2.26–3.25 (my trans.): "The fourth (the Sojourn) [and the] fifth (the Repentance) which is above (it, i.e., the Sojourn), [are the ones] you have come to know [as divine. The fourth, concerning that which] exists after the [somatic type] and nature [φύσις], that is, that which [is divided in] three. And you [were] [informed] about [these and that which is] in three [dimensions] by these [two (the fourth & fifth?)]. You [were informed that it] is incorporeal [...] and after [...] within [...]every [...] which [... and] the things within them. The [fifth], [concerning the] repentance [μετάνοια] [of] those that are within [it] and concerning those who sojourn in that place (the fourth?). But the sixth, concerning the self-generated ones [αὐτογέννητος], concerning the incorporeal being [οὐσία] that exists individually [κατὰ μέρος], together with those who abide in the truth of the All [in regard to] understanding [ἐπιστήμη] and stability." Codex Bruce, *Untitled* 263.16–23 (trans. Schmidt): "God created the aetherial earth [ⲡⲕⲁϩ ⲛ̄ⲁⲏⲣ], a dwelling-place for those who had come forth, that they should remain there until the establishment of those below them. After that, the true Sojourn [ⲡⲙⲁ ⲛϭⲟⲉⲓⲗⲉ ⲛⲁⲙⲉ = παροίκησις]; within this, the place of the Repentance [μετάνοια]; within this, the airy aeonic Copies [ⲡⲁⲛⲧⲓⲧⲩⲡⲟⲥ ⲛⲁⲉⲣⲟⲁⲓⲟⲥ = ἀντίτυπος]. Next the Sojourn [παροίκησις], the Repentance [μετάνοια], inside this, the self-generated aeonic Copies [ἀντίτυπος]. In that place, they were baptized in the name of the Autogenes, the one who is divine over them." See Carl Schmidt, *Plotins Stellung zum Gnosticismus und kirchlichen Christentum* (Leipzig: Hinrichs, 1900), 61–62; Michel Tardieu, "Les gnostiques dans la Vie de Plotin: Analyse du chapitre 16: Vie de Plotin," in *Porphyre, La Vie de Plotin, II: Études d'introduction, texte grec et traduction française, commentaire, notes complémentaires, bibliographie*, ed. Luc Brisson et al., HDAC 16 (Paris: Vrin, 1982), 527–28 n. 60; Mark Edwards, "The Cave of the Nymphs and the Gnostic Controversy," in *Christians, Gnostics and Philosophers in Late Antiquity*, VCS (London: Routledge, 2012), 98; John Turner, *Sethian Gnosticism and the Platonic Tradition* (Quebec: Presses Université Laval, 2001), 570.

4. Gos. Eg. NHC III 59.9–23 (trans. Böhlig and Wisse): "Because of this Metanoia came to be. She received her completion and her power by the will of the Father and his approval with which he approved of the great, incorruptible, immovable race of the great, mighty men of the great Seth, in order that he may sow it in the aeons which had been brought forth, so that, through her, the deficiency may be filled up."

guarded by glories, he eludes "the entire world and its thirteen aeons" with their angelic host.[5]

Thereupon Zostrianos exclaims:

> I traversed the aetherial [earth] and passed by the Aeonic Copies after immersing myself [there] seven times [in] living [water], once for each [of the] aeons without pausing until [I had traversed] them all at once. I ascended to the [truly] existent Sojourn; [I] was baptized, and [I abandoned the world] and [I] ascended to the truly existent Repentance [and was] baptized there [six] times. I passed through the sixth; [I was empowered from this very one] and I ascended to the [Self-generated] Aeons. (Zost. NHC VIII 5.17–6.2)[6]

Having entered the Self-generated Aeons, Zostrianos is baptized five more times and angelified in the name of the divine Autogenes. He then encounters a certain "Authrounios, the ruler on high," and asks him questions about the various kinds of souls and their relationship to the aeonic copies. On pages 8–9 of Zostrianos, Authrounios describes the creation

---

5. Leaving his physical body and perhaps the lower components of his soul on earth, he ascends with his angelic escort through the thirteen Aeons of the sublunary realm presided over by the archon of creation (Zost. NHC VIII 4.20–5.10; see also Gos. Eg. III 63.17–18). In his first baptism, evidently at the level of the moon, he is assimilated to the image of the glories (5.11–17). He next traverses the "airy/aetherial earth" and passes by the aeonic copies, perhaps the realm of the seven planets, since he is baptized there seven times (Zost. NHC VIII 5.17–23). When he then arrives and is baptized in the true Sojourn—likely the place where disembodied souls reside between periods of reincarnation—he abandons the cosmos and ascends to the true Repentance—perhaps the place where such disembodied souls make the choice that determines their next reincarnation—where he is baptized six times, is empowered, and ascends to the Self-Generated Aeons. Here he undergoes five baptisms administered by a traditional set of celestial Sethian powers in the name of the divine Autogenes and is transformed into various grades of angel and even becomes divine. In the presence of the Triple Male Child, he is baptized two more times by Youel in living water, and receives form, semblance, light, a holy spirit, and sight (Zost. NHC VIII 59.25–62.10). At this point the series of baptisms ends. Although he comes to stand before Protophanes as "truly existing," the remainder of the text gives no indication that he is ever actually baptized in the waters of Protophanes and Kalyptos. Instead, he is anointed by the Luminaries of the Barbelo Aeon, and, after their lengthy revelation, brought before Protophanes, empowered, inscribed in glory, sealed, and crowned, becoming all-perfect.

6. Translations of Zostrianos are my own.

of the world and the education (including punishment) of souls and the dual nature of the Aeons. It then becomes clear that Zostrianos's ascent to the Barbelo Aeon anticipates the final postmortem experience of all souls:

> And the pure [souls] are trained [γυμνάζειν] by the aeonic Copies [ἀντίτυπος], which receive a model [τύπος] of their souls while they still exist in the material world. They (the aeonic copies?) came into existence after the emanation of each of the aeons, and they (the soul copies) are taken, one after another, from the aeonic Copy [ἀντίτυπος] of the Sojourn [παροίκησις] to the Sojourn that truly exists, (and) from the Copy of Repentance [μετάνοια] to the Repentance that truly exists, and [from the] Copy of the Autogenes to the truly existent [Autogenes (aeons)], and so on. (*Zost.* NHC VIII 12.2–18)

This obscure passage gives valuable information about the makeup of the heavenly world. After traveling past an enigmatic "Aetherial Earth" (which is perhaps to be understood as the Moon), Zostrianos encounters six realms comprising the true Sojourn, Repentance, and Self-Generated Aeons as well as their inferior copies, regarded as a kind of training ground for the soul's entry into their truly existing archetypes.

The Hierarchy of Aeons in Sethian Thought

Zostrianos's ascent suggests the following aeonic hierarchy extending from the very highest principle to the earth itself:

Invisible Spirit / Unknowable One	*Exists*	Lives	Knows
The Triple Powered One/Eternal Life	Essentiality	*Vitality*	Mentality
The Aeon of Barbelo/First Thought (Intellect)	Being	Life	*Mind*

Kalyptos *contemplated intellect* (contains True Being) cf. the Living-Thing-That-Is

Protophanes *contemplating intellect* (contains the "Unified") cf. the *Nous kathoran*

Autogenes *planning intellect* (contains the "Individuals") cf. the *Nous dianooumenon*

Metempsychotic aeons that truly exist

The Autogenes Aeons (self-begotten individuals)

| The Repentance (strangers following ways of others) |
| The Sojourn (the repentance with sufficient knowledge) |

| The aeonic Copies (for pure souls = the Milky way?) |
| Copy of the Autogenes |
| Copy of the Repentance |
| Copy of the Sojourn |

| The Aetherial Earth (the Moon?) |

| The thirteen cosmic aeons (presided over by the Archon of creation) |

| The perceptible earth |

This hierarchy consists of four distinct ontological levels: (1) the highest is hypernoetic, that is, beyond the realm of any sort of determinate being, and is occupied solely by the supreme principle, the Unknowable One or "Invisible Spirit"; (2) the intelligible level, called the Barbelo Aeon, characterized by pure, incorporeal, eternal, and unchangeable determinate being; (3) the psychic realm of incorporeal entities subject to change and becoming; and (4) the corporeal realm of physical entities perceptible by the senses, subject to change and corruption.

The Intelligible Realm

At the intelligible and hyperintelligible levels, the supreme One's triple powers of existing, living, and thinking—called Existence or Essentiality, Vitality and Mentality—generate the divine intellect, the Barbelo Aeon, whose own tripartite structure is derived from an interpretation of Plato's description of cosmogenesis in Plato's *Timaeus*, "According, then, as Intellect [νοῦς] observes [καθορᾷ] Forms [ἰδέας] existing in the Living-Thing-that-Is [ὃ ἔστι ζῷον], such and so many as exist therein he planned [διενοήθη] that this world also should possess" (Plato, *Tim.* 39e3–40a2 [my trans.]). Thus, the Barbelo Aeon consists of three subintellects: first, one that is contemplated (νοῦς νοητός), called Kalyptos or "hidden," which contains the authentic existents (τὰ ὄντως ὄντα), roughly Plato's intelligible forms; second, one that contemplates those intelligible forms (νοῦς θεωρῶν), called Protophanes Nous or "first appearing" Mind; and a third, a demiurgic intellect (νοῦς διανοούμενος), called Autogenes or "self-generated" that confers those forms on the cosmos. As these terms suggest, the divine intelligence is at first "hidden" (*kalyptos*) in the supreme principle, then emerges as "first appearing" (*protophanes*) and is finally instantiated as "self-generated" (*autogenes*).

Moreover, these Sethian thinkers further surmised that the *activities* or *powers* of being and living that characterize the Living-Thing-That-Is (ὃ ἔστιν ζῷον) of *Tim.* 39e—now actually instantiated as Kalyptos—as well as the observing and planning intellection of the observing demiurgical Intellect—now respectively actively instantiated as Protophanes Nous and Autogenes—must have preexisted on an even higher, supranoetic level as the three *activities* of being, living, and intellection to be ascribed to the first principle as its triple powers of Existence, Vitality, and Mentality.

The Physical Realm of Nature

Beginning from the very lowest level of the ontological hierarchy lies the sensible realm of corporeal reality and its material substrate, sometimes called the realm of nature, the impermanent realm of coming into being and passing away inhabited by mortal humans and animals motivated by souls that are often characterized as imprisoned in physical bodies. The next higher realm is sometimes called the thirteen Aeons, a perishable realm whose acme is occupied by the ruler (archon) of creation and its remaining lower twelve levels by his angelic host (Zost. NHC VIII 4.20–5.10).[7] It is unclear whether this realm coincides with that of the seven planets plus the five subterranean levels of Hades that are mentioned in the Apocryphon of John and the Gospel of Judas, or whether it is in fact a sublunary and purely atmospheric realm, perceptible yet incorporeal, as suggested by Zostrianos.

The Metempsychotic Realms

Sandwiched between the intelligible levels and the lower thirteen Aeons of the aeonic hierarchy lie what one might call the psychic or metempsychotic realms, populated by disincarnate beings, angels, demons, and human souls in the process of transmigration. Like Zostrianos during his visionary ascent, so too the soul, on its postmortem departure from

---

7. These angelic powers are said to be nailed and overthrown by Jesus in Gos. Eg. NHC III 63.17–18; see also Gos. Jud. 46.2, 55.10–11.

the body, may anticipate traversing seven further Aeons on its way to the intelligible world: the Aetherial Earth; the inferior copies of the Sojourn, Repentance, and Self-Generated Aeons; and then the superior, truly existing Sojourn, Repentance, and Self-Generated Aeons.

This enigmatic aetherial/airy earth (*pkah ennaēr*) is mentioned in the Sethian treatises Marsanes, Gospel of the Egyptians, and the Untitled treatise of the Bruce Codex,[8] but most frequently in Zostrianos, especially in Authrounios's revelation about the demiurgic creation of the physical cosmos by the chief archon's own imagination aided by the dim reflection of the true eternal paradigm cast on primordial matter illuminated by Sophia's downward inclination rather than by the archon's direct vision:[9]

> And] the [great] pre-eminence Authrounios said [to me]: "The Aetherial Earth came into being by a rational principle, and it incorruptibly manifests generated and perishable things for the sake of the advent of the great judges (i.e., stars), lest they experience perception and be enclosed in the creation. But when they came upon it and thereby perceived the

8. For its part, the Sethian Gospel of the Egyptians characterizes the Aetherial Earth as "the receiver of God, where the holy men of the great light receive shape" (NHC III 50.10 = NHC IV 62.9: ⲡⲕⲁϩ ⲛⲁⲉⲣⲟⲁⲓⲟⲥ < *ⲅⲏ ⲁⲉⲣⲱⲇⲏ?). The Aetherial Earth is also mentioned in the Untitled treatise of the Bruce Codex (ch. 20) and apparently also in the Sethian treatise Marsanes (NHC X 2.21–26) as the place where "a sense-perceptible [power] will [hide] those who will rest, and they will be kept [from the] passion(s) and division [of the] (incarnational) union."

9. Zost. NHC VIII 9.16–10.20: "When Sophia looked [down], she saw the darkness, [illumining it] while maintaining [her own station], being [a] model [τύπος] for [worldly] things, [a principle (ἀρχή)] for the [insubstantial] substance [and the form]less form [...] a [shapeless] shape. [It makes room] for [every cosmic thing...] the All [...] the corrupt product. Since it is a rational principle [ϣⲁϫⲉ ≈ λόγος] that persuades] the darkness, [he sows from his] reason [ϣⲁϫⲉ ≈ λόγος], since it [is im] possible [for the archon] of [creation] to see any of the eternal entities. He saw a reflection [εἴδωλον], and with reference to the reflection that he [saw] therein, he created the world. With a reflection of a reflection [ⲉⲓⲁⲱⲗⲟⲛ ⲛ̅ⲧⲉ ⲟⲩⲉⲓⲁⲱⲗⲟⲛ] he worked upon the world, and then even the reflection of the appearance was taken from him. But Sophia was given a place of rest in exchange for her repentance. In consequence, because there was within her no pure, original image, either pre-existing in him or that had already come to be through him, he used his imagination [φαντάζεσθαι] and fashioned the remainder, for the image [εἰκών] belonging to Sophia is always corrupt [and] deceptive. But the archon—[since he simulates] and embodies by [pursuing the image (εἰκών)] because of the superabundance [that inclined downward]—looked downward."

works of the world, they condemned its ruler to a perishability that is a pattern for the world, since it is a [substance] and principle of matter, the dark, corrupt [product]." (Zost. NHC VIII 9.1–15; see also 5.17–18; 8.11; 130.1)

Although certain later authors such as Macrobius, Porphyry, Proclus, and Simplicius claim this "Aetherial Earth" as a common Platonic term for the moon, one must wonder whether it is also cognate with the similar term "new earth"—a phrase ultimately of biblical provenance (e.g., Isa 65:17 LXX; 66:22 LXX; 2 Pet 3:13; Rev 21:1)—which is mentioned in Plotinus's critique of terms such as "another," "new," or "strange" earth that he found in gnostic sources known to him.[10] Assuming that Plotinus equated the notion of this "new" or "strange" earth with the gnostic "Aetherial Earth,"

---

10. Macrobius, *Comm. somn.* 1.11.8 ("maluerunt enim mundum alii in elementa ter quaterna diuidere, ut in primo numerentur ordine terra aqua aer ignis, qui est pars liquidior aeris uicina lunae: supra haec rursum totidem numero sed naturae purioris elementa ut sit luna pro terra quam aetheriam terram a physicis diximus nominatam, aqua sit sphaera Mercurii, aer Veneris, ignis in sole"). Also Porphyry (*In Tim.* 1.147.6–13): γῆ μὲν γὰρ αἰθερία ἡ σελήνη; see also Simplicius, *Comm. cael.* 7.375.29. According to Proclus (*In Tim.* 2.16.1–7), Porphyry claims that the "Egyptians"-- whoever this means--consider the Moon to be an "aetherial earth" (γῆ αἰθερία) into which the Demiurge sows souls who gestate there for a certain period of time prior to their descent into bodies; in *In Tim.* 2.48.15–21, Proclus attributes to the "Pythagoreans" a similar doctrine in the form of an ostensibly Orphic fragment to the effect that the moon is an "immense Earth" with innumerable mountains, cities, and mansions. According to Plutarch's essay *On the Face in the Moon*, the earth is viewed as the source of bodies, the sun as the source of mind, and the moon—into which the sun has sown minds—as the repository of souls and producer of new souls. Upon one's death, while still on the earth, Demeter violently separates soul from body, whereupon the soul wanders in the space between earth and moon to purge the pollutions of embodiment. Those souls that have managed to subjugate their irrational passions to reason arrive at the moon, where, in "Hecate's cave," the affective part of the soul pays the penalties for its wrongdoings in its daemonic existence. At this point, Persephone gently detaches the "true self" from the soul, namely, the intellect (νοῦς) that strives toward the sun as the visible likeness of the good, leaving the substance of the soul on the moon, where it either withers away, or, in the case of those souls enamored of the body, is drawn away into another birth. This new earth is mentioned in Codex Bruce, Untitled (ch. 12: ⲡⲕⲁϩ ⲛⲃⲣⲣⲉ) and the Manichaean Kephalaia (§55 [BG 15996: ⲡⲓⲕⲁϩ ⲛ̄ⲃⲣ̄ⲣⲉ]). See Plotinus, *Enn.* 2.9 [33]. *Enn.* 4.26–32: τίς γῆ ἄλλη παρὰ ταύτην μετὰ τὴν ἐκεῖ γῆν; 5.24–25: τήνδε τὴν γῆν καινὴν αὐτοῖς γῆν φασι; 11.8–15: Ἔπειτα καὶ ὁ λογισμὸς ὁ τοῦ κόσμου, ἡ γῆ αὐτοῖς ἡ ξένη λεγομένη.

his indignation at these terms may have been motivated by his suspicion that the notion was derived from an inappropriate conflation of biblical or Sethian gnostic terminology with Plato's notion of a "true earth" that serves as an imperishable paradigm of our own earth in a mythical passage of the *Phaedo* (109e–111c).[11] The apparent gnostic demotion of this supernal new earth to an inferior level, perhaps that of the moon, would have struck Plotinus as a perverse interpretation of Plato. At any rate, one may regard the region in the vicinity of the moon—perhaps extending even to the sun—as the place of disembodied souls in the process of purification from bodily passions, a kind of staging area for souls about to undertake a postmortem or visionary ascent.

Next, between the Aetherial Earth and lower boundary of the intelligible realm of the Barbelo Aeon presided over by the divine Autogenes, there exist the metempsychotic Aeons, the "real" Sojourn, Repentance, and Self-Generated Aeons, as well as their inferior copies (ἀντίτυπος) or lower reflections. The revealer Authrounios specifies that it is in these lower copies of the metempsychotic aeons that souls are "trained" and "judged" by certain "eternal glories."

> And the aeonic Copies [ἀντίτυπος] exist as follows: While they did not obtain a form [εἰδέα] of a single power, they did, however, possess eternal glories. And they exist as judgment seats for each of the powers.... And [the] pure [souls] are trained [γυμνάζειν] by the aeonic Copies [ἀντίτυπος], which receive an imprint [τύπος] of their souls while they still exist in the physical world. These souls came into existence after the emanation of each of the aeons, and they are taken, one after another, from the aeonic Copy [ἀντίτυπος] of the Sojourn [παροίκησις] to the Sojourn that truly exists, from the Copy of Repentance [μετάνοια] to the Repentance that truly exists, and [from the] Copy of the Autogenes to the truly existent [Autogenes (aeon)], and so on. (Zost. NHC VIII 11.2–9, 12.2–17)

These aeonic copies seem to be the place of metempsychosis, yet located above the moon. In contemporary Platonic thought, the lunar vicinity was a common site for the process of reincarnation. Numenius and other later Platonists sug-

---

11. Here Socrates explains that the earth on which we live is but a miserable reflection of the "true earth" (*Phaed.* 110a1), which contains vastly superior, imperishable animals, plants, and minerals, as well as humans and gods who interact harmoniously with one another. See also Plotinus, *Enn.* 5.8 [31] 3 27–4.19.

gested the Milky Way is the place of reincarnation.[12] Thus Zostrianos's aeonic copies may constitute our galaxy, or perhaps the fixed stars in general, and the training of souls is their education between lives, which makes them "pure."

Various Kinds of Souls and Their Level of Aeonic Attainment

All of this raises the question of the individual afterlife, which must somehow depend on the lifestyle and character of the person anticipating it. Intriguingly, a lengthy section of Zostrianos offers an extensive taxonomy of types of souls, stratified hierarchically according to their respective postmortem destinations. According to this schema, the vast majority of people have dead souls, which, after bodily death, ascend out of the cosmos into the inferior, punitive domains, which include the Aetherial Earth and the aeonic copies, but do not achieve celestial immortality. Superior to these dead souls are three classes of immortal souls, who return after death to their celestial origin or root in successive intermediary domains, the Sojourn, the Repentance, and finally the Self-Generated Aeons. The last of these is attained only by the Sethian elect themselves, those souls who are said to possess "self-generated" power, perhaps acquired through baptismal rebirth. In this schema, the postmortem destination of each of these types of souls is in some way correlated with a differential capacity for revelatory knowledge or contemplative insight. Those who are *not* among the elect self-generated souls and who wind up in the Sojourn or Repentance are said to suffer from various degrees of sin associated with their previous attempts to obtain a vision of the transcendentalia without the benefit of revelation or contemplative insight uniquely bestowed on the elect. Thus on pages 24–25 of Zostrianos, the revealer named Ephesech informs Zostrianos about the salvific destiny of various kinds of souls based on their ability to apprehend increasingly transcendent levels of reality.

> On the one hand, one sees in a perfect soul those of Autogenes; on the other hand, in intellect, those of the Triple Male;[13] (and) in a pure spirit,

---

12. Numenius, frag. 12; Macrobius, *Comm. somn.* 1.9, 1.12; Porphyry, *Antr. nymph.* 28; Plutarch, *Fac.* 943e; Proclus, *Comm. in R.* 2.128.26–131.14; John Lydus, *Mens.* 4.32; see Christian Bull, *The Tradition of Hermes Trismegistus: The Egyptian Priestly Figure as a Teacher of Hellenized Wisdom*, RGRW 186 (Leiden: Brill, 2018), 327–31.

13. The Triple Male Child is a prominent figure in the Barbelo Aeon, closely related to the "individuals," the individual forms and souls that reside in the Autogenes Aeon,

those of the Protophanes. One hears about Kalyptos through the powers
of the Spirit which emerged in a vastly superior manifestation of the
Invisible Spirit. By the thought that now exists in Silence (and) by the
First Thought (one learns) about the Triple Powered Invisible Spirit; it
is, then, an audition and a power of silence which is purified in a vivifying spirit, perfect, first-perfect, and all-perfect. Therefore, glories are set
upon them, as nourishers. Those who have been truly baptized in knowledge and those who are worthy are guarded, but those who [are] not
from this kind [γένος] [are mere things] and they [return] to [their own
root. One deriving from] the fifth is [satisfied with those of the Aeonic]
Copies. [For each] of the aeons [there is] a baptism [of this sort]. Now if
[one] strips off the world and lays aside [nature], one is either a sojourner
[ϭⲁⲗⲏⲩⲧ] without dwelling place or power, following the practices of
others [ϩⲃⲏⲩⲉ ⲛ̄ⲧⲉϩⲉⲛⲕⲟⲟⲩⲉ], or one repents, having committed no sin,
and because knowledge [γνῶσις] was sufficient for him, he is without
concern for anything. (Zost. NHC VIII 24.1–25.8)

Here the basic distinction is between the souls of those who stand within
the Sethian tradition, whether by natural affiliation as "those who are
worthy"—the most frequent designation of the righteous seed of Seth—or
by initiatory baptism, and those who do not. While the first category has
both knowledge and protective guardians and thus the prospect of celestial
immortality, the latter does not, since they have not laid aside the natural
world; they are mere things, apparently completely materialistic persons
who return to their own root, which might be either the Aetherial Earth or
even the corruptible matter from which their bodies are made. Associated
with them are those who merely attain the aeonic copies, a destiny that is
apparently satisfactory for those who derive from some mysterious fifth
entity, perhaps the immediately subjacent Aetherial Earth as a locus of disembodied souls.[14] This suggests three classes: the truly baptized Sethians,
non-Sethians doomed to dissolve, and an intermediary class interested in
conversion, having laid aside the world but not yet fully converted.

---

as well as to "those who exist together," the undifferentiated forms and souls that reside
in Protophanes. Although his ontological level is unspecified, his function seems to be
that of a savior or mediator: he brings undifferentiated beings in the Aeon of Protophanes into differentiated existence in the Aeon of Autogenes and, conversely, helps the
differentiated beings in the Aeon of Autogenes to ascend to the Aeon of Protophanes.

14. If the term "the fifth" draws on Aristotle's identification of the aether as the
fifth element, it might denote the Aetherial Earth, which is apparently immediately
subjacent to the aeonic copies.

Destiny of Souls: Initial Classification

A bit later, on pages 26–29, Ephesech provides further details on the post-mortem destiny of these various sorts of souls. Here the basic distinction is between the three types of disembodied souls that achieve immortality by ascending beyond the aeonic copies to the truly existing Sojourn, Repentance, and Self-Generated Aeons, and those that do not, of which there are four species (εἶδος; see *Phaed.* 113d–114c) of disembodied souls that have "utterly perished" along with nine kinds (see Plato, *Phaedr.* 248 c–e) of souls that continue in their embodied earthly existence, each with its own "species" and "habit."[15]

> [Now] one (kind of person) [appears] in a [soul] and has [completely] perished; their [souls are disem]bodied. Another [who is within] his time [appears] for a time; their soul is [em]bodied. Now those who have completely [perished (ⲧⲁⲕⲏⲟⲩⲧ)] are four [species (εἶδος)], while those [within] time [χρόνος] are nine. Each one of them has its species and habit. Though similar, they are different; though distinct they are also stable. (Zost. NHC VIII 26.23–27.9)

In the meantime, the three kinds of "immortal souls" dwell—perhaps temporarily—among the "utterly perished souls" because of the fall of Sophia: "And other immortal souls associate with all these souls because of the Sophia who looked down. For there are three species of immortal souls" (Zost. NHC VIII 27.9–27.14).

At some point, the three kinds of immortal souls move from their initial staging area in the aeonic copies onward to their truly existing exem-

---

15. See Turner, who recalls the four kinds of souls in Plato's *Phaed.* 113d–114c, the nine kinds of mortal life in *Phaedr.* 248c–e, and the curable and incurable sins of *Gorg.* 252a–b, which would refer to sinners who "repent" and those who "perish," respectively. See Turner, *Sethian Gnosticism*, 602–3; John Turner, trans., "Zostrianos," in *The Nag Hammadi Scriptures: The Revised and Updated Translation of Sacred Gnostic Texts Complete in One Volume*, ed. Marvin Meyer and Elaine Pagels (New York: Harper, 2009), 540–41; also on Proclus, *In Tim.* 1.147.27–148.16, on Porphyry's account of the reincarnations of the soul. Yet none of the souls in *Phaed.* 113d–114c perish forever. One kind winds up in Tartaros for good, but it is not destroyed; the other three kinds are reincarnated. Similarly, the nine lives in the *Phaedrus* include the philosopher-king who, like the fourth, philosophical soul in the *Phaedo*, will transcend reincarnation and bodily existence; however, Zostrianos's nine types of temporal existence (27.2–7) are all subcategories of destructible, not "immortal," souls.

plars in the "true" Sojourn, Repentance, and Autogenes Aeons. Like the visionary Zostrianos, the ascending soul first encounters the truly existing Sojourn. This name may distantly stem from the condition attributed to resident aliens in the land of ancient Israel,[16] but in traditional Sethian thought it designates a temporary refuge for the righteous seed of Seth during the hostile creator God's attempts to destroy them by means of the primordial cosmic flood and conflagration through fire and brimstone as described in Gen 6–9 and 18–19.[17] Ephesech informs Zostrianos about the Sojourn Aeon as follows: "The ones who have taken root upon the Sojourn do not have self-generated power; they follow the ways of others. Now this is a single type, [self-contained]" (Zost. NHC VIII 27.14–21).

---

16. See Dylan Burns, *Apocalypse of the Alien God: Platonism and the Exile of Sethian Gnosticism* (Philadelphia: University of Pennsylvania Press, 2014), 102–5.

17. Rather than Noah's ark, the Apocryphon of John describes this refuge as a place where they are hidden from the biblical God's further attacks in a "luminous cloud": Ap. John NHC II 28.34–29.12: "Again he (Yaldabaoth) plotted, to bring a flood over the creation of the human. But the greatness of the Light (Epinoia) of Providence (Barbelo) taught Noah, and he preached to the whole seed, the children of men. And those who were strangers to him did not listen to him. Not as Moses said: 'They hid themselves in an ark'; rather, they hid themselves in a place. Not only Noah, but many other people from the immovable race entered a place and hid themselves in a luminous cloud." For the Apocalypse of Adam, the righteous who survive the flood enter and sojourn in safety among the heavenly seed of Seth that reside in the third Luminary Daveithai: Apoc. Adam NHC V 73.13–24: "Then others from the seed of Ham and Japheth will come, four hundred thousand (righteous) men, and enter into another land and sojourn [ϭοειλε] with those men who came forth from the great eternal knowledge (the angelic seed of the heavenly Seth). For the shadow of their power will protect those who have sojourned [ϭοειλε] with them from every evil thing and every unclean desire." The Gospel of the Egyptians calls that heavenly residence the "spring" (πηγή) or "plant" (τωϭε) of Gomorrah, from which the heavenly Seth transplanted his seed to an earthly place of safety called Sodom, no doubt as an interpretation of Gen 18:23's account of Abraham's entreaty that the biblical God spare the few righteous from his intention to destroy the wicked Sodomites: Gos. Eg. NHC III 60.9–18: "Then the great Seth came and brought his Seed. And it was sown in the aeons which had been brought forth, their number being the amount of Sodom. Some say that Sodom is the place of pasture of the great Seth, which is Gomorrah. But others (say) that the great Seth took his plant out of (the spring) Gomorrah (in the Luminary Daveithai) and planted it in the second place [IV 71.28 adds "even in a place of pasture"] to which he gave the name Sodom."

Next, the souls of those in the Repentance Aeon are immortal souls whose knowledge was sufficient to take the sins they commit seriously enough to either repent or at least intend to repent.

> Those that stand [upon the] Repentance [were not ambivalent about] sin, since knowledge is sufficient [for] them. Since they are neophytes, [they still sin]. Yet it (this type of souls) also has distinctions: there are [those] who have sinned; others [also who] have repented; and others [who only intended (to repent)]. (Zost. VIII 27.21–28.2)

The issue of repentance is also addressed in the Apocryphon of John, where it appears to apply to those who have no immediate claim to natural membership in Seth's primordial seed that dwells in the third Luminary Daveithai, but upon their repentance have a potential dwelling in the fourth Luminary Eleleth: "In the fourth aeon were established the souls of those who are ignorant of the Pleroma, and did not repent quickly, but persisted for a while and later repented. They came to exist beside the fourth luminary Eleleth. These are creatures that glorify the Invisible Spirit" (Ap. John NHC II 9.18–23). Indeed, the Gospel of the Egyptians confirms that an Aeon named Repentance was deployed to enable the repentance of the earthly seed of Seth as well as its heavenly counterpart that Seth was about to transfer from its original residence in the third Luminary to populate the antediluvian earth.[18] Finally, there is the third group, the "self-generated" souls in the Self-Generated Aeons presided over by the divine Autogenes.[19]

---

18. See Gos. Eg. NHC III 59.9–60.2: "Because of this (the creation of the earthly Adam) Metanoia came to be. She received her completion and her power by the will of the Father and his approval with which he approved of the great, incorruptible, immovable race of the great mighty men of the great Seth, in order that he may sow it in the aeons that had been brought forth, so that, through her the deficiency may be filled up. For she had come forth from above down to the world which is the image of the night. When she had come, she prayed for (the repentance of) both the seed of the archon of this aeon and (the) authorities who had come forth from him—that defiled (offspring) of the demon-begetting god which will be destroyed—and the seed of Adam and the great Seth, which is like the sun." The term *Repentance* probably derives from the Sethian tradition concerning Sophia's repentance; see Zost. VIII 10.7–9: "But Sophia was given a place of rest in exchange for her repentance." In the Apocryphon of John (NHC II 13.32–14.13), Sophia's repentance for bringing into being the ignorant world creator results in her restoration to the sphere of the Ninth, just below the periphery of the Pleroma.

19. The Untitled text of the Bruce Codex confirms that the Self-Generated Aeons constitute the level at which Zostrianos is baptized five times (Zost. NHC VIII 6.1–7.22;

Apparently these souls also have four kinds, perhaps corresponding to the four Luminaries that Zostrianos also locates in the Self-Generated Aeons:[20]

> The third (kind of soul) is that of the souls of the self-generated ones; they have a rational expression [λόγος] of the ineffable truth existing in knowledge as well as self-generated [power] and eternal [life]. [And] they have four distinctions in the same manner: the forms of angels, those who love the truth, those who hope, and those who believe. [Indeed], they [also] have [syzygies], and they exist [within them]. They exist [as four places of] the Self-generated ones. (Zost. VIII 28.10–25)

A Second Classification

However, after a lengthy digression on the intelligible contents of the Barbelo Aeon, on pages 42–44 of Zostrianos the revealer Ephesech goes on to offer an *alternative* classification of souls and their prospects for salvation. The earlier classification apparently distinguishes between immortal souls in the true Sojourn, Repentance, and Self-Generated Aeons who are guarded and baptized and thus candidates for celestial salvation, as opposed to certain souls that merely attain to the aeonic copies, or worse, other souls that are mere things who return to their root, perhaps their constituent material element, that undergo destruction. The second classification, while noting that all souls, whether capable of salvation or not, inhabit the realm of mortality by virtue of their incarnation in human bodies, distinguishes between those *able* to achieve salvation and immortality and those souls that *cannot* ultimately escape the mortal condition of embodiment.

53.15–56.23) in the name of Autogenes (which may reflect the Sethian baptismal rite known as the Five Seals). They contain the vast majority of the divine beings traditionally associated with the Sethian baptismal rite (such as Yesseus Mazareus Yessedekeus the Living Water and the spiritual baptizers Micheus, Michar) as well as the four Luminaries Armozel, Oroiael, Daveithai, and Eleleth (the celestial stations of Adamas, his mother Meirothea, Seth and his mother Plesithea, and Seth's offspring, his "Seed"), and the repentant and restored Sophia. Souls that reside in the Self-Generated Aeons are called "perfect individuals" who possess "a rational expression (Logos) of the ineffable truth" as well as self-generated power and eternal life.

20. Zost. NHC VIII 29.1–12: "the Four Lights exist [there] in the same way: [Arm]ozel [is set] over the first aeon, a desire for god [and] truth and a uniter of souls; Oroiael, a seer of truth, is set over the second; Daveithe, a vision of knowledge, is set over the third; Eleleth, an eager impulse and preparation for truth, is set over the fourth."

The lowest type of humanity condemned to mortality is demonic—perhaps corresponding to Origen's lowest ontological class of fallen souls—and appears to be destroyed by fire. It apparently belongs to lowest rank of utterly perished souls in the earlier classification:

> Now the [one who repents and] the sojourner [ⲥⲁⲗϩⲟⲩⲧ] [and the one inhabiting] the perceptible [world] live with what is dead. [They] all [resemble a single thing. They] attain salvation [apart from] the dead. Now [none] of them needed salvation initially, but salvation is [greater] when they are degraded. As for the (type of) person that is dead: its soul, [its mind] and its body [are] all [dead]. Undergoing [destruction], fathers of [material [ὑλικόν] men, they are demons that] the fire [consumes]. (Zost. NHC VIII 42.10–26)

Meanwhile, the second kind of humanity, despite having an immortal soul, seems also excluded from celestial salvation by pursuing materialistic concerns and thus associating with demons: "The second (type of) person is the immortal soul that inhabits dead things, concerning itself with itself; [for] it then [seeks] benefits in every situation [and it] experiences bodily suffering. It (the soul) [is treated corporeally], and it [forgets that it has] an eternal god; it associates with *daimons*" (Zost. NHC VIII 43.1–12). Of these two lower types of humanity, the first and lowest should be identified with the souls that "pass away" with the world, probably at the end of time, while the second type seems to be caught in the cycle of reincarnation. Both of these types would probably ascend to the moon or Milky Way after death, where they are either destroyed in fire or sent back to earth, respectively. The third type of humanity, since it avoids contact with wicked and possesses a discovery of the truth, is able to escape the prospect of reincarnation and comes to reside in the true Sojourn (παροίκησις): "Now (concerning) the humanity in the Sojourn: if it inwardly possesses a discovery of the truth, it is far from the deeds of others who live [wickedly] and [stumble]" (Zost. NHC VIII 43.13–19). The fourth type of humanity enters the Repentance, where it is exclusively concerned with true realities: "(Concerning) the (type of) person that repents [μετανοεῖν]: if he renounces dead things and desires real things—immortal mind and immortal soul—[he will] be zealous about them by first scrutinizing not just behavior [πρᾶξις] but its consequences" (Zost. NHC VIII 43.19–27). The fifth type of humanity is the elect who have entirely withdrawn into their divine selves, who apparently come to inhabit the Self-Generated Aeons:

Now the (type of) person that can be saved is the one that seeks himself
and his intellect and finds each of them. And how much power he has!
The person that has been saved is one who has not known about these
things (merely) as they exist, but one who is personally involved with
[the] rational faculty as it exists [in him]. He has grasped their [image
that changes] in every situation as though they had become simple
and one. For then this (type of person) is saved who can pass through
[χωρεῖν] [them] all; [he becomes] them all. Whenever he [wishes], he
again parts from all these matters and withdraws into himself, for he
becomes divine, having withdrawn into god. (Zost. NHC VIII 44.1–22)

The first classification on pages 24–28 is mainly devoted to an enumera-
tion of five possible postmortem *destinations* for various kinds of souls,
the Self-Generated Aeons, Repentance, and Sojourn for immortal souls,
while the aeonic copies receive souls caught in the reincarnational cycle
and the Aetherial Earth receives those souls destined for destruction.
The second classification on pages 42–44 proceeds from the perspective
of five *kinds* of souls—in this case, four of which are immortal and one
mortal—that will attain to these destinations.[21] However, in either classi-

---

21. These classifications resemble somewhat the short dialogue on the destinies
of various souls between the Savior and John Son of Zebedee in Ap. John NHC II
25.16–27.30; BG 8502.64.9–71.2. According to it, not all souls will be saved; it all
depends on which spirit descends on the soul and unites with it, the "Spirit of life"
conferred by the Mother Barbelo or the "counterfeit spirit" of lust supplied by the
ignorant creator Ialdabaoth, and on whether the soul accepts or rejects the saving
knowledge. This yields three basic categories. The first and highest category more or
less corresponds to those souls who attain the Self-Generated Aeons, since they are
by nature united with the Spirit of Truth. Their salvation seems to be undifferentiated
and immediate upon death; they are raised by their "receivers" to eternal imperishable life, having been purified from evil "in that place" (BG 65.311; 2.25.239), which
could be either in its premortem incarnation or perhaps within certain unspecified
Aeons subjacent to the Pleroma functioning as a sort of purgatory. Second comes that
category of incarnated souls on whom either the Spirit of Truth or the counterfeit
spirit may descend; if they do not succumb to the evil spirit they are instantly saved,
otherwise, they fall into ignorance and must undergo a process of reincarnation, to
be punished by evil authorities until, with the help of other elect souls, they attain
knowledge and thus escape further reincarnations. Until then, as the apocryphon's
concluding Pronoia monologue puts it (2.31.1625), one must protect oneself from
the angels of poverty and demons of chaos and be sealed with the Five Seals to completely disarm the power of death. This second category seems to correspond to the
Platonizing Sethian distinction between souls that enter the Aeons of the Sojourn and

fication, *the only group referred to as elect* are those in the Self-Generated Aeons who "withdraw to themselves" and become divine, that is, who practice contemplation.[22]

Cognitive Failure of the Elect

Yet there still remains a dilemma, namely, why even the Sethian elect themselves ever came to be incarnated in material bodies despite their elect status and self-generated power. Thus on pages 44–46 of Zostrianos, Ephesech goes on to explain that even the elect soul whose repeated contemplation of the transcendent realm grants it access to the Self-Generated Aeons can also experience temporary lapses in its contemplation, when its attention can incline away from the hypernoetic realm toward the merely intelligible realm in which it resides. As a result the soul can forfeit its lofty status and once again suffer reincarnation into a physical body tortured by evil spirits.

> I said to the child of the child Ephesech who was with me, "Can your wisdom instruct me about the dissipation of the (type of) person that is saved? What are the things mixed with it, and what are those that divide it, so that the living elect might know?" Then the child of the child Ephesech, [speaking] openly, told me: "When (this type of person) repeatedly withdraws into itself alone and is occupied with the knowledge of other things, since the intellect and immortal [soul] do [not] intelligize, it thereupon experiences deficiency, for it too turns, has nothing, and separates from it (the intellect) and stands [apart] and experiences an alien [impulse] instead of becoming a unity. So that (type of person) resembles many forms. And when he inclines, he comes into being, seeking those things that do not exist. And if he happens upon them in a thought [νόημα], he cannot understand them in any other way unless he be enlightened, and it becomes a physical entity [φύσις]. Thus this type of person accordingly descends into birth, and becomes irrational because

Repentance and their respective copies, a distinction unknown to the Apocryphon of John. The last category, souls who possessed the saving knowledge but then apostatized, enter into a poverty from which there is no repentance, to be kept for the day when all those who have blasphemed the Spirit of Life will suffer eternal punishment.

22. Turner ("Zostrianos," 555–56) rightly identifies the fifth type of humanity with the self-generated souls from 28.10–30. The phrase "finds itself" means, as he argues, that they live like philosophers. Like Zostrianos, they are divinized by a fifth baptism in the Autogenes (53.15–24).

of the passions and indefiniteness of matter. Although possessing eternal, immortal power, he is bound in the clutches of the body, [removed], and [continually] bound within strong bonds, lacerated by every evil spirit, until he once more acts and comes back to him[self] and begins again to enter it. Therefore, for their salvation, there have been appointed specific powers, and these same ones inhabit this world. And among the Self-generated ones there stand at each [aeon] certain glories so that one who is in the [world] might be saved alongside [them]. The glories are perfect living concepts [νόημα]; it is [im]possible that they perish because [they are] imprints [τύποι] of salvation, that is to say, anyone receiving them will be rescued to them, and being imprinted [τύπος] will be empowered by each (imprint), and having that glory as a helper, one thus transcends the world [and all the aeons]." (Zost. NHC VIII 45.1–46.31)

The reason for this contemplative failure, we learn elsewhere in Zostrianos, is that the unaided contemplative intellect is insufficient to maintain unbroken intellection of the essentially unknowable realities beyond even the intelligible realm without divine assistance. Fortunately for those that attain the Self-Generated Aeons, this assistance is available in the form of certain powers called glories that can permanently imprint (τύποι) on the soul. The glories are described as perfect living concepts (νόημα) that persist in the soul even when one's intense contemplation and self-withdrawal should lapse or become distracted by other, lower things. Thus, almost as in the case of Sophia, who, having fallen from the divine realm because of her own failed attempt to know the unknowable First Principle, eventually repented of her contemplative overreach and was restored to her divine status by the Self-Generated Child, so too the glories of the Self-Generated Aeons restore elect self-generated souls that experience similar contemplative overreach.

Interestingly, Zostrianos's situation bears an undeniable resemblance to Plato's own mythical description of reincarnated souls whose failure to apprehend the divine realities causes the soul to fall down into birth. The difference for Plato, however, is that the subsequent escape from embodiment is enabled not by the assistance of divine glories but rather by the philosophical contemplation of beauty:[23]

---

23. Zeke Mazur, "A Gnostic Icarus? Traces of the Controversy Between Plotinus and the Gnostics over a Surprising Source for the Fall of Sophia: The Pseudo-Platonic 2nd Letter," *IJPT* 11 (2017): 3–25, esp. 7–9.

And the rule of destiny is as follows: whichever soul should accompany the god and should gaze upon something among those that are true is unharmed until the next circuit, and if it is able to do this eternally, it is eternally uninjured. But when, being unable to follow, it does not see, and, subject to some chance occurrence, is filled with forgetting and evil, it is weighted down, and "moults," and falls down to earth, then, at that point, the law is that this [soul] is not implanted into any beast in its first birth, but the one having seen the most will come to be in the seed of man. (*Phaedr.* 248c2–d3)

As Zeke Mazur has pointed out,[24] the Platonic *Second Letter* also appears to attribute the origin of all evil to the soul's hubristic striving and failure to comprehend the "the King of All." That is, since the soul has no inherent kinship (συγγενῆ) with the transcendent principle, it has no mechanism for apprehending it.

And so the human soul yearns to learn about these things, of what sort they are, by looking towards those things that are akin to her, while none of them have sufficient [kinship]. The very King about which I spoke is not of the same kind [as the soul]. After this, then, the soul says, "but of what kind *is* it, really?" This is, O son of Dionysius and Doris, the question which is the cause of all evils; or rather, it is concerning this [question] that birth-pangs are born in the soul; and unless one should extricate oneself from it, one will never really attain the truth. (*Ep.* 2 [212e4–313a6])

But in the Sethian view, this kinship can be restored, literally reimprinted on the soul, by divine helpers sent from above.

Bibliography

Primary Sources

Bohlig, Alexander, and Wisse, Frederik. "The Gospel of the Egyptians." Pages 195–205 in *The Nag Hammadi Library in English*. Edited by J. Robinson. Leiden: Brill, 1984.

---

24. Zeke Mazur, *Introduction and Commentary to Plotinus' Treatise 33 (II.9) "Against the Gnostics" and Related Studies*, ed. Francis Lacroix and Jean-Marc Narbonne, CZ (Quebec: Presses de l'Université Laval, 2019), 51–52.

Mazur, Zeke. *Introduction and Commentary to Plotinus' Treatise 33 (II.9) "Against the Gnostics" and Related Studies.* Edited by Francis Lacroix and Jean-Marc Narbonne. CZ. Quebec: Presses de l'Université Laval, 2019.

Schmidt, Carl, ed. *The Books of Jeu and the Untitled Treatise in the Bruce Codex.* Leiden: Brill, 1978.

Turner, John. "Marsanes." Pages 629–50. In *The Nag Hammadi Scriptures: The Revised and Updated Translation of Sacred Gnostic Texts Complete in One Volume.* Edited by Marvin Meyer and Elaine Pagels. New York: Harper, 2009.

—— "Zostrianos." Pages 537–84 in *The Nag Hammadi Scriptures: The Revised and Updated Translation of Sacred Gnostic Texts Complete in One Volume.* Edited by Marvin Meyer and Elaine Pagels. New York: Harper, 2009.

Secondary Sources

Bull, Christian. *The Tradition of Hermes Trismegistus: The Egyptian Priestly Figure as a Teacher of Hellenized Wisdom.* RGRW 186. Leiden: Brill, 2018.

Burns, Dylan. *Apocalypse of the Alien God: Platonism and the Exile of Sethian Gnosticism.* Philadelphia: University of Pennsylvania Press, 2014.

Edwards, Mark. "Porphyry's Cave of the Nymphs and the Gnostic Controversy." Pages 88–100 in *Christians, Gnostics and Philosophers in Late Antiquity.* VCS. London: Routledge, 2012.

Mazur, Zeke. "A Gnostic Icarus? Traces of the Controversy between Plotinus and the Gnostics over a Surprising Source for the Fall of Sophia: The Pseudo-Platonic Second Letter." *IJPT* 11 (2017): 3–25.

Schmidt, Carl. *Plotins Stellung zum Gnosticismus und kirchlichen Christentum.* Leipzig: Hinrichs, 1900.

Tardieu, Michel. "Les gnostiques dans la Vie de Plotin: Analyse du chapitre 16: Vie de Plotin." Pages 503–63 in *Porphyre, La Vie de Plotin, II: Études d'introduction, texte grec et traduction française, commentaire, notes complémentaires, bibliographie.* Edited by Luc Brisson, Marie-Odile Goulet-Cazé, Richard Goulet, and Denis O'Brien. HDAC 16. Paris: Vrin, 1982.

Turner, John. *Sethian Gnosticism and the Platonic Tradition.* Quebec: Presses Université Laval, 2001.

Part 3
Hermeneutics and Methodologies

The Indefinite Dyad and The Platonic Equality of the Male and Female Ruling Principles

Danielle A. Layne

In each of us two powers preside, one male, one female.... The normal and comfortable state of being is that when the two live in harmony together, spiritually co-operating. The androgynous mind is resonant and porous; it transmits emotion without impediment; that it is naturally creative, incandescent and undivided.
> —Virginia Woolfe, *A Room of One's Own*

Doesn't this entail that the "always becoming offspring" will be taken over or (received by) archai who attend to this, either men or women both? The *archai* are shared by both women and men.
> —Socrates in Plato, *Resp.* 460b

Plato's "unwritten doctrines" concerning the One and the Indefinite Dyad are often associated with the Pythagorean first principles of the limit and the unlimited (or πέρας and ἄπειρον).[1] According to the reports of Aristotle, the Pythagoreans relegated the limit and the unlimited to their now-infamous table of opposites in which *limit, one, right, rest, straight, light, good,* and *male*

---

1. See Dmitri Nikulin, *The Other Plato: The Tubingen Interpretation of Plato's Inner-Academic Teachings* (New York: State University of New York Press, 2012); Hans Krämer, *Plato and the Foundations of Metaphysics: A Work on the Theory of the Principles and Unwritten Doctrines of Plato with a Collection of the Fundamental Document* (New York: State University of New York Press, 1990), 115–20; John N. Findlay, *Plato: The Written and Unwritten Doctrines* (New York: Routledge, 1974), 57–58, for comprehensive records of the passages alluding to Plato's unwritten doctrines and for their origin in Pythagorean and pre-Socratic philosophy. See also Geoffrey S. Kirk, John E. Raven, and Malcolm Schofield, *The Presocratic Philosophers*, 2nd ed. (Cambridge: Cambridge University Press, 1983), for the definitive collection of Pythagorean fragments.

(πέρας ἓν, δεξιὸν, ἠρεμοῦν, εὐθὺ, φῶς, ἀγαθὸν, ἄρρεν) and other corresponding terms are countered by *unlimited, many, left, motion, curved, darkness, bad,* and *female* (ἄπειρον, πλῆθος, ἀριστερόν, κινούμενον, εὐθὺ, σκότος, κακόν, θῆλυ; *Metaph.* 986a22–26). Of course, the relevance of this gendered dichotomy for feminist research on the masculinization of reason and virtue has not gone unnoticed. Many scholars and historians alike have turned to the table of opposites, lambasting it as one of the premier discourses within the history of Western thought that does not merely incidentally but essentially casts the feminine or female reality as the object of, at best, mere ridicule, and, at worst, the site of depravity that must be excised from the human (read: male) condition.[2] Indeed, much ink has been spilled emphasizing how Plato reproduces this seemingly sexist discourse not merely when characters such as Socrates discuss the traits of women in contrast to men, valorizing the latter at the expense of the former,[3] but, more notably,

---

2. For arguments that analyze the appearance of this binary in the classical Greek tradition while further tracing the inheritance of this gendered matrix throughout the course of Western metaphysics, see particularly Page Dubois, *Sowing the Body: Psychoanalysis and Ancient Representations of Women* (Chicago: University of Chicago Press, 1988); Genevieve Lloyd, *The Man of Reason: Male and Female in Western Philosophy* (London: Routledge, 1984); Judith Genova, "Feminist Dialectics: Plato and Dualism," in *Engendering Origins: Critical Feminist Readings in Plato and Aristotle,* ed. Bat-Ami Bar On (Albany: State University of New York Press, 1994), 41–54; Judith Butler, *Gender Trouble: Feminism and the Subversion of Identity* (New York: Routledge, 1990); Butler, *Bodies That Matter: On the Discursive Limits of "Sex"* (New York: Routledge, 1993). See also Brooke Holmes, *Gender: Antiquity and Its Legacy (Ancient and Moderns)* (Oxford: Oxford University Press, 2012), for a good historical account of the use of gender and gendered language and practices in antiquity. The volume edited by Jessica Elbert Decker, Danielle A. Layne, and Monica Vilhauer (*Otherwise Than the Binary: New Feminist Readings in Ancient Philosophy and Culture* [New York: State University of New York Press, 2022]) offers a variety of essays that attempt to trouble the binary categories deployed across genres in ancient discourse and especially in the Greek metaphysical tradition.

3. See Plato, *Resp.* 395d5–e3, 431b9–c3, 469d, 536b, 538d–e, 605c–607a; *Theaet.* 176b; *Gorg.* 527a; and *Apol.* 24b, where Socrates explicitly associates women or the feminine with lacking some kind of virtue or behaving in unbecoming ways. Alcibiades (*Symp.* 215c) or Thrasymachus (*Resp.* 350e) and even Glaucon's idea that women are weaker at 451d are good examples where other Athenian characters insist on disparaging views of women (nonetheless, how we conceive of the Platonic understanding of "weaker" will be challenged in this essay). Of course, the most troublesome example for my students (and students of my colleagues) is *Tim.* 42c1, where Timaeus nonchalantly mentions that men who do not live well, specifically those who

when Plato explicitly genders his metaphysical projects in works such as the *Timaeus*, where the Pythagorean narrator casts the two etiological principles of creation, the Demiurge and the Receptacle, as respectively male and female. As most feminist readers of Plato decry, the Receptacle appears to be a passive placeholder for Form, an unfortunate contingency, an unruly plastic material mother whose irrational motions frustrate the rational prerogatives of the demiurgic father.[4] Ultimately, Plato stands charged by these scholars of solidifying, as natural, a gendered and exclusionary binary that ensures that the feminine remains bound to the normative categories that deem her the problem that must be overcome if the project of being human (again, read: male) is to reach its telos.

Despite the popularity and persuasiveness of these arguments, the following will push back against the idea that the dialogues reproduce

---

are weak, will be reincarnated as a woman. In fact, this essay is dedicated to every woman, BIPOC, and LGBTQ+ student whose face becomes crestfallen when they read this passage. I remember the very moment I finally understood the implications of that passage when I was a young researcher devouring the dialogues of Plato like an eager disciple. I was sitting in the stacks of the Leuven library, chewing my pen and scribbling away, and then, well, I just wasn't anymore. I just stopped and stared out the window. I felt betrayed by the philosophy/philosopher I had come to admire and with whom I was beginning to identify. At that early stage in my career, I wondered whether I would have to deny myself, or the value of what it means to be a woman, to be a Platonist. Was this what Plato really meant? Or was there something else at play? Did Plato really think that gender was essential and could be punitive, and, moreover, does this passage and others entail the idea that one gender, female, is inherently worse than the other, male? I did not have a solution to these questions then, and, as so many young feminists do at that time in their research, I tabled it. Nonetheless, I did not ever let it go. Inspired by scholars such as John Finamore, who supported even oddballs like me, I held on to the faith (*pistis*) that I would sort these issues out, even if it meant acknowledging Plato's complicit role in the history of patriarchy. Hopefully, the product of that faith after almost two decades of questioning is neither an apologetic exercise nor a wind-egg of speculation. If either, the fault is my own, and I will dust off my big-girl britches and continue searching, examining, and doubting even those things I think I know.

4. Butler, *Bodies That Matter*; Elizabeth Grosz, *Space, Time, and Perversion* (New York: Routledge, 1995); Luce Irigaray, *Speculum of the Other Woman*, trans. Gillian C. Gill (Ithaca, NY: Cornell University Press, 1985), 305. See Emanuela Bianchi, "Receptacle/Chôra: Figuring the Errant Feminine in Plato's Timaeus," *Hypatia* 21.4 (2006): 26–130, 135–43; Bianchi, *The Feminine Symptom: Aleatory Matter in the Aristotelian Cosmos* (New York: Fordham University Press, 2014), for excellent arguments that are complimentary but counter to this image of the feminine within patriarchal regimes.

this patriarchal logic. Rather, the central arguments of this essay revolve around the possibility that Plato explicitly and repeatedly undermines the moral implications implied in the dichotomy between the limit and the unlimited, the masculine and the feminine. In short, Plato did more than simply appropriate wholesale the gendered metaphysical project of the Pythagorean tradition. Instead, he markedly repositioned the value of the unlimited via its transformation into the Indefinite Dyad, the equiprimordial principle alongside the One, of the great and small, the more or less, the excessive and deficient (*Metaph.* 987b).[5] As these corollaries indicate, the Dyad's nature is unlimited and indefinite—the great can always be greater, while the small can always be smaller,[6] and so the Dyad (in contradistinction to the One) reflects infinite possibility. Furthermore, unlike the One, which is wholly impassable, the Dyad is *necessarily* receptive of its other (qua its otherness to the unreceptive One),[7] producing from within itself relation, difference, and opposition so that all things are produced or generated from within the Dyad, constituting both unique, indepen-

---

5. The argument that there is a difference between the Pythagorean unlimited and the Indefinite Dyad beyond a mere change of names runs counter to Findlay, *Written and Unwritten Doctrines*, 61. See also *Metaph.* 988a, where Aristotle suggests that the term *participation* versus the apparently more Pythagorean term *imitation* is a mere "change of name," which suggests to me that Aristotle would have sided with Findlay and also would have seen Plato's shifting terminology from the unlimited to Indefinite Dyad as a mere "change of name." See, in contrast, Krämer, who argues that the shift in vocabulary reflects Plato's concern for dialectic, wherein we move from thinking from the binary of contradictories to contraries/corollaries, which can admit of middle terms (*Plato and the Foundations*, 78).

6. Aristotle, *Metaph.* 987b25; Sextus Empiricus, *Math.* 10.277. Simplicius, *In Phys.* 455.14: "[Plato] said that the dyad was unlimited by nature because the great and the small, or the greater and the lesser, have no bounds but contain the more and less, which proceed without limit" (trans. Krämer). See also *In Phys.* 453.30–35, where Simplicius reports Porphyry's views on the Dyad: "[Plato] assigns the more and the less and the intense and the gentle to the nature of the infinite. For where these are present, proceeding by increased and decreased tension, they neither are static nor limit what partakes of them, but they proceed into indefinite limitlessness."

7. The Dyad, as other to the One, is not merely the passive material principle but, as μεταληπτικός and μεθεκτικός (*Phys.* 209b11–17 and b33–210a2) indicate, it is the "grasping/apprehending" or the "participatory" principle. Particularly, the Dyad is that which grasps and receives the One and is, consequently, the ground for the necessity (or brute and ultimate fact) of *participation* or *connection* between all things (*Phys.* 207a29–32, 209b11–17 as well as 209b33–210a2). See also Sextus Empiricus, *Math.* 10.258–259.

dent and determinative kinds and contradictory, contrary, and correlative relations (Sextus Empiricus, *Math.* 10.265–274). Therein the Dyad is the space or place wherein which being(s) (both intelligible and sensible) live and move, dynamically reproducing the indefinite or infinite power of its cause,[8] receiving or discovering within itself the determinate in the indeterminate. This is a process described as imposing limit on the unlimited, providing a mean between the extremes, a process sometimes described as the equalization (ἰσάζω) of the unequal (*Metaph.* 1091a25).[9] So, the Dyad acts as the field of possibility, the matter or space of such determination, a determination caused by the Dyad's own movement and power to relate to its other, the One. Again, as an equiprimordial principle, the Dyad, like the One, is in some sense not-Being while being a co-constitutive cause of both Being and Becoming. In short, the Dyad is both the indeterminate space and inexhaustible power behind all of reality,[10] beguiling and

---

8. Aristotle, *Phys.* 209b11–17: διὸ καὶ Πλάτων τὴν ὕλην καὶ τὴν χώραν ταὐτό φησιν εἶναι ἐν τῷ Τιμαίῳ. τὸ γὰρ μεταληπτικὸν καὶ τὴν χώραν ἓν καὶ ταὐτόν. ἄλλον δὲ τρόπον ἐκεῖ τε λέγων τὸ μεταληπτικὸν καὶ ἐν τοῖς λεγομένοις ἀγράφοις δόγμασιν, ὅμως τὸν τόπον καὶ τὴν χώραν τὸ αὐτὸ ἀπεφήνατο. Λέγουσι μὲν γὰρ πάντες εἶναί τι τὸν τόπον, τί δ'ἐστίν, οὗτος μόνος ἐπεχείρησεν εἰπεῖν. See also Aristotle, *Metaph.* 988a, where he emphasizes that Plato "makes many things out of the matter and the form generates only once" (trans. Findlay) and then emphasizes that both intelligible and sensible are a determinate dyad before criticizing the idea that a material principle could be so productive. Here, I believe, Aristotle is unable to accept this position because he sees matter or the Dyad as a thing rather than a power, comparing the Dyad to a usable or serviceable woman who, like the raw material of a table, can only contribute to making one thing. This comparison clearly evidences one of the many glaring moments that Aristotle's sexism and heteronormativity inhabit his ability to think speculatively. See Simplicius (*In Phys.* 202b36), who reported comments wherein which he argues that there is an "infinite element both in sensible things and in Ideas" (trans. Findlay). See also Theophrastus, *Metaph.* 6a15–b17; Alexander, *Test. Plato.* 22b (56, 15–20), Alexander, 25013–20; Simplicius, *In Phys.* 454.3–9: οὐ γὰρ ἂν εἰς ἀδιαίρετόν γε ἔλθοιμέν ποτε μέρος τέμνοντες. συνεχὲς γάρ ἐστιν ὁ πῆχυς. τὸ δὲ συνεχὲς διαιρεῖται εἰς ἀεὶ διαιρετά. ἡ δὴ τοιαύτη ἀδιάλειπτος τομὴ δηλοῖ τινα φύσιν ἀπείρου κατακεκλεισμένην ἐν τῷ πήχει, μᾶλλον δὲ πλείους, τὴν μὲν ἐπὶ τὸ μέγα προϊοῦσαν τὴν δὲ ἐπὶ τὸ μικρόν. ἐν τούτοις δὲ καὶ ἡ ἀόριστος δυὰς ὁρᾶται ἔκ τε τῆς ἐπὶ τὸ μέγα καὶ τῆς ἐπὶ τὸ μικρὸν μονάδος συγκειμένη.

9. See Findlay, *Written and Unwritten Doctrines*, 62, 74–75.

10. See Krämer, who believes that this not-Being quality of the Dyad makes the Dyad in some sense "below being" (*Plato and the Foundations*, 79). Yet, to be sure, this runs counter to the Platonic conception of not-Being as relative Being wherein which that which is not is not absolute privation but relation qua contrary/corollary (see *Soph.* 257b–259b). In agreement, Dmitri Nikulin writes: "The indefinite dyad is not

perplexing all determination, frustrating being at all levels of reality while simultaneously nurturing and constituting the uniqueness of all things, providing all things with their own infinite motive/generative power, or the capacity to dynamically and creatively live, to be self-moved while inhabiting our own indeterminate space.

In short, unlike the Pythagoreans, Plato's conception of the Indefinite Dyad is not something to be avoided or controlled. It is not the bad simpliciter.[11] Insofar as the indefinite contains both extreme terms (the definite is in the indefinite, the limit in the unlimited), we are invited to see how, for Plato, the unlimited, the indefinite, the dark, the so-called weak, are necessary for human flourishing. In other words, Plato thought beyond the binary of the Pythagorean limit and the unlimited, and it is the contention of this paper that Plato, throughout his corpus, consistently makes use of masculine and feminine images, the exclusionary gender binary deployed by the Pythagoreans, so as to highlight how terms associated with the table of opposites—the manic, the irrational, the confused, the emotional, the dark, the weak, the empty or impoverished—must necessarily be incorporated into the flourishing life, must not be repressed or ignored as inessential. From this starting position, Plato playfully uses sex, gender, and sexuality in a variety of dialogues to evidence that one must recognize the equality of the male and the female, the masculine and the feminine as fluid and dynamic codetermining ruling principles of the soul because these *archai* in the soul never exist in isolation.

To evidence this very controversial interpretation of Plato, we will first turn to how the Dyad of the great and small, masculine and feminine, strength and weakness, the limit and the unlimited, appears in explicitly gendered images of the soul found in the *Timaeus* and the *Symposium*. Explicitly concerned with the mixture or the in-betweenness of Soul, be it the cosmic soul of the *Timaeus* or the particular eroticism of individu-

---

non-being per se (because non-being, properly, *is not*), ... but [is] an ideal principle of otherness and inequality that is further associated with motion." See Nikulin, ed., *The Other Plato: The Tubingen Interpretation of Plato's Inner-Academic Teachings* (New York: State University of New York Press, 2012), 17.

11. Contra Aristotle, *Metaph.* 1091b13–15; *Eth. Eud.* 1218a; *Elements of Harmony* 2.30–31; Krämer, *Plato and the Foundations*, 86; Thomas Szlezak, "The Idea of the Good as *Arkhe* in Plato's *Republic*," in Nikulin, *Other Plato*, 131. See also *Metaph.* 1072b–1073a and 1091b16–35, as well as Iamblichus, *Comm. Math. sc.* 4.15. 23–4.17.1, where Aristotle claims that Speusippus refuses to identify the Good with the One on pain that it would eliminate the Good from the Even, i.e., from the Dyad.

als in the *Symposium*, Plato repeatedly features the power of the so-called deficient feminine principle and the weakness of the so-called excessive masculine principle. Rather, these extreme terms, these gendered dyads, need mediation if their offspring is to be good or beautiful. These readings will allow us to turn to the *Republic* and the *kallipolis*, examining how Socrates's equality of men and women demands we go beyond the literal political interpretation and toward the psycho/philosophical implications for the city's analogy to the soul. Overall, we shall conclude that Plato, in the playful mixture of extremes, reminds readers that what appears to be the soul's weakness may rather be the site of the soul's unlimited and infinite power and, as such, should be acknowledged as a genuinely central, or equal, guiding principle in the philosophical life.

The Gendered Principles in the *Timaeus* and the *Symposium*

1. *Timaeus*

> Our task of filling the place of the absent one falls upon you and our friends here, does it not?
> —Plato, *Tim.* 17a

In response to learning that some illness (ἀσθένεια), literally some weakness, has befallen the fourth member of the not-so motley crew of friends, Socrates charges Critias, Timaeus, and Hermocrates with the work of filling (ἀναπληρόω) seemingly empty space while setting in motion (κινέω) or enlivening the city from Socrates's own speech advanced the day before. The task at hand in the *Timaeus* is that the men must create dynamic living images of *logoi*. As we all know, the response to Socrates's challenge is far from lackluster, as Critias and Timaeus provide two stunning images supporting the reality of the *kallipolis*, which assigns the same functions in ruling and war alike to women and men alongside holding women and children in common (*Tim.* 18c–d). The image offered by Critias, of course, is the infamous myth of Atlantis, wherein we are invited to view the current Athenian population as the product of a perfect race (γενεά) born of the land (χώρα) they now inhabit. Contemporary Athenians are described as "some little seed that happened to be left over [περιλειφθέντος ποτὲ σπέρματος βραχέος]" after millennia of deluges and restarts (*Tim.* 23c). Here, the allusion to a kind of smallness that contains a trace of perfection, of a people who could bravely battle even the larg-

est of foes despite their own meager size, should not be cast aside as a
mere literary trope. In other words, the explicit reminder of the equality
of men and women in the prelude of the speech as well as the demand
to set the city in motion, depicted in a battle of corollaries of seemingly
strong (Atlanteans) and weak (Athenians), seemingly potent and impotent, intentionally demands a reevaluation of the power of the opposing
terms, particularly the coming opposition between the Demiurge and the
Receptacle/Khora later in the text.

As mentioned, the *Timaeus* casts the causes of the cosmos in explicitly
gendered terms, with the speech's first half being the works of Reason/
Demiurge and the second half the works of Necessity/Khora before turning to their combined consequences, wherein we are repeatedly told that
the works of Reason/Necessity never occurred in isolation, there is no
time wherein which the Demiurge performed certain tasks and Khora
actualized others. Rather, the cosmos, the sensible living thing, is always
a mixture of the powers of both. In short, the speech already sets up a
dichotomy between extreme terms, the works of Reason and the works of
Necessity, so as to stress ultimately the soul's fusion of opposites. At first
blush, the Demiurge appears to reflect the determining/equalizing/limiting
power, while the Receptacle graces the stage as a kind of indefinite chaotic
material reflecting standard accounts of the Dyad.[12] Yet, the Demiurge and
Khora actually reflect a kind of excessiveness whose middle term, whose
mixture, most likens it as far as possible to the beauty of the intelligible
living thing. The Demiurge, as representing the extremity of the power of
the great and the small, is most "like" the intelligible living being, while
Khora/Receptacle reflects the deficiency (the small of the great and small)
and is most "unlike" the intelligible living being. She is indeed perplexing, a seeming nothingness, something grasped only by a form of bastard
reasoning, which is described as other than sensation and almost dreamlike (a description that will return when we discuss Socrates's constant
confessions of ignorance in the *Republic*). Nonetheless, Khora/Receptacle,

---

12. See Findlay, who fixates on the Receptacle as the Indefinite Dyad to the point
wherein it is also identified with the utterly nonexistent (*Written and Unwritten Doctrines*, 317–31). Findlay further reinforces her neediness and the idea that despite her
role in the coming-into-being of the cosmos, "The One is really responsible for everything," and later, "No serious heed need therefore be given to the state of Chora before
the Divine Doctor took her hand. Her weakness were the weaknesses of the impo-
tently possible which is nothing apart from its structuring Eide."

in her so-called deficiency, her otherness to the Demiurge, is oddly the *proper* or *fitting* space (χώρα) for life, for the totality of all things, internalizing extremes such as great and small so that in the so-called weak there is a power to grasp or take hold of the strong, in the seeming nothingness there is a capacity to bear all of reality, both infinite and finite, mortal and immortal. She is the *necessity* or power of relation between extremes, supporting and nourishing the life of the sensible living thing.[13] She, in her seeming nothingness, for she is not Being, is still the Nurse (τιθήνη) of Becoming—an indefinite field of possibility, a mad chaotic movement that fittingly can receive Demiurgic Form, limit, and can so tend to the unique and determinative life of their shared offspring, Soul.

Explicitly introduced in romantic and erotic terms, as one who yields to the intelligent persuasion of reason, the Receptacle is described as Necessity, and in this necessity she takes the form of the wandering cause (τὸ τῆς πλανωμένης εἶδος αἰτίας). Like the discussion of the Demiurge, Timaeus prefaces his discussion of this wandering cause by reminding his peers that this is a "likely account," and so he calls on god to act as a savior (48d3) that can bring them through an uncanny and strange discussion of that cause whose power and nature is difficult and obscure (ἀμυδρός). Primarily, she is to be both inviting host or receiver (ὑποδοχή) and nurse or supporter/caretaker (τιθήνη) of becoming, but then, later, she is described as a kind of mold (ἐκμαγεῖον) that can retain traces or impressions of the things that emerge from her (in her coordination with the other, the Demiurge). Finally, she is deemed mother who (due to her nature as invisible, unshaped, and all-receptive/inviting) "shares/partakes of," literally, grasps (μεταλαμβάνω), the mixtures of body and soul, giving them a place or space to live and move. Ultimately, she becomes the ever-existing space (τῆς χώρας ἀεί) that will not admit destruction, that is, she safeguards all that is in her, providing an abode (ἕδραν) for all that comes in to being and moves between extremes. Far from passive, the Khora/Receptacle necessitates that everything has a place, and anything outside

---

13. See Glenn R. Morrow, "Necessity and Persuasion in Plato's Timaeus," *PhilRev* 59 (1950): 147–63. Consider also the following from Bianchi: "While Plato uses figures of human work and technology, it is the distinctively feminine labors of nursing and grain sorting, and the distinctively feminine artifact of the woven basket, that give shape and name, or perhaps more strictly give motion qua 'life' to the strictly unknowable 'wandering cause' of the receptacle and chora, and thus to the cosmos itself" ("Receptacle/Chôra," 132).

her is nothing (τὸ οὐδέν). There is nothing outside her, and, as such, she is the indeterminate, fluctuating but inviting space, providing movement via transmitting her own shaking to all who enter.[14] Again, she herself is not absolute non-Being but that which *refuses* not-Being, as she will not admit (or invite in) destruction. Overall, like her corollary, Khora's indefinite unlimitedness is that which desires to secure a place for meaning, for being, for the Good, even in her so-called limited power, even in her own so-called nothingness. Ultimately, qua ὑποδοχή and χώρα she is both receptacle and host, both troubling and providing, nothing in herself but also all things in her activity of relation, connection and participation. As Emanuela Bianchi argues while analyzing Necessity's twin identities as Receptacle and Khora,

> Perhaps the most decisive distinction is itself topological: ὑποδοχή, receptacle, envelops with a boundary, it presents a kind of invagination, a cave, an opening into interiority, an invitation to filling, inscription, penetration. Chora denotes rather an exteriority, an opening out, giving room, dimension, depth, and magnitude—spacing—but also, as indicated by the related verb *chorizo*, separating, dividing, differentiating, and severing. Chora thus provides the possibility of distinguishing up and down, here and there, an originary separation and dispersal of Being into beings with position with respect to one another.... ὑποδοχή / χώρα thus discloses the interdependence and co-constitution of space and boundary, as well as a dual movement: inviting in, receiving, holding, appropriating on the one hand, and opening out, providing space, giving, dispersing on the other.[15]

This dual function of the Receptacle is often glossed over in favor of concentrating on the works of the Demiurge, but, again, the Demiurge and Receptacle belong together as the dyadic otherness in relation to the intelligible living being that must be brought into mixture, must be made equal or codeterminative, if it hopes to resemble the all-embracing intelligible model.

---

14. Here, the active reading of ὑποδοχή as "host" allows for an image of one who has the gift of making space for others, a party where all things are a bit indeterminate and in flux, but a party that once underway is carefully nourished by the host's power to unexpectedly shake things up, a shaking that provides the necessary but also novel rhythm to invite individuals to dance.

15. Bianchi, "Receptacle/Chôra," 131–32.

To clarify, the Demiurge, too, is part of the dyadic field where both the Demiurge and the Receptacle possess active and passive elements, both are needy of the other, and as such both necessarily express a kind of duality and excessiveness. Recall that the Demiurge is to create something beautiful; he *compelled* to fix his gaze always on the paradigm (πρὸς τὸ κατὰ ταὐτὰ ἔχον βλέπων ἀεί). Further, Timaeus leans on spatiotemporal metaphor to describe the activity of the Demiurge, that is, he seems to be *in* something or at least looking out or above himself. Further, the Demiurge is described as most good (τῷ ἀρίστῳ) and most fair (τὸ κάλλιστον), emphasizing his place on a spectrum in relation to an opposing corollary. Further, his activity is one wherein he constructs reason within soul and soul within body (διὰ δὴ τὸν λογισμὸν τόνδε νοῦν μὲν ἐν ψυχῇ, ψυχὴν δ' ἐν σώματι), reproducing the importance of creating or finding the fitting place *in which* things belong, even providing a place for reason and soul.

The intelligible living being is further described as that which embraces (περιλαμβάνω) and holds (ἔχω) all intelligible creatures, and as a consequence the Demiurge creates, as closely as possible, a living being that resembles this paradigm. Particularly striking is that the Demiurge fashions both body and soul whereby, on the one hand, body is constructed so that each term is relative to the other, that is, middle terms are interchangeable (*Tim.* 31c–32a), ensuring that while things have determinative power, they cannot dominate or take over the mixture (no element is Atlantean). On the other hand, the soul is also a mixture of intermediate Being, Sameness and Difference, which come to live and move, have a place, in Khora/Receptacle. Yet, to be sure, in this process the Demiurge shows himself to be dyadic. He, too, is both mixer and mixing bowl (κρατῆρα), both form and himself a kind of matter/space, an active desire and will to look to the paradigm and create, a creative process still subject to the necessity of relation and participation, still subject to the field of possibility provided by Necessity. He is not, despite his strength, all-powerful. He must bend to the necessity of Necessity, bend to the fact of his relation to otherness. In other words, in the weak there is the strong and in the strong there is weakness. Even in the extremes of the Demiurge and Khora, we find that they are already mixed.

So, in the end, it seems that Necessity reigns or rules in being both a determinate and indeterminate feature of the extremes of both Khora/Receptacle and the Demiurge. This necessary relation, existing between not only Khora/Receptacle and the Demiurge but also the two in relation to the intelligible living being, allows their offspring to be like the intelligible living thing but also unlike, slightly other or different but still related. Both are a combination of being and power, limit and unlimited. Like Critias and Timaeus, the task of Becoming, the offspring of the Demiurge and Khora, is to fill the gap (ἀναπληρόω) between the extremes of its parents, making present the absence, making something Good/beautiful not in spite of the absent/weak but partly because of it. Qua offspring of both extremes, the living cosmos is tasked with being the measure or mean of that which can be *both* ordered and chaotic, same and different, limited and unlimited, strong and weak, wherein the latter, its/our so-called weakness, may in fact be the space or abode of support/nourishment, it may be what *motivates* us. In other words, the excessive small or the excessive and disruptive feminine nothingness, a nothingness that refuses to admit of destruction, is the fitting space for movement that secures the power of lives that run between extremes, be it low or high, strong or weak, feminine or masculine. The image of the masculine and feminine principles of the Demiurge and Khora/Receptacle plays with a kind of gender essentialism but so as to emphasize that ultimately the good for Soul is in the mixture, in the relation, a relation that ultimately constitutes the beauty of being a neither/nor, something like the extremes of the father and mother of creation but also other to them.

As products of *both* the Demiurge and Receptacle, we, too, are dyadic. First, as those beings that inhabit bodies, individuals reflect the mixture of a strange reality, that regardless of our personal death, the Receptacle's power safeguards that we never come to suffer absolute destruction, as she refuses to admit of non-Being. We shall pass, again and again, into other lives, into other bodies, a one in a many. In the final section on reincarnation in Timaeus's speech, our narrator, perhaps unintentionally, reminds us that he is a Pythagorean, an identification that brings with it an explicitly sexist understanding of reality whereby the female and feminine are less than. We see this in his understanding of reincarnation when he comes to reinforce a kind of gender essentialism whereby the superior sex is explicitly demarcated as man (*Tim.* 41d) so that "men who prove themselves cowardly and spent their lives in wrong-doing were transformed, at their second incarnation, into women" (*Tim.* 90e). Yet, even this devaluation of the embodied life of a woman is overcome or surmounted from within Timaeus's speech, that is, like Athens there is a powerful and disruptive trait lying dormant in his speech. That is, when we remember that soul is a mixture of intermediate Being, Sameness and Difference, then we are invited to remember that the soul is a mixture of what the Pythagoreans would have gendered. If man is the limit and woman the unlimited, if man is determinate being and woman the indeterminate being, then in sensible reality, which is a combination of determinate and indeterminate Being, Sameness and Difference, there are no men and women, at least not absolutely so. Both body and soul are mixtures of these principles, principles often associated with binary gender whereby sameness and limit reflect the masculine product of the Demiurge while difference and unlimited the necessary unruly offshoot of feminine Khora.

Indeed, this understanding of the mixture of the soul/body that constitutes the beauty and good of the sensible living being is reinforced when Timaeus describes the male and female sex organs in such a way as to indicate the problems of a male and female principle isolated from its other, that is, excessive maleness or excessive femaleness. Despite being very heteronormative, these descriptions of extreme male and female indicate that if male and female or masculine and feminine are thought in isolation or as not mixed, sickness and vice will ensue. In other words, anything that attempts to neatly sit on one side of the binary will fail to do its productive work. For example, for Timaeus, the male sex organ (which is described as capable of providing seed) without the female will become unpersuadable (ἀπειθές), autocratic (αὐτοκρατὲς), disobedient or deaf (ἀνυπήκοον) to reason, filled with raging lusts and bent on dominating all things (πάντων δι᾽ ἐπιθυμίας οἰστρώδεις ἐπιχειρεῖ κρατεῖν; descriptions that gesture to the *Republic* and the image of the tyrannical man). Similarly, the female sex organ without its binary counterpart becomes sick (νόσους) with violent irritations that are hard to bear (χαλεπῶς ἀγανακτοῦν φέρει), wandering all over (πλανώμενον πάντῃ) so that she blocks pathways (διεξόδους ἀποφράττον) and throws everything into excessive perplexity (εἰς ἀπορίας τὰς ἐσχάτας ἐμβάλλει; descriptions that allude to or mirror, as we shall soon see, both Eros and the laboring soul of the philosopher in the *Symposium*). Ultimately, though, the wandering womb that indwells women, that is desirous of children (ζῷον ἐπιθυμητικὸν ἐνὸν τῆς παιδοποιίας), gestures back to the power of the dyad of both Demiurge and Khora, where sexual union with the other allows for "invisible smallness" to grow and become great (even in the weak or the hysterically mad, there is a trace of power, a trace that moves us to become otherwise or to grasp or take hold of something otherwise), ending in generation, a process that, Timaeus concludes, completes the living creature (*Tim.* 91a–d).

So, in all these ways, living things, both then and now, exchange with one another [διαμείβεται], possessing the power of transformation [κτήσει μεταβαλλόμενα] and the loss of reason or unreason [νοῦ καὶ ἀνοίας ἀποβολῇ].... For our Cosmos has seized [λαμβάνω] the mortal and immortal and has therein been filled up [συμπληρόω], a visible living being embracing [περιέχω] visible being, a perceptible God, an image of the intelligible, most great and good and fair and perfect, one heaven sole of its kind. (*Tim.* 92b–c)

Noting the language of seizing, embracing and filling as well as the extreme terms such as "greatest" (92c5, μέγιστος), we see that the offspring is indeed a mixture of dyadic power, a relation of extremes where the mean or middle, the new mixture, must transform and must move between extremes, gain and lose reason, fluctuate and remain fluid, never always one thing or the other insofar as both causes of the soul are equal, are codeterminative.

2. *Symposium*

In the *Symposium* we are again invited to observe an explicitly gendered dyadic set of relations that produce a particular kind of dyadic or mixed offspring, that is, masculine Plenty (Πόρος) and feminine Poverty. Interestingly, it seems that Plenty (explicitly associated with his mother, Μήτιδος) and Poverty (Πενία) are like the great and the small, expressing excessive extremes. The extremity is perhaps even more pronounced than in the presentation of the Demiurge and the Receptacle insofar as Plenty's abundance is to the point of drunken leisure (203b), while Poverty is described as destitute, begging (προσαιτήσουσα), needy to the point of thievery and violence (she takes from, arguably rapes, Plenty). Here, again, like the deficient terms of the *Timaeus*, we see that Poverty is not wholly impotent; she contains, like Athens/Khora, within herself a kind of resource, a trace of power. Recall that it is Poverty rather than Plenty who possesses the cunning and craftiness (she, too, appears like a child of Metis) to devise (ἐπιβουλεύουσα) the plan to bear a child. She actively lies down beside him (κατακλίνεταί) and conceives/brings forth (ἐκύησε) Eros, the attendant (ἀκόλουθος) of divine Aphrodite, her comrade in arms (θεράπων; two terms that will reappear in the *Republic*). Despite Poverty's so-called lack of resource or perplexity (ἀπορίαν)—she is not docilely abstinent but ravishingly libidinous—she comes to bear Eros while Plenty, in his needlessness, drinks too much of the divine nectar and ends up alone, dreaming and sleeping (εἰσελθὼν βεβαρημένος ηὗδεν) in the garden of Zeus. In other words, it is the resource in Poverty that constitutes the creation of the erotic alongside a kind of poverty in Plenty, a too-much-ness, whereby the plentiful has become excessive to the point that he appears not like himself, not plentiful but drowsy and uninterested in his own virility. Ultimately, like both his parents, Eros becomes a both/and, but a both/and that reinforces the possibility of connection between the extremes, discounting neither the one nor the other but always connecting the two. As Diotima suggests when discussing the spiritual as that which supplements both the mortal and the immortal, Eros is that which seems to fill (συμπληροῖ), like Critias and Timaeus's role in the *Timaeus*, the seemingly empty space between the two (*Symp.* 202e). Due to this in-betweeness, Plato, via a series of interrelated narratives that culminate in Socrates's perplexing account of a female foreign priestess, crafts a lovely and inspiring image of one who embodies strength despite typically being regarded as weak. Diotima qua both being a woman and a foreigner would be like the flute girl, one who would normally be dismissed, like *Timaeus's* absent and weak fourth, not be heard. Diotima, whose expertise is in love, articulates (as best as she is able: *Symp.* 201d) a peculiar account of the origin and being of Eros before discussing the activity or power of Eros in the pursuit of Beauty (*Symp.* 201e). In this account, Diotima articulates an uncanny measure or mean, the erotic way of life, which seems to move through excess and deficiency in such a way as to show the value of both.

Rather remarkably, the exegesis on the being of love begins with a mistake in reasoning on Socrates's part. His inexperience in matters of love makes him think in terms of exact contraries, that is, when told that Eros is not beautiful, Socrates thus assumes he must be ugly. In short, he neglects to notice the possibility of a middle term between the extremes of the beautiful and ugly. He fails to understand the field of possibility, the need of a space between, something that resides halfway (μεταξὺ), something that partakes or shares of both extremes. To explain more fully, Diotima infamously creates a different kind of table of opposites between terms such as wisdom/knowledge and ignorance, whereby true opinion moves between them, akin (or related) to knowledge insofar as it hits at the truth but akin (or related) to ignorance insofar as it is unreasoned (*Symp.* 202a). Rather interestingly, once Socrates agrees that true opinion resides between knowledge and ignorance, Diotima highlights that the good and bad are in complementary rather than contradictory terms, emphasizing that Socrates ought not compel or, more literally, necessitate that what is not beautiful be ugly or what is not good be bad (Μὴ τοίνυν ἀνάγκαζε ὃ μὴ καλόν ἐστιν αἰσχρὸν εἶναι, μηδὲ ὃ μὴ ἀγαθόν, κακόν). Further, she goes on to emphasize that Eros is not a god insofar as he lacks or is deficient (ἐνδεής) and, a little later, is without a share (ἄμοιρος) in possessing beautiful and good things, which makes it impossible to view him as a god because gods must possess the beautiful and good (*Symp.* 202d). Again, this leads Socrates to once again fail to notice the middle term insofar as he immediately concludes that the contrary term, *mortal*, must be applied to Eros.

Socrates does at least have the good sense to ask Diotima about the value of the between insofar as he wonders what that daimonic or spiritual is that lies between the divine and the mortal. She responds with the basic idea that the spiritual is that which interprets and transports human things to the divine and divine things to the human, a supplementing (συμπληροῖ, literally a filling up) of both (again, the same language as the *Timaeus*). For Diotima, it is only via the spiritual that contact between mortal and immortal is secured, and ultimately, like the various forms of divine madness in the *Phaedrus*, the priestess reassures Socrates that there are many forms of the daimonic, of that which is a product of the dyadic corollaries, but one of them is Eros.

Eventually turning to the parental lineage of Eros (discussed above), Diotima ultimately paints a portrait of Eros whereby the daimonic spirit is not a definite limit (or measure) in the way that the absolutely equal resides between the great and the small or excess and deficiency. Rather, Eros resembles his mother (*Symp.* 203d). He always dwells in want (ἀεὶ ἐνδείᾳ σύνοικος), moving between extremes as something whose power waxes and wanes, ascends and descends, something unlike his father, who has become complacent and drowsy, impoverished by his haughty arrogance (perhaps resembling someone like Alcibiades, who possesses great gifts but squanders them, who seems to suffer from the disease of the autocratic male genitalia of the *Timaeus*). Markedly, Eros is described as a philosopher, and as such Diotima positions him as one who stands between wisdom and ignorance, because the gods are not in need of wisdom while the ignorant fail to acknowledge their deficiency, a sad fact that reinforces the need for recognized ignorance. As Diotima says, "the person who does not suspect their lack has no desire for that which he does not suspect he lacks" (*Symp.* 204a, trans. Lamb, slightly adapted). In other words, Eros, the philosopher, the spiritual attendant to the divine, is that which traverses the space between wisdom and ignorance because of a recognized lack/deficiency, in this case ignorance. In short, there is a kind of power or a potential power in a peculiar form of ignorance. Recognized ignorance, then, is a powerful weakness of the soul without which one could never honor and internalize the erotic, daimonic pursuit of the beautiful and the good.[16]

The eroticism of the soul is the reality of the dynamic relation between contrary and correlative relations and lives, lives that must continuously associate and identify with the markedly feminine activities of pregnancy, painful labor, and the corresponding relief/beauty of giving birth. It is the power of the feminine that is highlighted and, in a very real sense, seems to constitute the wantonness of need, the striving and pining that arises in the so-called deficient term. The soul, as that which seeks after others who are similarly pregnant, needs to give birth to the plenty growing from within their need, from within the interior space of their mental lives, a process that is markedly described as "giving birth to the beautiful *in* the beautiful both with respect to body and soul" (ἔστι γὰρ τοῦτο τόκος ἐν καλῷ καὶ κατὰ τὸ σῶμα καὶ κατὰ τὴν ψυχήν). While often thought of as a strange way of phrasing the erotic practice of philosophy, the emphasis on a kind of *birthing in* becomes clearer when we recall the importance of dyadic space in the *Timaeus*, where the dyad of the Demiurge and Khora allows for the production of beauty (in both body and soul) in the khoratic and aporetic nothingness. Her indefiniteness, her confusing place, is again the fitting or proper space (χώρα) for the totality of all things to come into being. In other words, like Poverty, Khora may be impoverished or discordant, but this discordance or lack does not make her ugly or, as Diotima says, unfitting (ἀναρμόστῳ). Because of her own motions, in some sense, she was already pregnant with desire for a child (she possessed a seed or trace of her own infinite power), already exhibiting a kind of beauty that made her the fitting place for the Demiurge's own conceptions of body and soul. Because they fit, that is, despite their difference, they were able to give birth to that which comes-to-be, a divine cosmos both like and unlike the intelligible living thing.

Similarly, Poverty's and Plenty's offspring, Eros, is not a god, an absolute principle like Form, but rather Eros becomes "a different type" [τὸ δέ γε ἐρῶν ἄλλην ἰδέαν τοιαύτην ἔχον], something between the determinate and the indeterminate, a strange indeterminate determination allowing

---

16. See Danielle Layne, "Refutation and Double Ignorance in Proclus," *Epoché* 13 (2009): 347–62.

movement and the constant replenishment of ideas (*Symp.* 204b–c).[17] The parallel between the Demiurge and Khora and Plenty and Poverty as well as the definition of Eros as that which gives "birth to the beautiful in the beautiful" seems further confirmed when Diotima invokes a pair of deities as presiding over the relationship between the lover and the beloved (where the beloved also needs to be beautiful in the sense of fitting): "Consequently, Beauty presides over generation as Moira (Fate) and Ilithyia (goddess who both comes in need and of childbirth)" (*Symp.* 206d). Here, like Khora, who is Necessity, Eros's ability to unite extremes seems connected to the corresponding terms of Fate and need/birthing. Moreover, like the end of the *Timaeus*, where he advances images of unmixed extremes whereby isolated male and female sex organs are compared to animals, Diotima, too, describes animal desire to help elucidate the need to join/mix but also the lengths animals go to care for their young.

> What do you suppose is the cause of this love and desire? For don't you perceive how all animals when desiring to generate, are in a strange disposition [διατίθεται]? They are sick [νοσοῦντά] and amorously disposed [διατιθέμενα], first to have union one with another, and next to find nourishment [τροφὴν] for the new-born; on their behalf, they are ready to fight hard battles even the weakest against the strongest [ἕτοιμά ἐστιν ὑπὲρ τούτων καὶ διαμάχεσθαι τὰ ἀσθενέστατα τοῖς ἰσχυροτάτοις], and to sacrifice lives; to torture themselves with hunger, and yet still further doings, if they can but nourish [ἐκτρέφειν] their young. (*Symp.* 207a–b [Lamb])

Again, the allusion to animals is no accident. Diotima emphasizes (like Timaeus) the spectrum of animal extremes, from low to high, and emphasizes that over and above the union, the erotic process is also about caring for what has been born, and it is this caring that is the cause of love and desire. It is this nourishing, this imaging of Khora as a nurse or attendant, that sustains the life of her offspring, not in spite of but because of her erratic, protective movement. Particularly striking in this passage is how the weakest are the ones battling against the strongest, ready to run the risk of death in battle, or even ones (like Khora) who fail to provide for

---

17. See Findlay, *Written and Unwritten Doctrines*, 150.

themselves. Again, like Khora, these animals are in a strange state but a strange state that is ready to care for its offspring, come what may.

Ultimately, the parallel to nourishing (ἐκτρέφειν) is maintained when Diotima returns to Eros, qua spirit of the philosopher, who presides over the birth of ideas, those erotic offspring that *ever dwell in desire* within ourselves. Yet, unlike the divine ideas, which always remain our offspring, the children between knowledge and ignorance grow and perish due to forgetfulness and memory (the flux of movement between knowing and not knowing). As such, the philosopher is called to attend to or care for (μελέτη) knowledge via replacing old ideas with new ones, different but also similar to the old ideas, so that we experience a continuity in our sense of knowledge (*Symp.* 208a). As lovers of wisdom, as those who are "of another kind" from the divine (who possess the absolutely good and beautiful), the erotic soul must recognize when deficiency or lack arises. Diotima compares this to a kind of waning period, when we should accept that what seems departed or absent (τὸ ἀπιὸν) or decayed (παλαιούμενον) has still left behind a trace (ἐγκαταλείπειν; much like the Athenian khora and the small seed of the perfect race), and as such, with a little care, we can replace the old with the new (explicitly something other that is like the old or original; *Symp.* 208a–b). Ultimately, as we know, it is via eros and this constant, never-ending process whereby we may ascend to a vision of the Beautiful, a vision that *almost* enables the philosopher to touch or lay hold of Beauty itself (σχεδὸν ἄν τι ἅπτοιτο τοῦ τέλους), a laying hold of or reaching (ἐφάπτῳ) toward the end, which, if tended to or reared properly (τρέφω), constitutes divine friendship (θεοφιλεῖ). Yet, to be sure, what is required of the philosopher is a proper tending (τρέφω), caring (μελέτη), a reaching out (φαπτῳ) that demands that one remain in constant relation not only to the Beauty at the end but also to the trace of the beautiful motivating the beginning, the small resource in Poverty, the erratic but nourishing space of Khora, the nourishment that even the weakest animal attempts to bring, ready to battle against the strongest (possibly something/someone like the male sex organ or Alcibiades that has become autocratic, unpersuadable, bent on domination and disobedient to reason), all for the sake of producing and letting grow an offspring that resembles its parental causes.[18]

---

18. Of course, in many ways, we can see this erotic condition also in the image of the soul recounted in the *Phaedrus*. While not explicitly gendered as it is in the *Symposium*, the triad of charioteer and two horses is explicitly marked by the Pythagorean

The First and Second Wave of Paradox of *Republic* 5

Nowhere else in Plato's corpus is gender so conspicuous and taken so seriously than the relations between men and women infamously advanced in book 5 of the *Republic*.[19] Like the *Timaeus*, much ink has been spilled by feminists either defending or undermining the seriousness of Socrates's arguments for (1) the equality of men and women in the first wave of paradox alongside (2) his objectively strange organization of their sexual and reproductive lives in the second wave of paradox. Many have read the first two waves quite literally arguing that Plato was indeed offering a protofeminist vision,[20] and others have dismissed both waves as absurd, an absurdity meant to remind us that the *kallipolis* is not to be taken seriously. Socrates is being ironic.[21] Unlike these positions, the following will take into serious consideration two things: (1) the *kallipolis* is an explicitly crafted analogy for the soul (an analogy that does not discount the political implications but one that supplements them), and (2) Timaeus's and Diotima's use of masculine and feminine reproductive imagery is absolutely relevant for understanding Socrates's use of sex, gender, and

---

terms of light and dark. One horse immediately inclines to the heavens and is thus like the charioteer, a kind of leading demiurgic power, while the dark horse inclines downward, opening up an actual field of opposition. In other words, like the unruly Receptacle or desperate Poverty, the dark horse has a power and motion of its own, one that must be trained or exercised by the limiting principle of the charioteer.

19. See Julia Annas, "Plato's *Republic* and Feminism," *Philosophy* 51 (1976): 307–21; Gregory Vlastos, "Was Plato a Feminist?," in *Feminist Interpretations of Plato*, ed. Nancy Tuana (University Park: Pennsylvania State University Press, 1994), 133–43; Christopher C. W. Taylor, "The Role of Women in Plato's Republic," in *Virtue and Happiness: Essays in Honour of Julia Annas*, ed. Rachana Kamtekar (Oxford: Oxford University Press, 2012), 75–86.

20. See Vlastos, "Was Plato a Feminist?" Contra Annas, "Plato's *Republic* and Feminism."

21. For those who do not take Socrates's proposal seriously, see Allan Bloom, "Interpretive Essay," in *The "Republic" of Plato with Notes and Interpretive Essay*, ed. Bloom (New York: Basic Books, 1968), 305–436; Arlene Saxonhouse, "The Philosopher and the Female in the Political Thought of Plato," *PT* 4 (1976): 195–212; Elizabeth Spelman, "Hairy Cobblers and Philosopher Queens," in *Engendering Origins*, ed. Bat-Ami Bar-On (Albany: State University of New York Press, 1994), 3–24; Leo Strauss, *The City and Man* (Chicago: Rand McNally, 1964); Natalie Bluestone, "Why Women Cannot Rule: Sexism in Plato Scholarship," in Tuana, *Feminist Interpretations of Plato*, 109–30.

sexuality in his city in speech. Indeed, when these two things are taken into account, one must ask whether there may in fact be a very simple answer to these two seemingly paradoxical waves. Is it not possible and maybe even desirable to read the first two waves of paradox as offering a highly elaborate analogy for obtaining the proper measure between extremes, a measure that results in a kind of mixed offspring that, if properly reared and trained, lead the soul toward the just life or, as the third wave of paradox entails, the philosophical life, which explicitly ascends and descends, lives as that uncanny being that moves between extremes?[22]

In response to Adeimantus and Polemarchus's request to discuss how women and children will be held in common, like Timaeus, who admits the perplexity and confusion, his need even for a savior (483d3), before attempting to discuss the works of Necessity, Socrates hesitates before the "female drama" and admits his fears (*Resp.* 450a–b). Also, like Timaeus, Socrates mentions that such a discussion is like starting again from the beginning (ἐξ ἀρχῆς), a beginning that sets in motion (κινεῖτε) or awakens (ἐπεγείρετε) a swarm of debate (ἑσμὸν λόγων) and a vast multitude (πολὺν ὄχλον) of problems. Emphasizing that coming to the limit (περαίνειν) of the "female drama [γυναικεῖον [δρᾶμα]" [23] will not be easy because it admits of many doubts or, literally, incredulities (ἀπιστίας), Socrates expresses a reluctance to engage (ὄκνος τις αὐτῶν ἅπτεσθαι) for fear it is merely wishful opinion (εὐχὴ δοκῇ), and, further, he suspects his speech will become excessively long. Unbothered by the possible multitude of problems, the swarm of arguments before them, Thrasymachus, an unlikely friend, ironically jabs Socrates and says, "Do you think these people have come here now to prospect for gold, but not listen to our discussion?" (a retort that echoes both *Resp.* 1 and 4 and statements made by Socrates about Alcibiades in the *Symposium*, trans. Bury, slightly adapted). Socrates rejoins, "As long as it is a reasonable [μετρίων] length" (*Resp.* 450b). Provocatively, Glaucon responds that the measure for such devotion, the measure for philosophical dialogue, is a seeming excess, that is, one should spend the whole of one's life listening such discussion (Μέτρον δέ γ'[...] τοιούτων

22. Contra Findlay, who casually asserts that "the way that Socrates-Plato meet the first two waves do not merit very great attention" (*Written and Unwritten Doctrines*, 177).

23. The text actually seems to point to, having brought the male drama to its end/limit, it is now to time to bring the female (drama) *again* to its end/limit (μετὰ ἀνδρεῖον δρᾶμα παντελῶς διαπερανθὲν τὸ γυναικεῖον αὖ περαίνειν).

λόγων ἀκούειν ὅλο ὁ βίος νοῦν ἔχουσιν). Interestingly, there is an excess that is the right measure, a kind of rational excess.

Noting their support as well as further encouragement (θαρσύνω/ παραθαρρύνω), Socrates fears for his friends and the consequences of advancing doubtful and possibly misleading (σφάλλω, 451a2, a3, a4) arguments but agrees to run the risk (κινδυνεύειν) for the sake of the best, that is, to complete and tend to his conception of the city/soul, a conception that would defend or support the value of the just life over against the arguments that the unjust life is superior to the seemingly stronger or dominating/tyrannical rule. Overall, like Timaeus, who persists in attempting to unpack the role of Necessity, though it seems to require a bastard reasoning, Socrates admits he is not completely confident, and as such he fears the indefinite arguments may be harmful (*Resp.* 450e–451b). Nevertheless, he is willing to take the risk. Here, Socrates interestingly admits he cares less about invoking ridicule (γέλως), for that is childish, and consequently instigates the first of several moments wherein he distinguishes what is worthy of ridicule or laughter from what is not (*Resp.* 452a–e). Socrates emphasizes that despite the fact that others may laugh, others could ridicule him for speaking of something doubtful, this is actually something serious, because in discussing the doubtful he cares for the souls of his friends. Rather ironically, Glaucon notably laughs (γελάσας) at Socrates's confession of weakness (*Resp.* 451b) but encourages him to tell of the "female drama." So, Socrates proceeds along the unruly path, but just before commencing the discussion, he bows to Adrasteia (*Resp.* 451a)—again, a goddess of Necessity reminiscent of Diotima's erotic attendance with the Fates as well as Khora's association with Necessity.[24] This indeed may be a bastard form of reasoning, but one that will give birth to Socrates's own long-felt conceptions regarding the virtue and happiness of the just soul.

The first wave of paradox, the arguments for the equality of men and women, interestingly begins with Socrates imagining possible debate partners, ones who may be jokesters (φῐλοπαίγμων) and others more serious. Either way, ultimately these imagined interlocutors are credited with being the ones who expose the seeming contradiction in Socrates's argument, that is, men and women cannot do the same jobs if they have

---

24. For another reference to Adrasteia as that which compels us to ascent and descent, see also Plato, *Phaedr.* 248d–249b.

different natures. To this objection, Socrates playfully reminds his friends that this kind of objection was exactly what he feared but that, like persons who fall in either a small pool or the greatest ocean, they must swim nonetheless (κολυμβήθραν μικρὰν ἐμπέσῃ ἄντε εἰς τὸ μέγιστον πέλαγος μέσον, ὅμως γε νεῖ οὐδὲν ἧττον), hoping, much like Timaeus before his discussion of Necessity, for some other unlikely savior (ἄπορον σωτηρίαν; *Resp.* 453d). The way out, that is, what saves the perplexing and paradoxical argument, starts with Socrates demarcating between contradictory, contrary, and corollary terms (showing that he has indeed learned from Diotima about the need for middle terms). Socrates does this because he fears that he and his companions (as well as the imagined interlocutors) may have accidentally slipped into a form of argument that simply contradicts (via latching onto apparent difference), that is, like Socrates before Diotima, thinking that what is not immortal is mortal or what is not beautiful is ugly. In contrast, Socrates hopes to wield a method of argument that examines different kinds of differences (whether accidental or essential), a distinction that will tease out whether the function or work, that is, the power, of men and women could be shared (453e–456c). As will become pertinent, the distinction between eristic and dialectic[25] is advanced (454a), and as a consequence of using the latter Socrates is able to show that male and female exist as corollaries whereby one is weaker rather than stronger (451d, 455e, 456a, 457a–b), superior rather than inferior (455c–d). The two may be different insofar as the male "mounts" and the female conceives (τῷ τὸ μὲν θῆλυ τίκτειν, τὸ δὲ ἄρρεν ὀχεύειν), but this is not a difference of nature when it comes to their skill or business, that is, their powers or capacities. Rather, the difference is one of degree in

---

25. See Plato, *Meno* 75c5–d7, for a similar distinction between eristics and other methods that are marked by friendly inquiry that is more gentle and caring, more concerned with education than mere refutation via contradiction. See Dimitri El Murr for an account of the distinction between eristics and dialectic and its use in the equality of men and women in the *Republic*. El Murr, "Eristic, Antilogy and the Equal Disposition of Men and Women (Plato, *Resp.* 5. 453B–454C," *ClQ* 70 (2002): 85–100. El Murr, unfortunately, sees the distinction as a strange occurrence in this particular discussion, but, as the following will argue and as other forthcoming work will set out more clearly, this distinction between eristics and dialectic is the central point of book 5 insofar as most of the book is concerned with demarcating the rules for proper and effective dialectic—of course, El Murr can be forgiven for this oversight as the rules for proper dialectic with friends is cleverly hidden by Socrates under the guise of the city/soul analogy, or, at least, so I argue.

power; they are just weaker. To the chagrin of many feminist commentators, this weakness is not limited to just physical weakness but, strangely, a weakness in *all* capacities—even functions or work typically associated with women, as Socrates oddly asserts:

> Do you know of anything practiced [μελετώμενον] by human beings in which the male sex is not superior to the female in all these aspects? Or do we have to string it out by mentioning weaving and looking after the baking and the cooking where the female sex has a reputation, though if outclassed, they are the most absurd [καταγελαστότατόν] of all. (*Resp.* 455c)

Overall, we are given an explicit example where Socrates very clearly indicates that women's work should be easy, so easy, in fact, that even if men do not have a reputation for it, they should effortlessly be superior in these areas; otherwise they will be subject to ridicule. Again, like Diotima's insistence that the ignorant who do not recognize their ignorance will fail to search after the requisite knowledge they lack, Socrates accentuates that if men failed to be good at things such as baking or cooking, it would be because they failed to recognize a simple and correctable inability, they failed to seek out the knowledge that would allow them to be good at even "women's work," and so they would appear most absurd, having been bested by the seemingly inferior sex. So, while hyperbolically consigning women to an inferior position with respect to power in *all* areas, Socrates's emphasis on men's absurdity if they lost to a woman even in these areas shows that despite the weakness of women, they have capacities to best those who fail to acknowledge their lack. Moreover, Socrates's accent on the fact that women have the capacity to rule suggests that their weakness or supposed inferiority does not disqualify one from ruling. Perhaps, like Khora's erratic nature or Eros's Poverty, indeed, it may constitute the power of the feminine, the seemingly deficient term.

When read alongside the gendered images of the *Symposium* and the *Timaeus*, many of the oddities regarding Socrates's vision of the equality between men and women start to take on a different meaning altogether. Consider, first, Socrates's ad hoc mention of one of his imagined interlocutor's objections. Many would think it *ridiculous* for women to exercise naked alongside men (*Resp.* 452c–e), an objection that seems trivial in the face of the Athenian patriarchal regime. Would there not be much bigger concerns than the gymnasium, especially with the likes of Thrasymachus in attendance? Yet oddly, no one offers more pertinent objections. All are fine or in agreement that this is a fair objection. Yes, women would be laughed at in the gymnasium, their nakedness would be a source of ridicule before the ignorant, unaware of what is truly worthy of ridicule. Ultimately, Socrates argues that women exercising before men should not, like his own confessions of doubt, be ridiculed because, like his own doubtful speech, which tends to the good of his companions' souls, such womanly exercise is a good for the city. It makes the women and the city stronger. In other words, exercising the weak women (or Socrates's doubtful speech) is much like nurturing one's ideas in the *Symposium* or the erratic movements in Khora, which nourish or stimulate the movement of the soul. We must learn to train and exercise, nourish what appears weak or small or confused and rear them properly. Like Socrates, who risks looking ridiculous via advancing ideas that are not clear, women should exercise before all. As Socrates remarks with regard to those who thought it ridiculous to exercise naked in the first place,

> When it appeared better to those taking part in all this, I think, to undress rather than to cover up, then what was ridiculous [γελοῖον] to the naked eye vanished away when discussion of the matter showed it was best; and this showed that the man who thinks anything other than baseness is ridiculous [γελοῖον] is a fool. (*Resp.* 452d)

Like Diotima's eros, who is between ignorance and knowledge because it is aware of one's lack, the idea that it is better to undress than cover up harkens to Socrates's confessions of ignorance in marked contrast to those who cover up, those who pretend to know. In other words, what is weak should strip and exercise, be made stronger by working alongside the strong, the determinate alongside the indeterminate. In short, Socrates's confessions of perplexity before the female drama parallel the structure of his discussion of the seeming ridiculousness of women exercising, gesturing to the idea that our ignorance/perplexity can be exercised if it just strips, is laid bare before all. In these naked confessions regarding what is perplexing and doubtful, Socrates exercises said weakness alongside his strength, the things he knows. Socrates, one who is confident that the just life is better than the unjust while at the same time confused about how that is exactly so, is in the present moment with his friends and colleagues admitting he still needs such a conception to be worked out, that the details present him with perplexity. Like "weak" women who exercise naked with men, Socrates (throughout the dialogues) famously strips and bears his weakness before all, and in so doing he strengthens the indefinite power within.[26] In agreement with the *Timaeus* and the *Symposium*, there is a resource in admitting perplexity before the indeterminate.

Before starting the second wave, Socrates asks for support, claiming that he is not ready to talk about the *possibility* of holding children in common. Rather, he compares himself to the lazy (ἀργός) who feast on their thoughts, increasing their laziness, and concludes, "I, too, am giving into my weakness [μαλθακίζομαι]" (458b1), and, so, prior to the arguments for the *possibility* of rearing children in common, he turns to whether such a city/soul is *desirable*. As most know, Socrates seamlessly moves to the consequences of men and women sharing exercise and all other nourishment (ἄλλη τροφῇ) together. Socrates concludes that such naked wrestling and common nourishment would provoke in each of them a desire for sex and offspring. Here, if read analogically, we return again to an image of the value of one who marries opposing principles, knowing and not-knowing, and sees that there is something between, some power to give birth to the beautiful in the beautiful. As the arguments of the *Symposium* make clear, philosophy is erotic. To reason well is not blindly believing we know (dogmatism), nor haphazardly giving into not-knowing and practicing eristics (relativism). Rather, we must produce offspring that marry the reality of being beings who exist between, who are both/and. Socrates emphasized that this attraction will occur from *necessity* (ὑπ' ἀνάγκης) if both male and female exercise and nourish themselves together. He repeats, "Or do you not think that what I am saying follows from necessity?" (ἢ οὐκ ἀναγκαῖά σοι δοκῶ λέγειν). Gesturing to the *Timaeus* and the work of the Demi-

---

26. As Claudia Baracchi argues while discussing Socrates in contrast to the standard Greek hero in the *Apology*: "Let us conclude by calling attention to this adjective, *amêkhanon*, which amplifies the recurrence of the adverb *atekhnôs* variously emphasized earlier. Socrates seems to point to a certain non-technical, non-artful, ultimately non-volitional, excessive dimension of his inquiry and passion. The happiness here at stake is inconceivable in the sense that it cannot be devised or contrived. No skill, technical mastery, machination, or otherwise calculative resources pertain to it or may grant it. A certain lack of resource, or even powerlessness, seems to mark the philosopher and to distinguish him from the epic hero, who at least in Homer is characterized as wily and shrewd (paradigmatically, Odysseus is first said to be 'of many guiles,' *polumêkhanos*, in *Il.* II 173). The philosopher would, quite distinctively, do what he *can*, not what he *wants*." See Baracchi, "The 'Inconceivable Happiness' of 'Men and Women': Visions of an Other World in Plato's *Apology* of Socrates," *CLS* 43 (2006): 282.

urge, Glaucon contrasts this erotic necessity with a geometrical necessity (Οὐ γεωμετρικαῖς γε, ἦ δ'ὅς, ἀλλ' ἐρωτικαῖς ἀνάγκαις), jokingly emphasizing their difference while possibly highlighting, again, how the feminine aspect of ruling allows for a measure that is other than arithmetic (perhaps a measure that is a little less exacting—an erotic, dynamic, ever-creative measure). In any case, as a consequence of women's nakedness and sharing in meals with men, the erotic is born, resulting in the sacred marriages of the best of men and women; the ones who have done particularly well in war are rewarded with sex and the possibility of offspring. In other words, the mingling of the doubtful with the certain, the swarming multitude of perplexing arguments, when exercised, make the soul stronger. There are certain masculine and feminine ways of argument that win wars or debates, and these should be carefully brought together, for they will produce the best offspring, new arguments with new perplexities that tend to the health or justice of the soul. Like the erotic in the *Symposium* (or even midwifery in the *Theaetetus*), philosophy is that which gives birth to ideas and, as the restrictions on marriage and procreation in the *Republic* indicate, this is not something we should do haphazardly. Rather, we must precisely marry the one and the many, the limit and the unlimited, the certain and the doubtful. If we are not careful, we can produce wind-eggs that need to be either exposed (refuted—like the idea that justice is the advantage of the stronger) or moved to the thumetic or epithumetic class of desires.

The restrictions on procreation, understood this way, mirror the question of which ideas should we mate, how we are to bring together one's perplexity with one's sense of certainty, the many and the few, the different and the same. Which ideas in relation to their doubts, to the many ways we can view things, even to the differences between differences (as Socrates uses in discussing men and women's possible sameness or difference), lead to offspring or mixtures that reproduce justice? Here we should be reminded of that good offspring (or conceptions) are literally taken into care by the rulers or *archai*. "Doesn't this entail that the 'always becoming offspring' will be taken over or (received by) archai who attend to this, either men or women both? For the archai are shared by both women and men" (*Resp.* 460b).[27]

---

27. Οὐκοῦν καὶ τὰ ἀεὶ γιγνόμενα ἔκγονα παραλαμβάνουσαι αἱ ἐπὶ τούτων ἐφεστηκυῖαι ἀρχαὶ εἴτε ἀνδρῶν εἴτε γυναικῶν εἴτε ἀμφότερα; κοιναὶ γάρ που καὶ ἀρχαὶ γυναιξί τε καὶ ἀνδράσιν;

Emphasizing that both the male and female *archai* are responsible for
tending to the ceaseless supply of children, Socrates first focuses on how
that the children will be taken to the public nursery. There, mothers are
described as bearing overly full breasts (*Resp.* 460d), which nourish the
children "for a reasonable period of time" (καὶ αὐτῶν τούτων ἐπιμελήσονται
ὅπως μέτριον χρόνον θηλάσονται), recalling Glaucon's belief that the "reasonable measure" for discussing the "doubtful" was the whole of one's life.
Here, if this nourishment is the dyadic principle of perplexity/multiplicity,
one wonders whether the measure in this case is also excessive. No longer a
trifle detail or joke, this reference to overly full breasts takes on the important function of emphasizing the value and need for an excessive supply of
aporia as that which allows the philosophical soul to grow, to move toward
the beautiful and good in the *Symposium*. Another correspondingly dismissed detail, that the female ruling principles are explicitly described as
not having to do the dirty work of rearing children all the time—no sleep-
less nights, because other wet-nurses or attendants (τίτθαις τε καὶ τροφοῖς)
can perform those duties—also takes on new and relevant meaning. One
may think of Timaeus and his identification of Necessity with a wet-nurse
while further remembering that the speech was made because Socrates
claimed to be incapable of the tedious work of bringing his *kallipolis* into
motion, that is, Socrates is no cosmologist; others can and should attend to
that. In other words, we can give birth to ideas that we ourselves may not
attend to, as the work of rearing certain ideas belongs to others.

Nearing the end of the discussion of whether the commonality of
women and children is of benefit, Socrates sets up a corollary between an
image of the greatest good and greatest evil (*Resp.* 462a). The latter state,
not ruled by both women and men, leads to a city that is an indefinite
multiplicity, while the former state is a unity, but a unity that looks very different than one may expect. The unity is not a tyranny of reason, wherein
the city is frozen to behave and act in one set way. Rather, the description
of the city/soul as unified is a dramatic description of the city/soul experiencing a range of corollary emotions. As Socrates describes, the unified
city/soul would experience, as far as possible, almost equally in all its parts
(be it the rational, the spirited, or the appetitive aspect of city/soul), things
such as joy and grief alongside gains and losses (*Resp.* 462b), in almost
equal measure (ἀπολλυμένων παραπλησίως). In other words, the soul is not
grieving in one part while another part celebrates. Rather, the soul, as a
whole, is able to experience the totality of human emotions, even the so-
called bad or irrational ones such as grief. In other words, when both the

limit and the unlimited, sameness and difference, unity and multiplicity, the male and the female, rule the soul and are erotically combined so as to carefully nourish and rear the lives of new and novel reasoning principles (new offspring, which, as Diotima emphasizes, are other but also like the originary; *Symp.* 209c), the soul can experience a multiplicity of conflicting experiences while not becoming divided or akratic. Overall, the ruling principles of the city/soul are not masters or despots but guardians, saviors, and friends in battle (Σωτῆράς τε καὶ ἐπικούρους). The other parts of the city/soul, the spirited and appetitive, are not slaves but employees or those receiving recompense and attendants/nourishers (Μισθοδότας τε καὶ τροφέας). So, if the analogy holds, the passions and desires are not slaves of reason but, under the equality of the masculine and feminine (the definite and the indefinite, the one and the many, the strong and the weak), the spirited and appetitive parts of the soul receive their due. Recalling that Socrates is not hoping to make merely one part of the soul happy, that is, just caring for reason; the *kallipolis* must care for the compound creature, the mixture of itself qua also being embodied, desirous emotional beings. Yet, it is only when women rule equally, only when weakness, lack, the indefinite, the multiple, and so on, rules alongside the masculine strength, resource, definition, unity, that the soul can do the work of marrying and reproducing the harmonious mixture of extreme terms and ways of life. Such corulership reproduces erotic offspring that tend to the totality of what it means to be human, ruling in such a way that the nonrational can be not slaves but attendants, giving the soul in its emotional and embodied life the literal and metaphorical food we need to flourish.

In the end, Socrates concludes that the well-run state has as its cause "the holding in common of women and children," the sharing of the feminine indefinite or multiple that leads to erotic, dynamic offspring, connected in such a way that it constitutes the beauty of a truly unified and just life, in both body and soul. To be sure, the remaining aspects of book 5 turn away from the desirability of such a state to the possibility of this city/soul. In a complementary essay to this one, I argue that the details of proper training and warfare, which Socrates painstakingly outlines, remarkably detail the differences between eristic and dialectical debate. In other words, the response to *possibility* of this desirable erotic soul, which values both knowing and not-knowing, limit and unlimited, strength and weakness, sameness and difference, is, in short, proper dialectics. The third wave of paradox, philosophers should rule, responds to the cliffhanger of the second: the rules for war, that is, dialectic that protects the just soul—what makes dialectic itself desirable and possible? The answer is, of course, that philosophy/philosophers who believe in and study the Good must rule the soul. In other words, the third wave actually follows from the second if we see the first and the second as (1) the equality of the demiurgic/khoratic, plenty and poverty, the limit and the unlimited, the same and the different in the soul, and (2) the careful marriage of these so as to produce offspring that can properly engage others outside yourself, your own soul, in such a way that you are not being eristic or contradictory but rather carefully tending to the multiplicity of meanings and ideas that come to bear in dialectical conversation with others. This is only possible when philosophy rather than sophistry or the desire for power rules the soul. Ergo, in the third wave of paradox, Socrates must demarcate between the actual philosophers and the imitators, therein focusing on the activity or study of the philosopher, the Good beyond being.

To close, it might be fun to note that just before Socrates turns to the discussion of the differences between the imitators of philosophy who can mislead, he emphasizes that in order to respond to the question he needs to use an image (Ἐρωτᾷς ἐρώτημα δεόμενον ἀποκρίσεως δι'εἰκόνος λεγομένης). Adeimantus jokingly responds, "Really, I didn't think it was your practice to use images" (Σὺ δέ γε οἶμαι οὐκ εἴωθας δι' εἰκόνων λέγειν). Socrates in turn playfully banters back, "Well, are you mocking me after landing me in an argument which is difficult to prove?" (σκώπτεις ἐμβεβληκώς με εἰς λόγον οὕτω δυσαπόδεικτον) (*Resp.* 487e–488a). Here I like to imagine the company of Socrates's companions, all in on the joke, all knowledgeable that the previous discussion of the equality of men and women and the procreation and rearing of children was an elaborate image, one Socrates meant both psychologically and politically (albeit a political reading other than the literal one). This image of all the companions *in* on the actual intent also gestures back to the *Timaeus*, where one wonders whether Timaeus or Critias images reflect an understanding of Socrates's strange penchant for producing images that value the corollary field between extremes that constitutes the life of the soul. Like good assistants, they arrive the day after Socrates has apparently given a similar speech to the one advanced in the *Republic*; Timaeus and Critias know that they must set the *kallipolis* in motion, depict it in war, and, fantastically, both offer accounts that seem to be much more explicitly images/myths rather than literal political outlines that would resemble Socrates's utopia.

While this present essay is only a preliminary attempt to show Plato's deep appreciation for that which was typically excised from the human condition, the feminine or the so-called weak, it suffices to show that, unlike the Pythagoreans before him and Aristotle after him, Plato's feminine neither is essentialized, insofar as nowhere does it exist outside mixture in the spectrum of Being and Becoming, nor is impotent or merely weak. Rather, male and female exist but always only in relation, always only as a combination reproducing and creating unique offspring. Ultimately, the individual human soul is tasked with being the beings who must give birth and transform. We are the moving mean, the erotic measure. This is the task of philosophy—to desire both what is and what becomes, seeing that our being is not a static sameness, nor is it simply a becoming, a chaotic flux, a radical alterity always to be overcome. Rather, these two principles must and have always been in an embrace, never torn asunder at any level of reality. In short, we must recognize that to be a good or wise soul, to foster justice, is to see that we are a mixture of strong and weak, masculine and feminine, one and many. In possessing the capacity, the power to think otherwise than expected, to take risks into a form of bastard reasoning, we fall into the great ocean of perplexity. Nevertheless, we discovering the means, the uncanny saviors/arguments/images/stories that light the pathway in the dark. In this we are invited to read (or move) Plato (and any other suspected patriarchal thinker) toward something otherwise than they may have intended, reading them, perhaps despite themselves, as resistant to discourses that erase weakness or are resistant to discourses that hide perplexity, ignorance, or a life that, while being one, is also subject to being multiple. While being certain, we are also unsure. While being the same, things are always ever different and unique. Reality and appearance, arguments and myth, separation and connection all belong together, blended and birthed in the erotic soul that is tasked to move between the extremes. In this we must tend to the peculiar ways that we are all both strong and weak, knowing and not-knowing, one and many, showing how the so-called weakness, perplexity of it all not only is real and beautiful but also is the source of our greatest power. To the wise, what the ignorant think is ridiculous; that is, the feminine, the weak, the ignorant are all actually what open us up to the dyadic space of infinite possibility, a space that nurtures the divine seed of our greatness, our virtue, which reveals that in our admittances of ignorance we move toward knowledge, taking the risky way for the sake of nurturing and loving the beautiful, but often indeterminate and constantly transforming ambiguity, in us all.[28]

---

28. Thomas Szlezak, "The Indefinite Dyad in Sextus Empiricus's Report (*Adversus*

Bibliography

Primary Sources

Aristotle. *Aristotle's Physics*. Translated by Hippocrates G. Apostle. Bloomington: Indiana University Press, 1969.

———. *Metaphysics*. Translated by Hugh Tredennick. 2 vols. LCL. Cambridge: Harvard University Press, 1933.

Burnet, John, ed. *Platonis Opera*. Vols. 2–4. Oxford: Clarendon, 1903.

Cooper, John M. *Plato: Complete Works*. Indianapolis: Hackett, 1997.

Plato. *Lysis, Symposium, Gorgias*. Translated by Walter R. M. Lamb. LCL. Cambridge: Harvard University Press, 1925.

———. *Republic*. Translated by Chris Emlyn-Jones and William Preddy. 2 vols. LCL. Cambridge: Harvard University Press, 2013.

———. *Timaeus, Critias, Clitophon, Menexenus, Epistles*. Translated by Robert G. Bury. LCL. Cambridge: Harvard University Press, 1929.

Secondary Sources

Annas, Julia. "Plato's *Republic* and Feminism." *Philosophy* 51 (1976): 307–21.

Baracchi, Claudia. "The 'Inconceivable Happiness' of 'Men and Women': Visions of an Other World in Plato's *Apology* of Socrates." *CLS* 43 (2006): 269–84.

Bianchi, Emanuela. *The Feminine Symptom: Aleatory Matter in the Aristotelian Cosmos*. New York: Fordham University Press, 2014.

———. "Receptacle/Chôra: Figuring the Errant Feminine in Plato's *Timaeus*." *Hypatia* 21.4 (2006): 124–46.

Bloom, Allan. "Interpretive Essay." Pages 305–436 in *The "Republic" of Plato with Notes and Interpretive Essay*. Edited by Allan Bloom. New York: Basic Books, 1968.

Mathematicos 10.248–283) and Plato's *Parmenides*," in *Plato's Parmenides and Its Heritage*, ed. John Turner and Kevin Corrigan (Leiden: Brill, 2010), 91: "That we conceive of the *aoristos dyas* in such completely different ways surely has something to do with the contingencies of the tradition, but perhaps it also has to do with the hetera phusis itself; only the person who hopes to find this in one guise alone, forgets that it is other than the Form, that is, other than what is clear and unambiguous."

Bluestone, Natalie. "Why Women Cannot Rule: Sexism in Plato Scholarship." Pages 109–30 in *Feminist Interpretations of Plato*. Edited by Nancy Tuana. University Park: Pennsylvania State University Press, 1994.

Butler, Judith. *Bodies That Matter: On the Discursive Limits of "Sex."* New York: Routledge, 1993.

———. *Gender Trouble: Feminism and the Subversion of Identity.* New York: Routledge, 1990.

Decker, Jessica Elbert, Danielle A. Layne, and Monica Vilhauer, eds. *Otherwise Than the Binary: New Feminist Readings in Ancient Philosophy and Culture.* New York: State University of New York Press, 2022.

Dubois, Page. *Sowing the Body: Psychoanalysis and Ancient Representations of Women.* Chicago: University of Chicago Press, 1988.

El Murr, Dimitri. "Eristic, Antilogy and the Equal Disposition of Men and Women (Plato, *Resp.* 5. 453B–454C)." *ClQ* 70 (2002): 85–100.

Findlay, John N. *Plato: The Written and Unwritten Doctrines.* New York: Routledge, 1974.

Genova, Judith. "Feminist Dialectics: Plato and Dualism." Pages 41–54 in *Engendering Origins: Critical Feminist Readings in Plato and Aristotle.* Edited by Bat-Ami Bar On. Albany: State University of New York Press, 1994.

Grosz, Elizabeth. *Space, Time, and Perversion.* New York: Routledge, 1995.

Holmes, Brooke. *Gender: Antiquity and Its Legacy (Ancient and Modern).* Oxford: Oxford University Press, 2012.

Irigaray, Luce. *Speculum of the Other Woman.* Translated by Gillian C. Gill. Ithaca, NY: Cornell University Press, 1985.

Kirk, Geoffrey S., John E. Raven, and Malcolm Schofield. *The Presocratic Philosophers.* 2nd ed. Cambridge: Cambridge University Press, 1983.

Krämer, Hans. *Plato and the Foundations of Metaphysics: A Work on the Theory of the Principles and Unwritten Doctrines of Plato with a Collection of the Fundamental Document.* New York: State University of New York Press, 1990.

Layne, Danielle. "Refutation and Double Ignorance in Proclus." *Epoché* 13 (2009): 347–62.

Lloyd, Genevieve. *The Man of Reason: Male and Female in Western Philosophy.* London: Routledge, 1984.

Morrow, Glenn R. "Necessity and Persuasion in Plato's Timaeus." *PhilRev* 59 (1950): 147–63.

Nikulin, Dmitri, ed. *The Other Plato: The Tubingen Interpretation of Plato's Inner-Academic Teachings*. New York: State University of New York Press, 2012.

Saxonhouse, Arlene. "The Philosopher and the Female in the Political Thought of Plato." *PT* 4 (1976): 195–212.

Spelman, Elizabeth. "Hairy Cobblers and Philosopher Queens." Pages 3–24 in *Engendering Origins*. Edited by Bat-Ami Bar-On. Albany: State University of New York Press, 1994.

Strauss, Leo. *The City and Man*. Chicago: Rand McNally, 1964.

Szlezak, Thomas. "The Idea of the Good as *Arkhe* in Plato's *Republic*." Pages 121–41 in *The Other Plato*. Edited by Dmitri Nikulin. Albany: State University of New York Press, 2012.

———. "The Indefinite Dyad in Sextus Empiricus's Report (*Adversus Mathematicos* 10.248–283) and Plato's *Parmenides*." Pages 79–92 in *Plato's Parmenides and Its Heritage*. Edited by John Turner and Kevin Corrigan. Leiden: Brill, 2010.

Taylor, Christopher C. W. "The Role of Women in Plato's Republic." Pages 75–86 in *Virtue and Happiness: Essays in Honour of Julia Annas*. Edited by Rachana Kamtekar. Oxford: Oxford University Press, 2012.

Vlastos, Gregory. "Was Plato a Feminist?" Pages 133–43 in *Feminist Interpretations of Plato*. Edited by Nancy Tuana. University Park: Pennsylvania State University Press, 1994.

Soul in the Earliest Multilevel
Interpretations of the *Parmenides*

Harold Tarrant

The Plotinian Position and Its Limitations

Those who work on Plotinus are well used to his three hypostases, One, Intellect, and Soul, which he detected in Plato (*Enn.* 5.1.8), both in the *Second Epistle* (dubiously ascribed to him) and in the first three hypotheses of the final part of the *Parmenides*—an exercise in which Parmenides bombards young Aristoteles with strings of questions concerning the existence or nonexistence, and the unity or diversity, of the One. Plotinus's previous chapter (7) also relates the three hypotheses to the mythical triad of three rulers, Ouranos, Kronos, and Zeus, and perhaps less directly to the passage of Plato's *Cratylus* that discusses their names (*Crat.* 395e–396c);[1] however, to the extent that it does not suggest the relevance of numbers and counting, that dialogue will not be central to this contribution.

It is the mysterious *Second Epistle* (312e) that most obviously involves numbers. After postulating a king who is transcendent in various ways,

---

John F. Finamore has long promoted and stimulated interest in obscure and puzzling Platonic paths, offering helpful solutions to puzzles on soul in the framework of Platonist metaphysics. I constantly use his edition, with John Dillon, of Iamblichus's important but hard *De Anima*. To him I offer this contribution on soul in the pre-Plotinian *Parmenides*, suspecting that even he regards these paths as ones that angels fear to tread, but in the expectation that much remains to be said. I hope that John may forgive me for also remembering here another key influence, that of Tony Malim (1929–2005), who first taught me Greek and Plato, and later moved to and published on the discipline of psychology: for him, too, *psyche* mattered.

1. The etymologies connect Kronos with pure intellect and Zeus with the cause of life (and so perhaps with soul), and Ouranos perhaps with the source of intellect that may be glimpsed on high.

it follows this with something "second" (singular) that relates to second things (plural) and something "third" that relates to third things. That is where the numbering stops, making the triad seem to have special relevance. Again, what Neoplatonists knew as the third hypothesis of the *Parmenides* (but is often called deduction 2b in modern interpretation) starts off with the somewhat perplexing words: "Going on [ἔτι], let us state the third." It does not tell us whether it is a third "One," for the first two series of questions are both about "Ones," or a third argument, or what precisely. But the number invites the reader to associate what it introduces with *something* "third," and it seems that this had been sufficient for Plotinus to associate it with the third of the levels alluded to in the *Epistle* as well as with his third hypostasis. Accordingly, he is not much known for hypostases beyond that point, even though Porphyry's name for the relevant treatise (10) suggests that there might have been other less causative hypostases.[2] But since even the term *hypostasis* is Porphyry's, what we get from such titles or from his arrangement, which has the last three *Enneads* deal with Soul, Intellect, and the One, respectively, is Porphyrian insight into Plotinus's system. Nonetheless, it is Plotinus himself who tells us from where in the Platonic writings his triadic scheme supposedly derives, downplaying any originality of his own.

That there are these three levels is reaffirmed at *Enn.* 5.1.10.1–4, but 5.1.7.43–49 had already established that there were other things after soul; soul merely constituted the limit of the *divine* (καὶ μέχρι τούτων τὰ θεῖα). By drawing this sharp line between things divine and things otherwise, and by placing soul at the lowest level of things divine, Plotinus is virtually compelled to keep all soul together. So "therefore our soul too is something divine and of a different nature, just like the overall nature of soul" (*Enn.* 5.1.10.10–12). This entailed that there was no room for another level of soul below the third hypostasis, nor below the "third things" of *Second Epistle*, nor perhaps beyond the third hypothesis of the *Parmenides*. Certainly Porphyry thought that the Soul belonged firmly to the third hypothesis,[3] the hypothesis that Plotinus took to discuss neither "the first One that is more properly one," nor the second one called many, but a third "one *and* many." The problem for Plotinus's interpretation of

---

2. He calls it "On the three original hypostases" or "On the three dominant hypostases," depending on whether ἀρχικός is seen as relating to ἀρχή as "beginning" or as "rule."

3. See Proclus, *In Parm.* 1053.28–54.4, with the scholion.

the hypotheses of the *Parmenides* is that it cannot satisfy us until it offers a view about the remaining hypotheses. If these do not offer us further levels of the divine, then what lessons do they offer, and what are they supposed to present? And how many other arguments should we be counting, given that Plato has not given us any numbering except at the third level? It was left to Porphyry to sketch out a comprehensive interpretation that Plotinus might perhaps have been satisfied with and to establish the conventional number of nine hypotheses.

Amelius and Porphyry

It is book 6 of Proclus's *In Parmenidem* that tells us about various comprehensive metaphysical interpretations of the hypotheses that had preceded Syrianus. Most of these are not explicitly attributed to a named figure, though after those that we have reason to associate with Amelius, Porphyry, and Iamblichus, one is attributed to a mysterious "philosopher from Rhodes" and another explicitly to Syrianus's predecessor, Plutarch of Athens. Since the innovation of that "philosopher from Rhodes," whose identity is thankfully irrelevant to us here,[4] only five distinct metaphysical levels were required by those interpreting the hypotheses, corresponding to hypotheses 1–5, now known as deductions 1–4. Even so, the earliest multilevel interpretations known to Proclus sought metaphysical levels corresponding to everything counting as a hypothesis, eight reportedly in Amelius and nine in Porphyry and Iamblichus. The different number was perhaps arrived at by the refusal of Amelians to count hypothesis 9 (= deduction 8) separately, seeing it rather as a coda; there is otherwise a considerable overlap between these systems, including the eighth level, widely associated with the *quasiforms* reflected in the Platonic Receptacle: things lacking real being on close inspection. This in fact applies to Plotinus, even though Paul Henry and Hans-Rudolf Schwyzer's index[5] cites nothing beyond 160b2–3 at the beginning of hypothesis 5 (= deduction 4).

---

4. I have said enough on the topic, but I now look to Evagoras, plausibly from Lindos on the island of Rhodes, and an important figure in Syrianus, *On Hermogenes*. His associate Aquila is also known to have interpreted Plato during this period (Proclus, *In Tim.* 3.263.7), as did Peisitheus, a friend of Theodorus of Asine (Damascius, *in Phileb.* 1.3.1–2); Theodorus himself is favored by many, yet is known as "the philosopher from Asine."

5. Plotinus, *Opera*, ed. Paul Henry and Hans-Rudolf Schwyzer (Oxford: Oxford University Press, 1964–1984), *ed. min.*

While Plotinus presumably associates hypothesis 3 (= deduction 2B) with the entire hypostasis of soul, Porphyry does so more explicitly, supposedly correcting the interpretation that the scholiast[6] ascribes to Amelius, who took hypothesis 3 to be about rational soul *only* and hypothesis 4 (= deduction 3) to be about nonrational souls. It seems to me likely that, while Porphyry's interpretation had here followed Plotinus's lead, the Amelian position had been partially developed by others beforehand and come to the attention of Amelius relatively early in his career. The scholiast names Amelius here not because he was known to be its originator but because he is the figure with whom the commentary tradition, owing much to Porphyry, had most closely associated it.

Moderatus and the Problems Regarding Hypotheses 3 and 4

Proclus's account of the interpretation of the hypotheses does not go back earlier than the interpretation associated with Amelius. It was left to Eric Dodds's seminal 1928 article to suggest a prehistory of the metaphysical interpretation involving a fragment of the first-century Pythagorean Moderatus.[7] Since then, scholars who took the fragment from Simplicius (*Phys.* 230.34–231.24 = frag. 8 Lakmann) as being faithful to *Moderatus* rather than to *Porphyry* have been hampered by a lack of attention to the main purpose of this text. Most have been concerned to discover how far parallels for Plotinus could be discovered in the two preceding centuries: searching above all for any possible doctrine of a transcendent One, any possible doctrine of three hypostases. With a focus on Plotinus they could fail to ask questions about any level beyond the "third." Up to this point it looked as if the so-called fragment of Moderatus was too convenient to be reliable here, obliging Dodds with just about everything that he needed. But we must not neglect the basic need to understand both what Simplicius and what Porphyry were trying to present here. Neither is conveying this passage with the intention of elaborating a Moderatan doctrine of the One, a Moderatan triad, or a Moderatan interpretation of the *Parmenides*. Both are citing Moderatus as a source for a particular kind of theory of matter, Simplicius adding that the information came from the second

---

6. See Proclus, *Procli in Platonis Parmenidem Commentaria*, ed. Carlos Steel, vol. 3 (Oxford: Oxford University Press, 2007–2009), 393.

7. Eric R. Dodds, "The Parmenides of Plato and the Origin of the Neoplatonic One," *ClQ* 22 (1928): 129–42.

book of Porphyry's *On Matter*. According to the Amelian, Porphyrian, and Iamblichan interpretations, matter was tackled in later hypotheses: the fifth, sixth and seventh, sixth and seventh, and seventh, respectively. What preceded the fifth hypothesis would therefore be tangential for any discussion of matter in these interpretations, so absolute clarity was not a priority. It is, however, clear that Moderatus distinguished matter's paradigm (i.e., Plato's receptacle) from the bodily matter whose paradigm it was. This latter had been allegedly referred to by Pythagoras and Plato as τὸ πόσον ("the quantitative"?), and perhaps again from the matter in things sensed, which is described as "the non-being initially present in τὸ πόσον." Thus there are likely to be three kinds of matter (as in the Amelian interpretation) contributing to Moderatus's multilevel metaphysical theory: paradigmatic matter (= ποσότης, "quantity"), bodily matter (= τὸ πόσον), and the matter in things sensed (= nonbeing initially present in τὸ πόσον).

Accordingly, I once argued that the Amelian position was already present, in its essentials, in the Porphyrian paraphrase of Moderatus's theory of matter as reported in Simplicius.[8] More recently, by a careful study of Porphyry's manner of paraphrasing what we may call Neopythagorean material, I have been able to convince myself that this passage (= Moderatus frag. 8) is indeed recognizable as Porphyrian paraphrase of Moderatus,[9] provided only that Porphyry is making adjustments in presentation designed to assist readers more familiar with the Plotinian system. It is clear that fragment 8 postulated a transcendent One-above-being, a second one that embraced the forms, and a third thing that participates in the one and the forms. Yet, several other metaphysical levels were mentioned, with most attention being given to matter. A major difficulty in appreciating Moderatus's schema, and especially in relating it to more than three of the *Parmenides*'s hypotheses, is that Porphyry, wanting to concentrate on matter, seems to be simplifying the first part of the fragment, and in particular the third stage, which he identifies with "the psychical." It is easy for us, and for all those ancients more familiar with Porphyry's system, to think of this third stage as involving the Porphyrian hypothesis 3 alone. Amelius

---

8. Harold Tarrant, *Thrasyllan Platonism* (Ithaca, NY: Cornell University Press, 1993), 150–61.

9. The opposite case is argued by J. Noel Hubler, "Moderatus, E. R. Dodds, and the Development of Neoplatonist Emanation," in *Plato's Parmenides and Its Heritage*, ed. John D. Turner and Kevin Corrigan, WGRWSup 2–3, 2 vols. (Atlanta: Society of Biblical Literature, 2010), 2:115–28, but see my linguistic research in appendix 1.

had associated *two* hypotheses (3 and 4) with soul, rational and irrational souls respectively, and Moderatus seems to have done something similar. He associates "the psychical" with *participation in the one and the forms*, which the *Parmenides* associates with hypothesis 4 (*Parm.* 157b6–159b1) rather than with hypothesis 3 (*Parm.* 155e4–157e5). Seeing the discussion of soul split across hypothesis 3 and hypothesis 4 is a second way in which Moderatus anticipated Amelius, the first being the complexity that he read into the Pythagoro-Platonic theory of matter.

There were, I shall suggest, two sides to Moderatus's allocation of both hypothesis 3 and hypothesis 4 to soul. The first of these is a rather plausible reading of the hypotheses, a reading that linked hypothesis 3 (= deduction 2B) not with the second hypothesis *from which it is clearly separated by being labeled "third,"* but rather with the fourth: he saw it not, with most modern scholars, as a corollary to deduction 2 but as a *prelude* to deduction 3! Nor is he the only Greek philosophic author to do so, for something similar has been known for some time, through the continuation-commentary on the *Parmenides* present in Parisinus Graecus 1810, published by Victor Cousin and since by Leendert Westerink, attributed to George Pachymeres.[10] In this commentary, the only extant representative of the logical interpretation of the hypotheses, there were just six principal divisions, following a reading of *Parm.* 136a–b.[11] Its assumption is that

---

10. See Proclus, *Philosophi Platonici Opera Inedita*, ed. Victor Cousin (Hildescheim: Olms, 1864), 616.1257–1314. Leendert G. Westerink wrongly speculated that the continuation-commentary depends on a sixth-century Alexandrian text, but distinctively Alexandrian language is lacking, and the material is in George's handwriting. See Westerink, introduction to *George Pachymeres: Ypomnema Eis Ton Parmeniden Platonos [Anonymou Synecheia Tou Ypomnematos Proklou]*, ed. Thomas A. Gadra et al. (Athens: Akademia Athenon, 1989).

11. On this interpretation, outlined by Proclus at *In Parm.* 633.10–635.18, see Steel, "Proclus et l'interprétation"; see also Tarrant, *Plato's First Interpreters*, 187–89. The continuation-commentary nevertheless makes something of opposite arguments (1257.21C = 1.10W) such as an earlier polemical interpretation (*In Parm.* 631.4–633.9), and employs limited metaphysical language, e.g., τὸ τοῦ ἑνὸς ἀπειρογόνιμον (6.13–14W; given as ἀπειροδύναμον at 1262.30–31C), αὐτοὲν καὶ αὐτοὸν (1258.20–21C = 1.19W). See Mossmann Roueché, "Notes on a Commentary on Plato's Parmenides," *GRBS* 12 (1971): 553–56, for a reconstruction, based on various passages, especially 1288.4–1289.6C (= 36.19–29W). Linguistically and schematically, this reading is more reminiscent of Proclus's discussion of 136a–b at *In Parm.* 1001.11–28 than of the original passage. Might Proclus have already known this division from those who had interpreted the hypotheses as a logical exercise?

Parmenides's method examines the consequences both of the postulation of a given entity and of its rejection, and in either case it examines three sets of consequences: what emerges, what does not emerge, and what does and does not emerge (τίνα ἕπεται, τίνα οὐχ ἕπεται,[12] τίνα ἕπεται καὶ οὐχ ἕπεται). According to Mossmann Rouché, this system allots the whole of 155e–160b (hypotheses 3–5) to what does and does not emerge from the postulation of the one, and the whole of 164b–166c (hypotheses 8–9) to what does and does not emerge following the negation of the one: but with significant subdivisions between hypothesis 4 and hypothesis 5 and hypothesis 8 and hypothesis 9 separating the positive and negative consequences.[13] Proclus, in my view, already knew this system, associating it with the logical division of the hypotheses, so that its outline was probably available far earlier.[14] The key point is that it *requires* hypothesis 3 to lead seamlessly into hypothesis 4.

Consider Parmenides's final words in what we think of as hypothesis 3 or deduction 2B: "Then the one, if it is, would undergo [πάσχειν] all these happenings [παθήματα]." His first words of hypothesis 4 or deduction 3 are, "Shouldn't we investigate [σκεπτέον] what the others would properly undergo [πάσχειν], if the one is?"[15] Above all, the actual conditional clause

---

12. I take it that οὐχ ἕπεται does not just mean "does not follow" but "follows that not." The verb ἕπεται replaces parts of the verb συμβαίνειν at *Parm.* 136a1, a5, a9, b3, b8 (see also 137b4).

13. See especially 1313.4–10C = 61.30–62.2W. Westerink clearly understands the approach to hypotheses 8 and 9 somewhat differently but offers no schema (introduction, ix). This issue is irrelevant to soul.

14. As Rouché points out, Proclus refers to this at 1000.27 as τὸ λογικόν of the Eleatic method; Proclus introduces it continuing to use Plato's term συμβαίνειν at 1001.3, 5, 8, 9, 13, and it is not until 1001.15–16 that τὸ συμβαῖνον is divided into ἑπόμενον, μὴ ἑπόμενον and ἅμα καὶ ἑπόμενον καὶ μὴ ἑπόμενον. In the logical interpretation of the hypotheses, which dominated in the first two centuries of the empire. See Carlos Steel, "Proclus et l'interprétation 'logique' du Parménides," in *Néoplatonisme et philosophie mediévale* (Turnhout: Brepols, 1997), 67–92. On this interpretation (on which see Proclus, *in Parm.* 634.5–635.18), see Harold Tarrant, *Plato's First Interpreters* (London: Duckworth, 2000), 187–89.

15. The word translated "happenings" (παθήματα) occurs in this dialogue only here and at 141d4; the related verb for "undergo" (πάσχειν) occurs in the hypotheses at (hypothesis 1) 138b–e, 139e–140b; (hypothesis 2) 146b2, 147c6–148c; (hypothesis 3) 156c, 157b; (hypothesis 4) 157b, 158e–159b; (hypothesis 5) 159b, 160a; (hypothesis 7) 163e; (hypothesis 8) 164b, 165c. However, these cases at 157b4 and b6, plus one at 156c5, mean that hypotheses 3–4 contain three out of only five cases of present-

seems the same: "the one, if it is" and "if the one is." The continuity should have been unmistakable, given Parmenides's carefulness elsewhere to indicate when making a new start.[16] Any interpreter, in the ancient world or in ours, would need good reasons for making a strong division at this point.[17] Mere tradition, especially the conventional insertion of a blank line after 157b5, cannot be regarded as a valid reason. Accordingly, Moderatus would have had good textual justification for taking hypotheses 3 and 4 (= deductions 2B and 3) as *one continuous investigation* examining what will be the consequences, if the one is, (1) for the one and (2) for the others. There is a shift in *focus* at 157b from the one to the others, but not a switch to a substantially new investigation, for the whole hypotheses 3–4 sequence is an investigation into a *one and many*.[18]

Another factor that might have assisted Moderatus to allocate the whole of hypotheses 3–4 to soul is the way the *Timaeus* was interpreted

---

stem forms. The verb σκεπτέον, repeated in the response of Aristoteles, may have some minor transitional force, for it is found again twice at 160b6, the second line of hypothesis 6 (= deduction 5). However, in this later case Parmenides adds the words "after this" to make the transition more explicit.

16. This (157b, hypotheses 3–4) is the *only* transition between conventionally separate hypotheses not clearly marked as such. Often the transition involves going back to the beginning (expressions such as πάλιν and/or ἐξ ἀρχῆς or equivalents): hypothesis 1–2, hypothesis 4–5, hypothesis 6–7, hypothesis 8–9 (142b1, 159b2–3, 163b7, 165e2). The transition hypothesis 2 to hypothesis 3 involves both the numeral "third" and an opening ἔτι δὴ ("Furthermore then..."), and hypothesis 5 to hypothesis 6 involves the repetition of the particle εἶεν that elsewhere in *Parmenides* had only occurred at the opening of the first hypothesis at 137c. This clearly marks the transition from the consequences of One to the consequences of no One. The transition from hypothesis 6 to hypothesis 7 is marked by the two opening words ἔτι δὴ, thus mirroring the opening of hypothesis 3, and the only other conjunction of these words in the *Parmenides* is at the opening of hypothesis 9, together with the theme of going back to the beginning. Of twenty-one cases in the Platonic corpus where the two words are found together, not just 155e4 but also *Lach.* 198c9 and *Euthyd.* 277d1 couple them with τὸ τρίτον.

17. While the presence of a jussive λέγωμεν ("let us state") is used very soon after the start of hypothesis 2 (142c7), hypothesis 3 (155e4), hypothesis 5 (159b4–5), and hypothesis 8 (164b5–6), this is also found in the middle of hypothesis 7 (163e6), so that its presence at 157b7–8 is not conclusive. λέγωμεν at the start of hypothesis 7 (163c2) is not jussive.

18. It is not certain that Plotinus in earlier treatises, including *Enn.* 5.1, recognized a major switch here, for 5.1.8.26 calls the third object of inquiry in the *Parmenides* "one and many," which would allow hypothesis 3 to concentrate on this "one and many" qua one, while hypothesis 4 examined it qua many.

in the early empire. While the linking of hypotheses 3 and 4 was textually justified, with no clear break ever signaled by the author, the shift at 157b from "one" to "others" must still have involved a *more modest* distinction in the mind of the interpreter, so if soul were considered to be their over-all subject, we might expect to encounter two types or aspects of soul, one unitary and another involving greater multiplicity. A gulf between the rational (immortal: from the Demiurge) and nonrational soul (mortal: from the young gods) was perhaps a feature of Neopythagorean exegesis of Plato since Eudorus.[19] It is clear from *Didasc.* 25.24–32[20] that Alci-nous, too, welcomed a sharp distinction between two psychic substances (*ousiai*) so as to argue that only the rational soul was immortal (i.e., "one" over time!) while the irrational was mortal. Plutarch again, a younger con-temporary of Moderatus, made a great deal of use of the two (or not fewer than two) souls hinted at by *Laws* 10.896e4–7 (See Plutarch, *Is. Os.* 370f; *An. procr.* 1014d, 1015e). Hence understanding the metaphysics of Mod-eratus involves his understanding of soul as somehow double. This does not commit him to a theory of *twin souls*, most obviously espoused by Numenius, but suggests rather that he read the *Parmenides* alongside the much-studied *Timaeus* (especially 42a–b).[21]

Moderatus: Ones and Soul

Before examining the opening of fragment 8 in some detail, let us intro-duce an important point about any "ones" that may be found in this passage. Fragment 6 declares: "So too in the case of the first *logoi* and forms the Pythagoreans have done the same thing [sc. as the grammarians and geometricians]—not being able to pass down in speech the immate-rial forms and the first causes they resorted to illustrating them through

---

19. Eudorus (?) in Stobaeus, *Ecl.* 2.49.8–15, where the goal of assimilation to god according to what is possible is interpreted as meaning "according to wisdom." For Numenius, see frags. 44 and 52 (if *silvae anima* should be understood in this context).

20. Note especially the final words: μήτε τῆς αὐτῆς οὐσίας εἶναι ταῖς λογικαῖς, θνητάς τε καὶ φθαρτὰς εἶναι. In that case there would be two separate οὐσίαι of soul, a fact deriving from one kind being "mortal" (because of their creation by the younger gods at *Tim.* 41c2–7).

21. The *Parmenides* interpretation of Iamblichus at Proclus, *In Parm.* 1055.8–9, talks of the fifth hypothesis depicting "the second souls that get woven onto the ratio-nal ones," the verb προσυφαίνω being taken from Plato, *Tim.* 41d1–2: ἀθανάτῳ θνητὸν προσυφαίνοντες.

numbers." So, according to Moderatus, when the *Parmenides* speaks of a "One beyond being," we should not be taking that as the *definitive* name for the first principle but merely as a good way of illustrating what is beyond ordinary language. The language of Plato's character Parmenides is a useful way of conveying to the reader the basic principles of the universe, including the first *logoi* and *eidē*. This fragment goes on to speak of "the *logos* of oneness, sameness and equality, and cause of (i) the joint animation and joint experience of the whole and (ii) the preservation of that which is always in the same state" as having being described as "one"; and its opposite as a dyadic *logos* or "dyad." Nevertheless, the primary purpose here is simply to show how *mathematical terms were being used to describe metaphysical principles*.

I now turn to the fragment preserved by Simplicius. Once again Moderatus is supposedly setting out Pythagorean doctrine: this time doctrine concerning matter as characterized by mass, extension, and divisibility, and by each of these insofar as they lack the measure and determination that form can bring to it. However, the passage of most interest to scholars precedes this:

> It seems that the Pythagoreans were the first of the Greeks to have held this view concerning matter, and Plato after them, as Moderatus too records. For this person too (= Plato)[22] reveals [ἀποφαίνεται] that the first one is above being [τὸ εἶναι] and all substance [οὐσία]; whereas he says that the second one [i.e., what really is and is intelligible] is the forms, while the third [i.e., what concerns soul][23] partakes of the one and of the forms, while the furthest nature from this, being that of sense-objects [αἰσθητά],[24] does not even participate in them, but is arranged according to their reflections in it, a shading [σκίασμα][25] of the matter

---

22. I follow the assumption of Marie-Luise Lakmann in *Platonici Minores. 1.Jh.v.Chr.–2. Jh.n.Chr*, ed. Lakmann (Leiden: Brill, 2017), 625. So far Moderatus has only been depicted as giving his version of philosophic history, not his own theory (even though this latter must clearly be related to his version of history).

23. Here "i.e." stands for ὅπερ ἐστί, which, in the sense of "which means," is a specification technique reasonably widespread in Porphyry.

24. I have misgivings about translating αἰσθητά in such a way, because we seem not now to be dealing with objects that cause the sensation but with what actually is sensed, a visual representation, a sound or a taste, for instance. See below.

25. In Tarrant (*Thrasyllan Platonism*, 150), I take σκίασμα as the complement of the participle *ousēs*. Compare John Dillon, *The Middle Platonists* (London: Duckworth, 1977), 347, Lakmann, *Platonici Minores*, 625: "wobei die in ihnen befindliche

in them, which is non-being initially present in the quantitative [πόσον], and is even lower and more remote from this.[26] And Porphyry, setting these things out as the doctrine of Moderatus in the second book of his *On Matter* has written that... (Moderatus [Lakmann] frag. 8 = Simplicius, *In Phys.* 230.34–231.24 [Diels] = Porphyrios frag. 236 [Smith] = Dörrie and Baltes, no. 122)

Given the claim that Plato was the one to *reveal* this theory, it was relatively easy for Dodds to associate the first One to be mentioned here with what is described in the first hypothesis of the *Parmenides* (especially *Parm.* 141e), and I have no special qualms about Porphyry's reporting here. My problems begin with the second one, where Porphyry's explanation tilts Moderatus's theory in the direction of Plotinus's Nous, speaking of "the intelligible," whereas Moderatus's own language seems to consistently use the term "forms" (*eidē*). It is crucial for the theory of matter outlined below that the *heniaios logos*, which is presumably not other than "the *logos* of the One" in fragment 6, should embrace within itself *all the forms of things that are* (πάντας τοὺς λόγους τῶν ὄντων). It is the will of this unitary principle to establish the generation of reality from himself, separating off quantity (ποσότης) from all his own *logoi* and forms. Now, I take it that any principle that contains all the forms of things *that are* cannot be beyond *being*, and I would accordingly identify the unitary *logos*, or *logos* of the one, with the second one of which Porphyry had spoken, and so with the second hypothesis of the *Parmenides*, which possesses *ousia* (*Parm.* 142b, etc.). This one is playing a role rather like the Demiurge, and it is the same unitary principle that is contrasted with the dyadic principle that it produces.

Materie ein Schatten des Nicht-Seienden ist, das primär im Quantum ist." But good Greek would seem to require a genitive *skiasmatos* in such a case. Hence I now take σκίασμα to be accusative because it stands in apposition to "the furthest nature." The word is almost always used in discussions of eclipses up until early imperial times, of the moon's passing into the area shaded by the earth. It is very difficult to see the present case merely as an extension of that usage.

26. It is in my view important, in Amelian discussion of the entities signified by the hypotheses, that regarding the sensible bodies their so-called forms are actually inferior to their matter—a possibility that the Porphyrian reply explicitly fails to envisage (1053.16–19).

Moderatan Soul and Participation

But let us move onto what Porphyry calls the domain of soul (τὸ ψυχικόν). In this case the text does not specifically label it a "one," being content with calling it "the third" (τὸ τρίτον), rather like the text of *Parm.* 155e4 (ἔτι δὴ τὸ τρίτον λέγωμεν). We have to allow the possibility that this was quite deliberate. This "third" "partakes of the one and the forms," and partaking of the one is not what we should expect from anything that is *in its essence* a one. This third thing, besides needing two prior levels if it is to be "third," must be posterior not only to the one beyond being but also to the one that embraces the forms if it is itself to partake in those forms.[27] This is what we should expect from an entity that was a "one-and-many," as suggested by 155e5–6 and by Plotinus's description of the third level (*Enn.* 5.1.8.26). But the *Parmenides* itself does not suggest that the "one" described in hypothesis 3 participates in anything other than time (*Parm.* 155e–156a). Where then does Moderatus's emphasis on participation at the *third* level come from? Why would he mention such participation if it had not been explicit in the Platonic passage that he seeks to interpret?

The language of participation is recurrent in the *Parmenides* because of the very nature of the dialogue, but its importance diminishes after hypothesis 2. It is *non*participation that is relevant to hypothesis 5 (= deduction 4: 159d1–7, 159e6–160b) and hypothesis 7 (= deduction 6: 163c3–164a4). In hypothesis 6 (= deduction 5) the one-that-is-not participates in many other things (160e2, 161c9–d4), even in being as well as in nonbeing (161e3–162b8), but not of course in the one. There is no talk at all of participation in hypotheses 8–9. We are left with hypothesis 4 (= deduction 3), where I count a total number of sixteen participation terms.[28] Here, discussion of the participation of others in the one occurs first from 157e2 to 158b1, while talk of things "participating" (participle) continues to b9. At 158d8 and 158e4 we meet reference to these same things participating in limit (*peras*), which would surely be associated with form of some kind in the eyes of the Pythagoreans. The many "others" share limits

---

27. One may suspect that "in the one and the forms" is a convenient way of saying "in the first one and in the entity incorporating the forms," for the third hypothesis does indeed begin from the one as conceived in the first two hypotheses, and continues to be about a one.

28. μετέχειν: 157c2, d8, e3, e6, 158a3, a4, b1, b2, b6, b8, c4, d8, e4; μεταλαμβάνειν: 158b3, b9 x 2.

and differences with one another. Consequently, I had originally assumed that "Moderatus or his reporters or their scribes" had "somehow slipped from consideration of the third 'one' of hypothesis three into discussion of the 'others' of hypothesis four."[29]

There was no need to postulate such a lacuna. After brief consideration of an alternative explanation,[30] I concluded that Moderatus, like most modern scholars, had not considered hypothesis 3 as an independent exercise at all. Such a stance seems justified not so much because of hypothesis 3's brevity[31] but rather because of the singular emphasis on time, change, and the instant, which places it apart from the principal deductions. Yet adding it to hypothesis 2 as an appendix would be neither the only solution nor the best one, since it would have been philosophically possible and, as we saw, linguistically convincing to argue that it is a prelude to hypothesis 4—necessary because prior material has not adequately explained "the others" (*ta alla*), those things with which hypothesis 4 will be concerned from the outset. Only when the one has morphed into a plurality *that has ceased to be one* can the others be properly considered as separate entities. The neuter plural of *allos* is accordingly almost entirely absent from hypothesis 1.[32] The result of taking hypotheses 3 and 4 together, as *a single episode in Plato's exercise*, is that the reference to "the third" at the opening of hypothesis 3 ("Then let us go on to state the third") would cover hypothesis 3 plus hypothesis 4 (= deduction 2B + deduction

---

29. Tarrant, *Thrasyllan Platonism*, 154.

30. A first possibility was that Porphyry's introduction to Moderatus's theory of matter had glossed over some aspects of his wider metaphysical system—not too surprising if Moderatus, like Amelius, had located soul in both hypothesis 3 and hypothesis 4 (deduction 2B + deduction 3). So, if Moderatus anticipated Amelius in assuming that hypotheses 3 and 4 depicted different aspects or different kinds *of soul*, then Porphyry, influenced by Plotinus's treatment of soul as one continuous hypostasis, could combine what Moderatus had found in hypotheses 3–4, call it "the psychical," and ascribe to "the psychical" things said about the others of the lengthier hypothesis 4. So Porphyry could have been misleadingly brief out of a desire to get on to Moderatus's views on matter. Even so, Porphyry is ordinarily a careful and scrupulous reporter of those whom he paraphrases, and my own linguistic analysis (see appendix 1) shows that the style of the original still manages to shine through.

31. It is less than two OCT pages as opposed to more than six for hypothesis 1, eighteen for hypothesis 2, and more than two for hypotheses 4 and 6.

32. A rare exception is found at 138c8 in the phrase "other parts" and another at 140c5 (in relation to what the one could not be).

3). Moderatus's reference to "the third" would therefore *include* hypothesis 4, and the reference to the third's participating in the one and the forms would accord with Plato's text.

Did Moderatus recognize no transition at all as hypothesis 3 passed into hypothesis 4? I doubt that, because Plato's text, although it from the very beginning was talking of a "one and many" (*Parm.* 155e5) and of alternation between the two (156b1–4), quite obviously passes at 157b3–7 from what happens *to the one* to what happens *to others*. I would rather propose that Moderatus found two *aspects* or *phases* of soul behind hypotheses 3–4, one more unitary and the other involving greater plurality. Other independent evidence clearly shows that unity and plurality were both essential to the Moderatan soul, to which numeric ratios and the harmonization of otherness were of considerable relevance (frag. 11).[33] The unity might have been dominant in the cosmic souls as opposed to individual souls respectively, in divine as opposed to human and animal souls, or in rational as opposed to irrational soul, irrationality representing a failure of the harmonizing unity. Soul is the level at which *one and many belong together*, with a potential for human souls at least to shift between being more "one" and being more "many."

The Moderatan System and the *Timaeus*

Now we need to take stock, insofar as is possible, of *all* the metaphysical levels offered by fragment 8. So far, we have seen that, in the course of introducing Moderatus's theory of matter, Porphyry has first listed various *other* metaphysical levels that Moderatus postulated. So far, we have met the first one, above being. Next, a second one, identified by Porphyry as the intelligible, and possibly identical with the unitary principle (ἑνιαῖος λόγος) from later in the fragment. This *logos* embraced "all the principles of things that are" (πάντας τοὺς λογοὺς τῶν ὀντῶν),[34] much as Plotinian *nous* embraced

---

33. Fragment 11 involves Stobaeus's quotations from Iamblichus's *De anima*. These preserve, with some textual uncertainty, a Moderatan conception of soul as a "number embracing *logoi*," and as somehow involving a harmony "that renders contrasting things commeasurable and congruent." See Iamblichus, *De Anima: Text, Translation and Commentary*, ed. John F. Finamore and John Dillon (Leiden: Brill, 2002), 28–29. Finamore and Dillon tackle the textual issue on 83.

34. The term "forms" (*eidē*) is an alternative to *logoi* for the formal principles present in the *heniaios logos*.

the intelligibles. At a third level soul, said to "partake of the one and of the forms." Besides these, Porphyry now mentions "the final nature from this [τὴν ... ἀπό τούτου τελευταίαν φύσιν], that of sense-objects [*aesthēta*]" (Moderatus [Lakmann] frag. 8.5 = Simplicius, *In Phys.* 230.34–231.24 [Diels] = Porphyry frag. 236 [Smith] = Dörrie and Baltes no. 122). It is as if these sense-objects are at the end of a process of evolution.[35] They do not participate but are structured according to mere reflections of the forms (κάτ' ἔμφασιν ἐκείνων); they are thus a kind of "shading" (σκίασμα) upon that in which they appear.[36] The language strongly suggests their connection with hypothesis 8 in the *Parmenides*, and indeed in Proclus's *Commentary on the Parmenides* Plutarch of Athens's interpretation of hypothesis 8 accounts for shadow-language otherwise absent from that work.[37] Yet it also connects

---

35. This may be somewhat different from Amelius's "enmattered forms" and from Porphyry's own "enmattered forms viewed in the substrate" (Proclus, *In Parm.* 1054.6–7: περὶ τῶν ἐνύλων εἰδῶν ἐν τῷ ὑποκειμένῳ μέντοι θεωρουμένων), a description that makes its connection with the receptacle plain.

36. The relationship between reflection (ἔμφασις) and participation (μέτοχος or μετοχή) is prominent in Proclus (*Elem. theol.* 71.4–8; *In Tim.* 2.295.8; *In Parm.* 690.13–16, 839.16, 845.24, 846.19), though unnamed predecessors use the distinction at *In Tim.* 1.434.23–25, while others make *emphasis* a mode of *methexis* at 846.18–21. There is also a "Pythagorean" precedent in Iamblichus, *Comm. math. sc.* 93.26–94.2: ἢ κατὰ μετοχήν, ὅταν τῶν καθαρῶν λόγων οἱ ἐν ἄλλοις ὄντες λόγοι κατὰ τί μετέχουσιν ἐπισκοπῶμεν· ἢ κατὰ ἔμφασιν, ἡνίκα ἂν ἀμυδρὸν ἴχνος τοῦ μαθηματικοῦ ἐμφανταζόμενον περὶ τὰ αἰσθητὰ θεωρῶμεν. Plato does not use *emphasis*, but when talking of the "works of necessity," the receptacle, elements, and their effects on us, he uses the verb *emphanizein* (49a4, 61c5, and the verbal at 65c3), otherwise found in authentic works only at *Crat.* 438d6 and *Soph.* 218c1 and 244a5; so three close appearances in *Timaeus* require explanation. Proclus (*In Parm.* 1053.20) uses *emphasis* for Amelius's "matter that is unordered and has insubstantial reflections of the forms," while Damascius uses the term *emphasis* in relation to hypothesis 8 at *In Parm.* 315.9: ὅμως δὲ ἐπειδὴ ἔχει τινὰ ἔμφασιν τοῦ ἑνός. In Tarrant (*Thrasyllan Platonism*, 150), I take σκίασμα as the complement of the participle *ousēs*; see Dillon, *Middle Platonists*, 347, Lakmann, *Platonici Minores*, 625 (from Dörrie and Baltes, *Der Platonismus*, 177). Orthodox Greek would then require a genitive σκιάσματος. I now take σκίασμα to be accusative, in apposition to "the furthest nature." This word is usually used in discussions of eclipses until early imperial times, of the moon's passing into the area shaded by earth; I assume that it is not just a synonym for σκία ("shadow") here.

37. The only three uses of σκία (1059.28, 1060.16, 1060.21) occur in reports of Plutarch's interpretation of hypotheses 8 and 9; also important is the language of dreamlike imaginings (1059.28, 1060.1) and of "things sensed" that are "dreamlike and do not at all participate in [real] being or separation according to forms." Plutarch

with the *Timaeus*'s description of *how we see things*[38] at 49b1–50a4—as shifting qualities rather than form-possessing things. The matter in these things that are sensed, on which they are a kind of shading, is rather like a screen on which images are projected, where the screen that is more *real* than the images projected on it. Hence the material reflecting sense-objects is somehow prior to them; and indeed it is they rather than their matter that are said to be "last." At this point Porphyry goes on to consider Moderatus's theory of matter in the proper sense, introducing the two following types:

> Paradigmatic matter, clearly identified with universal receptacle of the Platonic *Timaeus*, and known as "quantity" [ποσότης].[39] Conceived by privation of all form, this has none of the forms found at the second level, but it is ready for receiving them.
>
> The matter in bodies, conforming to this paradigm and called πόσον, having the same character of formlessness in itself, and the same ability to be circumscribed by form. This matter, it seems, is genuinely *affected* by the form and number received, and hence participates; it cannot be identified with the matter of things sensed. (Modertus [Lakmann] frag. 8.15 = Simplicius, *In Phys.* 230.34–231.24 [Diels] = Porphyry frag. 236 [Smith] = Dörrie and Baltes no. 122)

It is natural, when thinking in hierarchical terms, to take both the "matter" that serves as a paradigm and the matter in bodies as posterior to the three levels first mentioned by Porphyry, but prior to the "matter" on which sense-objects are projected. Accordingly, we might associate the paradigm of matter with hypothesis 5 (where participation is denied), the matter of bodies with hypothesis 6 (where participation is affirmed), and the matter of mere sense-images with hypothesis 7 (where participation is again denied).[40] This is close to the Amelian interpretation, in which hypoth-

---

probably best understood the development of *Parmenides* interpretation, since it was he who "clarified what had been confusingly stated by his predecessors" (1061.15–16). In hypothesis 8 note (1) the absence of language of participation, (2) the language of mere appearance at 164d2, d7, e3, etc., including especially (3) φαντάσματα (165a5, d2), and (4) shade-paintings (ἐσκιαγραφημένα, 165c7).

38. Note δοκοῦμεν (49b8), ὁρῶμεν (c1), ὡς φαίνεται (c7), φανταζομένων (d1), and ἀεὶ ἕκαστα αὐτῶν φαντάζεται (e8).

39. This common term is also used by Moderatus when defining number in frag. 10, lines 4–5.

40. See above under "Moderatan Soul and Participation." Though *paradigm* is in the text, this might not be the primary way Moderatus conceived it. It cannot be

eses 3–4 represent types of soul (rational/irrational), hypothesis 5 pictures matter in readiness for receiving form, hypothesis 6 matter in receipt of form, and hypothesis 7 matter with neither form nor the aptitude to receive it.[41] While it may seem strange to postulate three such levels of matter, Speusippus had already been said, by Aristotle, to have postulated a different kind of matter for all his substance levels (οὐσίαι), and Speusippus is the earliest figure somehow connected with interpretation of the *Parmenides*.[42] Furthermore, we should consider how a theory of multiple matters might agree with what is read in the *Timaeus*.

The relevance of the *Timaeus* is made clear not only by Moderatus's references to the plurality of Plato's names for the receptacle but also by the fact that Moderatus introduces a quasidivine *logos* that embraces the forms of all things and desires to bring about coming-to-be, starting somehow from himself. This looks rather like an interpretation of the Platonic Demiurge, or like a variant of the role played by the *logos* in Philo's treatise on the creator. One might think also of the theory of a universal *logos* associated with Thrasyllus by Porphyry (*Comm. harm.* 12.18–28), where it appears at first sight to be associated with a *supreme* divinity.[43] Because

---

a paradigm in the usual Platonic sense, and its identity with universal matter seems assured given its identity with Plato's receptacle.

41. Importantly, since things sensed do not participate (sc. in the One and the Forms), Moderatus's matter of things sensed will have no aptitude for the reception of form.

42. See Aristotle, *Metaph.* 1028b21–24; in Leonardo Táran, ed., *Speusippus of Athens* (Leiden: Brill, 1981), this is frag. 29. The οὐσίαι mentioned here are numbers, magnitudes, and soul; sensible bodies may be added from *Metaph.* 1090b16–20 (frag. 37 in Táran, *Speusippus of Athens*). If that exhausts the list, then Speusippus postulated *four* types of matter, each being a different manifestation of his principle of plurality (πλῆθος); only in Plutarch, *Mor.* 1007a–b (frag. 60 in Táran, *Speusippus of Athens*) might a manifestation of plurality in Speusippus be called πόσον. Speusippus's treatment of the One as a minimum (frags. 49a, 49b in Táran, *Speusippus of Athens*) might have prevented his wider influence on imperial interpretation of the *Parmenides*. Speusippus is referred to in both the anonymous (or Porphyrian) Commentary on the Parmenides (1.20–21 = frag. 49b in Táran, *Speusippus of Athens*; see also frag. 48a = Damascius, *Princ.* 2.25–3.2) and Proclus, *In Parm.* (7.38.32–40.7K = frag. 46 in Táran, *Speusippus of Athens*). Luc Brisson needlessly argues that the material is fraudulent. See Brisson, "The Fragment of Speusippus in Column I of the Anonymous Commentary on the Parmenides," in Turner and Corrigan, *Plato's Parmenides and Its Heritage* 2:59–65.

43. But an allusion to (Plato) *Ep.* 6 (323d) hints that there might be a "cause" beyond the "god and leader of all."

the ultimate material principle is derived from this formal principle in Moderatus, albeit by separation from it, it must be posterior to this *logos*. However, the use of the *Timaeus* is at its most explicit and most striking when Moderatus asserts that *all* the key descriptions applied by Plato to the receptacle apply to this paradigmatic matter: terms and phrases including "all-receptive," "formless," "having participated in the intelligible in a very perplexing way," "grasped with difficulty by a bastard reasoning," and so on.[44] Could it be that his metaphysic has somehow resulted from an attempt to interpret the hypotheses of the *Parmenides* alongside the *Timaeus*, perhaps even as a kind of blueprint for the latter? Correspondence might proceed roughly as follows (table 11.1):

Table 11.1. Possible Correspondence between
Hypotheses and *Timaeus* in Moderatus

Hypothesis	Subject according to Moderatus	*Timaeus* episode	Introduced
1	One beyond Being	Demiurge and Good[45]	29a
2	one *Logos* embracing forms	Demiurge/ paradigm/Ideas	31a
3	souls [unitary]	cosmic and immortal Soul	35a
4	souls [divisible]	mortal souls	41b
5	paradigmatic *posotês*	universal receptacle	50b

---

44. See Plato, *Tim.* 51a7–b1, 52b2; it is important that none of these terms are from 49b2–50b5, which do not directly describe universal matter in this interpretation but illustrate it through the use of analogies.

45. Separating the first two stages is tricky. However, note Proclus's claim that for Numenius (whose second god was clearly the demiurgic force proper; frag. 21.4–5) the Demiurge is double, the first god and the second. This becomes intelligible if we understand him to be saying that in the *Timaeus* the Demiurge had been, according to Numenius, a composite character sharing features of his own first god (= the unmoved Good, like the world's *father*) and his second god (= the motive cause of creation, like the world's *maker*). It is entirely possible that Moderatus too should have seen the Platonic demiurgic as something similar.

6	*poson* of physical bodies	triangles and solids	53b; see also 50a
7	*poson* of things sensed	perceptual affections	61c etc.
8	qualities that are sensed	perceptual affections	61c, etc.

Moderatus has tried to see the evolution of the one and the others in the *Parmenides* as *mirroring* the evolution of universe as set out in the *Timaeus*'s more literal description. Only at the very end does this mirroring falter, but even the text of the *Timaeus* makes it clear at 61c–d that details of our bodies and mortal soul must already be assumed when tackling the origins of perceptual qualities.

Soul in the Amelian System

It cannot be expected that any interpreter is going to reproduce a predecessor's schema exactly, and the report in Proclus of what is supposed to be Amelius's interpretation is presented in slightly different terms (table 11.2):

Table 11.2. Possible Correspondence between
Hypotheses and *Timaeus* in Amelius

Hypothesis	Subject according to Moderatus	Possible *Timaeus* episode	Introduced
1	One	Good	29a
2	intellectual world	Demiurge and paradigm[46]	31a
3	rational souls	cosmic and immortal souls	35a
4	irrational souls	mortal souls	41b
5	matter ready for form	precosmic receptacle[47]	49a, 52d

---

46. The intelligibles are not outside the intellect for the mature Amelius (Porphyry, *Vit. Plot.* 18).

47. Proclus associates Amelius's matter-ready-for-form with the receptacle as described at 52d–53a, referring to its "insubstantial reflections of the forms" (*In Parm.*

6	matter structured	matter characterized[48]	50a, 53b
7	prime matter	receptacle free from all form[49]	50b
8	form in matter	triangles and solids	53c

I take it that Amelius could see that many details of Moderatus's schema fit the *Parmenides* quite well, but he preferred to adapt it to suit features of Plotinian doctrine. What had been particularly noteworthy in Moderatus, according to this investigation, was his insistence that there is no participation, in the one or the forms, in things sensed (what we saw, heard, tasted, etc.), seemingly considering them quite different from the actual physical objects that underlie our sensations. The latter are actual combinations of matter and form, while what is seen offers an appearance of form without participating in it. Porphyry was not so pessimistic about extracting form from our sensations, as the *Commentary on Ptolemy's Harmonics* (13.21–14.22) shows, and one must doubt whether Amelius would have been. At any rate it is now enmattered form that is associated with the eighth hypothesis on the grounds that it is the last remaining principle (ἀρχή) after matter (*In Parm.* 1053.5–7), and this argues for the greater reality of such form since a mere reflection cannot easily be seen as a principle.

I suspect Amelius believed there really was textual justification in the *Timaeus* for postulating these three grades of matter, in much the same way that he had found there, particularly at 39e and 30a–b,[50] three demiurgic minds, apparently inspired partially by Numenius's ingenuity. At least when Porphyry knew him he had accepted Plotinus's insistence on a single hypostasis of Intellect, which would have required him to keep any such intellectual triad wholly within the second hypostasis and therefore to find them only in hypothesis 2. However, Plotinus cannot have convinced him also to treat soul in a unified way, for it required no subtlety at all to find both an immortal and a mortal soul in the *Timaeus*, part of the

---

1053.20). Those same descriptions would also fit the picture of the material world as we see it at 49a–50a and the description of precosmic matter at 69b2–8.

48. While the ultimate universal receptacle must be free of all the forms that are to appear in it, the lump of gold referred to at 50a–b takes on various shapes while being already characterized as "gold" itself; much the same applies to the more stable conditions of the four basic elements, discussed from 53b.

49. The necessity of matter itself being cleansed of all that it must receive is a major theme from 50b to 51b.

50. These are found in Proclus, *In Tim.* 1.398.16–26, 3.103.18–23.

same plan, but fashioned by different makers. Furthermore, one cannot assume that Plotinus himself did not take hypotheses 3 and 4 together as a single "third" exercise, for we have scant evidence of his reading of any hypothesis after the first three.[51] What we do have is Plotinus's early exercise in how all soul could somehow be one in spite of its presumed divisions (*Enn.* 4.9), his insistence that the number of hypostases is three (*Enn.* 5.1.8), and his later reaffirmation of this number (*Enn.* 2.9.1.12–16), along with the overall unity of soul in spite of its diversity (*Enn.* 2.9.2.6–9). But its ability to be seen as both a unity and a plurality seems to have been something he never doubted. And if soul involved both a "one" and "others," then both hypothesis 3 and hypothesis 4 might still theoretically apply to soul—as one continuous exercise.

How Many Hypotheses?

How, then, did the familiar division of the hypotheses into nine come about? Porphyry used it, but did it exist beforehand? There appears to have been little interest in the significance of a particular number, beyond a natural curiosity over Plato's reference to a "third" at the beginning of hypothesis 3. Amelius almost certainly felt no need to assign any entity to the so-called ninth hypothesis because it seems to depict nothing at all. The other hypotheses (or whatever he called them) bear in Proclus the same numbers as their Porphyrian counterparts, but we cannot affirm that he regarded the division of hypothesis 3 from hypothesis 4 as comparable with that between hypothesis 6 and hypothesis 7, for instance.[52] Perhaps Porphyry was primarily responsible for the Neoplatonist division into nine. Porphyry had special motivation for reaffirming the key division insofar as he wanted to maintain a single hypostasis of soul, while organizing the whole sequence in an evolving order from highest to lowest.[53]

---

51. The *index fontium* of the *Editio Minor* makes no reference at all to 157b–159b (see Plotinus, *Opera*). I assume that Plotinus had no confidence on how the later hypotheses should be divided or what they were referring to. His main interest was elsewhere, and he left Amelius and Porphyry to quarrel over such hermeneutical issues.

52. It may have appealed to him to have an intelligible world that if one, a soul that is both one and many, and types of matter that display more serious divisions, under the influence of Speusippus.

53. It seems that the criticism of Amelius at *In Parm.* 1053.12–20 was traditional and probably went back to Porphyry.

Porphyry thus put an end to the tendency in Neopythagoreanism and Middle Platonism to distinguish sharply the natures of immortal and mortal souls. Consider Eudorus, who said that the Pythagoreans postulated a One over and above the One opposed to the Dyad, thus anticipating Moderatus's distinction between Ones. It was most likely his idea that "assimilation to the divine regarding that which is possible" should be interpreted as "regarding wisdom," that is, "regarding the rational soul."[54] This, too, suggests a rather sharp divide between rational and irrational soul, one that the *Timaeus* does not discourage. Moving a century forward rather than a century back from Moderatus, we should also note Numenius's remarkable doctrine that we do not just have rational and irrational *parts* of the soul but two souls, rational and irrational. Nor should one overlook the fact that Amelius appears to have been something of an expert on the doctrines of Numenius—deeply influenced by him in other respects, too, not least regarding the interpretation of *Tim.* 39e. Any line from Eudorus, through Moderatus, to Numenius, and to Amelius came to a halt. For the distinction between Middle and Neoplatonisms, soul matters a great deal.

Appendix 1: Statistical Analysis of Porphyry's Paraphrases

A cluster analysis of recurrent nontechnical vocabulary suggests that, out of a range of Porphyrian and Neopythagorean material, there is no block of analyzed text more akin to the paraphrase of Moderatus in Porphyry's *Life of Pythagoras* (48–53 = frag. 6) than his paraphrase of Moderatus preserved by Simplicius (*In. Phys.* 230.34–231.24 = frag. 8).[55] Porphyrian material included a selection from his *Commentary on Ptolemy's Harmonics*, all the essay *On the Cave of the Nymphs*, and all the *Life of Pythagoras*. Material (from Thrasyllus, Moderatus, Numenius, and Cronius) likely to be paraphrased was placed in separate files. Also present in the analysis were two files of Numenius's verbatim fragments, those from the metaphysical *On the Good*, and those from the historical work *On the Revolt of the Academics against Plato*.

---

54. Dillon, *Middle Platonists*, 122–23.

55. These files are SimplModer and VPythModer; the next most similar file is Numenius, frag. 30, from *Cave of the Nymphs*, while frags. 32–33 and passages that I ascribe to Thrasyllus in Porphyry's *Comm. harm.* (12.6–13.12; 13.21–14.28, both closed with διὰ μὲν δή) are next closest.

In all, the number of separate blocks analyzed was as follows:

Porphyry, *Commentary on Ptolemy's Harmonics*
- Two files before Thrasyllan material (HarmIntr1–2), eight after (HarmRemC1–8), mostly of 800 words
- Three files suspected (with decreasing probability) of being Thrasyllan paraphrase (HarmThrasLogB, HarmLog2B, HarmLog3)[56]

Porphyry, *On the Cave of the Nymphs*
- Three files with all material other than those listed as Cronius and Numenius
- Cronius, frag. 9
- Numenius, frag. 30
- Numenius, frag. 31
- Numenius, frags. 32–33

Porphyry, *Life of Pythagoras*
- All material other than the paraphrase of Moderatus
- Moderatus, frag. 6

Numenius
- Fragments from *On the Good*
- Fragments from *On the Revolt of the Academics against Plato*

Simplicius
- Moderatus, frag. 8 from *In Physica*, pp. 230–31

A cluster analysis applying Ward's method with standardized data, a method regularly used in the area of linguistic analysis, allocated the material in five clusters, producing the following results: Clusters 3 and 4 were the furthest removed from all the regular Porphyrian material and were somewhat related to each other. They consisted of:

Cluster 3
- Numenius, frag. 30

---

56. HarmThrasLogB = *Comm. harm.* 12.6–13.12; HarmLog2B = *Comm. harm.* 13.21–14.28; HarmLog3 = *Comm. harm.* 15.10–27.

◆   Moderatus, frags. 6 and 8 (rather more closely associated)

Cluster 6
◆   Numenius, frags. 32–33
◆   HarmLog2B and HarmThrasLogB (rather more closely associated)

Hence this branch of the analysis consisted *entirely* of Porphyrian *paraphrase*. The remaining branch consisted of clusters 1, 2, and 5. Regular Porphyrian material was divided between clusters 2 and 5, with four of the five regular files from the *Life of Pythagoras* (other than Moderatus, frag. 6) placed in cluster 5,[57] and all regular files from the other two Porphyrian works placed in cluster 2. Cluster 2, however, contained one noticeable subcluster containing Numenius, *On the Revolt of the Academics against Plato*, close to Numenius, fragment 31, plus (at a slightly greater distance) the file HarmLog3 (where some Thrasyllan influence might still linger) and one other file from the *Commentary on Ptolemy's Harmonics*. Finally, cluster 1 consisted of just two files, Numenius, *On the Good*, and Cronius, fragment 9. That Cronius, known as the companion (ἑταῖρος) of Numenius, should have a style similar in some respects is not unexpected. On the other hand, it is only mildly surprising for the fragments *On the Good* to be placed in a different cluster from those *On the Revolt of the Academics against Plato*, owing to a considerable difference in genre.[58]

My conclusion is that Porphyrian close paraphrase is usually detectable by the computer, sometimes but not always approximating the style of the original author; and that no text that I have so far found is closer in style to Moderatus, fragment 6 (in Porphyry's *Life of Pythagoras*), than fragment 8 (in Simplicius's *In Aristotelis Physicorum libros quattuor priores/posteriores*). Principal component analysis largely confirmed these conclusions. Here are the results for three principal components:

---

57. In analyses also involving the *Life of Plotinus*, that biography (or hagiography, perhaps) tends to be linked in style with the *Life of Pythagoras*, suggesting a distinct style for that genre.

58. A dendrogram giving a visual representation of this analysis is available at https://tinyurl.com/SBL4222a.

Table 11.3 Principal Component Analysis (Moderatan files italicized)

Block	PC1	Block	PC2	Block	PC3
NumenHistFrs	-8.54244	*VPythMod*	*-6.71902*	NumenFrr32&33	-4.0963
HarmIntr (1)	-3.18179	*SimplModeratus*	*-5.25033*	HarmRemC (1)	-3.06425
HarmRemC (6)	-2.46845	HarmRemC (1)	-2.77491	HarmRemC (7)	-2.97414
NumenGoodFrs	-2.13945	HarmLog3	-2.50418	HarmRemC (6)	-2.81561
CroniusFr9	-1.927	CroniusFr9	-2.03149	NumenFr31	-2.56238
HarmRemC (3)	-1.7753	NumenGoodFrs	-1.92352	NumenGoodFrs	-2.38828
VPythStart (2)	-1.72919	NumenFr30	-1.7537	HarmLog3	-2.06147
VPythStart (3)	-1.51305	HarmRemC (6)	-1.26616	NumenFr30	-1.86348
HarmRemC (1)	-1.13606	NumenHistFrs	-1.09055	CaveRem (2)	-1.24341
HarmRemC (2)	-1.10807	HarmIntr (2)	-1.05943	CaveRem (3)	-1.22603
VPythStart (4)	-1.05191	HarmRemC (2)	-1.03201	HarmRemC (8)	-1.05691
HarmIntr (2)	-1.0185	VPythStart (4)	-0.98409	VPythStart (1)	-0.58321
VPythStart (1)	-0.98935	HarmRemC (5)	-0.66186	HarmRemC (3)	-0.49178
VPythEnd	-0.86401	HarmRemC (3)	-0.47581	HarmRemC (2)	-0.33078
HarmRemC (4)	-0.3669	HarmRemC (7)	0.03275	CaveRem (1)	-0.27926
HarmRemC (7)	-0.31946	HarmRemC (8)	0.34277	HarmRemC (5)	-0.21527
CaveRem (1)	-0.27376	CaveRem (3)	1.14211	NumenHistFrs	0.21983
CaveRem (2)	0.09945	HarmRemC (4)	1.14439	VPythEnd	0.37172
HarmLog3	0.25313	HarmLog2B	1.1568	*SimplModeratus*	*0.41548*
HarmRemC (5)	0.87626	HarmIntr (1)	1.16563	HarmIntr (1)	0.66815
CaveRem (3)	1.08046	CaveRem (1)	1.22805	VPythStart (4)	0.71987
HarmRemC (8)	1.09448	NumenFr31	1.77247	HarmRemC (4)	0.94402
HarmThrasLogB	1.48225	CaveRem (2)	2.0252	HarmIntr (2)	1.11328
NumenFr31	1.49787	VPythStart (2)	2.49728	VPythStart (2)	1.45004
VPythMod	*3.24421*	HarmThrasLogB	2.5948	*VPythMod*	*2.79544*
SimplModeratus	*4.41943*	VPythStart (3)	2.64174	CroniusFr9	3.2822
HarmLog2B	4.57632	VPythEnd	2.79414	VPythStart (3)	3.3654
NumenFrr32&33	5.73976	VPythStart (1)	3.10767	HarmLog2B	5.00016
NumenFr30	6.04108	NumenFrr32&33	5.88126	HarmThrasLogB	6.90699

The two files offering Porphyrian paraphrase of Moderatus are closest together on component 1 (statistically the most important), closest together and at the extreme end of the minus-range on component 2 (the next most important), and relatively close together on component 3, too.

Appendix 2: Different Types of Matter

We still have to find sufficient explanation for the various kinds of matter, including both the matter of things sensed and the matter of bodies. The notion of a plurality of materials, however, may well have been detected at *Tim.* 69a6–8. This is how Richard Archer-Hind translates it: "Now therefore that the different kinds of causes lie ready sorted [διυλισμένα or διυλασμένα][59] to our hand, like wood [ὕλη] prepared for a carpenter, of which [ἐξ ὧν] we must weave the web of our ensuing discourse." The term translated "wood" was, for Moderatus, the familiar term for "matter," a sense he would have assumed to be pre-Platonic.[60] While that term appears only in the singular, the participle translated "sorted" implies a distinction between various kinds of cause. While it is open to us to associate this with the distinction between the true cause and the auxiliary cause from 46c–e, the words ἐξ ὧν might also have suggested different kinds of *material* cause to Moderatus.[61] Moderatus could with justification assume that the receptacle was not the only thing qualifying as an auxiliary cause. These had, at 46d, included processes such as cooling, warming, melting, and congealing, and also earth, air, fire, and water. The section on auxiliary causes (47e–69a) introduces not just the receptacle but also the construction of the four physical bodies (from 53c) and the way that this construction influences our senses (from 61c). At 69b2–c1

---

59. διυλισμένα (F) would normally mean something like "strained," but διυλασμένα (Y) is without parallel. In any case the context suggests that the second syllable should relate to ὕλη in some way (by pseudo-etymology, perhaps); the separate types of causes have apparently been distinguished by separate discussion in the discourse.

60. Pseudo-Pythagorean writers used the Doric form ὕλα regularly, including, importantly, "Timaeus Locrus" (205.9–206.18 *saepe*, 215.11, 14), and also Callicratidas, Metopus, Ocellus, and Pseudo-Archytas.

61. Talking of causes ἐξ οὗ would immediately be suggestive of matter in the eyes of early imperial philosophers; see Aristotle, *Metaph.* 1013a24; *Phys.* 194b24; Philo, *Cher.* 135; Sextus Empiricus, *Math.* 10.10; Origen, *Comm. Jo.* 17.103; see also Seneca, *Ep.* 65.5: *ex quo.*

"these things"[62] (plural) were initially in a state of disorder and had to be organized by the Demiurge before the establishment of the universe. To read the passage as postulating a plurality of matters was not unnatural. But why three kinds?

Here I sketch an answer. The matter of physical bodies is not easily identified with the receptacle, but, in the case of complex bodies, with earth, air, fire, and water; or, in the case of those bodies themselves, their constituent triangles. But what we see, hear, taste, smell, and touch do not seem to have the structure or stability of any such bodies, relying on the imagination to construct them on a different canvas. The nature of the receptacle was inferred from two different analogies: the first, at 49b6–50a3, compares the way that *we see* things, always seeming to undergo quite radical changes that defy their true nature, so that we should not speak of something being "this" but as being "suchlike" (49d5). We see only qualities that shift unstably. "The thing in which each of them keep arising and being imaged [φαντάζεται], and from which it again vanishes" is the only thing that can be called this or that, and that cannot be called by any of the qualitative terms used for the appearances. This is not a description of the universal receptacle, but it follows the same pattern. The second analogy, that of a lump of gold that can be molded into all sorts of separate shapes, likewise insists on the stable reality only of the underlying gold, not of the transient shapes (50a5–b5). This seems to be an obvious *bodily* illustration, the gold playing the role of the matter of bodies. Plausibly, then, the two illustrations (49b–50b) employ (1) the matter of sensations and (2) the matter of bodies as a means to illustrate the universal receptacle.

Bibliography

Primary Sources

Iamblichus. *De Anima: Text, Translation and Commentary*. Edited by John F. Finamore and John Dillon. Leiden: Brill, 2002.

Moderatus. *Platonici minores. 1.Jh.v.Chr.–2. Jh.n.Chr.* Edited by Marie-Luise Lakmann. Leiden: Brill, 2017.

---

62. 69b3: *tauta*; this could plausibly be taken to refer to the "kinds of causes" at 69a7, the last neuter plural, thus entailing that this referred only to kinds of auxiliary cause.

Pachymeres. *George Pachymeres: Ypomnema Eis Ton Parmeniden Platonos [Anonymou Synecheia Tou Ypomnematos Proklou]*. Edited by Thomas A. Gadra, Sion M. Honea, Patricia M. Stinger, and Gretchen Umholtz. Athens: Akademia Athenon, 1989.

Plato. *Platonis Opera*. Edited by John Burnet. Oxford: Oxford University Press, 1900–1907.

———. *The Timaeus of Plato*. Edited by Richard D. Archer-Hind. London: Macmillan, 1888.

Plotinus. *Opera*. Edited by Paul Henry and Hans-Rudolf Schwyzer. Oxford: Oxford University Press, 1964–1984.

Porphyry. *Porphyrii philosophi fragmenta*. Edited by Andrew Smith. Stuttgardt: Teubner, 1993.

Proclus. *Philosophi Platonici Opera Inedita*. Edited by Victor Cousin. Hildescheim: Olms, 1864.

———. *Procli in Platonis Parmenidem Commentaria*. Vol. 3. Edited by Carlos Steel. Oxford: Oxford University Press, 2007–2009.

Speusippus. *Speusippus of Athens*. Edited by Leonardo Táran. Leiden: Brill, 1981.

Secondary Sources

Brisson, Luc. "The Fragment of Speusippus in Column I of the Anonymous Commentary on the Parmenides." Pages 59–65 in *Plato's Parmenides and Its Heritage*. Vol. 2. Edited by John D. Turner and Kevin Corrigan. Atlanta: Society of Biblical Literature, 2010.

Dillon, John. *The Middle Platonists*. London: Duckworth, 1977.

Dodds, Eric R. "The Parmenides of Plato and the Origin of the Neoplatonic One." *ClQ* 22 (1928): 129–42.

Dörrie, Heinrich, and Matthias Baltes. *Der Platonismus in der Antike*. Vol. 4, *Bausteine 101–124*. Stuttgart: Frommann-Holzboog, 1995.

Hubler, J. Noel. "Moderatus, E. R. Dodds, and the Development of Neoplatonist Emanation." Pages 115–28 in *Plato's Parmenides and Its Heritage*. Vol. 2. Edited by John D. Turner and Kevin Corrigan. WGRWSup 2–3. 2 vols. Atlanta: Society of Biblical Literature, 2010.

Roueché, Mossmann. "Notes on a Commentary on Plato's Parmenides." *GRBS* 12 (1971): 553–56.

Steel, Carlos. "Proclus et l'interprétation 'logique' du Parménides." Pages 67–92 in *Néoplatonisme et philosophie mediévale*. Turnhout: Brepols, 1997.

Tarrant, Harold. *Plato's First Interpreters*. London: Duckworth, 2000.

———. *Thrasyllan Platonism*. Ithaca, NY: Cornell University Press, 1993.

Westerink, Leendert G. Introduction to *George Pachymeres: Ypomnema Eis Ton Parmeniden Platonos [Anonymou Synecheia Tou Ypomnematos Proklou]*. Edited by Thomas A. Gadra, Sion M. Honea, Patricia M. Stinger, and Gretchen Umholtz. Athens: Akademia Athenon, 1989.

Apuleius's Platonic Laboratory

Sara Ahbel-Rappe

Introduction: Plato's Self-Moving Myth

The *Phaedrus* myth is filled with paradoxes. It is a story about the origins of human consciousness and human embodiment while simultaneously being a story about the life of the gods. Socrates's palinode suggestively narrates how the aspirant to wisdom lifts his head and glimpses the realm of truth, a truth to which he assimilates and a truth that assimilates itself to him. Nonetheless, it is also a story about losing sight of the truth, about being in a condition of ignorance that may last ages. It is a story about gradual change, reincarnation, and the hope of attaining the life of the philosopher after endless wandering. This is the truth grasped or obtained only after struggle. Yet, even within this dialogue, we see the idea that truth is something one sees suddenly, an immediate vision or cognizance, hitherto unknown. Plato's strictures on knowledge—that it be of what is and always is, of what is eternally the same, suggest that such eternal knowledge cannot be attained over time. Yet, the soul's activity takes place in time; life is lived in time. Moreover, birth and death cycle through vast stretches of time. What are we to make of these internal puzzles and claims regarding the temporal and/or the eternal process by which one obtains truth?

This essay is dedicated with heartfelt gratitude to Professor John Finamore, whose work on the soul in Platonism is foundational. We in the International Society for Neoplatonic Studies owe John a debt of gratitude for all of his work as president of the society, his nurturing of young scholars from all over the world, his exemplary scholarship and translation, and his friendship to Platonists both young and old. I count myself fortunate to be one such old friend.

These two approaches to apprehending the truth, sudden and gradual, are both represented in Socrates's palinode, and the reception of Plato's *Phaedrus* markedly testifies that these two registers concerning the attainment of truth, that is, expansive seeing versus gradual decline and incremental restoration of vision, are in constant tension. Allusions to Plato's myth of the psychic chariot (*Phaedr.* 246), the incarnation of the soul after the molting of its wings, and its precarnate life in the supercelestial world are ubiquitous in the religious and philosophical texts of the Roman Empire. Apuleius of Madaurus, Philo of Alexandria, Origen of Caesarea, certain authors in the Nag Hammadi library, Numenius and Iamblichus of Syria, the Chaldean Oracles, and fourth-century Origenist monk Evagrius Ponticus all find ways to integrate the dialogue into their cosmological and soteriological speculations. Far from resulting in a unified narrative that merely repeats itself, what we find is that elements of the myth split off and colonize infrasectarian Platonic debates. Some philosophers or religious traditions emphasize the moment of the crash of the chariot itself—suggesting that human incarnation is a default state. Further, other authors are drawn to the story of the horses and even the chariot itself (i.e., the vehicle of the soul). Apuleius's *Golden Ass* features the dark horse's avatar, the wandering Lucius, transformed into a donkey while trying to acquire wings, and this ass continues to circulate in medieval, Renaissance, and even modern narratives: Pinocchio, *Midsummer Night's Dream*, and Cinderella all feature a version of the tale of Cupid and Psyche. Occasionally the ass even meets up with its celestial companion, the winged horse, as we find in Giordano Bruno's *Cabala of Pegasus*'s divine ass.

Overall, it seems that the *Golden Ass* is a highly influential part of the *Phaedrus*'s textual reception, showing how Platonism migrated to North Africa and became a part of a hybrid Latin/Greek philosophical translation, which was also simultaneously a transformation. Basically, the theme of the *Golden Ass* and the adventures of the black horse demand that readers inquire after a world in which we ask what happens when the charioteer takes a wrong turn. What is at stake in this reading of the *Golden Ass* turns on understanding how philosophy in the second century is practiced. Put otherwise, the narrative imitation of Plato's *Phaedrus* functions more like a laboratory for Platonism than a treatise composed of doctrines. The fictional world that Apuleius creates is a living experiment on creatures like us, mortal living beings who are simultaneously immortal. Apuleius's narrative deploys Phaedrean elements with allusions both subtle and obvious,[1] keeping the trajectory of the myth's cycle in view, as it tracks the progress of the runaway dark horse in the guise of the narrator, Lucius, and his transformation into the ass. In Apuleius's *Golden Ass*, we find the charioteer no longer driving the yoked team but mounted on a single white horse, utterly letting loose the reins, or else oddly fused with the dark horse,[2] keeping his humanity wholly disguised beneath and within his calamitous embodiment.

Much the way Plato works in the *Phaedrus*, where the narrative of the soul's descent is embedded within a greater discourse that touches on eros, beauty, and *logos*, Apuleius's larger narrative allows for a mirrorlike retelling of Lucius's transformation and thereby of Plato's myth in the embedded story of Cupid and Psyche (*Metam.* 4.28–5.24).[3] Thus the progress of Lucius and the stages of his embodiment in a world of suffering are complemented by the quasi-allegorical folktale of Cupid and Psyche, which inhabits an extra narrative space that might put us in mind of the hyperouranian topos in Plato's myth, in the sense that events on high interact with as well as reflect the earthly love affairs of mortal beings.[4] Psyche's story builds on moments of further, precipitous descent,[5] using the vertiginous contrasts of high and low, while the outer frame, the story of Lucius, employs the visceral elements of embodiment: sexuality, pain, and the flesh itself. By casting the embodiment of the narrator, Lucius, into a four-legged animal, Apuleius at once

---

1. For a survey of work that has been done on the *Golden Ass* as a reception of Plato's *Phaedrus*, see Claudio Moreschini, *Apuleius and the Metamorphoses of Platonism*, Nutrix 10 (Turnhout: Brepols, 2015), esp. chs. 2–3.

2. On the *candidus equus* of Lucius as Plato's white horse, and also for Lucius, the narrator himself, as embodying Plato's dark horse, see Jeffrey T. Winkle, "'Necessary Roughness': Plato's *Phaedrus* and Apuleius' *Metamorphoses*," *AN* 11 (2013): 93–131.

3. On the story of Cupid and Psyche in terms of its references to the Platonic myth of the charioteer, see Moreschini, *Apuleius and the Metamorphoses*, 87–115.

4. In using the phrase "mortal beings," I am alluding to Plato's own definition of the embodied individual at *Phaedr.* 246.

5. See below for a discussion of the narrative import of the tale of Cupid and Psyche. Commentators disagree as to whether this embedded tale represents a moment of redemption, through the immortalization of Psyche and her assimilation to the divine or rather the permanent rout of the soul outside the domain of the spiritual, represented by her everlasting union with Cupid, the god of sexual appetite. See John L. Penwill, "Slavish Pleasures and Profitless Curiosity: Fall and Redemption in Apuleius' Metamorphoses," *Ramus* 4 (1975): 49–82.

elevates the human station and forces a very uncomfortable repudiation of the body that is consonant with strongly dualistic forms of imperial Platonism.[6] We might ask whether the redemptive apotheosis of Psyche in the inner tale signals the triumph of dualism, in representing a stunning contrast to the world of Lucius, or rather subverts said dualism. After all, Lucius, too, meets with a redeeming goddess, and the toils of Psyche seem every bit as painful as the sufferings of Lucius the ass.[7] By following the novel's Phaedrean elements,[8] this essay will argue that we can read the *Golden Ass* alongside more overtly philosophical receptions of the *Phaedrus* contemporary with Apuleius, for example Origen's *On First Principles*, as meditations on the teleology of suffering, embodiment, and eros. These two narratives stand in bold contrast to a common genre of Middle Platonic philosophical production, the *placita*, the *expositio*, the *compendium*, or doxography: the list-like catalogues of Platonic *dogmata*. In contrast to the "potted Platonism" of works such as *de Platone et eius dogmate*, which offer a concise system of rules for Platonic thinking, the narrative forms of imperial Platonism tend to fuse with indigenous or imported religious traditions of the Roman Empire. No doubt inter-sect polemics in the Hellenistic world—that is, the rivalries between the Stoa, Peripatetics, and the Academy—nurtured the growth of a doxographic approach to Plato.[9] At the same time, slight variations

---

6. On the meaning of dualism in early imperial Platonism, many scholars point to Plutarch's interpretation of the world soul. This dualism is also present in Plutarch's *De Iside et Osiride*, a work that has significant importance as a subtext for the *Golden Ass*. For Plutarch, dualism consists in an understanding that there are two kinds of cause operative in the world, one the source of order and intelligence, the other irrational and source of passion. Plutarch not only sees this operating distinction within the individual soul but sees it operative in a cosmic source of irrationality, an irrational cosmic soul derived from his reading of *Laws*, *Timaeus*, and *Statesman*.

7. On the later books of the novel and especially book 11 of *Isis*, see Wytse H. Keulen and Ulrike Egelhaaf-Gaise, *The Isis Book: A Collection of Original Papers*, vol. 3 of *Aspects of Apuleius' Golden Ass* (Leiden: Brill, 2012).

8. For previous work on the novel as a reading of the *Phaedrus*, see Moreschini, *Apuleius and the Metamorphoses*.

9. See George Boys-Stones, *Platonist Philosophy, 80 BC to AD 250: An Introduction and Collection of Sources in Translation* (Cambridge: Cambridge University Press, 2018), on the importance of dialectical contexts for Middle Platonist philosophy. Bonazzi is emphatic about the importance of Middle Platonism as a system. He writes: "Indeed, what we call (Middle) Platonism is the result of this attempt to produce a Platonic system out of the dialogues, in opposition to the Hellenistic schools (and Aristotle) but

in specific doxographic formulations accompany this proliferation. Consequently, the following will outline how Platonism was not limited to a set of propositions or doctrinal truths. Instead, by concentrating on the Middle Platonic narrative of Lucius's journey, we may see how the late antique leitmotif of wandering, *plané*, is at work in the novel and how the novel's investigation of worldly sojourning parallels other contemporaneous Platonizing theories. To do this we will first discuss the textual and literary echoes of the *Phaedrus* in the novel as a whole with reference to the tale of Cupid and Psyche. Next, specific attention to the nature of the world such as we find it theorized in the novel will expose Apuleius's response to the tensions of Platonic psychology and the emergence of a world overrun by the dark horse. Overall, we will conclude by renewing the arguments surrounding the value of narrative, emphasizing how literary treatments of Platonic themes form an essential part of the Platonic tradition and that the effort to isolate doctrine from its larger contexts comes at the expense of a fuller comprehension of the meaning and nature of Platonism in the imperial period.

Apuleius Reads the *Phaedrus*

Michael Trapp has already noted the likely references to the *Phaedrus* in the opening lines of the preface:

> Now I shall weave colorful stories into that infamous Milesian Tale and seduce your ears to earn your favor with a charming whisper, if only you not disdain to gaze upon an Egyptian papyrus, inscribed with the message of a Nilotic pen, so that you marvel at the shapes and fortunes of human beings, transformed into the appearances of other creatures and then transformed back into themselves, in mutual interdependence. (at ego tibi sermone isto Milesio varias fabulas conseram auresque tuas benivolas lepido susurro permulceam—modo si papyrum Aegyptiam argutia

---

also under their influence and relying on their philosophical agenda. Today, many readers of Plato will surely argue against the legitimacy of such an attempt to systematize Plato: but that is precisely what happened. And when one considers that it is this form of Platonism that has influenced the reception of Plato over the centuries, its historical and philosophical importance becomes evident. The *Compendiosa expositio* provides a unique testimony for this period and for this way of conceiving and practicing philosophy." See Mauro Bonazzi, "Plato Systematized: Doing Philosophy in the Imperial Schools," *OSAP* 53 (2017): 221.

Nilotici calami inscriptam non spreveris inspicere—, figuras fortunasque
hominum in alias imagines conversas et in se rursus mutuo nexu refectas
ut mireris, *Metam*. 1.1 [Reilihan])

As Trapp interprets this passage, the Egyptian papyrus and its Nilotic
reed are most likely a reference to the *Phaedrus*'s story of Theuth and
invention of writing, where Socrates is also accused of inventing "Egyptian tales" for the sake of his own devices: his critique of writing is linked
to his critique of sophistry and an implicit criticism of Lysias.[10] For this
chapter, the opening lines raise the question of how texts themselves
receive agency in the process of writing. Recall that the myth of Theuth
at *Phaedr*. 275e goes on to develop the point that texts are alive and can
thus wander far from authorial intent, preserving only the appearance
of standing still/remaining the same.[11] The caution, "only if you do not
reject looking at an Egyptian papyrus," suggests that Apuleius's text is
also a product of this wandering, a medium through which the tale is
converted into "foreign images." This comment about the text and its
transmigrations continues with added emphasis as Apuleius mentions
the *exotici ac forensis sermonis* (exotic and vulgar speech) of the Latin language and the *ipsa vocis immutatio* (transformation of voice), which, he
claims is important to his task, to tell a Greek story. Further compound-
ing allusions to the *Phaedrus* and the charioteer's circuit are Apuleius's
initial mention of the transmigration of the soul. The preface itself, then,
will serve as an important thematic introduction, which is, after all, the

---

10. Plato, *Phaedr*. 279a3: "It seems to me that he is better by nature than the kind
of discourse surrounding the disciples of Lysias" (δοκεῖ μοι ἀμείνων ἢ κατὰ τοὺς περὶ
Λυσίαν εἶναι λόγους τὰ τῆς φύσεως). *Phaedr*. 275a: "This invention (writing) will furnish
forgetfulness in the souls of its disciples owing to their neglect of practice in memory,
through trust in writing" (τοῦτο γὰρ τῶν μαθόντων λήθην μὲν ἐν ψυχαῖς παρέξει μνήμης
ἀμελετησίᾳ, ἅτε διὰ πίστιν γραφῆς) (my translations).

11. *Phaedr*. 275e (Nehamas and Woodruff): "When it has once been written
down, every discourse roams about everywhere, reaching indiscriminately those with
understanding no less than those who have no business with it, and it doesn't know to
whom it should speak and to whom it should not. And when it is faulted and attacked
unfairly, it always needs its father's support; alone, it can neither defend itself nor
come to its own support." γραφῇ, κυλινδεῖται μὲν πανταχοῦ πᾶς λόγος ὁμοίως παρὰ τοῖς
ἐπαΐουσιν, ὡς δ᾽ αὕτως παρ᾽ οἷς οὐδὲν προσήκει, καὶ οὐκ ἐπίσταται λέγειν οἷς δεῖ γε καὶ
μή. πλημμελούμενος δὲ καὶ οὐκ ἐν δίκῃ λοιδορηθεὶς τοῦ πατρὸς ἀεὶ δεῖται βοηθοῦ· αὐτὸς
γὰρ οὔτ᾽ ἀμύνασθαι οὔτε βοηθῆσαι δυνατὸς αὑτῷ.

story of a text and its afterlife, its own extended episodes, and wanderings in the history of its own reception.[12]

Apuleius seems eager for his novel to be incorporated into some version of the Platonic tradition or at least to claim affinity with it. Consider the following remark in the paragraph just after the introduction: "Thessaly—for from here the roots of my maternal lineage stemming from that famed Plutarch and his nephew, the philosopher Sextus, bring us glory" ("Thessaliam—nam et illic originis maternae nostrae fundamenta a Plutarcho illo inclito ac mox Sexto philosopho nepote eius prodita gloriam nobis faciunt," *Metam.* 1.2). Here Apuleius uses the genealogical metaphor for philosophical lineage that Plato already introduces in the *Phaedrus*: the father of the *logos* (*Phaedr.* 275e4). By putting himself in the matrilineal line of descent from Plutarch, the narrator also begins to tug at the skein of the Platonic tradition. Plutarch's own teacher, Ammonius (as we know from Plutarch's essay *On the Delphic E*),[13] is also a strand of the same family into which Apuleius carefully inserts his own origin. *Inclitus*, "well-known," and *gloria*, "brilliance," mark the entire tale as conspicuously Platonic and arguably, together with the remarks in the preface, a reading of the *Phaedrus* in particular. In other words, this tale belongs in the lineage of writings that transform the *Phaedrus* and wander about restlessly in the shape of a new body, a new incarnation, if you will, forming a new offshoot in the noble branch of the Platonic family tree of philosophical *logoi*.[14]

To strengthen this affiliation with the *Phaedrus*, note that Apuleius immediately plunges us into the story of the charioteer and the two yoke mates, telling us that he was mounted on what he calls "equo indigena peralbo vehens peralbo" (a pure white horse, *Metam.* 1.2; see *Phaedr.* 253d, λευκὸς ἰδεῖν). He conspicuously dismounts from the horse and, what is worse, he "loosens the reins" (*frenos detraho*). Recalling 247b2, εὐήνια ὄντα

---

12. Michael Trapp, "Plato's Phaedrus in Second-Century Greek Literature," in *Antonine Literature*, ed. Donald A. Russell (Oxford: Oxford University Press, 1990), 141–73. On Trapp, see also Alexander Kirichenko, "Asinus Philosophans: Platonic Philosophy and the Prologue to Apuleius' 'Golden Ass,'" *Mnemosyne* 61 (2008): 112.

13. See John Whittaker, "Ammonius on the Delphic E," *ClQ* 19 (1969): 185–92.

14. Of course, it must also be duly noted that Apuleius makes the outrageous claim that this noble intellectual lineage originates not in Athens or indeed in Chaeronea but in Thessaly. Perhaps then we can already feel the word *originis* as the first in a series of allusions to the duality of the myth as a whole and to the yoked team with its mixed origins (*Phaedr.* 253) and dubious lineage.

ῥᾳδίως πορεύεται, the text gestures to the grasp on the reins of the divine chariots circumambulating within the hyperouranian topos and the lack of skill exhibited by the souls of mortals in controlling the horses: οὗ δὴ κακίᾳ ἡνιόχων πολλαὶ μὲν χωλεύονται (*Phaedr.* 248b1). *Frenos/ἡνία* are an example of what Apuleius refers to just a few lines above in the preface of his *ipsa vocis immutatio*, which alerts us to the ways that he will translate/ transform the myth. In the same lines, danger lurks up ahead as the human charioteer is confronted with what Plato calls "a noisy, sweaty struggle" (θόρυβος οὖν καὶ ἅμιλλα καὶ ἱδρὼς ἔσχατος γίγνεται, *Phaedr.* 248b1) in which nothing less than the destiny of one's life is decided. Again, Apuleius carefully recalls the struggle between the two horses in Plato's myth by writing that once his own charioteer has dismounted from the white horse, he must carefully wipe the sweat from the brow of the (white) horse ("equi sudorem frontem curiose effrico," *Metam.* 1.2.6). Once Lucius dismounts from the white horse and drops the reins, we will want to know the fate of its yoke mate, the dark horse, but so far this third figure is absent from the text. Conspicuously, we have only the white horse and the person who (formerly) held the reins.[15]

Now the narrator begins a second layer of the tale: he falls in with a storyteller, Aristomenes, who tells Lucius of his encounter with *Socratem contubernalem* (*Metam.* 1.6), that is, Socrates, a companion, tent-mate, fellow traveler, but one who appears sprawled on the streets half-clothed and emaciated. Like his self-donned attire in his first speech on love in the *Phaedrus*,[16] the Socrates of the *Golden Ass* is veiled, *capite velato* (*Metam.* 1.7). The bizarre appearance of Socrates in Aristomenes's tale, sordid, exposed, and having squandered his life in abject subjection to a Thessalian witch (and having run away to Thessaly, the very thing he vows to avoid in the *Crito*; see Θετταλίαν 45e) invokes a contradictory doppelganger of the philosopher. Commentators have referred to this least Socratic of eponymous doublets as a veritable unSocrates,[17] a Socrates

---

15. As I will argue below and as Winkle writes, it is Lucius himself who will come to represent the dark horse in his transformation into an ass, thus raising the question of where the charioteer goes in the remainder of the novel.

16. We read in *Phaedr.* 237a6: "I'll cover my head while I'm speaking" (ἐγκαλυψάμενος ἐρῶ, ἵν᾽ ὅτι τάχιστα διαδράμω τὸν λόγον καὶ μὴ βλέπων πρὸς σὲ ὑπ᾽ αἰσχύνης διαπορῶμαι).

17. Winkle develops the point that Apuleius's Socrates is the antithesis to the Platonic Socrates ("'Necessary Roughness,'" 97–98).

who represents the broken life of a voluptuary. In this exhaustion, having let go of the reins of appetite, enamored of the world soul and obedient to its own lusts, the rational soul (the fallen Socrates) comes under the spell of magic, of illusion. Socrates warns Aristomenes:

> She is a witch, a powerful divinity who can bring down heaven, lift up the earth, dry up the rivers, flatten the mountains, raise the dead, bury the gods, extinguish the stars, and light up Tartarus itself. ("saga" inquit "et divina, potens caelum deponere, terram suspendere, fontes durare, montes diluere, manes sublimare, deos infimare, sidera exstinguere, Tartarum ipsum inluminare," *Metam.* 1.8)

Again, the reader must ask, why this violence against an icon, and why the deliberate citations from the *Phaedrus*? Perhaps we can imagine this tale as portending a world utterly lacking a Socrates, a world in which even the most self-controlled of men falls prey to his own lusts—so much so that philosophy itself is not even present.

Our Socrates has fallen in with the wrong lover (*amator*, again an invocation of the *Phaedrus*) and the appetites of the paramour, who transforms into a wild beast (see *Phaedr.* 241d: "Do wolves love lambs? That's how a lover befriends a boy!"). The savage appetites of the predatory *erastes* are transferred with additional, magical elements to the Meroe of Apuleius's world. This falling under the spell of a magician's power is an integral aspect of Apuleius's text and has no equivalent in the *Phaedrus*, but Socrates in the *Symposium* casts Eros as, among other things, a magician (γόης, *Symp.* 203e). Notably, members of the later Platonist tradition address the ontological status of magic and explore its efficacy. For example, Plotinus devotes some important paragraphs to the topic of magic in *Enn.* 4.4 and 4.5. Plotinus writes:

> For everything that looks to another is under spell to that: what we look to, draws us magically. Only the self-intent go free of magic. Hence every action has magic as its source, and the entire life of the practical man is a bewitchment: we move to that only which has wrought a fascination upon us. This is indicated where we read "for the burgher of greathearted Erechtheus has a pleasant face [but you should see him naked; then you would be cautious]." For what conceivably turns a man to the external? He is drawn, drawn by the arts not of magicians but of the natural order which administers the deceiving draught and links this to that, not in local contact but in the fellowship of the philtre. (*Enn.* 4.4.43 [MacKenna])

For Plotinus, this natural attraction to the world of nature and becoming implicated in the natural order is the chief magical operation. Here we see the complex negotiation between freedom (hardly visible in the *Metamorphoses*) and magic, seduction, slavery, bondage, captivity, and karmic retribution, as well as the forces of passion, appetite, anger, and ignorance that beset the individual soul.[18] The irony of using the *Phaedrus* as a subtext for the *Golden Ass* resonates through the entire plot of the novel, which turns precisely on a more and more diminished expression of genuine agency in contradistinction to the *Phaedrus*, which defines the soul as self-moved. Although the debates about fate, free will, and voluntary action that would come to infuse first Stoic and then Platonist philosophy (through the meditation of Peripatetic arguments) were all centuries in the making, the simple declaration that begins the myth of the charioteer, that the soul is a self-mover, came to be seen as Platonic orthodoxy affirming human freedom and responsibility so that the images of such diminished capacity of human agency in the *Golden Ass* leave readers questioning the Platonic definition of the soul. Overall, the *Golden Ass,* read as an evaluation of what it means to be in the world, presciently responds to the academic questions concerning fate and human freedom raised by Middle Platonists in conversation with the Stoa. Aristomenes's degraded Socrates points in the direction of Middle Platonist musings on fate, on the causal nexus that governs action in the sublunary world. Indeed, later in the novel, Apuleius develops the Phaedrean conception of the cycle of birth and death, wherein beings are successively born and must inevitably return to their original incarnation every ten thousand years.[19] In the picaresque story of the miller's wife in book 9, comprising sequences borrowed from Roman comedy and from the genre of adultery mime, we find Lucius chained to

---

18. Winkle: "The Tale of Aristomenes shows us rather a world in which intellectual posturing has little effect, magic is no false charge but a horrifying reality, and the powers of evil have the upper hand: the witches prevail, and the forces of justice will be helpless to stop the real culprits, while there is a real threat that an innocent man will be condemned. Aristomenes, the man of 'excellent might' is unprepared for the forces of witchcraft; Socrates himself, the man of saintly virtue, is reduced to a slave of his bodily appetites. As a program piece for the novel as a whole, the Tale of Aristomenes is a grim warning of the unleashing of dark forces in the world" ("'Necessary Roughness,'" 97).

19. "Each soul cannot reach the place from whence it has come within [any less than] 10,000 years" (εἰς μὲν γὰρ τὸ αὐτὸ ὅθεν ἥκει ἡ ψυχὴ ἑκάστη οὐκ ἀφικνεῖται ἐτῶν μυρίων, *Phaedr.* 249e5).

a millwork, forced to pull, alongside a compendium of fellow bedraggled working animals, the weight of a heavy stone. The circuitous path of the threshing floor challenges the Platonic images of transmigration found in the *Phaedrus* but also the *Republic*'s whorl of necessity. Lucius narrates of his time imprisoned there:

> I was harnessed to what seemed to be the largest stone, and with veiled face I was forced along the curving track of its circular floor, as on a circumscribed orbit, ever retracing my steps, I traveled along in a fixed wandering. (molae quam maxima videbatur matutinus adstituor, et ilico velata facie propellor ad incurva spatia flexuosi canalis, ut in orbe termini circumflentis reciproco gressu mea recalcans vestigial vagarer errore certo, *Metam.* 9.11)

This description of the *errore certo*, the wandering that is fixed, will superbly describe the idea of fate that operates in the novel and in contemporaneous Platonisms. As George Boys-Stones writes of Apuleius, Albinus, and Plutarch:

> Platonists were engaged in a more sophisticated debate with the Stoics, which led them to think that fate was restricted to events under a particular description—namely, insofar as they are considered as the consequences of other events. My conclusion will be in fact that all relevant events, which means all events in the sublunary realm, are "fated" in this sense, because all arc the consequences of previous causes. To this extent, the Platonist theory of fate is considerably closer to the Stoic account than is generally acknowledged. It differs in one crucial respect, however. For while events within the cosmos follow one another with predictable regularity, Platonists (unlike Stoics) insist that the cosmos itself need not have been this way. This is how Platonists can at the same time say that no event (at least, again, no event in the sublunary realm) is fated absolutely.[20]

As we further explore the idea of the Platonic world and the path that an embodied being traces through this world, Apuleius's description of the mill-works presents a very negative understanding of this world: "There the endless gyrations of numerous beasts turned millstones of varying size, and

---

20. George Boys-Stones, "'Middle' Platonists on Fate and Human Autonomy," *BICS* 94 (2007): 432.

not only by day but all night long the ceaseless turning of the machines" (ibi complurimum iumentorum multivii circuitus intorquebant molas ambage varia, nec die tantum, verum perpeti etiam nocte prorsus instabili machinarum vertigine, *Metam.* 9.11). This mechanistic world order, powered by blinded captives, all forms of life in an endless cycle, forms a bleak and almost gnostic image. Of course, the image is merely set into a tale and is a literal description of the physical constraints that beset Lucius in his transformed state. Yet, this description, with its imprisoned, blind, enslaved inhabitants chained to an ever-repeating cycle, resonates within the larger fabric of the novel and the *Phaedrus*'s depiction of souls who were unable to glimpse the truth, those souls who are unable to see. There, Plato's Socrates admonishes the soul to strive to see reality, as "This is the law of Adrasteia: whichever soul attends upon a god in its sojourn and beholds some aspect of reality is free from harm until the next cycle (of one thousand years)" (*Phaedr.* 248c1). This "law declares that such a soul is prevented from entering into the form of a beast upon its first round of birth" (*Phaedr.* 248c1). However, after the second round of birth, it is possible to observe "a human soul entering into the life of a beast" (*Phaedr.* 249b4).

To offer a final orientation to the overall *locus amoenus* of Phaedrean erotic discourse set in the *Golden Ass*, consider the conclusion of Aristomenes's tale, which ends abruptly with his failure to rescue his boon companion, Socrates, from the ravages of eros. Aristomenes has put his friend up at an inn, determined to get him off the streets, where in the middle of the night, Meröe and Panthea steal into their hotel room, slice open Socrates's throat, drain and catch his blood in a basin, and remove his heart and replace it with a sponge. They depart, but not before uttering a curse on the sponge, one that distinctly recalls the Socratic palinode of the *Phaedrus*. Socrates cannot leave the shrine to Orythuia on the banks of the Illissos underneath the shade of the plane tree without offering his apologies to love: "When I was about to cross the river, good man, my *daimonion* and familiar sign came to me" (*Phaedr.* 242b–c).[21] Likewise, Panthia utters this curse over the sponge she inserts into the chest of the zombified Socrates: "You, Sponge, as you were born in the sea, take care not to cross the river" ("heus tu," inquit "spongia, cave in mari nata per fluvium transeas," *Metam.* 1.13). The magical interdict against crossing the

---

21. ἡνίκ᾽ ἔμελλον, ὠγαθέ, τὸν ποταμὸν διαβαίνειν, τὸ δαιμόνιόν τε καὶ τὸ εἰωθὸς σημεῖόν μοι γίγνεσθαι ἐγένετο.

river, as we will see, lands this dissipated Socrates in the river. There will be no recuperation of Socrates. Instead, in the remainder of the journey, as Aristomenes and Socrates make their way make back from the inn into a receding Phaedrean landscape, Socrates bends over a deceptively familiar stream to scoop water from a river, whereupon the cursed sponge leaps out of his chest: "Suddenly the sponge rolls out of him!" (spongia de eo repente devolvitur, *Metam.* 19.8). Our Socrates is a hollowed-out shell of a man (*corpus exanimantem*), and his interlocutor or companion an inveterate liar. It is a traumatic and impudent invocation of Socrates, one that further suggests that the inheritors, such as Plutarch, of the Platonic *logos* have entered into a dying and deceptive tradition.[22]

In the *Phaedrus*, Socrates and Phaedrus choose a setting that bears three distinctive landmarks: (1) a shrine to Orythuia on (2) the stream of the Illissus, under the shade of (3) plane tree (*Phaedr.* 229a). In the *Golden Ass*, Socrates and Aristomenes make good their escape from the inn as the Phaedrean landscape looms in the distance, complete with the signal plane tree and diaphanous stream. Here, we see the Latin rendering of the Greek language promised in the prologue in high relief. Apuleius writes, "Not far from the roots of a plane tree a gentle stream flowed lazily into a pool with a color like glass or silver in appearance" (et haud ita longe radices platani lenis fluvius in speciem placidae paludis ignavus ibat argento vel vitro aemulus in colorem. "En" inquam "explere latice fontis lacteo," *Metam.* 1.18). These lines loosely convey *Phaedr.* 229b, where Phaedrus directs Socrates's attention gestures to their surroundings saying, "Do you see that very tall plane tree?" (ὁρᾷς οὖν ἐκείνην τὴν ὑψηλοτάτην πλάτανον; *Phaedr.* 229a). Socrates's suggestion is to sit by the plane tree (ἐκεῖ σκιά τ᾽ ἐστὶν καὶ πνεῦμα μέτριον, καὶ πόα καθίζεσθαι ἢ ἂν βουλώμεθα κατακλινῆναι, *Phaedr.* 229b). Similarly, Aristomenes suggests to his own Socrates that they sit next to the plane tree: "iuxta platanum istam resida-

---

22. In book 10, Lucius invokes the figure of Socrates as an innocent victim of Athenian mob vengeance, but this invocation is absurdly colored by the fact that the *Asitis Philosophantis* has been the sexual partner of a Roman-era Pasiphae. It comes at a time when Lucius's career has reached its psychological nadir, as the bestial pleasures recommended by the dark horse seem to placate him (*Metam.* 10.33). On this absurdist invocation of Socrates and the ridiculous image of the ass philosophizing, see Krichenko, "Asinus Philosophans," 92. Krichenko writes, "We are urged to realize that Apuleius uses philosophy not to redeem but to intensify the bawdy humor of his fictions" (106).

mus aio" (*Metam.* 1.18). Again, the verbal echoes of the *Phaedrus* might suggest, as above in Apuleius's miller, a counterfactual world absent the saving influence of philosophy, one where the eponymous hero, Socrates, abandons his mission and escapes to Thessaly. Recalling Apuleius's invocation of Plutarch, Theuth, the horses, the veiled Socrates, and now the setting of the *Phaedrus*, we can begin to see how all the apparently random citations/gestures to the dialogue are elegant translations of the original Greek but also uncanny transformations.[23]

With this setting in place, having communicated to the reader both his connection to the larger Platonic tradition and to the *Phaedrus* in particular, Apuleius moves toward the central transformation signaled by both titles, the *Golden Ass* and the *Metamorphosis*, bringing Lucian's *Onos* into a distinctively Phaedrean drama. As we have seen, Lucius abandons the white horse and enters the precarious realm of Thessaly. From the viewpoint of late antique Platonism, magic, or *goeiteia*, is associated with the realm of becoming, the sublunary world that is determined by fate. Book 3 of the *Golden Ass* has Lucius become the palinode's dark horse,[24] associ-

---

23. To illustrate the *vocis immutatio* of Apuleius's tale, we can summarize the results in a way that juxtaposes the verbal echoes of the *Phaedrus* alongside their Latin equivalencies:

Phaedrus 229a8: ἣν ὑψηλοτάτην πλάτανον

AA 18: "Iuxta platanum istam residamus" aio.

Phaedrus 229b: καθίζεσθαι

Phaedrus 229b: χαρίεντα γοῦν καὶ καθαρὰ καὶ διαφανῆ τὰ ὑδάτια φαίνετα

AA 19: fluvius in speciem placidae paludis ignavus ibat argento vel vitro aemulus in colorem.

Phaedrus 237a6: ἐγκαλυψάμενος ἐρῶ

AA 6: faciem suam iam dudum punicantem prae pudore obtexit

Phaedrus 253d: λευκὸς ἰδεῖν

AA: in equo indigena peralbo vehens

Phaedrus 274c–d: ἤκουσα τοίνυν περὶ Ναύκρατιν τῆς Αἰγύπτου γενέσθαι τῶν ἐκεῖ παλαιῶν τινα θεῶν, οὗ καὶ τὸ ὄρνεον ἱερὸν ὃ δὴ καλοῦσιν Ἶβιν· αὐτῷ δὲ ὄνομα τῷ δαίμονι εἶναι Θεύθ. τοῦτον δὴ πρῶτον ἀριθμόν τε καὶ λογισμὸν εὑρεῖν καὶ γεωμετρίαν καὶ ἀστρονομίαν, ἔτι δὲ πεττείας τε καὶ κυβείας, καὶ δὴ καὶ γράμματα.

AA: modo si papyrum Aegyptiam argutia Nilotici calami inscriptam non spreveris inspicere

24. Again, this association has been well documented in the secondary literature. Probably the most detailed comparison between the dark horse of Plato's *Phaedrus* and Lucius-become-ass is Winkle, "'Necessary Roughness.'" My purpose here is not

ated with hubris, lust, unbridled appetite, and those features of the animal prevail in the novel's progression. As an ass, Lucius begins to relate to the world primarily as an embodied being; his rational nature is obscured and his agency severely diminished. This aspect of the novel ties into Middle Platonic theories of fate, providence, embodiment, and dualism more generally. The figure of the ass and Lucius's transformation have an unmistakably Phaedrean refrain but also rely on scattered Platonic remarks about asses together with elements of Egyptian mythology. For example, as has been noted by Jeffrey Winkle and Claudio Moreschini as well as earlier commentators,[25] at *Phaed.* 81e Plato writes of the fate awaiting souls who are not on guard against the vices of appetite, that they might enter "into the race of asses" (εἰς τὰ τῶν ὄνων γένη).

Alongside the allusions to asses, when Lucius attempts to imitate Pamphile's transformation, he anticipates the Cupid-and-Psyche story but also alludes to the *Phaedrus*'s winged eros: "for ever by a boon that I can never repay, and make me able to stand beside my Venus as a winged Cupid" (*Veneri Cupido pinnatus, Metam.* 3.22). This phrase echoes Plato's epigram: "Mortals call him winged Love, but the immortals call him The winged One, because he must needs grow wings" (Fowler; τὸν δ' ἤτοι θνητοὶ μὲν ῎Ερωτα καλοῦσι ποτηνόν, ἀθάνατοι δὲ Πτέρωτα, διὰ πτεροφύτορ' ἀνάγκην, *Phaedr.* 252c). Certainly the winged charioteer, his flight fueled by eros, lingers in the background, as well as the loss of wings associated with the triumph of the dark horse in the myth. Lucius's story of his transformation begins with the imagery of wings, "nec ullae plumulae nec usquam pinnulae," heavily negated (*Metam.* 3.24). Lucius is not about to fly anytime soon. What follows this failed attempt at growing feathers is his transformation into the ass, this time described in words that faintly recall the physiognomy of the dark horse. Here the verbal resonances of the two texts are in play around the central myth of the *Phaedrus*, the winged horses pulling the charioteer across the vault of the hyperouranian topos, the subsequent loss of plumage, and the place of love as well as the role of the two horses, one dark, one white, in restoring the wings of the soul. Initially, we can remark on strength of the image of the wings themselves; Plato uses three different compounds for *pteros*, "winged," at

---

to attempt or pretend to supersede the fine philological work Winkle accomplishes; rather, this chapter places Apuleius's reception of the *Phaedrus* into the context of Middle Platonic philosophy, considering in particular its narrative dimensions.

25. Winkle, "'Necessary Roughness'"; Moreschini, *Apuleius and the Metamorphoses.*

255d: ἀναπτερῶσαν, πτερῶν, πτεροφυεῖν. Would it be amiss to detect an echo of this same tricolon with *plumulae, crescent pinnulae, totil alis* at *Metam.* 3.21? Plato describes the effects of falling in love, the beauty that flows through the eyes in a stream that moistens the wings of the soul, softening the openings of the feathers, allowing the wings to regrow and thus the lovers to regain their place in the heavenly panoply. Plato writes that they "regain their wings and become weightless" (τελευτήσαντες δὲ δὴ ὑπόπτεροι καὶ ἐλαφροὶ γεγονότες, *Phaedr.* 256b). This is the Platonic paradigm, the growing of wings under the tutelage of love (*Phaedr.* 255d).[26] As the flow of beauty back into the beautiful boy proceeds through the eyes, which are by nature the avenue through which the stream of beauty arrives at the soul, it regrows its feathers.

Likewise, Lucius appears to witness the regrowing of love's wings in the figure of Pamphile, who transforms into an owl, the mascot of wisdom incarnate.[27] Nonetheless, after the molting of wings, Lucius's transformation ends in becoming the dark horse, the incarnation of lust and hubris.[28] Essentially, Apuleius compresses three elements of the Phaedrus's myth— the molting of the wings, rebirth in the form of successively lower beings, and the regrowth of the plumage through the nourishment of desire—into a single moment, where Lucius's physiognomy comes to resemble Plato's dark horse. Lucius finds himself σιμοπρόσωπος, *nares hiantes, os prolixum,* περὶ ὦτα λάσιος, *aures inmodicis horripilant auctibus,* πολύς, *enormis.*

---

26. οὕτω τὸ τοῦ κάλλους ῥεῦμα πάλιν εἰς τὸν καλὸν διὰ τῶν ὀμμάτων ἰόν, ᾗ πέφυκεν ἐπὶ τὴν ψυχὴν ἰέναι ἀφικόμενον καὶ ἀναπτερῶσαν.

27. "As they gently waved, a soft down sprouted, strong feathers grew, her nose bent back and hardened, and hooked claws solidified on her feet. Pamphile became an owl" (Quis leniter fluctuantibus promicant molles plumulae, crescunt et fortes pinnulae, duratur nasus incurvus, coguntur ungues adunci. Fit bubo Pamphile. Sic edito stridore querulo iam sui periclitabunda paulatim terra resultat, mox in altum sublimata forinsecus totis alis evolat, *Metam.* 3.21).

28. "Then I extended my arms, executed some practice flaps, and did my best to make like a bird. But fluff there was none, and feathers nowhere. Instead, my hair thickened into bristles, and my tender skin hardened into hide. On the edges of my palms, I saw the countable digits disappearing and melding into solid hooves. At the end of my spine, a big tail came forth. My face was already huge, with an elongated mouth, gaping nostrils, and dangling lips" (Iamque alternis conatibus libratis brachiis in avem similis gestiebam; nec ullae plumulae nec usquam pinnulae, sed plane pili mei crassantur in setas et cutis tenella duratur in corium et in extimis palmulis perdito numero toti digiti coguntur in singulas ungulas, *Metam.* 3.24).

Moreover, he is *voce privatus*, soon threatened with maiming (*debilem claudumque reddam*, 3.27) and a thrashing with goads (*fascem lignorum positum*). Finally, he shares the *tail* of the dark horse: *de spinae meae termino grandis cauda procedit.*

Having entered into this magical world, Lucius is driven by his overweening *curiositas* to become initiated into the dark arts of sorcery and transformation. Much has been written about the curiosity of Lucius and its significance particularly in a Platonic context. One can only commend DeFillipo's treatment of Latin *curiositas* as a translation of the Greek πολυποεῖν in the context of Plato's dialogues, which refers to an imbalanced soul not ordered by the principle of justice, ἑαυτό ποιεῖν (one that not just figures importantly in the *Republic* but also is characterized by the harmony of the hyperouranian topos in the *Phaedrus* myth).[29] Yet the desire to explore the world is intimately connected to the themes of wandering, distraction, getting lost in the details, becoming overwhelmed by experience, and, of course, suffering. Indeed, it is this correlation between wandering and errant desire that forms the basis of the Platonic analysis of the world as a place to encounter suffering.

Apuleius's World

Certainly, the story of Cupid and Psyche continues the theme of curiosity and errant desire but apparently illustrates, as does Plato's myth, the divinization of the soul under the tutelage of love. Keeping with DeFillipo's reading of *curiositas* as a translation for πολυπραγμασύνη, it is possible to see in Psyche's companion sisters the different parts of the soul, greed and envy (ἐπιθυμία and θυμός), separated from Psyche, who, left with curiosity, the desire to know, and eros, the desire for beauty and for giving birth in beauty, undergoes the harsh disciplines of love. Another resonance with Platonic teaching of Apuleius himself may be found in Psyche's journey to the court of her husband, Cupid, whose description seems to contain a reference to the language of the *Timaeus* and to the world as an icon or emblem of the divine ideas. Important to the description of Psyche's palace is the word *demiurge*. To study the Platonist associations of psyche's palace we can revert to Apuleius's own *De dogma Platonis*:

---

29. Joseph DeFilippo, "Curiositas and the Platonism of Apuleius' Golden Ass," *AJP* 111 (1990): 471–92.

On top of this, the world is characterized by both perpetual youth and inviolable health because nothing extra is left outside of it which can corrupt its natural disposition. Even if there were something left, it would not damage the world, especially since it was constructed and arranged within and from every part, so that things adverse and contrary to its nature and organization would not be able to harm it. For this reason, then, for the most perfect and most beautiful world, the divine craftsman sought the likeness of a beautiful and perfect sphere in order that the world may lack nothing; rather, covering and enclosing all things, that it may contain them, a world beautiful and marvelous, similar to itself and answering to itself. (*Dogm. Plat.* 1.7 [Fowler])

We are now in the world of the *Timaeus*, a dialogue that also elaborates the incarnation of the soul. Obvious parallels to the tale of Cupid and Psyche include the divine craftsmanship, the receptacle, and the Demiurge himself.[30] The doctrine of the world as a divinely wrought artifact that exhibits sustainability, self-motion, and rule by soul shares many features with the description of Psyche's palace in the *Metamorphoses*. The gold of the palace in the tale of Cupid and Psyche corresponds to the *Timaeus*'s Receptacle; in Cupid and Psyche, Apuleius produces a striking image of the demiurge at work on the receptacle: "a god had with his sublime and subtle artistry not tamed but literally brutalized all this metal" (*Metam.* 5.1).

The contemplative dimension of the text, the vision of divine beauty that leads to the restoration of the soul's spiritual identity, comes through vividly in the language of seeing. Psyche, about to wound Cupid on the advice of her sisters, now has her first glimpse of divine beauty: "as she glances often and often upon the beauty of the divine visage, her mind is gladdened" (dum saepius divini vultus intuetur pulchritudinem, recreatur animi, *Metam.* 5.22). Returning to Plato's text, we find that the language may resonate across the centuries and find its way into the Latin. For example, κάλλος δὲ τότ' ἦν ἰδεῖν λαμπρόν ... εἶδόν ("then beauty was a luminous form to gaze upon," *Phaedr.* 250b) corresponds closely to Apuleius's *divini*

---

30. "Domus regia est aedificata non humanis manibus sed divinis artibus; magno Iovi fabricatum caeleste palatium. Idcirco autem perfectissimo" (*Metam.* 5.1): "you first entered it, you recognized this as the resplendent, delicious retreat of some god" (Ruden).

"Et pulcherrimo mundo instar pulchrae et perfectae sphaerae a fabricatore deo quaesitum est, ut sit nihil indigens, sed operiens omnia coercensque contineat, pulcher et admirabilis, sui similis sibique respondens" (*Dogm. Plat.* 1.7).

vultus intuetur pulchritudinem ("she glances upon the beauty of the divine visage," *Metam.* 5.22), that is, Psyche's vision of Cupid's divine beauty, and Psyche's falling in love with love corresponds to the Platonic σέβεσθαι τὸ κάλλος or worship of beauty. The restoration of the feathers in Plato's story is now replaced through the winged god Eros himself. Just as the fall is dramatized and highlighted in the tale of Cupid and Psyche, so too the feathers of Eros feature prominently in Apuleius's version. Psyche's experiences when she sees the god of love are similar to the madness of the lover who worships beauty: "no longer mistress of herself: feeble, pale, trembling and powerless, sick with love, her heart was in turmoil in his lofty flight; trailing attendance through the clouds she clung on underneath, but finally in her exhaustion fell to the ground" (*Metam.* 5.24). The divine madness that ultimately helps to restore Psyche (Soul) to her rightful place as a member of the hyperouranian realm fuels the work of recovery and the tasks assigned to her suggest the presence of the virtues, wisdom especially, that the soul now needs to develop on her own.

At the same time, the novel is evidently pessimistic because, despite the efforts of the soul to comply with the dictates of the goddess, she ultimately succumbs to what Apuleius calls "infernus somnus ac vere Stygius" (*Metam.* 6.21), that is, the infernal sleep, the cloud of forgetfulness, common descriptors for the condition of the soul that we find so frequently in gnostic texts but also very much in Plato. Commentators are divided about the redemptive force of the episode as a whole.[31] The lack of memory, the condition of sleep itself as a dangerous contrast to wakefulness, the theme of the novel, explicitly described as belonging "to you," suggests that the entire story is about the nature of the self. As a refrain, the author suggests that the larger interpretive frame can only be understood by reference to oneself. It points toward the reader as the arbiter of meaning and as the final index. When we return to the larger narrative frame, that this story is told inside a cave to a prisoner in the cave seems relevant to the trajectory of the story, that the world surrounding the story is utterly unredeemed and that the Platonist tale that gives Charite comfort leads to complete misdirection.

At this point the fortunes of the ass follow a trajectory of embodiment, wherein the needs of the physical dominate the course of events. The progression is toward greater and greater identification with the body as well

---

31. Moreschini surveys the views (*Apuleius and the Metamorphoses*).

as toward a transmigration over different states and conditions, influenced by events outside the control of the embodied individual. The meaning of fortune, the determination of one's trajectory owing to sequences of cause and effect, provoking reaction and resulting in either well or ill being, is fundamentally alien to the real identity of the person. This understanding of the world as a deterministic system in which there is transmigration through varying conditions, as the soul assumes the form of births alien to the human condition, is conveyed in the misadventures of Lucius, the wrong turn and the wandering that the ass must undergo.

Images of wandering, blind fortune, entrapment, imprisonment, the cycle of cause and effect, all of these dominate the second half of the novel, after the asses' escape from the cave. It is as though he leaves the cave only to enter the larger cave, and his experiences in this realm definitely resonate with Middle Platonist theories of fate.

> There, ever so many work animals, on roundabouts with a whole range of circumferences, kept twirling the mills on an endlessly multiplied circuit. Not only in the daytime but throughout the night, in a whirl of machinery that allowed no loitering, they ground the wakeful flour by lamplight. (ibi complurium iumentorum multivii circuitus intorquebant molas ambage varia nec die tantum verum perperi etiam nocte prorsus instabili machinarum vertigine lucubrabant pervigilem farinam, *Metam.* 9.11 [Ruden])

Here the beasts of burden circulate day and night in a trap (*multivus*), caught in the perpetual (*instabili*) mechanical motion that enslaves them in a *circuitus* route: *ambage, circuitus, servitii*. A small respite granted by the owner of the machine (*otii saginaeque beatitudo*) is followed by a period of absolute bondage. We are reminded of Plato's warnings in the *Republic*'s Myth of Er that heavenly benefits (*beatitudo*) will run out. *Illico*, or "immediately," equates with the Platonic *exaiphnes*; the instantaneous change of condition attendant on the fact that the soul is still caught up (*propellor ad incurva spatia*) or rather "forced onto the circular path," that is, the rounds of birth and death, all owing to its ignorance. Apuleius uses the word *velata*, "veiled" or "blinded." Here the beast wanders in certain error (*vagarer errore certo*), and lest we miss allusions to Plato's cave, Lucius describes the human inhabitants at the mill in language that recalls the prisoners of *Resp.* 7: chained about the ankles (*pedes anulati*), their eyelids gnawed by the gloomy smoke of the murky fumes, which left them less able to access light at all (*Metam.* 9.12).[32] This image of the mill, the endless rounds of blind wandering, the shackles and darkness, the fixed path that only cycles back—all of these descriptors function in tandem with the earlier construction of Psyche's palace, divinely wrought, filled with perpetual motion, like the precosmic chaos of the Receptacle before it has received the imprint of the Demiurge.

In Plato's myth, souls that stay on the wheel of birth and death are subject to a power differential: "whether a farmer, or on the eighth birth a sophist or demagogue, on the ninth, a tryant" (ἢ γεωργικός, ὀγδόη σοφιστικὸς ἢ δημοκοπικός, ἐνάτῃ τυραννικός, *Phaedr.* 248e). Here the occupations of the embodied souls are listed in a numerical ranking that begins to descend to the banausic but then reverses order, listing the Sophist and the tyrant as occupying the lowest possible ranks for human birth. For our purposes, what closely connects the two texts is the transmigration into nonhuman animals, or entry into the life of a beast. Rebirths follow a reordering depending on the moral development of the soul, lasting for a ten-thousand-year cycle. Rebirth takes place every thousand years, with heavenly rewards or infernal punishments punctuating the incarnations. At the time of choice, Plato tells us, the human soul can enter into the life of a beast, and a beast once more can return to the life of a human being. But, Plato assures us, a soul who never had a glimpse of the truth can never attain this form.

We have seen that the cosmos is both created by the Demiurge as a magical abode, a wish-fulfilling gem that can respond to the desires of its inhabitant, Psyche, as well as a fearscape, in which suffering owing to unfulfilled desires combined with ignorance and malice, the subordination of the divine aspects of the soul to the other elements that is illustrated in the Psyche story and clearly developed in the stories that Lucius tells, is the essential element. Wandering through the cycles of birth and death in the trap, the machine, the path that goes nowhere, the darkness that is the experience of embodiment—all of this is the more negative way of characterizing the world.

Conclusion

Myth takes place in *illo tempore*, before time, in proximity to the *axis mundi*, among beings divine and semidivine. Simultaneously, this prox-

---

32. "Fumosis tenebris vaporosae caliginis palpebras adesi atque adeo male luminanti."

imity to the *axis mundi* and access to primordial time is shared for participants in the ritual life or afterlife of the myth; in rites of worship invoking the myth, or merely in the recitation or narration of the myth. In the case of the Phaedrean charioteer, the atemporal realm of the divine pleroma and the eternal bliss of contemplation enjoyed by the spiritual or intellectual beings there is one of equilibrium and perfection. What enters into that realm or arises from within that realm to cause differentiation, distance from the divine wisdom, and alienation? Whatever answer is discovered, whatever the cause of separation, the restoration or apokatastasis, the healing of this departure from the divine reality takes place over time. It is this introduction of the temporal dimension that adds all of the difficulty. For, of course, there is no time in the eternal; nothing can happen, and there can be nothing adventitious. Therefore, the other method of healing the departure, apart from the long conversion of the soul to God that takes place over the eons, is a sudden return, a recollection or vision, a contemplative turn that reveals the truth of nonseparation. The original myth of the Phaedrus and its deployment by the Middle Platonists provide difficulty for interpreters precisely because of these two registers, one of the soul, a being that necessarily participates in time, and the other of intellect, a being whose reality and activity are eternal and from which change is entirely absent. These two registers, temporal sequencing and eternal presence, come with a host of other disparities: individuality, corporeality, inequality, distance and proximity, better and worse, absence and presence, beginning and end. The entire story between the two points of separation and return, the drama that is the story of the soul, can only be seen between the slots of narrative that separate the entire panorama into still panels whose logic cannot ultimately align with the perspective of eternity. This paper has tried to demonstrate the importance of narrative to an appreciation of Middle Platonic philosophy. The long road of rebirth is lived by the reader, and the complete story of the soul, its embodiment and wandering, is studied in the moving narrative of the novel. The reader, after all, is the self-mover. In order to illustrate this fact about the soul, Apuleius offers a world that is opaque, at once filled with obscenity and disgrace, with every possible degradation, together with divine light and redemption. When we look at some of the great Middle Platonic authors—Philo Judaeus, Origen, Plutarch, and Apuleius himself—doctrine is not the only thing at stake. I would offer the example of Apuleius's *Golden Ass* as a mirror for the soul, an interactive adventure, a thought experiment or laboratory of Platonism.

Bibliography

Primary Sources

Apuleius. *De Platone et eius dogmate*. Translated by Ryan C. Fowler. In *Imperial Plato: Albinus, Maximus, Apuleius; Text and Translation, with an Introduction and Commentary*. Las Vegas: Parmenides, 2016.

———. *The Golden Ass*. Translated by Joel Reilihan. Indianapolis: Hackett, 2009.

———. *Metamorphoseon Libri XI*. Translated by Maaike Zimmerman. OCT. Oxford: Oxford University Press, 2012.

Plato. *Complete Works*. Edited by John Cooper and Douglas Hutchinson. Indianapolis: Hackett, 1997.

———. *Opera*. Vol. 2. Edited by John Burnet. Oxford: Oxford University Press, 1903.

———. *Phaedrus*. Translated by Alexander Nehamas and Paul Woodruff. Plato: Complete Works. Indianapolis: Hackett, 1997.

Plotinus. *Ennead IV*. Translated by Arthur H. Armstrong. LCL. Cambridge: Harvard University Press, 1984.

———. *Enneads*. Translated from the Greek by Stephen Mackenna. London: P. L. Warner, 1917–1930.

———.. *Opera*. Edited by Paul Henry and Hans-Rudolf Schwyzer. Oxford: Clarendon, 1964–1984.

Secondary Sources

Bonazzi, Mauro. "Plato Systematized: Doing Philosophy in the Imperial Schools." *OSAP* 53 (2017): 215–36.

Boys-Stones, George. "'Middle' Platonists on Fate and Human Autonomy." *BICS* 94 (2007): 431–47.

———. *Platonist Philosophy, 80 BC to AD 250: An Introduction and Collection of Sources in Translation*. Cambridge: Cambridge University Press, 2018.

DeFilippo, Joseph. "Curiositas and the Platonism of Apuleius' Golden Ass." *AJP* 111 (1990): 471–92.

Keulen, Wytse H., and Ulrike Egelhaaf-Gaiser. *The Isis Book: A Collection of Original Papers*. Vol. 3 of *Aspects of Apuleius' Golden Ass*. Leiden: Brill, 2012.

Kirichenko, Alexander. "Asinus Philosophans: Platonic Philosophy and the Prologue to Apuleius' 'Golden Ass.'" *Mnemosyne* 61 (2008): 89–107.

Moreschini, Claudio. *Apuleius and the Metamorphoses of Platonism.* Nutrix 10. Turnhout: Brepols, 2015.

Penwill, John L. "Slavish Pleasures and Profitless Curiosity: Fall and Redemption in Apuleius' Metamorphoses." *Ramus* 4 (1975): 49–82.

Trapp, Michael. "Plato's Phaedrus in Second-Century Greek Literature." Pages 141–73 in *Antonine Literature.* Edited by Donald A. Russell. Oxford: Oxford University Press, 1990.

Whittaker, John. "Ammonius on the Delphic E." *ClQ* 19 (1969): 185–92.

Winkle, Jeffrey T. "'Necessary Roughness': Plato's *Phaedrus* and Apuleius' *Metamorphoses.*" *AN* 11 (2013): 93–131.

Proclus Interprets Hesiod:
The Procline Philosophy of the Soul

John F. Finamore

One of the central features of Neoplatonic interpretation is the juxtaposing of various texts from different authors to expose the underlying truth inherent in all of them. Whether a Neoplatonic author is discussing Greek philosophical texts, poetic texts, or texts of ancient wisdom such as the *Chaldaean Oracles*, there will be a basic tenet of Platonic philosophy that underlies all of them. This being so, it is not at all surprising to find Proclus, in his commentary to the *Republic*, explicating a passage from Plato through the lens of Orphism and Hesiod's *Works and Days*. I wish to use this Procline text to highlight how the Athenian philosopher uses diverse texts to underscore an interpretation that is at once surprising and (when more carefully considered) natural for a later Neoplatonist.

In the thirteenth essay of his commentary, Proclus embarks on an eighty-page discussion of the discourse of the Muses in book 8 of the *Republic*.[1] In the essay, Proclus discusses the decline of the state and the problem of knowing the mathematical formula behind discovering the perfect number and so the perfect time for the mating of the guardians, a mating that will ensure the birth of children capable of governing properly. In section 42 (*Comm. in R.* 2.74.26–78.11), he tackles the meaning of the Platonic noble lie that the citizens in the ideal state were fashioned in the earth and that the best of them were blended with gold and would be

---

1. In books 8–9, Plato discusses the decline of the ideal state into the various inferior sorts of constitution. As he begins to discuss the decline into timocracy, Plato has Socrates invoke the Muses, asking how the conflict among the rulers first took place (545d5–545e3).

rulers, the second best with silver and would be auxiliaries, and the rest with bronze and iron (*Resp.* 3 [414b8–415d5]).[2]

Orpheus

Proclus begins his discussion of the myth of the metals with Orpheus. Orphic writings play a major role in Proclus's philosophy, especially evidenced in his *Platonic Theology*, and here too the role of the Orphic myths is meant to underscore the Platonic theory latent in them. According to Proclus, the Orphics laid out a tripartite system of the metaphysical universe, each layer of which was ruled over by its own god and was inhabited by races molded from a different metal. Proclus begins: "The theologian Orpheus proposed three races of humans. The first is gold, which he says Phanes established. The second is silver, over which the mighty Kronos ruled. Third is the Titanic [race] which he said that Zeus contrived from the limbs of the Titans"[3] (*Comm. in R.* 1.74.26–30). Proclus glosses over the fact that there are only two elements listed. The third race is marked not by its metal but rather by its formation from the bodies of the Titans that Zeus blasted with his thunderbolts. The significance is not in the physical makeup of the three races but rather in the kinds of lives that the three lived. Proclus explains:

---

2. As Plato has Socrates explain, he is searching for a deceptive device, "a certain noble one," a lie that would persuade the citizens of his city: "'What device,' he said, 'might there be for generating the necessary falsehoods, which we had been discussing just now, some single noble one to persuade the rulers themselves especially, but if not, the rest of the city?'" Τίς ἂν οὖν ἡμῖν, ἦν δ' ἐγώ, μηχανὴ γένοιτο τῶν ψευδῶν τῶν ἐν δέοντι γιγνομένων, ὧν δὴ νῦν ἐλέγομεν, γενναῖόν τι ἓν ψευδομένους πεῖσαι μάλιστα μὲν καὶ αὐτοὺς τοὺς ἄρχοντας, εἰ δὲ μή, τὴν ἄλλην πόλιν (414b8–c2). The myth of the metals, Socrates explains, is intended "to persuade first the rulers and the soldiers and then the rest of the city" (ἄρχοντας πείθειν καὶ τοὺς στρατιώτας, ἔπειτα δὲ καὶ τὴν ἄλλην πόλιν, 414d3–4) that "they were in truth fashioned and nourished in the earth ... and the earth, being their mother, brought them up" (ἦσαν δὲ τότε τῇ ἀληθείᾳ ὑπὸ γῆς ἐντὸς πλαττόμενοι καὶ τρεφόμενοι ... καὶ ἡ γῆ αὐτοὺς μήτηρ οὖσα ἀνῆκεν, 414e6–7 and e2–3). All the citizens are brothers and sisters, but the rulers had gold added to their mixture of elements, the auxiliaries silver, and the rest bronze and iron (415a4–7). All translations of Greek are my own.

3. Ὁ μὲν θεολόγος Ὀρφεὺς τρία γένη παραδέδωκεν ἀνθρώπων· πρώτιστον τὸ χρυσοῦν, ὅπερ ὑποστῆσαι τὸν Φάνητά φησιν· δεύτερον τὸ ἀργυροῦν, οὗ φησιν ἄρξαι τὸν μέγιστον Κρόνον· τρίτον τὸ Τιτανικόν, ὅ φησιν ἐκ τῶν Τιτανικῶν μελῶν τὸν Δία συστήσασθαι.

Now Orpheus understood that every form of human life is encompassed in these three defined groups. For a form of life is either intellectual and divine, since it is established among the very highest of the things that are, or else it has reverted upon itself and intelligizes itself and enjoys this sort of life, or else it looks toward what is inferior and wants to live with what is irrational.[4] (*Comm. in R.* 1.74.30–75.5)

Proclus is considering the "races" (or "classifications," γένη) of human beings in terms of their three possible ways of life. The first represents the human soul at its highest, Intelligible phase: it is attached to the Transcendent Intellect and is actively engaged in intellection. As Proclus explains: "the first [race] is from Phanes, who connects every [race] that engages in intellection to the intelligibles"[5] (*Comm. in R.* 1.75.6–8). Phanes, then, is the god who facilitates the soul's union with the Transcendent Intellect so that it can intelligize the intelligible reality.

Just as the Orphic myth indicates a decline in the lives of its individual members, so too the souls that inhabit the Neoplatonic cosmos descend from their highest form of life into a lower one. Proclus describes the decline of the silver race in this way: "The second [race] is from Kronos, who is (as the myth says) the first who is 'crooked of counsel' and who causes all to revert upon themselves"[6] (*Comm. in R.* 1.75.8–10). Kronos represents a god beneath the order of the Intellect, operating at the level of the human souls.[7] The adjective ἀγκυλομήτης ("crooked of counsel") is used of Kronos in both Homer and Hesiod (see Homer, *Il.* 2.205; *Od.* 21.415; Hesiod, *Theog.* 18) to highlight the cunning of Kronos. Proclus interprets the term differently, using ἀγκύλος more in the sense of

---

4. συννοήσας ὡς ἐν τρισὶν ὅροις τούτοις πᾶν εἶδος περιέχεται τῆς ἀνθρωπίνης ζωῆς. ἢ γὰρ νοερόν ἐστιν καὶ θεῖον, αὐτοῖς τοῖς ἀκροτάτοις τῶν ὄντων ἐνιδρυμένον, ἢ πρὸς ἑαυτὸ ἐπέστραπται καὶ νοεῖ ἑαυτὸ καὶ ἀγαπᾷ τὴν τοιαύτην ζωήν, ἢ πρὸς τὰ χείρονα βλέπει καὶ μετ' ἐκείνων ἐθέλει ζῆν ἀλόγων ὄντων.

5. τὸ μὲν πρώτιστον ἀπὸ τοῦ Φάνητός ἐστιν, ὃς πᾶν τὸ νοοῦν συνάπτει τοῖς νοητοῖς.

6. τὸ δὲ δεύτερον ἀπὸ τοῦ Κρόνου τοῦ πρώτου, φησὶν ὁ μῦθος, ἀγκυλομήτου καὶ πάντα πρὸς ἑαυτὰ ποιοῦντος ἐπιστρέφειν.

7. It is difficult to name this god in the Procline hierarchy. The set of gods (Phanes, Kronos, Zeus) seem to mirror the divinities in the Intellective Realm, the Heptad. If so, Phanes stands for the first triad (Cronus, Rhea, Zeus); Kronos for the second (Athena, Kore, Curetes); Zeus for the Monad (represented by the castration of Heaven by Kronos and of Kronos by Zeus). Alternatively, Proclus might be imagining them as hypercosmic or hypercosmic/encosmic gods, who act directly with souls. See Radek Chlup, *Proclus: An Introduction* (Cambridge: Cambridge University Press, 2012), 126.

"curved" or "pivoting, turning around," and so connects it with the concept of reversion (ἐπιστροφή). This is not, however, reversion to a higher cause (as would have been the case under Phanes), but rather a reversion to the soul's lower nature, where it makes use of rational thought (λογισμός) rather than intelligizing. The god counsels souls to turn about and return (ἐπιστρέφειν) to their rational level. Unlike Phanes, who guides souls upwards to Intellect, Kronos brings the soul down to a lower but still appropriate level. Thus the originally negative adjective ἀγκυλομήτης takes on a new significance, one that is not so negative.

The third and final and final phase draws the soul down further into the realm of Nature: "The third [form of life] is from Zeus, who teaches [the souls therein] to care for secondary entities and to bring inferior ones into order, for this is characteristic of demiurgic activity" (τὸ δὲ τρίτον ἀπὸ Διὸς τοῦ τῶν δευτέρων προνοεῖν καὶ διακοσμεῖν τὰ χείρονα διδάσκοντος· τοῦτο γὰρ ἴδιον δημιουργίας, *Comm. in R.* 1.75.10–12). Zeus, the demiurgic divinity, who destroyed the Titans with his thunderbolt, is thus interpreted as the god who leads souls down to care for things in the realm below. The lowest race of souls is engaged in creativity in the realm of generation and deals directly with matter. It is worth noting that none of these three modes of life is evil. Rather, they represent three different "natural" ways for souls to engage in the cosmos. The highest phase is of course the best, but the two lower phases are also part of the assigned duties of descended souls. In what follows Proclus will expand the lowest level to include the dangers of coming into contact with matter.

Hesiod

Proclus next moves on to consider the five races of human beings covered by Hesiod in *Op.* 110–201. This section of the commentary is prompted by Socrates's remark about Hesiod in book 8 of the *Republic*. After stating that the guardians who lose the ability to choose the correct times for marriages and the generation of children will bring less worthy rulers to power (*Resp.* 546c6–d8), Plato continues: "From these [faulty rulers] there will fail to arise rulers who are altogether careful to scrutinize the races of Hesiod and among you, [viz., those of] gold, silver, bronze, and iron"[8]

---

8. ἐκ δὲ τούτων ἄρχοντες οὐ πάνυ φυλακικοὶ καταστήσονται πρὸς τὸ δοκιμάζειν τὰ 'Ησιόδου τε καὶ τὰ παρ' ὑμῖν γένη, χρυσοῦν τε καὶ ἀργυροῦν καὶ χαλκοῦν καὶ σιδηροῦν.

(*Resp.* 546d8–a1). Once the races are mixed, strife arises in the ideal city (*Resp.* 546a2–4). Proclus continues by showing a connection between Hesiod's poem and both Orpheus and Plato.

The first problem Proclus faces is the number of races. There are three in Orpheus (as we have seen), but there are five in Hesiod. I will argue that Proclus's solution is to divide the third (lowest) race into three subsections. Here is how he begins, before tackling each of the five classifications individually: "In fact Hesiod does not make only three races, but first golden, then silver, then bronze, then a certain heroic race, then iron, extending the act of division into lives of more varied forms"[9] (*Comm. in R.* 1.75.12–15). Proclus's point is that Hesiod brings the three races into a set of five divisions, some of which can themselves be understood as finely divided subsections of the three, distinguished according to the forms of life that the souls in those subsets exhibit. Let us tackle each division one by one and see what Proclus does. According to Hesiod (*Op.* 110–126), the golden race appeared in the time of the reign of Kronos. They lived a carefree life. The earth provided them with its bounty without their labor. In the end, they became "pure, noble *daimons* on the earth, warding off evil [and were] guardians of mortal human beings"[10] (*Op.* 121–122).

Proclus interprets their purity as possessing "a certain intellectual life that is free from matter and pure" (νοεράν τινα ζωὴν ἄυλον καὶ ἄχραντον, *Comm. in R.* 1.75.16–17). Gold is a symbol of this life since it is "incapable, they say, of receiving rust and decay" (ἄδεκτος ὤν, φασίν, ἰοῦ καὶ σήψεως, *Comm. in R.* 1.75.17–18). Thus the individuals in this race are placed, as they were in the Orphic hierarchy, in the Intelligible. It is because of this pure, intellectual life, Proclus tells us, that the members of this golden race, after their time on earth, transfer into the order (τάξις, *Comm. in R.* 1.75.19) of daimons, an order "that exercises providence over the human race, preserving it and protecting it from evil" (προνοητικὴν καὶ φρουρητικὴν καὶ ἀλεξίκακον τοῦ ἀνθρώπων γένους, *Comm. in R.* 1.75.19–20). Assuming that Proclus is maintaining the strict Iamblichean distinction between the superior classes, Proclus is claiming that the reward of living a life separated from the material realm is the ability to descend to the daimonic

---

9. Ὁ δέ γε Ἡσίοδος οὐχὶ τρία τὰ γένη ποιεῖ μόνον, ἀλλὰ πρῶτον τὸ χρυσοῦν, εἶτα ἀργυροῦν, εἶτα χαλκοῦν, εἶτα ἡρωϊκόν τι γένος, εἶτα σιδηροῦν, εἰς πολυειδεστέρας ζωὰς τὴν τομὴν προάγων.

10. τοὶ μὲν δαίμονες ἁγνοὶ ἐπιχθόνιοι τελέθουσιν ἐσθλοί, ἀλεξίκακοι, φύλακες θνητῶν ἀνθρώπων.

level and work for the good of humanity. Thus the souls of the golden race are those who lived a pure life in the Intelligible and then descended to a lower level to work with and aid less fortunate souls. At this point a problem arises in the manuscripts. Instead of moving on to a discussion of the silver race, as one would have expected after a discussion of the golden-race daimons and which would have mirrored Hesiod's own structure, the manuscripts continue:[11]

> And while [this race] is in the realm of Becoming, he [i.e., Hesiod] says, it is nourished for one hundred years and brought to maturity by its parents. He has written, as it seems to me, a myth that is appropriate to the Muses and has demonstrated that while [this race] <acts> in accordance with Intellect, <it clings to> its parents[12] and has removed itself from human concerns, thereby living a life that returns it to its beginning.[13] (*Comm. in R.* 1.75.20–25)

The hundred-year period, as both Wilhelm Kroll in his 1901 edition and André Jean Festugière point out, belongs not to the golden but to the silver race (*Op.* 130–137).[14] The children of the silver race are raised by their parents for a hundred years, and they manage to live only for a short time thereafter because of their folly (ἀφραδία, line 134) of wrongdoing and ignoring the gods. It is difficult to know what to make of the placement of this passage. Did Proclus have a text before him with the lines transferred from their proper position to the passage about the golden race? Did he think that, in spite of the passage's position and its negative meaning, that it nonetheless referred back to the previous section of the poem? There is no evidence of any such transposition taking place in the manuscript tradition of Hesiod's poem, and it is most unlikely that Proclus would have

---

11. In the sentence that follows (75.25–28), Proclus connects the one hundred-year period to Plato (*Resp.* 8 [546c]) and to the nuptial number.

12. Wilhelm Kroll marks a lacuna of sixteen letters and conjectures: κατὰ νοῦν <ἐνεργοῦν ἐξῆπται τῶν> πατέρων καὶ τῶν ἀνθρωπίνων ἐξήρηται πολυπραγμοσυνῶν ἀποκαταστατικῶς διαζῶν.

13. καὶ ἐν τῇ γενέσει ὂν τρέφεσθαί φησιν ἑκατὸν ἔτη καὶ ὑπὸ τῶν πατέρων τελειοῦσθαι· μῦθον, ὡς ἐμοὶ δοκεῖ, μουσικὸν γράφων καὶ ἐνδεικνύμενος, ὅτι κατὰ νοῦν ... πατέρων καὶ τῶν ἀνθρωπίνων ἐξήρηται πολυπραγμοσυνῶν ἀποκαταστατικῶς διαζῶν.

14. Wilhelm Kroll, *Procli Diadochi in Platonis Rem Publicam Commentarii*, 2 vols. (Leipzig: Teubner, 1899); André Jean Festugière, *Proclus: Commentaire sur la République* (Paris: Vrin, 1970), 3:186 n. 1.

mistaken these lines as belonging to an earlier section of the poem. I would suggest that the problem is with our manuscript of Proclus's commentary. The text is out of place and should be moved to the section on the silver race. A careful consideration of what Proclus says about the silver race should help to show that this is the most probable solution to the problem.

The silver race, for Proclus, is characterized by the soul's reversion to the realm of Intellect and to discursive reasoning in the realm of generation, the latter downward reversion being similar to the case in the Orphic mythology. The souls in it, Proclus writes, proceed from the pure intellection of the golden race "to an activity that is both intellective and rational" (εἰς τὴν σύμμικτον κατά τε νοῦν καὶ λόγον ἐνέργειαν, *Comm. in R.* 1.75.29–30). For Proclus, silver is a symbol of this double power: silver becomes tarnished and so symbolizes the lower activity of *logos*, but it is also shiny and so reflects the intellective activity of the golden race: "On the one hand it possesses the brilliance of a life led in accordance with reason and exhibits a property of sometimes sharing in material rust and decay, but it also takes on another property in addition to these, and when it is placed next to [gold] it reflects the gold and does not act differently from gold" (*Comm. in R.* 1.75.30–76.5).[15] Proclus compares and contrasts the life of the silver race with that of the gold and finds that while the golden race engages in intellection only, the silver race engages in both intellection at one time (when it is in the Intelligible Realm) and in discursive reasoning at another (when it has descended into the realm of generation). Proclus concludes:

> Thus also the reason that belongs to the soul, even if it is filled with matter and material impurity, is nonetheless illuminated by intellect and, having been illuminated, produces for itself a single and common activity with it. (οὕτω γὰρ δὴ καὶ ὁ ψυχικὸς λόγος, εἰ καὶ ὕλης ποτὲ καὶ ὑλικῆς ἀκαθαρσίας ἀναπίμπλαται, ἀλλὰ καὶ ὑπὸ νοῦ καταλάμπεται καὶ καταλαμφθεὶς μίαν καὶ κοινὴν ποιεῖται πρὸς αὐτὸν ἐνέργειαν, *Comm. in R.* 1.76.5–8)

For Proclus, then, the silver race is, as it were, an imperfect reflection of the golden. The shininess of silver acts as a symbol for the reflec-

---

15. σύνθημα δὲ ταύτης ὁ ἄργυρος, τὸ μὲν λαμπρὸν ἔχων τῆς κατὰ λόγον ζωῆς καὶ φανὸν ἴδιον καὶ τὸ ἔστιν ὅτε τοῦ ὑλικοῦ μετίσχειν ἰοῦ καὶ σηπεδόνος, προσειληφὼς δὲ ἄλλο τι πρὸς τούτοις, τὸ καὶ ἐν τῇ παραθέσει περιλάμπεσθαι ὑπὸ τοῦ χρυσοῦ καὶ μὴ τοὐναντίον δρᾶν εἰς τὸν χρυσόν.

tion of the golden nature in it. Souls in the silver race too share in the activity of intellection. The other characteristic of silver, however, its tarnishability, indicates the other side of silver souls, their tendency to discursive reasoning.

It is at this point in the text that the earlier passage should be returned. Having explained that the silver race lives two sorts of lives, intellectual and rational, Proclus next explains the myth of the silver-age children. Their so-called parents are the members of the golden race in the Intelligible Realm. When the silver-age children engage in intellection, they are said to cling to their parents and cease from their lower-level activities. Proclus further interprets the hundred-year period during which the silver race is in this condition as "the period of the form of life that is characterized by sameness, similarity, and intellection" (τὴν ταὐτοῦ καὶ ὁμοίου καὶ νοεροῦ τῆς ζωῆς εἴδους περίοδον, *Comm. in R.* 1.75.27–28). Thus the silver race shares intermittently in the life of the golden race but also descends below to engage in discursive thought.[16]

Hesiod describes the bronze race as fierce and warlike (*Op.* 143–155). For Proclus their lives consist only of rational activities, not intellective ones (*Comm. in R.* 1.76.9–11). Bronze is symbolic of this level of thought): "Immaterial reason, therefore, existing as pure light free from the darkness of matter, possessing by itself a certain likeness to intellect because of its reversion to itself—just as bronze has a certain likeness to gold—defines the life of these [members of the bronze race]" (*Comm. in R.* 1.76.15–19).[17] The bronze race thinks at the level of discursive reason but never (as the silver race did) at the intelligible level. Like the silver race, the shiny surface of bronze can reflect the light of reason and so is not subject to the darkness

---

16. Proclus is, of course, putting a positive spin on Hesiod's words. For Hesiod, they are under parents' care for too long and so spoiled. They are foolish, immoral, and impious. Clearly Proclus would have allegorized these traits differently, perhaps arguing that time in the Intelligible makes one appear foolish down here (with an allusion to Plato's allegory of the cave) and that their immoral, impious behavior is only from the perspective of the hoi polloi in our realm. It is also worth noting that Hesiod says that after death of this race mortals honor them as blessed, secondary underworld beings (τοὶ μὲν ὑποχθόνιοι μάκαρες θνητοὶ καλέονται, δεύτεροι, 141), and this statement might have helped Proclus to support his positive interpretation.

17. λόγος οὖν ἄυλος καὶ καθαρὸν φῶς ὑπάρχων καὶ τῆς σκοτώδους καθαρεύων ὕλης, ἔχων δέ τινα καὶ καθ᾽ ἑαυτὸν ἀπεικασίαν πρὸς νοῦν διὰ τὴν πρὸς ἑαυτὸν ἐπιστροφήν, καθάπερ καὶ ὁ χαλκὸς πρὸς τὸν χρυσόν, ἀφορίζει τὴν τούτων ζωήν.

of matter (symbolized by iron[18]). This is our first hint that although this race is like that of the Orphic Titanic race, which also existed in the realm of nature and cared for what existed there, it is also engaged with Nature at a higher level than the mere material.

The next race is intermediate between the bronze and iron races. Proclus sees it as combining reason that marks the bronze race with the irrationality of the iron: "The fourth is the race of demigods, which turns reason toward a life that is entirely practical and receives in addition from its passion a certain motion of its irrational [elements] and an impulse in its actions since it is more eagerly attached to them" (*Comm. in R.* 1.76.22–25).[19] It is clear that this race possesses the reason of the previous one, but it is turned in a different direction. The reason of the bronze race, we were told, resembled Intellect "because of its reversion to itself" (διὰ τὴν πρὸς ἑαυτὸν ἐπιστροφήν, *Comm. in R.* 1.76.17–18). The reason of the demigods' race, on the other hand, reverts toward a practical life (ἐπιστρέφει τὸν λόγον εἰς τὴν πρακτικὴν ὅλον ζωὴν). This unusual use of ἐπιστρέφει for a reversion downward is intentional. Properly, reason (*logos*) should revert to Intellect, as would be the case in the silver race. In the bronze race, however, reason reverts to itself, which is to say that it is *logos* that thinks diachronically but not about the objects in nature. It is therefore thought concerning nonmaterial objects. Reason in the demigods' race is still diachronic as well, but it is also about material objects. Reasoning about material objects, however, involves the irrational soul and its use of images.[20] It is a lesser kind of reason. As Proclus will go on to say, this race of demigods shares in the reason in the race above it (bronze race) and in the irrationality of the race below it (iron race): "it has blended the mortal life of passion together with reason that has been allotted a divine essence" (τῷ λόγῳ θείαν εἰληχότι οὐσίαν συνέμιξεν τὴν θνητοειδῆ τοῦ πάθους ζωήν, *Comm. in R.* 1.76.28–77.1). It is

---

18. Hesiod says that they "had no black iron" (μέλας δ' οὐκ ἔσκε σίδηρος, 151), and Proclus echoes this at *Comm. in R.* 1.76.14–15. Bronze, a reflective material, therefore indicates that it can operate at a level of the merely material.

19. τὸ δὲ δὴ τῶν ἡμιθέων τέταρτον ὂν ἐπιστρέφει τὸν λόγον εἰς τὴν πρακτικὴν ὅλον ζωὴν καί τινα καὶ ἀπὸ τοῦ πάθους προσλαμβάνει κίνησιν τῶν ἀλόγων καὶ ὁρμὴν ἐν ταῖς πράξεσιν, προθυμότερον αὐτῶν ἐφαπτόμενον,

20. Proclus may have the divided line (*Resp.* 509d1–511e5) in mind here. Intellection is at the summit of the line, pure reason the next lower section, reason about material objects next, and images at the end.

this combination of reason and passion along with its downward attention that marks the demigods' race.

The iron race is the lowest of the five. Proclus says that it is empas-
sioned (ἐμπαθὲς, *Comm. in R.* 1.77.5), and passion, he says, is "difficult to
correct, hard to bend by reason, weighed down from behind, and having
(so to say) no share in reason, which is light" (δυσνουθέτητος οὖσα καὶ
λόγῳ δύσκαμπτος καὶ ὀπισθοβαρὴς καὶ ἄμοιρος ὡς εἰπεῖν λόγου, φωτὸς
ὄντος, *Comm. in R.* 1.77.8–10). Passion, like matter and iron itself, is dark
and black; reason and thought are light. Because of the iron race's proximity to matter and its association with the passions, it is tainted and lacks
even the reason of the two races above it. Proclus concludes: "Therefore
it is likely that this race is last and least in worth since it is bound fast in
the passions, risking degeneration into a way of life that is utterly bestial
and irrational, dimly procuring for itself the light of reason" (*Comm. in
R.* 1.77.11–14).[21] The iron race is furthest from the Intelligible and nearly
lost in the darkness of matter, a darkness for which black iron is a symbol.

Proclus has therefore described a threefold division of activity in the
realm of Nature. At best, souls use reason alone, thinking without the taint
of matter; second best involves reason but with some passions and imaging involved, as well as a looking away toward matter itself; at the lowest
level, the soul is intimately engaged in matter and so is filled with passions,
which render its reason useless or nearly so. This threefold division at the
end is a more careful working out of the lowest Orphic realm. Proclus is,
in effect, exposing the inner workings of that lowest stratum of reality for
human souls.

Plato

With this prolegomenon completed, Proclus comes to Plato's division of
the ideal state. First he considers the three classes and writes (*Comm. in R.*
1.77.19–26) that Plato had assigned gold (which is "undefiled and immaterial," ἀκήρατον ... καὶ ἄυλον, *Comm. in R.* 1.77.22–23) to the highest class
of the guardian rulers; silver to the auxiliary class ("since they are akin
to the golden rulers and receive their education and use of reason from
them," ὡς ἐκείνῳ συγγενεῖ καὶ ἀπ᾽ ἐκείνου λόγον προσλαβόντι καὶ παιδείαν,

---

21. εἰκότως ἄρα καὶ ἔσχατόν ἐστι τοῦτο καὶ ἀτιμότατον, ὡς ἐν πάθεσιν εἰλούμενον,
κινδυνεῦον ἐκπεσεῖν εἰς τὴν παντελῶς θηριώδη καὶ ἄλογον ζωήν, ἀμυδρὸν ἐπαγόμενον τὸ
τοῦ λόγου φέγγος.

Comm. in R. 1.77.23–25); and both bronze and iron to the lowest class of workers (which makes use of "material passions," πάθεσιν ὑλικοῖς, *Comm. in R.* 1.77.25).[22] In this way, Proclus makes clear that the metals are central to both Hesiod's and Plato's myths and continues his interpretation of the four elements as symbolic of the souls at each level.

Proclus next looks specifically at the lowest class, which we have seen is akin to the three lowest levels of Hesiod's myth: "There is in a certain way an altogether better and worse analog to those [two metals] in this [lowest class]. The bronze preserves an analogy of the better part in the lowest class to gold, while the iron [preserves an analogy of the worse part] to silver" (*Comm. in R.* 1.77.26–29).[23] As he had done with his interpretation of the lower three strata of Hesiod's myth, Proclus differentiates the inhabitants of Plato's lowest class by reference to the symbolic elements of bronze and iron. The better part of the lower class (which would be equivalent to the members of the Hesiodic bronze age) are as similar to the ruling class as bronze is to gold. This is to say that the shiny nature of bronze allows for an impaired but nonetheless recognizable reflection of the intellection of the rulers. As we have seen above, the similarity is in their use of reason, which is, as it were, a weak reflection of intellection. This is the best that the lowest class can manage. Iron, on the other hand, as we also learned from Proclus's interpretation of Hesiod, is black and does not reflect well. Whereas the silver in the auxiliaries reflects well (but partially) the intellection of the rulers, the iron reflects poorly the shine of the already reflected gloss of silver in the auxiliaries—and most probably sometimes it does not reflect it at all. The lowest subsection of the lowest class, then, is a very poor reflection of what is essentially already a reflection of the activities of the souls in the Intelligible. Proclus sees them as he does the members of the Hesiodic iron age, mired in passions and barely able (if at all) to reason.

Since the lowest class is so inferior to the upper two classes, Proclus tells us, the Muses are right to say that the classes should be kept separate and not be mixed together (*Comm. in R.* 1.77.29–78.3). This is a reminder that within the ideal state the gene pool must remain untainted so that the

---

22. For Plato's use of these four metals and their correspondence with the three classes in the ideal city, see *Resp.* 3 (415a2–7).

23. ἔστι γάρ τι καὶ ἐν τούτῳ πάντως ἄμεινον καὶ χεῖρον ἀνάλογον ἐκείνοις, καὶ ὁ μὲν χαλκὸς τὴν πρὸς τὸν χρυσὸν ἀναλογίαν διασώζει τοῦ κρείττονος ἐν αὐτῷ, ὁ δὲ σίδηρος τὴν πρὸς τὸν ἄργυρον.

rulers can continue to arrange society rightly. Proclus then returns to his interpretation of the metals, now with an eye to preserving the state:

> Through these metals the two [authors] indicate differences about the forms of life, which must be preserved whether someone were to distinguish them into five divisions, as Hesiod does, or into two divisions of two each, as Plato does. For [the Muses add that] the mixture does not preserve the gold pure but from the mixture of other [metals] becomes rusted and decayed and that iron no longer preserves its own rank but wishes to perform the tasks of silver because of its mixture, even though it is earthy but not fiery and dark but not light.[24]

These final two sentences bring the myths of Hesiod and Plato together under the spotlight of the Orphic passage. Plato's tripartite state, now seen as bipartite with each half being bipartite as well, is equivalent to Hesiod's five ages. Both myths tell us something about the individual human soul's forms of life. We have learned that the soul lives at different levels. Applying that knowledge to statecraft, it is important to keep the differences between souls in mind so that the state can function properly and survive. If you mix gold (pure intellection) with a baser metal (*logos* with irrationality), the amalgam (unlike gold) will be subject to decay. Proclus imagines a mixture between an auxiliary (silver) and a worker (iron), and the result would be disastrous for the state. Workers add the dark nature of iron to the silver sheen of auxiliaries. Just as the new metallic compound partakes of an earthiness instead of fire and is dark instead of light, so too the child of such mixed parentage loses its ability to intelligize and performs instead a darker sort of blend of reason and irrationality. This child would no longer have knowledge of the Forms and so could not rule justly or make sound laws.

The Platonic myth of the metals, therefore, is in Proclus's interpretation about the very nature of the souls of the citizens of the ideal state. Gold represents the shiny, clear vision of intellection, silver the less shiny

---

24. παρ' ἀμφοτέροις γὰρ διαφορότητες εἰδῶν ζωτικῶν σημαίνονται διὰ τῶν ὑλῶν τούτων, ἃς ἀκράτους διατηρητέον, εἴτε οὕτως αὐτὰς διαστήσαιτό τις ὡς ὁ Ἡσίοδος πενταχῶς, εἴθ' οὕτως ὡς Πλάτων διχῇ διχῶς. τὴν γὰρ σύμμιξιν μήτε τὸν χρυσὸν ἀκήρατον ἔτι σώζειν, ἀλλ' ἐκ τῆς τῶν ἄλλων μίξεως ἰούμενον καὶ σήψεως ἀναπιμπλάμενον ἀποτελεῖν, μήτε τὸν σίδηρον ἔτι τὴν ἑαυτοῦ φυλάττοντα τάξιν, ἀλλὰ τὰ ἀργύρου πράττειν ἐθέλοντα διὰ τὴν μῖξιν, καὶ ταῦτα χθόνιον ἀλλ' οὐ πύριον ὄντα, καὶ σκοτεινὸν ἀλλ' οὐ φανόν (*Comm. in R.* 1.78.3–12).

and clear reason without irrationality, bronze the duller reason mixed with some irrationality, and iron the dark, dull state of the irrational taking precedence over the rational. The hierarchy of metals must be maintained in statecraft. Mixing the metals (or the three classes in the state) will lead to the destruction of the state. Orpheus, Hesiod, and Plato share the same message. Leaders must be philosopher-rulers capable of accessing the Forms and applying them to the world of generation.

Bibliography

Chlup, Radek. *Proclus: An Introduction*. Cambridge: Cambridge University Press, 2012.

Festugière, André Jean. *Proclus: Commentaire sur la République*. Vol. 3. Paris: Vrin, 1970.

Kroll, Wilhelm. *Procli Diadochi in Platonis Rem Publicam Commentarii*. 2 vols. Leipzig: Teubner, 1899.

Part 4
Ritual Contexts, Inspiration, and Embodied Practices

Julian and Sallust on the Ascent of the Soul and Theurgy

Crystal Addey and Jay Bregman

Others attribute the goal of the descent to the demonstration of divine life. For this is the will of the gods: to show themselves as gods through the souls. For the gods come forth in the open and show themselves through the pure and immaculate lives of souls.
—Iamblichus, *De an.* 379.23–26 (Finamore and Dillon)[1]

Introduction: Julian, Theurgy, and the Ascent of the Soul

The emperor Julian (ca. 331–363 CE), the last pagan Roman emperor and one of the most fascinating figures in Roman history, preferred Plato's account of creation in the *Timaeus* to that of Moses in Genesis. The original creation involved the generation of many (rather than one) human beings: "the gods who rule over generation brought them forth receiving their

We would like to thank Sara Ahbel-Rappe for organizing and hosting the excellent and congenial conference "Soul Matters: Plato and Platonists on the Nature of the Soul" in celebration of the seventieth birthday of John Finamore (December 2019, University of Michigan), at which an initial draft of this paper was presented. We also thank Danielle Layne for her assistance with this essay. We dedicate this chapter to John F. Finamore, with the deepest gratitude and thanks for his extensive and important work on Iamblichus, Proclus, theurgy, and Neoplatonism, which has consistently inspired our own research, his exemplary leadership of the International Society for Neoplatonic Studies, and most especially for his friendship, encouragement, and support over many decades. If friendship is important to philosophy (as most ancient philosophers considered it to be), John exemplifies and embodies this friendship.

1. Οἱ δὲ εἰς θείας ζωῆς ἐπίδειξιν τὸ τέλος ἀναφέροντες τῆς καθόδου. Ταύτην γὰρ εἶναι τὴν βούλησιν τῶν θεῶν, θεοὺς ἐκφαίνεσθαι διὰ τῶν ψυχῶν· προέρχονται γὰρ εἰς τοὐμφανὲς οἱ θεοὶ καὶ ἐπιδείκνυνται διὰ τῶν ψυχῶν καθαρᾶς καὶ ἀχράντου ζωῆς. The authors would like to thank Brill for permission to reproduce this quotation as an epigraph. All quotations and translations from *De anima* are from this edition.

souls from the Demiurge from eternity" (οἳ καὶ προήγαγον αὐτούς, ἀπὸ τοῦ δημιουργοῦ τὰς ψυχὰς παραλαμβάνοντες ἐξ αἰῶνος; *Frag. Ep.* 292c9–d1).[2] In good Platonic fashion, Julian emphasizes the importance of investigating the nature and faculties of the soul and its relationship to the body, as well as investigating all that precedes soul and is nobler and more divine, beginning from the traditional Delphic maxim "Know yourself":

> First, let us begin with "Know Thyself," since this precept is divinely inspired. It follows that he who knows himself will know about his soul and will know his body also. And it will not be enough to know that a human being is a soul employing a body, but he will also investigate the essential nature of the soul and then trace out its faculties. And not even this alone will be enough for him, but he will investigate whatever exists in us nobler and more divine than the soul, that something which we all believe in without being taught and regard as divine, and all in common supposed to be established in the heavens. (*Or.* 6.4.1 [183a7–c2])[3]

Julian interprets the Delphic maxim in a philosophical, specifically theurgic, sense: to know oneself is to know oneself as a soul *and* to understand one's body—an idea that reflects the inclusivity of the theurgic worldview—and to understand the nature of the soul, its faculties, and its divine causes through an ordered, ascending, and ever-deepening pattern of investigation. This essay aims to examine Julian's and Sallust's accounts of the nature of the soul and its ascent to the divine by means of theurgic rituals. *Theurgy*, literally meaning "god-working" or "divine work," designates a set of polytheistic ritual practices, especially those using several kinds of inspired divination such as oracles and statue animation for divinatory purposes (τελεστικά), coupled with a way of life based on ethical

---

2. Translation from Julian, *Letter to a Priest*, in vol. 2 of *The Works of the Emperor Julian*, ed. and trans. Wilmer Cave Wright (Cambridge: Harvard University Press, 1913), with slight modifications.

3. Ἀρξώμεθα δὲ πρῶτον ἀπὸ τοῦ «Γνῶθι σαυτόν», ἐπειδὴ καὶ θεῖόν ἐστι τοῦτο τὸ παρακέλευσμα. Οὐκοῦν ὁ γιγνώσκων αὐτὸν εἴσεται μὲν περὶ ψυχῆς, εἴσεται δὲ καὶ περὶ σώματος. Καὶ τοῦτο οὐκ ἀρκέσει μόνον ὡς ἔστιν ἄνθρωπος ψυχὴ χρωμένη σώματι μαθεῖν, ἀλλὰ καὶ αὐτῆς τῆς ψυχῆς ἐπελεύσεται τὴν οὐσίαν, ἔπειτα ἀνιχνεύσει τὰς δυνάμεις· καὶ οὐδὲ τοῦτο μόνον ἀρκέσει αὐτῷ, ἀλλὰ καὶ εἴ τι τῆς ψυχῆς ἐν ἡμῖν ἐστι κρεῖττον καὶ θειότερον, ὅπερ δὴ πάντες ἀδιδάκτως πειθόμενοι θεῖόν τι εἶναι νομίζομεν, καὶ τοῦτο ἐνιδρῦσθαι πάντες οὐρανῷ κοινῶς ὑπολαμβάνομεν. All translations of this work are drawn from Julian, *Oration VI: To the Uneducated Cynics*, in vol. 2 of Wright, *Works of the Emperor Julian*, with modifications.

and intellectual practices.[4] The goal of theurgy was the cumulative contact, assimilation, and ultimately union with the divine—the gods and the One—and thereby the divinization of the theurgist; or, in other words, the ascent of the soul to the divine realm and the consequent and spontaneous manifestation of the divine in embodied, human life (*De an.* 379.23–26).[5] It has often been noted that the emperor Julian follows Iamblichus closely in his endorsement of theurgy. Despite this, Julian's commitment to theurgy and its implications for and impact on his own religiosity and his imperial religious program (361–363 CE) are contested.[6] In an experimental and pluralistic style that we think that John Finamore would appreciate given his consistent encouragement of a diversity and plurality of voices in research and scholarship, this chapter also contains several voices. Drawing particularly on the prologue of Julian's *Hymn to King Helios, Hymn to the Mother of the Gods*, and several of his letters, Crystal Addey examines in the first half of the essay Julian's understanding of the relationship between the soul, theurgy, and traditional religious practices, all of which informed the emperor's religious restoration in the fourth century CE. In the final half of this essay, Jay Bregman explores Julian's and Sallust's approach toward myth, especially that of Cybele and Attis, and some of the ways in which their explication and defense of traditional myth supported the restoration of religious Hellenism.

Julian: Restorer of the Temples and Theurgist

Upon becoming emperor, Julian began his program of restoring traditional religion across the Roman Empire by restoring the temples and traditional rites, including the rites of sacrifice (Ammianus Marcellinus, *Res gest.* 22.5.2).[7] Any evaluation of the relationship between Julian's imperial

---

4. Crystal Addey, *Divination and Theurgy in Neoplatonism: Oracles of the Gods* (Farnham, UK: Ashgate, 2014), 3, 24.

5. See Addey, *Divination and Theurgy*, 25.

6. See Sean Tougher, *Julian the Apostate* (Edinburgh: Edinburgh University Press, 2007), 54–55, 58–62; Ilinca Tanaseanu-Döbler, *Theurgy in Late Antiquity: The Invention of a Ritual Tradition* (Göttingen: Vandenhoeck & Ruprecht, 2013), 136–37.

7. *AE* 1983: 285 (Thessalonica) (cited in Tougher, *Julian the Apostate*, 102) hails Julian as "restorer of the temples"; *CIL* 8.18529 (Cassae, Numidia) addresses Julian as "restorer of liberty and of the Roman religion." See Tougher, *Julian the Apostate*, 58–59, 102; Rowland Smith, *Julian's Gods: Religion and Philosophy in the Thought and Action of Julian the Apostate* (Abingdon: Routledge, 1995), 210–11.

pagan program of religious restoration and theurgy depends on the way(s) in which theurgy is defined, interpreted, and understood. Theurgy stands in a close relationship to traditional Mediterranean polytheistic religious traditions and practices and implies "a real religious commitment"—in our view, it does not represent the "invention of a ritual tradition," as Ilinca Tanaseanu-Döbler describes it, but rather the codification, preservation, and protection of a range of Mediterranean polytheistic ritual traditions— Egyptian, Chaldean or Assyrian, Greek, and others.[8] For later Neoplatonist philosophers, these traditional religions needed codifying, defending, and preserving because of the growing threat posed by the progressive Christianization of the empire through the fourth and fifth centuries CE, which increasingly threatened and marginalized traditional pagan religious practices and those who adhered to them. Thus, for Iamblichus and Proclus, theurgy was a restoration of the old ways, a way of following the ancestors and their modes of polytheistic, pagan ritual worship.[9] Iamblichus's *De mysteriis* draws a range of traditional, polytheistic religious practices— including the consultation of oracles, the use of dream incubation and divination, and the offering of sacrifices, to name but a few—under the aegis of theurgy.[10] Furthermore, Iamblichus identifies three levels or stages of worship appropriate for human beings at different stages of development in accordance with each human soul's level of ascent to the divine: (1) an immaterial form of worship for the most advanced humans who are purified from all generation, (2) a level or stage that is proper to souls who are not yet released from generation, and (3) a mixed form of worship

---

8. On theurgy as "a real religious commitment," see Jay Bregman, *Synesius of Cyrene: Philosopher-Bishop* (Berkeley: University of California Press, 1982), 47. On theurgy as the codification, preservation, and protection of traditional Mediterranean polytheistic religions, see Addey, *Divination and Theurgy*, 278–80. For the notion that theurgy was "the invention of a ritual tradition," see Tanaseanu-Döbler, *Theurgy in Late Antiquity*, 12–13 (and the title of this work).

9. For Proclus's piety and commitment to the stringent observance of ancestral rites and festivals of different polytheistic peoples and cultures as part of his theurgic practice, see Marinus, *Proclus or On Happiness*, in *Neoplatonic Saints: The Lives of Plotinus and Proclus by Their Students*, trans. Mark Edwards (Liverpool: Liverpool University Press, 2000), 18–19; see also Addey, *Divination and Theurgy*, 278–80.

10. For Iamblichus's commitment to and account of traditional religious practices and rituals, see *Myst.* 3, 5; dream incubation and divination: *Myst.* 3.2–3; divine inspiration and possession: *Myst.* 3.4–8; the use of divine possession in the rituals dedicated to the Korybantes, Sabazios, and the Great Mother (Cybele): *Myst.* 3.9; traditional oracles: *Myst.* 3.11; sacrifice: *Myst.* 5.

for humans at an intermediate stage of development (*Myst.* 5.15 [219.1–220.1]; 5.18). On this basis, Iamblichus defends the importance of sacrifice for all peoples, and thus defends the importance of all forms of traditional religious worship, which activate and catalyze human contact with the gods and the theurgic ascent of the soul:

> So, if one does not grant some such mode of worship [i.e., material and corporeal] to cities and peoples not freed from the fated processes of generation and from a society dependent on the body, one will contrive to fail of both types of good, both the immaterial and the material; for they are not capable of receiving the former, and for the latter they are not making the right offering. (*Myst.* 5.15 [220.1–5])[11]

Iamblichus then confirms that cultic, ritual action must be performed according to the level of development of the worshiper and that one should not overstep the measure proper to the sacrificing agent (*Myst.* 5.15 [220.5–7]). He also argues that sacrificial ritual must be offered in the appropriate form (either material or immaterial) according to the nature of the god worshiped; thus, theurgic ritual has to involve the worship of every level of gods in due order, including the cosmic gods who guard and preside over the material world, and thus material forms of ritual will be important even for the most developed and advanced theurgist (*Myst.* 5.14, 5.15 [220.8–4], 5.16–17, 5.19 [226.3–14], 5.20, 5.21 [229.10–230.11]). The philosophical rationale for this ordered worship of every type of god (cosmic, intermediate, and hypercosmic) is the total unity of spirit and action that must characterize theurgic ritual, according to Iamblichus, in imitation of the unbroken coherence and continuity of the cosmos, which necessarily entails a model of piety and respect for traditional religious practices (*Myst.* 5.26 [240.9–14]). Iamblichus envisages the cosmos as an inextricably connected community of gods and humans (and all other beings, including angels, *daimones*, heroes, animals, and plants) bound together

---

11. All translations of this work are drawn from Iamblichus, *De Mysteriis*, ed. and trans. Emma C. Clarke, John M. Dillon, and Jackson P. Hershbell, WGRW 4 (Atlanta: Society of Biblical Literature, 2003). τὰ δ' ἔνυλα καὶ σωματοειδῆ καὶ διὰ μεταβολῆς συνιστάμενα, οἷα τοῖς ἔτι κατεχομένοις ὑπὸ τοῦ σώματος ἁρμόζει. Πόλεσι τοίνυν καὶ δήμοις οὐκ ἀπολελυμένοις τῆς γενεσιουργοῦ μοίρας καὶ τῆς ἀντεχομένης τῶν σωμάτων κοινωνίας εἰ μὴ δώσει τις τὸν τοιοῦτον τρόπον τῆς ἁγιστείας, ἀμφοτέρων διαμαρτήσει, καὶ τῶν ἀύλων ἀγαθῶν καὶ τῶν ἐνύλων· τὰ μὲν γὰρ οὐ δύναται δέξασθαι, τοῖς δὲ οὐ προσάγει τὸ οἰκεῖον.

by divine love (θεία φιλία; *Myst.* 1.8 [28.1–6, 28.11–29.3], 1.9 [31.9–32.15], 1.12 [42.5–11], 1.14 [44.8–45.3], 1.19 [59.11–61.5], 3.20 [149.9–150.2], 5.9 [209.9–11], 5.10 [211.12–14], 5.14 [217.4–5], 5.20 [227.1–10]). In order to fulfill the theurgic goal of the manifestation of the divine in human life, the theurgist had to cultivate and develop an all-encompassing friendship (φιλία) and care for humanity (φιλανθρωπία), which includes the provision of effective cultic worship for all humanity (Iamblichus, *Myst.* 5.1 [199.5–10], 5.18, 5.22 [231.2–4], 5.26 [240.9–14]).[12]

In this sense, it is clear that the emperor Julian—with his imperial program for the restoration of traditional religion and his enthusiasm for sacrifice—was a devoted theurgist who followed Iamblichus closely. Julian's religious restoration is inextricably related to his theurgic approach and follows the inclusive approach toward theurgy evident in the philosophy of Iamblichus. It is also vital to appreciate the full implications of the fact that Julian had been educated and trained directly by theurgists who were the philosophic descendants of Iamblichus—Aedesius (Iamblichus's philosophic successor), and then Chrysanthius of Sardis and Maximus of Ephesus, who were the pupils of Aedesius and Sosipatra (Eunapius, *Vit. soph.* 7.1.5).[13] Eunapius relates the details of Julian's philosophic education prior to his becoming Caesar and then emperor. While Julian was a student of philosophy in Athens, he actively sought out the teaching and instruction of Aedesius, Iamblichus's direct philosophic successor. Julian traveled to Pergamon (the location of Aedesius's and Sosipatra's philosophical school) to ask Aedesius to teach him (*Vit. soph.* 7.1.8–13). After attending some of Aedesius's lectures, Aedesius (on account of his old age) sent Julian to his own pupils, Eusebius of Myndus and Chrysanthius of Sardis, to attend their philosophy classes (7.2.1). Based on Eusebius's recounting of Maximus of Ephesus's performance of theurgic ritual where he animated a statue of the goddess Hekate in her temple, Julian then

---

12. See Addey, *Divination and Theurgy*, 78–280.

13. It is important to note that Eunapius's reluctance throughout his work to use the term *theurgy* was undoubtedly related to historical circumstances at the time that he composed this work (ca. 396–405 CE)—when traditional pagan religious practices had been made illegal and many of the temples throughout the empire were being destroyed by the Christians, such as the Temple of Serapis at Alexandria, whose destruction Eunapius describes. Eunapius explicitly comments on Chrysanthius's expertise in divination, indicating his expertise in theurgy, and the theurgic nature of Maximus's activities are well-known.

actively sought out Maximus and was subsequently taught by him (7.2.2–13).[14] Moreover, both teachers played central roles in Julian's religious restoration—he appointed Chrysanthius as the high priest (ἀρχιερεύς) of Lydia, while Maximus acted consistently as his adviser (23.2.7–8).[15]

It is also interesting to note that during his time as a student in Pergamon, Julian visited Athens and conversed with the hierophant of the mystery cult at Eleusis (*Vit. soph.* 7.3.1–4). Although Eunapius does not name this hierophant, displaying the typical piety and reserve of an initiate of the mysteries, the approximate dating and timing of the episode confirms with almost certainty that this hierophant was Nestorius (hierophant of Eleusis, ca. 355–380 CE), a seer as well as a priest, who was either the father or the grandfather of Plutarch of Athens.[16] The identification is further supported by Eunapius's description of the hierophant's prophetic, mantic powers and predictions, given that Nestorius was known as a seer who is reported to have constructed a statue of Achilles and conducted telestic rites to save Athens from earthquakes.[17] This Nestorius apparently passed on his theurgic and ritual expertise to Plutarch, who then taught them to his own daughter Asclepigeneia, who subsequently trained Proclus in theurgic ritual.[18] Indeed, the Athenian school held Julian in great reverence; Marinus, for example, explicitly dates Proclus's death to the 124th year since Julian's imperial reign, indicating that the Athenian school used his accession specifically for recording significant events and as a form of chronology within the school (see Marinus, *Procl.* 36).[19]

---

14. See Polymnia Athanassiadi, *Julian: An Intellectual Biography* (Abingdon: Routledge, 1981), 32–33.

15. See Athanassiadi, *Julian: An Intellectual Biography*, 34.

16. See Marinus, *Procl.* 12, 28; Eunapius, *Vit. soph.* 7.3.1–5; Zosimus, *Hist. nov.* 4.18; Kevin Clinton, "The Sacred Officials of the Eleusinian Mysteries," *TAPS* 64.3 (1974): 43; Walter Burkert, *Ancient Mystery Cults* (Cambridge: Harvard University Press, 1987), 50, 85, 113–14; Smith, *Julian's Gods*.

17. See Zosimus, *Hist. nov.* 4.18.2–5, who attributes this account of Nestorius to Syrianus.

18. Marinus, *Procl.* 12 (trans. Edwards): Plutarch of Athens named as the son or grandson of Nestorius and takes Proclus into his home as his lodger; 28: Asclepigeneia trains Proclus in theurgy; Marinus states that "she alone preserved the rituals and the whole process of theurgy, passed on to her by her father from the great Nestorius."

19. I would like to thank Carlos Machado and Arsen Nisanyan for first bringing

Theurgy in Julian's Hymns

Two key sources for Julian's account of the nature and the theurgic ascent of the soul are his *Hymn to King Helios* (*Or.* 4), a work that tells us much about Iamblichus's lost work on the gods and is dedicated to his friend Sallust,[20] and his *Hymn to the Mother of the Gods* (*Or.* 5). Both are theurgic hymns and include prayers to the deities concerned (Julian, *Or.* 4 [145d]; direct prayer to Helios). Julian composed his *Hymn to the Mother of the Gods* by closely observing the *kairos*, which was a central element of theurgic ritual: he tells us that he wrote this hymn at the season (*kairos*) of her sacred rites (i.e., March at the spring equinox; *Or.* 5 [161c]). In doing so, Julian puts into practice Iamblichus's emphasis on the observation of the *kairos* as crucial for the efficacious performance of theurgic ritual: Iamblichus maintains that the Egyptians recommend that we ascend through the practice of sacred theurgy to the higher realms bringing nothing to bear but the critical time for action (*kairos*; Iamblichus, *Myst.* 8.4 [267.6–10]).[21] Moreover, Julian composed this hymn in Pessinus in Phrygia (while on his way to Persia in 362 CE), the very region where the cult of Cybele (the mother of the gods) originated.[22] Thus, Julian observes the *kairos* in a theurgic manner in its broadest sense in his composition of this hymn: that is to say, he composed the hymn at the most appropriate (kairotic) time, place, and context. In this sense, Julian demonstrates his theurgic expertise and follows Iamblichus closely, given that the latter construes the concept of the *kairos* in its widest sense to refer to the appropriate timing, place, *and* context of ritual (*Myst.* 8.4 [267.6–10], 5.23 [233.9–13]).[23]

---

to my attention Marinus's comment and its potential significance. See Smith, *Julian's Gods*, 23.

20. Citation of Iamblichus: Julian, *Or.* 4 (146a–b). Dedication to Sallust: see Julian, *The Works of the Emperor Julian*, trans. Wilmer Cave Wright (Cambridge: Harvard University Press, 1913), 1:351.

21. See also Eunapius, *Vit. soph.* 5.2.1–2, who reports that Iamblichus waited for the appropriate moment (*kairos*) before performing a ritual where he evoked two spirits, Eros and Anteros, from the baths at Gadara. See Crystal Addey, "Divination and the *kairos* in Ancient Greek Philosophy and Culture," in *Divination and Knowledge in Greco-Roman Antiquity*, ed. Crystal Addey (Abingdon: Routledge, 2021), 154.

22. Composition of the hymn in Pessinus, Phrygia: see Wright, *Oration VI*, 441.

23. See Addey, "Divination and the *kairos*," 154–55.

At the close of the *Hymn*, Julian prays directly to the goddess to grant him true knowledge of the gods as a fruit of his ritual worship and practice and to make him perfect in theurgy (Julian, *Or.* 5 [180b–c]).[24] In his *Hymn to Helios*, Julian claims that he is a follower of Helios and serves the god, thereby claiming that Helios-Apollo is his leader god, a profoundly theurgic idea. In a broader sense, Julian's claim also draws on Plato's portrayal of divine-human relationships in the myth of the *Phaedrus* (whereby each soul has a leader god or goddess whom he or she follows), and, more specifically, on Iamblichus's portrayal of Pythagoras as specially connected with Apollo in his *On the Pythagorean Way of Life* (discussed further below).

Both hymns discuss traditional religious practices in a theurgic and philosophical manner. The *Hymn to Helios* describes the essence, powers, and energies of the sun god, as well as his gifts to the intelligible and intellectual worlds and the material world of sense perception. It is structured according to Neoplatonic metaphysics and ontology, particularly the tripartite classification of being into essence-power-energy (see *Or.* 4 [132b]). Herein, Julian discusses Greek and Roman religious practices, as well as referring to Egyptian, Chaldean, and Phoenician religions in the manner of Iamblichus. Furthermore, a focus on divination, as an emanation of the forethought and providence (πρόνοια) of Helios-Apollo, permeates the hymn: both oracles of Apollo and astrology lie at the center of this hymn, and the importance of divination is centralized in accordance with theurgic practice.[25] Julian also relates Cybele's key role to the bestowal of providence (as will be discussed further below), thereby characterizing Helios-Apollo and Cybele as the mother and father deities of providence. The *Hymn to the Mother of the Gods* begins with the ritual of purification for the goddess (in the prologue) and then describes the introduction of her cult from Phrygia into Athens, alongside or together with the mysteries of the great mother, after the Athenians initially rejected Gallus and

---

24. See also 166a, where Julian states that Cybele—as the source of the intellectual and creative gods, who in turn guards the visible (cosmic) gods—brings to perfection all things that are made.

25. Julian, *Or.* 4 (144b), identifies or closely relates Helios to Apollo: "Apollo is the interpreter for us of the fairest purposes that are to be found with our god. Further Helios, since he comprehends in himself all the principles of the fairest intellectual synthesis, is himself Apollo the leader of the Muses," a clear reference to Apollo's divination. See also 144c. Unless otherwise noted, translations of this work are drawn from vol. 1 of Wright, *Works of the Emperor Julian*.

the cult (*Or.* 5 [158d–159a]). In an oracle, the Pythia at Delphi advises the Athenians to propitiate the consequent anger of the mother of the gods (159b). Then, Julian relates how Apollo, in another oracle, advised the Romans to bring the statue of the goddess from Phrygia as an ally for their war against the Carthaginians and gives an account of the arrival of the cult statue into Rome (ca. 204 BCE; *Or.* 5 [159c]).[26] As the people and Senate of Rome, including all the priests and priestesses, go to the Tiber to meet the boat carrying the statue, Julian tells us:

> But the goddess, as though she desired to show the Roman people that they were not bringing a lifeless image from Phrygia, but that what they had received from the Phrygians and were now bringing home possessed greater and more divine powers, stayed the ship directly she touched the Tiber, and she was suddenly as though rooted in mid-stream.[27] (*Or.* 5 [160a–b; Rochefort 2.15–20])

Julian then relates that the Romans tried both to tow the ship and to push it, as well as bringing every possible device to move the statue and the boat, but the goddess remained immovable. After a while the Romans began to blame Claudia, who held the most sacred office of priestess in Rome, and accused her of being impure—when Claudia saw that this charge was growing and gaining strength, she took off her girdle and fastened it around the ship and then prayed to the goddess, begging her to let the priestess tow the ship if innocent of the charges; Claudia then managed to move and tow the ship singlehandedly. Further to his earlier comment about the cult statue, Julian concludes from this episode that the goddess showed the Romans that her statue was "not human,

---

26. In order to explicate Julian's description of the efficacy of the image of Cybele upon her arrival at Rome, Thomas Taylor notes his friend "Sallust's (*On the Gods and the World*) theory of statues, designed according to divine imitation and similitude; he contrasted this sharply to the false theory of images of Saints; the former being 'beautifully pious' the latter '… impious … full of delusion.'" Thomas Taylor, *Two Orations of the Emperor Julian* (repr. Kila, Montana, 1932), 103. See also Sallustius, *On the Gods and the World*, trans. Thomas Taylor (London: Facsimilie Reprint, 1976).

27. All translations of this work are taken from vol. 1 of Wright, *Works of the Emperor Julian*. Ἡ δὲ ὥσπερ ἐνδείξασθαι τῷ Ῥωμαίων ἐθέλουσα δήμῳ ὅτι μὴ ξόανον ἄγουσιν ἀπὸ τῆς Φρυγίας ἄψυχον, ἔχει δὲ ἄρα δύναμίν τινα μείζω καὶ θειοτέραν ὃ δὴ παρὰ τῶν Φρυγῶν λαβόντες ἔφερον, ἐπειδὴ τοῦ Τύβριδος ἥψατο, τὴν ναῦν λαβόντες ἔφερον, ἐπειδὴ τοῦ Τύβριδος ἥψατο, τὴν ναῦν ἵστησιν ὥσπερ ῥιζωθεῖσαν ἐξαίφνης, κατὰ τοῦ Τύβριδος.

but truly divine, not lifeless clay but a thing possessed of life and divine powers" (*Or.* 6 [161a; Wright]).[28] Julian also draws the conclusion that the goddess revealed to the Romans that none of them could be good or bad without her knowing, thereby connecting appropriate forms of ritual practice with the prerequisite of virtue and ethics in a typically theurgic manner, highlighting the close relationship between ethics and theurgy. Note that for both the Greeks and Romans, an oracle commands them to introduce the cult of the goddess and that Julian mentions the divine nature, powers, and life of the cult statue several times in his account. Both ideas, of course, are fully in line with the key idea of the theurgists that the gods themselves advise the appropriate ritual modes of worship in oracles and that cult statues are not lifeless but full of the divine.[29] Here, we see that theurgy and traditional religion are intimately related, even synonymous, with theurgy lying at the heart—the center—of traditional religious practices.

Julian on the Nature and Theurgic Ascent of the Soul

In the same work, Julian exhorts the reader to purify the eyes of the soul, suggesting that the proper catharsis in order to do so consists in a conversion of the soul to itself—a turning inward—and a perception that soul is a kind of mold or likeness of the Forms that are embodied in matter, the place of forms in potency, not in actuality, until independent from matter, fully developed, and illuminated by Intellect, she achieves perfect actuality (*Or.* 5 [163a–165a]). More interesting than the standard Platonism outlined above is the connection of the soul with the Chaldean Oracles and theurgic rites, the goal of which was the ascent of the soul to the divine via the cumulative contact, assimilation, and union with the gods and ultimately with the One.[30] For example, when quoting the Oracles directly, Julian states, "Through the holy rites not only the soul, but even the body is thought worthy of much help and salvation: 'Save also the mortal covering of bitter matter,' the gods announce to the

---

28. οὐδὲ ὡς ἀνθρώπινον τοῦτον, ἀλλὰ ὄντως θεῖον, οὐδὲ ἄψυχον γῆν, ἀλλὰ ἔμπνουν τι χρῆμα καὶ δαιμόνιον

29. On Iamblichus's approach toward the use of statue animation and divination by statues, which Julian follows closely, see Iamblichus, *Myst.* 5.23 (233.9–234.4); *Vit. Pyth.* 28.151; Addey, *Divination and Theurgy*, 252–55.

30. See Tanaseanu-Döbler, *Theurgy in Late Antiquity*, 138–40.

most holy of the theurgists when they are encouraging them" (Chald. Or. frag. 129 [Majercik]).[31] In *Or.* 5, Julian quotes this oracle as confirmation of the ways in which the salvation of the soul saves and gives health to the body as well:

> For when the soul abandons herself wholly to the gods, and entrusts her own concerns absolutely to the greater kinds, and then follows the sacred rites—these too being preceded by the divine ordinances—then, I say, there is nothing to hinder or prevent—for all things reside in the gods, all things subsist in relation to them, all things are filled with the gods—straightaway the divine light illuminates our souls. And thus, endowed with divinity, they impart a certain vigour and energy to the breath [πνεῦμα] implanted in them by nature, and so that breath is hardened as it were and strengthened by the soul and gives health to the whole body.[32] (*Or.* 5 [178b–c; Rochefort 18.14–24; trans. Wright, with modifications)

Julian's words echo Iamblichus's terminology of the divine illuminating human souls almost verbatim; further, he echoes Iamblichus's point that works of theurgy are established in intellectual laws, and thus inferior, or posterior, levels of reality are neutralized by a greater order and power (*Myst.* 8.8). In the same work, Julian comments explicitly on the theurgic rituals established by Julian the Chaldean to celebrate the god of the seven rays and his elevation or uplifting of human souls to the invisible, intelligible realm:

> And if I should also touch on the secret teaching of the Mysteries, in which the Chaldean, divinely frenzied, celebrated the God of the Seven Rays, that god through whom he lifts up the souls of humans, I should be

---

31. ὅτι διὰ τῆς αγιστείας οὐχ ἡ ψυχή μόνον, ἀλλὰ καὶ τὰ σώματα βοηθείας πολλῆς καὶ σωτηρίας ἀξιοῦται, "σώζετε καὶ τὸ πικρᾶς ὕλης περίβλημα βρότειον," οἱ θεοὶ τοῖς ὑπεράγνοις παρκελεθυόμενοι τῶν θεουργῶν κατεπαγγέλονται.

32. "Ὅταν γὰρ ἡ ψυχὴ πᾶσαν ἑαυτὴν δῷ τοῖς θεοῖς ὅλα τὰ καθ' ἑαυτὴν ἐπιτρέψασα τοῖς κρείττοσιν, ἑπομένης, οἶμαι, τῆς ἑαυτὴν ἐπιτρέψασα τοῖς κρείττοσιν, ἑπομένης, οἶμαι, τῆς ἁγιστείας καὶ πρό γε ταύτης τῶν θείων θεσμῶν ἡγουμένων, ὄντος ὐδενὸς λοιπὸν τοῦ ἀπείργοντος καὶ ἐμποδίζοντος—πάντα γάρ ἐστιν ἐν τοῖς θεοῖς καὶ πάντα περὶ αὐτοὺς ὑφέστηκε καὶ «πάντα τῶν θεῶν ἐστι πλήρη»—αὐτίκα μὲν αὐταῖς ἐλλάμπει τὸ θεῖον φῶς, θεωθεῖσαι δὲ αὗται τόνον τινὰ καὶ ῥώμην ἐπιτιθέασι τῷ συμφύτῳ πνεύματι, τοῦτο δὲ ὑπ' αὐτῶν στομούμενον ὥσπερ καὶ κρατυνόμενον σωτηρίας ἐστὶν αἴτιον ὅλῳ τῷ σώματι,

saying what is unintelligible, indeed wholly unintelligible to the common herd, but familiar to the blessed theurgists. (Julian, *Or.* 5 [172d–173a2; Rochefort 12.28–32; trans. Wright with slight modifications]) [33]

That Julian's account faithfully reflects the Chaldean system is confirmed by the injunction in fragment 110 of the Oracles to seek out the "channel" or "solar" ray of the soul (ψυχῆς ὀχετόν) and to discover how to elevate the soul through this solar ray by using ritual action. Helios-Apollo—the god of the seven rays—is most especially related to the theurgic elevation of the soul in this passage; and, of course, it is Apollo who is the god of both divination and philosophy, the means by which the soul can attain assimilation to the divine by becoming like the divine and thus come to see and know the gods. In theurgic terms, it is the sun god who enables the eyes of the soul to see. Paradoxically, the soul who has developed its eyes most fully is also the soul who sees all things for "what they really are" in Platonic terms—the philosopher does not see the object as purely material but as enformed matter expressing immaterial Forms. Further, all things are seen as connected with the divine, and the theurgist no longer considers anything purely matter: for the theurgist, the statue is not just wood and precious metals but the showing forth of the goddess, an animated and inspired divine epiphany. This is exemplified in the hymn by the immovability of the statue of Cybele and the showing forth of the goddess through the temporary, superhuman strength of the priestess Claudia.

---

33. εἰ δὲ καὶ τῆς ἀρρήτου μυσταγωγίας ἁψαίμην, ἣν ὁ Χαλδαῖος περὶ τὸν ἑπτάκτινα θεὸν ἐβάκχευσεν, ἀνάγων δι᾽ αὐτοῦ τὰς ψυχάς, ἄγνωστα ἐρῶ, καὶ μάλα γε ἄγνωστα τῷ συρφετῷ, θεουργοῖς δὲ τοῖς μακαρίοις γνώριμα· See Anne Sheppard, *Studies on the Fifth and Sixth Essays of Proclus' Commentary on the Republic*, HH 61 (Göttingen: Vandenhoeck & Ruprecht, 1980), 156–57. Sheppard briefly discusses Julian's description of the Chaldean Oracles, in *Or.* 5 (172d), as ineffable mystery teachings, and, in *Or.* 7 (215c–216d), Julian's division of philosophy into branches of which theology is the highest, concerned with initiation and mysteries. Sheppard states that within the same work (235a ff.), "Julian describes his own education in philosophy in terms of initiation into the mysteries. It is this education which, he claims, has made him adopt the right attitude to myths and poetry" (*Studies on the Fifth and Sixth Essays*, 156). Following Iamblichus, then, Julian has already anticipated "all the elements of Proclus' use of mystery language ... although not systematically organised or developed in detail" (156–57).

The emperor Julian, referring to his namesake Julian the Chaldean (ὁ Χαλδαῖος), characterizes the Chaldean tradition as a mystery cult. Several fragments of the Oracles explicitly refer to theurgic ritual practices and characterize the praxis using mystery cult terminology (frags. 132, 133, 135).[34] Furthermore, the Suda characterizes Julian the Chaldean as the preserver and safeguard of "the Chaldean initiations" (τὰ τελεσιουργικὰ Χαλδαϊκά, Suda 2.641.33–34 [no. 433]). Eunapius presents Sosipatra, a female philosopher, prophetess, and theurgist who married Iamblichus's student Eustathius, as trained and initiated by Chaldean prophets, who characterize the Chaldean tradition as a mystery cult (Vit. soph. 6.7.1–2, 6.7.8–9). Proclus also frequently describes the Chaldean tradition as a mystery cult using the terminology of "initiations and mysteries" (see, e.g., Proclus, Comm. in R. 6.1, 110). This view of the Chaldean Oracles correlates closely with the Neoplatonic views of theurgy as a mystery cult.[35] Indeed, Julian himself describes Iamblichus as a "hierophant" (ἱεροφάντης).[36] In a historical sense, theurgy was influenced by the soteriological focus of (some) mystery cults, but in a psychological sense theurgy was seen as the paradigm of all mystery cults, as embodying a higher religious wisdom derived from divinatory messages of the gods. For Iamblichus and his followers, theurgy entailed real contact with the gods and elicited a religious experience that was held to be similar or identical to that experienced by the initiate in mystery cults.

Sallust and Julian on the Ascent of the Soul and the Myth of Cybele and Attis

Sallust further explicated and worked out Julian's ideas concerning the nature and destiny of the individual soul in his handbook of religious

---

34. Scholars who have worked most extensively on the Chaldean Oracles have placed them within the context of a mystery cult: see Hans Lewy, Chaldean Oracles and Theurgy: Mysticism, Magic and Platonism in the Later Roman Empire (Paris: Études Augustiniennes, 1978), 38–39, 177, 210–11; Ruth Majercik, ed. and trans., The Chaldean Oracles (Leiden: Brill, 1989), 5; Tanseanu-Döbler, Theurgy in Late Antiquity, 31.

35. See, e.g., Proclus, Comm. Crat. 100.20–101.5; Julian, Or. 5 (172d5–173a, 2180b); see also Addey, Divination and Theurgy, 33–34.

36. Julian, frag. 4, in The Works of the Emperor Julian, vol. 3, Letters; Epigrams; Against the Galileans; Fragments, trans. Wilmer Cave Wright (Cambridge: Harvard University Press, 1923), 297.

(polytheistic) Hellenism titled *On the Gods and the Cosmos*, sometimes referred to as the "catechism of the pagan empire."[37] In chapter 8, subtitled "Concerning Intellect and Soul and that the Soul is immortal," he places a power—the intellectual nature (*he noera physis*)[38] below being (*ousia*) but above soul, which derives its noeric status from the noetic but completes the soul—as the sun completes the eyes in allowing them to realize their potential. Thomas Taylor considered Sallust's work suited to the intermediate class of souls, neither noetics nor hylics but rather psychics, who are able to reach the level of discursive reason—and perhaps, if they accept the axioms without grasping them, are able to infer that the noetic exists, but not how or why. These stages of the soul's development draw on and clearly match those set out by Iamblichus (as discussed above; Iamblichus, *Myst.* 5.15 [219.1–220.1], 5.18).

Sallust posits different orders of gods to create the rational and irrational souls. The soul is connected with and worships its proper gods. When irrational, the soul lives the life of sense and imagination. When rational, it lives the life that controls sense and imagination and uses reason (Sallust, *Diis mund.* 8.39.1–3, 40.1). He delineates five powers of the soul: intellect, discursive reason, opinion, the "image-making" faculty or imagination (*phantasia*), and sense (8.38–40). He attempts a basic proof of the soul's immortality: "But it is necessary that the rational soul should be immortal, because it knows the gods; for nothing mortal knows that which is immortal" (8.41.7–11). This of course draws on the demonstrations of Julian regarding the soul's likeness to the Forms because it can apprehend them, taken ultimately from Plato's argument from similarity (often referred to as the affinity argument) as a proof for the immortality of the soul in the *Phaedo* (*Phaed.* 78b–84b). The soul is not in the body but uses it as an instrument. If the soul is made to err by the body, that is not surprising, for the arts cannot perform their work when the instruments are defective.

Julian's cosmos is an ensouled being, but he does not have much to say about the world soul. Focused on Helios as center of the intellectual gods and his demiurgic functions, the activities of goddesses attached to Helios, such as Athena and Aphrodite, interpreted Neoplatonically, are much like those attributed to the world soul (*Or.* 4 [142a, 149b–150c]). Sallust, in chap-

---

37. See, e.g., Wright, *Oration VI*, 351, quoting F. Cumont.

38. See Proclus, *Elements of Theology* 20; Sallustius, *On the Gods and the World*, trans. Gilbert Murray, in *Five Stages of Greek Religion*, by Gilbert Murray (Oxford: Clarendon, 1925), 198 n. 6.

ter 6, titled "Concerning the Hyper-Cosmic and Cosmic Gods," provides a clear, compressed, and cogent account of this form of Iamblichean allegory.

Sallust's cosmic gods are composed of four groups—each of which has a beginning, middle, and end—creator gods, vivifying, harmonizing, and guardian gods: (1) creators—Zeus, Poseidon, Hephaistos; (2) vivifying—Demeter, Hera, and Artemis, who function at the cosmic level of the world soul; (3) harmonizing—Apollo, Aphrodite, and Hermes; and (4) guardian gods—Hestia, Athena, and Ares (perhaps to be thought of as also at the level of Nature—the lower world soul, as it were; Sallust, *Diis mund.* 6.28–30). The Olympians (at this level) are intellectual (noeric) gods. The creators, like Attis, are at the cusp of the visible cosmos and therefore close to the world soul. Zeus confers being, Poseidon presides over matter (the waters), Hephaistos informs matter, as fire energizes. The animating goddesses perform the basic work of soul, animating the cosmos as one living being: Demeter as the life of the cosmos, derived from Life itself; Hera as the Air; and Artemis, identified with the moon, presides over the sublunary natural world. The harmonizing and guardian divinities, also noeric, may also be thought of as closely associated with the World Soul.[39]

So what has this to do with ritual and its value? Sallust explains the Platonic principle of myth: these narratives never occurred at a particular time but *always are* and as such must be honored via the soul's reenactment, a process of becoming like the divine. Mind sees all things at once, but discursive reason expresses some first, others after.[40] Our ritual—like the myth, that accords with the cosmos—imitates the cosmos. We fallen souls live in despondency and so we must recreate, in ritual, the lives of individual deities such as Cybele, the venerated mother of the gods in Julian's work, and Attis, her unfortunate lover.

In the myth, Cybele sees Attis by the River Gallus and falls in love with him, places a starry cap on his head (interpreted as the Milky Way by

---

39. The twelve Olympians also contain other gods; Dionysius in Zeus, Asclepius in Apollo, and the Graces in Aphrodite. Dionysius and Apollo are, according to Julian, savior figures who descend to earth. John Finamore argues that Asclepius is a perfect soul, akin to the soul of a perfect human, such as Romulus and Heracles, rather than a god. See Finamore, "Julian and the Descent of Asclepius," *JNS* 7.2 (1999): 82, 86.

40. Sallust, *Diis mund.* 4.20.3–10: "because they have a perpetuity of subsistence." See Taylor's note, "This explanation of the fable is agreeable to that of the Emperor Julian in his Oration to the mother of the gods, my translation of which let the reader consult" (*On the Gods and the World*, 20).

Julian and Sallust), and lives together with him. But Attis descends into a cave, falls in love with a nymph, and deserts Cybele in order to live with the nymph. Cybele causes Attis to become insane, and he cuts off his genitalia, which he leaves with the nymph and then returns to Cybele (*Or.* 5 [165b–166a]; Sallust, *Diis mund.* 4.27–32). In the ritual to celebrate the Magna Mater—the Great Mother, Cybele (the Metroac rites)—in Rome, the descent and ascent of the individual embodied soul corresponds to the descent of Attis into the cave and his return to Cybele. The infamous tree-cutting indicative of the rites of Cybele in Rome, discussed by Julian, invokes the invaluable nature of fasting and withholding further generation.[41] Julian interprets the sacred felling of the pine tree allegorically—as a symbolic teaching of the gods to humans to "pluck the fairest fruits from the earth, namely, virtue and piety, and offer them to the goddess to be the symbol of our well-ordered constitution here on earth" and to strive upward to reach the goddess, just as the tree strives upward in its growth (*Or.* 5 [169a3–c1]). After that, the surviving texts mention the feeding on milk, a likely symbol for being born again; finally, in the Hilaria ritual, there is feasting, rejoicing, and garlands, as it were, and, as such, a symbolic return to the gods.[42] Julian's Attis is the "third Demiurge," who (like the world soul) contains the separate *logoi* of the forms embodied in matter. He is functionally almost indistinguishable from the world soul or perhaps the "lower part" thereof, Nature (*Or.* 5 [161d–162a; see also 162a–165a]). In said ritual, he returns to the mother.

Beyond Attis, though, is Cybele, the mother of the gods, who is the source of the demiurgic and intellectual gods governing the visible gods (*Or.* 5 [166a]). Mother and spouse, hypostasized and enthroned with Zeus, she is a kind of demiurge. Mistress of life and cause of all generation, she easily perfects the things that are made and painlessly generates, with Zeus, and molds the things that are (*Or.* 5 [166a]). Having received all the divine causes, noetic and hypercosmic, she is the source (πηγή) of the noeric gods. Julian explains the meaning of the rites according to Neoplatonic allegory. As mentioned above, the ritual orients us to reap the virtue

---

41. A pine tree sacred to Attis was cut down on 22 March and carried to the temple of Cybele. See Wright, *Oration VI*, 271 n. 1.

42. On 25 March (the spring or vernal equinox), the return of Attis to Cybele and the freeing of our souls from generation was celebrated by the feast of the Hilaria: see Wright, *Oration VI*, 471 n. 5.

and piety of our constitution (πολιτεία) on earth and to strive upward to the goddess, principle of life (ζωογόνον; *Or.* 5 [169b–c]).

During the part of the ritual called *arbor intrat* ("the tree enters"), the Romans cut down a pine tree. The following day of the festival involved the castration of the Galli, the priests of Attis, which symbolizes and reenacts the castration of Attis, and—following this—trumpet sounds functioned as a recall for Attis and for all souls, awakening the Attis-like soul to its descent or fall (*Or.* 5 [169c2–5]). Attis, then, functions like the world soul, in moving/falling or descending and thus making possible time, space, and motion. But, having fallen too far, he turns back to the mother of the gods and then—ultimately—to the One. So, our fallen souls, imitating this divine pattern, turn back from the unlimited toward the hypostases—*nous*-defined and unified—and even the One (*Or.* 5 [169c2–d9]). The sounding of the trumpet within the theurgic ritual acts as an acoustic reminder of the divine causes, stimulating the desire to return to them (*Or.* 5 [168c10–11, 169c2–d1]). As he says of Attis:

> And never did this happen save in the manner that it happens now; but forever is Attis the servant and charioteer of the Mother; forever he yearns passionately towards generation; and forever he cuts short his unlimited course through the cause whose limits are fixed, even the cause of the forms. In like manner the myth says he is led upwards as though from our earth, and again resumes his ancient sceptre and dominion: not that he ever lost it, or ever loses it now, but the myth says he lost it on account of his union with that which is subject to passion and change.[43] (*Or.* 5 [171c7–d7])

Julian himself is grateful to all the gods but above all to Cybele, the mother of the gods, for not disregarding him when he walked in darkness, an allusion to his early days as a Christian in his childhood and early youth (*Or.* 5 [174b9–c3]; *Or.* 4 [131a]). She did not ask him to cut off a part of his body but only the superfluous and vain irrational desires and motions of the psyche, through the intellectual cause subsisting prior to our souls (i.e., Attis; *Or.* 5 [174c3–9]). In Julian's final summary of the myth and ritual,

---

43. Καὶ οὐδέποτε γέγονεν ὅτε μὴ ταῦτα τοῦτον ἔχει τὸν τρόπον ὅνπερ νῦν ἔχει, ἀλλ' ἀεὶ μὲν Ἄττις ἐστὶν ὑπουργὸς τῇ Μητρὶ καὶ ἡνίοχος, ἀεὶ δὲ ὀργᾷ εἰς τὴν γένεσιν, ἀεὶ δὲ ἀποτέμνεται τὴν ἀπειρίαν διὰ τῆς ὡρισμένης τῶν εἰδῶν αἰτίας. Ἐπαναγόμενος δὲ ὥσπερ ἐκ γῆς τῶν ἀρχαίων αὖθις λέγεται δυναστεύειν σκήπτρων, ἐκπεσὼν μὲν αὐτῶν οὐδαμῶς οὐδὲ ἐκπίπτων, ἐκπεσεῖν δὲ αὐτῶν λεγόμενος διὰ τὴν πρὸς τὸ παθητὸν σύμμιξιν.

Attis is the immediate creator of the material world, who descends to the lowest limits and is checked by the demiurgic motions of Helios, as he reaches the equinox (*Or.* 5 [175a1–b2]). The castration means the suspension (ἐποχή) of the limitless, by the summoning and resurrection of Attis to the elder (πρεσβυτέρας) and seminal ruling causes (ἀρχηγικωτέρας). The aim (σκοπός) of the sacred rite is the ascent (ἄνοδος) of our souls (*Or.* 5 [175b2–8]).[44]

Conclusion

Julian's commitment to theurgy affected his religious pagan restoration greatly. In following Iamblichus's emphasis on the inclusivity of theurgy as a set of practices both necessary and suitable for all humans and human communities, Julian held that the codification, preservation, and protection of traditional Mediterranean polytheistic religious practices was central to theurgic praxis. Julian's theurgic hymns, especially the *Hymn to the Mother of the Gods*, relate the nature, destiny, and ascent of the human soul to theurgic practice, and his *Hymn to King Helios* characterizes theurgy as a mystery cult. Yet within these works, Julian's approach is to include traditional religious practices within the ambit of theurgy, such as the introduction of the cult of Cybele into Rome and the movement of her statue, and the myth of Cybele and Attis, which in allegorical terms is conceived as symbolizing the related and dynamic nature of procession and reversion, both metaphysically (hypostatically) and in relation to the descent and ascent of the soul.[45]

In the works of Julian and Sallust, the myth of Cybele and Attis is about the fall and rise of the soul, both in the sense of hypostatic procession and reversion and its recapitulation within the individual soul. We are each of us an intelligible world. Like all the myths, it hides the truth from the uninitiated, behind enigmatic Platonic allegorical symbolism. Allegories of myth began early in the classical period but intensified and changed their function in later times. In Plato's world, Homer had no serious competition (*pace* the Mysteries). He permeated that world, and the radical Plato could criticize him and suggest that he should be banned from Kallipolis, the ideal *polis*. At the same time, Plato, who seems to have

44. See Athanassiadi, *Julian: An Intellectual Biography*, 145.
45. See Athanassiadi, *Julian: An Intellectual Biography*, 142–46.

had an agonistic relationship with the poets, wrote his own dialogue, tragedy and comedy, made up his own myths, and employed mystery language and Orphic eschatology. But in late antiquity Homer, as scripture, had to be right on some level. Neoplatonist philosophers, such as Porphyry and Proclus, knew that an important element in preserving Hellenism was allegorizing Homer. Rather than kick him out of the city, revalorization was the order of the day.[46] Proclus, in the tradition of Julian and Sallust, was careful to find clever ways to reinterpret the passages on Homer and Plato's intention in his *Commentary on the Republic*.[47] During the religious

---

46. Two useful works that explicate the allegorical approach of late antique Neoplatonists to myths, mysteries, and revelatory texts are Luc Brisson, *How Philosophers Saved Myths: Allegorical Interpretation and Classical Mythology*, trans. Catherine Tihanyi (Chicago: University of Chicago Press, 2008), and Sheppard, *Studies on the Fifth and Sixth Essays*. Brisson argues that later Platonist philosophers rescued and revalorized myth using mystical forms of allegory that were "rooted in the conviction that myths and mysteries should be looked upon as two complementary means used by God to reveal truth to religious souls" (*How Philosophers Saved Myths*, 2). He also outlines the transition from Stoic to Platonic forms of allegory (56–86), which move from physical and ethical to mystagogic, metaphysical, and "mysterial," beginning with Philo of Alexandria and the Middle Platonists, including Plutarch, and the (neo-)Pythagorean philosophers Numenius and Cronius, through to Plotinus and Porphyry (61–63). Brisson argues that Plutarch of Chaeronea represents the transition from Stoic to Platonic forms of allegory (63–71). On Porphyry's use of allegory in his treatise *On the Cave of the Nymphs*, see also Addey, *Divination and Theurgy*, 43–71. It is also important to note that although Iamblichus does not allegorize Homer in his extant works, he does offer allegorical explanations of Egyptian symbols, specifically the god sitting on a lotus and the sun god sailing across the sky in the solar barque: see *Myst.* 7.22 (250.10–251.13; 251.14–253.1).

47. Brisson analyzes Proclus's use of allegory within the wider context of the Neoplatonic School of Athens and concludes, "The ambition of Proclus ...was to organize the life of his school, its curriculum, and the production of its works, so as to keep up the spiritual vitality of paganism and prepare for the future. Proclus attempted to reach this objective by seeking the harmony between Platonic theology and all the other Greek and Barbarian theologies" (*How Philosophers Saved Myths*, 106). The emperor Julian and Sallust, following Iamblichus, display some of the systematic approach later developed in much greater detail by Proclus, although Brisson does not analyze their allegorical accounts and exegesis. Sheppard, on the other hand, briefly analyzes Julian's approach in *Or.* 5: see n. 34 above (*Studies on the Fifth and Sixth Essays*, 156–57). She also examines Proclus's approach toward allegory and his use of mystery language. In particular, she answers in the affirmative her own question as to whether Iamblichus and Proclus really thought of progress in philosophy as a kind of progress in the mysteries: "When Iamblichus describes progress in philosophy as progressive initiation

crisis of the fourth century and beyond, the Neoplatonic interpretation and revalorization of myth, undertaken in the service of the restoration of pagan religious traditions and ritual, was a central and urgent task for these late antique theurgic Hellenes.

Bibliography

Primary Sources

Adler, Ada, ed. *Suidae Lexicon*. 4 vols. Leipzig: Teubner, 1928–1938.

Ammianus Marcellinus. *History*. Vol. 2, *Books 20–26*. Translated by John C. Rolfe. Cambridge: Harvard University Press, 1940.

The Chaldean Oracles. Edited and translated by Ruth Majercik. Leiden: Brill, 1989.

Eunapius. *Lives of the Philosophers and Sophists*. Translated by Wilmer C. Wright. Cambridge: Harvard University Press, 1921.

———. *Lives of the Philosophers and Sophists* (*Vitae Sophistarum*). Edited by J. Giangrade. Rome: Polygraphica, 1956.

Iamblichus. *De Anima*. Edited and translated by John F. Finamore and John M. Dillon. Leiden: Brill, 2002.

———. *De Mysteriis*. Edited by Éduoard Des Places. Paris: Belles Lettres, 1966.

———. *De Mysteriis*. Edited and translated by Emma C. Clarke, John M. Dillon, and Jackson P. Hershbell. WGRW 4. Atlanta: Society of Biblical Literature, 2003.

---

into the mysteries in *Vita Pythagorica* Ch. 17 he is following the traditional use of such language, although his belief in theurgy would give it a special meaning for him" (156). In conclusion, she succinctly sums up Proclus's worldview: "Proclus saw the traditional mystery language of Greek philosophy with the eyes of one who believed in the practice of theurgy and in the possibility of mystical experience. The metaphor therefore had a precise meaning for him and he used it in a variety of ways. In Proclus' thought everything really does reflect everything else. Like a modern structuralist he finds the same underlying pattern in the mysteries, in theurgy, in philosophy, in language, in myth, and in the world as a whole. The principles behind the use of *symbola* in theurgy are also the principles behind Proclus' interpretation of poetic myths and so he can transfer language from the one sphere into the other and use mystery-language to provide a terminology for allegory" (161).

——. *On the Pythagorean Way of Life (De Vita Pythagorica)*. Edited and translated by John M. Dillon and Jackson P. Hershbell. Atlanta: Scholars Press, 1991.

Julian. *Letter to a Priest*. Edited and translated by Wilmer Cave Wright. In *The Works of the Emperor Julian*. Vol. 2. Cambridge: Harvard University Press, 1913.

——. *Letters. Epigrams. Against the Galileans. Fragments*. Translated by Wilmer Cave Wright. In *The Works of the Emperor Julian*. Vol. 3. Cambridge: Harvard University Press, 1923.

——. *Oration IV: Hymn to King Helios; Oration V: Hymn to the Mother of the Gods*. Edited and translated by Gabriel Rochefort. In *L'empereur Julien: Oeuvres complètes*. Vol. 2.1. Paris: Les Belles Lettres, 1963.

——. *Oration VI: To the Uneducated Cynics*. Edited and translated by Wilmer Cave Wright. In *The Works of the Emperor Julian*. Vol. 2. Cambridge: Harvard University Press, 1913.

——. *Orations I–V*. Translated by Wilmer Cave Wright. In *The Works of the Emperor Julian*. Vol. 1. Cambridge: Harvard University Press, 1913.

——. *Two Orations of the Emperor Julian*. Translated by Thomas Taylor. Repr., Kila, MT, 1932.

Marinus. *Proclus or On Happiness*. Translated by Mark Edwards. In *Neoplatonic Saints: The Lives of Plotinus and Proclus by Their Students*. Liverpool: Liverpool University Press, 2000.

——. *Proclus ou Sur le bonheur*. Edited and translated by Henri-Dominique Saffrey and Alain-Philippe Segonds. Paris: Les Belles Lettres, 2001.

Origen. *Against Celsus*. Edited and translated by Henry Chadwick. Cambridge: Cambridge University Press, 1980.

Plato. *Phaedo*. In *Euthyphro, Apology, Crito, Phaedo, Phaedrus*. Edited and translated by Harold North Fowler. Cambridge: Harvard University Press, 1914.

Porphyry. *Contra Christianos*. In *Porphyrius, Gegen die Christen*. Edited by Adolf von Harnack. Berlin: Reimer, 1916.

Proclus. *The Elements of Theology*. Edited and translated by Eric R. Dodds. Oxford: Clarendon, 1933.

——. *In Platonis Cratylum commentaria*. Translated by Francesco Romano. Rome: Bretschnieder, 1989.

——. *In Platonis rem publicam commentaria*. Edited by Wilhelm Kroll. 2 vols. Leipzig: Teubner, 1899–1901.

Sallustius. *Concerning the Gods and the Universe* (*De Diis et Mundo*). Edited and translated by Arthur Darby Nock. Cambridge: Cambridge University Press, 1926.

———. *On the Gods and the World*. Translated by Gilbert Murray. Pages 191–212 in *Five Stages of Greek Religion*, by Gilbert Murray. Oxford: Clarendon, 1925.

———. *On the Gods and the World*. Translated by Thomas Taylor. London: Facsimile Reprint, 1976.

Zosimus. *New History*. Edited by Ludwig Mendelsohn. Leipzig: Teubner, 1887.

———. *New History*. Translated by Ronald T. Ridley. Canberra: Australian Association for Byzantine Studies, 1982.

Secondary Sources

Addey, Crystal. "Divination and the *kairos* in Ancient Greek Philosophy and Culture." Pages 138–73 in *Divination and Knowledge in Greco-Roman Antiquity*. Edited by Crystal Addey. Abingdon: Routledge, 2021.

———. *Divination and Theurgy in Neoplatonism: Oracles of the Gods*. Farnham, UK: Ashgate, 2014.

Athanassiadi, Polymnia. *Julian: An Intellectual Biography*. Abingdon: Routledge, 1981.

Bidez, Joseph. *La vie de L'empereur Julien*. Paris: Belles Lettres, 1930.

———. *Vie de Porphyre, Le philosophe neo-platonicien*. Hildesheim: Olms, 1913.

Bregman, Jay. *Synesius of Cyrene: Philosopher-Bishop*. Berkeley: University of California Press, 1982.

———. "Synesius of Cyrene." Pages 520–37 in *The Cambridge History of Philosophy in Late Antiquity*. Edited by Lloyd P. Gerson. Cambridge: Cambridge University Press, 2010.

Brisson, Luc. *How Philosophers Saved Myths: Allegorical Interpretation and Classical Mythology*. Translated by Catherine Tihanyi. Chicago: University of Chicago Press, 2008.

Burkert, Walter. *Ancient Mystery Cults*. Cambridge: Harvard University Press, 1987.

Clark, Gillian. *Christianity and Roman Society*. Cambridge: Cambridge University Press, 2004.

Clinton, Kevin. 1974. "The Sacred Officials of the Eleusinian Mysteries." *TAPS* 64.3 (1974): 1–143.

Finamore, John. "Julian and the Descent of Asclepius." *JNS* 7.2 (1999): 63–86.

Lewy, Hans. *Chaldean Oracles and Theurgy. Mysticism, Magic and Platonism in the Later Roman Empire*. Paris: Études Augustiniennes, 1978.

Sheppard, Anne. *Studies on the Fifth and Sixth Essays of Proclus' Commentary on the Republic*. HH 61. Göttingen: Vandenhoeck & Ruprecht, 1980.

Smith, Rowland. *Julian's Gods: Religion and Philosophy in the Thought and Action of Julian the Apostate*. Abingdon: Routledge, 1995.

Tanaseanu-Döbler, Ilinca. *Theurgy in Late Antiquity: The Invention of a Ritual Tradition*. Göttingen: Vandenhoeck & Ruprecht, 2013.

Taylor, Thomas. *Two Orations of the Emperor Julian*. Repr. Kila, Montana, 1932.

Tougher, Sean. *Julian the Apostate*. Edinburgh: Edinburgh University Press, 2007.

The Optimal Times for Incarnation:
Let Me Count the Ways

Dirk Baltzly and Dorian Gieseler Greenbaum

Introduction

Supposing there were a city as well-governed as Kallipolis in Plato's *Republic*, how would it ever fall? Plato chooses to explain the kinds of civic and psychic orders that are inferior to the best city and the best soul by means of a narrative of political decline. Thus books 8 and 9 chart the degeneration of Kallipolis into timocracy, oligarchy, democracy, and ultimately into tyranny as if this were a historical progression, with the faults of the preceding civic and psychic orders explaining how the next stage in the decline occurs. This may be an effective way of illustrating the defects of the inferior constitutions—whether political or psychic—but it invites the question: How can the *best* state ever fall?

Plato's answer is not given directly by Socrates in the dialogue—though this fact has occasioned little comment among modern interpreters. Rather, the answer is put in the mouth of the Muses, who are called in to explain, in the spirit of Homer, "How factional strife first came among them" (*Resp.* 545d7–e1), for it is factionalism among the guardians that is the most proximate cause of the transition from aristocracy to timocracy (*Resp.* 547b2–c5). But this factionalism itself has an earlier cause, and it is the natures of the men and women who are born to the previous generations of guardians: these children are neither talented nor fortunate (*Resp.* 546d2). This, in turn, has a further cause: the previous generations of guardians arrange for the breeding of the next generation at the wrong time, having made a mistake about "the geometric number" that controls better and worse births (*Resp.* 546b4). While the guardians are wise, the determination of the right times for reproduction involves *sense perception*, as well as reasoning, and they will make a mistake. Plato's spokeswomen, the Muses, give us a mathematical description of a cycle or period for "that which is divine and generated" that is contained in the "perfect (or complete) number." They also provide a cycle for human beings, "the entire geometric number" that is lord over better and worse births (*Resp.* 546c6–7). The description of these numbers was legendarily obscure even in antiquity (see Cicero, *Ep.* 136). Leaving aside the details of the numbers the reader is instructed to calculate, what is the connection between this high-flown obscurity and the births of children who are not up to the task of perpetuating the civic order of the ideal *polis*?

Plato's earliest interpreter and critic, Aristotle, took Socrates's point to be that *everything* is cyclic. Nothing is permanent, and everything changes in a certain cycle. Accordingly, sometimes nature produces people who are just born bad and thus immune to the effects even of the very best education (*Pol.* 1316a1–9). In effect, Aristotle's reading of Plato's speech of the Muses is that the practice of eugenics—which serves as an essential complement to Kallipolis's educational system—cannot be sustained indefinitely. Presumably this is because either the changing universe does not permit *any individual thing* in the sublunary realm to go on forever or, even if this were possible in theory, it is not within the limits of human intelligence to realize this possibility. Such a reading fits nicely with *some* of what the Muses have to say, for at *Resp.* 546a1–8 the Muses are made to assert that "everything that is born must perish." This point is combined with a reminder about the reproductive cycles of plants and animals. It is a reading that makes sense of some of Plato's text.

A whole host of modern interpreters follow Aristotle on this point. The complex mathematical description of the geometric number is just window dressing for the basic point that nothing down here in the realm of Becoming lasts forever. As Nickolas Pappas puts it:

> The gratuitously obscure language of this passage, that business of squares of numbers and dates of birth, make the point sound complicated. For Plato it is depressingly simple. The good city will only exist given human interventions into the natural order to breed natures attuned to society's needs. Because these interventions ultimately fail, some gap will always remain between the natural order (how people behave) and the moral order (how they ought to).[1]

---

1. Nickolas Pappas, *Plato and the Republic*, 2nd ed. (London: Routledge, 1995), 164.

Let us call this the "deflationary reading" of the speech of the Muses at the opening of *Resp.* 8. Note, however, that the deflationary reading fails to give any *specific* sense to the Muses' claim that it is the guardians' reliance on reason *together with perception* that leads to errors. The Muses explicitly say: "Those whom you have educated to be leaders in your city, though they are wise, still will not, as their reason is involved with sense perception, achieve the right production and non-production of your race" (*Resp.* 546a8–b3 [Grube]). A defender of the deflationary reading might insist that this is merely a way of contrasting the perceptible and temporal world of Becoming in general with the invisible and eternal world of Being. But surely Plato's point is not merely that the polis will not last because *nothing in time* lasts, but rather that perception leads the guardians to make a mistake about *timing*. Dwelling on this aspect of Plato's text invites the following questions: What specifically could establish the *right time* (*kairos*) to hold the marriage festivals at which future generations of guardians are produced? Moreover, what could establish this opportune moment in such a way that a failure that *specifically involves perception* could lead to getting the timing wrong? These are not questions that modern interpreters of Plato typically pose.[2]

Our purpose in this paper is not to give an account of how *Plato* supposed that there was some mathematically cosmic specification of opportune and inopportune moments for the conception of children that would require the guardians to mobilize both reason and perception to apprehend. Rather, it is to describe how subsequent ancient *Platonists* supposed that this was possible. The short answer we propose is that it was by means of astrology and in particular the holy grail of Hellenistic astrological practice—conception astrology. This is how you get the right souls in the right bodies at the right time.

---

2. In a note, Mark McPherran registers the lacuna but suggests that it is perhaps an intimation of the disorderly cause in the *Timaeus* or the evil soul in the *Laws*: "The *Republic* does at least make clear that human evil is a consequence of our having souls that are maimed by their association 'with the body and other evils' (611c1–2; cf. 611b–d, 353e; *Phaed.* 78b–84b; *Theaet.* 176a–b; *Leg.* 896c–897c); e.g., not even the *Republic*'s rulers are infallible in their judgments of particulars, and so Kallipolis will fail as a result of the inability of the guardians to make infallibly good marriages (given their need to use perception; 546b–c)." McPherran, "The Gods and Piety of Plato's Republic," in *The Blackwell Guide to Plato's Republic*, ed. Gerasimos Santas (Malden, MA: Blackwell, 2006), 84–103

Late Antique Platonism and Astrology: A Match Made in Heaven?

Few modern interpreters would suppose that Plato himself thought of the failure of the guardians in relation to the calculation of the number for human births in *Republic* as a failure of astrological practice. The not-quite-consensus is that the practice of astrology was introduced to Greeks in the Hellenistic period.[3] Certainly post-Hellenistic Platonists knew a lot about astrology and either sought to integrate it into their understanding of Platonism or at least sought to reconcile the perceived predictive successes of astrology with their versions of Platonism. In this section, we will briefly review some of the evidence for Platonic engagement with Hellenistic astrology and then discuss some features of Plato's works that would have made some sort of engagement with astrology seem natural for anyone who purported to be a follower of Plato.

The interweaving of Platonism with astrology is at least as old as the modern Platonic corpus. The current arrangement of Platonic works into tetralogies comes from Thrasyllus, who, in addition to being a philosopher, was astrologer to the emperor Tiberius (42 BCE–37 CE).[4] Now, in spite of his role in arranging the works of Plato, Thrasyllus might well be thought of as a Pythagorean as much as a Platonist. It is certainly true that astrology found other practitioners among Pythagorean philosophers. Earlier than Thrasyllus we have Nigidius Figulus (ca. 98–45 BCE), who was identified as a Pythagorean philosopher and also as an expert in astrol-

---

3. The dissenting voice is Robin Waterfield, "The Evidence for Astrology in Classical Greece," *CC* 3.2 (1999): 3–15. He includes several passages from Plato as part of his evidence, including the descriptions of the planetary circles from the Myth of Er in the *Republic*. On the use of the nuptial number, he says, "Plato envisages that the guardians of his ideal state will use arithmological (and probably astrological) knowledge to pick the auspicious times within a lifetime for conception to occur in such a way as to guarantee good offspring" (9). He designates this as an example of "theoretical research and speculation on astrological matters" (4–5). He also comments on the arithmology and astrological implications of the nuptial number in his translation of the *Republic*, Robin Waterfield, *Plato: Republic* (Oxford: Oxford University Press, 1993), 432–34 (commentary on 546b–d). As noted above, we suspend judgment on the question of Plato's intentions with respect to astrological knowledge in the marriage number and the speech of the Muses. We note, however, that all the reasons why later Platonists regarded Platonism and astrology as a match made in heaven could surely have appealed to Plato himself with equal force *had he been aware of* such a science.

4. Harold Tarrant, *Thrasyllan Platonism* (Ithaca, NY: Cornell University Press, 1993).

ogy (see Lucan, *Bell. civ.* 1.639–672). The question of the relation between the reemergence of dogmatic forms of Platonism in the early Roman Empire and the connection to Pythagoreanism is made problematic by the nature of our evidence. Summarizing the extant evidence of commentaries on Plato's dialogues as well as introductions to or summaries of Plato's thought from the early Imperial period, Harrold Tarrant observes:

> One feature recurs in all these genres, and that is the assimilation of Plato to Pythagoras, partially but not wholly resulting from the *Timaeus*. The period seems to have given rise to various Pythagorean works from "Timaeus Locrus" on physics, to Ps.-Archytus *On Categories*, to a host of ethical fragments attributed to persons with Pythagorean names but bearing the hallmarks of post-Classical philosophy.[5]

It thus seems plausible to us that astrology becomes an issue for subsequent Platonists partly as a consequence of Pythagorean interest and involvement in astrology. It is true that the reemergence of forms of dogmatic Platonism also involved cross-pollination with Stoicism. Moreover, Stoicism has long been credited with providing the philosophical basis for astrological practice. However, Long's examination of Stoic engagement with specifically astrological forms of divination casts some doubt on the truism that Hellenistic astrology's philosophical home was principally among the Stoics.[6] While the Stoic doctrine of cosmic sympathy provides one possible causal mechanism through which the heavenly bodies might signify, or even cause, events in the sublunary region, there are also obvious affinities with the Pythagorean tradition. In the latter tradition we find, in the most general terms, a philosophy that is concerned with celes-

---

5. Harold Tarrant, "From Fringe Reading to Core Curriculum: Commentary, Introduction and Doctrinal Summary," in *The Brill Companion to the Reception of Plato in Antiquity*, ed. Harold Tarrant et al. (Leiden: Brill, 2018), 114.

6. Anthony A. Long, "Astrology: Arguments Pro and Contra," in *Science and Speculation*, ed. Jonathan Barnes et al. (Cambridge: Cambridge University Press, 1982), 171–72: "Manilius and others claimed the Stoics as allies. But the modern consensus on unqualified Stoic support for astrology has alarmingly frail foundations." More recently, see Giuseppe Cambiano, "Astronomy and Divination in Stoic Philosophy," in *A Brill Companion to Hellenistic Astronomy: The Science in Its Contexts*, ed. Alan C. Bowen and Francesca Rochberg (Leiden: Brill, 2020), 614–18. Cambiano similarly argues that early Stoic acceptance of divination must be distinguished from deep engagement with astrology.

tial matters and committed to the importance of quantitative symbolism. It is a philosophical tradition that is at least as congenial to astrology as Stoicism, and perhaps more so.[7]

Whatever its relationship to Pythagoreanism, the transition from the Roman republic to the early empire seems to be an important turning point for the *political significance* of the practice of astrology in the Greco-Roman world. This matters for the history of Platonism. Tamsyn Barton makes the case that astrology gained a political significance that it had not previously had.[8] With the transition to the imperial period, horoscopic astrology became associated with the struggle for individual power and the pursuit of its legitimation. The apotheosis (as it were) of the political use of astrology is marked by Augustus's use of the sign of Capricorn on coins, representing its importance in his birth chart.[9] This change in the political significance of astrology is relevant to its standing for Platonists. The Platonic corpus provides ample connections between the true art of ruling and philosophy. To the extent that astrology entered into the toolkit of actual rulers, philosophers who fancied themselves in possession of the true art of ruling had reason to determine the proper value of astrology. A Platonist was obliged to decide. Did astrology really figure into the art of the statesman (as Thrasyllus surely supposed), or was it no part of the political art since its claims were said to be baseless (as Cicero argues in *Div.* 2.42–7)?

Plenty of features of Plato's dialogues suggest a positive answer to this question. Both *Timaeus* and *Epinomis* commend the study of the heavens

---

7. Walter Burkert uses late evidence for Philolaus to suggest a role for him in the incorporation of geometric elements in place of the Babylonian tablets in astrological practice. See Burkert, *Lore and Science in Ancient Pythagoreanism*, trans. Edwin Minar (Cambridge: Harvard University Press, 1972). "In the melange of myth and φυσιολογία which Philolaus' astronomy proves to be, we also find the first traces of astrology; though here the Babylonian tables are replaced by the idea of the angle—the graphic, geometrical, that is to say, the specifically 'Greek' element" (350). See also Wolfgang Hübner, "Die geometrische Theologie des Philolaos," *Phil* 124 (1980): 18–32. Hübner gives a perceptive and thorough examination of Philolaus's geometric theology and its astrological content concerning various polygons and aspects, including the triangle, square, dodecagon, etc., and their relationships to elements and deities.

8. Tamsyn Barton, *Power and Knowledge: Astrology, Physiognomics, and Medicine under the Roman Empire* (Ann Arbor: University of Michigan Press, 1994), 40–47.

9. See A. M. Lewis, "Augustus and His Horoscope Reconsidered," *Phoenix* 62 (2008): 308–37, for the latest arguments on what Capricorn could have represented in the nativity of Augustus.

as a means toward wisdom and happiness. That, of course, is not yet to specifically recommend the theory or practice of astrology. *Timaeus* 90a–d, however, connects the motion of the heavens with the motions within the soul and, importantly, equates the highest aspect of the soul, which is blessed and immortal when attuned to these celestial motions, to a daimon. This personal daimon might reasonably be imagined to have some affinity with the daimon that is assigned to each soul in the Myth of Er at the end of the *Republic* (629d–e). Similarly, *Epinomis* identifies Ouranos or the heavens as the god who bestows on us the greatest blessing (namely, knowledge of number) but goes on to populate the world with the intermediaries between gods and men: daimons. In fact, the *Epinomis* is the most important Platonic impetus to the rich tradition of theories and typologies of daimons in post-Hellenistic Platonism.

These two elements—the heavens as a source of wisdom and the importance of daimons of various sorts—were also features of Greek astrological theory and practice.[10] So if Pythagoreanism—with its preoccupations with the symbolic significance of number and its celestial orientation—was fertile ground for cross-pollination with astrology, forms of Platonism that emphasized the importance of daimons were an even more fitting philosophical complement to astrology. Accordingly, it should come as no surprise that Neoplatonic philosophers in particular produced handbooks on astrology and integrated astrological concepts into their works on Plato and Aristotle. To the extent that it does come as a surprise, this is probably because modern scholars have sought to avert their eyes from the evidence of Platonic philosophy's love affair with this most unscientific (from the modern point of view), and therefore unsuitable (from the modern scientistic point of view) consort. Let us briefly review the evidence of Platonic philosophy's late antique dalliance with astrology.

Plotinus is, as often, the odd man out among the Neoplatonists. Porphyry reports that he had acquaintance with some astrological methods and was not impressed with their basis (*Vit. Plot.* 15.21–26). Plotinus's own writings reveal repeated and nuanced engagements with the philosophical implications of astrologers' *success* in predicting future events, though not with the details of their practice. His principal concerns, then, are not with incorporating astrological theory into the body of Platonic wisdom but

---

10. Dorian Gieseler Greenbaum, *The Daimon in Hellenistic Astrology: Origins and Influence, Ancient Magic and Divination* (Leiden: Brill, 2016).

with protecting key Platonic theses from the seeming implications of successful astronomical practice. He is keen to "safe-guard human autonomy and astral benevolence" while still acknowledging that, in some sense, the stars cause some events and do not merely signify them.[11] Unlike subsequent Platonists, however, our evidence suggests that he did not engage in any detailed way with astrological theory or practice.

Porphyry is perhaps more typical of the Platonic tradition. His works show the same concern we find in Plotinus about accommodating human autonomy with the presumption of successful astrological practice. But Porphyry was much better acquainted with the details of the theory and practice of astrology. While the authorship has sometimes been questioned, there is an introduction to Ptolemy's *Tetrabiblos* attributed to Porphyry.[12] Importantly for our purposes, Porphyry's essay *On the Cave of the Nymphs*—a work whose authorship is not open to question—exhibits interest in both astrological concepts and the entry of the soul into the body.[13] The principal connection between astrology and Porphyry's Pla-

---

11. Peter Adamson, "Plotinus on Astrology," *OSAP* 35 (2008): 265–91. On the topic of Plotinus's views of astrology (*Enn.* 2.3, "On Whether the Stars Are Causes"), see also John Dillon, "Plotinus on Whether the Stars Are Causes," *ResOr* 12 (1999): 87–92; Marilynn Lawrence, "Who Thought the Stars are Causes? The Astrological Doctrine Criticized by Plotinus," in *Metaphysical Patterns in Platonism*, ed. John F. Finamore and Robert M. Berchman (New Orleans: University Press of the South, 2007), 17–33.

12. Accepted by Joseph Bidez, *Vie de Porphyre: Le philosophe Néo-Platonicien* (Leipzig: Teubner, 1913); Andrew Smith, *Porphyrius*, ed, *Philosophi Fragmenta* (Stuttgart: Teubner, 1993); denied by Giuseppe Bezza, "Astrological Considerations on the Length of Life in Hellenistic, Persian and Arabic Astrology," *CC* 2.2 (1998): 3–15. A recent article by Levente László reexamines evidence for genuine versus nongenuine chapters, still attributing some of them to Porphyry, albeit his main source of information was not Ptolemy but Antiochus of Athens. See László, "Revisiting the Authenticity of Porphyry's *Introduction to Ptolemy's 'APOTELESMATICS*,'" *CP* 116 (2021): 392–411.

13. K. Nilüfer Akçay sums up Porphyry's general orientation in the following terms: "The treatise is also a clear manifestation of Porphyry's great interest in the association and dissociation of the soul and body…. In *De Antro*, he provides a wide range of philosophical and astrological explanations of these processes through the concepts of pneuma (πνεῦμα), genesis (γένεσις), apogenesis (ἀπογένεσις), and the gates of heaven (πύλαι οὐρανοῦ), including the gates of the Sun, the gates of the Sun and the Moon, and the solstitial gates." See Akçay, *Porphyry's On the Cave of the Nymphs in Its Intellectual Context* (Leiden: Brill, 2019), 6–7.

tonism is via the concept of an individual's personal daimon. As noted, this notion has its clearest Platonic articulation in *Resp.* 629d6–e1 in the Myth of Er, where, after each soul has selected its life, Lachesis assigns an individual daimon "as the guardian of the person's life and the one who fulfills his choice." This individual daimon both Porphyry and Iamblichus seem to treat as equivalent to the *oikodespotēs* or "house master" identified in astrological theory and practice—though it seems that the two philosophers disagreed about whether this personal daimon was better sought through astrology or through theurgy.[14]

The authenticity of the paraphrase of Ptolemy's *Tetrabiblos* and the commentary on it that are attributed to Proclus are widely doubted. But his work on the *Syntaxis* or *Almagest* is certainly authentic, and—even if he is hostile to many of Ptolemy's claims where they conflict with Plato— there can be no question that he possessed deep familiarity with Ptolemy's astronomical text.[15] Even if the paraphrase and the commentary on Ptolemy's astrological text, the *Tetrabiblos*, is not that of Proclus, there is little reason to doubt that Proclus knew astrology and regarded it a body of wisdom to be aligned—where possible—with Plato.[16]

Similarly in Alexandria, we find Platonist philosophers guiding students into the intricacies of astrology. Olympiodorus lectured on the *Introduction to Astrology* of Paul of Alexandria.[17] His *Commentary on the Gorgias* defends the same delicate balance between the claim that some events in our world are fated by the stars (39.1) and the claim that our moral lives are up to us (48.5).

---

14. Dorian Gieseler Greenbaum, "Porphyry of Tyre on the *Daimon*, Birth and the Stars," in *Neoplatonic Demons and Angels*, ed. Luc Brisson, Seamus O'Neil, and Andrei Timotin (Leiden: Brill, 2018), 102–39.

15. It is perhaps significant that Proclus rejected Ptolemy's idea of the precession of the equinoxes on the basis that astrologers have no need of the innovations of tropical astrology in order to successfully practice their art. See Proclus, *Book 3, Part II, Proclus on the World Soul*, vol. 4 of *Commentary on Plato's Timaeus*, trans. Dirk Baltzly (Cambridge: Cambridge University Press, 2009), 24–28.

16. For another examination of Proclus's interests in astrology, see Marilynn Lawrence, "Astral Symbolism in Theurgic Rites," in *Divination and Knowledge in Greco-Roman Antiquity*, ed. Crystal Addey (London: Routledge, 2021), 278–81.

17. Leendert G. Westerink, "Ein astrologisches Kolleg aus dem Jahre 564," *ByzZ* 64 (1971): 6–21; Jean Warnon, "Le commentaire attribué à Héliodore sur les εἰσαγωγικά de Paul d'Alexandrie," *RPL* 1 (1967): 197–217; Dorian Gieseler Greenbaum, *Late Classical Astrology: Paulus Alexandrinus and Olympiodorus* (Reston, VA: ARHAT, 2001).

To sum up the results of this section: We have ample evidence of Platonist philosophers' engagement with astrology. They sought to correlate key ideas in Plato's dialogues, such as the personal daimon and the idea that observation of the heavens is somehow linked with human happiness, with notions in astrology.[18] They also sought to understand the nature and limits of astrological practice in ways consistent with their understanding of fate, providence, and what is up to us. One locus for this cross-fertilization between astrology and the Platonic dialogues was the Myth of Er.

We have yet to consider the nuptial number from the speech of the Muses in relation to astrology. In the next section we consider what kind of astrology a Platonist might reasonably suppose would be relevant to the task of the guardians in arranging the marriage festivals as part of a eugenics program. In the final section, we will turn to astrological elements in Proclus's exegesis of the nuptial number.

Natal Astrology and Conception Astrology

Suppose you aimed to produce the best and brightest who would—after their excellent education and extended practical apprenticeship—eventually become the future leaders of Kallipolis. Moreover, suppose you thought that the stars played *some* role in shaping the kinds of people who would be born. What kind of astrology would you need to practice in order to carry out your eugenics program?[19] The answer to this question turns on the nature and character of the relations between celestial influences and the innate talent of children. Is it celestial configurations at *birth*

---

18. In this presentation, we have stressed these two affinities—the daimon and the significance of the heavens—in explaining the attractions of astrology for those in the Platonic tradition. Another story of convergence would note the long-standing association between medicine and philosophy, for astronomical and astrological ideas were part of ancient medicine. As in the case of many Platonists, the views of the physician Galen as regards astrology are complex—a rejection of some forms but an embrace of others. See Dorian Gieseler Greenbaum, "Hellenistic Astronomy in Medicine," in *A Brill Companion to Hellenistic Astronomy: The Science in Its Contexts*, ed. Alan C. Bowen and Francesca Rochberg (Leiden: Brill, 2020), 364–67; also Greenbaum, "Divination and Decumbiture: Katarchic Astrology and Greek Medicine," in Addey, *Divination and Knowledge*, 109–37.

19. On the kinds of Hellenistic astrology and their deployment, see Dorian Gieseler Greenbaum, "The Hellenistic Horoscope," in Bowen and Rochberg, *Brill Companion to Hellenistic Astronomy*, 448–50.

that matter? Or is it celestial configurations at the moment of *conception*? Or do *both* play a role? Moreover, given that the marriage festivals that you organize involve sacrifices and hymns (*Resp.* 459e), as well as prayers offered by priests and priestesses (*Resp.* 461a), you might reasonably suppose that there are opportune moments for such things even independent of the question of their relation to the offspring conceived at the marriage festivals. This hieratic aspect of the eugenics program would be even more important if the daimon assigned to the offspring mattered to their suitability to become philosopher-rulers. So how does one determine the opportune moment for such rites?

The practice of astrology offered branches corresponding to all these possibilities. Then, as now, *natal astrology* or the practice of horoscopy based on the time of an individual's birth was predominant. But there was also a practice of *conception astrology* that was, in extant documents, mostly retrospective in practice. Based on the positions of the relevant celestial bodies at the time of conception, it added to information obtained from the birth chart. Finally, there was *katarchic astrology*, a branch of which sought to determine the opportune moment for beginning an undertaking—whether it be the crossing of the Rubicon or the seeking of an oracle.

Ptolemy's *Tetrabiblos*, which provides techniques for natal astrology rather than conception astrology, claims that the latter would be better *if it were practical*.

> Since the chronological starting-point of human nativities is naturally the very time of conception, but potentially and accidentally the moment of birth, in cases in which the very time of conception is known either by chance or by observation, it is more fitting that we should follow it in determining the special nature of body and soul, examining the effective power of the configuration of the stars at that time.... But if they do not know the time of conception, which is usually the case, we must follow the starting-point furnished by the moment of birth and give to this our attention, for it too is of great importance and falls short of the former only in this respect—that by the former it is possible to have foreknowledge also of events preceding birth. (*Tetr.* 3.1 [Robbins])[20]

---

20. See Sextus Empiricus, *Math.* 5.55.3–65.1 for similar skepticism about whether the time of conception can be known with the precision that astrologers would require for conception horoscopy.

The "events preceding birth" that Ptolemy mentions include the duration of the pregnancy itself. The ancients realized that not all pregnancies were of a single, standard duration. This is why you cannot simply work back from the date of birth to the date of conception in order to know the stars at that earlier moment. Nonetheless, ancient accounts of the types of pregnancies and their various durations owed more to numerological considerations than to empirical study.[21] The accounts of the nature of children born as a consequence of pregnancies of different lengths show that this, too, would have been a relevant concern for would-be eugenicists.

There were, in fact, works and practices of conception astrology, though these have been less studied.[22] Among the techniques for conception astrology was the so-called rule of Petosiris that putatively allowed the practitioner to know the astrologically significant ascendant at the moment of conception from the location of the moon at the time of birth and vice versa—to know the moon at the time of conception from the ascendant at the time of birth. This sort of technique, then, looks salient to the eugenic task of the guardians. Yet while these techniques for conception astrology were discussed in some texts,[23] we have almost no examples outside literary horoscopy. Katrin Frommhold concludes:

> Apart from the fictitious conception chart of Romulus handed down by Plutarch and the two sample charts which the astrologers Vettius Valens

---

21. Ann Ellis Hanson, "The Eight Months' Child and the Etiquette of Birth: Obsit Omen!," *BHM* 61 (1987): 589–602. For a concise overview of the ancient doctrine of conception in astrology in the Mediterranean *oikoumene*, see Mladen Popović, *Reading the Human Body: Physiognomics and Astrology in the Dead Sea Scrolls and Hellenistic-Early Roman Period Judaism*, STDJ (Leiden: Brill, 2007), 145–50; Stephan Heilen focuses on the various significant numbers (3, 7, 9, 40) associated with this doctrine. See Heilen, "The Doctrine of the Third, Seventh and Fortieth Days of the Moon in Ancient Astrology," *MHNH* 12 (2012): 179–98.

22. The most thorough investigation is Katrin Frommhold, *Bedeutung und Berechnung der Empfängnis in der Astrologie der Antike* (Münster: Aschendorff, 2004).

23. Including Porphyry, in the *Introduction to the Tetrabiblos* 37–38, which mentions conception astrology techniques; see also Frommhold, *Bedeutung und Berechnung*, 51, 71, 175–76, 184–86. He furthermore refers to a conception chart in his *Philosophy from Oracles* (166.20–167.5). See Porphyry, *De philosophia ex oraculis haurienda*, ed. Gustav Wolff (Berlin: Springer; Hildesheim: Olms, 1856). See commentary on this passage in Crystal Addey, *Divination and Theurgy in Neoplatonism: Oracles of the Gods* (Farnham, UK: Ashgate, 2014), 122–23. We thank Crystal Addey for this last reference.

and Hephaistion provided for their own conception dates to illustrate the rule of Petosiris, not a single original conception chart in Greek or Roman astrology has survived. This form of horoscopy as a competing method to natal horoscopy was obviously not able to establish itself practically.[24]

So, to sum up, while the positions of the heavenly bodies both at the time of conception and at the time of birth were at least *theoretically* accorded significance in Hellenistic astrology, the extant evidence suggests that most *actual practice* focused on the easier case of natal astrology. This is hardly surprising since the time of birth is, after all, much, much easier to determine. In the next section, we will see some evidence that Proclus supposed the guardians to be masters of the more difficult task of conception astrology—until, of course, they aren't.

Astrology in Proclus's Exegesis of the Nuptial Number

Wilhelm Kroll's edition of Proclus contains one tantalizing but incomplete hint at the centrality of conception astrology in the Platonists' understanding of the nuptial number. Proclus's commentary on the speech of the Muses and the nuptial number is transmitted to us only in the badly damaged manuscript in the Vatican library. We can see that it was originally composed of forty-five sections, but the first nine are missing. Kroll printed the first two pages of that which is missing from the Vatican manuscript on the basis of a sixteenth-century copy that was made prior to the damage to the Vatican manuscript. On the basis of these two pages, we can see that—as one would expect—Proclus dedicated the first part of *Essay 13 on the Speech of the Muses* to general comments about the decline of the ideal city and the appropriateness of the Muses as divinities to tell us about this. He argues that the sequential decline from the best *polis* is characteristic of natural processes that occur in continuous and gradual steps (*Comm. in R.* 2.21–25). Since the decline from the ideal originates from a lack of *harmony* among the guardians, the *Muses* are the divinities who are best placed to tell us about it. At the point at which we might expect a general overview of the sources from which such disharmony and dissension springs, the text breaks off. When it picks up again, we are in the midst of a more detailed analysis:

---

24. Frommhold, *Bedeutung und Berechnung*, 241 (our translation).

> From such couplings are introduced births of children who are "neither
> of the right nature nor of good fortune" [*Resp.* 546d2]. From this it is
> clear that Plato intends that some such birth results from some such
> starting point [*katarchē*] of conception, but not only that conception is
> the beginning of the pregnancy and of the life of the child but also that
> [the life of the child] is also dependent on [its conception] and has a
> continuity with it. (*Comm. in R.* 2.4.25–5.5)

It would be very nice to know what originally preceded this remark, which
seems so pregnant with meaning (so to speak). It is especially intriguing
since a scholiast on our manuscript comments at *exactly* this point:

> For the astrologers say that the hour of conception signifies that the
> pregnancy will be of this or that sort, while the hour of release[25] signi-
> fies the form of life. But the divine Plato says that the hour of conception
> makes clear not only what is regarded as the origin of the pregnancy,
> but also of the things that result together with the pregnancy. (scholion,
> *Comm. in R.* 2.377.7–12)

Where did the scholiast derive the notion that there was a significant difference between the way the divine Plato thought about these matters
and the way that most astrologers did? We cannot, of course, say with
any certainty, since the identity and time period of the scholiast remains
a mystery: he is either contemporaneous with the creation of the codex or
subsequent to it (unless, perhaps, the scribe also transferred notes from
the margin of the text he was copying). Since the codex dates from the
ninth or tenth century, he is far distant from Plato. One attractive hypothesis is that the missing sections of Proclus's *Commentary* itself reinforced
the superiority of "Plato's" commitment to conception astrology in opposition to what Proclus characterized as the more common practice of natal
astrology in his time. This fact perhaps struck the scholiast as sufficiently
important that he felt the need to reinforce this point in the margin of the
text. Is this suspicion borne out by what remains of Proclus's remarks on
the marriage number?

---

25. ἐκλύσεως, which Kroll marks with (?). Presumably the scholiast means the
release of the child from the womb or birth. The usual word in ancient astrology for
the time of delivery of the fetus from the womb is ἐκτροπή (e.g., in Valens, Ptolemy,
Paul of Alexandria).

We think that there are two related but nonetheless distinct agendas in Proclus's handling of astrological material in *Essay 13*. One of these agendas moves at a high level of generality. In it, Proclus seeks to show that concepts used by astrologers have a mathematical "fit" with the soul itself. Proclus's exegesis of the geometric number covers the full spectrum of modes in which quantity is manifested: arithmetic, geometric, musical, and *astronomical* (*Comm. in R.* 2.36.3–5).[26] In each of these readings of the geometric number whose compressed and complex specification is given by the Muses at *Resp.* 546b3–c7, Proclus relates the numbers in the Muses' formula to both numbers in the cosmos and in the soul. The astronomical/astrological reading does the same thing and, from Proclus's point of view, the recurrence of the same numbers in each reading exhibits the parallels between the cosmos ruled by just gods, the ideal city-state ruled by just rulers, and the healthy soul ruled by reason.

The second agenda is more specific and detailed. As part of that agenda, we have a quite detailed presentation in §§37–38 of the rule of Petosiris, which sits conveniently alongside Proclus's treatment of differing opinions on the various lengths of pregnancy. These are all relevant to the task of implementing conception astrology. In addition, we find Proclus adapting Nestorius's method for locating the chronocrator for the year to the task of finding the ruling divinity for the conception of a birth of seven or nine months. In short, the second agenda is to exhibit the sorts of techniques that would allow the guardians to choose the moments to mate the very best of their younger peers so as to produce auspicious stellar configurations at *conception*, with an optimal *length* of pregnancy to achieve auspicious stars at *birth*, with the hieratic bonus of daimons appropriate for the ideal future offspring. The insanely complex task of coordinating conception, duration, moment of birth, and divine rulers for the births explains how it would be possible for even the wisest of rulers to make inaccurate observations that would lead to a mistake. Moreover, the consequences of such a mistake, Proclus supposed, would not be fully manifest for three generations.[27]

---

26. See Theon, *De utilitate mathematicae* 17.14–18.2, for the linkage between the mathematical sciences; Nicomachus, *Arith.* 1.4 for the priority of arithmetic. Recall that while moderns—for whom astrology is anathema—regard astronomy as wholly distinct, in late antiquity astrology was merely applied astronomy.

27. See Finamore's essay in this volume.

As an illustration of the first, more general agenda, let us consider Proclus's initial arithmetic reading, which establishes symbolic connections between, on the one hand, aspects of Plato's formulas for computing the numbers in question and, on the other, the nature of the cosmos in general and the soul in particular. Thus Proclus decodes the instructions in *Resp.* 546b5–c6 in terms of the construction of a continuous geometric proportion between cubic end terms. This mirrors the way in which the intermediate elements of air and water, conceived as terms in a continuous geometric proportion, bind the extremes of fire and earth in the construction of the body of the world at *Tim.* 31c1–32c4. Of course, such continuous geometric proportions are also present in the composition of the world soul since the Demiurge inserts such means between the initial portions of the psychic stuff that is mixed in the storied mixing bowl (*Tim.* 35b4–36b6). So the arithmetic reading of the nuptial number in the *Republic* in terms of continuous geometric proportion connects—in a rather vague but suggestive manner—the binding into unity of the souls of future Guardians. The ideal city is, of course, a microcosm of a universe that is similarly held together by geometric proportion.[28]

It is important, though, to emphasize that these different ways of reading and interpreting the symbolism of the nuptial number—the arithmetic, geometric, musical, and astrological—are not chosen extraneously but are, in Proclus's view, the four best ways of understanding the relationship of the cosmos to the creation of human beings. All of these approaches are necessary to contextualize the creation of human beings ensouled and living within a cosmic system made up of harmonious numbers, geometric figures, and harmonious musical intervals, along with the astronomical organization of the spheres based on elements, and their associated letters and numbers. Here the meaning of the word *stoicheion*, which has connotations with all three—letters, numbers, and elements—and also, in some circumstances, the zodiacal signs, is the foundation of the created cosmos, and the created human.

Nor is Proclus eccentric in this regard. Here it is relevant to bring up an earlier interpreter of the arithmetic, geometric, and musical components,

---

28. One finds a similar deployment of geometric proportion to elucidate the way in which the tripartite soul is unified in Proclus's *Essay 7* on the virtues in *Resp.* 4. See Dirk Baltzly, "Civic Virtues and the Goal of Likeness to God in Proclus' *Republic Commentary*," in *Early Christianity and Late Antique Philosophy*, ed. Eva Anagnostou-Laoutides and Ken Perry (Leiden: Brill, 2020), 197–217.

namely, Aristides Quintilianus (fl. probably late third century),[29] in his *De musica*. His examinations of these topics are often so directly relevant to what Proclus says that one could reasonably suppose that Proclus had read them. For example, Aristides specifically discusses the 3-4-5 right triangle (see below) in relation to the births of children including seven- and nine-month births, and the musical ratios of 3:2 and 4:3 (3.18); the seven tones of the planets, their male and/or female nature, and assignment of the letter ε to the moon, planet of generation (3.21); and the connection of the zodiac to these right triangles, as well as the concordant harmonic divisions associated to the aspects between zodiacal signs (3.23).[30] The *epitritos* (4:3 ratio, the musical fourth) and *hēmiolios* (3:2 ratio, the musical fifth) are called concordant intervals by Aristides Quintilianus, and the 3-4-5 triangle, with its sides adding up to twelve (the twelve signs of the zodiac!), is the first with exclusively rational sides.[31] Similarly, the opening moves in Proclus's astronomical reading of the nuptial number look for ways in which these numbers are represented in the heavens. Thus it is taken as significant, for instance, that *five* of the seven planets (distinct from the sun and moon) have their own direct and retrograde motion (*Comm. in R.* 2.43.24–26). Of the *five* standard aspects, the trine aspect (*three*)—which connects signs that are *five* signs apart from one another (e.g., Aries to Leo to Sagittarius)—was determined as the best (*Comm. in R.* 2.43.26–27). *Three* is also connected to the elemental triplicities (*four* elements containing *three* signs each), and there are *four* signs each in the groups of *three* cardinal, fixed, and mutable signs. Thus even the commonplaces of astrological mechanics manifest the 3-4-5 right triangle that Proclus supposes to be the key to unlocking the Muses' description of the geometric number. In its very nature, the fundamentals of astrological mechanics promote an adherence to Pythagorean notions of number and their value in cosmology both celestial and earthly.

---

29. Barton, *Power and Knowledge*, 2, 392.

30. The critical edition is Reginald P. Winnington-Ingram, *Aristides Quintilianus: De musica libri tres* (Leipzig: Teubner, 1963). For translations of these, see Andrew Barker, *Harmonic and Acoustic Theory*, vol. 2 of *Greek Musical Writings*, ed. John Stevens and Peter le Huray, CRLM 2 (Cambridge: Cambridge University Press, 1989), 518–26.

31. Barker, *Greek Musical Writings*, 23, 524. See also Frommhold, *Bedeutung und Berechnung*, 208–9.

None of this material suggests any specific connection with astrological practice that might fail due to the role of perception in the guardians' eugenic task. We think that this aspect of Proclus's engagement with astrology is thus parallel to his engagement with the text of Homer in *Essay 6*: he wants to show that all these sources of wisdom coincide and that the Chaldeans' practice of astrology was familiar to Plato and, indeed, hinted at by his text, so that those in the know may know that Plato was similarly in the know. Moreover, this confluence of wisdom between Plato and the astrologers responds to an underlying presence of number in all things. Call this arm of Proclus's project the synoptic arm. In it, he wants to show how Plato's text actually organizes and refers cryptically to all branches of knowledge that are worthwhile. To do this he must, of course, pursue (or invent) allusions, parallels, connections, and so on. This creative interpretation is a version of what Dirk Baltzly, John Finamore, and Graeme Miles elsewhere call "Platonic literacy": the capacity to read the world in terms of Plato's divinely inspired texts.[32] As such, this part of Proclus's agenda moves largely at the level of generalities and is open-ended enough to invite the drawing of further connections by those with the relevant background knowledge.

Other parts of Proclus's engagement with astrology in *Essay 13*, however, are quite specific and reasonably detailed. Beginning at 54.25, he makes it clear that he expects the guardians to plan the timing of their marriage festivals, which are de facto conception festivals, by using the methods of astrology.

> If there is this number,[33] then it is both made manifest in the universe and brought to completion by the [astrological] configurations and motions that are in them, since things that are general or universal are always the leaders of things that are particular or partial. And this was stated previously: that this number is rendered consubstantial both within the partial souls—for they live in accordance with it [sc. the number]—and within the universe which produces the cycles of fertility and sterility, just as each of the ways of life (e.g. being a philosopher) is both in the souls themselves and in the corresponding configuration of the universe,

32. Proclus, *Commentary on Plato's Republic*, trans. Dirk Baltzly, John Finamore, and Graeme Miles, 2 vols. (Cambridge: Cambridge University Press, 2018, 2022), 1:125.

33. Sc. the geometric number the Muses have specified through two harmonies (*Resp.* 646c2) represented (as Proclus supposes) by 10,000 and 7,500.

so too is each of the other [traits]). If, as I was saying, it is therefore possible to see this double number that has control over better or worse
births within the cosmos, then it is necessary for the rulers who look to
the universe to make their judgements on the matters concerning the
consummations of marriages to do so through the things that are visible,
determining which cosmic order is productive of a better life and which
order is productive of a worse one. The Fate that includes the numbers
[of these lives] shows their differences through the motions that are visible to the eye. The question of whether these are merely signs of things
to come or whether they are things that are brought about in coopera-
tion with the souls (because Fate makes the parts after the whole) does
not matter for present purposes.[34] Instead it is merely necessary for the
rulers who have authority over the consummations to be clear-sighted
when it comes to the times for procreation to see if these times have a
preponderance of better or worse numbers. After all, the configurations
of the cosmos at the time of birth follow upon those at the time of conception, and the lives of those born follow upon these, becoming either
better or worse, and becoming like or unlike those of their parents, so
that it is possible for there to be a change in the political order. (*Comm.
in R.* 2.55.7–24 [Baltzly, Finamore, and Miles])

In the previous section of Proclus's commentary, the double number
specified by the Muses was read arithmetically and geometrically as symbolizing various aspects about the biformed nature of the human soul,
tending both toward the intelligible and the sensible. In this section, however, Proclus reads it astrologically. The double number in this context
is a human soul number that corresponds to a number in stellar configurations at the *kairos*, the "right time" of conception. The idea of the
katarchē reflecting the right time is not mentioned here but is taken up
in *Essay 16*, "On the Myth of Er" (*Comm. in R.* 2.186.25–26), when the
souls are trying to determine their future lives. Here, in this passage, the
soul number and the stellar number must be in conformity. A parallel to
this situation of choosing the right time can, interestingly, be found in a
passage from second-century astrologer Vettius Valens, where he tells us
that when an astrologer chooses a time to begin an endeavor (this is the
subbranch of elections in katarchic astrology), this time and the heavenly
configuration must "be in harmony" (ἐναρμόνιον ... τυχεῖν) to make the

---

34. See Porphyry, 271F43–51 on the contrast on the ways in which astrological
facts are related to what occurs. Porphyry's view is that the astrological facts are signs—
not causes—of that which will come about (see Greenbaum, "Porphyry of Tyre," 130).

event successful—and this is not a foregone conclusion, as Valens discovered through personal experience (Vettius Valens, *Anth.* 9.12.28–31).[35] *Katarchē* and *kairos* must be synchronized. Significantly for topics we are focusing on in this essay, the daimon and astrology, Valens considers that the *daimonion* (the word he uses), not the human, is the agent who must be followed in choosing moments that align with the right cosmic configuration (*Anth.* 9.12.31).[36] For Proclus, it is important, in addition to getting "the right soul into the right body," to make sure the daimon is also involved in this process. The importance of the correct daimon is clear from this remark in his *Alcibiades Commentary*: "The daimon alone moves all, governs all, orders all our affairs…. And this one being is king of all that is in us and all that has to do with us, steering our whole life" (*In Alc.* 6 [O'Neill]). Astrological knowledge, in turn, is essential to securing the right daimon: "One particular cause determines [the daimon and fortune]: the Sun and Moon, respectively, because the Lots of Daimon and Fortune are found from these gods in our nativities, which is clear to those trained in astrology" (*Comm. in R.* 2.299.2–28 [Greenbaum]). And just as it was for Valens, this daimon is a crucial guide for Proclus in discovering the *kairos* itself:

> Godlike men subordinately aim at the right moment [τοῦ καιροῦ] … the gods intelligently and divinely determining the measure of right time [τὰ μέτρα τῶν καιρῶν], men seeking to find it by scientific knowledge, and others again making their quest thereof by the inspiration of their daimon [κατὰ τὴν δαιμονίαν ἐπίπνοιαν].

> And guide of this concurrence is the good daimon, who determined for Socrates the precise moment [τὸν καιρὸν] of association.[37] (*In Alc.* 1.121.3–4, 5–7; 1.124.5–7 [O'Neill])

---

35. He examines the relationships between fate, astrology, knowledge, "right moments" (*kairoi*), and the daimon in two places in his book, 5.2 and 9.12. See an analysis of this material in Greenbaum, *Daimon in Hellenistic Astrology*, 40–43.

36. Valens alludes to his *daimonion* four times in his book. Note that the same word is consistently used by Plato in denoting Socrates's *daimonion*, a point noticed by Crystal Addey, "Divination and the *kairos* in Ancient Greek Philosophy and Culture," in Addey, *Divination and Knowledge*, 159.

37. These passages are part of a general discussion on *kairos*, gods, daimons, and humans in *In Alc.* 1.121–124. We thank Crystal Addey for pointing out this discussion to us. See also Addey, "Divination and the *kairos*," 142–43, 156–58.

From 56.15 to 58.16 Proclus enumerates a vast number of other factors that the rulers will need to attend to in order to realize all their eugenic goals. These include the more precise subdivisions (decans) within the sign that is rising at the moment of birth as well as those signs that are at the other cardinal points that play a central role in horoscopes, and in particular at the ascendant. They must also attend to the positions of planets. These are all factors that are discussed in Ptolemy as well. But the guardians must go further and attend to the signs and celestial bodies that co-rise or set together with those signs. This is the science of the *paranatellonta* discussed by Teucer of Babylon, and it gives Proclus's audience an indication that the guardians must be masters of every astrological technique.

Importantly, at 59.3–11 Proclus provides a statement of the rule of Petosiris, which correlates the position of the moon at the time of conception with the sign of the zodiac that is in the ascendant position at birth.

> The Egyptian school of Petosiris and Zoroaster maintain—and Ptolemy concurs—that the ascendant at the time of conception comes to be the place of the Moon at birth, while the Moon's place at conception comes to be the ascendant at birth. If this is true, then someone who knows where the Moon was at the time of conception is also able to know the ascendant at birth and vice versa. Understanding these matters, one needs to consider whether the delivery occurs at seven months or at nine months and how and in how many ways each of the two is produced, so that one may thus know in advance the nativities of those that have been conceived. (*Comm. in R.* 2.55.7–24 [Baltzly, Finamore, and Miles])

At first glance, this lays the groundwork for a katarchic use of astrology to determine the optimal time for the guardians to hold a marriage festival. If one can know how long the pregnancy will last,[38] then one could theoretically arrange a time for conception and a time for birth that are both propitious for producing future rulers who are "gifted and fortunate." Interestingly, there seems to be a precedent for this sort of deployment of the rule of Petosiris in the third book of Hephaestio's *Apotelesmatica* at 3.10.1–5. This book is dedicated to katarchic astrology, which concerns

---

38. Accordingly, this topic of the durations of pregnancies and the ways in which this may be known is taken up shortly after this passage and dominates Proclus's discussion of the "astronomical reading" of Plato's text until *Comm. in R.* 2.61.14, when he turns to factors in the sublunary realm that influence the conception and birth of children.

specific events and often their timing. One subdivision is "elections," or when to initiate a course of action. In the passage from Hephaestio the action in question is sexual intercourse leading to conception, and it seems plausible that Proclus has in mind a similarly katarchic use of the rule of Petosiris in order for the guardians to schedule mating under the best conditions.[39]

Proclus, or perhaps the copyist, has grouped all these astrological considerations into a single numbered section, §37 (*Comm. in R.* 2.54.25–64.4). Immediately following is a much shorter section whose technical details we may (mercifully!) largely pass over. Proclus goes back to a technique for drawing a diagram that was discussed in the preceding §37. Previously it was used to predict the duration of a pregnancy. But now Proclus tells us how Nestorius used this diagram to discover the divinity who is the ruler or custodian of either the seven-month or the nine-month pregnancy. This involves correlating letters with the signs and stars (i.e., planets) to yield a name for the divinity through which it may be summoned: "One must make use of these [names] in every annual cycle, but particularly in periods of pregnancies (whether of the seven-month or nine-month kind, reckoning from the time of conception until the time of birth), summoning through them [sc. the names] *those who are productive of good births*" (*Comm. in R.* 2.64.10–14).

The zodiac signs falling on the sides of the inscribed triangle he mentioned in §37 now furnish the letters correlated with them, and from these letters the divine names are produced (*Comm. in R.* 2.64.14–65.3).[40] Proclus does not divulge the correlations between signs and stars, but we find various systems of correlation in other writers, so the practice was not wholly novel. It is interesting to note, however, that Proclus associates vowels and consonants with planets and signs respectively, then again with soul and body. This not only introduces again the general idea of a parallel between the celestial order and the political order—an idea that dominates much of Proclus's commentary on the *Republic*—but it is also specific to

---

39. See the appendix, section 1, for a list of astrological components desirable for selecting the best time for conceptions.

40. See the appendix, section 2, for a diagram and brief description on how this works. The analysis of Frommhold, with diagrams, on the method Proclus describes, as well as the description of the procedure by Gersh, have been helpful here. See Frommhold, *Bedeutung und Berechnung*, 210–17; Stephen Gersh, *Being Different: More Neoplatonism after Derrida* (Leiden: Brill, 2014), 215–16.

the context at hand. Those unfit for the guardian role are described as lacking in harmony, and this may include the harmony between body and soul that is cultivated through the twin educational disciplines of *gymnastikē* and *mousikē*.

> It is also necessary to include in addition the elements/letters/signs [*stoicheia*] of these [planets] to interweave them with those of signs of the zodiac in a harmonious way, stringing together the benefics and accepting them to a greater extent, whilst doing so much less with their opposites. After all, the [letters] that belong to the signs of the zodiac are analogous to bodies, while those that belong to the stars are analogous to souls; for the latter are vowels, while the letters that belong to the zodiac signs are consonants. But it is impossible for a body to live without soul, but it is possible for a soul to live without body, so that is parallel to the case where consonants are not naturally able to be pronounced apart from vowels, but vowels are able to be pronounced independently of consonants. (*Comm. in R.* 2.65.9–16)

Without going into too much arcane detail, it is relevant to point out how this doctrine of letters in connection with planets and the zodiac, as well as the use of arithmological techniques in an astrological context, can be found in a number of late antique sources—musical, magical, and religious as well as astrological.[41] Important cosmological connections can also give us some indications as to why Proclus would consider this necessary in his

---

41. We have seen the musical in Winnington, *Aristides Quintilianus*, xx, nn. 29–30; see also Ptolemy, *Harmonics*, trans. John Solomon, MnemSup (Leiden: Brill, 2018), esp. 3.8–9, 14–16; and Nicomachus of Gerasa, *Manual of Harmonics*, in Barker, *Greek Musical Writings*, 247–69, and *Excerpta ex Nicomacho*, in Carl Jan, *Musici Scriptores Graeci: Aristoteles, Euclides, Nicomachus, Bacchius, Gaudentius, Alypius* (Leipzig: Teubner, 1895), excerpt 6, pp. 276–78; see translation in Stephen Gersh, *From Iamblichus to Eriugena* (Leiden: Brill, 1978), 295, and commentary by Dirk Baltzly, *Proclus: Commentary on Plato's Timaeus*, vol. 4 (Cambridge: Cambridge University Press, 2009), 46–47; also Joseph Crane, "Ptolemy's Digression: Astrology's Aspects and Musical Intervals," *CC* 11 (2007): 211–27. For magical, among other spells, see *PGM* XIII. 776–781, 824–910; CI. 308; see also Patricia Cox Miller, "In Praise of Nonsense," in *Classical Mediterranean Spirituality*, ed. A. Hilary Armstrong (New York: Crossroads, 1986), 481–505. For religious, gnostic doctrines such as those of Marcus the Valentinian documented in Irenaeus, *Against Heresies*, see Juan Acevedo, *Alphanumeric Cosmology from Greek into Arabic* (Tübingen: Mohr Siebeck, 2020), 156–61; see also Auguste Bouché-Leclercq, *L'astrologie grecque* (Paris: Leroux, 1899), 150 n. 1, 320 n. 1; Franz Boll, *Sphaera: Neue griechische Texte und Untersuchungen zur Geschichte*

exegesis on the nuptial number. These cosmological implications involve *stoicheia*, a polyvalent word, as we have seen above, which can mean "letters" but also "elements" and even refer to zodiacal signs/constellations.[42] The *stoicheia* are bound up in the creation of the cosmos both figuratively and literally.[43] The idea of heavenly writing informing the cosmos is Babylonian as well as Greek,[44] and clearly compatible with an astrological sensibility for finding meaning and correspondence between heaven and earth. Franz Dornseiff has laid out an important exposition on the relationships between the alphabet and the heavens and their interpretation for human life.[45]

An interesting parallel to Proclus's image of the interweaving of the vowels of the planets with the consonants of the zodiac signs, and with his characterizing the vowels as belonging to the soul but the consonants to the body, appears in two scholia to Dionysius Thrax, a grammarian whose brief *Ars grammatica* inspired more than 650 pages of subsequent commentary.[46]

> 1. Just as the seven planets in heaven have the sovereignty in the administration of the observable motions, never leaving the zodiac signs, but remaining always above them and revolving as they go through the visible heaven, thus do the vowels have the sovereignty of the written speech, as they are given shape and are combined with the consonants without ever transgressing the characters of the twenty-four letters, but rather by always being among them and through them, they bring into being the ever recurring wholeness of the written speech....[47]

---

der Sternbilder (Leipzig: Teubner, 1903), 471; Franz Dornseiff, *Das Alphabet in Mystik und Magie*, 2nd ed. (Leipzig: Teubner, 1925), 82.

42. See Acevedo, *Alphanumeric Cosmology*, 13 and n. 46; Dornseiff, *Das Alphabet in Mystik*, 15 n. 1, 88–90.

43. In reference to them as elements, Aristides also notes the importance of the four elements (and their four qualities) in *De musica* 3.14, 19, 21 in Barker, *Greek Musical Writings*, 515, 519, 521.

44. See, e.g., Francesca Rochberg, *The Heavenly Writing: Divination, Horoscopy, and Astronomy in Mesopotamian Culture* (Cambridge: Cambridge University Press, 2004).

45. Dornseiff, *Das Alphabet in Mystik*, 81–91.

46. Dionysius Thrax's probable dates are ca. 170–90 BCE (*OCD*, 479). The scholia are collected in Alfred Hilgard, *Scholia in Dionysii Thracis artem grammaticam* (Leipzig: Teubner, 1901), and cover ten centuries. The dates of these examples are uncertain. However, they show evidence of interest the kinds of ideas Proclus is discussing.

47. Hilgard, *Scholia in Dionysii Thracis*, 491.30–492.4; trans. Acevedo, *Alphanumeric Cosmology*, 28–29.

2. ... The vowels resemble the soul, and the consonants the body. Just as the soul, even though it can exist outside the body, needs the body to produce the compound of life, just so the vowels, even though they can be used and uttered on their own, need the addition of the consonants in order to produce the written speech.[48]

The use of letters in astrology is not widespread, though examples do exist.[49] Vowels are assigned to planets, but their order is not always consistent.[50] One scheme uses the Chaldean order of the planets, an order often associated with astrology (here it begins with the Moon and ends with Saturn):[51]

Moon	Mercury	Venus	Sun	Mars	Jupiter	Saturn
α	ε	η	ι	ο	υ	ω

Several astrological texts connect each sign to two letters: the first sign, Aries, with the first and thirteenth letters, α and ν, the second sign, Taurus, with β and ξ, and so on. In an excerpt from Teucer of Babylon, Rhetorius includes them in his descriptions of the zodiac signs.[52]

---

48. Hilgard, *Scholia in Dionysii Thracis*, 198.19–22, trans. Acevedo, *Alphanumeric Cosmology*, 30.

49. See, e.g., Bouché-Leclercq, *L'astrologie grecque*, 150 n. 1, 320 n. 1; Boll, *Sphaera*, 469–72; Wilhelm Gundel and Hans George Gundel, *Astrologumena: Die astrologische Literatur in der Antike und ihre Geschichte* (Wiesbaden: Steiner, 1966), 33–34, 186–87 (mentions Proclus, *In Platonis rem publicam commentarii*); Jesús Luque Moreno, "Letras, Notas y Estrellas," *MHNH* 11 (2011): 506–17; Moreno, "Letras, Notas y Estrellas. 2ª Parte," *MHNH* 12 (2012): 506–17.

50. Dornseiff, *Das Alphabet in Mystik*, 82–83; Moreno, "Letras, Notas y Estrellas," 510–12, mentioning Plutarch, Porphyry, and John Lydus.

51. Hilgard, *Scholia in Dionysii Thracis*, 198.4–6; Nicomachus, excerpt 6, in Jan, *Musici Scriptores Graeci*, 276–78.

52. *On the Twelve Signs*, excerpted by Rhetorius from Teucer of Babylon, in Franz Boll, ed., *Catalogus Codicum Astrologorum Graecorum* (Brussels: Lamertin, 1908), 7:194–213; see translation in James Holden, *Rhetorius the Egyptian* (Tempe, AZ: American Federation of Astrologers, 2009), 167–88. Other texts include *Epistula Petosiridi supposita*, in Boll, *CCAG* 7:161–62; and the Byzantine *An Oracle Devised by Valens*, in Domenico Bassi et al., trans., *Catalogus Codicum Astrologorum Graecorum* (Brussels: Lamertin, 1903), 4:146–49. While the attribution to Valens is false, the text gives instructions for finding the answer to a question by ascribing the corresponding number value to each letter of the first word of the question, and using values associated with the aspects to these signs.

♈		♉		♊		♋		♌		♍	
α	ν	β	ξ	γ	ο	δ	π	ε	ρ	ζ	σ

♎		♏		♐		♑		♒		♓	
η	τ	θ	υ	ι	φ	κ	χ	λ	ψ	μ	ω

Furthermore, because numbers in Greek are denoted by letters (so that α, β, γ, δ, ε are respectively 1, 2, 3, 4, 5, and so on; the same is true in Hebrew and Arabic),[53] letters and their particular numeric values can be used together. This is the case in the Byzantine astrological text on finding the answer to a question mentioned in note 52, falsely ascribed to Vettius Valens. The method is arcane but is evidence of at least possible practice.[54] The examples provided here give some context for Proclus and the use of letters in his astrological exposition.

Proclus then adds that he has adopted Nestorius's technique for discovering the ruler at the time of birth to a similar discovery at the time of conception, since this is "something useful for those who will be looking after births" (*Comm. in R.* 2.66.4). In thus expanding the guardians' presumed eugenic toolkit to include the summoning of the divine beings who rule over both births and conceptions, Proclus doubtless takes himself to be perfectly in accord with Plato's text, since at 459e, Socrates mentions that sacrifices and hymns will accompany the weddings, while 461a mentions sacrifices again and adds prayers offered by priests and priestesses. The hieratic aspect of the guardians' task is thus not a gratuitous reading-in from Proclus's point of view.

> [I have done this] so that they might not merely keep an eye on the universe for the appropriate time for consummating marriages and thus render the geometric number actual, but in order that they might also supply the opportune moments that they choose with effectiveness according to a sacred method. And this is consistent with the things stipulated by Plato, since he said that the consummations of marriages are to be made along with sacrifices and prayers. If, therefore, you accept this [technique] for discovering the name [of the chronocrator] along with the former [teachings on the geometric number], then you will truly have the sacred method [*hieratikos tropos*] of arranging marriages

---

53. See Acevedo, *Alphanumeric Cosmology.*
54. See the exposition in Dornseif, *Das Alphabet in Mystik,* 84–88.

according to Plato, augmented with sacrifices, with divine names and with prayers. (*Comm. in R.* 2.66.5–15)

While the astrological texts involving letter and number systems that we have considered in other authors have more mundane goals, for Proclus the use of letters (vowels for the planets and consonants for the zodiac signs) allows, in addition to the astrological means of finding a (planetary) ruler for a seven- or nine-month birth, a way to discover the divine names for the ruler as the divinity that can be used in the prayers and or rites accompanying the marriage festivities. Thus the triangle superimposed on the conception chart fulfills two functions, one astrological and one hieratic. We take Proclus's interest in the latter function to indicate his idea of the importance of the identity of the guardian daimon overseeing the pregnancy, and thereby the prenatal life of the child. After all, we know of Proclus's abiding interest in *daimones* and of previous Neoplatonists such as Porphyry exploring the idea of an astrological means of identifying such a daimon. Such an interest would certainly be consonant with the remark of the scholiast that we noted at the outset who took "Plato" to differ from the normal practice of natal astrology in treating the moment of conception as important. It may be that our missing pages from Proclus's commentary contained some more explicit statement from Proclus—read by our scholiast but lost to us—recommending some connection between the astrological and hieratic importance of the time of conception. This, after all, would explain why the timing of the marriage festivals is so important and why perception could lead even such wise rulers as the guardians astray in finding the *kairos* for such moments.

Conclusion

Though modern interpreters of Plato are not likely to endorse it, Proclus's reading of the multiple significances of the nuptial number does at least make sense of Plato's claim at 546b1–2 that the downfall of the state ultimately stems from the fact that the reasoning of even the wise guardians is mixed with *perception*. Among the many things that are communicated to us through the Muses' mathematical symbolism is the idea that the guardians engage in one of the most difficult and demanding forms of astrology: katarchic conception astrology. Moreover, the method of Nestorius that Proclus adapts to the time of conception serves to connect all their astrological endeavors to the practice of sacred rites and the summoning of the divinities that oversee good births. Even if the guardians' *theory* of all these complex matters is perfect, they must nonetheless read the heavens *through perception* in order to apply the theory, and given the difficulty of the task at hand, it is inevitable that something will go wrong.

Proclus's exegesis of the mathematical passage at 546b3–d1 is not exhausted by this interpretation in terms of astrology. Proclus interprets the nuptial number in several modes: arithmetically, geometrically, musically, astronomically, and dialectically (*Comm. in R.* 2.36.2–6). If we can abstract from the welter of detail, Proclus's general understanding of the passage is that it symbolically conveys a wide range of important information about the nature of the human soul and particularly about its descent into Becoming. Each mode of exegesis points to different ways in which numerical patterns are present both in the cosmos and in the microcosmos that is the human soul. While the astrology of conception horoscopy involves perhaps the most concrete and practical specification of this general parallel between the cosmos and the human soul, it is far from the only one. The first, more general agenda in Proclus's astrological reading is of a piece with the strong parallels between the cosmic, psychic, and political order that is the central thread uniting Proclus's various essays on the *Republic*.

We noted at the outset that Aristotle, along with modern readers, treats the nuptial number as merely a way of conveying the idea that nothing in the sensible realm remains forever in the same condition. Proclus would doubtless agree with the thesis that the sensible is the realm of everlasting coming-to-be. But were a reader of Plato to think that the speech of the Muses merely serves to make this point in a dramatic way, Proclus would suppose that such a reader misses the many layers of meaning that Socrates's spokeswomen convey symbolically through the nuptial number. Even if it strains the bounds of credibility to follow Proclus in supposing that Plato had in mind a failure of katarchic conception astrology, it is perhaps not absurd to suppose that the guardians fail in their eugenic project because—somehow—they manage to read some sort of natural signs wrongly. If this is so, then the downfall of Kallipolis results from an epistemic failure. Now, this epistemic failure may, in turn, be a consequence of the nature of what is imperfectly known: perhaps the sensible realm is such that it does not permit knowledge that is inevitably accurate. But this is a very different thing from saying that the ideal city-state degenerates simply because of its metaphysical status as part of the sensible (and thus perishable) realm. Rather, the downfall of Kallipolis is occasioned by epistemic limitations (of some sort), and while those limitations may in turn be partly explained by the metaphysical status of that which the guardians seek to know, they are not one and the same thing. Even if we hesitate to follow Proclus in his specific understanding of *what signs* the guardians miss, he is surely right that their missing them is an essential part of the Muses' account of the degeneration of the ideal city-state.

Appendix 1: The Best Astrological Qualities for Conception

For Proclus, the goal is to choose an astrological chart for conception that will produce the best human beings to rule Kallipolis. To accomplish this, he must therefore choose the best components for that chart. To demonstrate what these qualities are, and following what Proclus mentions as important, we will list what any ancient astrologer would use in electing a chart for the best moment to conceive a child. The three most important items are the right planets in the best condition, emphasizing the right zodiac signs, and in the best places of the chart. The condition of the planets also includes the aspects they make. These will be followed by other techniques Proclus mentions.

Citations from *In Platonis rem publicam commentarii* and astrological texts are given as needed. Hephaestio Thebanus gives instructions for a conception chart, and its components are also noted.[55]

1. Planets

1.1. Luminaries

Since the sun and moon, and their cycles, are associated with generation and birth, their status in the chart is a primary consideration (*Comm. in R.* 2.13.15–18; 2.34.3–24; 2.44.18–22; 2.58.10–13)

---

55. Other general techniques and mechanics of astrology such as rulerships, aspects, qualities of planets, places, and signs can be found in Dorian Gieseler Greenbaum, *The Daimon in Hellenistic Astrology: Origins and Influence, Ancient Magic and Divination* (Leiden: Brill, 2016), 399–414; Hephaestio, *Apotelesmatica* 3.10, in Hephaestio, *Hephaestio Thebanus Apotelesmaticorum libri tres*, ed. David Pingree (Leipzig: Teubner, 1973).

1.1.1. Sun (*Comm. in R.* 2.58.1–5)

- increasing in light (beginning in Capricorn, where daylight begins to increase; *Comm. in R.* 2.32.15)
- increasing in light in its daily cycle (moving toward the meridian; *Comm. in R.* 2.58.1–5)
- in propitious places (esp. 1, 9, 10, 11; also 5; Valens, *Anth.* 2.5–16)
- in a solar sign (from Leo–Capricorn; Ptolemy, *Tetr.* 1.17)
- signs of greatest heat and warmth (Cancer and Leo; Ptolemy, *Tetr.* 1.17)
- fertile seasons (spring and summer)

1.1.2. Moon (*Comm. in R.* 2.57.26–29): The Moon is the most associated with fertility, generation, and nutrition.

- waxing phase of her cycle: new to full moon (also increasing in light at these times)
- fast in motion
- in her own sign or exaltation (Cancer or Taurus)
- in a good relationship to the ascendant
- in a lunar sign (from Aquarius to Cancer; Ptolemy, *Tetr.* 1.17)
- unaspected by malefics
- avoid signs of detriment or fall (Capricorn or Scorpio)
- avoid unpropitious places (2, 6, 8, 12)

1.2. Benefic Planets (*Comm. in R.* 2.57.13–25, 29–30)

Venus and Jupiter should be in good condition, well-positioned in the chart and make good aspects, especially to the sun and moon and/or to the ascendant and its ruler.

1.2.1. Venus

- in own signs or exaltation (Taurus and Libra, or Pisces), own triplicity (earth), term or decan
- in a propitious place (1, 10, 7, 4, esp. 5 [her joy], 11)
- in a waxing phase, "evening" Venus (rising after the sun)
- making trines or sextiles to moon, Jupiter, ascendant or ascendant ruler
- not retrograde

1.2.2. Jupiter

  ♦   in own signs or exaltation (Sagittarius and Pisces, or Cancer), own
      triplicity (fire), term or decan
  ♦   in a propitious place (1, 10, 7, 4, esp. 11 [his joy], 5)
  ♦   in a waxing phase, especially waxing trine
  ♦   making trines or sextiles to sun, moon, Venus, ascendant or
      ascendant ruler
  ♦   not retrograde

The other planets, Mercury, Mars, and Saturn, will be involved if they
are connected to, for example, the ascendant sign, or ruling another
important part of the chart. If so, they should be in good condition and
waxing in phase (*Comm. in R.* 1.58.25–59.3). Mercury, rising in the
east and aspected by Venus and/or Jupiter, produces "fortunate, well-
educated and happy" offspring (εὐτυχῆ καὶ εὐπαίδευτα καὶ εὐδαίμονα;
Hephaestio, *Apot.* 3.10.4)
Mars and Saturn, as the malefic planets, should be avoided when
weaving them together with the letters of the zodiac signs (*Comm. in
R.* 2.65.9–10).

1.2. Signs (58.5–10)

  ♦   Increasing in light: Capricorn to Gemini (*Comm. in R.* 1.32.15,
      1.58.5–10)
  ♦   Fertile signs: Capricorn is the first of the fertile signs; most fertile
      signs for conception are Aries, Taurus ("extremely fertile," Ptol-
      emy, *Tetr.* 1.17), Gemini and Cancer (*Comm. in R.* 2.32.10–20).
      Other fertile signs are Libra ("extremely fertile," Ptolemy, *Tetr.*
      1.17), Scorpio and Pisces ("fecund," in Ptolemy, *Tetr.* 1.17)

1.3. Places

  ♦   Cardines: Ascendant (1), Midheaven (10), Setting (7), and Under-
      ground (4)
  ♦   Succedent places fifth ("Good Fortune"; joy of Venus), eleventh
      (Good Daimon; joy of Jupiter)
  ♦   Cadent places third (moon goddess) and ninth (sun god)

- ◆ Avoid the succedent places eighth (Hades or Death) and second (Gate of Hades); also cadent places sixth (Bad Fortune) and twelfth (Bad Daimon; Hephaestio, *Apot.* 3.10)

1.4. Ascendant

Ruler of the Ascendant free of aspects from malefic planets and in propitious places (Hephaestio, *Apot.* 3.10).

1.5. Lot of Fortune

Best placed in the eleventh, fifth, tenth (Midheaven), or ninth (Hephaestio, *Apot.* 3.10).

1.6. Sphere of the Fixed Stars (*Comm. in R.* 2.56.15–18)

Paranatellonta and Decans (*Comm. in R.* 2.57.1–12)

Rhetorius transmits an excerpt from Teucer of Babylon in which each of the signs is described (*CCAG* 7.194–213). It combines the *paranatellonta*, constellations that co-rise with planets or stars/groups of stars and the decans, the subdivisions of each sign into three ten-degree segments each ruled by a god or daimonic divinity, and later associated with a planetary god.[56] For example, Athena and the Tail of Cetus, among other stars, rise with the first decan of Aries. The techniques covered in this excerpt are similar to those Proclus mentions here. Whether consulting this particular text or one similar to it, possibly Proclus could be relying on it as a source of astrological practices used in finding the best ruler of the conception. Incidentally, this excerpt also contains letters assigned to each zodiac sign.

---

56. Decans and horoscopes are related in astrological, Hermetic, and philosophical texts (e.g., Porphyry's *Letter to Anebo*); see Dorian Gieseler Greenbaum and Micah T. Ross, "The Role of Egypt in the Development of the Horoscope," in *Egypt in Transition: Social and Religious Development of Egypt in the First Millennium BCE*, ed. Ladislav Bareš, Filip Coppens, and Kveta Smolarikova (Prague: Faculty of Arts, Charles University in Prague, 2010), 158–64. For the decans' connections to daimonic entities in astrological settings, see Greenbaum, *Daimon in Hellenistic Astrology*, 224–29.

Decans and horoscopes also have a connection to daimonic entities in astrological texts.[57]

Appendix 2: Proclus's Adaptation of Nestorius

This involves finding the ruler of a conception chart, depending on the length of the pregnancy, and the divine names associated with it (*Comm. in R.* 2.64.14–66.1).

This is one of the more difficult and arcane procedures described by Proclus. Because of the need to prepare for both seven- and nine-month births, procedures for both must be described. The angles of the right triangle are 90° (vertical side), 120° (horizontal side), and 150° (hypotenuse). Proclus associates different sides of the triangle with different durations of pregnancy:

> vertical + horizontal = seven-month birth (90+120 = 210 days)
> horizontal + hypotenuse = nine-month birth (120+150 = 270 days)

Proclus does not specify the letters associated with each sign or with the planets, since he says he has given them elsewhere (64.27–65.3, 18–20).[58]

The following steps are outlined by Proclus and summarized here:

---

57. For analysis of this topic, see Greenbaum, *Daimon in Hellenistic Astrology*, 210–11, 224–25, 227–28, 234–35.

58. One wonders, since at *Comm. in R.* 2.65.2–3, he refers to the "letters" of the signs "as they have been distributed in the sacred art [ἐν τῇ ἱερατικῇ τέχνῃ]," whether he literally meant his treatise *On the Sacred Art*, which today exists only in a fragment of two pages edited by Bidez, *Vie de Porphyre*, and translated into Latin by Marsilio Ficino. An English version is in Brian Copenhaver, "Hermes Trismegisthus, Proclus, and the Question of a Philosophy of Magic in the Renaissance," in *Hermetism and the Renaissance: Intellectual History and the Occult in Early Modern Europe*, ed. Ingrid Merkel and Allen G. Debus (Washington, DC: Folger Books, 1988), 102–5; Copenhaver, *Magic in Western Culture from Antiquity to the Enlightenment* (Cambridge: Cambridge University Press, 2015), 91–94. Later on in 2.65, Proclus refers to the fact that he has written about letters associated with planets and signs: "We have said elsewhere what letters belong to what signs and what letters to what planets and how the seven vowels have been divided among the seven planets, and the seventeen consonants among the twelve signs" (*Comm. in R.* 2.65.17–20).

- use a right triangle in the proportions 3-4-5
- inscribe the right triangle in the zodiacal circle with the right angle on the ascendant
- the vertical side is the right angle (square), placed above the ascendant
- the horizontal side is the trine (120°), placed below the ascendant
- the hypotenuse (150°) connects the vertical and horizontal sides
- zodiac signs connected with each side have letters used to make the divine names of the ruler
- place the planets in the chart according to the best moment chosen for conception
- using the vowels for the planets and consonants for the signs, interweave them with the consonants harmoniously, emphasizing the vowels of the benefics and minimizing those of the malefics
- in combining the vowels with the consonants, begin and end with the vowels
- for a seven-month birth, use the letters for the planets and signs on the vertical and horizontal sides
- for a nine-month birth, use the letters for the planets and signs on horizontal and hypotenuse sides
- use a rough breathing for the benefics but a soft breathing for the malefics

The accompanying example diagram shows how such a chart might have looked. It contains the inscribed 3-4-5 right triangle with right angle on the ascendant.

- Signs Scorpio, Libra, Virgo, and Leo are the vertical side
- Signs Scorpio, Sagittarius, Capricorn, Aquarius, and Pisces are the horizontal side
- Signs Leo, Cancer, Gemini, Taurus, Aries, and Pisces are on the hypotenuse side
- Planets included for illustration purposes

Note that Proclus does not specify the letters associated with each sign; those used here for illustration are the letter assignations given by Rhetorius, *On the Twelve Signs* (*CCAG* 7.194–213), an excerpt said to be originally from Teucer of Babylon (this same excerpt reports on *paranatellonta* and decans; see above, section 1).

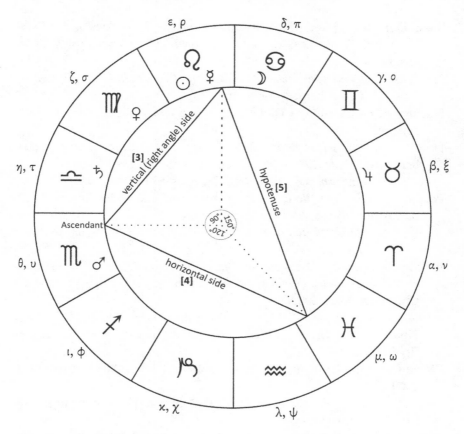

Diagram after Katrin Frommhold, *Bedeutung und Berechnung der Empfängnis in der Astrologie der Antike* (Münster: Aschendorff, 2004), 215.

Bibliography

Primary Sources

Barker, Andrew. *Harmonic and Acoustic Theory*. Vol. 2 of *Greek Musical Writings*. Edited by John Stevens and Peter le Huray. CRLM 2. Cambridge: Cambridge University Press, 1989.

Boll, Franz, ed. *Catalogus Codicum Astrologorum Graecorum*. Vol. 7. Brussels: Lamertin, 1908.

———. *Sphaera: Neue griechische Texte und Untersuchungen zur Geschichte der Sternbilder*. Leipzig: Teubner, 1903.

Bassi, Domenico, Franz Cumont, Emidio Martini, and Alessandro Olivieri, trans. *Catalogus Codicum Astrologorum Graecorum*. Vol. 4. Brussels: Lamertin, 1903.

Hephaestio. *Hephaestio Thebanus Apotelesmaticorum libri tres*. Edited by David Pringree. Leipzig: Teubner, 1973.

Hilgard, Alfred. *Scholia in Dionysii Thracis artem grammaticam*. Leipzig: Teubner, 1901.

Jan, Carl, ed. *Musici Scriptores Graeci: Aristoteles, Euclides, Nicomachus, Bacchius, Gaudentius, Alypius*. Leipzig: Teubner, 1895.

O'Neill, William. *Proclus: Alcibiades I*. The Hague: Nijhoff, 1965.

Porphyry. *De philosophia ex oraculis haurienda*. Edited by Gustav Wolff. Berlin: Springer; Hildesheim: Olms, 1856.

———. *Philosophi Fragmenta*. Edited by Andrew Smith. Stuttgart: Teubner, 1993.

Proclus. *Book 3, Part II, Proclus on the World Soul*. Vol. 4 of *Commentary on Plato's Timaeus*. Translated by Dirk Baltzly. Cambridge: Cambridge University Press, 2009.

———. *Commentary on Plato's Republic*. Translated by Dirk Baltzly, John Finamore, and Graeme Miles. 2 vols. Cambridge: Cambridge University Press, 2018, 2022.

Ptolemy. *Harmonics*. Translated by Jon Solomon. MnemSup. Leiden: Brill, 2000.

———. *Tetrabiblos*. Translated by Frank E. Robbins. LCL. Cambridge: Harvard University Press, 1940.

Vettius Valens. *Anthologiarum libri novem*. Edited by David Pingree. Leipzig: Teubner, 1986.

Winnington-Ingram, Reginald P. *Aristides Quintilianus: De musica libri tres*. Leipzig: Teubner, 1963.

Secondary Sources

Acevedo, Juan. *Alphanumeric Cosmology from Greek into Arabic*. Tübingen: Mohr Siebeck, 2020.

Adamson, Peter. "Plotinus on Astrology." *OSAP* 35 (2008): 265–91.

Addey, Crystal. "Divination and the *kairos* in Ancient Greek Philosophy and Culture." Pages 138–73 in *Divination and Knowledge in Greco-Roman Antiquity*. Edited by Crystal Addey. London: Routledge, 2021.

———. *Divination and Theurgy in Neoplatonism: Oracles of the Gods*. Farnham, UK: Ashgate, 2014.

Akçay, K. Nilüfer. *Porphyry's On the Cave of the Nymphs in Its Intellectual Context*. Leiden: Brill, 2019.

Baltzly, Dirk. "Civic Virtues and the Goal of Likeness to God in Proclus' *Republic Commentary*." Pages 197–217 in *Early Christianity and Late Antique Philosophy*. Edited by Eva Anagnostou-Laoutides and Ken Perry. Leiden: Brill, 2020.

———. *Proclus: Commentary on Plato's Timaeus*. Vol. 4. Cambridge: Cambridge University Press, 2009.

Barton, Tamsyn. *Power and Knowledge: Astrology, Physiognomics, and Medicine under the Roman Empire*. Ann Arbor: University of Michigan Press, 1994.

Bezza, Giuseppe. "Astrological Considerations on the Length of Life in Hellenistic, Persian and Arabic Astrology." *CC* 2.2 (1998): 3–15.

Bidez, Joseph. *Vie de Porphyre: Le philosophe Néo-Platonicien*. Leipzig: Teubner, 1913.

Bouché-Leclercq, Auguste. *L'astrologie grecque*. Paris: Leroux, 1899.

Burkert, Walter. *Lore and Science in Ancient Pythagoreanism*. Translated by Edwin Minar. Cambridge: Harvard University Press, 1972.

Cambiano, Giuseppe. "Astronomy and Divination in Stoic Philosophy." Pages 607–18 in *A Brill Companion to Hellenistic Astronomy: The Science in Its Contexts*. Edited by Alan C. Bowen and Francesca Rochberg. Leiden: Brill, 2020.

Copenhaver, Brian. "Hermes Trismegistus, Proclus, and the Question of a Philosophy of Magic in the Renaissance." Pages 79–110 in *Hermetism and the Renaissance: Intellectual History and the Occult in Early Modern Europe*. Edited by Ingrid Merkel and Allen G. Debus. Washington, DC: Folger Books, 1988.

———. *Magic in Western Culture from Antiquity to the Enlightenment*. Cambridge: Cambridge University Press, 2015.

Crane, Joseph. "Ptolemy's Digression: Astrology's Aspects and Musical Intervals." *CC* 11 (2007): 211–27.

Dillon, John. "Plotinus on Whether the Stars Are Causes." *ResOr* 12 (1999): 87–92.

Dornseiff, Franz. *Das Alphabet in Mystik und Magie*. 2nd ed. Leipzig: Teubner, 1925.

Frommhold, Katrin. *Bedeutung und Berechnung der Empfängnis in der Astrologie der Antike*. Münster: Aschendorff, 2004.

Gersh, Stephen. *Being Different: More Neoplatonism after Derrida*. Leiden: Brill, 2014.

————. *From Iamblichus to Eriugena*. Leiden: Brill, 1978.

Greenbaum, Dorian Gieseler. *The Daimon in Hellenistic Astrology: Origins and Influence, Ancient Magic and Divination*. Leiden: Brill, 2016.

————. "Divination and Decumbiture: Katarchic Astrology and Greek Medicine." Pages 109–37 in *Divination and Knowledge in Greco-Roman Antiquity*. Edited by Crystal Addey. London: Routledge, 2021.

————. "Hellenistic Astronomy in Medicine." Pages 350–80 in *A Brill Companion to Hellenistic Astronomy: The Science in Its Contexts*. Edited by Alan C. Bowen and Francesca Rochberg. Leiden: Brill, 2020.

————. "The Hellenistic Horoscope." Pages 443–71 in *A Brill Companion to Hellenistic Astronomy: The Science in Its Contexts*. Edited by Alan C. Bowen and Francesca Rochberg. Leiden: Brill, 2020.

————. *Late Classical Astrology: Paulus Alexandrinus and Olympiodorus*. Reston, VA: ARHAT, 2001.

————. "Porphyry of Tyre on the *Daimon*, Birth and the Stars." Pages 102–39 in *Neoplatonic Demons and Angels*. Edited by Luc Brisson, Seamus O'Neil, and Andrei Timotin. Leiden: Brill, 2018.

Greenbaum, Dorian Gieseler, and Micah T. Ross. "The Role of Egypt in the Development of the Horoscope." Pages 146–82 in *Egypt in Transition: Social and Religious Development of Egypt in the First Millennium BCE*. Edited by Ladislav Bareš, Filip Coppens, and Kveta Smolarikova. Prague: Faculty of Arts, Charles University in Prague, 2010.

Gundel, Wilhelm, and Hans Georg Gundel. *Astrologumena: Die astrologische Literatur in der Antike und ihre Geschichte*. Wiesbaden: Steiner, 1966.

Hanson, Ann Ellis. "The Eight Months' Child and the Etiquette of Birth: Obsit Omen!" *BHM* 61 (1987): 589–602.

Heilen, Stephan. "The Doctrine of the Third, Seventh and Fortieth Days of the Moon in Ancient Astrology." *MHNH* 12 (2012): 179–98.

Holden, James. *Rhetorius the Egyptian*. Tempe, AZ: American Federation of Astrologers, 2009.

Hübner, Wolfgang. "Die geometrische Theologie des Philolaos." *Phil* 124 (1980): 18–32.

László, Levente. "Revisiting the Authenticity of Porphyry's *Introduction to Ptolemy's 'APOTELESMATICS.'*" *CP* 116 (2021): 392–411.

Lawrence, Marilynn. "Astral Symbolism in Theurgic Rites." Pages 270–94 in *Divination and Knowledge in Greco-Roman Antiquity*. Edited by Crystal Addey. London: Routledge, 2021.

———. "Who Thought the Stars Are Causes? The Astrological Doctrine Criticized by Plotinus." Pages 17–33 in *Metaphysical Patterns in Platonism.* Edited by John F. Finamore and Robert M. Berchman. New Orleans: University Press of the South, 2007.

Lewis, A. M. "Augustus and His Horoscope Reconsidered." *Phoenix* 62 (2008): 308–37.

Long, Anthony A. "Astrology: Arguments Pro and Contra." Pages 165–92 in *Science and Speculation.* Edited by Jonathan Barnes, Jacques Brunschwig, Myles Burnyeat, and Malcolm Schofield. Cambridge: Cambridge University Press, 1982.

McPherran, Mark. "The Gods and Piety of Plato's Republic." Pages 84–103 in *The Blackwell Guide to Plato's Republic.* Edited by Gerasimos Santas. Malden, MA: Blackwell, 2006.

Miller, Patricia Cox. "In Praise of Nonsense." Pages 481–505 in *Classical Mediterranean Spirituality.* Edited by A. Hilary Armstrong. New York: Crossroads, 1986.

Moreno, Jesús Luque. "Letras, Notas y Estrellas." *MHNH* 11 (2011): 506–17.

———. "Letras, Notas y Estrellas. 2ª Parte." *MHNH* 12 (2012): 506–17.

Pappas, Nickolas. *Plato and the Republic.* 2nd ed. London: Routledge, 1995.

Popović, Mladen. *Reading the Human Body: Physiognomics and Astrology in the Dead Sea Scrolls and Hellenistic–Early Roman Period Judaism.* STDJ. Leiden: Brill, 2007.

Rochberg, Francesca. *The Heavenly Writing: Divination, Horoscopy, and Astronomy in Mesopotamian Culture.* Cambridge: Cambridge University Press, 2004.

Tarrant, Harold. "From Fringe Reading to Core Curriculum: Commentary, Introduction and Doctrinal Summary." Pages 101–14 in *The Brill Companion to the Reception of Plato in Antiquity.* Edited by Harold Tarrant, Dirk Baltzly, Danielle Layne, and François Renaud. Leiden: Brill, 2018.

———. *Thrasyllan Platonism.* Ithaca, NY: Cornell University Press, 1993.

Warnon, Jean. "Le commentaire attribué à Héliodore sur les εἰσαγωγικά de Paul d'Alexandrie." *RPL* 1 (1967): 197–217.

Waterfield, Robin. "The Evidence for Astrology in Classical Greece." *CC* 3.2 (1999): 3–15.

———. *Plato: Republic.* Oxford: Oxford University Press, 1993.

Westerink, Leendert G. "Ein astrologisches Kolleg aus dem Jahre 564." *ByzZ* 64 (1971): 6–21.

Prophets and Poets:
Plato and The Daimonic Nature of Poetry

Elizabeth Hill

In book 10 of Plato's *Republic*, Socrates speaks of an "an ancient quarrel" (ὅτι παλαιὰ μέν τις διαφορὰ φιλοσοφίᾳ τε καὶ ποιητικῇ, *Resp.* 607b)[1] between poetry and philosophy. He cites several (presumably) well-known adages: poetry is referred to as "the [bitch] yelping and shrieking at its master,"[2] "great in the empty eloquence of fools" (λακέρυζα πρὸς δεσπόταν κύων, *Resp.* 607b), and the craft of "the subtle thinkers, beggars all" (μέγας ἐν ἀφρόνων κενεαγορίαισι, *Resp.* 607b–c). The precise origin of these quotes is unknown, but their sentiment is clear: poetry is the product of hubristic and ignorant people, rendering it foolish, empty, and useless. While Socrates is only quoting others in this passage, books

As a member of the International Society for Neoplatonic Studies, I entered Dr. Finamore's orbit at the beginning of my academic career. From the moment I was introduced to him, he made me feel accepted and welcome within the Neoplatonic community, and this encouraged me to persist in my scholarly pursuits. Over the last several years, I have witnessed Dr. Finamore's many exceptional qualities. These include, but of course are not limited to, the depth, breadth, and richness of his scholarly work; his kind and welcoming demeanor; the trust and excellence he inspires in his students; and his outstanding adeptness at getting scholars together to talk about ideas. Dr. Finamore has made a lasting and invaluable impact on the scholarly community, but he has also made a lasting impact on our personal lives as an enduring example of kindness and wisdom.

1. All English translations are taken from *Plato: Complete Works*, ed. John M. Cooper (Indianapolis: Hackett, 1997), except where I note another translation, my own translation, or my own amendments to those translations given in Cooper. All Greek text is from the OCT.

2. This particularly vicious, but not inaccurate, amendment to Grube's translation is brought out by Robert Lloyd Mitchell in "That Yelping Bitch: On Poetry in Plato's Republic," *Arion (Boston)* 24.2 (2016): 69–90.

2 and 3 of *Republic* contain a protracted discussion on the use of poetry in education, the conclusion of which is that they must banish much, if not most, of the traditional Greek canon of poetry from Kallipolis. As Socrates puts it, "hymns to the gods and eulogies to good people are the only poetry we can admit into our city" (μόνον ὕμνους θεοῖς καὶ ἐγκώμια τοῖς ἀγαθοῖς ποιήσεως παραδεκτέον εἰς πόλιν, *Resp.* 607a).

Consequently, Socrates seemingly rejects the works of the comics and tragedians, and he dismembers the works of Homer and Hesiod, casting large portions of their oeuvre out of his Eden. By book 10, poetry in Kallipolis has had its wings sufficiently "clipped";[3] all that is left of the ancient Greek literary corpus are those few texts deemed sufficiently safe and morally edifying. Hence, perhaps, Plato finds some truth in the claim that poetry, or at least most poetry, is merely "great in the empty eloquence of fools" (λεπτῶς μεριμνῶντες, *Resp.* 607b) and nothing more, and many contemporary scholars have argued as much. As Robert Lloyd Mitchell puts it, "it is hard to recall, or even imagine, a more brutal attack upon poetry than Socrates['s]."[4] Suzanne Stern-Gillet describes Plato's view of poetry in the *Ion* as "anti-poetry," and Susan Levin states that Plato gives a "systematic critique of poetry."[5] John Ferrari claims that Plato "is uncompromisingly hostile towards [poetry]," and Andrew Ford states that Plato offered "aberrant moral attacks" against poetry that subsequently burdened Aristotle with its redemption.[6]

Despite the accounts given in the quotes above, Plato's position on poetry is not straightforwardly negative. Plato himself had a broad and deep knowledge of Homer, Hesiod, Pindar, Simonides, Aeschylus, Euripides, and Aristophanes, which was on full display in his own works. The dialogues are liberally peppered with quotations from and references to the poets, demonstrating that Plato himself was well-read and that he saw value in the relationship between poetry and philosophy. If we consider

---

3. John Ferrari, "Plato and Poetry," in *The Cambridge History of Literary Criticism*, ed. George Alexander Kennedy (Cambridge: Cambridge University Press, 1990), 1:110.

4. Mitchell, "That Yelping Bitch," 69.

5. Suzanne Stern-Gillet, "On (Mis)interpreting Plato's *Ion*," *Phronesis* 49 (2004): 190; Susan B. Levin, *The Ancient Quarrel between Philosophy and Poetry Revisited: Plato and the Greek Literary Tradition* (Oxford: Oxford University Press, 2000), 6.

6. Ferrari, "Plato and Poetry," 92; Andrew Laughlin Ford, *The Origins of Criticism: Literary Culture and Poetic Theory in Classical Greece* (Princeton: Princeton University Press, 2002), 3.

only Plato's uncontested and completed dialogues, there is not a single one that does not have at least one quote or reference to at least one of the poets. He most often invokes Homer. Furthermore, in many places, Plato depicts poetry as the product of poets who are divinely inspired, possessed by the Muses, and, as he tells us in the *Laws* and *Republic*, the divine can only be the source of good things.[7]

Accordingly, Plato appears to express conflicting views on poetry throughout his body of written work. The reader is left to wonder whether poetry is the product of ignorant thinkers, "beggars all," and therefore likely to corrupt the minds of those who hear it, or whether it is a divine gift resulting from holy possession, a conduit through which the divine communes with and nourishes mortal souls.[8] While a comprehensive answer to this question is beyond the scope of the present paper, I submit that one may find a resolution to it by understanding poetry, for Plato, as daimonic. First, this chapter will briefly explain how, in Plato's thought, there is a compatibility between reason and suprarational experience, and both are useful for the pursuit of true knowledge (*noēsis*). Second, this study will give a brief account of the daimonic in Plato's corpus, demonstrating that he has a consistent account of daimonic activity as that which mediates the divine-human relationship. Third, it will present the case for the daimonic nature of poetry for Plato, focusing primarily on an exegesis of the *Ion*. Fourth and finally, this chapter will conclude by briefly looking

---

7. *Leg.* 907a: "aren't all the gods the most supreme guardians of all, and don't they look after our supreme interests?" (ἀλλ᾽ οὐ πάντων φυλάκων εἰσὶ μέγιστοι καὶ περὶ τὰ μέγιστα ἡμῖν οἱ πάντες θεοί;) *Resp.* 379c: "Therefore, since a god is good, he is not—as most people claim—the cause of everything that happens to human beings but of only a few things, for good things are fewer than bad ones in our lives. He alone is responsible for the good things, but we must find some other cause for the bad ones, not a god" (οὐδ᾽ ἄρα, ἦν δ᾽ ἐγώ, ὁ θεός, ἐπειδὴ ἀγαθός, πάντων ἂν εἴη αἴτιος, ὡς οἱ πολλοὶ λέγουσιν, ἀλλὰ ὀλίγων μὲν τοῖς ἀνθρώποις αἴτιος, πολλῶν δὲ ἀναίτιος· πολὺ γὰρ ἐλάττω τἀγαθὰ τῶν κακῶν ἡμῖν, καὶ τῶν μὲν ἀγαθῶν οὐδένα ἄλλον αἰτιατέον, τῶν δὲ κακῶν ἄλλ᾽ ἄττα δεῖ ζητεῖν τὰ αἴτια, ἀλλ᾽ οὐ τὸν θεόν). On poets as divinely inspired, see *Apol.* 22c, 23c; *Leg.* 682a; *Phaedr.* 265b; *Meno* 99d; and throughout the *Ion*. On poets as possessed by the muses, see *Phaedr.* 243a and throughout the *Ion*.

8. One could solve this problem by demonstrating a shift in Plato's thought on inspiration from early dialogues to late ones. However, no such shift appears to be present, or at least not one that would sufficiently address the apparent inconsistency completely. Divine inspiration is named in relation to the poets across the Platonic corpus from early to late dialogues. For examples, see footnote 7 above.

at how the daimonic account of poetry can resolve the apparent contradictions among Plato's various remarks on the value of poetry.

The Suprarational in Plato

Much of the scholarship over the last century has treated Plato as an arch-rationalist in the Cartesian sense.[9] Hence, many have assumed that Plato could not have valued suprarational experiences as part of the philosophical life. As John Cocking puts it, for Plato, "the ideal state would be one in which citizens of high intelligence would freely reason their way towards the good."[10] In other words, in the human quest for truth and knowledge, we need no divine or otherwise transcendent interventions; all we need is our own ability to contemplate reality according to the objective principles of reason. Knowledge is reducible to propositional truth claims. Poetry, divination, ritual, and interpersonal attachments either lack such claims or present them with too much unnecessary varnish.

Nevertheless, other scholars, including myself, view the rationalist approach as anachronistic because it reads an essentially early modern notion of reason into Plato's thought. Furthermore, it fails to account for the numerous references to suprarational experiences throughout Plato's work. Most problematically, however, the rationalist approach fails to properly situate human reason within the broader context of Plato's account of reality. It thereby misses the compatibility between the suprarational and the rational in Plato's cosmos. Briefly, Plato's metaphysical schema begins with the Good, which is that from which Being emanates. Therefore, the Good is beyond Being itself.[11] From the Good we get Being, or the eternal and static mode in which the Forms exist. Next is Becoming, the mode of existence inhabited by the sensible world; Plato characterizes it as a mixture of Being and non-Being, allowing motion and time to take place. In

---

9. In this context, *rationalist* connotes the belief that knowledge obtained through "reason" (i.e., the calculative, systematic processes of the mind) is superior to, distinct from, and even opposed to knowledge gained through experience, emotion, or revelation. The strict rationalist denies that experience, emotion, and revelation are sources of knowledge at all.

10. John Cocking, *Imagination: A Study in the History of Ideas*, ed. Penelope Murray (New York: Routledge, 1992), 10.

11. *Resp.* 509b: "the good is not being, but superior to it in rank and power" (οὐκ οὐσίας ὄντος τοῦ ἀγαθοῦ, ἀλλ᾽ ἔτι ἐπέκεινα τῆς οὐσίας πρεσβείᾳ καὶ δυνάμει ὑπερέχοντος).

Becoming, a thing can be both beautiful to the extent that it participates in the Form of Beauty and not beautiful to the extent that it does not participate in the Form of Beauty, but the Form of Beauty itself is never anything other than identical with itself.

To truly understand the Forms is to understand the whole of reality instantaneously and as a unity, because to completely understand one thing, one must completely understand everything. Thus, to know one Form is to know them completely and all at once, which is the kind of knowledge that Plato tells us the gods enjoy (*Phaedr.* 228a). Plato contrasts divine *noēsis* with mortal *dianoia*, which is knowing in the mode of a human being who must go "through thought" (δια + νόος). Human reason is therefore not the highest form of knowledge; instead, it is a kind of moving image of *noēsis*, which, in contrast to *dianoia*, is not in motion but comprehends all instantaneously and therefore a-temporally. The pursuit of divine knowledge, *noēsis*, is the human being's true, ever-present, yet never fully satisfied goal for Plato.[12] Discursive human reason is merely a tool to be used in pursuit of this goal.

We appear to have a prerational intuition of the Good and its products, as "every soul pursues the good and does its utmost for its sake" (ὃ δὴ διώκει μὲν ἅπασα ψυχὴ καὶ τούτου ἕνεκα πάντα πράττει, *Resp.* 505e). Nevertheless, while we have the Forms and the Good in our sights, we cannot hit the mark on our own. We cannot, to echo Cocking's verbiage, freely reason our way to the Good. The allegory of the cave makes our impotence vividly apparent. Plato describes the beginning of the prisoner's journey using the passive voice. The prisoner must be "freed and suddenly compelled to stand up" (λυθείη καὶ ἀναγκάζοιτο ἐξαίφνης ἀνίστασθαί, *Resp.* 515c). She is then "dragged ... away from there by force, up the rough, steep path" by someone who will not "let [her] go until [she] had dragged [her] into the sunlight, wouldn't [she] be pained and irritated at being treated that

---

12. I am in agreement with the central claims found in Arnold Herman, *To Think Like a God: Pythagoras and Parmenides, the Origins of Philosophy* (Las Vegas: Parmenides, 2004). Herman argues that the pre-Socratics mark a shift in thinking about the divine wherein the gods are relieved (somewhat) of their anthropomorphism and are consequently identified with those who know reality absolutely. As Herman puts it, "Deity ... had to *know*, and had to know *objectively*; it was obliged to maintain a direct, uninhibited kinship with truth" (5). The introduction of basic concepts of logic through *Parmenides*'s work on contradiction results in the basic principles of verifying human thought and the hope of attaining divine knowledge (7–11). I see Plato as a continuation of this new goal that is found in the pre-Socratics.

way?"[13] (*Resp.* 515e). Once she is outside the cave, the language changes to the active voice. As her eyes begin to adjust to the light, the prisoner starts actively studying this world outside the cave (*Resp.* 516a). The allegory is clear: we cannot initiate ourselves into the path toward knowledge; something or someone from outside of us must first shock us out of our ignorant stupor and make us aware of the sun's light.

Notably, the prisoner returns to the cave to bring others back out, so there is a temptation to see the message as an endorsement of Socrates's own pedagogical methods and therefore as an affirmation of our ability to reason our way to the Good via discourse. While this conclusion is not wrong, it does not tell the whole story, for we must ask, "How did Socrates himself (or the first prisoner) exit the cave?" If we want to avoid an infinite regress, we must acknowledge that something other than bare human reason got the first prisoner out of the cave. Furthermore, given that Socrates describes his own philosophical education as, at least in part, indebted to Diotima, who taught him "the things of eros" (*Symp.* 201d)[14]—and who tells us that the path to the soul's ascent is through erotic experience—it is reasonable to read the allegory of the cave as a nod to the need for the daimonic in our initiation into knowledge. In other words, human beings can only exit the cave because of the divine gift of daimonic mediation, whether via Eros or some other daimonic entity or activity.

Apart from Eros, Plato also repeatedly references Socrates's *daimonion*—his "divine sign"—as a vital component of Socrates's own philosophical path. The divine sign provides Socrates with revelatory prohibitions (*Alc.* 1.103a; *Apol.* 40a), rebukes (*Phaedr.* 242b–c), and even guides his pedagogical practices (*Theaet.* 151a). In the *Phaedrus*, Plato depicts religious madness as divinely given and valuable,[15] and in the *Apology* Socrates seriously ponders the utterances of the Delphic Oracle (*Apol.* 21b–23b). Finally, Socrates describes himself as a mantic.[16] In short,

---

13. εἰ δέ, ἦν δ' ἐγώ, ἐντεῦθεν ἕλκοι τις αὐτὸν βίᾳ διὰ τραχείας τῆς ἀναβάσεως καὶ ἀνάντους, καὶ μὴ ἀνείη πρὶν ἐξελκύσειεν εἰς τὸ τοῦ ἡλίου φῶς, ἆρα οὐχὶ ὀδυνᾶσθαί τε ἂν καὶ ἀγανακτεῖν ἑλκόμενον.

14. Translation mine: τὰ ἐρωτικά.

15. *Phaedr.* 244a: "the best things we have come from madness, when it is given as a gift of the god" (νῦν δὲ τὰ μέγιστα τῶν ἀγαθῶν ἡμῖν γίγνεται διὰ μανίας, θείᾳ μέντοι δόσει διδομένης).

16. *Phaedr.* 242c: "In effect, you see, I am a seer, and though I am not particularly good at it … I am good enough for my own purposes" (εἰμὶ δὴ οὖν μάντις μέν, οὐ πάνυ δὲ σπουδαῖος, ἀλλ' ὥσπερ οἱ τὰ γράμματα φαῦλοι, ὅσον μὲν ἐμαυτῷ μόνον ἱκανός).

one cannot deny the frequent presence of suprarational experiences as a method by which the human being is made aware of her soul's true goal.

Furthermore, such respect for the daimonic within Plato's body of work was widely acknowledged and embraced as a necessary part of Platonic philosophy by those in antiquity.[17] The suprarational was an integral part of being a Platonist. Crystal Addey points to this historical reality by stating:

> [The] view of Socrates as sage and mystic does not contradict or conflict in any way with the view of Socrates as a rationalist or as the philosopher par excellence. Both roles are attributed to Socrates by Neoplatonists and are seen as vital to the role of philosophy as a way of life leading toward self-knowledge and, consequently, toward knowledge of the cosmos.... Within Neoplatonism, the dialectician must be a mystic, and the mystic must be a dialectician. In this sense, Socrates exemplifies the culmination of the philosophical life—the enlightened mystic who lives and acts in assimilation to the divine.[18]

Addey is not alone in this claim. Stephen Halliwell appears to agree, stating, "Those competing demands [between discursive reason and 'intensely heightened and transformed consciousness], together with the aspiration to find a way of unifying them, run through Plato's conception of philosophy as a whole."[19] Pauliina Remes also agrees:

> One may wonder ... whether opposing the argumentative or dialectical to the literary and non discursive is necessary, fruitful or even possible. Socrates, Plato, as well as their late ancient interpreters were all lovers

---

17. See, for one example, Proclus, *In. Alc.* 1.60–85. Though Plato only spends about one sentence on the *daimonion* at 103A, where Socrates states that he was held back from engaging erotically with the youth by some *daimonion* (τι δαιμόνιον), Proclus nonetheless takes the time to give a lengthy commentary on the nature of daimons within Plato's philosophy as a whole. Proclus clearly thinks that, in order to fully grasp the dialogue as a whole, one must not only take this reference to the *daimonion* seriously, but also one cannot neglect to grasp it within the larger context of a Platonic demonology as a whole.

18. Crystal Addey, "The *Daimonion* of Socrates: *Daimones* and Divination in Neoplatonism," in *The Neoplatonic Socrates*, ed. Danielle A. Layne and Harold Tarrant (Philadelphia: University of Pennsylvania Press, 2014), 52.

19. Stephen Halliwell, *Between Ecstasy and Truth: Interpretations of Greek Poetics from Homer to Longinus* (Oxford: Oxford University Press, 2011), 159.

of argument, and just as an analytic-argumentative reading cannot
yield a fair picture of what goes on in Plato, so the literary approach
cannot stand alone: within Plato, the performative relies and strives
for values and ideals that are elsewhere argued for. And of course the
erotic activity in the Platonic context is the activity of dialectic.... Just
as there is no dialectic without a motivation and desire for goodness
and knowledge, there is no Platonic erotic without an intellectual or
rational content. In here, I find Addey close to the target: rational is
not opposed to irrational, divinational, or even to suprarational, but in
subtle ways related to them.[20]

Addey further elucidates why this "mutual inclusivity" between the rational and the suprarational works for the Platonist, pointing out that it
"derives from their metaphysical system and epistemology, whereby rationality is not in opposition to religious states of inspiration but operates on
a continuum with suprarationality and divine inspiration."[21]

The tendency to dismiss the value of the suprarational in Plato is something of a contemporary phenomenon. The reason for such a dismissal
among recent scholarship lies, I submit, in a perceived incompatibility
between human reason and suprarational states and experiences. While
most scholars will agree that such experiences are present throughout the
dialogues, they also tend to see them as something that Plato merely toler-
ated, as Cocking exemplifies when quoting Dodds, who says:

While [Plato] thus accepted (with whatever ironical reservations) the
poet, the prophet, and the "Corybantic" as being in some sense channels of divine or daemonic grace, he nevertheless rated their activities
far below those of the rational self, and held that they must be subject to
the control and criticism of reason, since reason was for him no passive
plaything of hidden forces, but an active manifestation of deity in man, a
daemon in its own right.[22]

Dodds, in my estimation, makes three errors here. He is correct in claiming
that Plato viewed reason as the manifestation of the divine in humanity.
However, this is the case because it is the part of us that most closely images
divine *noēsis* and not because it single-handedly affords us all we need to

---

20. Pauliina Remes, "Book Review: *The Neoplatonic Socrates*," NDPR (2015): n.p.
21. Addey, "*Daimonion* of Socrates," 52.
22. Dodds quoted in Cocking, *Imagination*, 288.

achieve our desired ends. Next, Dodds indicates that this "*daemonic* grace" is untrustworthy, but, as stated above, Plato makes it clear, especially in the *Laws* and the *Republic*, that the divine is utterly benevolent and is only the cause of good for human beings.[23] Finally, in claiming that "these [suprarational] activities are far below those of the rational self," Dodds conflates the reliability of the knowledge gained with esteem. While suprarational experiences require a great deal of responsible interpretation and therefore uncertainty on our part, they nonetheless reveal that which is to be held in the highest esteem: a divine glimpse of reality. The suprarational is both the beginning and end of our quest, functioning as the catalyst for our rational examinations and as the goal of those examinations. As Addey further explains, "Rationality and reason are themselves seen as *ultimately* gifts of the gods, which, when used appropriately, can lead to suprarational, mystic states of being, thought, and action."[24] Discursive reason, then, is the middle step in our journey. It works as an antidote to our hubris and ignorance, letting us interpret the workings of the divine earnestly and not according to our own conceits.

Toward a Strictly Platonic Demonology

Unlike many of his Neoplatonic successors, Plato does not have a systematic demonology. Concerning the identity of daimons, Plato is inconsistent, describing them as gods, the children of the gods (*Apol.* 27d), the spirits of great people who help the living after death (*Resp.* 469a; *Crat.* 398b–c), or the rational element within our own psyches.[25] The first option appears to be a living debate in Socrates's time, as he is aware of it in the *Apology* when he asks the court: "Do we not believe spirits [δαίμονας] to be either gods or the children of gods" (τοὺς δὲ δαίμονας οὐχὶ ἤτοι θεούς γε ἡγούμεθα ἢ θεῶν παῖδας, *Apol.* 27d). The *Symposium* comes down on the side of the daimons being the children of the gods, depicting Eros as the bastard child

---

23. As Socrates states in *Resp.* 382e: "the daemonic and the divine are in every way free from falsehood" (πάντη ἄρα ἀψευδὲς τὸ δαιμόνιόν τε καὶ τὸ θεῖον). This does not mean that there is no danger to be found in our encounters with the daimonic, but more will be said on this later.

24. Addey, "*Daimonion* of Socrates," 52.

25. *Tim.* 90a: "now we ought to think of the most sovereign part of our soul as god's gift to us, given to be our [*daimon*]" (τὸ δὲ δὴ περὶ τοῦ κυριωτάτου παρ' ἡμῖν ψυχῆς εἴδους διανοεῖσθαι δεῖ τῇδε, ὡς ἄρα αὐτὸ δαίμονα θεὸς ἑκάστῳ δέδωκεν).

of Poros and Penia (Poverty and Plenty; *Symp.* 203b–d). Other dialogues, such as the *Timaeus*, affirm this position,[26] while the *Phaedrus* comes down on the other side, with Socrates rhetorically asking Phaedrus, "Don't you believe that Love is the son of Aphrodite? Isn't he one of the gods?" (τὸν ἔρωτα οὐκ Ἀφροδίτης καὶ θεόν τινα ἡγῇ, *Phaedr.* 242d). From early dialogues to late ones, Plato never achieves any consistency regarding the identity or origins of daimons.

However, Plato does demonstrate consistency regarding the function of the daimonic; he always depicts daimons as intermediaries bridging the gap between divine and mortal existences. Thus, it appears that Plato's use of the term correlates to its early use according to Burkert, who states that "*daimon* does not designate a specific class of divine beings, but a peculiar mode of activity."[27] While the dialogues depict various daimonic tasks— the guardians of individual souls (*Resp.* 617c), of particular activities such as desire (*Symp.* 203a), or of whole cities or land areas (*Leg.* 747e)—they all consistently adhere to the central task of mediation. This task is perhaps most famously articulated in the *Symposium*:

> Everything spiritual [πᾶν τὸ δαιμόνιον] … is between god and mortal … [*daimons*] are messengers who shuttle back and forth between the two, conveying prayer and sacrifice from men to gods, while to men they command from the gods and gifts in return for sacrifices. Being in the middle of the two, they round out the whole and bind fast the all to all. (*Symp.* 202e)[28]

No matter what else Plato indicates about daimons, they always play the role of a go-between connecting two otherwise separate modes of existence. This mediating role is essential to the human journey toward divine

---

26. *Tim.* 40d: "As for the other spiritual beings [περὶ δὲ τῶν ἄλλων δαιμόνων], it is beyond our task to know and speak of how they came to be. We should accept on faith the assertions of those figures of the past who claimed to be the offspring of gods" (περὶ δὲ τῶν ἄλλων δαιμόνων εἰπεῖν καὶ γνῶναι τὴν γένεσιν μεῖζον ἢ καθ' ἡμᾶς, πειστέον δὲ τοῖς εἰρηκόσιν ἔμπροσθεν, ἐκγόνοις μὲν θεῶν οὖσιν, ὡς ἔφασαν, σαφῶς δέ που τούς γε αὐτῶν προγόνους εἰδόσιν).

27. Walter Burkert, *Greek Religion Archaic and Classical*, trans. John Raffan (Oxford: Blackwell, 1985), 180.

28. *Symp.* 202e: ἑρμηνεῦον καὶ διαπορθμεῦον θεοῖς τὰ παρ' ἀνθρώπων καὶ ἀνθρώποις τὰ παρὰ θεῶν, τῶν μὲν τὰς δεήσεις καὶ θυσίας, τῶν δὲ τὰς ἐπιτάξεις τε καὶ ἀμοιβὰς τῶν θυσιῶν, ἐν μέσῳ δὲ ὂν ἀμφοτέρων συμπληροῖ, ὥστε τὸ πᾶν αὐτὸ αὑτῷ συνδεδέσθαι.

understanding, for, we are told, "gods do not mix with men; they mingle and converse with us through spirits instead, whether we are awake or asleep."[29] The daimonic, therefore, functions as a lifeline allowing human beings to bridge an otherwise untraversable cosmic gap.

For example, Diotima explains that the daimon Eros succeeds in driving us toward divine truth because "he is in between wisdom and ignorance" (σοφίας τε αὖ καὶ ἀμαθίας ἐν μέσῳ ἐστίν, *Symp.* 203a). As per Diotima's description, this in-between status is the nature of the daimonic in general and explains its ability to initiate us into the pursuit of knowledge without actually bestowing knowledge on us. The mediation is explained with particular clarity in the case of Eros, who is said to be "a lover of wisdom" and thus between wisdom and ignorance (*Symp.* 204b). By the intervention of Eros, we are made aware both of what we lack and what we desire, a crucial role because "no one … who is wise already [desires] wisdom," and "no one who is ignorant will [desire] wisdom either," because no one will want what they do not think they need.[30] Hence, the task of the daimonic is to alert us to what we are missing by giving it to us in such a way that we both have it and do not have it so that we begin the pursuing it. In essence, the human psyche is starved of its essential nutrient,[31] and the daimonic presents us with just enough of it to remind us of our voracious hunger. This hunger can only be satisfied through our pursuit of divine truth, so we start our journey thanks to the ministrations of Eros's daimonic grace.

However, the daimonic in Plato extends beyond the scope of Eros alone, for Diotima tells us that "through [daimons] all divination passes, through them the art of priests in sacrifice and ritual, in enchantment, prophecy, and sorcery."[32] These are all activities that follow the same pattern

---

29. *Symp.* 203a: θεὸς δὲ ἀνθρώπῳ οὐ μείγνυται, ἀλλὰ διὰ τούτου [δαιμόνων] πᾶσά ἐστιν ἡ ὁμιλία καὶ ἡ διάλεκτος θεοῖς πρὸς ἀνθρώπους, καὶ ἐγρηγορόσι καὶ καθεύδουσι.

30. *Symp.* 204a: θεῶν οὐδεὶς φιλοσοφεῖ οὐδ' ἐπιθυμεῖ σοφὸς γενέσθαι—ἔστι γάρ— οὐδ' εἴ τις ἄλλος σοφός, οὐ φιλοσοφεῖ. οὐδ' αὖ οἱ ἀμαθεῖς φιλοσοφοῦσιν οὐδ' ἐπιθυμοῦσι σοφοὶ γενέσθαι ... οὔκουν ἐπιθυμεῖ ὁ μὴ οἰόμενος ἐνδεὴς εἶναι οὗ ἂν μὴ οἴηται ἐπιδεῖσθαι.

31. *Phaedr.* 248b–c: "The reason there is so much eagerness to see the plain where truth stands is that this pasture has the grass that is the right food for the best part of the soul, and it is the nature of the wings that lift up the soul to be nourished by it" (οὗ δ' ἕνεχ' ἡ πολλὴ σπουδὴ τὸ ἀληθείας ἰδεῖν πεδίον οὗ ἐστιν, ἥ τε δὴ προσήκουσα ψυχῆς τῷ ἀρίστῳ νομὴ ἐκ τοῦ ἐκεῖ λειμῶνος τυγχάνει οὖσα, ἥ τε τοῦ πτεροῦ φύσις, ᾧ ψυχὴ κουφίζεται, τούτῳ τρέφεται).

32. *Symp.* 202e–203a: διὰ τούτου καὶ ἡ μαντικὴ πᾶσα χωρεῖ καὶ ἡ τῶν ἱερέων τέχνη τῶν τε περὶ τὰς θυσίας καὶ τελετὰς καὶ τὰς ἐπῳδὰς καὶ τὴν μαντείαν πᾶσαν καὶ γοητείαν.

as the erotic. They begin with the divine reaching down to convey a truth we could not ascertain by our own power, and they demand a response from us to bring our understanding of this truth to any kind of fruition. Socrates models this response to the daimonic each time his divine sign makes itself known. In all cases, it gives Socrates an impression, a hint at knowledge beyond the scope of Socrates's understanding, and a warning that he should amend his course of action accordingly. However, Socrates is still responsible for deciding on the correct action in response to this daimonic prompt. Socrates similarly models the interpretation of oracles to us in the *Apology* when he recounts the Pythia's statement that no one is wiser than he. While he treats the oracle as necessarily true, having come from Apollo, he still recognizes that determining the way in which it is true is his responsibility. Appropriately, he ultimately interprets the words as a call to recognize the futility of human reason in the face of divine knowledge (*Apol.* 21a–23b).

This call-and-answer structure depicted between Socrates and the daimonic is essential to the compatibility between suprarational experience and the workings of reason for Plato. As Danielle Layne points out:

> Throughout the dialogues Socrates' prophecies, oracles and the like are not mantras to be taken at face value or immediately accepted, they are, as we discussed earlier, enigmas to be clarified and continuously reinterpreted. Moments of divine inspiration, even the Delphic oracle, have to be tested and scrutinized. For Socrates, his main duty in the face of such "divine" wisdom is a testing and examining. Even his daemon, while offering him divine wisdom, only offers a "sign" that Socrates must interpret in order to understand. In this, Socrates demonstrates how testing and examining is his human work in gracious response to such divine gifts.[33]

To gain anything from this divine gift, something is required of us in response. This requirement undoubtedly carries with it the grave risk of misinterpretation. If we are not humble and honest about where our own knowledge begins and ends, we stand to miss the opportunity that is afforded in the moment of revelation and instead fall further into the ignorance of our own ignorance. Yet, Socrates's repeated modeling of the

---

33. Danielle A. Layne, "From Irony to Enigma: Discovering Double Ignorance in Plato's Dialogues," *Méthexis* 23 (2010): 84.

appropriate response indicates that Plato does think daimonic activities are worthwhile.

A Reading of the *Ion*

In order to address the daimonic nature of poetry, I will first give a reading of Plato's early dialogue, the *Ion*. It stars Socrates, of course, and Ion, a Homeric rhapsode, and it deals primarily with the question of the nature of the rhapsode's—and the poet's—knowledge. Socrates meets Ion coming from the festival of Asclepius in Epidaurus, where Ion has just won first prize. Socrates confides in Ion that he has often envied rhapsodes for their ability to understand the poets: "a rhapsode must come to present the poet's thought to his audience; and he can't do that beautifully unless he knows what the poet means."[34] Ion, flattered, agrees and states that he speaks "more beautifully than anyone else about Homer" (οἶμαι κάλλιστα ἀνθρώπων λέγειν περὶ Ὁμήρου, *Ion* 530c). However, when questioned about whether Ion speaks as well on other poets, he answers in the negative: "When someone discusses another poet I pay no attention, and I have no power to contribute anything worthwhile: I simply doze off. But let someone mention Homer and right away I'm wide awake and I'm paying attention and I have plenty to say."[35] Given that Ion presents rhapsody as his profession and, therefore, a genuine skill, Socrates is puzzled; the poets primarily speak on the same subject matter, so why is Ion only able to speak on Homer? Ion responds by saying that, on shared subjects, he speaks of both Homer and Hesiod "just the same" (ὁμοίως ἂν περί γε τούτων, *Ion* 531a).

Socrates, of course, leads Ion to see that the practical content of Homer's works cannot be the reason that Ion is able to speak of Homer so eloquently but not the other poets: "Take all the places where those two

---

34. *Ion* 530b–c: ἀναγκαῖον εἶναι ἔν τε ἄλλοις ποιηταῖς διατρίβειν πολλοῖς καὶ ἀγαθοῖς καὶ δὴ καὶ μάλιστα ἐν Ὁμήρῳ, τῷ ἀρίστῳ καὶ θειοτάτῳ τῶν ποιητῶν, καὶ τὴν τούτου διάνοιαν ἐκμανθάνειν, μὴ μόνον τὰ ἔπη, ζηλωτόν ἐστιν. οὐ γὰρ ἂν γένοιτό ποτε ἀγαθὸς ῥαψῳδός, εἰ μὴ συνείη τὰ λεγόμενα ὑπὸ τοῦ ποιητοῦ. τὸν γὰρ ῥαψῳδὸν ἑρμηνέα δεῖ τοῦ ποιητοῦ τῆς διανοίας γίγνεσθαι τοῖς ἀκούουσι· τοῦτο δὲ καλῶς ποιεῖν μὴ γιγνώσκοντα ὅτι λέγει ὁ ποιητὴς ἀδύνατον.

35. *Ion* 532c: ὅταν μέν τις περὶ ἄλλου του ποιητοῦ διαλέγηται, οὔτε προσέχω τὸν νοῦν ἀδυνατῶ τε καὶ ὁτιοῦν συμβαλέσθαι λόγου ἄξιον, ἀλλ' ἀτεχνῶς νυστάζω, ἐπειδὰν δέ τις περὶ Ὁμήρου μνησθῇ, εὐθύς τε ἐγρήγορα καὶ προσέχω τὸν νοῦν καὶ εὐπορῶ ὅτι λέγω;

poets speak of divination, both where they agree and where they don't:
who would explain those better and more beautifully, you, or one of the
diviners if he's good?"[36] As Halliwell puts it:

> Socrates … proceeds on the basis that a good interpreter of poetry would
> need to be expert in each and every domain of knowledge (such as arith-
> metic and medicine) which has an independent existence outside poetry
> but might be reflected within its images and narratives of life. This pre-
> supposes that poetic subject matter is nothing but a collection of things
> each of which belongs to a specific domain of knowledge or expertise.
> That supposition makes absurd, however, the idea of being an expert
> interpreter of poetry as such: the interpreter would need to be expert
> in everything, since Socrates himself suggests that poetry can range
> across the affairs of the entire cosmos (from Olympus to Hades, 531c) in
> what might be called its world-picturing scope. But the supposition also
> makes poetry itself extremely problematic: either the poet would need
> to be a polymathic expert (a current idea explicitly mocked by Socrates
> in the *Republic*) or his work will be purely parasitic on all the existing
> domains of knowledge, its significance fragmenting into ersatz bits of
> other activities and lacking any coherent identity of its own.[37]

Obviously, if Ion is able to speak beautifully on Homer and not the other
poets, it cannot be in any way related to the content of Homer's work,
in which he depicts contemporary *technē* (generalship, naval warfare, soldiering, divination, leadership, etc.). If it did, then those skilled in those
technē themselves would be better able to speak on Homer than Ion and
would be equally able talk about any other poet who depicts those *technē*.

Ion counters that the source of Homer's special power (and thus Ion's
ability to speak about Homer so well) results from the fact that, while the
poets generally write about the same subjects, they do not "do it the way
Homer did" (οὐχ ὁμοίως πεποιήκασι καὶ Ὅμηρος, *Ion* 531d). The other
poets may have spoken of the same *technē*, but Homer did it much better.
To this, Socrates levels the critique that a comprehensive knowledge of a
particular skill entails being able to pick out both the good and the bad:
"Well now, Ion, dear heart, when a number of people are discussing arithmetic, and one of them speaks best, I suppose someone will know how

---

36. *Ion* 531b: ὅσα τε ὁμοίως καὶ ὅσα διαφόρως περὶ μαντικῆς λέγετον τὼ ποιητὰ
τούτω, πότερον σὺ κάλλιον ἂν ἐξηγήσαιο ἢ τῶν μάντεών τις τῶν ἀγαθῶν.
37. Halliwell, *Between Ecstasy and Truth,* 170.

to pick out the good speaker.... Will [the one who can pick out the good speaker on math] be the same person who can pick out the bad speakers, or someone else?" (*Ion* 531d–e).[38] Ion agrees that it would be the same person. Socrates then asks, "And that will be someone who has mastered arithmetic, right?" (*Ion* 531e). The takeaway is that if the quality of poetry is determined by its ability to skillfully depict various *technē*, then those who practice those various skills would be most qualified to speak on Homer's depictions, not a rhapsode.

Yet, another conclusion implied in this passage is that Homer is nothing special, for however well he depicts generalship, an actual general will always be better. Thus, by Ion's assertion that he speaks most beautifully on Homer because Homer is the best at depicting all the subjects of poetry, he is unwittingly admitting to a three-tiered technical world in which his own profession (and even Homer's) comes out looking entirely superfluous. For example, there is the diviner, then the poet, who represents the art of divination, then the person who speaks about the poet's representation of the art of divination. In this hierarchy, the latter two positions are unnecessary, for the diviner is best able to explain divination and best able to determine who is speaking on it best.

Disturbed by the conclusion thus far, Ion asks how Socrates can explain the rhapsode's own experience of Homer. When other poets are being discussed, he is bored to death, dozing off, and powerless to contribute anything worthwhile. But when Homer is the poet of discussion, he is suddenly energized, excited, and has much to say. Ion's point here is entirely valid. If Homer is superfluous in general, then why does he have this power to affect Ion so, and why is this power, for Ion, specific to the poetry of Homer? The answer could be trivial: perhaps Ion just likes Homer for reasons of personal taste; accordingly, his experience of Homer versus the other poets holds no more importance than my preference for cream and sugar in my coffee as opposed to drinking it black. However, Socrates does not make any recourse to personal taste. Instead, he recognizes Ion's experience as both very real and consequential by stating that, while Ion is "powerless to speak about Homer by means of technical skill or professional knowledge" (*Ion* 532c), Ion is nonetheless experiencing something profound, for "a divine power moves you [Ion], just as if

---

38. *Ion* 531d–e: οὐκοῦν, ὦ φίλη κεφαλὴ Ἴων, ὅταν περὶ ἀριθμοῦ πολλῶν λεγόντων εἷς τις ἄριστα λέγῃ, γνώσεται δήπου τις τὸν εὖ λέγοντα;

[you] were in the presence of a magnetic stone" (*Ion* 533d).[39] Therefore, while Plato denies the rhapsode's skill, he affirms the legitimacy of Ion's *experience*. In this nuanced situation, Socrates draws our attention to the difference between experience and expertise. Ion's experience is valid. He is divinely inspired and experiences a kind of power in relation to Homer that Socrates, at no point in the Ion, denies. Nevertheless, this experience is external to Ion and in no way corresponds to the possession of any real expertise on Ion's part.

If Ion's ability came from expertise, he would not be limited to Homer but would be able to speak equally well on other poets, for "there is an art of poetry as a whole" (ποιητικὴ γάρ πού ἐστιν τὸ ὅλον, *Ion* 532c). Interestingly, in this section, Socrates sticks only to examples involving the arts, asking Ion, "Have you ever known anyone who is clever at showing what's well painted and what's not in the work of Polygnotus, but who's powerless to do that for other painters?"[40] Ion answers in the negative. The conclusion is that no one "is clever at explaining" (δεινός ἐστιν ἐξηγεῖσθαι, *Ion* 533b) what is good about one artist's work—be it sculpture, painting, lute or cithara playing, or even rhapsody itself—who cannot similarly apply the same technical expertise to explain the work of any other artist of that medium. Thus, in contrast to the preceding section wherein the skill of the poet was attributed to her ability to depict various *technē* well, Socrates is now arguing that poetry must have a unified *technē*: "Take the whole of any other subject: won't it have the same discipline throughout?"[41] Given the preceding passage, I take Socrates to be pointing out that the *technē* of poetry cannot be every *technē* it depicts (such as those of generalship, soldiering, and divination altogether), but rather something that we can point to throughout a work and across several works regardless of subject matter. John Ferrari concurs that "Socrates does not actually deny that poetry and rhapsody are arts; he denies that what poets and rhapsodes say (as professionals) is said with

---

39. Translations mine: τέχνη καὶ ἐπιστήμη περὶ Ὁμήρου λέγειν ἀδύνατος εἶ (*Ion* 532c); θεία δὲ δύναμις ἥ σε κινεῖ, ὥσπερ ἐν τῇ λίθῳ ἣν Εὐριπίδης μὲν Μαγνῆτιν ὠνόμασεν (*Ion* 533d).

40. *Ion* 532e–533a: ἤδη οὖν τινα εἶδες ὅστις περὶ μὲν Πολυγνώτου τοῦ Ἀγλαοφῶντος δεινός ἐστιν ἀποφαίνειν ἃ εὖ τε γράφει καὶ ἃ μή, περὶ δὲ τῶν ἄλλων γραφέων ἀδύνατος; Poetry, painting, music, and sculpture are all mentioned.

41. *Ion* 532d: οὐκοῦν ἐπειδὰν λάβῃ τις καὶ ἄλλην τέχνην ἡντινοῦν ὅλην, ὁ αὐτὸς τρόπος τῆς σκέψεως ἔσται περὶ ἁπασῶν τῶν τεχνῶν;

art and understanding on their part."[42] Halliwell, with reference to the *Apology*, agrees, stating:

> Contrary to many readings of the passage [on the poets in the *Apology*], Socrates does not deny poets *technê* or craft-knowledge altogether: he implies that they have a skill or craft of poiêsis which is manifest in the verbal structures and textures of their works. What he questions is their possession of knowledge or wisdom of a more far-reaching kind, a kind which the poets' audiences might learn to bring to bear on their lives as a whole.[43]

However, Halliwell appears to think that the *Ion* does not say as much, claiming that "Socrates ... seems to slip, without explanation, between different models of poetry as either a kind of secondary vehicle for other forms of expertise, or an art and expertise in its own right."[44] In this respect, I diverge from Halliwell's reading of the *Ion*, and I argue that Socrates has clearly delineated the two views. He first addresses and then rejects the idea that the poet's *technē* is a kind of polymathy, and he then addresses the idea the poet's *technē* is something else related to the skill of composition itself. The second view is affirmed as a claim in itself, but it is rejected as an explanation for the original problem of the dialogue, which was the question of Ion's unique experience of Homer.

To get an answer to the real question of the dialogue, the source of Ion's asymmetrical genius, we must take Socrates at his word regarding divine inspiration when he, rather uncharacteristically, obliges Ion with a straightforward account of the experience in question:

> I'm going to announce to you what I think [this means]. As I said earlier, that's not a subject you've mastered—speaking well about Homer; it's a divine power that moves you, as a "Magnetic" stone moves iron rings.... This stone not only pulls those rings, if they're iron, it also puts power in the rings, so that they in turn can do just what the stone does—pull other rings—so that there's sometimes a very long chain of iron pieces and rings hanging from one another. And the power in all of them depends on this stone. In the same way, the Muse makes some people inspired herself, and then through those who are inspired a chain of

---

42. Ferrari, "Plato and Poetry," 95.
43. Halliwell, *Between Ecstasy and Truth*, 163.
44. Halliwell, *Between Ecstasy and Truth*, 170–71.

other enthusiasts is suspended. You know, none of the epic poets, if they're good, are masters of their subject; they are inspired, possessed, and that is how they utter all those beautiful poems. The same goes for lyric poets if they're good. (*Ion* 533c–534a)[45]

Ion can speak about Homer this way because he is connected to the great chain suspended from the Muse. Furthermore, Socrates does not deny that Ion has a genuine power in regard to Homer; he simply denies that Ion has it on the basis of his own knowledge or mastery. Ion truly does possess power, but it is not his own. Crucially, Diotima herself distinguishes between those who are wise daimonically and those who are wise through *technē*: "He who is wise in any of these ways is a man of the spirit, but he who is wise in any other way, in a [*technē*] or any manual work, is merely a mechanic."[46] Diotima describes the daimonic as that which bestows knowledge and power without *technē*, and this is precisely how poetry is described in the *Ion*.

It is here that I must address the fact that many scholars have argued that the *Ion* is meant to be read as an attack on the value of poets and poetry wholesale. Ferrari, for example, sees the image of the magnet in less than a positive light, despite the eloquence of its depiction, stating, "Socrates' strategy in conversation with the rhapsode Ion is to get him to see that poetic inspiration is not a prerogative of the poets alone ... but is transmitted by them to intermediaries, such as actors and rhapsodes, enabling them to perform the poetry; and so the contagion spreads to its final carrier, the enthusiastic audience."[47] Rather than seeing the image of the magnet as something like the poetic equivalent of Diotima's ladder,

---

45. *Ion* 533c–534a: ἔρχομαί γέ σοι ἀποφανούμενος ὅ μοι δοκεῖ τοῦτο εἶναι. ἔστι γὰρ τοῦτο τέχνη μὲν οὐκ ὂν παρὰ σοὶ περὶ Ὁμήρου εὖ λέγειν, ὃ νυνδὴ ἔλεγον, θεία δὲ δύναμις ἥ σε κινεῖ, ὥσπερ ἐν τῇ λίθῳ ἣν Εὐριπίδης μὲν Μαγνῆτιν ὠνόμασεν, οἱ δὲ πολλοὶ Ἡρακλείαν. καὶ γὰρ αὕτη ἡ λίθος οὐ μόνον αὐτοὺς τοὺς δακτυλίους ἄγει τοὺς σιδηροῦς, ἀλλὰ καὶ δύναμιν ἐντίθησι τοῖς δακτυλίοις ὥστ' αὖ δύνασθαι ταὐτὸν τοῦτο ποιεῖν ὅπερ ἡ λίθος, ἄλλους ἄγειν δακτυλίους, ὥστ' ἐνίοτε ὁρμαθὸς μακρὸς πάνυ σιδηρίων καὶ δακτυλίων ἐξ ἀλλήλων ἤρτηται: πᾶσι δὲ τούτοις ἐξ ἐκείνης τῆς λίθου ἡ δύναμις ἀνήρτηται. οὕτω δὲ καὶ ἡ Μοῦσα ἐνθέους μὲν ποιεῖ αὐτή, διὰ δὲ τῶν ἐνθέων τούτων ἄλλων ἐνθουσιαζόντων ὁρμαθὸς ἐξαρτᾶται. πάντες γὰρ οἵ τε τῶν ἐπῶν ποιηταὶ οἱ ἀγαθοὶ οὐκ ἐκ τέχνης ἀλλ' ἔνθεοι ὄντες καὶ κατεχόμενοι πάντα ταῦτα τὰ καλὰ λέγουσι ποιήματα, καὶ οἱ μελοποιοὶ οἱ ἀγαθοὶ ὡσαύτως.

46. *Symp.* 203a: καὶ ὁ μὲν περὶ τὰ τοιαῦτα σοφὸς δαιμόνιος ἀνήρ, ὁ δὲ ἄλλο τι σοφὸς ὢν ἢ περὶ τέχνας ἢ χειρουργίας τινὰς βάναυσος.

47. Ferrari, "Plato and Poetry," 93.

Ferrari sees it as a "contagion." Barry Dixon's approach to the *Ion*, for example, is a fairly representative one among scholars who dismiss poetry in the *Ion* due to Socratic irony. Dixon states that Socrates's speech on poetic inspiration "is a perfect example of an ironic speech given how it seems to be offering praise but is actually degrading both the rhapsode's and poet's art, by taking from them any claim to knowledge."[48] Given such perspectives on the dialogue and its central importance to my claims, I ought to explain why I do not take the inspiration hypothesis to be ironic.

First, Dixon's argument, like many arguments from irony, begs the question. He claims that the speech is ironic because it "seems" to offer praise while "actually" degrading, but such a claim already assumes an ironic reading in which Socrates says one thing but means another, and it assumes to know which things he means and which he does not. If we set aside these assumptions and begin from the ground up, we have to ask ourselves whether an ironic reading is necessary for understanding the passage. In fact, there is no inherent contradiction in the speech on inspiration. Socrates can be praising the poets as conduits of divine inspiration (which I think he is) while simultaneously degrading them for thinking that they actually know about the things they are gifted. Layne highlights this nuance when she points out that, in the *Apology*, while Socrates does find "that [the poets] possess their ability by nature [φύσει] and divine inspiration ... they, through conceit of possessing the mere natural gift of poetry, unwittingly disgrace themselves by thinking they know when they do not."[49] Plato can acknowledge the divine inspiration of the poets while simultaneously finding them wanting for their hubris and inability to understand the source of their power, leading the poets to believe they have wisdom when they do not.

Curiously, Dixon comes close to acknowledging that the *Ion* only works if Socrates means what he says throughout. He states: "Socrates succeeds in taking from the rhapsodes and poets any claim to knowledge by using divine inspiration, an ironic speech which Ion eventually embraces."[50] Dixon is correct in stating that Socrates does take their claims to knowledge away, but why must the argument regarding inspiration then be ironic? In fact, Dixon's argument here (and the argument of the *Ion* as a whole) only works if Socrates *means what he says* regarding divine inspiration. If the

---

48. Barry Dixon, "Phaedrus, Ion, and the Lure of Inspiration," *PLATO* 8 (2008): 7.
49. Layne, "From Irony to Enigma," 82.
50. Dixon "Phaedrus, Ion, and the Lure of Inspiration," 6.

poets and rhapsodes are not the sources of their own power, then we have an explanation for how they can say such moving things and yet have no real knowledge or expertise. However, if Socrates is insincere in his invocation of divine inspiration, then the actual argument of the *Ion* falls apart.

Furthermore, if, as Dixon argues, Plato's treatment of poets and rhapsodes involves a much larger attack on the pedagogical and cultural norms of the times involving the public performance of poetry,[51] then Plato has hardly chosen the best path for success. It is true that Ion can leave this discussion humbled by the realization that he has no expertise or knowledge, but he can also be conversely heartened by the idea that he is a divine conduit channeling the power of the gods through the muse to the poet to the rhapsode to the people. Dixon thinks that "inspiration achieves Plato's task in the most efficient and suitable way for the type of interlocutor [i.e., an ignorant rhapsode] at hand."[52] Yet if Plato's task is to undermine the public recitation of Homer, Socrates's approach, contra Dixon, is a dismal failure. Even if Ion walked away from the conversation entirely converted to everything Socrates has said thus far, there is no reason to think he would stop being a rhapsode, only that he would speak differently about his own knowledge. However, if Plato's task is to reframe the way in which his contemporaries think about the nature of poetry and the knowledge of the poets, then his approach is potentially successful and requires no deception on his end.

Accordingly, I see no benefit to reading the *Ion*'s remarks on inspiration as ironic. As Halliwell puts it: "The dialogues betray a recurrent tension, embodied above all in the persona of Socrates, between attraction and resistance to the possibilities of poetic experience."[53] This tension is embodied well in a dialogue in which "Socrates undertakes an almost scornful questioning of the poets' pretensions and supposed wisdom," and yet "nevertheless, he does not suggest that their works are without value."[54] The nuance of this tension stands well enough on its own without appealing to irony as a hermeneutical device. The *Ion* can already sustain both the conclusion that the poets and rhapsodes are not knowledgeable or experts and the conclusion that divine inspiration is real and at play without ever diving into the weeds of which parts are sincerely meant and why.

---

51. Dixon, "Phaedrus, Ion, and the Lure of Inspiration," 6.
52. Dixon, "Phaedrus, Ion, and the Lure of Inspiration," 6.
53. Halliwell, *Between Ecstasy and Truth*, 159.
54. Halliwell, *Between Ecstasy and Truth*, 164.

Therefore, assuming sincerity, I derive three conclusions from the dialogue. First, Socrates does appear to deny that Ion himself has a *technē*. If Ion truly had the *technē* he claims, he would not feel particularly able to speak on Homer yet powerless to speak on Hesiod. Whatever Ion is experiencing, it cannot be a *technē*, for it does not apply to the art of poetry as an entire discipline. Second, poets and their critics appear to have the same *technē*. It is through familiarity with the art of poetry as a whole that the rhapsode (in theory if not in practice) expertly speaks on which poet is good and which poet is bad. This, of course, demands the question: What sets poets apart from their critics? The fact that, throughout the passage on the *technē* of poetry as a whole, Socrates is speaking about the ability to "cleverly explain" artistic *technē* rather than the ability to produce them is key; it indicates that he acknowledges a distinction between the artist and the critic, and acknowledges that, while the critic (in theory, if not in practice) may be intimately acquainted with the *technē* belonging to the artistic medium in question, she lacks something that allows her to produce them. The poet's skill, which is apparently far from fully realized (*Ion* 533e–534a), is actually secondary to the most important component of the poet's work, which is this divine inspiration (533e–534a). Thus, we come to the third conclusion: good poetry (i.e., the kind of poetry capable of stirring the soul of people, such as Ion) is not the product of human skill but of divine intervention into the human project of creation.

Poetry as Daimonic

I will now bring my reading of the *Ion* to bear on my claim that poetry is daimonic for Plato. My arguments are based primarily on my reading of the *Ion* in consort with the *Symposium*'s description of the daimonic in general. While it is true that the *Ion* never explicitly uses the term *daimonic* to describe poetry, Plato nevertheless describes poetry in a manner that can only be daimonic as per the description given of the daimonic in the *Symposium*. Furthermore, both in the *Ion* and elsewhere Plato repeatedly speaks of poetry alongside other daimonic practices, indicating that he places poetry among them.

We learn from the *Symposium* that the gods do not deal directly with humans but rather that daimons mediate the relationship. We can conclude from this alone that if Plato claims that the poet is receiving something from the gods, he is necessarily claiming that they are receiving it via the daimonic, for, as quoted above, "gods do not mix with men." Given that poetic inspiration is clearly attributed to the Muses, who are not described as daimons themselves, one might wonder how poetry could be daimonic. However, the inclusion of prophecy within the scope of daimonic activities should alleviate this question, for prophecy comes from Apollo, and yet it is also listed among the daimonic activities. This implies that it comes to humans from Apollo by way of the daimonic. Accordingly, we can presume that poetry comes to us from the Muses via daimonic mediation.

Furthermore, the poets themselves are described in terms quite similar to daimons. Socrates states that the "poets are nothing but [messengers] [ἑρμηνῆς] of the gods, possessed by whoever possesses them" (οἱ δὲ ποιηταὶ οὐδὲν ἀλλ᾽ ἢ ἑρμηνῆς εἰσιν τῶν θεῶν, *Ion* 535a) which mirrors Diotima's language of the daimons as "messengers [ἑρμηνεῦον]" going between gods and mortals (ἑρμηνεῦον καὶ διαπορθμεῦον θεοῖς τὰ παρ᾽ ἀνθρώπων καὶ ἀνθρώποις τὰ παρὰ θεῶν, *Symp.* 202a). Halliwell brings out how this kind of in-between knowledge is present in Socrates's treatment of the poets, noting that, while Socrates does affirm that there are "many beautiful things" found in the works of the poets, "Socrates does not himself explain how he recognizes [them]. Still less does he explain how he can recognize them without knowing (the whole of) what they mean."[55] But if we take poetry as a daimonic activity, then Halliwell's puzzle here is resolved, for, in the *Symposium*, Diotima connects the daimonic in general, and Eros in particular, to the power of true opinion. As discussed above, Eros is described as "something in between wisdom and ignorance ... [which is] judging things correctly without being able to give a reason" (τὸ ὀρθὰ δοξάζειν καὶ ἄνευ τοῦ ἔχειν λόγον δοῦναι οὐκ οἶσθ᾽, *Symp.* 202a), and those who participate in daimonic activities in general (be they divination, priestly arts, sacrifice and ritual, enchantment, prophecy, and sorcery) are described as those who are wise in ways other than having systematic knowledge (i.e., they are opposed to those with *technē*). Thus, The problem that Halliwell identifies regarding Socrates's treatment of the poets in which he is able to recognize "many beautiful things" without being able to give a systematic account of how or why further substantiates the connection between the poetic and the daimonic, as the daimonic is elsewhere connected directly to true opinion, or the power to judge things correctly without being able to give a reason. The connection between true opinion, daimonic activities, and poetry is further found in the *Meno*, where the

---

55. Halliwell, *Between Ecstasy and Truth*, 165.

power of true opinion via divine gift is attributed to soothsayers, prophets, poets, and (oddly enough) statesmen (*Meno* 99a–100a).

Throughout the Platonic corpus, Plato draws clear connections between poetry and other activities that are identified as daimonic. One such example appears in the *Ion* when Socrates places the poets and their divine madness alongside prophets and godly diviners (*Ion* 534a–c). Importantly, we know from the *Symposium* that divination and prophecy are named alongside the erotic as daimonic activities (*Symp.* 203a). Thus, in the *Ion*, Plato claims that the same power and divine madness that enables daimonic activities also enables poetry. In the *Phaedrus,* poetry is named alongside three other types of divine madness, including the madness of oracles, mystic rites, and Eros (*Phaedr.* 244a–245b). Furthermore, these connections between the poetic and the daimonic would have been missed by Plato's contemporary audience. As Yulia Ustinova remarks, "the poet is … compared to seers, who were distinguished by their divinely inspired knowledge of the past, present, and future."[56] Furthermore, the connection between poetry and mantics (who are daimonic) was already common among ancient thinkers.[57]

Furthermore, in the *Ion*, Socrates also states that "a poet is an airy thing, winged and holy, and he is not able to make poetry until he becomes inspired and goes out of his mind and intellect is no longer in him. As long as a human being has his intellect in his possession he will always lack the power to make poetry or sing prophecy."[58] Again, we see the parallel between poetry and prophecy, with the indication that they are enabled by the same divine power. However, there is also the description of the poet as "winged and holy," which cannot but call the *Phaedrus* to mind. The poet, much like the winged soul, seems to come into contact with the beautiful in some way that bears her aloft in a unique and powerful way.

---

56. Yulia Ustinova, *Divine Mania: Alteration of Consciousness in Ancient Greece* (London: Routledge, 2018), 266.

57. Ustinova, *Divine Mania*, 266: "Later poets assume the role of manteis in their poetry, and Pindar even refers to himself as 'a prophet of the Muses in verse.'… According to Plutarch, the Muses were the 'assessors of prophecy' at Delphi. Apollo the divine patron of prophecy and poetry was frequently called Musagetês." Nevertheless, Ustinova does affirm that the "most thorough explanation of the nature of inspired poetic manticism is given in Plato's *Ion*" (268).

58. *Ion* 534b–c: κοῦφον γὰρ χρῆμα ποιητής ἐστιν καὶ πτηνὸν καὶ ἱερόν, καὶ οὐ πρότερον οἷός τε ποιεῖν πρὶν ἂν ἔνθεός τε γένηται καὶ ἔκφρων καὶ ὁ νοῦς μηκέτι ἐν αὐτῷ ἐνῇ· ἕως δ' ἂν τουτὶ ἔχῃ τὸ κτῆμα, ἀδύνατος πᾶς ποιεῖν ἄνθρωπός ἐστιν καὶ χρησμῳδεῖν.

It is clear from the *Ion* that Plato views poetry as connecting the divine to humans and that in this way humans are drawn upward toward the divine, as is shown in the image of the magnet. This description of poetry aligns with the function of the daimonic, which is to make the divine known to mortals and initiate them into the pursuit of divine *noēsis*. Socrates describes the purpose of poetic madness in the *Ion* thus:

> On account of these things the god, removing the intellect of these poets, uses them as servants like he uses oracles and diviners. He does this in order that we who hear these things know that it is not these poets—for whom the intellect is absent—who are saying such very worthy things; rather, it is the god himself who is speaking. So, through these poets, the god speaks to us loud and clear. (*Ion* 534b–c)[59]

Poets are inspired, again, like prophets and diviners, in order to point humans toward the divine. Thus, poetry, like prophecy, is given to humanity in order to make us aware of divine reality.

Reframing Poetry in the Platonic Corpus

The reader may still find herself wondering what one is to do about all those passages wherein Plato has less flattering things to say about poetry. How does understanding poetry as daimonic alleviate the tensions between two apparently contradictory sets of quotations from the Platonic corpus? To fully alleviate this tension would be a monumental, perhaps impossible, task; however, I believe that thinking of poetry as daimonic takes us in the right direction because it allows us to reframe our readings of those passages in which Plato expresses concerns over the dangers of poetry.

First, while it is tempting to read Plato's less positive comments on poetry as critiques of bad poetry, this approach does not solve our problem. Plato's comments in the *Republic*, for example, are not concerned with aesthetically bad poetry but rather with how particularly good poetry can move us deeply but in the wrong direction. Instead, I submit that the solution is to frame all of Plato's comments on poetry in the same way that we frame his comments

---

59. *Ion* 534c–d, translation mine: διὰ ταῦτα δὲ ὁ θεὸς ἐξαιρούμενος τούτων τὸν νοῦν τούτοις χρῆται ὑπηρέταις καὶ τοῖς χρησμῳδοῖς καὶ τοῖς μάντεσι τοῖς θείοις, ἵνα ἡμεῖς οἱ ἀκούοντες εἰδῶμεν ὅτι οὐχ οὗτοί εἰσιν οἱ ταῦτα λέγοντες οὕτω πολλοῦ ἄξια, οἷς νοῦς μὴ πάρεστιν, ἀλλ᾽ ὁ θεὸς αὐτός ἐστιν ὁ λέγων, διὰ τούτων δὲ φθέγγεται πρὸς ἡμᾶς.

on other daimonic activities. Poetry does not present us with a special case regarding the dangers of the daimonic. We must view the danger of poetry in the same way that we view the danger of the erotic or the oracular: they connect us to the divine, but we must know how to engage with them. For example, while Plato views erotic relationships as initiatory to philosophical contemplation, he also expresses concern over how these relationships can go wrong; this is demonstrated by the fact that the erotic dialogues spend so much time on the question of what the proper lover actually looks like.

A similarly dangerous yet divine situation is present in Plato's treatment of religious activities such as prophecy, rites, and divination. Plato gives us Diotima and Socrates; both described as mantics or mantic-like and both clearly viewed in a positive light as philosophers. But he also gives us the image of Euthyphro, a mantic who does not engage in philosophical contemplation. Euthyphro is, in some ways, the anti-Socrates in his treatment of the oracular. Whereas Socrates contemplates the Pythia's utterances, turning them over in his mind with humility and diligence, Euthyphro presents himself as a veritable expert on piety itself. Unlike Socrates, who knows that he does not know when presented with the oracle's words, Euthyphro assumes that he *does* know. This is why Euthyphro's reception of daimonic activity will never result in true divine knowledge; it will only present him with fleeting intuitions that will remain unconsummated. The case is the same with the poets, as Layne notes regarding Plato's treatment of them in the *Apology*, wherein she contrasts their reception of divine inspiration with that of Socrates: "Unlike the poets in the *Apology*, Socrates recognizes that his mantic moments or divine intuitions must be meditated with the particularly human work of examination in order to appropriate, even appreciate, what human knowledge may arise or be understood in such intuitions."[60] Thus, the danger lies not in poetry itself but rather in the orientation of the poets (and the general people) toward poetry as something that has the potential to inspire us in the direction of the divine. The dangers of the daimonic in general come from our own hubris and ignorance, not from the goodness of the daimonic itself. Still, this does not mean that daimonic activities are safe. Plato is clear that they are not. Nevertheless, to the initiated, they are indeed an aid to the soul.

Proclus, in addressing the very question of how "false oracular pronouncements" are given, states that "the falsehood is not in those giving

---

60. Layne, "From Irony to Enigma," 84.

the oracles but in those who receive the oracular pronouncements."[61] In other words, the immediate experience in which the divine bestows revelation is entirely reliable, but the interpretation is another matter. Proclus's point is directly supported by the *Timaeus*, wherein Socrates agrees with an ancient proverb that "Only a man of sound mind may know himself and conduct his own affairs" (τὸ πράττειν καὶ γνῶναι τά τε αὑτοῦ καὶ ἑαυτὸν σώφρονι μόνῳ προσήκειν, *Tim.* 72a–b), and states, "This is the reason why it is customary practice to appoint interpreters to render judgment on an inspired divination. These persons are called 'diviners' by some who are entirely ignorant of the fact that they are expositors of utterances or visions communicated through riddles. Instead of 'diviners,' the correct thing to call them is, 'interpreters of things divined.'"[62] Socrates's roles demonstrate that the problem lies not in the reality of divine inspiration, or even in its goodness or theoretical usefulness, but in the particular disposition toward it which is fostered by his contemporaries and which is liable to misuse the daimonic in dangerous ways.

In sum, if we think of poetry as daimonic alongside the erotic and the mantic or oracular, we can better understand how dialogues such as the *Ion* and the *Republic* are consistent. It makes sense that Plato depicts daimonic activities in an ambiguous light. They are obviously good insofar as they come from the gods, but they are supremely dangerous insofar as they must be interpreted by fallible humans with a tendency to take the easy way out. They are meant for those who are ready to respond to the divine hand reaching down with her own raised hand reaching back up in response.

Bibliography

Primary Sources

Plato. *Alcibiades I.* Translated by Douglas S. Hutchinson. Pages 557–95 in *Plato: Complete Works.* Edited by John M. Cooper. Indianapolis: Hackett, 1997.

---

61. Proclus, *Commentary on Plato's Republic*, ed. and trans. Dirk Baltzly, John F. Finamore, and Graeme Miles (Cambridge: Cambridge University Press, 2018), 112–16.
62. *Tim.* 72a–b: ὅθεν δὴ καὶ τὸ τῶν προφητῶν γένος ἐπὶ ταῖς ἐνθέοις μαντείαις κριτὰς ἐπικαθιστάναι νόμος: οὓς μάντεις αὐτοὺς ὀνομάζουσίν τινες, τὸ πᾶν ἠγνοηκότες ὅτι τῆς δι' αἰνιγμῶν οὗτοι φήμης καὶ φαντάσεως ὑποκριταί, καὶ οὔτι μάντεις, προφῆται δὲ μαντευομένων δικαιότατα ὀνομάζοιντ' ἄν.

———. *Apology*. Translated by George M. A. Grube. Pages 17–36 in *Plato: Complete Works*. Edited by John M. Cooper. Indianapolis: Hackett, 1997.

———. *Ion*. Translated by Paul Woodruff. Pages 937–49 in *Plato: Complete Works*. Edited by John M. Cooper. Indianapolis: Hackett, 1997.

———. *Laws*. Translated by Trevor J. Saunders. Pages 1318–1616 in *Plato: Complete Works*. Edited by John M. Cooper. Indianapolis: Hackett, 1997.

———. *Meno*. Translated by George M. A. Grube. Pages 870–97 in *Plato: Complete Works*. Edited by John M. Cooper. Indianapolis: Hackett, 1997.

———. *Phaedrus*. Translated by Alexander Nehamas and Paul Woodruff. Pages 506–56 in *Plato: Complete Works*. Edited by John M. Cooper. Indianapolis: Hackett, 1997.

———. *Republic*. Translated by George M. A. Grube and revised by C. David C. Reeve. Pages 971–1223 in *Plato: Complete Works*. Edited by John M. Cooper. Indianapolis: Hackett, 1997.

———. *Symposium*. Translated by Alexander Nehamas and Paul Woodruff. Pages 457–505 in *Plato: Complete Works*. Edited by John M. Cooper. Indianapolis: Hackett, 1997.

———. *Theaetetus*. Translated by M. Jane Levett and revised by Myles Burnyeat. Pages 157–234 in *Plato: Complete Works*. Edited by John M. Cooper. Indianapolis: Hackett, 1997.

———. *Timaeus*. Translated by Donald J. Zeyl. Pages 1224–91 in *Plato: Complete Works*. Edited by John M. Cooper. Indianapolis: Hackett, 1997.

Proclus. *Commentary on Plato's Republic*. Edited and translated by Dirk Baltzly, John F. Finamore, and Graeme Miles. Cambridge: Cambridge University Press, 2018.

Secondary Sources

Addey, Crystal. "The *Daimonion* of Socrates: *Daimones* and Divination in Neoplatonism." Pages 51–72 in *The Neoplatonic Socrates*. Edited by Danielle A. Layne and Harold Tarrant. Philadelphia: University of Pennsylvania Press, 2014.

Burkert, Walter. *Greek Religion Archaic and Classical*. Translated by John Raffan. Oxford: Blackwell, 1985.

Cocking, John. *Imagination: A Study in the History of Ideas.* Edited by Penelope Murray. New York: Routledge, 1992.

Dixon, Barry. "Phaedrus, Ion, and the Lure of Inspiration." *PLATO* 8 (2008): 1–12.

Ferrari, John. "Plato and Poetry." Pages 92–148 in *The Cambridge History of Literary Criticism.* Vol. 1. Edited by George Alexander Kennedy. Cambridge: Cambridge University Press, 1990.

Ford, Andrew Laughlin. *The Origins of Criticism: Literary Culture and Poetic Theory in Classical Greece.* Princeton: Princeton University Press, 2002.

Halliwell, Stephen. *Between Ecstasy and Truth: Interpretations of Greek Poetics from Homer to Longinus.* Oxford: Oxford University Press, 2011.

Herman, Arnold. *To Think Like a God: Pythagoras and Parmenides, the Origins of Philosophy.* Las Vegas: Parmenides, 2004.

Layne, Danielle A. "From Irony to Enigma: Discovering Double Ignorance in Plato's Dialogues." *Méthexis* 23 (2010): 73–90.

Levin, Susan B. *The Ancient Quarrel between Philosophy and Poetry Revisited: Plato and the Greek Literary Tradition.* Oxford: Oxford University Press, 2000.

Mitchell, Robert Lloyd. "That Yelping Bitch: On Poetry in Plato's Republic." *Arion (Boston)* 24.2 (2016): 69–90.

Remes, Pauliina. "Book Review: *The Neoplatonic Socrates.*" *NDPR* (2015): n.p.

Stern-Gillet, Suzanne. "On (Mis)interpreting Plato's Ion." *Phronesis* 49 (2004): 169–201.

Ustinova, Yulia. *Divine Mania: Alteration of Consciousness in Ancient Greece.* London: Routledge, 2018.

Part 5
Christian and Pagan Perspectives

The Soul in Bardaisan, Origen, and Evagrius:
Between Unfolding and Subsumption

Ilaria L. E. Ramelli

In this essay I set out to study how the soul and its development is conceived by three ancient Christian Platonists: Bardaisan of Edessa (whom
I have proposed to view as a Christian Middle Platonist[1]), Origen of
Alexandria (between Middle and Neoplatonism), and Evagrius (strongly
influenced by pagan and Christian Neoplatonism). I also draw on Philo
of Alexandria and Paul as antecedents and sources of inspiration. I will
point out how Bardaisan (more briefly) and Origen and Evagrius (in a

This project has benefited from a Research Professorship in Patristics and Church
History (KUL) I have been awarded, within the Initiative of Excellence program # 028/
RID/2018/19. It is a joy and a great honor to dedicate this essay to such a distinguished
and admired scholar and colleague, Professor John Finamore. I have been inspired over
the years by a number of his scholarly contributions, including those on Proclus and
Iamblichus, his studies and his translations and editions, such as that of the fragments
of Iamblichus's *De anima* with John Dillon in Iamblichus, *De anima: Text, Translation,
and Commentary*, ed. and trans. John Finamore and John Dillon, PhA 192 (Leiden:
Brill, 2002). I studied, referred to, and reflected on them. We have chaired together,
and often along with Svetla Slaveva-Griffin, many panels on the soul in the Platonic
tradition, so-called pagan as well as Christian, Jewish, and Islamic, in various sessions
at International Society for Neoplatonic Studies conferences (including on the soul-
body relation, the soul and soteriology, and the soul and the ascent to God). I have thus
contributed to some volumes that contain selected studies from the conferences (such
as *Mysticism, Apocalypticism, and Platonism* and *Porphyry and the Motif*).

1. As I argue in Ilaria L. E. Ramelli, *Bardaisan of Edessa: A Reassessment of the
Evidence and a New Interpretation* (Piscataway, NJ: Gorgias, 2009; Berlin: De Gruyter,
2019); Ramelli, "Bardaisan of Edessa, Origen, and Imperial Philosophy: A Middle Platonic Context?," *Aram* 30 (2018): 337–53; further in Ramelli, *Bardaisan on Free Will,
Fate, and Human Nature: The Book of the Laws of Countries* (Tübingen: Mohr Siebeck,
forthcoming).

more elaborate way) conceived of an initial unfolding of the intellect or *nous* in rational creatures into soul and body, and posited a final subsumption of body into soul and soul into *nous*. This perspective helps to correct some widespread views, for instance, that of the destruction of bodies in Evagrius: we should think not of the elimination of something bad but of a subsumption into a superior order.

A general presupposition for this movement of unfolding from *nous* and subsumption into *nous* lies in the theory that the intellectual soul is opposed both to the inferior faculties of the soul, which are liable to passions, and to the body. These are the three components of the human being: body, inferior soul, and intellectual soul or intellect (as we shall see, such tripartition arguably contributes to explaining why Bardaisan opted to include fate in his tripartition of forces active in human beings: nature, fate, and free will). The latter is the main and noblest faculty of the soul.

This is the case in most of the Platonic tradition, for example, in Numenius, Plotinus, and Porphyry, who maintain that the soul is essentially intellect or *nous* (*C. Boeth.* 243, 254) and in his *Against Boethus* argues that the *nous* is the core component of the human being, which makes it similar to God. This view was certainly shared by Platonizing thinkers such as Philo and Origen. This is also why Porphyry claimed that the perfection of the human being qua human being consists in voluntary actions (this corresponds to Evagrius's πρακτική), but the perfection of the human being qua divine being and intellect consists in contemplation (this corresponds to Evagrius's θεωρία). According to Porphyry, only the intellect (νοῦς) and the intellectual reason (νοερὸς λόγος), or the logos with its thoughts or Ideas, as thoughts of the *nous*, are incorporeal entities that subsist separately from any body (*Sent.* 42). Here I will examine three Christian Platonists, from a very early one and close to early imperial Platonism, Bardaisan (d. 222), to Origen, a fellow disciple of Plotinus at Ammonius Saccas's school, and Evagrius, who was strongly influenced by Origen and Gregory of Nyssa but also knew Plotinus and Porphyry.

Bardaisan of Edessa

Bardaisan could be regarded, as mentioned, as a Christian Middle Platonist, who for the elaboration of his own Christian philosophical ideas could rely on Paul, the Gospels, and Genesis as well as on Platonism and Stoicism. It is an interesting question whether he knew Philo of Alexandria—also close to so-called Middle Platonism—and, if so, how much of his oeuvre.[2] Bardaisan, like Origen later, upheld the Body-Soul-Nous/Intellect tripartition, which was widespread among Middle and Neoplatonists and late Stoics.[3] It was present in Paul of Tarsus in two variants: the body-soul-intellect and the body-soul-spirit tripartition: σῶμα–ψυχή–νοῦς or σῶμα–ψυχή–πνεῦμα.[4] Early Christians, including most gnostics, will remember Paul's tripartition into σωματικοί, ψυχικοί, and πνευματικοί—a distinction of natures against which Origen polemicized all his life long, claiming that there is one single nature (φύσις, οὐσία) for all rational creatures. This tripartition coexisted with the tripartition σῶμα–ψυχή–νοῦς, clear in Evagrius but already evident in Bardaisan and Origen. All can be deemed Christian Platonists: this is the backdrop against which such tripartition must be considered.

Philo also expresses an idea that could inspire the Christian Platonic notion of the subsumption of the components of a person into the *nous* alone. This is very interesting, given that Origen, Gregory of Nyssa, and Evagrius, besides probably Bardaisan, were well acquainted with Philo. In *Mos.* 2.288, Philo describes the death of Moses in the following way: Moses "was summoned by the Father, who subsumed his twofold nature of body and soul [δυάδα ὄντα, σῶμα καὶ ψυχήν] into a single unity [εἰς μονάδος ἀνεστοιχείου ὅλον], rearranging his entire body into the brightest and most ethereal *nous* [μεθαρμοζόμενος εἰς νοῦν ἡλιοειδέστατον]."[5] This notion, as suggested by the reference to ἀναστοιχείωσις (ἀνεστοιχείου), was probably influenced by the Stoic theory of ἐκπύρωσις in Philo,[6] but his idea later affected the concept, developed in Christian Platonism, of the

---

2. See Ilaria L. E. Ramelli, "Philo as One of the Main Inspirers of Early Christian Hermeneutics and Apophatic Theology," *Adamantius* 24 (2018): 276–92.

3. See Ilaria L. E. Ramelli, "Tricotomia," in *Enciclopedia Filosofica*, ed. Virgilio Melchiorre (Milan: Bompiani and Centro di Studi Filosofici di Gallarate, 2006), 12:11772–76; Ramelli, "Origen," in *A History of Mind and Body in Late Antiquity*, ed. Sophie Cartwright and Anna Marmodoro (Cambridge: Cambridge University Press, 2018), 245–66.

4. On which see George van Kooten, *Paul's Anthropology in Context: The Image of God, Assimilation to God, and Tripartite Man in Ancient Judaism, Ancient Philosophy and Early Christianity*, WUNT 232 (Tübingen: Mohr Siebeck, 2008); Jörg Frey and Manuel Nägele, *Der νοῦς bei Paulus im Horizont griechischer und hellenistisch-jüdischer Anthropologie*, WUNT 464 (Tübingen: Mohr Siebeck, 2021).

5. Translations always mine, unless otherwise stated.

6. As suggested by Stefan Nordgaard, "Paul's Appropriation of Philo's Theory of Two Men in 1 Corinthians 15.45–49," *NTS* 57 (2011): 363–64.

subsumption of body into soul and this into *nous*, with the simplifica-
tion of the composite human nature into the simple *nous*. We shall now
analyze this notion in some remarkable Christian Platonists who read
Scripture in light of Platonism.

In Bardaisan, the Intellect-Soul-Body tripartition appears in several
texts, such as the *Liber legum regionum*,[7] as well as in a fragment preserved
by Ephrem, *Hymn* 1.9. The latter claims that the human being is "equipped
with three forms." As will be clear from what follows, these forms are, in
ascending order, body, soul, and intellect (*nous*).

Like Origen, his younger contemporary, Bardaisan thought that a
soul results from the descent of a *nous*. In the most articulate and significant passage, Bardaisan states: "According to this process and order, the
intellects are transformed in their *descents* to *souls*, and the souls are transformed in their descents to *mortal bodies*."[8] This corresponds to Origen's
idea.[9] Bardaisan argues that the abovementioned transformation is related
to fate (which for him is not conceived as an absolute power, in the Stoic
manner, but as depending on God; this is why I do not capitalize *fate* in the
case of Bardaisan): "And precisely this transformation [*sc.* of *nous* into soul
into body] is called fate and horoscope of this compound, which is sifted
and purified, for the assistance to every being that by God's kindness and
grace has been assisted and will be assisted, until the end of the universe."
The latter reference is a hint of the doctrine of apokatastasis or universal
restoration, supported by Bardaisan: Bardaisan, Clement, and Origen are
among the very first Christian thinkers who, to various degrees, espoused
the theory of apokatastasis (see below).

The hierarchical tripartition, in descending order, between intellectual soul or intellect, vital soul, and body is also the reason why the soul is
declared by Bardaisan to be unable to grasp God. For this is a privilege of
the intellect—which is the divine part in each human being, as an important fragment from Bardaisan's *De India*, preserved in Porphyry's *De Styge*,
makes clear[10]—and not of the inferior soul. This is attested by Ephrem in

---

7. *BLC* 5 and 9 in Ramelli, *Bardaisan on Free Will* = François Nau, *Bardesanes: Liber legum regionum*, Patrologia Syriaca 1.2 (Paris: Firmin-Didot, 1907), cols. 551, 572.
8. *BLC* 10 in Ramelli, *Bardaisan on Free Will* = Nau, *Bardesanes*, col. 574.
9. I endeavored to reconstruct it in Ramelli, "Origen."
10. I examined it in Ramelli, *Bardaisan of Edessa: A Reassessment*; Ilaria L. E Ramelli, "The Body of Christ as Imperishable Wood: Hippolytus and Bardaisan of Edessa's Complex Christology," in *Proceedings of the Twelfth Symposium Syriacum*

Hymn 54.3: the followers of Bardaisan "say that the soul, too, is constituted on the basis of the 'beings,' but that *it cannot grasp the Being* that is its source and root." The beings are the primordial elements created by God; the Being is God the Creator. The vital soul cannot grasp God.

Unlike the *nous*, which is the rational and divine component of the human being, the vital soul does not possess knowledge: "The *Logos*, they say, is the *unknown yeast* hidden in the *soul*, which is *deprived of knowledge* and a stranger both to the mortal body and to the Logos. If things stand so, the body, being *earthly*, cannot adhere to the soul, nor can the soul adhere to the Logos, who is *divine*" (Ephrem, *Haer.* 29.4–5; *PR* 2.158.20RF.). Al-Biruni in his eleventh-century *Chronology*, provides a testimony, albeit in a way misleading, on Bardaisan's anthropology, which confirms that Bardaisan regarded the *nous*/intellect/spirit/Logos as divine and distinct from the vital soul: "Bardaisan was convinced that God's light had sought a place in his heart" (207.5–12 [Sachau]). Bardaisan did not refer to his own heart, as hostile sources may have conveyed, but to all human intellects, the true dwelling places of God's image.

If the *nous* descends and becomes a soul and further a mortal body, the reverse process is contemplated in the return to God or apokatastasis. Indeed, Bardaisan is one of the very first Christian authors to support the doctrine of apokatastasis, probably just before Origen (although the sources on Bardaisan's thought, from the *Book of the Laws of Countries* onward, are later than Bardaisan's lifetime), as I argued in detail elsewhere.[11] In this connection, I remark as a very significant datum that the main supporters of the descent of *nous* to soul and body, and its reascent into the "unified *nous*" within Christian Platonism (especially Bardaisan, Origen, Gregory of Nyssa, Evagrius, and Eriugena, who rightly traced this doctrine back to Gregory), all embraced the doctrine of apokatastasis.[12] Bardaisan was no exception.

2016, ed. Emidio Vergani, OrChrAn 311 (Rome: Pontifical Oriental Institute, 2022), 447–58.

11. Ilaria L. E. Ramelli, "Origen, Bardaisan, and the Origin of Universal Salvation," *HTR* 102 (2009): 135–68.

12. Ilaria L. E. Ramelli, *The Christian Doctrine of Apokatastasis: A Critical Assessment from the New Testament to Eriugena*, VCSup 120 (Leiden: Brill, 2013); on Eriugena see Ramelli, "From God to God: Eriugena's Protology and Eschatology against the Backdrop of His Patristic Sources," in *Eriugena's Christian Neoplatonism and Its Sources in Patristic and Ancient Philosophy*, ed. Ramelli (Leuven: Peeters, 2021), 99–123.

Bardaisan's trichotomic anthropology, which gave rise to his theory of unfolding from the intellect and subsumption into the intellect, arguably also explains his theory of the three forces that govern human beings: nature, fate, and free will—as expressed primarily in the *Book of the Laws of Countries*, which reflects his own *Against Fate*[13]— each force having as a sphere of influence, respectively, the body, the vital soul, and the intellectual soul or *nous*. Diodore of Tarsus, who probably depended on Bardaisan's work and his doctrine of free will, attacked Bardaisan in one single respect: for failing to get rid of the notion of fate completely. Diodore's treatise *Against Fate* is preserved in a summarized form by Photius (*Bibl.* 223) and attacks fatalistic determinism, exactly as Bardaisan had done. Diodore, indeed deeply acquainted as he was with Origen as well, praises Bardaisan because he freed the soul from Fate, only criticizing him for keeping the name of "fate":[14]

> In chapter 51, in which he demolishes the belief in Fate, [Diodore] also criticizes Bardaisan's doctrine. This doctrine, indeed, is partially insane [ἡμιμανής], so to say, and left midway [ἡμίτομος]. For, to be sure, Bardaisan liberates the soul from Fate and the so-called horoscope, and keeps its free will safe. However, he submits to the government of Fate the body and what concerns it, that is, richness and poverty, illness, life and death, and all that does not depend on us, and he teaches that all this is a work of Fate.

Diodore wrote *Against Fate*, Κατὰ εἱμαρμένης, which bears the same title as Bardaisan's own work, in the form transmitted by Epiphanius and Theodoret. Both Bardaisan and Diodore upheld free will against fatalistic determinism. Diodore criticizes Bardaisan only in chapter 51 for having kept the name of "fate," although he did subordinate it to Providence. Diodore's long treatise refutes not Bardaisan but Fate and astrological determinism, its full title being *Against Astronomers, Astrologers and Fate*, Κατὰ ἀστρονόμων καὶ ἀστρολόγων καὶ Εἱμαρμένης,[15] which is what Bardaisan had also argued. As I contend elsewhere,[16] Diodore rests exactly on Bardaisan's arguments against fatalistic determinism and even

---

13. As I argued extensively in Ramelli, *Bardaisan of Edessa: A Reassessment*.
14. Analysis in Ramelli, *Bardaisan of Edessa: A Reassessment*, 142–60.
15. Suda, s.v. "Diodore of Tarsus."
16. Ramelli, *Bardaisan of Edessa: A Reassessment*, 142–60.

displays revealing details, such as that of the "Lazians," a detail also present in the *Book of the Laws of Countries* (according to my emendation of "Zazians"—a nonexistent people and very probably a scribal mistake—into "Lazians"), which make it virtually certain that it depended, directly or indirectly, on Bardaisan's argument. Diodore states that the elements (στοιχεῖα) are creatures (col. 833), like Bardaisan in *BLC* 4: God is "their creator," and they are subjected to God.[17] Diodore refuted the same "climatic" theory of Fate that was rejected by Bardaisan. Bardaisan inspired Diodore's argument that the heavenly bodies cannot influence the course of nature (col. 840). In book 6, chapter 44, Diodore takes over Bardaisan's argument to prove that human *nous*, not stars, determine the customs and laws of the nations.

That Diodore's argument was identical to that of Bardaisan is clear even from Photius's version (col. 861): Diodore proves even closer to Bardaisan in chapter 45, in which Diodore responds to the same astrological objection concerning the climatic zones, each governed by a star, to which Bardaisan had replied. Diodore responds to this objection exactly like Bardaisan: he produces the same examples concerning the Jews and the Christians, who keep their laws in different regions of the earth. The most disparate peoples in every zone have converted to Christianity and submitted to the law of Christ. The words that introduce Diodore's treatment of the Christians, "our race [γένος], I mean that of the Christians," are an echo of the phrase with which Bardaisan introduced his own example of the Christians: "the new race of us Christians." It even seems that Diodore is citing from the Syriac text, not from Eusebius's Greek translation, which has αἵρεσις, not γένος. Bardaisan's adjective *new*, in reference to race, and his whole satisfaction about the expansion of Christianity in his day in *Book of the Laws of Countries* (and in his works on India and Armenia), also corresponds to Diodore's sentence—adapted to his own time—that Christianity in four hundred years has conquered the whole world. Bardaisan, like Diodore later, rejoiced in the fact that Christianity had already spread "in every land and in all regions." Some precise details, such as of the "Lazians" and of the Christian γένος, make me think that Diodore did not simply use Eusebius's excerpts but a full text of good quality, either Syriac or Greek. The second argument adduced by Diodore concerns the peoples who,

---

17. *BLC* 4 in Ramelli, *Bardaisan on Free Will* = Nau, *Bardesanes*, col. 551.

conquered by the Romans, change their laws and customs and assume those of the Romans. This argument is very likely inspired by that of Bardaisan on peoples altering their laws on the decision of their governors; what is more, it even echoes the example adduced by Bardaisan concerning Abgar the Great, who, after his conversion to Christianity, forbade a pagan ritual mutilation. All this confirms that Diodore was resting on Bardaisan's antifatalistic and antiastrological arguments, in defense of human free will, which in turn depends on *nous* (within an ethical intellectualistic framework).

There is simply one thing for which Diodore reproaches Bardaisan: keeping the name of fate without getting rid of it completely. I suspect that Bardaisan did so ultimately because of his trichotomic anthropology, culminating in *nous* and, as seen, moving between the movement of unfolding from *nous* and that of subsumption into *nous*. Diodore wanted Bardaisan to be more radical in his antifatalistic refutation and eliminate Fate altogether. Indeed, Bardaisan is criticized for this single point, in one chapter, within this bulky eight-book work.

Bardaisan maintained the notion of fate together with nature and free will as the three forces that influence human life, although his conception of fate is depleted, diluted, and depending on divine Providence, as befits a Christian philosopher. I suspect that Bardaisan posited these three forces, without reducing them to two (by abolishing fate), in order to keep the notion of the stars as mediators of the divine economy, as Origen also did, and especially in order to maintain the parallel between the three forces (nature, fate, and free will) and the three anthropological levels of the human being: body, animal soul, and *nous*.[18] For he regarded the vital, inferior soul, which vivifies the body, to be subject to fate, which brings about fortunes or misfortunes, beauty or ugliness, money or poverty, and the like (what the Stoics called ἀδιάφορα or morally indifferent things), whereas what is free from fate is *nous*, which exercises free will in what depends on us (τὰ ἐφ᾽ ἡμῖν), and many bodily facts are governed by Nature, such as birth, nutrition, death, and the like. Thus, the correspondence that Bardaisan constructs seems to be the following, in ascending order: Nature > body; Fate > vital, inferior soul; free will > intellectual, superior soul or intellect/*nous*.

---

18. See Ramelli, *Bardaisan of Edessa: A Reassessment*, 142–60 on Diodore.

Origen's Trichotomy, Unfolding and Subsumption, and
Some Parallels with Pagan Neoplatonism

Origen, who presents many congruities with Bardaisan,[19] elaborates on the body-soul-*nous* tripartition and the movement from *nous* to soul and body, as well as the movement back in the process of apokatastasis. Like Bardaisan, Origen also suggests a movement from the *nous* to a tripartite development in the human being and, backwards, a final subsumption into the *nous*, for instance in *Princ.* 2.8.3. Here, he indicates that the soul, once emended and purified, will become again *nous*, as it was originally, before cooling down and losing the fire of love for God (Origen followed the etymology of ψυχή from ψῦξις, which was already used by the Stoics and had become traditional, but Origen attached to it his whole theory of descent; see *Princ.* 1.8.4; *Comm. Jo.* 13.16; *Comm. Matt.* 17.30; *Hom. Ezech.* 13.2; *Hom. Lev.* 9.11).

That *nous* is above soul (or can be conceived as soul's highest part), that its fall degraded it to the level of soul and had it unfold into soul and then body, and that its restoration will elevate soul to the level of *nous* (and ultimately of God, in deification or *theōsis*, which in Christian Platonism is the culmination of apokatastasis and *epistrophē*), is something that Christian Platonists such as Bardaisan and Evagrius also maintained, as is emerging from this essay. A strong parallel also obtains with the pagan Platonist Plotinus, Origen's fellow disciple at Ammonius Saccas's school (the so-called Socrates of Neoplatonism), who in his protology posited Nous as the second hypostasis and Soul as the third, inferior to it and derived from it (his triad, unlike that of Origen and especially of the Origenian Cappadocians, is hierarchic or strongly subordinationistic); the reversion or *epistrophē* of Soul in Platonism elevates it to the level of Nous (and ultimately the One).[20] The tripartition of the human into *nous*, soul, and body is inscribed in Plotinus's protology: *nous* and soul correspond to the second and third Hypostasis (the first being the One, which part of the

---

19. As argued in Ramelli, "Bardaisan of Edessa, Origen, and Imperial Philosophy."

20. See Ilaria L. E. Ramelli, "The Father in the Son, the Son in the Father in the Gospel of John: Sources and Reception of Dynamic Unity in Middle and Neoplatonism, 'Pagan' and Christian," *JBR* 7 (2020): 31–66. For Bardaisan and Evagrius, see Ilaria L. E. Ramelli, *Evagrius's Kephalaia Gnostika: A New Translation of the Unreformed Text from the Syriac,* WGRW 38 (Atlanta: SBL Press, 2015); for reversion in Platonism, a study on Platonist reversion/apokatastasis is in the works.

pagan Platonic tradition and of the Christian Platonic tradition identified with God). The body is the last expression of the descending activity, from the One down. Before the individual soul joins a human body, the world soul creates an outline in advance (a προϋπογραφή): "like illuminations running on before into matter, and the soul which carries out the work [follows] traces of this kind and [makes] by articulating the traces part by part, and each individual soul [becomes] this to which it came in shaping itself" (*Enn.* 6.7.7.8–15). The body is like "a beautiful and richly various house.... It possesses a soul, not as a possession [οὐχ αὐτοῦ], but it is present to it [αὐτῷ]; the body is mastered [κρατούμενος]: it is not the master; it is possessed [ἐχόμενος]: it is not the possessor" (*Enn.* 4.3.9.34–38).

Origen adheres to a trichotomic anthropology of body, soul, and spirit (σῶμα, ψυχή, πνεῦμα, *Princ.* 4.2.4; *Dial.* 6), which he also attributes to Christ (*Dial.* 7), but, as just seen in his unfolding-and-subsumption movement, also deploys prominently the body, soul, and intellect tripartition (σῶμα, ψυχή, νοῦς).[21] Both trichotomies go back to Paul, who is a main authority for Origen in many respects, in theology, allegorical exegesis, ethics, and so on.[22] Some scholars detect an influence of the Stoic doctrine of material πνεῦμα in Origen's notion of πνεῦμα. That Origen knew the Stoic theory of πνεῦμα is clear; that he embraced its materialism, however, is improbable, given his transcendental, Platonic perspective—which he also used, for example, when he insisted that God is πνεῦμα, νοῦς, and immaterial, at the beginning of *De Principiis* and elsewhere. Origen also knew the Stoic theory of apokatastasis, conceived as a cyclical reiteration of aeons, but he refuted it and explicitly opposed to it his own, Christian Platonic doctrine, as compatible with his theology of freedom.

The notion of a trichotomic anthropology, on which Origen builds his conception of unfolding and subsumption of the *nous*, also seems to rest on the theory of the inner and the outer human being. Such a concept was present already in Plato in the form of "inner man" (ὁ ἐντὸς ἄνθρωπος, *Resp.* 9 [589a]), as well as in Philo of Alexandria, and Paul used both forms—inner and outer human—in Rom 7:21–23 (κατὰ τὸν ἔσω ἄνθρωπον, related to "the law of my mind," τῷ νόμῳ τοῦ νοός μου, as

---

21. See Ramelli, "Tricotomia"; Kooten, *Paul's Anthropology in Context*, 20.

22. Case study in Ilaria L. E. Ramelli, "The Reception of Paul in Origen: Allegoresis of Scripture, Apokatastasis, and Women's Ministry," in *The Pauline Mind*, ed. Stanley Porter and David Yoon (New York: Routledge, 2023).

opposed to "the law of my limbs") and 2 Cor 4:16 (ὁ ἔξω ἡμῶν ἄνθρωπον, which is ruining, in contrast to ὁ ἔσω ἡμῶν, which is renewed day by day). This use was followed by Eph 3:17 (whether it is by Paul or not; Origen of course deemed it Pauline): εἰς τὸν ἔσω ἄνθρωπον, related to the πνεῦμα of God. This is a typical conception of Origen, who based it on both Paul and Platonism (*Cels.* 6.63; *Comm. Cant.* prol.; *Comm. Jo.* 20.22; *Comm. Rom.* 1.19; 7.4; *Hom. Gen.* 1.13; *Dialogus cum Heraclide*; *Princ.* 4.4.9). But it is a Platonic, Pauline, and Philonic heritage taken over not only by Origen but also by Plotinus (*Enn.* 1.1.10.5–15).[23] Plato, like Origen, was of course familiar with the Greek usage of νοῦς: "possessing *nous*" meant to be intelligent, and not possessing it meant to be stupid. Speaking of a person who possesses *nous* in *Resp.* 591c1, Socrates, in Plato's elaboration, notes that such a "noetic" person "will always cultivate the harmony of the body for the sake of the *symphony* of his soul"; this will enable her to be "musical" (μουσικός, 591d4–5).[24]

Connected to Origen's concept of *nous* in a human is the notion of spiritual senses, which pertain to the inner human being. Origen focuses on them on many occasions, especially in his *Dialogue with Heraclides*, which in 16–20 focuses on the spiritual or interior senses. They are here analyzed one by one. As Origen explains, both human beings, inner and outer, have a set of senses, which are in turn inner and outer. The outer human has eyes, ears, nostrils, tact, and so on, and the inner human has too. So, in addition to the outer senses, there is an inner sight, an inner hearing, an inner touch, an inner smell, and an inner taste.

This double set of senses is also found in Scripture. Origen insists on the Bible's spiritual meaning (μυστικόν, πνευματικόν, *Dial.* 15). This is why he "anguishes" about speaking or not speaking: he wants to speak for those who are "worthy" (ἀξίους, an important category for Origen, which he applies not only to exegesis but to all of his theology) of the spiritual meaning but not the unworthy, who remain at the level of bodily senses. Origen includes spiritual or noetic senses under allegore-

---

23. See Christoph Markschies, "Die platonische Metapher vom "inneren Menschen,"" *ZKG* 105 (1994): 1–17; Kooten, *Paul's Anthropology in Context*, 358–74; Karl-Wilhelm Niebuhr, "Jakobus und Paulus über das Innere des Menschen," *NTS* 62 (2016): 22–30, esp. on Rom 6–8.

24. For the importance of this notion in Plato and the Platonic tradition, see Ramelli, *Christian Doctrine of Apokatastasis*; Ilaria L. E. Ramelli, "Soma (Σῶμα)," *RAC* 30:814–47.

sis as opposed to physical senses under the *littera*.[25] Thus, he applies the inner and outer human, and the couple of physical and spiritual senses, to the exegesis of Scripture.

This application also intersects with the double way of considering Christ, as human or divine. Origen parallels the sense-perceptible level of reality (Christ's human nature, which corresponds to the *littera* of Scripture) and the intelligible, noetic level (Christ's divine nature, which corresponds to the spiritual sense of Scripture; *Hom. Lev.* 1.1; *Comm. ser. Matt.* 27). Not all of Scripture has a literal meaning, but all of Scripture has an allegorical, spiritual, noetic meaning: "Do you think these are myths? Do you think the Holy Spirit in Scriptures just tells stories?[26] This is rather teaching for souls, spiritual instruction…. All that is written in Scripture is mysteries," that is, allegories, noetic senses (*Hom. Gen.* 10.2). As we read the Bible, Origen notes, considering his own practice of assiduously reading and meditating Scripture, "a heap of symbolic meanings increases before us … such an immense sea of mysteries!" (*Hom. Gen.* 9.1). The interpretation of the accounts of Jesus's earthly life—as modern New Testament scholars also warn, although often for different reasons—requires "much investigation" (πολλὴ ἐξέτασις, *Cels.* 1.42), especially to discern both historical and spiritual senses. The use of φιλομαθής and related terms concerning "love for learning" is profuse in Origen's oeuvre, with reference to exegesis (e.g., *Comm. Jo.* 6.213; *Ep. Afr.* 23; *Cels.* 4.51; *Philoc.* 6.2; etc.).

The Logos, the Mind of God (corresponding in many ways to Plotinus's Nous[27]) inspired all of Scripture—Moses, the prophets, the apostles—and likewise inspired Greek philosophers (especially Plato), and is also that which is "incarnate" in Scripture and became incarnate in Jesus, and, again, is also the Logos that inspires the philosophical exegete who has

---

25. On Origen's spiritual senses, see Mark McInroy, "Origen," in *The Spiritual Senses*, ed. Paul Gavrilyuk and Sarah Coakley (Cambridge: Cambridge University Press, 2012), 20–35; on their role in Origen's esotericism, see Ilaria L. E. Ramelli, "Esoteric Interpretations of Scripture in Philo (and Hellenistic Judaism), Clement, and Origen," in *Esoteric Cultures of Scripture*, ed. Toby Mayer (Oxford: Oxford University Press, forthcoming).

26. This is reminiscent of Paul's support of allegoresis in his oxen passage, the allegory of Hagar and Sarah, and so on. See Ilaria L. E. Ramelli, "The Role of Allegory, Allegoresis, and Metaphor in Paul and Origen," *JGRChJ* 14 (2018): 130–57.

27. Ilaria L. E. Ramelli, "The Logos/Nous One-Many between 'Pagan' and Christian Platonism: Bardaisan, Clement, Origen, Plotinus, and Gregory of Nyssa," *StPatr* 102 (2020): 175–204.

to interpret the Bible. Likewise, Clement had deemed the same Logos, who inspired Scripture, also its true "exegete," by whom the interpreter is enlightened (*Strom.* 1.26.169). The Logos warrants the unity of Scripture and the coherence of its interpretation. This is why Origen, when philosophically interpreting Scripture, which is a "zetetic" work, feels inspired by the Logos as both a philosopher and an exegete. Christ-Logos-Wisdom, indeed, illuminates the exegete's and philosopher-theologian's intellect (*Hom. Jer.* 19.11; *Comm. Cant.* 3.11.17–19: *Verbum illuminat mentem*; see also 1.1.14; *Hom. Cant.* 1.7). Origen describes the toil of the exegete—primarily himself: this is one of his many but indirect autobiographical hints[28]—as helped by the Logos: if "one has done everything in one's own power, and has exercised one's senses to distinguish good and evil," then God takes away the veil of allegory (*Cels.* 4.50). The senses mentioned in this declaration are the spiritual, noetic senses of the inner human being: the senses of the *nous*.

De principiis 1.1.7 speaks indeed of "intellectual senses" or "senses of the mind" (*sensus mentis*), namely, noetic senses. This discourse goes on in 1.1.8, with an explicit scriptural reference to John 1:18 on God as "invisible" and the equation between invisibility and unknowability. *De principiis* 1.1.9 in turn refers to Matt 5:8 on "seeing" God and points again to all spiritual senses. In *Comm. Rom.* 4.5.138–145, Origen insists that, if the spiritual, noetic senses do not grasp God, there results the death of the (intellectual) soul. Indeed, if these senses are the senses of the mind, and these do not grasp God, who is the life of the *nous* or intellectual soul, this will die. This, as Origen insists, is not an ontological death—as Philo probably had postulated—but a moral death.[29] Origen interprets "the dead" in Rom 4:17 in the sense of those who are dead in their souls due to sin, (wrongly) chosen by their soul:

> "God who vivifies the dead and calls the beings that are not just as those which are." As for "the dead," we must understand here those who are dead on account of the sin of their soul, because, as Scripture says, "The soul that sins will die" [Ezek 18:4].... A man who has lost his spiritual

28. Ilaria L. E. Ramelli, "Autobiographical Self-Fashioning in Origen," in *Self, Self-Fashioning and Individuality in Late Antiquity: New Perspectives*, ed. Maren Niehoff and Joshua Levinson (Tübingen: Mohr Siebeck, 2019), 273–92.

29. Ilaria L. E. Ramelli, "Philo's Doctrine of Apokatastasis: Philosophical Sources, Exegetical Strategies, and Patristic Aftermath," *SPhiloA* 26 (2014): 29–55.

senses in his soul, so that he cannot see God, nor hear the words of God, nor perceive Christ's sweet perfume, nor taste the sweet Logos of God; and his hands do not touch the Logos of life—well, this kind of people are called "dead," and rightly so. (*Comm. Rom.* 4.5.138–145)[30]

The most serious kind of death is the death of the *nous* away from God. A full list of all the possible meanings of *death* in Scripture is provided by Origen both in his *Dialogue of Heraclides*—where Origen lists the death of the body, the death of the soul, which is a big evil, and the death to sin, which is always very good—and, in a still completer form, in his *Commentary on Romans*:

"Death" in Scriptures is one single name, but has many meanings. Indeed, the separation of the body from the soul is called "death," but this cannot be said to be either evil or good, since it is in the middle, what is called "indifferent." Again, the separation of a soul from God is named "death," which comes about through sin. This death, which is also called "the wages of sin," is clearly evil.... And again, the author himself of this death, the devil, is called "death," and he is the one who is said to be the very last enemy of Christ, bound to be destroyed [1 Cor 15:26]. But hell, in which souls are imprisoned by death, this too is called "death." And in yet another sense, that death is called praiseworthy by which a person dies to sin and is buried together with Christ; thanks to this, a soul is improved and acquires eternal life. (*Comm. Rom.* 6.6.29–43)[31]

---

30. "Qui uiuificat mortuos et uocat ea quae non sunt tamquam quae sunt. Mortuos hic secundum animae peccatum intellegimus, quoniam anima inquit, quae peccat ipsa morietur ... qui spiritales sensus in anima perdiderit ut non uideat Deum neque audiat uerba Dei neque suauem odorem capiat Christi neque gustet bonum Dei uerbum neque manus eius pertractent de uerbo uitae, huiusmodi homines merito mortui appellantur."

31. "Mors in Scripturis unum quidem nomen est, sed multa significat. Etenim separatio corporis ab anima mors nominatur. Sed haec neque mala neque bona dici potest; est enim media, quae dicitur indifferens. Et rursus separatio animae a Deo mors appellatur quae per peccatum uenit. Haec aperte mala est, quae et peccati stipendium nominatur.... Et iterum ipse auctor mortis huius diabolus mors appellatur et ipse est qui dicitur inimicus Christi nouissimus destruendus. Sed et inferni locus in quo animae detinebantur a morte etiam ipse mors appellatur. Dicitur uero illa mors laudabilis qua peccato quis moritur et Christo consepelitur, per quam emendatio fit animae et uita aeterna conquiritur."

Three of these meanings (bodily death, as an indifferent thing in the sense of the Stoic ἀδιάφορα, spiritual death, and death to sin) are the same as those that are classified by Origen in his *Dialogue* and again in *Comm. Rom.* 6.5.35–41: "this common death" (*mors ista communis*), that is, bodily death; "the death caused by sin, since 'The soul that sins will die' [Ezek 18:4]" (*peccati mors, quoniam anima quae peccat ipsa morietur*), and "the death by which we die to sin together with Christ (*istam mortem qua cum Christo peccato morimur*).

Evagrius, too—to whom we shall return below—uses *death* to indicate physical death, spiritual death, or death to sin. The last kind of death is reflected in *To the Monks* 21, where death to sin is identified with dying the death of Christ, and in *Chapters of the Disciples of Evagrius* 58: the intellect or *nous*, that is, the "interior human being" (ὁ ἔσω ἄνθρωπος), dies to sin when it separates itself from "intellections of passions" (ἐμπαθῆ νοήματα). As Origen had taught, the "death to sin" on the part of the *nous* is an excellent kind of death and does not prevent but facilitates the subsumption of the whole human being into *nous* and eventually into God. This is Evagrius's ideal, which will be taken over later by the Christian Neoplatonist Eriugena.[32]

According to Origen, *nous* unfolds initially into soul and body, and eventually all human components are subsumed again in *nous*, which will in turn be deified. But such components are always there. As I extensively argue elsewhere,[33] body and *nous* in rational creatures seem to be always united, according to Origen, from the creation of the rational creature (*logikon*) as an independent substance onward (the only doubt for Origen concerns the final deification, since God is immaterial, although, if deification affects more will than substance, it opens up the possibility of a continual existence of a spiritual body).

In the fall, owing to the misuse of one's freedom—a pivotal concept in Origen's theology of freedom[34]—and a lessening intensity of one's activity

---

32. See Ramelli, "From God to God."

33. Ramelli, "Origen," 2; for aspects of Origen's immediate aftermath, see Ilaria L. E. Ramelli "Origen on the Unity of Soul and Body in the Earthly Life and Afterwards and His Impact," in *The Unity of Soul and Body in the Earthly Life and After*, ed. Jörg Ulrich, Anna Usacheva, and Siam Bhayro (Leiden: Brill, 2021), 38–77. I argue, among other points, that none of the passages adduced by scholars entails disembodied souls who receive a body only as a result of sin, and some, such as *Princ.* 2.9.1–2, clearly gainsay this hypothesis.

34. Analysis in Christian Hengstermann, *Origenes und der Ursprung der Freiheitsmetaphysik* (Münster: Aschendorff, 2015); Ilaria L. E. Ramelli, *Social Justice and*

of contemplation and love for God in such an activity, the *nous*'s original unity unfolds into three components. As the *logika* fall, they take on souls and bodies in accordance with the state of their *nous* and become angels, humans, and demons. All rational creatures or *logika*, according to Origen, possess the very same nature, to the point that they can even change status and rank between aeons according to their moral choices, becoming angels, humans, or demons (understood as fallen angels) or vice versa. *Logika* can become demons but also revert to their original condition, as is explained in the final sentence of *Princ.* 1.6.3: "Every rational creature can pass from one order to another and reach all, one by one, because each rational creature, by virtue of its free will, makes progresses or regresses depending on its movements (of the will) and impulses." Therefore, in *De Principiis* 1.8.4 Origen remarks: "We see some humans progress until they are assumed into the order of angels," and in *Comm. Cant.* 4.3.21: "By means of free will it is possible that each rational creature passes to another class, either to the part of God if the change is an improvement, or, if it is a change for the bad, to the rank of demons."[35] In *Princ.* 3.1.23, Origen expresses the same concept: "I deem it possible that the soul, which I have repeatedly described as immortal and eternal, through infinite spaces and innumerable and different times, either will fall from the supreme Good to the deepest evil, or will be restored from the deepest evil to the highest Good," noting that some "can reach such a degree of evilness as to become hostile powers."

Nevertheless, in Origen's system, even these hostile powers, namely, demons, by education and purification, can be restored to the Good. In *Princ.* 3.6.3, Origen argues for the apokatastasis or restoration of the devil and his angels on the grounds of an eventual universal harmony and unity. Thus, he concludes that not even demons will be in disagreement with the rest of the restored creation or be excluded from the eventual perfect unity and harmony, an ideal that is both Platonic and based on John 17.[36] Thus, "Once things have begun to rush toward the ideal state in which all

---

the *Legitimacy of Slavery: The Role of Philosophical Asceticism from Ancient Judaism to Late Antiquity* (Oxford: Oxford University Press, 2016), 172–211.

35. "Per arbitrii libertatem possibile est unumquemque ex parte alterius transire, vel ad partem Dei si melius, vel si nequius ad daemonum portionem."

36. See Ilaria L. E. Ramelli, "Harmony between *arkhē* and *telos* in Patristic Platonism and the Imagery of Astronomical Harmony Applied to the Apokatastasis Theory," *IJPT* 7 (2013): 1–49.

are one, just as the Father is one with the Son, as a logical consequence we must believe that, when all are one, there will be no divergence any more" (*Princ.* 3.6.4). This does not mean that Origen envisages a final state in which there will be no distinction or differentiation at the metaphysical, ontological level, but he thinks of the eventual apokatastasis as a state in which there will be "no divergence" in the sense of "no opposition" at the level of will. Origen is not imagining a confusion of substances but is foreseeing a unity and harmony of will, in that the wills of all rational creatures will be oriented toward the Good. Divine Providence extends to demons as well, who, after a long purification and illumination, will no longer be powers of evil but will return to their angelic state and ascend the angelic hierarchies:

> Both in these visible and temporal aeons and in those invisible and otherworldly, God's Providence operates in favor of all with measure and discernment, with regard to order and merit. Therefore, some first and then others, and yet others in the very last times, by means of heavier and more painful sufferings, long and undergone, say, for many aeons, in the end all, renewed by instruction and severe corrections, will be restored first among angels, then in superior hierarchies; thus all will be gradually received higher and higher, until they arrive at the invisible and eternal realities, after running, one by one, the offices of the heavenly hierarchies to be instructed. (*Princ.* 3.6.4)

Instruction is primarily noetic: it concerns *nous*.

Origen anticipates, here and elsewhere, later conceptions of angelic hierarchies. Higher-ranking angels instruct lower-ranking ones, so that the latter "may be able to return and be restored to their former state of blessedness" (*Princ.* 1.6.2). Angels, in their intermediary role between humans and God, ascend through the angelic hierarchy, "bringing the prayers of men into the purest heavenly region of the universe, or even to places purer than these beyond the heavens" (*Cels.* 5.4).[37] The hierarchic conception of angelic ranks, and of their operations upwards and down-

---

37. On prayer in late antiquity, both pagan and Christian, see Andrei Timotin, *La prière dans la tradition platonicienne, de Platon à Proclus* (Turnhout: Brepols, 2017); see also Ilaria L. E. Ramelli, review of *La prière dans la tradition platonicienne, de Platon à Proclus*, by Andrei Timotin, *BMCR*, 17 April 2020; and, on the relation between prayer and divination, see Timotin, *Trois théories antiques de la divination: Plutarque, Jamblique, Augustin* (Leiden: Brill, 2022).

wards, was to be developed especially by Pseudo-Dionysius the Areopagite (who arguably knew Origen well and built on his thought)[38] in his *Heavenly Hierarchy* (*De caelesti hierarchia*) and his whole thought. Dionysius used many words, including newly coined ones, related to hierarchy and many terms finishing in –αρχία,[39] including ἀγαθαρχία and θεαρχία, very probably influenced—as I suspect—by Origen's notion of God the Trinity as the three ἀρχαί, as elaborated in Περὶ ἀρχῶν.

Moral choices for rational creatures are inevitable and determine their rank as angels, humans, or demons in Origen's view and bring about the details of their unfolding from *nous* and their eventual subsumption into *nous*. For God alone is substantial Good; creatures participate in it to a lesser or greater degree, and this is why they can fall away from it (*Princ.* 4.6.2; see also 1.7.2, 1.8.3). For, being created out of nothing, they are mutable, unlike their Creator, who is essential Good. The good that was initially in the intellectual creatures was a gift from God; it did not belong to them by nature and was thus open to being lost, depending on "the souls' movements": these derive from "the power of free and voluntary action," bestowed on them by God, that "the good that was in them might become their own, being preserved by the exertion of their free will" (*Princ.* 2.9.2). Indeed, the theory of the soul consists in knowing "what is soul and *how it moves* [*qualiter moveatur*]: its substance [*substantia*] and its affections [*affectibus*]" (*Comm. Cant.* 2.5.1–2 [Baehrens 143]). By means of free will (which depends on *nous*), through their movements, the intellectual creatures fell away from the Good, while only their adhesion to the Good, through their knowledge of it, will eventually produce their deification, since the supreme Good is God.

The Valentinians speculated about Christ's pneumatic, psychic, and hylic body; Origen, as the Neoplatonists also did, postulated various

---

38. As I argued in Ilaria L. E. Ramelli, "Origen and Evagrios," in *Oxford Handbook of Dionysius the Areopagite*, ed. Mark Edwards, Dimitrios Pallis, and Georgios Steiris (Oxford: Oxford University Press, 2022), 94–108, and, with further methodological points on the double references to pagan and Christian Platonism, often with references to both Proclus and Origen, in Ramelli, "'Pagan' and Christian Platonism in Dionysius: The Double-Reference Scheme and Its Meaning," in *Byzantine Platonists 284–1453*, ed. Frederick Lauritzen and Sarah Klitenic Wear, TSBPCP (Washington, DC: Catholic University of America Press, 2021), 92–112.

39. E.g., Κυριαρχία, ἱεραρχία (*Cael. hier.* 8.1 [240B]), ἐναρχία (*Div. nom.* 2.4 [641A], etc.), οὐσιαρχία (*Div. nom.* 5.1 [816B], etc.), ἐξουσιαρχία, ἀγαθαρχία (*Div. nom.* 1.5 [593C], 3.1 [680B], etc.), and θεαρχία.

degrees of corporeality and kinds of bodies for rational creatures—as well as for Christ—conceived as united with the intellectual soul or *nous*.[40] Porphyry employs the same notion of "skin tunic" (*Abst.* 2.46; 1.31) as Origen and Scripture do: Jakob Bernays and Eric Dodds suggest an influence of Valentinian exegesis of the skin tunics in Gen 3:21 as fleshly body.[41] Origen's influence seems possible as well, all the more so in that Porphyry likely studied with Origen and surely knew (a part of) his works well.[42] Both Origen and Porphyry posited a light, invisible body as the vehicle of the soul that can become thicker and visible, enabling the apparitions of the dead as ghosts (*Antr. nymph.* 11; *Abst.* 2.47). This is the same explanation as Origen's—the αὐγοειδὲς σῶμα allows dead to appear (*Cels.* 2.60)—later taken over by Gregory of Nyssa in *De an.* 88. Iamblichus attributes the theory that the soul cannot exist without a body to "the school of Eratosthenes, the Platonist Ptolemy, and others," who thought that souls did not receive a body for the first time when they began to ensoul the *mortal* body but from the beginning had "finer" (λεπτότερα) bodies (*De. an.* 26; see 54.5–6).[43] This appears to have been Origen's stance as well.

Plotinus also posits a "finer" body (λεπτότερον), as the vehicle of the soul (*Enn.* 3.6.5), but denies that a soul possesses such a body from the beginning: unlike Origen, Plotinus maintains the preexistence of disembodied souls

40. See Ilaria L. E. Ramelli, "Conceptualities of Angels in Late Antiquity: Degrees of Corporeality, Bodies of Angels, and Comparative Angelologies/Daemonologies in 'Pagan' and Christian Platonism," in *Inventer les anges de l'Antiquité à Byzance: conception, représentation, perception*, ed. Delphine Lauritzen (Paris: CNRS – Collège de France, Centre d'Histoire et Civilisation de Byzance, 2022), 115–72. On the Valentinians see Einar Thomassen, *The Spiritual Seed: The Church of the Valentinians* (Leiden: Brill, 2008).

41. Eric R. Dodds, *Proclus: The Elements of Theology* (Oxford: Clarendon, 1963), 308.

42. See Ilaria L. E. Ramelli, "Origen, Greek Philosophy, and the Birth of the Trinitarian Meaning of Hypostasis," *HTR* 105 (2012): 302–50; Ramelli, "Origen's Allegoresis of Plato's and Scripture's Myths," in *Religious Competition in the Greco-Roman World*, ed. Nathaniel Desrosiers and Lily Vuong, WGRWSup 10 (Atlanta: SBL Press, 2016), 85–106; Ramelli, "Porphyry and the Motif of Christianity as παράνομος," in *Platonism and Its Legacy: Selected Papers from the Fifteenth Annual Conference of the International Society for Neoplatonic Studies*, ed. John F. Finamore and Tomáš Nejeschleba (Lydney, UK: Prometheus Trust, 2019), 173–98.

43. On λεπτότερα for bodies in Iamblichus, see Ilaria L. E. Ramelli, "Iamblichus, De anima 38 (66,12-15 Finamore/Dillon): A Resolving Conjecture?," *RhM* 157 (2014): 106–11.

and metensomatosis. For Plotinus, souls acquire this light, finer body only during their descent, and later they acquire "earthlier and earthlier bodies," and very probably drop them during their subsequent reascent (*Enn.* 4.3.15; 4.3.24). This movement parallels that of the unfolding and the eventual subsumption of the human components from *nous* and into *nous* in Bardaisan, Origen, and Evagrius. Initially, according to Plotinus, humans were "pure souls," some even gods (*Enn.* 6.4.13). Some daimons have bodies, others are bodiless, as detailed in *Enn.* 3.5.6, within a commentary on Plato's Poros myth, which Origen assimilated to Genesis's Eden account.[44] Here, Plotinus uses δαίμονες as "spirits," rational creatures sharing the same φύσις/οὐσία and distinct from the gods, although they are occasionally called "gods." Likewise, Origen's *logika* share the same φύσις/οὐσία and are different from God, albeit being also called gods. For Plotinus, daimons participate in matter, but not "corporeal matter," since they are not sense perceptible. They assume "airy or fiery bodies," but "earlier" (πρότερον), being pure, had no bodies, "though many opine that the substance of the spirit qua spirit [δαίμων] implies some body [τινος σώματος], whether airy of fiery" (*Enn.* 3.5.6.40–42). These "many" may include Origen ("Origen" is reported to have composed a treatise *On Spirits/Daimones*, Περὶ δαιμόνων).[45] In this case, Plotinus would refer again to Origen's theory, but without taking it up. On the other hand, it is virtually sure that Origen's demonology inspired Porphyry's demonology and even subsequent pagan demonology such as that expounded in Martianus Capella.[46]

According to Origen, intellectual creatures or *noes* possessed a fine body from the beginning of their creation as independent substances (not in their eternal preexistence in the Mind of God) and keep this after the death of the earthly body—which is the same as the risen body as for individual identity—and in the eventual apokatastasis or restoration. Porphyry sides with Plotinus, against Origen, teaching that the light body is not with soul from the beginning or forever but is acquired during soul's descent (*Sent.* 13.8; *Gaur.* 11.3), being gathered from the heavenly bodies, and finally discarded by the rational soul during its ascent (*apud*

---

44. See Ramelli, "Origen's Allegoresis of Plato's and Scripture's Myths," 85–106.

45. Discussion in Ilaria L. E. Ramelli, "Origen, Patristic Philosophy, and Christian Platonism: Re-thinking the Christianisation of Hellenism," *VC* 63 (2009): 217–63; further in ongoing works.

46. Argument in Ilaria L. E. Ramelli, "Martianus Capella," in *The Encyclopedia of Ancient History*, ed. Roger Bagnall et al. (Oxford: Wiley-Blackwell, 2021).

Proclus, *In Tim.* 3.234.18–26). The same line is later represented by Macrobius (*Comm. somn.* 1.11.12, 1.12.13).[47] Origen's perspective, that the luminous, light body *always* accompanies the soul, was rather continued within Neoplatonism by Iamblichus (*De an.* 38), Hierocles, and especially Proclus, as mentioned. This, of course, does not mean that Proclus derived the widespread theory of the ὄχημα of the soul from Origen, as seems to have been misunderstood by some scholars,[48] but Proclus may have been acquainted with Origen's anthropology as well as his protology.[49] Damascius will also theorize a gradation of bodies, mortal to pneumatic to luminous, but—like Plotinus—will identify the ideal state with disembodiment (*In Phaed.* 1.551).

In Origen's view, no creature can ever live as a pure *nous*, completely disembodied. Only the Creator-Trinity is absolutely incorporeal, while all creatures need a body, whether spiritual or mortal, to live; bodies can be separated from *logika* only theoretically, not actually:

> If it is absolutely impossible to claim that any other nature besides the Father, Son, and Holy Spirit can live without body, the argument's coherence compels to understand that *logika* were created as the principal creation, but material substance [*materialem substantiam*] can be separated from them—and can thus appear to be created before or after them—only theoretically and mentally [*opinione et intellectu solo*], because *they can never have lived, or live, without matter* [*numquam sine ipsa*]. For *only the Trinity can be correctly thought to live incorporeally* [*incorporea vita existere*]. Therefore … the material substance, capable by nature of being transformed from all into all, when dragged to inferior creatures is formed into a *dense, solid body* … but when it serves more perfect and blessed creatures, it shines forth in the splendor of heavenly bodies and adorns with a *spiritual body* both God's angels and the resurrected. (*Princ.* 2.2.2)

---

47. Ilaria L. E. Ramelli, "Macrobius: Astrological Descents, Ascents, and Restorations," *MHNH* 14 (2014): 197–214.

48. Cristina D'Ancona, "Mind and Body," *SGA* 10 (2020): 387; contrast Johannes van Oort, "Mind and Body," *VC* 73 (2019): 594; Daniel Tolan, "Mind and Body," *JTS* 70 (2019): 857–59.

49. As I suggest in Ilaria L. E. Ramelli, "Some Overlooked Sources of the Elements of Theology: The Noetic Triad, Epistrophé-Apokatastasis, Bodies, and the Possible Reception of Origenian Themes," in *On Causes and the Noetic Triad*, vol. 3 of *Reading Proclus and the Book of Causes*, ed. Dragos Calma, SPNPT 28 (Leiden: Brill, 2022), 406–76.

Origen makes this point again, for example, in *Princ.* 1.6.4: "I cannot understand how so many substances could live and subsist incorporeally, whereas it is a prerogative of God alone ... to live *without material substance and any union with corporeal elements.*" In this passage, built up with a zetetic attitude, Origen argues that eventually there will be "no total destruction or annihilation of material substance [*substantiae materialis*], but a change of quality [*immutatio qualitatis*] and transformation of habit [*habitus transformatio*]." He is pointing to the transmutation of bodies from mortal into spiritual.[50] Origen syllogistically argues that it is impossible for any creature to live without a body: if any can, all will be able, but then corporeal substance would be useless; therefore, it would not exist. But it does exist. Therefore, all creatures must have a body (*Princ.* 2.3.2), including noetic/rational creatures.

First Corinthians 15:53 denies that it is possible for any creature to live without a body: "This same corporeal matter, which is now corruptible, will put on incorruptibility, when the perfect soul, instructed on the incorruptible truths, begins using the body" at resurrection: incorruptibility and immortality are God's Wisdom, Logos, and Justice (all *epinoiai* or conceptualizations of Jesus Christ), which will wrap the soul as its body (*Princ.* 2.3.2–3). The objection in *Princ.* 2.3.3 comes from people who—like most "pagan" Platonists and "gnostics"—taught that intellectual creatures can live disembodied. Origen repeatedly denied such a possibility, asserting that only God can live incorporeally: "no one is invisible, incorporeal [*incorporeus*], immutable, and without beginning or end but the Father, the Son, and the Holy Spirit" (*Hom. Exod.* 6.5). The substance of the Trinity is neither corporeal nor endowed with a body but absolutely incorporeal (*Princ.* 4.3.15).

This was also the position of another Christian (Middle) Platonist, Clement of Alexandria, but with a difference concerning Christ: even angels and the Protoctists need a body; "not even the Son can exist without form, shape, figure, and body [ἀσώματος]" (*Exc.* 10.1). Origen insists that the Son, qua God, needs no body at all, although Christ, in his human component, does have a body, as all *logika* have. Clement also contemplated degrees of corporeality. Stars are incorporeal (ἀσώματα)

---

50. Ilaria L. E. Ramelli, "Matter in the Dialogue of Adamantius: Origen's Heritage and Hylomorphism," in *Platonism and Christianity in Late Ancient Cosmology: God, Soul, Matter*, ed. Johannes Zachhuber and Anna Schiavoni, APR (Leiden: Brill, 2022), 74–124.

and formless (ἀνείδεα) compared with earthly things but are measurable and sensible bodies (σώματα μεμετρημένα, αἰσθητά) in comparison with Christ, as the Son is also measured and corporeal in comparison with the Father (*Exc.* 11.3). Clement here uses *incorporeal* relatively; Origen stresses the Son's absolute incorporeality qua divine hypostasis but largely employs the relative conception of bodies in his discourse concerning the bodies of all creatures.[51]

Again and again, Origen argues that noetic creatures always need bodies: as long as they exist, there has been and will be bodily nature (*semper erit natura corporea*), for them to make use of the "corporeal garment/tunic" (*indumento corporeo*) they need (*Princ.* 4.4.8). They need it because they are mutable from their creation: their goodness or evilness is not essential; "because of this mutability and convertibility, the rational nature *necessarily had to use a corporeal garment of different kind*, having this or that quality according to the deserts of rational creatures" (*Princ.* 4.4.8). Only God, being immutable, requires no such garment. Therefore, rational creatures were endowed with a body from the outset of their substantial existence, when God created them and matter:

> The noetic nature *must necessarily use bodies* [*necesse erat uti corporibus*], because, qua created [*facta*], it is mutable and alterable [*commutabilis et convertibilis*]. For what was not and began to exist [*esse coepit*] is for this very reason mutable by nature [*naturae mutabilis*] and possesses good or evil, not substantially, but accidentally…. The rational nature was mutable and alterable so that, according to its deserts, it could be *endowed with a different body as a garment* [*diverso corporis uteretur indumento*] of this or that quality [*illius vel illius qualitatis*]. Therefore, God, foreknowing the different conditions of souls or spiritual powers, *created the corporeal nature too* [*naturam corpoream*], which, according to the Creator's will, could be *transformed, changing qualities* [*permutatione qualitatum*] as needed. (*Princ.* 4.4.8)

Spiritual bodies changed qualities after the fall, becoming mortal from immortal in the case of humans.

Matter for the bodies of noetic creatures made the latter's volitional movements and diversification possible, since "there cannot be diversity without bodies" (*Princ.* 2.1.4). God, "receiving all those germs and causes

---

51. Ramelli, "Conceptualities of Angels."

of variety and diversity, according to the diversity of the intellects [*mentes* = νόες], i.e., rational creatures [*rationabiles creaturae*]..., rendered the world varied and diversified" (*Princ.* 2.9.2). For the cause of diversity in the world is "the variety of movements and falls of those who have abandoned the initial unity" (*Princ.* 2.1.1). Before the diversification, matter had already been created, for *logika* to be equipped with their bodily vehicles from the beginning of their existence as substances.[52] God created matter along with rational creatures: "God created all 'by number and measure': we shall correctly refer 'number' to *rational creatures or minds* ... and 'measure' to *bodily matter*.... These we must believe were *created by God in the beginning, before anything else*" (*Princ.* 2.9.1). Bodies were created with intellects, to serve them in the movements of their free will as vehicles. Origen often insists that each soul has a body in accordance with its spiritual progress and deserts (this is part of his conception of the aeons, constituting the time of creation, conceived as an essentially moral system): "each soul that takes up a body does so in accordance with its merits and former character ... all bodies conform to the habits of their souls" (*Cels.* 1.32–33). God alone needs no body-vehicle to sustain God's movements of free will or moral choices, since God, being essential Goodness, is immutable in the Good.

Thus, we have seen that the Trinity alone (the three ἀρχαί of Origen's Περὶ ἀρχῶν or *First Principles*) is incorporeal, according to Origen, who indeed defines God as *nous* in *First Principles*—the only *nous* without a body (while all creatures, including rational creatures and angels, do have a body). Porphyry, who knew Origen, also claims that only Plotinus's Triad,[53] the three ἀρχαί, are incorporeal in *Aneb.* 3. All other beings have bodies, ethereal (gods), aerial (daimons), or earthly (souls). In his debate with a pagan Middle Platonist, in *Cels.* 7.32, Origen similarly claims that the soul, per se incorporeal (ἀσώματος), always needs a body suited

---

52. The hypothesis that for Origen rational creatures had from the beginning a spiritual body is shared, e.g., by Manlio Simonetti, "Osservazioni sull'interpretazione origeniana di Genesi 2,7;3,21," *Aevum* 36 (1962): 370–78; Henryk Pietras "L'inizio del mondo materiale," in *Origeniana Nona*, ed. György Heidl and Robert Somos (Leuven: Peeters, 2009), 653–68; Benjamin Blosser, *Become Like the Angels: Origen's Doctrine of the Soul* (Washington, DC: Catholic University of America Press, 2012), 176–80.

53. On the identification of the three ἀρχαί in Origen and Plotinus-Porphyry and Origen's influence on Porphyry, see Ramelli, "Origen, Greek Philosophy." I examine the difference between Plotinus's Triad as hierarchic and Origen's and the Cappadocians' Trinity as less or not in "The Father in the Son."

(σώματος οἰκείου) to the place/state where it happens to be according to its spiritual progress; "a soul inhabiting corporeal places must necessarily use bodies suited to the places where it dwells" (*Hom. Ps.* 1 *apud* Pamphilus, *Apol.* 141). Souls can become thicker or finer, depending on their moral choices: the soul, sinning, becomes thicker and, "so to say, fleshly," while virtue refines a soul; we have thickened our soul, while we should exit flesh (*Hom. Ps.* 2 38.8). Souls must use a body even after death (*apud* Photius, *Bibl.* 234.301a): while all risen bodies are spiritual and immortal, the blessed will possess a luminous, glorious body; those in the torments of hell will have bodies adapted to suffering, obscure, and reflecting their intellect's "darkness of ignorance" on earth (*Res.* 2, *apud* Pamphilus, *Apol.* 134; *Princ.* 2.10.8), according to their moral quality.

In his zetetic attitude, Origen considers whether "becoming divine" will entail becoming bodiless, as God is (*Princ.* 3.6.1, 2.3.3–5). But this state relates only to the final deification and is but one alternative; the other is keeping a spiritual body: the corporeal substance will continue to stick even to the purest and most perfect spirits and, transformed into an ethereal state, shine forth in proportion to the merits and conditions of those who assume it (*Princ.* 2.3.7). This is consistent with Origen's conception—shared by Bardaisan, Gregory of Nyssa, Evagrius, and Eriugena—of the subsumption of body into soul into *nous* as opposed to the simple destruction of bodies and as the path back from the initial unfolding from *nous* to soul to body. Rational creatures will maintain spiritual bodies in the final restoration: the subsumption of bodies into a higher level will entail their transformation into spiritual bodies: "all this corporeal substance of ours will be brought to that state when every being will be restored to be one and God will be all in all.... Once all rational souls will have been brought to this condition, then the nature of this body of ours, too, will be brought to the glory of the spiritual body" (*Princ.* 3.6.6).

The role of *nous* is paramount in the ascent to God, both in this life and eschatologically speaking, in the eventual apokatastasis, when the composite human being will be subsumed into *nous*, and this will be deified in God and "become God." The very contemplation of God takes place through *nous*. Addressing a Platonic and/or Christian Platonic public in *Cels.* 6.69.13–15, Origen identifies what the Bible calls "heart" with what Plato and the Platonic tradition call "intellect/*nous*": God can be contemplated by a pure heart, which means by a pure *nous* (so also *Cels.* 6.69, 7.33). This concept will become paramount in Evagrius, as we will see in the final section. The body, which, as pointed out above, is always joined to the *nous* in a rational creature, is the vehicle of the soul's recovery or restoration of its former status as *nous* (*Princ.* 2.8.3).

Faithful to his hierarchy of *nous*, soul, and body in descending order, Origen, in his heuristic spirit, notes that Paul in 1 Cor 14:15 associates intellect (νοῦς), and not soul (ψυχή), with the Spirit (πνεῦμα), so as to put *nous* in direct relation with God. He warns, zetetically as often, that his argument will be "not a truth of faith, but an object of examination and discussion … more an object of readers' investigation than an exact definition" (*Princ.* 2.8.4–5). Origen's heuristic method was particularly justified in the case of psychology, which in *De principiis* prologue 6 is included among the issues left unclarified by Scripture and apostolic tradition. Consequently, Origen applies rational investigation in the tradition of philosophical psychology, especially of Plato and Middle Platonism, including Plutarch, whose lost *On the Soul* he cites in *Cels.* 5.57.[54]

Evagrius: Trichotomy, Descent and Subsumption, and Resurrection-Restoration

Evagrius, who was profoundly influenced by Origen and Gregory of Nyssa,[55] has a very clear anthropological tripartition into body, soul, and *nous*, in which *nous* is the highest faculty. It is the faculty for knowing God directly, an idea that owes much to Plato, Origen, and Gregory Nyssen. Its health depends on its orientation toward God and its exercise of love, virtue, and knowledge. While πρακτική (what we can call asceticism) works on the purification and perfecting of the soul through apatheia, θεωρητική strives towards the perfection of *nous*, which is knowledge (but not disjoined by love, which is the apex of apatheia). Evagrius also posits an initial unfolding from *nous* to soul and body and a final subsumption of body into soul into *nous*. In light of this, we can conceive not a destruction of the body but its sublimation.

---

54. See Ilaria L. E. Ramelli, "Gregory of Nyssa on the Soul (and the Restoration) From Plato to Origen," in *Exploring Gregory of Nyssa: Historical and Philosophical Perspectives*, ed. Anna Marmodoro and Neil McLynn (Oxford: Oxford University Press, 2018), 110–41.

55. As I argue in Ilaria L. E. Ramelli, "Gregory Nyssen's and Evagrius' Biographical and Theological Relations: Origen's Heritage and Neoplatonism," StPatr 84 (2017): 165–231; Ramelli, "Gregory and Evagrius," StPatr 101 (2020): 175–204.

In *Probl. gnos.* 6.49, Evagrius theorizes the passage from πρακτική, that is, the purification of the inferior faculties of the soul, to knowledge and contemplation (γνῶσις, θεωρία, thence the θεωρητική discipline), which involves the intellectual soul or *nous*. This purification-knowledge scheme, which is very prominent in Evagrius, was common to Neoplatonism, and Plotinus insisted on the preliminary purification (κάθαρσις) of the part of the soul subject to passions (τὸ παθητικόν; *Enn.* 3.6.5.22–29). Nyssen, like Evagrius later, presents the sequence purification => seeing God, based on the beatitude in Matt 5:8 that the pure in heart will see God. Gregory interprets that the pure in heart will see God in the divine Beauty that will shine forth in their purified soul, which is God's image:

> I think that in this short saying the Logos expresses some such counsel as this: there is in you, human beings, a desire to contemplate the true Good. But when you hear that the divine majesty is exalted above the heavens, that its glory is inexpressible, its beauty ineffable, and its nature inaccessible, do not despair of beholding what you desire. It is indeed within your reach; you have within yourselves the standard by which to apprehend the divine. For He who made you did at the same time endow your nature with this wonderful quality. For God imprinted on it the likeness of the glories of His own nature, as if molding the form of carving into wax. But the evil that has been poured all around the nature bearing the divine image has rendered useless to you this wonderful thing that lies hidden under vile coverings. If, therefore, you wash off by a good life the filth that has been stuck on your heart like plaster, that beauty which is in the image of God will again shine forth in you.... Hence, if a person who is pure of heart sees herself, she sees in herself what she desires; and thus she becomes blessed, because when she looks at her own purity, she sees the archetype in the image. (*Beat.* 6)

Evagrius seems to rely on this cluster of notions of Nyssen, who has recently been argued to have represented a major source of inspiration for Evagrius.[56]

Arguing for the priority of the intellectual soul—the seat of the image of God—within the human being, Gregory (in the person of Macrina in the

---

56. Ilaria L. E. Ramelli, "Evagrius and Gregory: Nazianzen or Nyssen? A Remarkable Issue That Bears on the Cappadocian (and Origenian) Influence on Evagrius," *GRBS* 53 (2013): 117–37; Ramelli, "Gregory Nyssen's and Evagrius' Biographical and Theological Relations."

dialogue *De anima et resurrections* or *On the Soul and the Resurrection*) states that "what sees and what hears is the intellect [νοῦς]" (*De an.* 32ab), and attributes this principle to "one of the learned from outside," that is, a pagan philosopher. She endorses this principle as true and rightly enunciated, and indeed Gregory insists on the same principle, that *nous* works through sense perception, in *De opif. hom.* preface 10 as well. Macrina may be referring to Porphyry in the *De anima* passage. Porphyry attributed this maxim to Pythagoras: "Pythagoras thought that what sees and what hears is the intellect alone, while everything else is blind and deaf" (*Vit. Pyth.* 46). This is a tenet of Platonism, which Macrina develops at length and demonstrates with examples in *De anima*, and which Gregory endorses. The Middle Platonist popular philosopher Maximus of Tyre, *Diss.* 11.9, probably known to Origen, attributed this maxim to "the Syracusan," Epicharmus. The same maxim was quoted by other Middle and Neoplatonists (e.g., Plutarch, *Fort.* 98d; *Alex. fort.* 336b; Porphyry, *Abst.* 3.21; Iamblichus, *Vit. Pyth.* 32.228).

Gregory seems to have influenced to a great extent Evagrius's theories of the threefold resurrection (of body, soul, and *nous*) and of the subsumption of body into soul and soul into *nous*—the so-called unified *nous*.[57] The Christian Neoplatonist Eriugena was right to trace the latter doctrine back to Gregory of Nyssa, as we shall see. Evagrius's theory of the unfolding of the three anthropological components from *nous* and their subsumption into *nous* is closely linked to his conception of the resurrection as threefold, each kind of resurrection referring to each anthropological component:

Unfolding (↓):	Subsumption (↑):	Resurrection (↑↑):
nous	body	of the body (= immortality)
> soul	> soul	of the soul (= *apatheia*)
> body	> *nous*	of the *nous* (= knowledge)

---

57. Argument in Ramelli, "Gregory Nyssen's and Evagrius' Biographical and Theological Relations." On Evagrius's threefold notion of resurrection, see the full commentary on *Probl. gnos.* 5.19, 22, 25, and see Ilaria L. E. Ramelli, "The Reception of Origen's Ideas in Western Theological and Philosophical Traditions," in *Origeniana Undecima: Origen and Origenism in the History of Western Thought*, ed. Anders-Christian Jacobsen, BETL 279 (Leuven: Peeters, 2016), 443–67; Kevin Corrigan, "Mind, Soul, and Body in Plotinus, Gregory of Nyssa and Evagrius of Pontus," in *Lovers of the Soul and Lovers of the Body: Philosophical and Religious Perspectives in Late Antiquity*, ed. Svetla S. Griffin and Ilaria L. E. Ramelli, HS (Cambridge: Harvard University Press, 2022), 253–76.

Like Gregory (and like Origen, who already posited both a physical and a spiritual resurrection), Evagrius insisted that the resurrection-restoration involves not only the body but also the soul and the *nous* (that is, the inferior faculties of the soul and the intellectual soul). (1) The resurrection of the mortal body is a passage from a bad quality—mortality, corruptibility, liability to passions, genderedness, weakness, liability to illnesses, and so on—to an excellent quality,[58] as is described in Gregory's *De anima et resurrectione*: immortality, incorruptibility (opposed to the present need to replace deaths with births[59]), impassivity, strength, glory, and the like. (2) The resurrection of the soul is the return from the condition of vulnerability to passions to the condition without any passions,[60] that is, to *apatheia*, which was from the beginning in God's plan for humanity and all rational creatures.[61] (3) The resurrection of the intellect or *nous* is the passage from ignorance to knowledge of the truth.[62] These three closely related definitions, each in a *kephalaion* in the same book, the fifth, of *Problematica gnostica*, demonstrate that Evagrius, like Origen and Nyssen, entertained a holistic conception of the resurrection: it is not only the resurrection of the body but of all the components of the human being (those that resulted from the initial unfolding of the *nous*): the body, the soul in its inferior parts, and the superior faculty of the soul, the *nous*.

The latter is the superior faculty of the soul after its unfolding, but both originally and in the end (after the subsumption of body and soul in *nous*) it is the rational creature tout court. In the first of these three *kephalaia*, Evagrius concentrates on the resurrection of the body. The mortal body will pass from a bad quality to a good one, from mortality to immortality, from corruptibility to incorruptibility, from illness to health, from ugliness to beauty, and so on. This is the set of characteristics that Gregory

---

58. *Probl. gnos.* 5.19: "The resurrection of the mortal body is a passage from a bad quality (lit. mixture) to an excellent quality (lit. mixture)."

59. So, "once the former humans have died, others replace them," as opposed to the eternity and irreplaceability of the three divine Persons (see *Ad Graecos ex communibus notionibus* in *Opera dogmatica minora, Pars 1*, ed. Frederick Mueller, GNO 3.1 [Leiden: Brill, 1958], 24.1–25.24).

60. *Probl. gnos.* 5.22: "The resurrection of the soul is the return from the condition of vulnerability to passions to the condition without any passions."

61. On *apatheia* in Evagrius, see Monica Tobon, *Apatheia and Anthropology in Evagrius of Pontus* (London: Routledge, forthcoming).

62. *Probl. gnos.* 5.25: "The resurrection of the intellect is the passage from ignorance to knowledge of the truth."

of Nyssa listed at the very end of his *De anima* (section 9) as the properties of human nature, as God intended them before the fall. They will be
recovered again at the final resurrection-restoration:

> Therefore, once passions have been purified and have disappeared,
> thanks to the opportune, attentive cure through the therapy of fire,
> instead of such defects [i.e., weakness, dishonor, corruption, and so on],
> there will follow each one of the respective realities that are conceived in
> a positive sense: incorruptibility, life, force, honor, grace, glory, and every
> other similar prerogative which we conjecture it is possible to contem-
> plate both in the Divinity itself and in its image, which is human nature.
> (*De an.* 9 Ramelli)

Evagrius is on the line of Origen and of Adamantius in the *Dialogue of
Adamantius* in maintaining that the individual body remains the same in
the resurrection, from the mortal to the risen body, and does not become
another body in its individual identity, but what is transformed are rather
its qualities.[63] Evagrius likewise identifies the resurrection of the body
with the transformation of the same body from one "mixture" to another,
keeping the same elements.[64] As Gregory of Nyssa also suggests, the body
remains the same, but its texture is finer; the elements are still there, but
their composition and mixture change. It is also from Origen that Evagrius
derived the close correspondence and dependence of the kinds of body
and soul one has from the choices of one's *nous*.[65]

After explaining what the resurrection of the body is, namely, a passage
from bad qualities or a poor arrangement of elements to good qualities or
a fine arrangement of elements, Evagrius clarifies what the resurrection
of the soul is (*Probl. gnos.* 5.22): it is likewise a passage, not to a different
soul but from liability to passions to *apatheia*, which is the ethical ideal of
Evagrius just as it is of Clement, Origen, and Gregory of Nyssa. This pertains to πρακτική, the ethical and ascetic practice. It is to be noticed that
Evagrius does not simply speak of a "passage" to *apatheia*, but he mentions
a "return" proper. The reference is clearly to the ἀνάστασις or resurrection
understood as ἀποκατάστασις, the restoration to the original state, in which

---

63. Ramelli, "Matter in the Dialogue of Adamantius."

64. The Syriac noun means "mixture"; from different mixtures of elements come
different qualities. Thus, Evagrius also maintains that the risen body has different
qualities—becoming spiritual—but it is not a different body from the dead one.

65. For Origen, see Ramelli, *Christian Doctrine of Apokatastasis*.

the soul was not liable to passions. This definition is a tenet of Gregory of Nyssa's connection between the resurrection and the restoration.[66] From this connection Evagrius clearly derived his own idea of resurrection-restoration. Gregory of Nyssa, indeed, in his dialogue *On the Soul and the Resurrection* defines the resurrection (ἀνάστασις) as "the restoration of our nature, i.e., human nature, to its original state" (ἡ εἰς τὸ ἀρχαῖον τῆς φύσεως ἡμῶν ἀποκατάστασις). This entails not only the resurrection of the body but also purification from sin, impassivity, illumination, and knowledge. Gregory's definition already includes in the restoration the resurrection of the three components of the human being, not of the body alone but of body, soul, and *nous*.

Indeed, the restoration of the soul is its restoration to life after death, and Evagrius is clear in *Probl. gnost.* 1.41 that the death and illness of the soul are posterior to its life and health: "If death comes after life, and illness after health, it is clear that also evil comes after virtue. For it is evil that is the death and the illness of the soul, but virtue comes even before the intermediate state (between virtue and evil)." The restoration of the soul, therefore, will be a return to its primeval condition of life, a return to being *nous*. This is why it is its resurrection from death. Note that the movement of subsumption of body and soul into *nous*—the opposite of the unfolding from *nous*—is apokatastasis. This is the definitive liberation from evil.

Indeed, *Probl. gnost.* 1.41 is a corollary of *Probl. gnost.* 1.40, with the priority of Good over evil, a tenet of Evagrius's ontological monism and the premise to his doctrine of apokatastasis (the universal restoration to the Good): "There was a time when evil did not exist, and there will be a time when, likewise, it will no more exist, whereas there was no time when virtue did not exist, and there will be no time when it will not exist. For the germs of virtue are impossible to destroy." Evagrius follows Origen in his twofold conception of death, both physical and spiritual. The same is the case with his twofold conception of resurrection: physical (the resurrection of the body, with its transition to incorruptibility, the "superior quality") and spiritual, that is, the resurrection of the soul in both its superior part and its inferior one. The superior part is the intellect, the *nous*, whose resurrection is said to be the passage from ignorance to knowledge, since gnosis is the perfection of *nous*. The inferior parts, in accord with

66. See Ilaria L. E. Ramelli, "Christian Soteriology and Christian Platonism. Origen, Gregory of Nyssa, and the Biblical and Philosophical Basis of the Doctrine of Apokatastasis," *VC* 61 (2007): 313–56; Ramelli, "Gregory of Nyssa on the Soul."

Plato's division, adopted also by Gregory of Nyssa in his dialogue *On the Soul and the Resurrection*, are the ἐπιθυμητικόν or concupiscible/appetitive faculty, and the θυμικόν or irascible faculty (in *Probl. gnos.* 5.27 and many other loci, Evagrius clearly takes over this classification[67]). Since these parts are vulnerable to passions, their resurrection consists in their passage to impassivity. But the resurrection of *nous* is the passage from ignorance—"the shadow of evil(ness)" according to Evagrius, *Probl. gnost.* 4.28—to gnosis.

Thus, the concept of resurrection is very rich and complex in Evagrius: it involves the whole of the human being, not merely one's body. In his *Letter on Faith* as well, in addition to his *Problemata gnostica*, Evagrius reflects on the resurrection of the intellect, taking Jesus's promise of resurrecting his saints as a reference precisely to the resurrection of *nous*:

> What does Jesus say in the Gospel? "And I will resurrect him on the last day," meaning by "resurrection" [ἀνάστασις] the transformation from material knowledge to *immaterial contemplation*, and calling "the last day" that knowledge [γνῶσις] beyond which there is no other (knowledge). Our mind has been resurrected and risen to the height of blessedness only when it shall contemplate the Logos as Monad and Henad.

The resurrection of *nous* takes place in the telos, when it attains perfect and ultimate knowledge (in deification: for God the Trinity is constantly called by Evagrius "substantial knowledge"), but has its anticipation here and now. Regarding the above definition of the Logos as "Monad and Henad," which Augustine Casiday finds "a decidedly odd expression,"[68] it must be observed that is in fact a further proof that Evagrius is following Origen *ad litteram*. For "Monad and Henad," μονάς τε καὶ ἑνάς, is Origen's definition of God, ὁ θεός, in *Princ.* 1.1.6: given the technical nature of this expression, Rufinus in his translation preserved the original Greek in this point. That "Monad and Henad" is the definition of God is clear from another passage of Evagrius's *Letter on Faith*: "The Monad and Henad indicates the simple and incomprehensible substance" of God (2.41–42).

---

67. *Probl. gnos.* 5.27: "The irascible faculty, when it is troubled, blinds the seer; the concupiscible / appetitive faculty, when bestially moved, hides the visible objects."

68. Augustine Casiday, *Reconstructing the Theology of Evagrius Ponticus* (Cambridge: Cambridge University Press, 2013), 214.

The strong assertion of the eventual resurrection of the entire human being, in all of its faculties and component parts, perfectly corresponds to the conviction—which Evagrius shares, again, with Origen—that death cannot be the ultimate reality, whether it is physical or spiritual. One of Origen's arguments in this connection was drawn from Rom 8:38: death will not be able to separate anyone from God forever. And this applies not only to physical death, but above all to spiritual death, namely, the death of sin, which separates the soul from God: "Death, as (Paul) says, must be understood as the enemy of Christ that will have to be destroyed as the last [1 Cor 15:26–28], as I have explained above. Now, this enemy is called 'death' because, just as this common death separates the soul from the body, likewise it endeavors to separate the soul from the charity-love of God: and this is precisely the death of the soul" (*Comm. Rom.* 7.10.48–53).[69] Now, Paul avers that not even this death will ever be able to separate Christians from God's love. Thus, even after such a death there will be a resurrection, not physical in this case but spiritual.

It is evident again from *Probl. gnost.* 5.19, 5.22, and 5.25 that Evagrius adheres to the threefold conception of the human being, divided into body (σῶμα), soul (ψυχή), and intellect (νοῦς) or spirit (πνεῦμα), which was Platonic in its origin (*Tim.* 30b4–5) and was typical of Paul (e.g., 1 Thess 5:23), Origen, and several Middle Platonists and Roman Stoics, such as Marcus Aurelius. This is why, after speaking of the resurrection of the body (*Probl. gnos.* 5.22), he treats here that of the soul (the πρακτική soul, which strives to liberate herself from the passions that besiege its inferior parts, the θυμικόν and ἐπιθυμητικόν) and finally, in *Probl. gnost.* 5.25, of that of *nous*, the highest faculty of the soul (between the unfolding from *nous* and the subsumption of body and soul into *nous*).

From Origen, this conception passed on to Gregory of Nyssa and Evagrius. Among Origen's writings, one of the many passages that display this anthropological trichotomy (which also corresponds to the three-fold interpretation of Scripture theorized by him in *Princ.* 4) is *Comm. Rom.* 1.12.16–21, where Origen grounds this tripartition precisely in Paul, 1 Thess 5:23 (with *pneuma* in the place of *nous*): "That these three components are found in the human being, Paul makes it clear in his letter to

---

69. "Mors, quod dicit ille, accipiendus est quem supra exposuimus inimicum Christi destruendum nouissimum dici. Qui utique propterea mors dicitur, quia sicut haec communis mors animam separare a corpore, ita ille contendit animam separare a caritate Dei, et haec utique est animae mors."

the Thessalonians, when he states: 'That your body, soul, and spirit may be preserved intact in the day of our Lord Jesus Christ.'"[70] And in *Comm. Rom.* 1.21.40–47 Origen ascribes this threefold vision of the human being to the whole of Scripture: "We often find in Scripture that the human being is said to be spirit, body, and soul. In fact, when it is said that the flesh has desires that are opposite to the spirit, and the spirit has desires that are opposite to the flesh, the soul without doubt is posited in the middle, so as to either yield to the desires of the spirit or incline to the concupiscence of the flesh."[71] Both Origen and Evagrius are acquainted with both anthropological trichotomies: body-soul-*nous*, which is the tripartition on which we are concentrating, and body-soul-spirit.

The aim of the resurrection of the *nous* according to Evagrius, namely, the knowledge of truth, is also said by Scripture to be the will of God for all human beings according to 1 Tim 2:4: "God wants all human beings to be saved and to reach the knowledge of truth." This is the goal of the *logika*'s life. Evagrius explicitly appeals to this scriptural passage in *Probl. gnost.* 22: "The gnostic must be neither sad nor intimidating. For the former (being sad) is tantamount to ignorance of the *logoi* of things which have come into existence; the latter (being intimidating) does not want 'all humans to be saved and come to knowledge of the truth'" (1 Tim 2:4).

Now, Evagrius's three levels of resurrection-restoration are not unrelated to one another. For Gregory and, more in detail, Evagrius envisaged as an ideal the subsumption of body into soul and soul into *nous*—the so-called doctrine of the unified *nous*. The Origenian Neoplatonist Eriugena interestingly traced this core doctrine of Evagrius back to Gregory of Nyssa, thus pointing to Evagrius's indebtedness to Gregory. Indeed, Evagrius conceived of the eschatological transformation of body into soul and soul into *nous*, and this finally into God at the stage of θέωσις and unity (*Ep. Mel.* 22; *Probl. gnos.* 2.17, 3.66, 3.68, 3.15, 1.65), in *Ep. Mel.* 22, building on John 17:21–23. He constructed his eschatological notion of unification (ἕνωσις), with the subsumption of body to soul to *nous*:

---

70. "Haec enim tria esse in homine designat ad Thessalonicenses scribens cum dicit: ut integrum corpus uestrum et anima et spiritus in die Domini nostri Iesu Christi seruetur."

71. "Frequenter in Scripturis inuenimus ... quod homo spiritus et corpus et anima esse dicatur. Uero cum dicitur quia caro aduersus spiritum concupiscit, spiritus autem aduersus carnem, media procul dubio ponitur anima, quae uel desideriis spiritus adquiescat uel ad carnis concupiscentiam inclinetur."

And there will be a time when the body, the soul, and the intellect will cease to be separate from one another, with their names and their plurality, since the body and the soul will be elevated to the rank of intellects; this conclusion can be drawn from the following words: "That they may be one in us, just as you and I are one" [John 17:22]. And thus there will be a time when the Father, the Son, and the Spirit, and their rational creation, which constitutes their body, will cease to be separate, with their names and their plurality. And this conclusion can be drawn from the words, "God will be all in all" [1 Cor 15:28]. (*Ep. Mel.* 22)

This notion of the subsumption of body into soul and soul into *nous*, according to Eriugena—who made the most of it—comes from Gregory, who was Evagrius's inspirer along with Origen and the two other Cappadocians. It is significant that Eriugena chose to cite Gregory of Nyssa's theory, taken over by Evagrius, in reference to the eventual deification (which in Gregory's view will be universal, like the resurrection-restoration): "Likewise Gregory, without doubt, posited the transformation of the body into soul at the time of the resurrection, the transformation of the soul into *nous*, and the transformation of *nous* into God" (*Periph.* 5 [987c]). The body will become soul, the soul *nous*, and *nous* (in the eventual deification) will become God. This is an important element of inspiration provided by Gregory to Evagrius. The idea of the subsumption of what is inferior into what is superior with a view to unification—body into soul and soul into *nous*—which is so clear in Evagrius, and came from Gregory, became prominent in Maximus the Confessor, who was profoundly influenced by Nyssen in turn, and especially in Eriugena himself, who followed both Nyssen and Maximus closely.[72]

Gregory indeed inspired Evagrius with the idea of unified *nous*—when the *nous* has the soul subsumed in itself, and the soul the body—especially in his dialogue *De anima* (which Evagrius might have brought to Egypt, thus contributing to its very early translation into Coptic[73]): "When the soul becomes simple [ἁπλῆ], unitary [μονοειδής], and perfectly similar to God [θεοείκελος], it will find the truly simple and immaterial Good" (*De an.* 93C). The unified soul is a unified *nous*—its loftiest component—that has subsumed everything else into it. This is Evagrius's view as well, and

---

72. For the conceptions of subsumption and resurrection in Eriugena, see, respectively, Ramelli, "Some Overlooked Sources," 406–76; and Ramelli, "From God to God," 99–123.

73. See Ramelli, "Evagrius and Gregory."

within this concept of the unified *nous* it is necessary to read Gregory's and Evagrius's notion of the subsumption of body into soul and soul into *nous*. Gregory's concept that the superior component assimilates the inferior to itself (so does intellect with soul, and soul with body in turn) was already espoused by Origen (Origen, *Dial.* 12 and *passim*): within the human being, the inferior nature must assimilate itself to the superior, which is in the image of God. This idea will return prominently in Evagrius, as seen, and later in Eriugena, in connection with apokatastasis.[74] For Nyssen, too, the assimilation of human nature to the divine will take place at apokatastasis: "The two must become one, and the conjunction will consist in a *transformation into the better nature* [τὸ κρεῖττον]" (*Beat.* 7). Nyssen's idea of unified soul as *nous*, which strongly influenced Evagrius, must be read against the backdrop of Origen's aforementioned notion of souls as a result of the decadence of intellects (*noes*) and their future return to the level of intellects (*Princ.* 2.8.2–3). This theory, which, as pointed out at the beginning, was also shared by Origen's older contemporary Bardaisan, another Christian Platonist, was clearly taken over by Evagrius.

Regarding the nature of *nous*, Gregory argues as follows at *De opif. hom.* 9.149.24: "mind [νοῦς] ... is an intellectual and incorporeal thing." This corresponds to Gregory's definition of the soul in *De anima et resurrectione*, from which it is clear that *nous* belongs to the very definition of the soul and designates the highest, intellectual, and most authentic part of the soul. The soul, as Macrina explains here to Gregory, is "a created, living, and noetic/intellectual substance [οὐσία νοερά], which through itself infuses a faculty of life and apprehension of perceptible objects into an instrumental body equipped with organs of perception [σώματι ὀργανικῷ καὶ αἰσθητικῷ], as long as the nature that can receive these faculties subsists," that is, as long as the mortal body continues to live.[75] The

---

74. See Ramelli, *Christian Doctrine of Apokatastasis*, 773–815.

75. Οὐσία γεννητή, οὐσία ζῶσα, νοερά, σώματι ὀργανικῷ καὶ αἰσθητικῷ δύναμιν ζωτικὴν καὶ τῶν αἰσθητῶν ἀντιληπτικὴν δι᾽ ἑαυτῆς ἐνιεῖσα, ἕως ἂν ἡ δεκτικὴ τούτων συνεστήκῃ φύσις (*De an.* 15.6–9). George Karamanolis in his first edition expressly follows here my reading ἐνιεῖσα in the edition included in *Gregorio*: ἐνιεῖσα derives from ἐνίημι, which has manuscript support, instead of Migne's correction, ἐνιοῦσα (my reading is now also kept in Andreas Spira's edition). See Karamanolis, *The Philosophy of Early Christianity* (Durham: Acumen, 2013), 279. Karamanolis translates: "a created substance, living, intellectual, which through itself provides a faculty of life and a faculty of cognition of perceptible things in a body equipped with organs and potentially perceiving, as far as nature can admit" (206). Only ἕως ἂν ἡ δεκτικὴ τούτων συνεστήκῃ

expression σῶμα ὀργανικόν was used by Aristotle in his own definition of soul as "first form of a natural organic body [σώματος φυσικοῦ ὀργανικοῦ]" (*De an.* B1 [412ab]). Tertullian also described the body as the instrument of the soul (*An.* 40.3, a definition that would dovetail with the notion of body as vehicle or ὄχημα of the soul, widespread in both pagan and Christian Platonism[76]). In Gregory's definition, the clause "as long as the nature that can receive these faculties subsists" means "as long as the mortal body continues to be alive." After the latter's death, the soul continues to exist as a living and noetic substance, but it ceases to infuse life and sense perception in the mortal body. While the mortal body is alive, instead, the intellectual soul or *nous* infuses life and sense perception into the body. This is why, as I have pointed out above, Macrina states that "what sees and hears is the intellect," taking over a Pythagorean-Platonic tenet. After its death, the mortal body will need to be resurrected, and this resurrection, as Gregory emphasizes, must be conceived within the restoration of the whole human being. Evagrius will develop this conception.

Evagrius's theory of subsumption of the body into the soul and the intellect means the body's elevation and transformation with a view to unification, not necessarily its destruction, as is often assumed. A more positive evaluation of the body in Evagrius is in order, which is supported by many arguments,[77] and does not surprise in a follower of Gregory. Eriugena was therefore right to trace Evagrius's doctrine of the subsumption of body into soul and soul into intellect back to Gregory. This is far from being the only derivation of Evagrius's ideas from those of Gregory: for example, Evagrius inherited from Gregory—and, through him, from Origen—the theory of apokatastasis, which, as argued above, is closely linked to the subsumption of all human components into *nous*, and the latter's deification (θέωσις).

Eriugena not only traced back to Gregory the doctrine of the subsumption of body into soul and soul into *nous* but also highlighted the

---

φύσις does not exactly mean "as far as nature can admit," but "as long as the nature that can receive these faculties subsists." The new edition has now corrected these points. See Karamanolis, *The Philosophy of Early Christianity*, 2nd ed. (London: Routledge, 2021), 187–88.

76. Ramelli, "Soma (Σῶμα)."

77. Pointed out in Ilaria L. E. Ramelli, "Evagrius Ponticus, the Origenian Ascetic (and Not the Origenistic 'Heretic')," in *Orthodox Monasticism, Past and Present*, ed. John A. McGuckin (New York: Theotokos, 2014), 147–205.

continuity that in this respect there obtains between Gregory and Maximus the Confessor. In *Periph.* 5.8 he quotes Maximus in this connection: "At the resurrection, through the grace of the incarnate Son, the flesh will be absorbed by the soul." For Maximus, too, as for Gregory and Origen, the resurrection is the holistic restoration of body, soul, and *nous*. Maximus followed Gregory also in deeming passions such as pleasure, grief, desire, fear, and so on adventitious for human nature and not part of its original creation and its "natural rationale" (λόγος τῆς φύσεως), apart for love and desire for God and pleasure in the presence of God (Maximus, *Quaest. Thal.* 61). After the fall, passions entered human nature with the consequence of corruption, death, and social inequality, but the original λόγος τῆς φύσεως will be restored at apokatastasis.[78]

Gregory probably inspired Evagrius's concept of the subsumption of body into soul and soul into *nous*, that is, the subsumption of the inferior into the superior, also from another perspective: namely, with his theory of the subsumption of the (inferior) human nature into the (superior, infinite) divine nature in Christ (*Eun.* 3.3.68; see also his *Letter to Theophilus*).[79] In Gregory just as in Evagrius, the superior element undergoes no change or diminution; only the inferior does, by its elevation to the superior level. Evagrius remarks that *nous* is hindered from knowing God by tempting thoughts, "which attack it from the irascible and the concupiscible/appetitive faculties of the soul, which assail it, going against what properly belongs to (human) nature" (*Probl. gnos.* 6.83). Evagrius conceives of these tempting thoughts to be inspired by demons, availing himself of a notion and terminology already found in Origen.[80] But the idea that λογισμοί and passions, coming from the θυμικόν and the ἐπιθυμητικόν,[81] are against

---

78. See also Ramelli, *Christian Doctrine of Apokatastasis*, 737–57. This was exactly Gregory's theory, as I argue in Ramelli, "Gregory of Nyssa on the Soul."

79. For the role of divine infinity in Gregory and partial roots in Origen, see Ilaria L. E. Ramelli, "Apokatastasis and Epektasis in *Hom. in Cant.*: The Relation between Two Core Doctrines in Gregory and Roots in Origen," in *Gregory of Nyssa: In Canticum Canticorum. Commentary and Supporting Studies. Select Proceedings of the Thirteenth International Colloquium on Gregory of Nyssa (Rome, 17–20 September 2014)*, ed. Giulio Maspero, Miguel Brugarolas, and Ilaria Vigorelli, VCSup 150 (Leiden: Brill, 2018), 312–39.

80. For instance: "sunt ergo huiusmodi cogitationes [λογισμοί] quae a daemonibus iniciuntur cordibus hominum" (*Comm. Cant.* 4.3.4).

81. Evagrius often follows Plato's terminology for the tripartition of the soul into rational, irascible, and concupiscible or appetitive: see also, e.g., *Probl. gnos.* 1.53, 1.68, 1.84, 3.35, 3.59, 4.73, 4.79, 5.27, 5.39, 5.66, 6.41, 6.84, 6.85.

human rational nature was especially developed by Nyssen in *De anima*. Given that it is one's *nous* that, by means of free will, gives the assent to temptations,[82] Evagrius insists that evil or demonic thoughts depend on one's *nous*, when it is moved in a passionate way. "A demonic thought is an *image* of the sensible human being put together in discursive thinking, an incomplete image, with which the *nous* being moved in a passionate way does or says something lawlessly in hiddenness in relation to the *image being formed successively by it*."[83]

In *Probl. gnost.* 6.85, Evagrius follows again Nyssen concerning the secondary, later, and adventitious nature of the inferior faculties of the soul liable to passions. Gregory uses terms such as ἐπιγεννήματα in this regard, speaking of the soul's 'accretions' to be shed (*De an.* 52–56, 64), an image stemming from Plato, *Resp.* 10 (611d): "barnacles, seaweed, and stones," which encrust the soul. These correspond to Plotinus's "additions" (προσθῆκαι, *Enn.* 4.7.10, 5.5.2), which do not enrich but impoverish the soul (*Enn* 6.5.12),[84] and already to Numenius's προσφυόμενα/προστιθέντα (F34) and Basilides's προσαρτήματα (*apud* Clement, *Strom.* 2.20.113). These are all expressions for later additions or accretions.

Such adventitious elements are, according to Gregory, parts of those "animal" elements that invaded human life after the fall, when it became mortal and shared in bestial life, as Gregory puts it: human beings after the fall assumed, instead of the angelic life, the irrational life of beasts. Likewise Evagrius: "If it is true that all those faculties that we have in common with animals belong to the mortal corporeal nature, it is evident that the irascible and appetitive faculties do not seem to have been created together with the rational nature before the movement," namely, in Origenian terms, the movement of will that determined the fall. The inferior faculties of the soul, just as mortality, did not exist before the movement of free will toward evil and will not exist in the ultimate end, the telos. The irascible faculty of the soul (θυμός, θυμικόν) and the concupiscible, appetitive, or desiderative faculty (ἐπιθυμητικόν), characterized by greed and lust, are

---

82. See esp. Richard Sorabji, *Emotion and Peace of Mind: From Stoic Agitation to Christian Temptation* (Oxford: Oxford University Press, 2000).

83. λογισμὸς γὰρ δαιμονιώδης ἐστὶν εἰκὼν τοῦ αἰσθητοῦ ἀνθρώπου συνισταμένη κατὰ διάνοιαν, ἀτελής, μεθ᾽ ἧς ὁ νοῦς κινούμενος ἐμπαθῶς λέγει τι ἢ πράττει ἀνόμως ἐν τῷ κρυπτῷ πρὸς τὸ μορφούμενον ἐκ διαδοχῆς εἴδωλον ὑπ᾽ αὐτοῦ (*Logism.* 25.52–56).

84. See also Plotinus's description of the body as "attached" or "added" to the soul (προσηρτημένον, *Enn.* 1.4.4.27).

the two main headings under which passions are (Platonically) classified. Evagrius calls them "bestial" in *Probl. gnost.* 5.27 ("The irascible faculty, when it is troubled, blinds the seer; the concupiscible, when bestially moved, hides the visible objects") in that the irrational movements and faculties of the soul assimilate humans to animals. This notion was dear to Nyssen, who developed it in *De anima*, and is taken over by Evagrius also in *Ep. Mel.* 46.

To Evagrius's mind, then, just as to Nyssen's, the ideal of *apatheia* or eradication of passions or bad emotions (πάθη) is closely related to the conception of passions as adventitious in rational creatures, secondary, and against nature (in the order of ἀλλοτρίωσις vs. οἰκείωσις), unlike *nous*, which is natural to humans. This theory must be seen against the background of Evagrius's notion of the three human components as the unfolding from the unified *nous* and their eventual subsumption into *nous*. Evagrius argues that, since all the faculties that humans have in common with animals belong to the mortal corporeal nature, then clearly the irascible and concupiscible faculties were not created together with the rational nature before the movement of will that determined the fall (see *Probl. gnos.* 6.85). Indeed, they do not belong to the unified *nous*. They are adventitious; they do not pertain to the authentic human nature, which is the prelapsarian nature of *logika*, the unified *nous*. Evagrius declares them to be "against nature," that is, against the authentic human nature (*Probl. gnos.* 6.83). Their major fault is that they produce *logismoi* that prevent the intellect from knowing God. Intellects were created by God so that they might know God: this is their nature. Whatever impedes this knowledge or makes it difficult is therefore against nature. This is why, since passions were not at the beginning—being not included in God's plan for rational creatures—they will not endure in the end.

Evagrius makes a great deal of the concept of "bare intellect" or "bare *nous*," sometimes also translated "naked intellect," meaning an absolutely pure intellect—pure from all garments. This concept finds parallels not only in Plotinus (e.g., *Enn.* 6.8.4–5) but especially in Gregory of Nyssa, for example in *Hom. Cant.* 10. Here, Gregory observes that, when the intellectual soul "rejoices in the contemplation of what really exists," it can "receive the vision of God with pure and bare *nous*." Likewise, in *Probl. gnost.* 3.6 Evagrius explains that a bare *nous* is "that which, by means of the contemplation that regards it, is joined to the knowledge of the Trinity." In *Probl. gnost.* 3.8 Evagrius explains how a *nous* that dons "the last garment" is: it "knows the contemplation only of all secondary beings." This is not yet perfection: the bare *nous*, after shedding even the last garment, that is, the contemplation of creatures, enjoys the knowledge of God. Indeed, the *theōria* of secondary beings is inferior to that of primary (i.e., intelligible) beings and God, which pertains to the bare *nous*. Origen and Nyssen, too, used the imagery of the garment/tunic (χιτών) of the intellectual soul in connection with the skin tunics/garments mentioned by Genesis as the clothes given by God to the protoplasts after their fall. A philosopher who was well acquainted with Origen's ideas and works, and in turn was known to Evagrius, Porphyry, as I have pointed out above, also used the expression and concept of the last garment of the soul and identified it with the skin tunics. Evagrius equates the last garment of the soul with the contemplation of secondary beings, that is, corporeal beings, which is the postlapsarian condition of humans. The contemplation of primary beings is a prerogative of the *nous* in its more perfect condition of bare *nous*. The primary being par excellence is God, who is "substantial knowledge."

The final contemplation of God, requiring a bare *nous*, will be unified, as the intellect itself will at that point be—the *nous* as a "unified *nous*"— and consequently will be no longer dispersed in many thoughts and, in the case of God, the economic *epinoiai*. Indeed, in the telos, the divine *epinoiai*, such as rock, gate, or shepherd, will vanish, since they exist exclusively for the sake of the salvific economy (*Ep. Mel.* 24–25). Evagrius derived this conviction from Origen (e.g., *Princ.* 4.4.1) and Nyssen, but Nyssen, like Evagrius, spoke more of *epinoiai* of God than of *epinoiai* of Christ alone. This is one of the cases in which Evagrius seems to adhere specifically to Nyssen more than to Origen. Evagrius attributes to God the *epinoiai* of Christ in *Probl. gnost.* 6.20 as well, just as Nyssen had done:

> Before the movement, God was good and powerful and wise, and creator of incorporeal beings, and father of rational creatures, and omnipotent. But after the movement, God has become creator of bodies, and judge and ruler and physician and shepherd and teacher, and merciful and patient, and also door/gate, way, lamb, high priest, together with the other epithets that are said in modes. But Father and Principle he is also before the creation of the incorporeal beings: Father of Christ, Principle of the Holy Spirit.

God has both pre-economic, intra-Trinitarian *epinoiai* (such as Father of Christ, Principle of the Holy Spirit) and economic *epinoiai*, which in turn are divided into prelapsarian ones (omnipotent, father of the *logika*, etc.) and postlapsarian ones (creator of [mortal] bodies, judge, ruler, physician,

shepherd, etc.). If Christ's *epinoiai*—such as the postlapsarian ones of physician, shepherd, teacher, door/gate, way, lamb, high priest, and so on—are
presented by Evagrius as God's *epinoiai*, this obviously means that Christ
is God.

On this point, Evagrius follows Origen and the Cappadocians, as his
Letter on Faith and a correct interpretation of some of his *Problemata
gnostica* shows.[85] Origen, far from being the inspirer of the Arians, was the
inspirer of the Cappadocians', and especially Nyssen's, Trinitarian theology
and anti-Arianism.[86] Evagrius followed in their footsteps, not only regarding aspects of Trinitarian thought and eschatology (primarily the cluster
of notions related to apokatastasis) but also and especially with reference
to the notion of unified *nous*, the unfolding of the human anthropological
components from it and their eventual subsumption into it, and, related
to this theory, the threefold notion of the resurrection, each for one of
the human components: body, soul, and *nous*. Both the subsumption of
the inferior component into the unified *nous* and the resurrection of the
nous—concepts that in the end coincide in Evagrius—are open to the last
step, already theorized by Origen: the deification or θέωσις of the *nous*.

Bibliography

Primary Sources

Baehrens, Wilhelm Adolf, ed., *Homilien zu Samuel I, zum Hohelied und zu
den Propheten, Kommentar zum Hohelied in Rufins und Hieronymus'
Übersetzung*. Vol. 8 of *Origenes Werke*. Berlin: De Gruyter, 1925. Repr.,
2012.
Dodds, Eric R. *Proclus: The Elements of Theology*. Oxford: Clarendon, 1963.
Gregory of Nyssa. *De anima et resurrectione: Opera dogmatica minora,
Pars 3*. Edited by Andreas Spira. GNO 3.3. Leiden: Brill, 2014.
———. *Opera dogmatica minora, Pars 1*. Edited by Frederick Mueller.
GNO 3.1. Leiden: Brill, 1958.

---

85. I have endeavored to offer such an interpretation in Ramelli, *Evagrius' Kephalaia Gnostika*, e.g., lxv–lxvi, 323–24 especially on *Probl. gnos.* 6.14, and Ramelli, "Gregory and Evagrius."

86. Ilaria L. E. Ramelli, "Origen's Anti-subordinationism and Its Heritage in the
Nicene and Cappadocian Line," *VC* 65 (2011): 21–49; and new arguments in Ramelli,
"The Father in the Son."

Iamblichus. *De anima: Text, Translation, and Commentary.* Edited and translated by John Finamore and John Dillon. PhA 192. Leiden: Brill, 2002.

Nau, François, *Bardesanes: Liber legum regionum.* Patrologia Syriaca 1.2. Paris: Firmin-Didot, 1907.

Ramelli, Ilaria L. E. *Evagrius' Kephalaia Gnostika.* Atlanta: SBL Press, 2015.

Sachau, Edward C., ed. and trans. *The Chronology of Ancient Nations: An English Version of the Arabic Text of the Athâr-ul-Bâkiya of Albîrûnî.* London: Oriental Translation Fund, 1879.

Secondary Sources

Blosser, Benjamin. *Become Like the Angels: Origen's Doctrine of the Soul.* Washington, DC: Catholic University of America Press, 2012.

Casiday, Augustine. *Reconstructing the Theology of Evagrius Ponticus.* Cambridge: Cambridge University Press, 2013.

Corrigan, Kevin. "Mind, Soul, and Body in Plotinus, Gregory of Nyssa and Evagrius of Pontus." Pages 253–76 in *Lovers of the Soul and Lovers of the Body: Philosophical and Religious Perspectives in Late Antiquity.* Edited by Svetla S. Griffin and Ilaria L. E. Ramelli. HS. Cambridge: Harvard University Press, 2022.

D'Ancona, Cristina. "Mind and Body." *SGA* 10 (2020): 372–92.

Frey, Jörg, and Manuel Nägele, eds. *Der νοῦς bei Paulus im Horizont griechischer und hellenistisch-jüdischer Anthropologie.* WUNT 464. Tübingen: Mohr Siebeck, 2021.

Hengstermann, Christian. *Origenes und der Ursprung der Freiheitsmetaphysik.* Münster: Aschendorff, 2015.

Karamanolis, George. *The Philosophy of Early Christianity.* Durham: Acumen, 2013. 2nd ed. London: Routledge, 2021.

Kooten, George van. *Paul's Anthropology in Context: The Image of God, Assimilation to God, and Tripartite Man in Ancient Judaism, Ancient Philosophy and Early Christianity.* WUNT 232. Tübingen: Mohr Siebeck, 2008.

Markschies, Christoph. "Die platonische Metapher vom 'inneren Menschen.'" *ZKG* 105 (1994): 1–17.

McInroy, Mark. "Origen." Pages 20–35 in *The Spiritual Senses.* Edited by Paul Gavrilyuk and Sarah Coakley. Cambridge: Cambridge University Press, 2012.

Niebuhr, Karl-Wilhelm. "Jakobus und Paulus über das Innere des Menschen." *NTS* 62 (2016): 1–30.

Nordgaard, Stefan. "Paul's Appropriation of Philo's Theory of Two Men in 1 Corinthians 15.45–49." *NTS* 57 (2011): 348–65.

Oort, Johannes van. "Mind and Body." *VC* 73 (2019): 594.

Pietras, Henryk. "L'inizio del mondo materiale." Pages 653–68 in *Origeniana Nona*. Edited by György Heidl and Robert Somos. Leuven: Peeters, 2009.

Ramelli, Ilaria L. E. "Apokatastasis and Epektasis in *Hom. in Cant.*: The Relation between Two Core Doctrines in Gregory and Roots in Origen." Pages 312–39 in *Gregory of Nyssa: In Canticum Canticorum. Commentary and Supporting Studies. Select Proceedings of the Thirteenth International Colloquium on Gregory of Nyssa (Rome, 17–20 September 2014)*. Edited by Giulio Maspero, Miguel Brugarolas, and Ilaria Vigorelli. VCSup 150. Leiden: Brill, 2018.

———. "Autobiographical Self-Fashioning in Origen." Pages 273–92 in *Self, Self-Fashioning and Individuality in Late Antiquity: New Perspectives*. Edited by Maren Niehoff and Joshua Levinson. Tübingen: Mohr Siebeck, 2019.

———. *Bardaisan of Edessa: A Reassessment of the Evidence and a New Interpretation*. Piscataway, NJ: Gorgias, 2009; Berlin: De Gruyter, 2019.

———. "Bardaisan of Edessa, Origen, and Imperial Philosophy: A Middle Platonic Context?" *Aram* 30 (2018): 337–53.

———. *Bardaisan on Free Will, Fate, and Human Nature: The Book of the Laws of Countries*. Tübingen: Mohr Siebeck, forthcoming.

———. "The Body of Christ as Imperishable Wood: Hippolytus and Bardaisan of Edessa's Complex Christology." Pages 447–58 in *Proceedings of the Twelfth Symposium Syriacum 2016*. Edited by Emidio Vergani. OrChrAn 311. Leuven: Peeters, 2022.

———. *The Christian Doctrine of Apokatastasis: A Critical Assessment from the New Testament to Eriugena*. VCSup 120. Leiden: Brill, 2013.

———. "Christian Platonists in Support of Gender Equality: Bardaisan, Clement, Origen, Gregory of Nyssa, and Eriugena." Pages 313–50 in *Otherwise than the Binary: Towards Feminist Reading of Ancient Greek Philosophy, Magic and Mystery Traditions*. Edited by Danielle Layne and Jessica Elbert Decker. New York: State University of New York Press, 2022.

————. "Christian Soteriology and Christian Platonism. Origen, Gregory of Nyssa, and the Biblical and Philosophical Basis of the Doctrine of Apokatastasis." *VC* 61 (2007): 313–56.

————. "Conceptualities of Angels in Late Antiquity: Degrees of Corporeality, Bodies of Angels, and Comparative Angelologies/Daemonologies in 'Pagan' and Christian Platonism." Pages 115–72 in *Inventer les anges de l'Antiquité à Byzance: conception, représentation, perception.* Edited by Delphine Lauritzen. Paris: CNRS – Collège de France, Centre d'Histoire et Civilisation de Byzance, 2022.

————. "Esoteric Interpretations of Scripture in Philo (and Hellenistic Judaism), Clement, and Origen." In *Esoteric Cultures of Scripture.* Edited by Toby Mayer. Oxford: Oxford University Press, forthcoming.

————. "Evagrius and Gregory: Nazianzen or Nyssen? A Remarkable Issue That Bears on the Cappadocian (and Origenian) Influence on Evagrius." *GRBS* 53 (2013): 117–37.

————. "Evagrius Ponticus, the Origenian Ascetic (and Not the Origenistic 'Heretic')." Pages 147–205 in *Orthodox Monasticism, Past and Present.* Edited by John A. McGuckin. New York: Theotokos, 2014.

————. *Evagrius's Kephalaia Gnostika: A New Translation of the Unreformed Text from the Syriac.* WGRW 38. Atlanta: SBL Press, 2015.

————. "The Father in the Son, the Son in the Father in the Gospel of John: Sources and Reception of Dynamic Unity in Middle and Neoplatonism, 'Pagan' and Christian." *JBR* 7 (2020): 31–66.

————. "From God to God: Eriugena's Protology and Eschatology against the Backdrop of His Patristic Sources." Pages 99–123 in *Eriugena's Christian Neoplatonism and Its Sources in Patristic and Ancient Philosophy.* Edited by Ilaria L. E. Ramelli, Leuven: Peeters, 2021.

————. "Gregory and Evagrius." StPatr 101 (2020): 175–204.

————. "Gregory Nyssen's and Evagrius' Biographical and Theological Relations: Origen's Heritage and Neoplatonism." StPatr 84 (2017): 165–231.

————. "Gregory of Nyssa on the Soul (and the Restoration): From Plato to Origen." Pages 110–41 in *Exploring Gregory of Nyssa: Historical and Philosophical Perspectives.* Edited by Anna Marmodoro and Neil McLynn. Oxford: Oxford University Press, 2018.

————. "Harmony between *arkhē* and *telos* in Patristic Platonism and the Imagery of Astronomical Harmony Applied to the Apokatastasis Theory." *IJPT* 7 (2013): 1–49.

———. "Iamblichus, De anima 38 (66,12-15 Finamore/Dillon): A Resolving Conjecture?" *RhM* 157 (2014): 106–11.

———. "The Logos/Nous One-Many between 'Pagan' and Christian Platonism: Bardaisan, Clement, Origen, Plotinus, and Gregory of Nyssa." StPatr 102 (2020): 175–204.

———. "Macrobius: Astrological Descents, Ascents, and Restorations." *MHNH* 14 (2014): 197–214.

———. "Martianus Capella." In *The Encyclopedia of Ancient History*. Edited by Roger Bagnall, Kai Brodersen, Craig Champion, Andrew Erskine, Sabine Huebner, and Arietta Papaconstantinou. Oxford: Wiley-Blackwell, 2021.

———. "Matter in the Dialogue of Adamantius: Origen's Heritage and Hylomorphism." Pages 74–124 in *Platonism and Christianity in Late Ancient Cosmology: God, Soul, Matter*. Edited by Johannes Zachhuber and Anna Schiavoni. APR. Leiden: Brill, 2022.

———. "Mysticism, Apocalypticism, and Platonism." Pages 201–26 in *Platonic Pathways: Selected Papers from the Fourteenth Annual Conference of the International Society for Neoplatonic Studies*. Edited by John Finamore and Danielle Layne. Bream, UK: Prometheus Trust, 2018.

———. "Origen." Pages 245–66 in *A History of Mind and Body in Late Antiquity*. Edited by Sophie Cartwright and Anna Marmodoro. Cambridge: Cambridge University Press, 2018.

———. "Origen and Evagrios." Pages 94–108 in *Oxford Handbook of Dionysius the Areopagite*. Edited by Mark Edwards, Dimitrios Pallis, and Georgios Steiris. Oxford: Oxford University Press, 2022.

———. "Origen, Bardaisan, and the Origin of Universal Salvation." *HTR* 102 (2009): 135–68.

———. "Origen, Greek Philosophy, and the Birth of the Trinitarian Meaning of Hypostasis." *HTR* 105 (2012): 302–50.

———. "Origen on the Unity of Soul and Body in the Earthly Life and Afterwards and His Impact." Pages 38–77 in *The Unity of Soul and Body in the Earthly Life and After*. Edited by Jörg Ulrich, Anna Usacheva, and Siam Bhayro, Leiden: Brill, 2021.

———. "Origen, Patristic Philosophy, and Christian Platonism: Re-thinking the Christianisation of Hellenism." *VC* 63 (2009): 217–63.

———. "Origen's Allegoresis of Plato's and Scripture's Myths." Pages 85–106 in *Religious Competition in the Greco-Roman World*. Edited by Nathaniel Desrosiers and Lily Vuong. WGRWSup 10. Atlanta: SBL Press, 2016.

———. "Origen's Anti-subordinationism and Its Heritage in the Nicene and Cappadocian Line." *VC* 65 (2011): 21–49.

———. "'Pagan' and Christian Platonism in Dionysius: The Double-Reference Scheme and Its Meaning." Pages 92–112 in *Byzantine Platonists 284–1453*. Edited by Frederick Lauritzen and Sarah Klitenic Wear. TSBPCP. Washington, DC: Catholic University of America Press, 2021.

———. "Philo as One of the Main Inspirers of Early Christian Hermeneutics and Apophatic Theology." *Adamantius* 24 (2018): 276–92.

———. "Philo's Doctrine of Apokatastasis: Philosophical Sources, Exegetical Strategies, and Patristic Aftermath." *SPhiloA* 26 (2014): 29–55.

———. "Porphyry and the Motif of Christianity as παράνομος." Pages 173–98 in *Platonism and Its Legacy: Selected Papers from the Fifteenth Annual Conference of the International Society for Neoplatonic Studies*. Edited by John F. Finamore and Tomáš Nejeschleba. Lydney, UK: Prometheus Trust, 2019.

———. "The Reception of Origen's Ideas in Western Theological and Philosophical Traditions." Pages 443–67 in *Origeniana Undecima: Origen and Origenism in the History of Western Thought*. Edited by Anders-Christian Jacobsen. BETL 279. Leuven: Peeters, 2016.

———. "The Reception of Paul in Origen: Allegoresis of Scripture, Apokatastasis, and Women's Ministry." In *The Pauline Mind*. Edited by Stanley Porter and David Yoon. New York: Routledge, 2023.

———. Review of *La prière dans la tradition platonicienne, de Platon à Proclus*, by Andrei Timotin. *BMCR*, 17 April 2020.

———. "The Role of Allegory, Allegoresis, and Metaphor in Paul and Origen." *JGRChJ* 14 (2018): 130–57.

———. *Social Justice and the Legitimacy of Slavery: The Role of Philosophical Asceticism from Ancient Judaism to Late Antiquity*. Oxford: Oxford University Press, 2016.

———. "Soma (Σῶμα)." *RAC* 30:814–47.

———. "Some Overlooked Sources of the Elements of Theology: The Noetic Triad, Epistrophé-Apokatastasis, Bodies, and the Possible Reception of Origenian Themes." Pages 406–76 in *On Causes and the Noetic Triad*. Vol. 3 of *Reading Proclus and the Book of Causes*. Edited by Dragos Calma. SPNPT 28. Leiden: Brill, 2022.

———. "Tricotomia." Pages 11772–76 in *Enciclopedia Filosofica*. Vol. 12. Edited by Virgilio Melchiorre. Milan: Bompiani and Centro di Studi Filosofici di Gallarate, 2006.

Simonetti, Manlio. "Osservazioni sull'interpretazione origeniana di Genesi 2,7;3,21." *Aevum* 36 (1962): 370–78.

Sorabji, Richard. *Emotion and Peace of Mind: From Stoic Agitation to Christian Temptation.* Oxford: Oxford University Press, 2000.

Thomassen, Einar. *The Spiritual Seed: The Church of the Valentinians.* Leiden: Brill, 2008.

Timotin, Andrei. *La prière dans la tradition platonicienne, de Platon à Proclus.* Turnhout: Brepols, 2017.

———. *Trois théories antiques de la divination: Plutarque, Jamblique, Augustin.* Leiden: Brill: 2022.

Tobon, Monica. *Apatheia and Anthropology in Evagrius of Pontus.* London: Routledge, forthcoming.

Tolan, Daniel. "Mind and Body." *JTS* 70 (2019): 857–59.

Proclus, Hermias, and Cyril of
Alexandria on the Embodied Soul

Sarah Klitenic Wear

Introduction

Cyril of Alexandria,[1] a rough contemporary of Syrianus in the fifth century, presents arguments in his *Scholia on the Incarnation* that may be viewed in light of Platonist teachings on the tripartite soul: here, the Logos and the rational soul of Jesus are distinct natures that interact as a "union without confusion" (*asynchytos henosis*) in the body of Jesus. For Cyril, Jesus incarnate has natures distinct with their own properties, and yet these share substance and are said to have one activity. That is, the two natures always act in concert such that actions cannot be ascribed to either nature as if

John Finamore's work on the tripartite soul in the Platonic tradition, as well as his recent translation of Proclus's *Commentary on the Republic*, have inspired this essay. I would like to thank him for his groundbreaking work on the soul in Iamblichus and Proclus. We in the world of classics owe him a debt of gratitude. I would also like to thank Sara Ahbel-Rappe for providing me with two venues to debut this article (her conference Soul Matters in Ann Arbor in December of 2019 and her SCS panel in January 2020). I would also like to thank Matthew Crawford for reading over drafts of this article and providing comments. All of the mistakes in this article are my own fault.

1. Syrianus (fl. 432); Proclus (412–485); Cyril of Alexandria (375–444). Syrianus accepted Proclus as a student in 412, the same year Cyril was made bishop of Alexandria. It is difficult to trace a direct relationship between Cyril and Proclus, or even Syrianus, his closer contemporary. However, it should be remembered that Proclus studied in Alexandria for a short time in his career. The school of Alexandria in the fifth century was known to have included Hellenes and Christians who studied simultaneously. While we do not have direct evidence about the school of Olympiodorus the Elder (fifth century CE), of which Proclus was a member, we have evidence of mixed populations of Christians and Hellenes in the school of Hypatia in the 380's–410's, as well as the schools of Hierocles, Ammonius, and Horapollon between 430–520.

they were a concrete entity. The rational element of the incarnate Jesus, moreover, interacts with the irrational portions (the emotions and the body) to create harmony. Cyril's description of the incarnation here, as in his other works, shares a framework with the language of Proclus and Hermias on the embodied soul. While Cyril focuses his language of essence and activity with respect to the two natures of the embodied soul of Christ, Proclus and Hermias focus on the language of essence (*ousia*)[2] and activity (*energeia*) with respect to each part of the soul. They teach that the embodied soul has three parts that share substance, yet each part has distinct properties; however, unlike Cyril's account of the two natures, the distinct properties are associated with activities particular to each part. Still, the embodied soul acts in some way as one unit, also, insofar as one sees the result of the activity through a person's singular action. In the seventh essay of Proclus's *Commentary on the Republic of Plato* (1.206.1–235.21), Proclus explains that each of the three parts of the embodied soul share essence, and yet each has its own activity particular to its own nature: the rational part (*logos*) accomplishes its work when it lives a purified and contemplative life;[3] spirit (*thymos*) takes vengeance or reacts to supposed fears; and the appetite (*epithymia*) speaks to a desire for pleasure. In the body, however, these three elements form a unity so that the three parts "are united without confusion" (*tōn asōmatōn asynchtyōs henōmenōn*) (*Comm.*

---

2. Proclus and Hermias refer to a soul's essence as its *ousia* and its activity as *energeia*. Sometimes *eidos* is used as a synonym for *ousia*; other times *eidos* refers to the structure of the soul according to its properties. On this debate, see Sarah Klitenic Wear, "Hermias on the Activities of the Soul: A Commentary on Hermias, *In Phdr.* 135.14–138.9," in *Studies in Hermias's Commentary on Plato's Phaedrus*, ed. John Finamore, Christina-Panagiota Manolea, and Sarah Klitenic Wear (Leiden: Brill, 2020), 105. These terms are important in late antique Platonic debates on the changing nature of the soul. Stemming from a rejection of Plotinus's view that part of the soul remains undescended, Proclus and Hermias argue that activities take place in time and place and are changeable, while substance remains eternal (Proclus, *In Tim.* 2.131.23–25; *Elem. Theol.* 191; Hermias, *Comm. Phaedr.* 1135.15–17.) Activities can be affected by numerous elements when the soul descends, including emotions, which eventually need to be controlled for the soul to reunite with a series god. While emotions and activities change, however, they do not alter the substance of the soul. Thus, powers and activities can be corrupted, but the substance of the soul cannot be corrupted (Proclus, *Mal. sub.* 39). There is a debate among Platonists on whether or not the substance of the soul changes. See Wear, "Hermias on the Activities of the Soul."

3. This is D. Gregory MacIssac's phrasing in "The Soul and the Virtues in Proclus's *Commentary on the Republic of Plato*," *Philosophie antique* 9 (2009): 119.

in R. 1.234.15). Essentially, Proclus, as with his contemporary Hermias, shows that soul is divided into a divine *logos* and irrational parts ordered by *logos*.[4] Hermias in his *Commentary on the Phaedrus* (135.14–138.9) shows that the embodied soul has a rational part (with a divine origin) and an irrational element (connected to the passions and emotions) that share substance but differ in properties and activities. Thus, Proclus, Hermias, and Cyril discuss an individual soul consisting of distinct properties that unify under one substance. This paper, thus, argues that Proclus and Hermias's discussions of the embodied soul share a framework similar to the one Cyril uses as he reflects on the incarnation. Obviously, notable differences exist: while Proclus and Hermias argue that the embodied soul must control emotions attached to the irrational soul for ultimate divinization, Cyril says that Jesus's experience of emotions raise and sanctify emotions for the individual soul.

Proclus and Hermias

For the Platonists, the soul is divided into parts (the chief being the rational [the *logos*] and irrational elements [*epithymia* and *thymos*]), each of which relate with one another to create a united soul in a body. The Platonists arrive at this theory based on a reading of Plato's *Republic* where there are three elements in the soul (the rational, spirited, and appetitive) (436b8–9). In the *Timaeus* (696–71a3), Plato identifies the three elements within various locations of the body; Plato's primary point is to show how these three parts interrelate for a harmonious soul; in a harmonious soul, the spirit and appetites are under the control of reason. The later Platonists interpret these three parts as having two states: an independent state, prior or subsequent to life in a body, and a state within the body (Proclus, *Comm in R.* 1.207.20–23). Proclus and Hermias elaborate upon the lives of the rational and irrational soul that exist before falling into a body; even the irrational soul will retain a life (albeit shorter than the rational soul) outside of the body.

In his seventh essay on the *Commentary on the Republic*, Proclus concerns himself with how these parts bear a mutual relation that reflects at once their activity in their own state, as well as their activity in an embodied state where each element works with the other parts for a harmonious

---

4. MacIssac, "Soul and the Virtues," 137.

unity. In his *Commentary on the Republic*, Proclus explains that the *logos* (whose activity in isolation is *phronesis*) regulates and creates standards for *epithymia* and *thymos*. *Epithymia* (whose virtue in itself is temperance) uses temperance to turn toward *logos* and regulate desires, while *thymos* (whose own virtue is courage) accepts the standards set by *logos* and keeps *epithymia* in check (1.11.26–212.20; 213.28–214.7).[5] Thus, when they exist in the soul, the three parts no longer exist in isolation; they must join together to form a single life (*mian zoen*) (1.208.29–209.2).[6] Each part is in some way in the other, and each reflects the activity of the other, with *logos* ruling over the irrational parts (1.208.19). At the crux of his theory of internal unity—despite the natural differences of the parts—is Proclus's view of the substance of soul. Proclus describes the embodied soul as having one *ousia* that is internally complex so that each part of the soul carries out different activities reflecting its relationship to its shared *ousia*. It is the relationship between each of the three parts that makes a soul truly human. Were a soul to lack reason, spirit, or appetite, it would cease to be human; without reason, it would be an animal; without spirit or appetite, it would become divine. It is the latter that becomes the goal of the Platonist's soul, which must ultimately purify itself of its irrational elements.

The tradition of Proclus and Hermias on the parts of the soul begins with the teachings of Porphyry and Iamblichus on the soul, especially how parts of the soul exhibit different powers in the soul's embodied state. While the parts share *ousia*, the rational and irrational parts of the soul maintain different functions: the rational element controls the soul and connects it to its divine origin, while the irrational element is affected by the passions and is connected to the body. Porphyry and Iamblichus argue that the soul has powers that differ while being extended throughout the whole soul when disembodied; once embodied, the powers are located in specific parts. Porphyry, for instance, says that one substrate can have different powers, all unified in one entity: "For example now, all of the powers of an apple are in a single apple, but the parts [of the apple] are separated, some in one place, others in another" (*Concerning the Powers of the Soul*, 253F.68–70 [Finamore and Dillon]).[7] Thus, powers need not be distinguished into parts, although they can be associated with a particular

---

5. MacIssac, "Soul and the Virtues," 127.

6. MacIssac, "Soul and the Virtues," 119.

7. See the commentary on Iamblichus, *De an.* 11 in John Finamore and John Dillon, *Iamblichus De Anima: Text, Translation and Commentary* (Leiden: Brill, 2002).

element of the soul (for instance, Iamblichus associates reason with the power of the ruling element).[8] For Porphyry, the soul does not have parts *per se*, but powers that can be likened to qualities. These powers exhibit different activities. The body receives multiple powers in distinct places, a feature continuing even when the rational soul is embodied. Porphyry's rational soul is a separate and immortal entity when it is embodied; such a state allows it to be released at the time of death.[9] The activities of the rational soul are like those of the divine minds.[10] Likewise, in his *De anima* commentary, Iamblichus says that various powers existing within a soul correspond to different elements within the soul. The soul is a single power with rational and irrational powers present at different times; the rational soul has irrational powers that can be actualized when the soul is embodied.[11] Iamblichus disagrees with Porphyry on a key issue regarding the powers of the soul. Where Iamblichus thinks that the whole irrational life exists even when separated from the body and reasoning, Porphyry says that irrational faculties do not exist in a purified soul (Iamblichus, *De an.* 48).

Proclus and Hermias posit that the rational and irrational parts of the soul can exist in an unembodied state. Even in an unembodied state, each of the three parts of the soul has an activity naturally arising from its essence (*Comm. in R.* 1.208.4–5).[12] When embodied, however, the parts of the soul are unified by the rational part, which is essentially intelligible, having arisen from a more divine essence.[13] Below the rational soul is the irrational soul or lower soul, the very image of the rational soul. This

---

8. See Finamore and Dillon, *Iamblichus De Anima*, 104.

9. John Finamore, "Hermias and the Ensoulment of the Pneuma," in *Studies in Hermias's Commentary on Plato's Phaedrus*, ed. John Finamore, Christina-Panagiota Manolea, and Sarah Klitenic Wear (Leiden: Brill, 2020), 38.

10. Finamore, "Hermias and the Ensoulment of the Pneuma," 37.

11. Finamore and Dillon, *Iamblichus De Anima*, 117.

12. MacIssac, "Soul and the Virtues," 119.

13. Proclus, *Comm. in R.* (1.234.17–25) (Finamore): "Nevertheless there is also another way that Plato's account is able to gain leeway, when he says that reason arises from a more divine essence but the irrational from another is much inferior, and that the former preserves and orders while the latter is preserved and ordered. Just as Form when it is associated with matter introduces unity to it (and we have no need for any other thing to unite these with one another), in the same way also reason, which holds the rank of Form, itself unifies the irrational life, and does not require any third thing to bind both." Finamore, "Hermias and the Ensoulment of the Pneuma," 45.

lower soul is connected to irrational life. However, rational souls contain the summits of the lower life when they are housed in a pneumatic body, that is, before they are in a corporeal body. The pneumatic body (or vehicle) is associated with the irrational soul; it is material, although it lives long. This vehicle is important; when the rational soul reincarnates, it receives a new corporeal body, but it can reuse its irrational soul and pneumatic body from a previous life (Proclus, *In Tim.* 3.6.24.1–5).[14] Thus, the pneumatic vehicle stands as a kind of bridge between the luminous vehicle of the rational soul and the material body. This is why the passions and emotions can affect the thinking of the rational soul when it is in a body (*In Tim.* 3.284.16–285.16).[15] Hence, the lower or irrational soul is ordered by its rational counterpart to produce a unified soul.[16] Thus, the soul in a body has a number of parts, with the highest being the rational element that engages in intellection, created by the Demiurge (*Comm. in R.* 1.234.26–30). The soul also has lower elements in its embodied state: the spirited element and the irrational element, both of which are ordered by its rational element. These parts form a unity in relation to each other (1.208.14–25).[17] They relate because the Demiurge was the primary cause of the rational soul, as well as the source of the coherence (*sunexeian*) and unity (*henōsin*) between the three elements (234.26–30).[18] However, it is important to point out that while each part relates to the other, the *energeia* of the rational part is "higher" than that of the lower elements.[19] Of the rational and irrational elements, Proclus says: "These two [*thymos* and *epithymia*] have the same father, while *logos* has a different father; these two are mortal and either exist or do not exist together, while *logos* is immortal; these two cannot receive knowledge, while *logos* by nature

14. Jan Opsomer, "Souls and Their Bodies in the Philosophy of Proclus," in *A History of Mind and Body in Late Antiquity*, ed. Anna Marmodora and Sophie Cartwright (Cambridge: Cambridge University Press, 2018), 133.

15. Finamore, "Hermias and the Ensoulment of the Pneuma," 45.

16. John F. Finamore, "Proclus and the Tripartite Soul in Plato's Republic," in *The Byzantine Platonists*, ed. F. Lauritzen and Sarah Klitenic Wear (Franciscan University Press, 2021), 70.

17. Finamore, "Proclus and the Tripartite Soul," 70.

18. Finamore, "Proclus and the Tripartite Soul," 70.

19. MacIssac, "Soul and the Virtues," 120, citing *Comm. in R.* 1.209.6–210.5. Here MacIssac discusses the issues that each element of the soul has a double activity: that is, the activity within itself and the activity in relation to that which is outside itself (above or below it).

is cognitive" (1.215.4–7 [MacIssac]). The irrational and rational soul are connected insofar as the nonrational soul consists of faculties and emotions that are images of the rational soul (cf. 1.235). Still, although the rational soul is immortal, the lower elements of the irrational soul can survive until the soul meets its final permutation after a cycle of lives. In his *In Tim.* 3.236.31–237.9, Proclus describes how the immortal soul is preserved after the corruption of the mortal body. At this time, the soul is punished in the afterlife in an effort to liberate it from its irrational passions. Here, the body is ensouled by the nonrational soul that makes it possible for soul to be connected with body.

Thus, while the rational and irrational elements have different activities particular to their unique properties, they share *ousia*. In the seventh essay of the *Republic Commentary*, Proclus describes the soul as having one *ousia* that unfolds itself into a complexity. *Logos, thymos,* and *epithymia* differ with respect to *ousia* (*kat'ousian*); that is, with respect to their own understanding of that same *ousia*. The single *ousia* contains a differentiated multiplicity *kat'ousian*, an issue Proclus returns to not only in the *Commentary on the Republic* (1.207.9–10, 1.224.18), but also in the *Commentary on the Timaeus* (2.47, 2.147.19–257.29).[20] Thus, the soul can be called *polydynamos*, with its parts indicating different activities and powers,[21] but these different activities and powers are attributed to one, unchanging being that is shared among the parts of the soul.

Hermias comes from a tradition on the parts of the soul that is similar to that of Proclus. In his *Commentary on the Phaedrus* (135–138), Hermias describes how, when the immortal rational soul descends into creation, it takes on irrational powers (the irrational soul) in its embodied state. In the. *Comm. Phaedr.* 135.18, Hermias describes what it means for the soul

---

20. There is some debate on what Proclus means by *kat'ousian*. MacIssac ("Soul and the Virtues," 123), Finamore ("Hermias and the Ensoulment of the Pneuma"), and Wear ("Hermias on the Activities of the Soul") interpret that the soul for Proclus has one substance that does not change nor does one part of the soul have a different substance from another part. Matthias Perkams offers the interpretation that the soul does have different substances: the rational soul differs from the irrational soul in substance, although the entire soul still remains unified. See Matthias Perkams, "An Innovation by Proclus: the Theory of the Substantial Diversity of the Human Soul," in *Proklos: Methode, Seelenlehre, Metaphysik: Aketen der Konferenz in Jena am 18.–20. September 2003*, ed. Matthias Perkams and Rosa Maria Piccione (Leiden: Brill, 2006), 167–85.

21. Perkams, "Innovation by Proclus," 179.

to be "swept into generation"; when the soul descends, it has a rational soul, as well as an irrational soul, the part of the soul that deals with the passions of the body. The passions of the body can be purified at the level of the irrational soul; the passions, moreover, only affect the faculties and acts, never the essence (*ousia*), which is unchanging. Hermias indicates that activity for the soul is in the context of how the soul administers the universe (135). That is, every part of the universe is administered by a certain soul that is akin to it insofar as they share particular characteristics (*idiomata*). However, the soul itself undergoes no substantial change. While passions of the body affect faculties, they do not affect the rational soul. Thus, as with Proclus, Hermias argues that the soul remains the same in its essence, despite its varying activities and engagement with its irrational parts. Proclus argues this in *In Tim.* 2.131.17–25:

> It is not sufficient, then, to say that the soul is generated in virtue of the activity of its parts, but one must see how this character pre-exists in the essence of soul. For every activity naturally depends upon an essence that contains in advance the cause of this activity. (Wear)

Within the nature of the essence of the soul are its activities. The potential faculty within the soul's essence becomes an activity when it is enacted. When Hermias describes the irrational soul and its relation to the body, the soul at that point is in a state of generation, and it exhibits different acts that do not affect its essence. Properties of souls may affect their actions but not their essences.[22]

Hermias agrees with Proclus that the passions of the body reach only faculties and acts; these passions can be purified at the level of the irrational soul, but they do not alter the immortal rational soul.[23] He clarifies his position on this in 102.13–15, where he says that when Plato says soul he means rational soul, not the irrational soul. This is because the rational soul is unchanging and immortal, unlike the irrational soul that is affected by the activities and properties of the soul (136.3). Thus, for Hermias, when souls

---

22. Rather, it is the properties (*idiomata*) of souls that affect the actions of souls. Hermias explains that "each of the divine causes of the whole universe bestows attention according to its own properties: the sun solarly, Ares in a war-like manner, and the others similarly" (136.1–3). That is, property is shared in a series but in different degrees. He elaborates that each divine cause pays attention to the universe according to distinct properties just as a general pays attention to his army.

23. Wear, "Hermias on the Activities of the Soul," 101.

administer the universe according to their own *idiomata*, some descend gradually, experiencing a change. The soul experiences a change in its *eidos*; this change in form reflects a change in the structure of its substance—the arrangement of its properties—but not in the substance itself. This idea is reflected in Proclus's *In Parm.* 707.5–31 where *ousia* affects property that then shapes activity; for example, intellect takes part in things intellectually. Thus, soul can shape its essence by assimilating to higher or lower worlds. This change in structure is most likely the addition of the irrational soul that allows the soul to be connected to the body during its ascent.[24]

Finally, both Proclus and Hermias have a doctrine that describes how and why the irrational powers must be purified. Proclus and Hermias maintain that the irrational soul is housed around the soul in something known as the "vehicle of the soul." Hermias says that when the souls have lost their wings, they are borne along until they reach something solid—our bodies (136.7). Irrational souls "hang on" to these bodies that contain the "taint of generation." Proclus in *In Tim.* 3.237.15–31 says that our souls (i.e., rational souls) have irrational life weaved onto our vehicles by the gods. These lower vehicles create perceptions and desires in our earthly bodies (137.9–13). Living beings need purification to be rid of these perceptions and desires (137.13). Proclus, likewise, maintains that the incorporeal life—separate and against the irrational soul—is what is proper to souls (*In Alc.* 256.11–14; *Comm. in R.* 2.349.20–26).[25] Souls affected by passions cannot imitate the gods or see the forms; they can only descend (157.5–158.3). Thus, the emotions, passions, even elements of *thymos*, need to be purified from the soul. For Proclus, purification from the passions takes place in different ways depending on where the soul rests in the hierarchy of virtues, whether our soul is at the level of the civic virtues or purificatory virtues or higher. At the level of civic virtues, negative emotions must be eradicated and good emotions must be used in accordance with the reasoning aspect of the soul. At the level of the purificatory virtues, the soul is in the process of separating from the body and irrational souls. At higher levels, this separation has already taken place. The irrational soul must be purified of bad emotions; once the rational soul is separated from the irrational soul, any remaining good emotions benefit the individual.[26]

---

24. Perkams, "Innovation by Proclus," 179.

25. MacIssac, "Soul and the Virtues," 139.

26. I would like to thank John Finamore for his clarification on the emotions at different levels of the hierarchy. Robbert Van den Berg explains the different place of

Cyril

Cyril describes the incarnation in a manner that accounts for the embodied soul as it concerns all late Platonists: namely, a rational soul, emotions, and body that interact in a harmony. For Cyril, of course, the embodied soul is fully human and fully divine, meaning that divinity permeates and redeems all three parts in its embodied state. Also, Cyril shares a basic framework with the later Platonists insofar as he uses language such as "union without confusion," which we saw with Proclus: this time, however, the elements that share *ousia* and yet have distinct properties when housed in a body are the natures of Jesus as man and Jesus as divine. Unlike the later Platonists, who focus on the parts of the soul sharing *ousia*, the different elements within Jesus (again, Cyril's concern here is with the natures of man and divinity) share one activity. Finally, when Cyril discusses how the reason principle coexists with irrational elements, his concern is not with the subduing of these elements, but with their redemption. Ultimately, however, it must be remembered that while Proclus and Hermias discuss human souls in the passages discussed above, Cyril discusses a soul that is fully human and fully divine. Still, the latter's understanding of the soul of Jesus (particularly how the reason principle relates to the emotions) adheres in many ways to the description of Proclus and Hermias on the parts of the individual soul. Differences in understanding of the soul occur because the soul of Jesus is already divinized—insofar as it experiences emotions, for instance, it divinizes those emotions for the experience of every human soul. What is of interest in the comparison is that Cyril understands the incarnation as a soul united, but with distinction in roughly the same way as Proclus and Hermias account for the parts of the soul that are distinguishable, but fully unified. Thus, when we discuss Proclus and Hermias, we are discussing parts of the soul interacting; when we discuss Cyril, we discuss two separate interactions: (1) the interaction of the divine and human natures and (2) the interaction of the reason principle, emotions, and body with the divine and human soul of Christ in the incarnation.

---

emotions at the civic level and purificatory level: "In fact, on the Neoplatonic scale of virtues, the political virtues in general are identified with the Peripatetic ideal of metriopatheia (measured emotions), as opposed to the subsequent purifying virtues which aim at apatheia (no emotions at all)." See Robbert Van den Berg, "Proclus and Damascius on φιλοτιμία: The Neoplatonic Psychology of a Political Emotion," *Philosophie antique* 17 (2017): 157.

In section 8 of his *Scholia on the Incarnation*, Cyril explains that Jesus has two natures, and yet these natures are united (*henosis*) (PG 75:1376C).[27] Cyril affirms and reaffirms throughout the *Scholia* that God as Logos underwent no change (*metabolē*) in nature at the incarnation. At this point of the *Scholia on the Incarnation*, Cyril offers and discounts Stoic terminology of mixture and combination. Thus, what Cyril describes here happening at the incarnation is not a conjunction because at the incarnation two entities occupy one place without undergoing change. Cyril explains this process using the term *asynchytos* in section 11, where the Word comes to a union with humanity so the two elements are united, yet remain unconfused. He uses this term in section 13, where he says that "the nature or hypostases remained in an unconfusion," and again in section 13, where "Jesus Christ is one and the same, even though we recognize the difference of natures and keep them unconfused with each other." This terminology was also used (as seen above) by Proclus in his

---

27. The Greek fragments of the *Scholia on the Incarnation* are available in PG 75:1369–1412; the complete translation in Latin is printed in PL 48:1004–1040. The standard edition is E. Schwartz, *Acta Conciliorum Oecumenicorum*, vol. 1.5.1 (Berlin; de Gruyter, 1924), which gives both the Greek fragments and the Latin text. There is a translation in English in John Anthony McGuckin, *St. Cyril of Alexandria: The Christological Controversy* (Leiden, Brill, 1994), 294–335. All quotations in this article from the *Scholia* are McGuckin's. The text is known in Greek fragments, Latin, Syriac, Coptic, Arabic, Georgian, and Armenian. Cf. references in M. Geerard, *Clavis Patrum Graecorum* vol. 3: A Cyrillo *Alexandrino ad Iohannem Damascenus* (Corpus Christianorum; Turnhout; Brepols, 1976) sub numero; M. Geerard and J. Noret, *A Cyrillo Alexandrino ad Iohannem Damascenus*, vol. 3 of *Clavis Patrum Graecorum*, Corpus Christianorum (Turnhout: Brepols, 1988), sub numero. In this treatise, Cyril considers and rejects Stoic terms that describe the union between Logos and the rational soul of Christ. While my primary aim is to show that his discussion is based in Platonist language of union (as opposed to Stoic), Cyril's discussion here is also steeped in the Aristotelian commentary tradition. See Steven A. McKinion, *Words, Imagery and the Mystery of Christ: A Reconstruction of Cyril of Alexandria's Christology* (Leiden: Brill, 2000), 59–67. For discussions of Aristotelian language on mixture used more generally by Patristic sources on the incarnation, see Iain R. Torrance, *Christology after Chalcedon: Severus of Antioch and Sergius the Monophysite* (Norwich: Cantebury Press, 1988), esp. 59–74; Harold H. Joachim, *Aristotle on Coming-to-be and Passing Away* (Oxford: Oxford University Press, 1922); Harry Austryn Wolfson, *The Philosophy of the Church Fathers* (Cambridge: Harvard University Press, 1964), 372–86, John M. Rist, "Pseudo-Ammonius and the Soul/Body Problem in Some Platonic Texts of Late Antiquity," *AJP* 109 (1988): 402–15.

Commentary on the Republic (1.233.29–234.17), where he describes the parts of the soul interacting as a union without confusion.

What is at stake with the term *asynchytos* is that in a fusion (*synchusis*) the two entities fused form a *tertium quid* as neither of the elements fused can be retrieved. While Platonists, such as Proclus and Hermias, affirm the phenomenon—that two distinct entities can share one *ousia*—this was a teaching of the Platonists against Stoics, such as Chrysippus. Thus, while the intelligible entities can occupy the same place, they must do so through a juxtaposition of one thing running through the other. Cyril grapples with this problem in *Schol.* 13:

> So when we see things that happen to be dissimilar [*oux homoian*] in nature [*physin*] brought into unity by composition [*pros henoteta kata synthesin*], when perhaps the one is said to indwell the other, we must not divide this into two, even if we can still name each of the two united entities separately, whatever they might be. To divide them would be to dishonor the consilience into unity.

Here, Cyril engages in a thought experiment: if things appear dissimilar in nature, but they are united through *synthesis*, the two items can be recognized but must not be removed from each other or the composition will cease to be a composition. But the unity of Christ is indissoluble. In *Schol.* 25, in a portion extant in Greek, he says:

> He [Christ] is understood entirely as one thing within another [*heteron en heterō*]. That which indwells, that is the divine nature in the manhood, does not suffer any mixing [*phyrmos*], confusion [*anachysin*] or change [*metastasin*] into something that formerly it was not. Something that is said to dwell within something else does not become what that thing is in which it dwells, rather it is understood to be one thing in another thing. But in respect to the nature of the Word and the nature of manhood this difference indicates to us only the distinguishing of natures, for we also understand that there is one Christ, from out of both. And so, as I have explained, even though the non-confusedness [*to asynchyton*] was preserved, the evangelist tells us that the Word dwelt among us, for he knows that there is only one Only Begotten Son who was incarnated and made man.

Cyril's description of what is united between these two entities when embodied bears a similarity to what Proclus and Hermias describe when the parts of the soul are embodied. Cyril describes the incarnation as a mutual sharing of capacities (*dynameis*) and powers (*energeia*) and natural properties (*idiomata*).[28] For Cyril, a free exchange of properties exists allowing for whatever is characteristic of the divine to be attributed to humans and whatever is characteristic of humans be attributed to the divine. Proclus makes a similar statement about the union between parts of the soul in insofar as each bears some of the characteristics of each, although in their own way (*Elem. Theol.* prop. 28; *Comm in R.* 1.229.9–230.5, where opposed terms [here, different parts of the soul] are joined by means, all of which share terms). The union of the natures cannot be said to be without their own properties, nor can they be severed from each other (*Ep.* 46 [PG 77.237–245]; *1 Succ.* 6). Cyril argues this in his *2 Succ.* 3. Here Cyril says that the incarnation "does not imply there was any consequent mixture [*phyrmon*] or confusion [*synchousin*].… This does not mean as they would suppose that he has been mixed.… No, each nature is understood to remain in all its natural characteristics … though they are ineffably and inexpressibly united [*henothesis*]." Cyril uses the language of *asynchytos* and *henosis* to describe what takes place at the incarnation throughout his corpus.[29] His explanation for these terms rests on his understanding of the substance shared between man and divinity in the incarnation. Just as the Procline soul is at once unified and diverse because of the complex nature of *ousia*, so does Cyril say the incarnation is at once both simple and complex based on the complexity of *ousia* itself; the soul unfolds itself while retaining one substance. For Proclus, *logos, thymos,* and *epithymia* are distinct parts carrying out different activities, all related within one *ousia*. Cyril explains that the simultaneous simplicity and diversity at the incarnation is possible through the communication of idioms, whereby man and divinity can interpenetrate without either losing their nature. The transference of properties from the Son to the Logos and from the Logos to the Son allows Christ to be equally man and God. This communication of idioms, moreover, is not merely an accidental exchange of properties, but it affects Christ's mode of being.

The rational soul of Jesus, thus, remains a distinct element of Christ in the incarnation, as does the Logos. In section 10, Cyril says that "the

---

28. Bernard Meunier, *Le Christ de Cyrille d'Alexandrie: L'Humanitie* (Paris: Beauchesne, 1997), 258 and Alois Grillmeier, *Le Christ dans la tradition chrétienne: L'Église de Constantinople au VI siècle* (Paris: CERF, 1993), 589.

29. *Schol.* 9; *Letter to the Monks* 12; *1 Succ.* 7; *Explanation of the Twelve Chapters* 13, *inter alia*.

incorporeal Godhead became a body, that is flesh endowed with a rational soul."[30] What Cyril means by rational soul, however, at times changes; sometimes the body seems to be conflated with the rational soul of Jesus. The passions, at other times, seem to be located in the rational soul such that Cyril says the rational soul houses emotion and intellectual functions, all of which are called body by Cyril.[31] *Henosis* then for Cyril is between flesh endowed with a rational soul, the passions, and the Word—Cyril says that those who speak of two natures understand it this way (*Letter to Eulogius*, *Ep*. 45 [PG 77.228–237]). The first nature is the nature of Jesus—a rational soul housed in a body (*empsychōmenēs noerōs*)—and the second is the Word. Cyril points out that these two natures come together without confusion or change in an indivisible union (1 *Succ*. 6 [PG 77.228–237]). Cyril underscores that what is important at the incarnation is the union of the rational soul (as well as its relationship to the emotions and passions which are reliant upon his physical body) with the Word (Cyril, *Expl*. 12).[32] It is important, Cyril explains in *Quod unus sit Christus*, for Jesus to retain a rational soul and his emotions because Jesus needs to act as humanity's redeemer of both (728b).

Cyril's theory of body complicates his understanding of the way the rational soul of Jesus and Logos interact at the incarnation, particularly with respect to the emotions and passions. Looking again at section 8 of the *Scholia*, Cyril draws a comparison between the way Logos experiences suffering to the way soul appropriates suffering of the body. He says, "for the soul appropriates the things of the body even though in its proper nature it is apart from the body's natural passions [*pathon pyschikoon*], as well as those which impinge on it from without." This view, however, is difficult because of an argument he makes a few sections later concerning his understanding of body (*sarx*). At the beginning of *Schol*. 10, he defines body as "flesh endowed with a rational soul." When discussing the passions, he uses examples from Scripture to outline the importance of

---

30. Thomas G. Weinanday, "Cyril and the Mystery of the Incarnation," in *The Theology of Cyril of Alexandria. A Critical Appreciation*, ed. Thomas Weinandy and Daniel A. Keating (London: T&T Clark, 2003), 182. See *Comm. Jo*. 9.27, where "*sarx*" means soul. See also G. Joussard, "Impassibilité du Logos et impassibilité de l'âme humaine chez saint Cyrille de'Alexandrie," *Recherches de science religieuse* 45 (1957): 209–24.

31. McGuckin, *St. Cyril of Alexandria*, 206.

32. God the Father assumes the flesh and its sufferings. God takes on the properties of man and makes them his own.

emotions and how they are connected to the body at the incarnation. In section 25 of the *Scholia*, Cyril seems to conflate the passions of the body and soul with the term for body itself. He says that body refers to Jesus (rational soul, body, and human emotions) arguing that flesh in Scripture merely designates part of the animal; the term body, he says, has reference to the soul for God did not give salvation to soulless bodies or mere fleshly things. He states that, whenever we hear that "the Word was made flesh," we understand that it means soul and body. For the Word, who is God, became perfect man, assuming a body that was endowed with reason and soul, which he united to himself. He argues a few lines later that because the soul has a habitual communion and union with the body it cannot practically be seen as a different thing from the body.

In addition, for Cyril, the activity of the rational soul of Jesus and Logos are shared. Unlike Proclus and Hermias who attribute different activities to parts of the soul, Cyril reserves discussion of activities to the two natures of Christ; Jesus renders an activity that is shared by his divine nature according to its mode of being. However, despite his insistence that the two share activity, Cyril also notes some separation between the Logos and rational soul of Jesus with respect to the emotions. Here, there is one activity—emotion—but experienced in two different ways. This is best seen in a description of how the soul of Jesus can experience emotions in a human way while the Logos experiences them in an impassible way. In his *Commentary on the Gospel of John*, Cyril discusses Jesus's emotions, saying that the Logos is not subject to the passions but is moved (*kinoumenē*) in a way known only to itself (PG 74:136B). In *Schol.* 8, Cyril uses the example of the body being struck by a sword to show how soul appropriates suffering: the soul would suffer because its own body is suffering, but in its nature, it would not suffer. The soul appropriates the sensations of the body by virtue of the union that has bound it to a body.[33] He likens this relationship to the union at the incarnation. He says when the Word was united to the flesh endowed with a rational soul, when the flesh suffered, God was aware of what was happening, although God did not suffer (*Ad Nest.* 3, anathema 12). Still, God appropriated the weakness of his own body—that is to say, the Word does not ignore the passions he assumes, but remains impassible in his knowledge of the passions.[34] In this

---

33. Marie-Odile Boulnois also discuss this passage in "Patristique grecque et histoire des dogmes," *Annuaire EPHE, Sciences religieuses* (2016): 168.

34. Boulnois, "Patristique grecque et histoire des dogmes," 169.

way, Cyril's theory of the emotions is in some ways similar to Proclus and Hermias on the irrational soul housing the emotions; emotions, for both, are connected to the body and (in some way) separate from the divine part of the soul (which Cyril says experiences emotions, but in an "impassible way"). Still, Cyril offers a different position on the emotions, connecting them to the body, but also to the rational soul of Jesus insofar as he at times lumps together the rational soul of Jesus with the body and emotions.

The experience of emotion—even as emotions are connected to the body and the rational soul of Jesus—does not indicate a change of activity between Word and rational soul of Jesus. It seems that Cyril connects the passions with the rational soul of Jesus because the rational soul is something that in some way reacts to or appropriates the passions. Yet Logos also permeates the lower functions of Jesus. At the end of section 8, Cyril says that just as a body is of a different nature from the soul, still from both results man; likewise, God the Word and humanity come to form Christ. Cyril says, "the Word appropriates the affairs of his own flesh because it is his body. And he communicates, as his own flesh, the operations of his own powers." And yet the lower functions of the soul are connected to the Logos. Here body in section 8 seems to comprise the lower functions of the soul—the passions—that receive divine *energeia*. This is seen also in section 9, where the Word of God transforms what he assumes (that is, the things of the body, the passions) "into his own glory and operations."[35] Thus, when Cyril uses the term body and its relation to soul, he means the rational soul housing intellectual and emotional functions that react to physical body but that are mixed with Logos.

This argument responds to the Alexandrian Apollinaris, who claims that the subject of the incarnation is the Logos fused to the body. For Apollinaris, the soul of the Logos replaces the soul of Jesus at the incarnation.[36] Thus, Apollinaris argued that because Christ had no rational soul (here, connected to the emotions), he suffered only with respect to his corporeal

---

35. Boulnois says that Nemesius takes up a position against the Eunomians for whom the Word and the flesh are not united according to substance, but according to powers and faculties; the divine powers unite to the powers of the body identical to the senses. She interprets this to mean that the senses are not powers proper only to the body, but to the body and soul ("Patristique grecque et histoire des dogmes," 170).

36. C. E. Rave, *Apollinarism* (Cambridge: Cambridge University Press, 1923) and Ekkehard Muhlenberg, *Apollinaris von Laodicea* (Gottingen: Vandenhoeck & Ruprecht, 1969).

existence. The flesh had no ontological reality of its own; for Apollinaris, the Logos was fused to it in such a way that it was not changed by it.[37] In his *Oratio ad Pulcherium et Eudocuiam augustas de fide*, Cyril argues against Apollinaris who thought that the Logos inhabited a body soulless and mindless (section 44 [*ACO* 1.1.5]). He says:

> It is therefore wholly evident that the only begotten Son has become man in taking on a body, not without a soul or mind, but on the contrary, a body animated by a rational soul and having the perfection of what comes to it by nature. And just as he has made his own all bodily properties, just so he made his own all those of the soul. (Welch)

This letter, along with his *Second Letter to Succensus*, predicates suffering of body and soul. Thus, to oppose the opinion of Apollinaris, Cyril is careful to use language of union without confusion to explain the relationship between rational soul, passions, and Logos. For him, these primary entities undergo interpenetration at the incarnation. The human psychology of Christ at the incarnation appears at its foremost in the *Scholia on the Incarnation*.[38] For Cyril, the body is understood as belonging to the rational soul and passions. Throughout his writings, Cyril uses flesh to denote passions, rational soul, and physical body; for him, the emphasis is not on the physical body as a place for the union between Logos and man, but rather Cyril stresses that the physical body is something to which the passions must respond.[39]

The experience of emotions and passions need not be purified from the soul itself for deification. When Jesus experiences emotions, he perfects suffering and the experience of emotions for humankind. Jesus's suffering raises human nature to a transcendent condition (*hyper physin*).[40] In his *Comm. Jo.* 8 (PG 74:92D), Cyril explains the importance of Jesus's emotions:

---

37. See Apollinaris, frag. 107; Hans Lietzmann, *Apollinaris von Laodicea und seine Schute* (Tübingen: Mohr, 1904).

38. Lawrence J. Welch, *Christology and Eucharist in the Early Thought of Cyril of Alexandria* (New York: International Scholars Publications, 1993), 42.

39. See *Thesaurus* 24 (PG 75:397C); *Comm. Jo.* 12.27: "The affections of his flesh were aroused, not that they might have the upper hand as they do indeed in us, but in order that they might be thoroughly subdued by the power of the Word dwelling in the flesh, the nature of man thus undergoing a change for the better" (Randell).

40. *Commentary on the Gospel of John* (PG 73:153); *Dial.* 4 (PG 75:881). See McGuckin, *St. Cyril of Alexandria*, 222.

Moreover, just as death was brought to naught in no other way than by the death of the Saviour, so also with regard to each of the passions of the flesh. For unless Christ had felt cowardice, human nature could not be freed from cowardice; unless He had experienced grief, there would never have been deliverance from grief; unless he had been troubled and alarmed, no escape from these feelings could have been found. And with regard to every human experience, you will find exactly the corresponding thing in Christ. The passions of his flesh were aroused [*kekinēmena*], not that they might have the upper hand as they do in us, but in order that when aroused they might be thoroughly subdued by the power of the Word dwelling in the flesh, the nature thus undergoing a change for the better.[41]

Thus, emotions in Jesus are redemptive precisely because they are in some way ruled by the justice of the Logos. This description shares features with Proclus's description of the soul whose parts are harmonious when *logos* controls them. However, unlike Proclus's description of the interrelation of the rational and irrational parts of the soul, emotions (which Hermias and Proclus would attribute to the soul's irrational parts) are necessarily redemptive. For Proclus, the soul can only achieve unity with the One when its rational element controls the emotions. Emotions for Proclus and Hermias can be helpful once the irrational soul is separated from the rational soul, but only if the emotions are good, and aid in the individual in becoming moral and thus happy.

Conclusion

Cyril describes the incarnation using principles of Platonist teachings on the embodied soul. Proclus and Hermias structure the complex unity of the embodied soul in a way that can be likened to Cyril's understanding of union without confusion of natures in the incarnation. For Cyril and Proclus and Hermias, the emotions and passions—those connected to the lower functions of the soul—do not need to be purified from the soul if they are good emotions. For Cyril, in fact, emotions aid, rather than counter, the deification not just of this one particular entity, but all of humankind. Proclus describes the embodied soul as having one *ousia* that is internally complex so that each part of the soul carries out different

---

41. Andrew Mellas, "'The Passions of His Flesh': St Cyril of Alexandria and the Emotions of the Logos," *Phronema* 29 (2014): 95.

activities reflecting its relationship to its shared *ousia*. It is the relationship between each of the three parts that makes a soul truly human. Cyril posits the soul of Jesus and the Logos in the body as having one complex *ousia* with two natures that each have distinct properties, but share one activity. Cyril shows that it is the relationship between the soul of Jesus, the Logos, and the irrational functions (the emotions and passions) that makes Jesus simultaneously wholly man and wholly God.

Bibliography

Primary

Cyril. *Scholia on the Incarnation*. Edited by J.-P. Migne. PG 75. Paris: Garnier Fratres et J.-P. Migne Successores, 1863.

Finamore, John F., and John M. Dillon. *Iamblichus De anima: Text, Translation and Commentary*. Leiden: Brill, 2002.

Geerard, M., and J. Noret. *A Cyrillo Alexandrino ad Iohannem Damascenus*. Vol. 3 of *Clavis Patrum Graecorum*. Corpus Christianorum. Turnhout: Brepols, 1976.

Kroll, Wilhelm. 1899. *Procli Diadochi in Platonis Rem Publicam* Commentarii. 2 vols. Leipzig: Teubner

Lucarini, Carlo M., and Claudio Moreschini. *Hermias Alexandrinus: In Platonis Phaedrum Scholia*. Berlin: De Gruyter, 2012.

Pusey, P. E. *Sancti Patris nostril Cyrilli archiepiscopi Alexandrini: Epistolae tres oecumenicae*. Oxford: Clarendon, 1875.

Schwartz, E. *Acta Conciliorum Oecumenicorum*. Vol. 1.5.1. Berlin: Gruyter, 1924.

Secondary

Boulnois, Marie-Odile. "Patristique grecque et histoire des dogmes." *Annuaire EPHE, Sciences religieuses* (2016): 143–50.

Finamore, John F. "Hermias and the Ensoulment of the Pneuma." Pages 35–49 in *Studies in Hermias's Commentary on Plato's Phaedrus*. Edited by John Finamore, Christina-Panagiota Manolea, and Sarah Klitenic Wear. Leiden: Brill, 2020.

———. "Proclus and the Tripartite Soul in Plato's Republic." Pages 63–75 in *The Byzantine Platonists*. Edited by F. Lauritzen and Sarah Klitenic Wear. Steubenville: Franciscan University Press, 2021.

Grillmeier, Alois. *Le Christ dans la tradition chrétienne: L'Église de Constantinople au VI siècle* Paris: CERF, 1993.

Joachim, Harold H. *Aristotle on Coming-to-be and Passing Away*. Oxford: Oxford University Press, 1922.

Joussard, G. "Impassibilité du Logos et impassibilité de l'âme humaine chez saint Cyrille de'Alexandrie." *Recherches de science religieuse* 45 (1957): 209–24.

Lietzmann, Hans. *Apollinaris von Laodicea und seine Schute*. Tübingen: Mohr, 1904.

MacIssac, D. Gregory. "The Soul and the Virtues in Proclus's *Commentary on the Republic of Plato*." *Philosophie antique* 9 (2009): 115–43.

McKinion, Steven A. *Words, Imagery and the Mystery of Christ: A Reconstruction of Cyril of Alexandria's Christology*. Leiden: Brill, 2000.

McGuckin, John Anthony. *St. Cyril of Alexandria and the Christological Controversy*. Leiden: Brill, 1994.

Mellas, Andrew. "'The Passions of His Flesh': St Cyril of Alexandria and the Emotions of the Logos." *Phronema* 29 (2014): 81–100.

Meunier, Bernard. *Le Christ de Cyrille d'Alexandrie: L'Humanitie*. Paris: Beauchesne, 1997.

Muhlenberg, Ekkehard. *Apollinaris von Laodicea*. Gottingen: Vandenhoeck & Ruprecht, 1969.

Opsomer, Jan. "Souls and Their Bodies in the Philosophy of Proclus." Pages 129–50 in *A History of Mind and Body in Late Antiquity*. Edited by Anna Marmodora and Sophie Cartwright. Cambridge: Cambridge University Press, 2018.

Perkams, Matthias. "An Innovation by Proclus: The Theory of the Substantial Diversity of the Human Soul." Pages 167–85 in *Proklos: Methode, Seelenlehre, Metaphysik; Aketen der Konferenz in Jena am 18.–20. September 2003*. Edited by Matthias Perkams and Rosa Maria Piccione. Leiden: Brill, 2006.

Randell, T. *Commentary on the Gospel according to S. John, vol. II, S. John IX–XXI*. London: Smith, 1885.

Rave, C. E. *Apollinarism*. Cambridge: Cambridge University Press, 1923.

Rist, John M. "Pseudo-Ammonius and the Soul/Body Problem in Some Platonic Texts of Late Antiquity." *AJP* 109 (1988): 402–15.

Torrance, Iain R. *Christology after Chalcedon: Severus of Antioch and Sergius the Monophysite*. Norwich: Cantebury Press 1988.

Van den Berg, Robbert M. "Proclus and Damascius on φιλοτιμία: The Neoplatonic Psychology of a Political Emotion." *Philosophie antique* 17 (2017): 149–65.

Wear, Sarah Kiltenic. "Hermias on the Activities of the Soul: A Commentary on Hermias, *In Phdr.* 135.14-138.9." Pages 100–115 in *Studies in Hermias's Commentary on Plato's Phaedrus.* Edited by John Finamore, Christina-Panagiota Manolea, and Sarah Kiltenic Wear. Leiden: Brill, 2020.

———. *The Teachings of Syrianus on Plato's Timaeus and Parmenides.* Leiden: Brill, 2011.

Weinanday, Thomas G. "Cyril and the Mystery of the Incarnation." Pages 23–54 in *The Theology of Cyril of Alexandria: A Critical Appreciation.* Edited by Thomas Weinandy and Daniel A. Keating. Edinburgh: T&T Clark, 2003.

Welch, Lawrence J. *Christology and Eucharist in the Early Thought of Cyril of Alexandria.* New York: International Scholars Publications, 1993.

Wolfson, Harry Austryn. *The Philosophy of the Church Fathers.* Cambridge: Harvard University Press, 1964.

Christian and Pagan Neoplatonism

Gregory Shaw

Christianism lives myths deliberately, insisting they are not myths, and this has dreadful paranoid consequences.

—James Hillman, *Inter Views*

One cannot think, at one and the same time, as a Neoplatonist and as a Christian.

—Etienne Gilson, *Being and Some Philosophers*

The Problem

While attending a session on Platonism and Neoplatonism at the American Academy of Religion, I listened to a paper on deification according to Maximus the Confessor and Thomas Aquinas. At its conclusion, I witnessed this exchange:

Questioner: Were these Christians even familiar with Neoplatonism?
Speaker: Yes, they read Dionysius the Areopagite and other Christian Platonists.
Questioner: It just seems like the Christians lost Neoplatonism.
Speaker: I would say, rather, that they perfected it.
Questioner: That's the problem![1]

I am delighted to contribute to this volume in honor of John Finamore. He has been my constant companion in the study of Iamblichus since the late 1980s. John's impeccable scholarship, his generosity, and his good humor in leading the Neoplatonic community of scholars is matched by no one. We are all in his debt.

1. I happened to meet this mysterious questioner a few days later. He is Richard Pokorny, a student of esotericism as taught by Oscar Ichazo.

I would like to understand what kind of thinking leads one to say that Christianity perfected Neoplatonism. With the questioner, I also believe that presuming Christianity perfected Neoplatonism *is* the problem. It seems to me that Christianity's conviction of its exclusive possession of truth and its literalist reading of myth results in a kind of fundamentalist thinking that is the antithesis of Neoplatonism.

The idea that Platonism needed to be perfected by Christianity is expressed by Augustine in his *Confessions*. Although he was inspired by Victorinus's translation of Plotinus, Augustine was unable to attain unity with the divine as described in the *Enneads*. He explained his incapacity—not as a personal deficiency—but as due to the inescapable defect shared by all human beings: our original sin caused by the fall of Adam. Because of that fall, Augustine believed that human beings were incapable of reaching God without the incarnation of Christ. Thus, despite the inspiration he found in Plotinus, Augustine concludes that without Christ Platonists were incapable of reaching God. In his view, Christian revelation perfected the merely human efforts of the Platonists to reach God. He promoted a Platonism *perfected* by Christian revelation. Yet Augustine's Platonism is not the Platonism of Plotinus, Iamblichus, and Proclus, nor even of Plato. Augustine's highest principle is a Supreme Being and Creator, while the highest principle for the Platonists is not a being at all but an ineffable principle called "the One," which is as much present in the material world as in the spiritual. Their respective metaphysical structures, therefore, could not have been more different.

What Is at Stake?

I want to explore the difference between Christian Platonism and pagan Platonism as taught in the Neoplatonic schools. I want to ask, What was at stake then, and what is at stake for us today? As I have reflected on this question, I realize that my initial assumption that Christian Neoplatonism fails to be Neoplatonic is more applicable to Latin Christianity than to Greek Christianity. As Wayne Hankey explains, Latin theology is more Aristotelian, conceptually rigid, and dualist. It separates the natural world from the supernatural.[2] This is far less characteristic of Greek patristic

---

2. Wayne Hankey, "Augustine in the Twentieth-Century Revival of Neoplatonism in France," lecture given at the Catholic University of America, Washington, DC, 2006, 10.

theology, which is more Platonic than Aristotelian.[3] The theologies of
Dionysius the Areopagite and the Cappadocians trace a mystical itinerary
reflective of Platonic philosophy. The legacy of Augustinian spirituality in
the Roman Church followed a different course.[4] Augustine incorporated
and transformed the metaphysics of Neoplatonists into a theology that,
in the view of Jean Trouillard and Henri de Lubac, cut Western Christianity off from the transcendent.[5] Yet Augustine's Platonism became the
underlying framework of Christian theology, and unfortunately it is the
Platonism we have inherited today. Under his influence, Platonism is now
seen as a metaphysical dualism that separates the spiritual and material
worlds. Augustine saw Plotinus's Platonism as merely deficient (*Conf.*
7.21),[6] but he condemned Neoplatonic theurgy as the conjuring of evil
demons. Of theurgic rites he said, "Let us abominate and avoid the deceit
of such wicked spirits and listen to sound doctrine" (*Civ.* 10.10 [Dodds]).[7]

We have been listening to his sound doctrine for a long time. So, when
we are challenged to make sense of Neoplatonism, our default map has
been a metaphysical dualism that portrays nature as a realm from which
the soul must escape—that is, *we read Platonism through the mythology of
Christianity*. Rooted in its apocalyptic vision of a fallen world, the early

---

3. Hankey, "Augustine in the Twentieth-Century Revival," 10.

4. Jean Trouillard observes that "certain Christian authors speak of the presence
of the divine in the same terms as the Neoplatonists, leading some to assert an influence or spontaneous convergence" of thinking. Yet identical language, he cautions,
can "mask heterogeneous thoughts [*recouvrir pensées hétérogènes*].... Beneath similar
verbal formulas a veritable transubstantiation of content can occur." See Trouillard,
L'un et l'âme selon Proclos (Paris: Bude, 1972), 5.

5. Hankey, "Augustine in the Twentieth-Century Revival," 1–29. Trouillard says
that of the Latin theologians Augustine's "theme of illumination" comes closest to a
Platonic metaphysics, but since it lacks a "radical negative theology," it falls short of the
insights of the Neoplatonists (*L'un et l'âme selon Proclos*, 4).

6. He says the Platonists caught merely a glimpse of divinity but did not find the
way to reach it. The pride of the Platonists, says Augustine, kept them from submitting
to Jesus Christ.

7. Augustine's demonization of theurgy stands in stark contrast to Dionysius the
Areopagite, who spoke of theurgy as an integral part of the sacramental life of the
church. For a discussion of their respective attitudes about theurgy, see Gregory Shaw,
"Neoplatonic Theurgy and Dionysius the Areopagite," *JECS* 7 (1999): 573–99. See also
John M. Rist, "Pseudo-Dionysius, Neoplatonism, and the Weakness of the Soul," in
From Athens to Chartres, Neoplatonism and Medieval Thought, ed. Haijo Jan Westra
(Leiden: Brill, 1992), 135–61.

church believed that the saved would *rise up* to meet their Lord in the heavens, their sins forgiven and freed from the burdens of the body and death.[8] The *mythos* of Christianity, with its fallen world weighed down by the sin of Adam, is a profoundly different vision of human existence from that of the Neoplatonists. According to Trouillard, Henry Duméry, and other French Neoplatonic scholars, Augustine's theology separates God from nature, and this is antithetical to the Platonic and Pythagorean vision of the continuity and interpenetration of spirit and matter.[9]

When Christian theologians such as Augustine appropriated Platonism, they found Plato's description of an eternal world of Being and a mortal world of Becoming a confirmation of their dualism. They *literalized* what Platonists read as metaphor and created what has come to be known as Christian Platonism.[10] Unfortunately, this is the Platonism that is taught in universities today, and it is no small irony that contemporary theologians often blame Plato for infecting Christianity with dualism.[11]

---

8. 1 Thess 4:17: "After that, we who are still alive and are left will be caught up together with them *in the clouds to meet the Lord in the air. And so we will be with the Lord forever*" (NIV).

9. Hankey, "Augustine in the Twentieth-Century Revival," 12–15. According to Hankey, de Lubac argues that contemporary atheism is the consequence of Western Christianity, "which he knew to be Augustinian through and through" (10). Once God is separated from the natural world, de Lubac believed the world eventually would be taken over by secularism, denying God in our society, culture, and relationships (9).

10. As Jean Trouillard states: "We constantly run the risk of slipping into a scholarly Platonism that would double the world of objects by taking for a definitive system the mythic presentation of the theory of the Ideas. But Plato himself had vigorously criticized this interpretation." See Trouillard, *La mystagogie de Proclus* (Paris: Les Belles Lettres, 1982), 135. Reading the body as tomb (*sōma=sēma*), "riveted to the soul by sense experience" (*Phaed.* 83d), is a good example of this literalizing. For the later Platonists, the body is the vehicle through which the soul realizes its demiurgic activity and is deified. The metaphor of being riveted was taken, and is still taken by many scholars today, to mean the body is only a prison. But for Iamblichean Platonists, the body is the enclosure (*peribolos; Crat.* 400c) *through which it is saved*. The sense is that through embodiment (which is no doubt fraught with suffering and pain) the soul perfects itself and becomes divine.

11. Christian theologians maintain that the incarnation, the transformation of human flesh by the embodiment of Christ, is manifestly nondual. Yet the fact that Jesus is the *unique* exception to the human condition of being fallen simply confirms dualism and our fallen condition. In the face of this hopeless situation, the church—representing the body of Christ—provides our only escape from perdition. This is a dualist orientation. An exception to this tendency can be seen in the theology of

After centuries of absorbing this worldview, we are now habitually dualists, so it is difficult for us to see what was most important for the later Platonists, namely, *to become incarnations of divinity*. In our classrooms there is no room for supernatural Platonic sages, for deified philosophers, and certainly not for embodied gods. Yet this is an essential part of the Platonic tradition when freed from the distorting lens of Christian dualism. In a lucid exploration of the later Platonic schools, Dominic O'Meara explains how philosophers become gods. "We must … put aside an exclusivist, monotheistic notion of 'God' and remember the generous Greek sphere of the divine, which includes many different types and ranks of gods."[12] Assimilation to god, O'Meara explains, can range from becoming a god to a less intense imitation of divine life. He describes an entirely different notion of sanctity, divinity, and holiness among Greek philosophers from what developed in the Christian world. O'Meara argues that scholars have not recognized the embodied dimension of Neoplatonic philosophy because we continue to see it through the lens of an otherworldly dualism—largely inherited from Augustine.[13] We therefore fail to see how these philosophers became gods while remaining mortal human beings, yet this was their experience. This is what was at stake for the later Platonists, and their tradition was hardly perfected by Augustine or other theologians who failed to grasp the principles of their philosophy. Christians following Augustine misunderstood Platonic metaphysics because they failed to grasp the One beyond being; their theology was shaped by the myth of a fallen world requiring a savior to redeem us from sin.

Here, perhaps with some degree of irony, I turn to a Catholic priest, Jean Trouillard, to support my critique.[14] Trouillard was a student of Etienne Gilson, the preeminent historian of theology who understood the tension between Christian and Neoplatonic metaphysics. Gilson

---

John Milbank, who recognizes the nondual element in Neoplatonism and seeks to appropriate it to an incarnational theology. See Gregory Shaw, *Theurgy and the Soul: The Neoplatonism of Iamblichus*, foreword by John Milbank and Aaron Riches, 2nd ed (Kettering, Ohio: Angelico Press, 2014), v–xvii.

12. Dominic O'Meara, *Platonopolis* (Oxford: Oxford University Press, 2003), 31.

13. O'Meara, *Platonopolis*, 157. Or, more recently, because of our "flat reductionist physicalism" where there *is* no divine principle to which one might be assimilated (205).

14. I am indebted to Jean Trouillard, who generously initiated me to the world of Neoplatonism.

490 Gregory Shaw

recognizes that for Neoplatonists the One is the first principle and "being comes next as the first of its creatures." For a Christian, however, this is unacceptable, since Being cannot be a creature; "it has to be the Creator Himself, namely God."[15] Thus, Gilson concludes: "One cannot think at one and the same time, as a Neoplatonist and as a Christian."[16] Trouillard, a student of the philosopher Maurice Blondel, took Gilson's remark to heart. He and other theologians like Blondel had recognized the increasing alienation of a world separated from God, for which Catholic theology seemed to have no effective response. Trouillard, Duméry, and Stanislas Bréton turned to Neoplatonic metaphysics to reinvigorate their tradition.[17] They no longer imagined God as a Being but as the Unity from which Being is born; for them, the Neoplatonic One of Plato's *Parmenides* and Plotinus's *Enneads* trumps the creator God of traditional Thomistic theology. As Hankey puts it, "Trouillard boldly proposed that philosophy and Christian theology should turn from its Augustinian and Thomist science of God as Being, *ipsum esse subsistens*, to God represented as the One and Good, *to hen*."[18] Trouillard, who is largely responsible for the flowering of Neoplatonic scholarship in Paris in the late twentieth century,[19] maintained that to be a Neoplatonist one must engage the dialectic of Plato's *Parmenides* and the paradoxes of the One. He argues that this ineffable principle communicates itself to us more intimately and effectively than the Creator as conceived by

15. Etienne Gilson, *Being and Some Philosophers* (Toronto: Pontifical Institute of Medieval Studies, 1952), 30–31.

16. Gilson, *Being and Some Philosophers*, 31. I was led to Gilson's remarks by Jan Aertsen, "Ontology and Henology in Medieval Philosophy (Thomas Aquinas, Master Eckhart and Berthold of Moosberg)," in *On Proclus and His Influence in Medieval Philosophy*, ed. Egbert P. Bos and Piet A. Meijer (New York: Brill, 1992), 120–21.

17. More recently, John Milbank has made the same move for precisely the same reasons. His radical orthodoxy promotes a Neoplatonic theology in which God is integrated with material life. For example, see John Milbank and Aaron Riches, "Foreword: Neoplatonic Theurgy and Christian Incarnation," in *Theurgy and the Soul*, by Gregory Shaw (University Park: Pennsylvania State University Press, 1995), v–xvii.

18. Wayne Hankey, "Neoplatonism and Contemporary Constructions and Deconstructions of Modern Subjectivity: A Response to J. A. Doull's 'Neoplatonism and the Origins of the Older Modern Philosophy,'" in *Philosophy and Freedom: The Legacy of James Doull*, ed. David Peddle and Neil Robertson (Toronto: University of Toronto Press, 2003), 262.

19. See Wayne Hankey, "Aquinas' First Principle: Being or Unity?," *Dionysius* 4 (1980): 133–72.

the church.[20] Since the One penetrates the material world and is the anterior principle of all existence, this allows for a sacramental/theurgic integration of our natural life within the supernatural order.[21]

For Trouillard, neither Augustine nor Aquinas were Neoplatonists because they did not engage the dialectic of Plato's *Parmenides*.[22] They did not enter the mystery of the One prior to being.[23] Yet there were exceptions among Western theologians, most notably John Scotus Eriugena, who, Trouillard says "without having read the *Parmenides* ... divined the

20. Jean Trouillard, "Un (Philosophies de l')," in *Encyclopedia Universalis* (Paris, 1968), 16:461–63. On the need to engage the dialectic and paradox of the ineffable One as the necessary criterion of one's Platonism: "Même s'ils divergent dans l'interprétation des hypotheses, tous professent que nul n'est platonicien s'il n'a affronté dans ce dialogue le mystère de l'un." See also Trouillard, *L'un et l'âme selon Proclos*, 111. On the greater intimacy given by henological theology: "Les néoplatoniciens trouvaient dans ce modèle [henotheistic] une procession plus radicale que dans le scheme artisanal, *une intériorté plus stricte entre les dérivés et le principe, comme entre le nombre et l'unité.*" See Jean Trouillard, "Procession néoplatonicienne et création judéo-chrétienne," in *Néoplatonisme, Mélanges Offerts à Jean Trouillard* (Fontenay aux Roses: E.N.S., 1981), 9.

21. As Trouillard puts it, "The superiority of the supernatural is thus an anteriority. The beyond (*au-delà*) is equivalent to within (*en-decà*); *huper* [above] is better expressed by *pro* [before]" ("Procession néoplatonicienne," 14). Contrasting the consequences of ontic versus henadic models, Trouillard says: "To produce being is to form a product *extrinsic to its author*, it is to make its production passive and bear the weight of its finitude. *To act by mode of unity, on the contrary, is to keep the derivative in the spontaneity of the its principle*" (*La mystagogie de Proclus*, 97). Of this One he says, "The One is superior to Being: a) because expansion by the mode of unity is more perfect than every production of being; b) because the unity identical to the good is the law of every realization. Unity is not a property of the Principle *but its way of acting*" (96, emphases added). Thus, for Trouillard and later Platonists, we enter the One as an activity that rises from within.

22. Jean Trouillard, "Néo-Platonisme," in *Encyclopedia Univeralis*, 11:681.

23. I am now persuaded by Eric Perl that although Aquinas uses the vocabulary of onto-theology, he understands the highest principle in the syntax of henology: "What Aquinas means by *esse tantum* or *ipsum esse* is thus closely similar to what Plotinus means by the One: not any being (*ens*), nor the being (*esse*) of this or that distinct thing, but the 'power' or enabling condition by which there are any beings at all." See Perl, "Neither One nor Many: God and the Gods in Plotinus, Proclus, and Aquinas," *Dionysius* 27 (2010): 185. Wayne Hankey also finds this henological syntax in Thomas and suggests that the Persons of Aquinas function analogously to the henads of Proclus. See Hankey, "Divine Henads and Persons. Multiplicity's Birth in the Principle in Proclus and Aquinas," *Dionysius* 37 (2019): 168.

essence of it."[24] The charge that Christian Platonists fail to be Neoplatonic cannot be applied to Eriugena, to Meister Eckhart, or to the Greek patristic theologians. Their engagement with the highest principle in us and over-coming the separation of God from our world is entirely consistent with Neoplatonism. Eckhart's statement that "the eye through which I see God, is the same eye through which God sees me; my eye and God's eye are one eye"[25] evocatively captures the Neoplatonic experience of union with the ineffable principle within us, the One of the soul.[26] Yet it is reveal-ing that theologians such as Eckhart and Eriugena were condemned as heretics precisely because of this. Their integration of God and nature runs counter to the theology of the church, which *separates* God from the natural world. For traditional Western theology, the notion that God is in all things is characterized as pantheism and is wholly unacceptable.[27] With the distinction of Neoplatonism from the theology of the church, therefore, one must also distinguish henological and ontological forms of Christian theology. Henotheistic theology sees God as ineffable and per-vasive Unity; it expresses a kind of pan-en-theistic (Neoplatonic) vision of God.[28] Ontological theology, on the other hand, rivets its attention on a

---

24. Trouillard, "Néo-Platonisme," 681. Trouillard says, "la philosophie de l'Un au-déla de l'Etre coincide avec le néoplatonisme. On entend par cette denomination, non pas n'importe quel platonisme, mais une école déterminée de commentateurs pla-toniciens, dont les grands maîtres sont Plotin…, Porphyre, Jamblique, Proclos, Dam-ascios, Jean Scot dit Erigène. Leur ensieignement est caractérise par la place centrale qu'ils accordant au *Parménide* de Platon."

25. Raymond B. Blakney, *Meister Eckhart: A Modern Translation* (San Francisco: Harper & Row, 1941), 241.

26. Trouillard, "Un (Philosophies de l')," 463 (my translation).

27. *Unacceptable* is a euphemism for the regard in which pantheism has been held in the history of Western religion and philosophy. Pantheism, especially for Chris-tian thinkers, is a "monstrous" belief leading to the destruction of all morality, values, logic, and certainly to the loss of God in one's life. For an excellent exploration of the history of pantheism see Mary-Jane Rubenstein, *Pantheologies: Gods, Worlds, Mon-sters* (New York: Columbia University Press, 2018), 1–28.

28. Rubenstein's reflections on pantheism are illuminating. I introduce the term *pan-en-theism* to distinguish God as an ineffable *unity* that is the source of beings but is *not* a being, and a pantheistic theology that reduces God to phenomenal existence. However, if the addition of "en" leads one to reify and separate God from the world, this is *precisely opposite the understanding of the Neoplatonists*. For them, the One is more fully present in the world as its anterior condition than is the Being of onto-theology (Rubenstein, *Pantheologies*, 4).

supreme being "above" the world, a being who makes his singular appearance in the incarnation of Jesus. Neoplatonic and pan-en-theistic theology can be seen in Dionysian apophatic reflections on God and, by implication, God's everywhereness. This is also evident in Eriugena, whose God does not even exist and comes to *be* only through the created world. Pope Honorius III, speaking for the Latin church, condemned Eruigena's theology as "pullulating with worms of heretical perversity."[29]

Trouillard notes that Eruigena is "perhaps more Neoplatonist than Judeo-Christian,"[30] for his God is not a supreme being but ineffable nothingness from which being and the world arise. In other words, Eruigena's God functions like the One of Neoplatonism, and henotheism turns traditional Christian onto-theology on its head. It subverts the ontological hierarchy and its mirror on earth, the imperial church. The divine principle in Neoplatonism is not an exalted and imperial being but an ineffable and unifying *activity* that is revealed at all levels of reality from the most spiritual to the most material.[31] Trouillard explains the influence on Neoplatonists of the One in the *Parmenides*:

> According to their interpretation of the second part of this dialogue, the One passes above affirmation if it is seen in its absolute purity, ... and it falls below [affirmation] if it dissolves into pure diversity. But these two functions, *in themselves impossible to affirm, are indispensable to construct reality,* which is made of the graduated combinations of the One and the Many.[32]

For Neoplatonists, reality is both one *and* many, and each soul manifests its combinations. It is this mixing of the ineffability of Unity and the

---

29. Rubenstein, *Pantheologies*, 194.

30. Hankey, "Augustine in the Twentieth-Century Revival," 19.

31. The overcoming of dualism is also seen in theologians such as Maurice Blondel, with whom Trouillard studied. Blondel saw human life as a form of *théergie*, a "synthesis of man with God," an activity that transcends our conceptual grasp. See Blondel, *L'Action (1893): Essai d'une Critique de la Vie et d'une Science de la Pratique* (Paris: Presses Universitaires de France, 1950), 352. Reading Plotinus into Blondel, Trouillard entered the Neoplatonic vision in which *nature becomes the manifestation of the supernatural*. While in agreement with Eruigena's theology, this would be deemed heretical by the church.

32. Trouillard, "Un (Philosophies de l')," 462, emphasis added.

ineffability of Multiplicity that creates our world and which Iamblichus translated into theurgic rites.

Neoplatonic Metaphysics versus Christian Metaphysics

From their reflection on Plato's *Parmenides*, the Neoplatonists knew that the One was *never* revealed as a singular one but as measures of Unity and Multiplicity—and it was thus the practice of the sacred races, as Iamblichus called them, to *reveal and veil* their teachings in these symbolic measures.[33] To hold to one true revelation would turn the metaphysics of the One upside down. It would create a conceptual idol in place of living symbols of the Ineffable.[34] This is why Iamblichus dismisses the Christians of his time as atheists who "do not deserve to be mentioned in discussions about the gods ... [for they] are ignorant of the first principles [of theology]" (*Myst.* 179.10–180.3).[35] He was right. Christians such as Augustine had not engaged the dialectic of the *Parmenides* and the mystery of the ineffable One.[36] Their presumption to possess a singular revelation and saving truth betrays a core principle of Platonic metaphysics. By the late

---

33. For the "one" revealed/hidden as "many," see Plato, *Parm.* 141d–142. The use of the *symbolon* to reveal what must always remain hidden was absorbed into later mystical traditions. Sufi scholar William Chittick says, "The veil conceals the secrets, *but no secrets can be grasped without the veil.*" See Chittick, "The Paradox of the Veil in Sufism," in *Rending the Veil: Concealment and Secrecy in the History of Religions,* ed. Elliot Wolfson (New York: Seven Bridges, 1999), 60, emphasis added. Iamblichus explains the nature of cosmogony and its metaphysics of inversion by quoting Heraclitus: "neither speaking nor concealing but *signifying* [*sēmainontes*]," to explain how the gods both perform demiurgy and provide the means for divination through their creation (*Myst.* 136.1–4).

34. Iamblichus maintained that the "entire system of Pythagorean mystagogy was enshrined in symbols ... [but] like the oracles of the Pythian god they are hard to understand or follow for those who consult the oracle in a superficial manner." Iamblichus, *On the Pythagorean Life,* ed. John Dillon and Jackson Hershbell (Atlanta: Scholars Press, 1991), 247.

35. I have rephrased Dillon's translation.

36. As Hankey observes, it may be that the difference in Christian theologies, following Pseudo-Dionysius or Augustine, reflects the difference between Iamblichean Neoplatonism that holds the One as *beyond* Being and Porphyrian Neoplatonism that identifies the One with Being. As Hankey points out, the Porphyrian position, which collapses the One into Being, was followed by the Augustinians (Hankey, "Aquinas' First Principle," 139–40).

fourth century, Christianity had been empowered by the state to promote its singular revelation, even to punish the noncompliant, seen, for example, in Augustine's ordering of imperial troops against the Donatists.[37] For Iamblichus, Proclus, and Damascius revelation can never be singular; it is cosmogonic activity rising from an *ineffable* source that appears in *multiple* forms and diverse traditions. Edward Butler captures this difference: "The Christian God [he says] is not the Platonic One, because the latter is inseparable from polytheism."[38]

Pagan Neoplatonists were, as Bréton puts it, "inspired by self-criticism";[39] they erased their conceptual certainties through Socratic aporetics. Their revelations, therefore, were not considered true as facts but true as symbols. Iamblichus says revelation functions *symbolically* (συμβολικῶς), "neither revealing nor concealing" (*Myst.* 136.1–3 [Clarke, Dillon, and Hershbell]), and this allowed theurgists to enter its activity, to recognize that their embodiment was a σύνθημα that both shows and hides the divine (*Myst.* 136.4–7 [Clarke, Dillon, and Hershbell]). To see revelation in this way allows for a variety of expressions. Thus, for pagan Neoplatonists, polytheism and recognizing the authority of diverse revelations is intrinsic to their identity.[40] In a soteriological sense, the differences between Neoplatonists and Christians could not have been greater. In their exclusive possession of the Truth, Christians would have seemed like a man who claims the sun shines *only* in his own backyard. One can understand Iamblichus's reluctance to engage them. In their unique *possession* of revealed truth, in their insistence that their symbols are facts, Christians excluded themselves from entering the paradox of divine revelation.

---

37. As Peter Brown puts it, "Augustine may be the first theorist of the Inquisition." See Brown, *Augustine of Hippo* (Berkeley: University of California Press, 1969), 240.

38. Edward Butler, review of *Pagans and Philosophers: The Problem of Paganism from Augustine to Leibniz*, by John Marenbon, *WWBJ* 5 (2018): 63.

39. Hankey, "Augustine in the Twentieth-Century Revival," 15, quoting Stanislas Bréton.

40. Adrian Mihai has recently argued that Damascius's approval of various religious systems near the end of his *De principiis* (3.159.6–167.25) is not a defensive posture against Christian hegemony, nor is it missionary zeal, but an attempt to show that the multiplicity of expressions of divine revelation is "presque épistémologique," as Damascius's Neoplatonic metaphysics would require. See Mihai, "Comparatism in the Neoplatonic Pantheon of Late Antiquity: Damascius, *De Princ.* III 159.6–167.25," *Numen* 61 (2014): 457–83.

Neoplatonists did not assert saving truths. They did not possess infallible dogmas, and they did not rely on metaphysical certitudes delivered by a Magisterium.[41] In fact, the method of the Platonists, originating with Plato himself, was to enter deeper and deeper levels of unknowing, paradoxical impossibilities; they passed through the initiation of Socratic aporia. It is not metaphysical certitude that was encouraged by Platonists but the careful undermining of certitude and through this to enter and embody the mysteries of the One.[42] How might we define this? We cannot. But, like the later Platonists, we can evoke it through poetry. D. H. Lawrence, in *The Sound of a Man Who Has Come Through*, writes:

Not I, not I, but the wind that blows through me!
A fine wind is blowing the new direction of Time.
If only I let it bear me, carry me, if only it carry me!
If only I am sensitive, subtle, oh, delicate, a winged gift!
If only, most lovely of all, I yield myself and am borrowed
By the fine, fine wind that takes its course through the chaos of the world
Like a fine, an exquisite chisel, a wedge-blade inserted;
If only I am keen and hard like the sheer tip of a wedge
Driven by invisible blows,
The rock will split, we shall come at the wonder, we shall find
the Hesperides.[43]

The importance of aporetic loss and catharsis cannot be overemphasized for Platonists. In terms of the Eleusinian rites, where lesser mysteries prepare the soul for the greater, the shedding of discursive convictions prepared philosophers to receive the mysteries of the One and to enter, as Lawrence puts it, the garden of the Hesperides. In contrast, the Christians' possession of infallible Truth is like Callicles in the *Gorgias*, to whom Socrates says, "You are lucky in having been initiated into the Greater

---

41. In its catechetical indoctrination, the church understands such certitude as an "infallible assent of the mind to the propositions of dogma." This is the antithesis of the Neoplatonic path. Polymnia Athanassiadi refers to the "l'hérésie de l'intellectualisme" against which Iamblichus directed his efforts. See Athanassiadi, *La lutte pour l'orthodoxie dans le platonisme tardif: de Numénius à Damascius* (Paris: Les Belles Lettres, 2006), 213.

42. In apophatic terms, they "know" by tracing the paths of "unknowing."

43. D. H. Lawrence, *Selected Poetry* (New York: Penguin, 1986), 72. Lawrence emphasizes the experience of receptivity, of our being *carried*, borne by the wind to another world.

Mysteries before the Lesser; I didn't think it was permitted" (*Gorg.* 497c). Of course, it was not, and Callicles's presumption to know what he did not know was precisely the mental illness that Socratic aporia is designed to address. Later Platonists recognized it as the double ignorance (*Alc.* 1 [117e–118a])[44] of the *Alcibiades*,[45] the state not only of being ignorant of the truth but of being ignorant of one's ignorance. Only those aware of their ignorance can learn. Those convinced they possess infallible truth cannot.

So, how is it that coming to terms with our ignorance initiates the soul into the ineffable principle the Neoplatonists call the One? How is it that the paradox of self-awareness reflects the paradox—the showing and hiding—of a first principle that both is and is not? For Neoplatonists, the One is the principle that underlies all metaphysics. It is the glyph that reveals at once the mysteries of immanence and transcendence that are realized through our experience of being simultaneously myself *and* a

---

44. Socrates refers to "those who do not know but think that they do." He characterizes this as the "discreditable sort of stupidity."

45. The Anonymous Prolegomena to Platonic Philosophy, a sixth-century CE introduction to Platonism, states that Iamblichus established the curriculum for studying the dialogues of Plato. It was a progressive reading, moving from lesser to greater mysteries, and it began with the *Alcibiades* "because it teaches us to know ourselves, and the right course is to know oneself before knowing external things, for we can scarcely understand those other things so long as we are ignorant of ourselves" (Westerink and O'Neill). In the language of the later Platonists, Christian theologians were disabled by their "supreme ignorance" (*megistē agnoia*), "when a man knows that he does not know but *owing to the emotional appeal* of the opposite belief refuses to give up his ignorance" (Anonymous Prolegomena 16.24–28). See Danielle A. Layne, "The Reception of Plato in the *Anonymous Prolegomena to Platonic Philosophy*," in *Brill Companion to the Reception of Plato in Antiquity*, ed. Harold Tarrant et al. (Leiden: Brill, 2017), 533–54; Layne, "The Virtue of Double Ignorance in Olympiodorus," in *Olympiodorus of Alexandria: Exegete, Teacher, Platonic Philosopher*, ed. Albert Joosse (Leiden: Brill, 2021), 95–115. James Hillman is far more explicit. Describing Christian versus Greek myths, he says: "Greek myths bring Greek consciousness, the entire project of know-thyself [the Socratic *aporia*]. They bring psychology. They bring a subtle awareness of the complications of life because of all the Gods and Goddesses. And they bring dimensions Christianity doesn't want to deal with, really, like Aphrodite, like Hades, like Mars.... Christianism means simplicity, trust, childlikeness.... Christianity doesn't require consciousness at all. I am afraid of it. In my bones, I am afraid of Christian unconsciousness." See Hillman, *Inter Views: Conversations with Laura Pozzo on Psychotherapy, Biography, Love, Soul, Dreams, Imagination, and the State of the Culture* (Dallas: Spring, 1983), 84.

divine other.[46] As Plotinus puts it, in one of his exalted moments: "How could I, even now, descend; how has my soul come to be in the body?" (*Enn.* 4.8.1.1–10; O'Meara, modified). Neoplatonists wrestle with the paradox of the One *existentially*.

They ask themselves fundamental questions. What is self-consciousness? How do we come to grips with an attention that splits itself? For, to be self-aware, to know that I know, reflects a fundamental division. As Alan Watts states:

> Knowing that one knows generates a confusion of echoes in which the original sound is lost.[47]... [Our sense of I] seems to be without any tangible foundation. It springs from the void.[48] It stands alone: a light illuminating the world, but not illuminating the wires that connect it with the world, since they lie immediately behind it. I am therefore to myself a stranger in the earth, facing and meeting the world, but not really belonging.[49]

And, of course, we want to belong; we do not want to feel divided, but the very nature of self-consciousness is to be divided.

In the *Symposium* Plato tells us that "our nature was not what it is now.... The shape of each human being was completely round with back and hands in a circle" (*Symp.* 189e). But our circles now are broken; we are divided, fragmented, alienated; so, we seek sanctuary in something unbroken and undivided, a condition untouched by our self-divided awareness. To become undivided and whole seems impossible to us. It *is* impossible, but we yearn to recover undivided awareness, as if we once possessed it. Yet we never did, for to possess is to be divided. The solution, then, for the Neoplatonists, was not to try to possess wholeness but to discover it in our

---

46. I recommend the brilliant exploration of this theme in late antique religions by Charles Stang in *Our Divine Double* (Cambridge: Harvard University Press, 2016).

47. Alan Watts, *Beyond Theology: The Art of Godmanship* (New York: Vintage, 1973), 3.

48. I am reminded of Damascius's reference to the ineffable first principle. When we speak of it, he says, "we are stepping into the void (*kenembatein*)." See Damascius, *Problems and Solutions*, 71. See the exploration of this theme in Damascius by Marilena Vlad, "Stepping into The Void: Proclus and Damascius on Approaching the First Principle," *The International Journal of the Platonic Tradition* 11 (2017): 44–68.

49. Watts, *Beyond Theology*, 4. D. H. Lawrence explores the same paradoxes in us in his poem *Only Man* (Lawrence, *Selected Poetry*, 242–43).

dividedness. To try to escape from fragmentation is self-deception. The solution of the later Platonists, therefore, is to be both whole *and* divided, to belong *and* to feel abandoned, to be inside *and* outside at the same time. These kinds of contradictions make up Iamblichus's definition of the soul. For him, the soul is mediating activity that imitates the Demiurge's weaving of opposites; the soul is cosmogonic.[50] Iamblichean theurgy transforms even the passions (*pathē*) of our embodied life into vehicles of deification *and* cosmogenesis.[51]

To transform the soul, to discover wholeness in dividedness, requires our acceptance of opposites. The soul, Iamblichus says, is in essential contradiction: "it simultaneously remains and proceeds"; "stays itself and ... becomes other"; and "it is *never free from these oppositions*" (95.1, 241.11–12, 6.4–5 [Hayduck]). As Iamblichus put it, "that which is immortal in the soul is filled completely with mortality and no longer remains only immortal" (90.21–23 [Hayduck]).[52]

To be a later Platonist was to accept these impossibilities. Perhaps the most difficult is that the soul is "made other to itself";[53] yet even this is part of our demiurgic activity as we mediate opposites. What may be reflected here is Iamblichus's meditation on the One as participated by the soul. For the

---

50. Iamblichus, *Nicom. arithm.* 78.22–24. Iamblichus says, "There is nothing in existence in which opposition is not present" (73.4–5 [my trans.]). Iamblichus translated the Pythagorean principle of mean terms to the existential situation of souls, allowing us, in theurgy, to demiurgize opposing principles within us. As he put it, the *allēlouchia* (the weaving together of opposed principles) is performed dispassionately by the Demiurge and creates the continuity of numbers and orders in the cosmos. For human souls, *allēlouchia* is experienced passionately (*meta pathous*; *Myst.* 196.8–10), reflecting our condition in the sublunary realm.

51. Iamblichus's solution to our alienation is thus Tantric, for both theurgy and Tantra deify the soul by incorporating the very things that alienate us from divinity. See Gregory Shaw, "Platonic Tantra: Theurgists of Late Antiquity," *QSI* 10 (2017): 269–84.

52. See also *De an.* 14.7–8: "The definition of these matters is difficult because the soul is one and many in essence." See also 223.28–32; Priscianus, *Metaphr.* 32.13–19, which describes the soul as embracing permanence and change simultaneously; Iamblichus, *De anima: Text, Translation and Commentary*, trans. John F. Finamore and John Dillon (Leiden: Brill, 2002), 240–41.

53. Hayduck: "[the soul] is alienated by verging outside itself" (*allotriōthen dia tēn exō rhopēn heautou*, 223.26). Pseudo-Simplicius also says that according to Iamblichus the embodied soul is also "made other to itself" (*heteroiousthai pros heautēn*, 223.31).

One is also an impossibility. It is one only by becoming many: to reveal itself, unity must be inverted into what it *is not*—multiplicity (*Parm.* 141e–142e).

This principle of inversion is fundamental to Neoplatonic metaphysics and is reflected at every level of the cosmos. In this metaphysics, material reality is not deficient; it is the organ through which immaterial powers are revealed.[54] What is unique about the human soul is that our participation in this *procession* becomes "disrupted"; we become self-divided and alienated, yet even this mirrors the One.[55] Just as the timeless instant, the *exaiphnēs* of the *Parmenides,* pivots between the One that is and the One that is not, somehow, impossibly, being both (*Parm.* 155–156), human souls are also called to realize this impossibility.[56] To enter these mysteries requires passing through the aporia of Socrates, who says he has "no wisdom great or small" (*Apol.* 23b), and this, too, mirrors the One, which also has "no wisdom great or small" (*Parm.* 157b). The later Platonists follow the path of Socrates who, as Sara Ahbel-Rappe puts it, "lived in the wake … of this One."[57]

---

54. Iamblichus explains the nature of the cosmogony and its metaphysics of inversion by quoting Heraclitus: "Neither speaking nor concealing but *signifying* [σημαίνοντες],*" to explain how the gods perform demiurgy while providing the means for divination through their creation (*Myst.* 136.1–4 [Clarke, Dillon, and Hershbell]). In his critique of Porphyry's dualist conception of the gods, believing their transcendence separates them from the material realm, Iamblichus says: "Indeed, what is it that prevents the gods from proceeding in any direction and what hinders their power from going further than the vault of heaven?" (27.7–9). As regards Porphyry's contention that the gods cannot be found in matter Iamblichus replies: "In fact, the truly real, and that which is essentially incorporeal, is everywhere that it wants to be.… As for me, I do not see in what way the things of this realm could be fashioned and given form, if the divine creative force and participation in divine forms did not extend throughout the whole of the cosmos" (27.10–28.3, modified slightly). Put succinctly, Iamblichus says, "The immaterial is in matter immaterially" (232.12).

55. Carlos Steel, *The Changing Self,* trans. E. Haasl (Brussels: Paleis der Academien, 1978), 69. Iamblichus sees the soul as reflecting the paradoxes of the One. The soul, he says, "simultaneously remains as a whole and proceeds as a whole [*homou holē kai menei kai proeisi*]," just as the power of the One "simultaneously remains and proceeds [*hama menei kai proeisin*]," thus creating continuity [*to syneches*] by "extending through all things" and distinction (*to diōrismenon*) since "it stops at each of the forms and defines it" (90.20 [Hayduck]).

56. Steel, *Changing Self,* 98–102. Ahbel-Rappe notes that Damascius describes "the instant," as the one of the soul, the faculty or center of the soul (*Damascius: Problems and Solutions,* 168). It is also identified as our "attention" (προσεκτικόν).

57. Sara Ahbel-Rappe: "When in the *Apology* we meet Socrates at the age of seventy, he has fully developed and found a way to live in the wake, so to say, of this One;

Christian Platonists did not. Their perfecting of Platonism did not require the catharsis of Socratic aporia. Instead of shedding themselves of conceptual propositions, they embraced them. They believed in dogmas that promised security to the very self that Platonists wanted to erase. Christian and pagan Neoplatonists had profoundly different mythical orientations. Pagan Neoplatonists become transparent to the cosmos and enter demiurgic activity.[58] For them the cosmos is the shrine of the Demiurge (*Tim.* 37c), and nature is a theophany that reveals the gods. Far from being fallen, nature is the symbolic revelation of the divine; it *incarnates* a multiplicity of divine realities. In the Christian myth, however, nature is fallen and needs redemption. The incarnation of God is necessary to redeem nature and the material order. For Iamblichus, the sacramental power of matter does not require the incarnation of Christ. The material realm is, and has always been, unilaterally and intrinsically filled with gods. Here the Christian and Platonic myths plainly diverge. *The Platonic myth is cosmocentric, the Christian anthropocentric.* For the Neoplatonist there is no need for a new creation, no need to be redeemed *from* a fallen nature, for *nature itself is the body of our salvation.* In contrast, the Christian soul preserves itself *against* nature and seeks to dominate or redeem it.[59]

Perhaps the Christian formula was better suited to the empire of Rome, which had eclipsed the vitality of local communities. The polytheism of pagan traditions to which the later Platonists were aligned was

---

he understands the highest possible wisdom as the realization that he has no wisdom." See Ahbel-Rappe, "Socrates' Esoteric Disclosure in Plato's *Apology*: A Comparative Religions Approach" (unpublished paper, 2014), 3.

58. The goal of theurgy for Iamblichus is for the soul to be "fully established in the demiurgic god" (*Myst.* 292.12–13 [Clarke, Dillon, and Hershbell]). For the Neoplatonists, the Demiurge is not an entity fixed in a metaphysical hierarchy. The Demiurge is an *activity*, specifically the activity that divides the One and unifies the Many. For Platonists, the Demiurge is the weaving of opposites, the endless pulse of procession and return that creates our world. To borrow a Hindu metaphor, only when the soul becomes a jewel in Indra's Cosmic Net, with each jewel mirroring every other, does it begin to share in this demiurgy. As Proclus put it, "all things are in all, but in each in an appropriate way" (*Elem. theol.* 103).

59. The theme of separating oneself from and dominating the cosmos pervades Christian Scriptures. The Christian soul puts on "the whole armor of God ... to stand against the wiles of the devil ... for we wrestle ... against principalities, against powers, against the *rulers of the darkness of this world*, against spiritual wickedness in high places" (Eph 6:11–12 KJV). The Christian seeks to be saved *from* the world; the Neoplatonist, in contrast, sees the world as theophany and seeks to enter its divine activity.

perhaps not as well suited to the Roman imperium as was the monotheism of Christianity.[60] However true that might be, the Platonism of the Christians was, as Tuomo Lankila says, "alien to the Neoplatonic spirit."[61] "Proclus' concept of metaphysical faith and Damascius' ineffable conjecture are not [he says] easily reconciled with a conception of religiosity where a formal confession of faith is taken as the most serious criterion for redemption."[62] Under the Roman imperium, Lankila explains, diverse religious traditions were replaced by "an ideological apparatus for distributing grace ... backed by a theocratic state."[63] Imperial Rome and the church became partners in a powerful hegemony.

For Platonists, this kind of hegemony is exemplified in Alcibiades's hunger for empire building. Alcibiades wants to fill the entire world with his name, yet he has not yet undergone catharsis (*In. Alc.* 149.17–150.22). Proclus does not disparage Alcibiades's desire for power, for this is seeded into all of us by the gods. The problem is that we do not know how to express it. Proclus explains:

> The ineffable names of the gods fill the entire cosmos, as the theurgists say.... [64] The gods, then, have filled the whole world both with themselves and their names, and having contemplated these names before birth, and yearning to resemble the gods, but not knowing how ... souls become lovers of command and long for the mere representation of those realities and to fill the whole human race with their name and power.... The aspirations of such souls are grand and admirable but when put into practice they are petty, ignoble and vaporous because they are pursued without insight.... Their grand ideas arise from ... what has been

---

60. It is precisely this social dimension and its influence on later Platonism that is the focus of Radek Chlup, *Proclus: An Introduction* (Cambridge: Cambridge University Press, 2012). Chlup observes that as local leaders ascended up the imperial hierarchy, so holy men—both Christian and a few pagan—ascended to the One *above* the cosmos (the dualist form of Platonism seen in Porphyry and to some degree Plotinus). Chlup contrasts the world-affirming Neoplatonism of Iamblichus to that of Plotinus (255–78).

61. Tuomo Lankila, "Post-Hellenistic Philosophy, Neoplatonism and the Doxastic Turn in Religion," *Numen* 63 (2016): 163.

62. Lankila, "Post-Hellenistic Philosophy," 163.

63. Lankila, "Post-Hellenistic Philosophy," 163.

64. Proclus refers to the Chaldean Oracles, frag. 108, which states "For the Paternal Nous has sown symbols throughout the cosmos." See Ruth Majercik, *The Chaldean Oracles: Text, Translation and Commentary* (Leiden: Brill 1989).

inseminated into us, so their desire is natural and appropriate, ... but their expression of it is unconscious and ignorant. (150.4–23 [Westerink, slightly modified])

Without the aporetic undermining of self-idolatry, the soul blindly exalts itself and the community with which it identifies. For members of the imperial church this was encouraged, but it is the antithesis of Neoplatonism.

Conclusion: Christian Sacraments and Neoplatonic Theurgy

It might seem that Iamblichus was aligned with Augustine in their recognition of the limits of philosophy. Both turned to ritual to reach the divine, but their critique of the philosophical approach is entirely different. As a Platonist, Iamblichus had been initiated into the intellectual rigors of the *Parmenides* and Socratic aporetics. He understood that everything is rooted in an utterly ineffable principle, and therefore he recognized the need for a principle in us that transcends the mind, namely, the One in us—the trace (ἴχνος) of the ineffable—by which we realize our participation in it.[65] Iamblichean theurgy was not at odds with the rigors of Platonic philosophy but was its logical outcome. As James M. P. Lowry argues, by introducing theurgic rites, Iamblichus developed the "mystical side of Plotinus more systematically than Plotinus himself had done."[66] Ritual theurgy was coherent with philosophical ascesis.

With Augustine, the situation is different. He did not undergo the dialectical catharsis of the *Parmenides*. Unlike Greek patristic thinkers, whose apophatic theology transcended all intellectual formulations, Augustine

---

65. Speaking of the ineffable One, Damascius says, "As for us, how could we make any suppositions of any kind at all about it, if there were not within us also some trace [*ichnos*] of it, which is as it were striving towards it? Perhaps, then, one should say that this entity, ineffable as it is, communicates to all things an ineffable participation, in virtue of which there is in each of us some element of ineffability" (24.24–25.9 [Dillon]).

66. James M. P. Lowry continues: "It could be argued that Iamblichus, in trying to make sense out of Plotinus, developed philosophical principles which make possible mystical unity with the divine. By doing this he could then be said to have showed that this unity was not primarily philosophical. This should perhaps be the position that any Neoplatonist, especially Plotinus, should have made explicit." See Lowry, *The Logical Principles of Proclus' STOICHEIÔSIS THEOLOGIKÊ* (Amsterdam: Rodopi, 1980), 20–21.

became identified with dogmatic formulas that, from a Neoplatonic view, were simply conceptual idols.[67] Augustine and the imperial theologians did not pass through the henotheistic mystagogy of the Neoplatonists. They worshiped a Supreme Being who offers forgiveness for the sin of being human. Neoplatonists, however, did not need to be forgiven. For them, to be human was an invitation to share in divine activity, in what Blondel later described as a *théergie* that integrates the divine and human, "a synthesis of man with God."[68] Theologians of the imperial church created a caricature of Platonism that, however well suited it was for empire building, remains alien to the essence of Platonism.

Bibliography

Primary Sources

Anonymous/Olympiodorus. *Anonymous Prolegomena to Platonic Philosophy*. Translated by Leendert G. Westerink. Reprint, Wiltshire, UK: Prometheus Trust, 2011.

Augustine. *The City of God*. Translated by Marcus Dodds. New York: Modern Library, 1950.

Damascius. *Problems and Solutions Concerning First Principles*. Translated by Sara Ahbel-Rappe. Oxford: Oxford University Press, 2010.

Iamblichus. *Chalcidensis: In Platonis Dialogos Commentariorum Fragmenta*. Leiden: Brill, 1973.

——— *De anima: Text, Translation and Commentary*. Translated by John F. Finamore and John Dillon. Leiden: Brill, 2002.

——— *In Nicomachi Arithmeticam Introductionem*. Edited by Ermenegildo Pistelli and Ulrich Klein. Stuttgart: Teubner, 1975.

——— *On the Mysteries*. Translated by Emma Clarke, John Dillon, and Jackson Hershbell. WGRW 4. Atlanta: Society of Biblical Literature, 2003.

---

67. In the language of the later Platonists, some Christian theologians were disabled by their "supreme ignorance" (*megistē agnoia*), "when a man knows that he does not know but *owing to the emotional appeal* of the opposite belief refuses to give up his ignorance" (Anonymous Prolegomena 16.24–28; see Layne, "Reception of Plato," 533–54).

68. Blondel, *L'Action (1893)*, 352; Hankey, "Augustine in the Twentieth-Century Revival," 6.

—— *On the Pythagorean Way of Life.* Translated by John Dillon and Jackson Hershbell. SBLTT 29. Atlanta: Scholars Press, 1991.

Majercik, Ruth. *The Chaldean Oracles: Text, Translation and Commentary.* Leiden: Brill 1989.

Proclus. *Commentary on the First Alcibiades.* Translated by Leendert G. Westerink and William O'Neill. Reprint, Wiltshire, UK: Prometheus Trust, 2011.

Simplicius. *De Anima.* Edited by Michael Hayduck. Berlin: Reimeri, 1882.

Secondary Sources

Aertsen, Jan A. "Ontology and Henology in Medieval Philosophy (Thomas Aquinas, Master Eckhart and Berthold of Moosberg)." Pages 120–40 in *On Proclus and His Influence in Medieval Philosophy.* Edited by Egbert P. Bos and Piet A. Meijer. New York: Brill, 1992.

Ahbel-Rappe, Sara. "Socrates' Esoteric Disclosure in Plato's *Apology*: A Comparative Religions Approach." Unpublished paper, 2014.

Athanassiadi, Polymnia. *La lutte pour l'orthodoxie dans le platonisme tardif: de Numénius à Damascius.* Paris: Les Belles Lettres, 2006.

Blakney, Raymond B. *Meister Eckhart: A Modern Translation.* San Francisco: Harper & Row, 1941.

Blondel, Maruice. *L'Action (1893): Essai d'une Critique de la Vie et d'une Science de la Pratique.* Paris: Presses Universitaires de France, 1950.

Brown, Peter. *Augustine of Hippo.* Berkeley: University of California Press, 1969.

Butler, Edward. Review of *Pagans and Philosophers: The Problem of Paganism from Augustine to Leibniz,* by John Marenbon. *WWBJ* 5 (2018): 62–67.

Chittick, William. "The Paradox of the Veil in Sufism." Pages 59–84 in *Rending the Veil: Concealment and Secrecy in the History of Religions.* Edited by Elliot Wolfson. New York: Seven Bridges, 1999.

Chlup, Radek. *Proclus: An Introduction.* Cambridge: Cambridge University Press, 2012.

Dillon, John. "Damascius on the Ineffable." *AGP* 78 (1996): 120–29.

Gilson, Etienne. *Being and Some Philosophers.* Toronto: Pontifical Institute of Medieval Studies, 1952.

Hankey, Wayne. "Aquinas' First Principle: Being or Unity?" *Dionysius* 4 (1980): 133–72.

—— "Augustine in the Twentieth-Century Revival of Neoplatonism in France." Lecture given at the Catholic University of America, Washington, DC, 2006.

—— "Divine Henads and Persons. Multiplicity's Birth in the Principle in Proclus and Aquinas." *Dionysius* 37 (2019): 164–81.

—— "Neoplatonism and Contemporary Constructions and Deconstructions of Modern Subjectivity: A Response to J. A. Doull's 'Neoplatonism and the Origins of the Older Modern Philosophy.'" Pages 250–78 in *Philosophy and Freedom: The Legacy of James Doull*. Edited by David Peddle and Neil Robertson. Toronto: University of Toronto Press, 2003.

Hillman, James. *Inter Views: Conversations with Laura Pozzo on Psychotherapy, Biography, Love, Soul, Dreams, Imagination, and the State of the Culture*. Dallas: Spring, 1983.

Lankila, Tuomo. "Post-Hellenistic Philosophy, Neoplatonism and the Doxastic Turn in Religion." *Numen* 63 (2016): 147–66.

Lawrence, D. H. *Selected Poetry*. New York: Penguin, 1986.

Layne, Danielle A. "The Reception of Plato in the *Anonymous Prolegomena to Platonic Philosophy*." Pages 533–54 in *Brill Companion to the Reception of Plato in Antiquity*. Edited by Harold Tarrant, Danielle A. Layne, François Renaud, and Dirk Baltzly. Leiden: Brill, 2017.

—— "The Virtue of Double Ignorance in Olympiodorus." Pages 95–115 in *Olympiodorus of Alexandria: Exegete, Teacher, Platonic Philosopher*. Edited by Albert Joosse. Leiden: Brill, 2021.

Lowry, James M. P. *The Logical Principles of Proclus' STOICHEIŌSIS THEOLOGIKĒ*. Amsterdam: Rodopi, 1980.

Mihai, Adrien. "Comparatism in the Neoplatonic Pantheon of Late Antiquity: Damascius, *De Princ.* III 159.6–167.25." *Numen* 61 (2014): 457–83.

Milbank, John, and Aaron Riches. "Foreword: Neoplatonic Theurgy and Christian Incarnation." Pages v–xvii in *Theurgy and the Soul*, by Gregory Shaw. University Park: Pennsylvania State University Press, 1995.

O'Meara, Dominic. *Platonopolis*. Oxford: Oxford University Press, 2003.

—— *Plotinus*. Oxford: Clarendon, 1993.

Perl, Eric. "Neither One nor Many: God and the Gods in Plotinus, Proclus, and Aquinas." *Dionysius* 27 (2010): 167–92.

Rist, John M. "Pseudo-Dionysius, Neoplatonism, and the Weakness of the Soul." Pages 135–61 in *From Athens to Chartres, Neoplatonism and Medieval Thought*. Edited by Haijo Jan Westra. Leiden: Brill, 1992.

Rubenstein, Mary-Jane. *Pantheologies: Gods, Worlds, Monsters*. New York: Columbia University Press, 2018.

Shaw, Gregory. "Neoplatonic Theurgy and Dionysius the Areopagite." *JECS* 7 (1999): 573–99.

———. "Platonic Tantra: Theurgists of Late Antiquity." *QSI* 10 (2017): 269–84.

——— *Theurgy and the Soul: The Neoplatonism of Iamblichus*. Foreword by John Milbank and Aaron Riches. 2nd ed. Kettering, Ohio: Angelico Press, 2014.

Stang, Charles. *Our Divine Double*. Cambridge: Harvard University Press, 2016.

Steel, Carlos. *The Changing Self*. Translated by E. Haasl. Brussels: Paleis der Academien, 1978.

Trouillard, Jean. *La mystagogie de Proclus*. Paris: Les Belles Lettres, 1982.

———. "Néo-Platonisme." *Encyclopedia Universalis*. Pages 681–82 in *Encyclopedia Universalis*. Vol. 11. Paris, 1968.

———. "Procession néoplatonicienne et création judéo-chrétienne." Pages 1–30 in *Néoplatonisme, Mélanges Offerts à Jean Trouillard*. Fontenay aux Roses: E.N.S., 1981.

——— *L'un et l'âme selon Proclos*. Paris: Bude, 1972.

———. "Un (Philosophies de l')." Pages 461–63 in *Encyclopedia Universalis*. Vol. 16. Paris, 1968.

Vlad, Marilena. "Stepping into The Void: Proclus and Damascius on Approaching the First Principle." *The International Journal of the Platonic Tradition* 11 (2017): 44–68.

Watts, Alan. *Beyond Theology: The Art of Godmanship*. New York: Vintage, 1973.

Contributors

Crystal Addey is a lecturer in the Department of Classics at University College Cork, Ireland. She is the author of *Divination and Theurgy in Neoplatonism: Oracles of the Gods* (2014) and the editor of *Divination and Knowledge in Greco-Roman Antiquity* (2021).

Sara Ahbel-Rappe has taught in the Department of Classical Studies, University of Michigan, Ann Arbor, for over thirty years. She is the author of books and articles on Plato and the Platonic tradition.

Dirk Baltzly is emeritus professor at the University of Tasmania, Australia. His most recent books include *Hermias On Plato's Phaedrus*, volumes 1–2 (2018, forthcoming), with Michael Share, and *Proclus on Plato's Republic*, volumes 1 and 2 (2018, 2022), with Graeme Miles and John Finamore.

Robert Berchman is an academic fellow of Il Foro di Studi Avanzati/ Roma, Italia, and senior fellow of the Institute of Advanced Theology, Bard College, Annandale-on-Hudson, New York. He is author of *Thinking on Thinking: Studies in Mind, Meaning and Subjectivity* (2021).

Jay Bregman is emeritus professor of history and religious studies and part-time professor of music at the University of Maine. Recent publications include "The Platonist as Music Lover," in *Defining Platonism: Essays in Honor of the Seventh-Fifth Birthday of John M. Dillon*, edited by John F. Finamore and Sarah Klitenic-Wear (2017), and "Synesius of Cyrene: Body, Soul, Cosmos," in *A History of Mind and Body in Late Antiquity*, edited by Sophie Cartwright and Anna Marmodoro (2018).

Luc Brisson, director of research emeritus at the National Center for Scientific Research, Centre Jean Pépin (Paris – Villejuif, UMR 8230 CBRS-ENS, PSL), is known for his works on both Plato and Plotinus, including bibliographies, translations, and commentaries. He has also published numerous works on the history of philosophy and religions in antiquity.

Kevin Corrigan is Samuel Candler Dobbs Professor of Interdisciplinary Humanities in the Department of Middle Eastern and South Asian Studies at Emory University in Atlanta, Georgia. His recent publications include *Love, Friendship, Beauty and the Good: Plato, Aristotle, and the later tradition* (2018); *Plotinus. Ennead VI 8, On the Free Will of the One* (with John D. Turner, 2017); *A Text Worthy of Plotinus: The Correspondence of A. H. Armstrong, Paul Henry SJ, Hans-Rudolph Schwyzer, E. R. Dodds, Jean Trouillard, Jésus Igal, 1952–1989* (with Suzanne Stern-Gillet and José Baracat, 2020); and *Plotin. Oeuvres complètes, Traités 30–33, Tome 2. Collection des Universités de France. Série grecque, 482* (with Jean-Marc Narbonne, Lorenzo Ferroni, John D. Turner, Zeke Mazur, and Simon Fortier, 2021).

John Dillon is Regius Professor of Greek (emeritus) in Trinity College, Dublin, Ireland. His chief works include *The Middle Platonists* (1977; 2nd ed., 1996); *Alcinous, the Handbook of Platonism* (1993); Iamblichus, *De Anima* (with John Finamore, 2000); *The Heirs of Plato* (2003); *The Roots of Platonism* (2018); and three volumes of collected essays.

John F. Finamore is Emeritus Professor of Classics at the University of Iowa. He is the author (with Dirk Baltzly and Graeme Miles) of *Proclus: Commentary on Plato's Republic*, volumes 1 and 2 (2018, 2022), and editor of *The International Journal of the Platonic Tradition*.

Lloyd P. Gerson is professor of philosophy in the University of Toronto, Canada. He is the author of many books and articles on ancient philosophy, including the forthcoming *Plato's Moral Realism* (2023). He is the editor of *The Cambridge History of Philosophy in Late Antiquity* (2010) and editor and cotranslator of *Plotinus: The Enneads* (2018).

Dorian Gieseler Greenbaum is a postgraduate tutor at the University of Wales Trinity Saint David, UK. Recent publications include "Hellenistic Astronomy in Medicine" and "The Hellenistic Horoscope," in *Hellenistic Astronomy: The Science in Its Contexts* (2020) and "Divination and Decumbiture: Katarchic Astrology and Greek Medicine," in *Divination and Knowledge in Greco-Roman Antiquity* (2021).

Elizabeth Hill is a visiting instructor in the Department of Philosophy at Colby College in Waterville, Maine. She is the author of "Alcibiades, the Bad Lover: A Defense of the Ethics of Plato's Erotic Philosophy," in *Platonic Interpretations: Selected Papers from the Sixteenth Annual Conference of the International Society for Neoplatonic Studies*, edited by John F. Finamore and Eric D. Perl (2020).

Sarah Klitenic Wear is professor of classics at the Franciscan University of Steubenville. She is the author of books and articles on Neoplatonism, including *Syrianus' Teachings on Plato's Timaeus and Parmenides* (2011). Her latest book is *Patience and Salvation in Third Century Carthage* (2023.) She coedits the book series Theandrites: Studies in Byzantine Philosophy and Christian Platonism with Frederick Lauritzen (Franciscan University Press).

Danielle A. Layne is professor of philosophy and director of the MA program in philosophy at Gonzaga University, Spokane, Washington. She has published widely on Plato and the Platonic Tradition, including *Plotinus: Ennead I.5, "On Whether Well Being Increases With Time": Translation, with an Introduction and Commentary* (2022), and with Jessica Decker and Monica Vilhauer the edited volume *Otherwise Than the Binary: New Feminist Readings of Ancient Greek Philosophy and Culture* (2022).

Ilaria L. E. Ramelli, FRHistS, is professor of theology and patristics and senior fellow/member (Durham University, UK; Sacred Heart University, Angelicum, USA-IT; KUL, Poland; Princeton University; Bonn University, Germany; University of Cambridge, UK). Recent books include *Social Justice* (2016), *A Larger Hope?* (2019), *Bardaisan* (2009, 2019), *Patterns of Women's Leadership* (editor, 2021), *Eriugena's Christian Neoplatonism* (2021), *Terms for Eternity* (2007, 2022), and *Lovers of the Soul, Lovers of the Body* (coeditor, 2022).

Gregory Shaw is professor of religious studies and theology at Stonehill College, Massachusetts. He is the author of *Theurgy and the Soul: The Neoplatonism of Iamblichus* (1995, 2014), coeditor of *Practicing Gnosis* (2013), and author of a number of articles on the later Neoplatonists and on Iamblichus in particular. He is currently working on a book titled *Hellenic Tantra* that explores the embodied aspects of later Platonic philosophy and its similarity to the tantric traditions of South Asia.

Svetla Slaveva-Griffin is associate professor of classics at Florida State University. She is the author of *Plotinus on Number* (2009); coeditor, with Pauliina Remes, of *The Routledge Handbook of Neoplatonism* (2014); and, with Ilaria L. E. Ramelli, coeditor of *Lovers of the Soul, Lovers of the Body: Philosophical and Religious Perspectives in Late Antiquity* (2022).

Suzanne Stern-Gillet is professor of ancient philosophy emerita at the University of Bolton and honorary research fellow in the Department of Classics and Ancient History at the University of Manchester (UK). Her current research focuses on the epistemology and moral psychology of Plotinus, on whose tractate *On the Virtues* she is preparing a translation and commentary for Parmenides Publishing.

Harold Tarrant, emeritus professor at the University of Newcastle, Australia, taught classics, especially Greek, in Australian universities for many years. He is author of *The Second Alcibiades: A Dialogue on Prayer and on Ignorance* (forthcoming) and *Proclus: Commentary on Plato's Timaeus*, volumes 1 and 6 (2007, 2017).

Van Tu, assistant professor of philosophy at California State University, San Bernadino, has written articles on both Aristotle and Plato.

John D. Turner † was Cotner Professor of Religious Studies and Charles J. Mach University Professor of Classics and History at the University of Nebraska-Lincoln. He was the author of *Sethian Gnosticism and the Platonic Tradition* (2002) and a principal figure in an international team, centered at Laval University in Quebec, that produced the definitive editions of major gnostic texts (in *Bibliothèque Copte de Nag Hammadi*— especially *Zostrien* and *Marsanès* in 2000, *L'Allogène* in 2004). He also authored, with Kevin Corrigan, *Plotinus: On the Free Will of the One; Ennead VI.8, Translation, Introduction, and Commentary* (2017), contributed to *Plotin: Oeuvres complètes, Traités 30–33, Tome 2* (2021), and edited *Platonisms: Ancient, Modern, and Postmodern* (2007), *Plato's Parmenides and Its Heritage* (2010), and *Religion and Philosophy in the Platonic and Neoplatonic Traditions* (2012). He was honored in *Gnosticism, Platonism, and the Late Ancient World: Essays in Honour of John D. Turner*, edited by Kevin Corrigan and Tuomas Rasimus (2013).

Ancient Sources Index

Modern Authors Index

Subject Index

Printed in the USA
CPSIA information can be obtained
at www.ICGtesting.com
JSHW020630291223
54424JS00003B/36